Commonsense Care: Parenting Gender-Confused Kids with Truth & Love
35 Transcripts from the Video Series

Erin Brewer, Ph.D. & Maria Keffler, M.S.Ed.

D1522269

ABOUT THE AUTHORS

Erin Brewer who developed a "transgender" identity as a child grew up in Salt Lake City where she had inspiring high-school teachers who took the time to teach her more than academics. She went on to earn a B.S. from Hampshire College. After getting her Master's and Ph.D. from Utah State University, she was a stay-at-home mom and homeschool teacher for about ten years. During this time she also volunteered at a number of local agencies and ran her own produce business. She is co-founder of Advocates Protecting Children and the Compassion Coalition, an international group for those fighting to ban invasive, harmful, unproven medical interventions for gender-confused children. Her blog can be found at: http://www.chooseyourowndiagnosis.com

Maria Keffler is a co-founder of Advocates Protecting Children. Ms. Keffler is also a co-founder of the Arlington Parent Coalition, a watchdog group in Arlington, VA, which works to safeguard parents' rights and children's safety in public education. An author, speaker, and teacher with a background in educational psychology, Ms. Keffler has fought to protect children from unethical activism and dangerous policies around sexuality and transgender ideology since 2018. She lives in Arlington, Virginia (USA), with her husband and three teenage children.

Commonsense Care: Parenting Gender-Confused Kids with Truth & Love
35 Transcripts from the Video Series

Advocates Protecting Children
P.O. Box 41981
Arlington, VA 22204

advocatesprotectingchildren@gmail.com
www.advocatesprotectingchildren.org

Names have been changed to protect privacy. Some quotes, conversations, and information have been edited for brevity, grammar, or clarity, but all have been preserved accurately to the best of the author's ability.

Information presented in these transcripts is not a substitute for the advice of a licensed medical professional or mental health provider, nor for the counsel of a licensed attorney. Users of this information accept the sole responsibility to conduct their own due diligence on information presented and to consult licensed medical, legal, and other professionals for their individual concerns. We make no warranties or representations on the information presented, and users of this production acknowledge that we are not responsible nor liable, whether directly or indirectly, for any damages or loss caused or alleged to be caused by or in connection with use or reliance on any information, content, products, or services available on or through this site. We are not responsible for the content of any websites or organizations that are referenced or accessible from these transcripts.

TABLE OF CONTENTS

ACKNOWLEDGMENTS

Deepest thanks go to the many people whose experiences, research, support, and wisdom seeded and watered the creation of *Commonsense Care: Parenting Gender-Confused Children with Truth & Love*. From our parents and children, to our college professors, to our colleagues who are fighting to protect children from unethical activism, to the millions of parents who are struggling to save their children, we could not possibly name all of the people who deserve credit for teaching and guiding us.

We considered acknowledging the many voices who saw the gender train-wreck coming down the tracks long before the rest of us even knew it was a thing. But as we started trying to name all of them—such as Janice Raymond and Ryan Anderson—we realized we'd certainly miss someone in that lofty list of names.

As we were compiling the Thank-You list that we eventually abandoned, we realized that we owed debts of gratitude to people on all stations of the political spectrum: Democrat and Republican, conservative and liberal, left and right. We were reminded again that we have become politically homeless. With respect to nearly every cultural issue, the left has gone off the rails in some places, and the right has gone off the rails in others.

So we pledge our gratitude to and solidarity with all those who formerly considered themselves Democrats or Republicans, conservatives or liberals, leftists or righties, and who now wander the culture like tribeless vagabonds. You are our people. We have met the emperor, and not only is he naked, he knows it and is having the time of his life making everyone around him pretend he's not.

When this nightmare—where children are stolen from their parents and turned into lifelong medical customers—is over, may our friendships remain.

Nil carborundum illegitimi.

DEDICATION

To all of the parents and caregivers who were blindsided by their child's
out-of-the-blue transgender announcement.

You're not alone, you're not crazy, and you're not wrong
in recognizing that your children have been indoctrinated into a cult.

Our love and prayers are with you as you fight to save your children.

x

FOREWORD

If Commonsense Care had existed when we first began our long journey, I am certain our lives—and our son's life—would be very different than it is today.

Our family was dragged into the transgender nightmare when my son was still in college. I cried for hours after his big announcement. I wrestled with the thought that I must have been a bad mother, as I replayed his childhood over and over. What signs did I miss? What had I done wrong? How could this have possibly happened?

How I wish I'd had *Episode 1: My Child Announced a Transgender Identity. Now What?* and *Episode 4: Parent Support: Getting Help & Avoiding Harm.*

Now I know that my son made a self-diagnosis after being influenced on social media sites such as Deviant Art and Reddit.

Erin & Maria clearly outline how this happens in *Episode 27: Social Media & Gender Dysphoria.*

My husband and I began researching for any information we could get. There was little information available. At that time, the "experts" told us we must affirm our child if we didn't want him to be suicidal. We felt like we were the only ones in this world living this nightmare.

If only we'd had Episodes 7, 8, and 9, on dealing with all the different people, institutions, and organizations that impact this terrible ideology.

We began to realize other young people who identify as transgender have similar characteristics as my child. My child is on the autism spectrum, he's gifted and talented, he's socially awkward, and he suffered trauma as a child. He also suffers depression and spends too much time on the internet.

Episode 10: Autism & Gender Dysphoria

Episode 11: Trauma & Gender Dysphoria

Episode 12: Depression & Gender Dysphoria

Doctors and therapists ignored several important details including his previous bouts of depression, that he suffered multiple concussions, and that he was molested by a peer. In the first therapy session, he was told he needed to transition medically in order to prevent being suicidal. He is currently taking an antidepressant. Without having a mental health assessment, he was prescribed high dose female hormones after he signed an informed-consent form. The therapist and physician's assistant should have seen red flags.

Would that we had seen *Episode 5: Finding Trustworthy Support for Your Child* before we trusted therapists who would lead our son further down this nightmare of a path.

Potential irreversible harms were never discussed by the doctor, physician's assistant, therapist or clinic. His mental illness has never been appropriately addressed. He was fast-tracked into becoming a patient for life: a cash cow for the therapist, the surgeon, the gender clinic, and the pharmaceutical companies.

I know now that this is a manufactured diagnosis, which serves no one but the doctors and pharmaceutical companies who are raking in money hand over fist by transing children. Had I only seen *Episode 15: Problems with Medicalizing Children* back then.

We have been called transphobic, angry, and hateful since we do not affirm him as being female. We have been made to feel guilty by being asked, "Wouldn't you rather have a live daughter than a dead son?" as if our only choice is to celebrate our child's transgender identity or expect our child to kill him or herself. We will not participate in this lie.

Now I recognize what Erin and Maria illuminate in *Episode 7: The Cultic Aspects of Gender Ideology*. This is a cult.

How many more children will be harmed before this is stopped? My question for anyone who doubts this is happening is, "What if your son/daughter was told he/she needed to mutilate his/her body in order to become mentally healthy or happy?"

I am grateful to Erin and Maria for their dedication toward helping others navigate this issue. As you read *Commonsense Care: Parenting Gender-Confused Children with Truth & Love*, I hope you find it to be a valuable resource as you struggle through this issue.

—Mae Lyle, Co-Founder of Advocates Protecting Children

INTRODUCTION

During a leadership team meeting at our organization, which had been formed to fight transgender ideology in order to protect children and families from its predatory activism, an idea hit me. I said, "I'd like to do some videos for parents, to talk about this ideology and how to respond to it, in order to either keep children out of it, or to pull them out of it if they've already gotten sucked in."

Erin's eyes lit up. "Can I do it with you?" she asked.

That day, *Commonsense Care: Parenting Gender-Confused Kids with Truth & Love* was born.

Erin and I thought we'd do maybe seven or eight videos. By the time we felt we'd adequately covered all the necessary material, we had 35.

Working with Erin over the many months it took to create this series was a delight, despite the horrors of the topic we were tackling, and the difficulties of navigating something that was so dangerous to children and families, yet had been overwhelming accepted by the culture at large. I learned—and continue to learn—so much from Erin, and I'm grateful to her for all she's doing to fight for children's protections and women's rights.

As we began to compile the transcripts of our videos into this book, we struggled to balance a desire to present them exactly as they aired with the need to polish up the spoken language so it reads more easily. We have, therefore, edited the raw transcripts to take out extraneous words ("you know," "and so," *etc.*), as well as to correct any places where we misspoke (*e.g.*, using the word "conscious" when we meant "conscience"). We have also done some light-to-intermediate editing on the flow of sentences, in order to better reflect what we were trying to say when we were video-taping without a script or post-production editing.

We strove to maintain the integrity of the transcripts, so that nothing unnecessary was added, and nothing important was removed.

This series reflects our best effort to provide families a roadmap for navigating a world that preys upon children, trying to turn them into fodder for the gender industry's medicalization machine. This ideology has been intentionally manufactured, bountifully funded, and strategically maneuvered into every aspect of society: entertainment, the marketplace, schools, and even government policy. Why? Among other reasons, because it is massively profitable. According to multiple market reports, sex-reassignment surgery *alone* is projected to be a $1.5 billion industry by 2026.

By marketing it as a "civil right," gender has been deceptively slipped in under the LGB (lesbian, gay, bisexual) umbrella, a place where it does not belong. "Trans rights" are actually trans privileges which obliterate the rights and protections of the LGB community, as well as those of women and children.

There is nothing true, right, or healthy for anyone within transgender ideology. Humans cannot change sex, medicalization always comes with negative repercussions (even when it is a necessary alternative to doing nothing, which it is not in this case), and no one's lives are improved in the long-term by people pretending to be something they are not.

One day—hopefully very soon—the transgender house of cards will tumble, and everyone will see this malignant ideology for what it is. Until then, we continue to fight to protect children and families, and to turn a light into the dark places that transgender-rights activists don't want any-one to see.

Thank you for educating yourself on this topic, and for doing everything you can to keep children and families safe from transgender-rights activism and policies.

Our very best to you and your family.

—Maria Keffler
Co-Founder of Advocates Protecting Children

Episode 1: My Child Announced a Transgender Identity. Now What?

https://youtu.be/QsoIRpVWMEw

Maria Keffler (00:04):

Welcome to Commonsense Care: Parenting Gender-Confused Kids with Truth & Love, brought to you by Advocates Protecting Children. So-called affirmative care is the gender industry's one-size-fits-all answer for any and all children and youth who struggle with their identity. In no other area of medicine, psychology or education is one treatment plan assigned to all people. At Advocates Protecting Children we believe that each child should be treated as an individual and given the care and support that's most appropriate for him or her.

Today, we're here to talk about, "My child just announced a transgender identity. What now?" I'm Maria Keffler.

> **"I think I might want to take powerful drugs that will delay my development and affect me for the rest of my life." That's basically what they're saying when they announce that they're questioning their gender identity.**

Erin Brewer (00:45):

And I am Erin Brewer. Boy, that is a big question. What do we do? Because some parents might think, "This is no big deal," and not understand. It's akin to a child coming home and saying, "I think I might want to take powerful drugs that will delay my development and affect me for the rest of my life." That's basically what they're saying when they announce that they're questioning their gender identity: that they're a fairly dangerous path.

Maria Keffler (01:17):

Often what you hear—what parents are told—is, "It's just social transition. You know, it's just a haircut. It's just different clothes. It's just a different pronoun. It's just a different name. There's nothing permanent about it."

But what we are finding is that kids who start on a social transition—who start with those sorts of superficial changes—almost inevitably move into the next step: girls wearing the binder, boys starting estrogen, and girls starting testosterone.

Those kids who detransitioned or desisted (those kids who had claimed a transgender identity for a while, but then change their minds) say that it's like you never quite get to where you're happy. They think, "If I socially transition, that'll make me happy." Well, that doesn't do it. "Let me try the binder. Let me try the packer. Let me—oh, that didn't do it either. Okay. Maybe hormones will do it. We'll try that."

It's a slippery slope and it leads almost inevitably to irreversible medical changes. Kids who have desisted and detransitioned are just horrified at what they've done to their bodies.

If you can deal with this at the outset—get it dealt with right now and try to get kids back on a healthier path—there's just better long-term outcomes associated with that.

Erin Brewer (02:56):

I don't want to scare parents, but I do want to get into it a little bit for parents who are brand new to this, and haven't even heard of transgender. Let's talk about some of these things.

You mentioned that a lot of kids say, "It's just going to be a social transition." These kids are going to change their hair. They're going to wear different clothes, and they're going to go by a different name and pronouns. That also sounds pretty benign. But I wanted to get into this a little bit. You talked about packers and binders. Can you explain those?

Maria Keffler (03:25):

Chest binders are a corset-like device that girls wear to flatten their breasts. They are strong. They are powerful. They are crushing. Women in China used to bind their feet, because having small feet was considered a beauty standard. It broke their toes by curling their toes under. It damaged their bodies. And we look at that and say, "That's horrible. Why would you ever do that to someone?"

These chest binders are not much different. Girls who've worn them for a long time have damaged breast tissue. They've had cracked ribs. It causes breathing problems. The longer they wear these crushing devices, the more damage is done.

Packers are—I'm trying to find a family-friendly way of describing this— it's a fake penis that is made to put in a girl's underwear. I'm horrified to say that they make these for little girls as young as four and five years old as well, to put in their underwear, to look like they have a penis when they don't.

Erin Brewer (04:40):

This isn't just like a sock to make it look like you have a bulge there. They are designed to look very much like an actual penis. For any girl to put something like that in our panties—to me, it's disturbing that a child would do this. Even for a teenager, it is disturbing.

The other thing that we talked about were the drugs that are given to kids who want to transition. Generally, they start with puberty blockers, and those can be given as young as eight years old.

Puberty blockers sound pretty innocuous. I know that a lot of people say, "It's just a pause on puberty."

Do you want to talk about whether it is just a pause? Are we just giving these kids a little bit of time? Or is it more sinister than that?

> **There's no research backing up that you can pause puberty. In fact, there's ample research from endocrinologists that puberty is a finite window.**

Maria Keffler (05:27):

It's a lot more sinister than that. You'll hear a lot of people in the gender industry use that phrase, that "We're putting a pause button on puberty" to give kids time to figure out who they are, but that's really disingenuous. There's no research backing up that you can pause puberty. In fact, there's ample research from endocrinologists who say that puberty is a finite window.

This is a time of big changes to your body and your brain. There is a window for it, and if you miss that window, it's closed and it doesn't open up again. Kids who've been on puberty blockers like Lupron, which is one of the main drugs that's prescribed—have so much damage. It damages bone density, it retards brain growth, it retards physical growth.

You have stopped this child's maturation. It's not, "We're just going to pause it for a little bit and it can restart again." We know the longer that a child is on Lupron, the less likely that child is to ever attain full growth.

Erin Brewer (06:38):

It strikes me that as parents we tend to be very concerned about the development of our children. We make sure that they're meeting those very important developmental milestones. It sounds like what this does is induce developmental delays.

Maria Keffler (06:53):

It does. Looking at parents who've been terribly worried about things like: is your child walking on time? Is your child meeting language goals on time? Is your child keeping up with his or her class at school? To suddenly pathologize puberty and say, "Puberty is an uncomfortable, painful thing we need to stop"—

Puberty is a painful time for a lot of people. It's a hard time. It's a time of huge growth and change. It's been uncomfortable for people—and I might say especially for girls—for millennia. That's a normal thing that we need to go through in order to become adults.

To pathologize puberty that goes against the grain of the rest of education, of child development, and of saying, "My goal for this child is to attain adulthood in a healthy, productive way." I want my children to grow into adults who are physically healthy, mentally healthy, emotionally healthy, and can contribute productively to society. Putting a halt on something as significant in your developmental path, as puberty. That's indefensible.

Erin Brewer (08:11):

It's confusing. Then on top of that, these kids often want to go on wrong-sex hormones: estrogen for boys, testosterone for girls. Can you just give an overview of what those do?

Maria Keffler (08:24):

Those also create some painful changes for kids who have later desisted. Regarding estrogen for boys and testosterone for girls, they help to cosmetically alter that child's physical appearance so that they look more like the opposite sex. Estrogen creates breast growth in boys. It will create larger hips. It puts fat on in places that boys don't typically have on fat.

Testosterone is particularly insidious. It will lower the register of a girl's voice, to make her sound like she has a man's voice. It will start hair growth on her face. She will typically have hair loss on her head. Girls who've been on testosterone for a while will have that receding hairline, and thinning hair on the head.

Many of those changes do not go away. The voice change—that will probably not go away. If the girl decides that she wants to go off testosterone—once the vocal cords have thickened, they do not thin up again. That's the difference between the higher feminine voice and the lower masculine voice—the thickness of the vocal cords. The facial hair does not go away. That is likely to continue for the rest of her life.

Erin Brewer (09:43):

I've also heard that it can impact fertility and cause the reproductive organs to atrophy, which sounds pretty serious.

Maria Keffler (09:53):

It is. I think I heard this from you, when we were talking another time: You gave the analogy that giving wrong-sex hormones is like putting diesel gas into an automobile engine that uses unleaded gas. Our bodies were not designed to handle the wrong-sex hormones. Girls who've been on testosterone for a while—their uterus, fallopian tubes, and ovaries will tend to atrophy because they're not being restored and cared for by estrogen, which is what the female body was designed to run on. They'll often have to have a radical hysterectomy.

> **Giving wrong-sex hormones is like putting diesel gas into an automobile engine that uses unleaded.**

If you've been on puberty blockers and cross-sex hormones for a while, you will probably not have children. It does damage to so many systems in the body. That's a particularly painful one because I don't think many kids say, "I can't wait to be a parent."

Some do. Some kids are like, "I want to be a mom. I want to be a dad." But most of us—I know when I was younger, I thought, "Yeah, I'll probably have kids someday. I don't know. I don't really like kids."

But once you pass through puberty, you grow into adulthood. Your brain finishes its development around the age of 25. Our brains don't finish developing until that time. You have radically different ideas about who you are and what you want from your life at 25 than you did at 15.

Putting kids on a path of no return at 15, 16, 17, is just unconscionable.

Erin Brewer (11:30):

Then you compound that with these kids who want surgeries. Girls as young as 13 want their breasts removed and doctors are doing this. Surgeons are willing to do this. Removing the breasts—for boys getting castrated, having their testicles removed. I mean, that is irreversible. There's no doubt about that.

Any kind of elective cosmetic surgery should be questioned in anybody, but especially in children who are grappling with these identity issues.

Maria Keffler (12:04):

Yes. I hear people say, "You can go back and get breasts again." A particular gender industry therapist has been caught on video saying, "If a girl decides that she wants breast again, she can just go get them."

No, they're not the same. Once you get your breasts removed, sure, you can have reconstructive surgery at a very expensive cost, but they will never nurse a baby with those breasts. The milk ducts have been severed; they're not coming back. They will never have a pleasurable sexual sensation with their breasts.

> **A gender industry therapist has been caught on video saying, "If a girl decides that she wants breasts again, she can just go get them." No, they're not the same.**

With the reconstructive genital surgeries, they have so many issues with infection, inability to urinate well, and with sexual dysfunction. They will never have normal sexual function down there, because we cannot reproduce what nature created, and damaging that for cosmetic reasons in childhood is just unethical. That's just one of the most unethical things to do to children that I can think of.

Erin Brewer (13:24):

Something that is important, people who are part of the transgender movement suggest that those who don't support children in their gender identity are being hateful. They say that they're potentially putting their children at risk because they're not affirming their child.

Yet based on the information that I have and what we've talked about today, it's very clear to me that if a child starts down that path, it's a path towards dysfunction, developmental delays, and long-term side effects— basically medicalizing a child for the rest of his or her life.

This isn't about affirming a child. It's about looking out for the best interests of a child and what's healthy.

Generally speaking, experts and parents don't try to affirm a child in something that's going to damage them. That's what this is all about. It's not about saying that your child has to be gender-conforming. It's suggesting that going down this transgender path has significant negative long-term outcomes.

Maria Keffler (14:32):

I agree with everything you said, Erin. When a child announces a transgender identity, they do need support and they do need affirmation of their feelings. These are real, genuine struggles that these kids are having. They need compassion, they need support—but they also need parents and experts who are looking after their long-term good, not just conforming to momentary social pressure to do a particular thing.

So as we look at our own children, we want to ask, "Okay, what's going on? Why is my child feeling this way? How can I validate that? Yeah, you're really struggling. I see that you're suffering. Let's talk about how we can help you."

How do we be those kinds of parents? How do we address our kids' real, heartfelt, serious needs, while looking at the whole child and saying, "Let's find the best path for you, that's going to bring you into a place of healing."

I would love to hear from you because you have so much history and knowledge about what this path looks like. I'd like to hear your thoughts on that.

Erin Brewer (15:52):

For those who don't know—I had a transgender identity as a kid. I was very adamant that I was a boy and wanted my teachers to treat me like a boy, and call me by my boy's name. I was very determined to convince the world that I was a boy.

Kids have magical thinking and they can get into a mindset where they can first flirt with the idea, and then believe that they're something that they're not. In my case, I had therapists and parents and teachers who did not affirm me, and they didn't tease me, and they didn't dismiss me.

That's important. Parents might hear this, and some parents might just say, "That's ridiculous. My kid's not a boy, or my daughter's not a boy. My son's not a girl. What are you talking about? This makes no sense." And they dismiss it.

It's important to take this seriously, because this is coming from very strong feelings that a child has at the same time. I'm so very grateful that my school sent me to the school psychiatrist to assess me and figure out what was going on and come up with a treatment plan.

These days, if you send your child to the school psychiatrist or school counselor, it's not unlikely that counselor will say, "You think you're a boy. You are a boy," and then go ahead and affirm that child, which means allowing them to use the boy's bathroom. If they're a girl, it's allowing them to use the opposite sex locker room facilities. It's calling them by the name they want and the pronouns that they want. What this does is reaffirms these ideas in a child's head.

So rather than questioning it in a kind and compassionate way, you're just saying, "Okay. If that's what you believe, we'll go for it."

A lot of this is from kindness and the belief that this is the right thing to do, without the understanding of the implications of affirming that we talked about earlier.

It's important to take this seriously. Don't dismiss it, but also do not affirm it. Also don't completely freak out, because if kids see a parent freaking out, that does a lot of weird things to the dynamic.

This is asking a lot of parents. We know it's asking a lot, because we're saying that you get this heavy bomb dropped on you, but you have to respond in this compassionate, kind, caring way. Don't overreact. Don't under-react.

I'm curious what some of the experts have to say about this.

Maria Keffler (18:37):

I love what you said about not putting a child on a path of automatic affirmation, because we know from an educational and child development background that what you tell a child, a child will believe. Children believe trusted adults. I believe it was Johann Von Goethe who said, "Treat a man as he is, and he will remain what he is. Treat him as he ought to be,

> **"Treat a man as he is, and he will remain what he is. Treat him as he ought to be, and he'll become what he ought to be."** What the people around you reflect to you reinforces what you believe about yourself.

and he'll become what he ought to be." What the people around you reflect to you reinforces what you believe about yourself.

That's just basic social psychology. Let's say you're suffering from anorexia and the people around you are telling you, "Yes, you are fat. I agree with you. You should get your stomach stapled. You should take some diet pills." That person will die from that advice. You would never do that to an anorexic.

What we tell kids about themselves is vitally important to what they believe about themselves, and the decisions that they will make in the future.

I also just wanted to say that I love what you said to parents about just being calm: be patient, don't freak out. It is okay to say to your child, "I don't understand this. I'm, I'm completely at a loss. I need you to tell me more. I need to hear from you. I need you to explain this to me, and I need some time to think about this and to try to understand it. Please be patient with me as I try to understand, because I want to get what you're going through."

Erin Brewer (20:25):

I know that there were times as a child where I felt stupid. If I had gone to my teacher and said, "I'm stupid," and she said, "You're right. You are stupid," that would not have been helpful. Kids go through stages where they feel stupid, they feel ugly. They feel unloved. We do not suggest that teachers or parents or other adults in these kids' lives affirm those feelings.

Yet, in this case, this very strange case, we're saying that even though this potentially can lead to lifelong damage, it should be affirmed. It's a very strange thing that this transgender movement is suggesting.

I was wondering if you wanted to hear from Sasha Ayad? She is a therapist who works with teenagers and has some really good insights about how you should respond when a child comes to you and says that they're questioning their gender identity.

Sasha Ayad (21:23):

Parents have to recognize that their child is undergoing one of the most confusing periods in their life. Very lovingly, very kindly, say, "Look, I see that this is a struggle you're going through. And I don't know what this means, but we're going to get through this together. I'm here for you."

Erin Brewer (21:41):

Parents can do lots of things to strengthen relationships. Sometimes all that a child needs is just some time with their parents.

I know that we're told that the most important relationships in a child's life are their peers. But experts are starting to question that now. A lot of parents have abdicated their role as parents because they think, "Their peers are more important now. I don't really need to parent." That's just not true in this case. In most cases, teenagers do need parent figures in their lives to guide them.

Maria Keffler (22:15):

They do. We're focusing especially on that period because there are so many kids who are announcing this during adolescence and puberty.

This time in their lives is so formative for them because it's the time they're starting to leave the den and move into the forest. They're starting to grow up and prepare to leave home. And so those outside influences— their peers and people outside the home—do start to become more important for them. Their focus often shifts that direction, but they still very much need that safe, secure home base.

> **This time is so formative for them because it's the time they're starting to leave the den and move into the forest. They're starting to grow up and prepare to leave home. So those outside influences-their peers and people outside the home-do start to become more important for them. Their focus often shifts that direction, but they still very much need that safe, secure home base.**

In an ideal world, the children are close enough with their parents, and in a trusting relationship with their parents, that the child can venture out into the forest and start interacting with it. But the parents are still there watching. If the parent sees the child is going in a direction he or she shouldn't, the parent pulls the child back to the den and says, "Hey, this is not a healthy thing. Here's what I see happening. We're not going to let that happen."

Because until children are 18, they are still legally under the care of their parents, and parents have that right and responsibility to say, "No, this particular thing is not healthy. I'm not going to let you go there."

Then the child goes out in another direction, that's a healthy direction. The parents say, "That's great. You're doing a fantastic job there. I love the grades you're getting. I love the way you're working at that part-time job."

It is the parents' responsibility and privilege to guide their kids away from unhealthy paths and toward healthy paths, all the way until the children are fully functioning adults in their own right.

Erin Brewer (24:10):

It reminds me of a child who's self-harming. If a child had some issues and was doing some significant self-harm, and a parent just ignored that— or even affirmed that—we would realize that's problematic. We don't do that. If parents can shift their thinking about this—that this isn't about affirming a child in their "true self," but it's affirming self-harming behavior, because that's the road this leads to.

We wouldn't affirm if children wanted to cut themselves or starve themselves. We wouldn't say, "That's okay." As we mentioned in the case of anorexia, or in engaging in dangerous behaviors, parents' responsibility is to pull the kid back in and help to guide them. It is a time when parents can have a huge influence on a child.

We have some questions from some parents who have had children who have gone down the transgender path. We asked them, "What would you have liked to have known when you first encountered this?" This can be informative to parents who are just coming into this the first time, or maybe who just don't know what might walk in the door. It's always good to have some information about what parents should know about this if a child does come in and say, "I think that I'm transgender."

Maria Keffler (25:44):

The question that we got relates very well to Sasha Ayad's counsel. The parent asks, "What should my primary goal be? What is the most important thing to focus on first?"

The first thing is your relationship with your child. You don't want to damage the relationship by freaking out or ignoring the problem.

Probably a parent's first instinct when this happens is like, "I've got to stop this. What are the right words? What's the right logic? What's the right thing to do to make this stop right now?" But unfortunately, it's probably not going to stop quickly, because this is such a deep, heart issue with the child.

You do want to try get your child realigned with your family because, unfortunately, schools, social media, and what's going on out in the world are really disaffirming the importance of the family. They're telling kids, "If your parents don't automatically tell you, 'It's great that you're transgender,' they're homophobic, transphobic, hateful, bigoted, toxic."

> **You want to try to realign your child with your family because, unfortunately, schools, social media, and what's going on out in the world are really disaffirming the importance of the family.**

Those are just lies that are separating kids from the primary relationship in their lives. The most important people to protect and care for them are their parents. Parents have to do double work and help their children see, "You know what? Mom and Dad are actually not hateful. They're not toxic. They love me a lot. They care about me."

One way you can do that is by trying to shift the focus a little bit away from the transgender identity issue and focus on things you can do with your kids. If your child has an activity that he or she loves, try to do it with them: take them roller skating, take a cooking class with them, try to establish that you are their friend. You are there for them more than the world is. Strengthen that relationship.

Erin Brewer (27:52):

What you said is so important because I've seen both ends where parents completely ignore the problem and think it will just go away on its own. I've also seen parents who have freaked out so much that they become incapacitated to build that relationship with their child. As you said, this is not something that's likely going to resolve in a couple of days, a week, a couple months, maybe not even for years.

So you have to steel yourself for the long haul. If you're in the middle of a crisis and just completely freaking out about this, then you're not going to be able to build that relationship with your child.

It's like when the bomb goes off, rather than like running away or just pretending like it's not there, you have to say, "Okay, this is a new reality that we have to deal with. I'm strong and I can handle this. I need to focus on my child because if I let myself freak out, I'm not going to be able to parent the child the way the child needs me to."

<u>Maria Keffler (28:54):</u>

It would be understandable to freak out. I don't want parents to feel like they're being judged, because this is a huge thing. Self-care and finding support for yourself is going to be so important. We're going to talk about that in a later episode, about how to get support for yourself, and to self-care as parents.

I know someone who found a good therapist for her child. (And we're going to talk in a later episode too about how to find a responsible therapist.) This therapist met with the child and then said to the parent, "I think your child's going to be fine. I think your child's going to come through this, but I think it's going to take longer than you're comfortable with."

<u>Erin Brewer (29:39):</u>

The next question that we have is, "I discovered my child's trans identity on her social media account, which she doesn't know I can see, but she hasn't come out to us yet. Should I bring it up with her or wait until she brings it up?" That's a great question.

<u>Maria Keffler (29:58):</u>

That's a tough one. My first gut reaction is to ask how important is it to you that your child doesn't know that you can see their social media. If you need to maintain that spy-hole there, so that you can keep an eye on social media with your child, then know that you're probably going to have a harder time bringing it up.

If you're willing to out yourself, you can say, "You know, I actually can see what's going on in your social media. I saw this and I'm concerned. Can you tell me more about this?"

The way you phrase it is always so important with kids. If you can ask more questions than you make statements, I think you're going to have a little bit more success, rather than coming to the child and saying, "Hey, I saw this on social media. What's going on?" But if you can just say, "I have to admit, I've been lurking on your social media. I saw this thing that I really don't understand. Can you tell me more about that?"

> **That's a good phrase to keep in your toolkit: "Can you tell me more about that?"**

That's a good phrase to keep in your toolkit: "Can you tell me more about that?"

Erin Brewer (31:10):

If you don't feel comfortable admitting it, then again, use those skills to start strengthening your relationship with your child, and start spending more time with them. Start asking general questions, because as you said, if you start asking questions and you have a good solid relationship with your child, they might start opening up to you and then you don't have to out yourself.

There are two approaches here and it just depends on how you think your child's going to react. I know that some children will completely freak out if they feel like their parents have been spying on them. It could really undermine the relationship as well. And as you said, you might lose the insights that you're getting from lurking on that social media.

There are other children who might be like, "I had no idea. Let me tell you about this."

Part of it is just judging your child and figuring out how they're going to react, because what you want to do here is build that relationship. So you want to move forward with that. If you think that outing yourself is going to undermine your ability to do that, then you might want to think of some other strategies.

Maria Keffler (32:21):

Another thing that's important to keep in mind, especially during adolescent and teen years, is that it can really feel like your kids hate you and want nothing to do with you. They're good at communicating that, but that's not the truth. They want a relationship with their parents. They want to feel cared for. They want to feel known. They want to feel seen. And just like with small children, they need the discipline. They need the authority. They need the watching. It provides them a sense of safety.

Older kids do too, and sometimes even more, because they feel themselves moving out of the den and into the forest and that can freak

> **It can feel like your kids hate you and want nothing to do with you. They're really good at communicating that, but that's not the truth. They want a relationship with their parents. They want to feel cared for, known, and seen.**

them out. They can go in five minutes from, "I am an adult and I am in charge of my destiny and I need no help," to "I just want my mom to tuck me in and make cocoa." That's part of what's so hard for teenagers—they're flipping back and forth between those things.

But at the end of the day, they want relationship with their parents. They want to be known. They want to be seen. They want to be loved and cared for. I think keeping that goal in mind means asking, "What will this do to my child's relationship with me? Will this improve it? Or will this damage it?" That will help guide a lot in your decision-making. You may be the only one who is going to save your child from going down a unhealthy path.

I'm sorry to say that you're probably going to be alone in this for a while until you find some other support, and some other gender-critical people (those who are questioning the gender narrative) to support you on this.

You are going to have to steel yourself. You're going to have to get ready for some opposition, and you're going to have to be ready to just make a stand for your child, and say, "This is what I'm going to do with my child to protect him or her."

Erin Brewer (34:22):

There are resources out there. I'll list some in the description of this video. One of them is Advocates Protecting Children. If you go to our website, there's a lot of information there.

There's support out there. You just have to work to find it.

Maria Keffler (34:51):

In our next episode, we're going to talk about having some of those conversations with your child. We're going to talk about validation and invalidation as well as critical thinking, and how to approach this in a way that affirms your child's feelings, but does not affirm wrong thinking, and how to approach that as, as a parent, having those conversations with your child.

Erin Brewer (35:16):

I want to end this just by giving parents hope. We've given a lot of information. Some of it's disturbing and maybe scary, but there is hope.

Maria Keffler (35:27):

You need help. You need support and you need a roadmap. We're in the business of trying to write some road maps.

Episode 1 Resource List

If Your Child Says S/he Is Transgender:
https://arlingtonparentcoa.wixsite.com/arlingtonparentcoa/if-your-child-says-s-he-s-transgend

Parents of ROGD Kids: https://www.parentsofrogdkids.com/

Compassion Coalition:
https://www.facebook.com/groups/507342576879277

Parent Guide, Understanding the Transgender Issue:
https://genderresourceguide.com/

Sasha Ayad, Inspired Teen Therapy: https://inspiredteentherapy.com/

Episode 2: Facts vs. Feelings: Validation/Invalidation/Critical Thinking?

https://youtu.be/tNM7SaDA1ag

Maria Keffler (00:04):

Today's topic is facts vs. feelings, validation, invalidation, and critical thinking.

Erin Brewer (00:12):

I want to preface what we're going to talk about by saying that this isn't going to be easy. I know a lot of times people say, "Just validate their feelings. Just do this, just do that." They make it seem like a very easy thing to do, but this takes practice.

As human beings, we're going to make mistakes. Parents aren't perfect. We're going to get into some ideas about how to help validate your child's feelings if he or she come to you and say he or she is transgender.

I also just want to let you know that this is going to take practice and you're not going to get it right the first time or maybe the second time. But this is how you start to build a relationship with your child and understand the feelings that are motivating gender confusion.

Maria Keffler (01:05):

It's imperative to start parsing out the difference between a feeling and a fact. You want to validate feelings. Feelings are never wrong. Feelings just *are*. They work like red flags to let you know, "Hey, I'm uncomfortable. Something feels wrong here. I need to figure out why." Or, "This feels great. I really like this. I want more of this."

So that's the purpose of feelings. Feelings themselves are never wrong. They're something that you need to look at and ask yourself, "Okay, why am I feeling this? Am I creating an appropriate response to this feeling?"

Whereas facts are facts. Facts are things that we know are true, that we know are real. Facts are either right or wrong. And unfortunately, in our society today, we have gotten into a postmodernist philosophical era where the postmodernists would say, "There's no such thing as ultimate truth. All truth is truth. Your truth is true and my truth is true. Everybody has truth. And there's no such thing as truth."

One of the best apologists that I ever heard talking about postmodern theory said, "If someone tells you there's no such thing as truth, they're asking you not to believe them." In other words, that can't be a true statement if there's no such thing as truth.

> ## "If someone tells you there's no such thing as truth, they're asking you not to believe them."

There is truth. There are facts. To figure out where you should validate a child and where you should correct a child's thinking you have to be able to parse those things out.

Erin Brewer (02:54):

I have a question about that. If your daughter comes to you and says, "Mom, I'm a boy." And you say, "Well, let's go get you a genetic test to find out," is that going to be an effective way of addressing that? Just to show her the fact that she is actually a girl?

Maria Keffler (03:14):

I don't think it will be. It *should* be because sex is biological. Sex is factual. We have chromosomes which determine our sexual identity as male or female.

But unfortunately the gender industry has substituted that word, "gender" for sex. Gender is a word that is a linguistic term. It applies to nouns in certain languages. But it's been co-opted into this gender ideology and is being conflated with sex.

So gender ideologists will tell you, "It doesn't matter what your body says. It matters what you think and feel inside." So even if that genetic test comes back and says "XX chromosomes—there's no deviation and there's nothing unusual about you," the child will probably still say—because she has been taught to say—"It doesn't matter what my body is saying. It matters what I feel inside."

That's why it's so important to be able to differentiate between feelings and facts. Does that make sense?

Erin Brewer (04:33):

Definitely. So if you try to fix somebody's feelings with facts, it sounds like that's not going to work.

Maria Keffler (04:41):

I don't think so, because feelings are not the same as facts, and feelings can absolutely fly in the face of facts, which is what's happening with gender ideology.

My feelings are that I'm not exactly like a girl or I'm not exactly like a boy. It's based so much on stereotypes—these harmful, regressive stereotypes about what it means to be a girl or what it means to be a boy.

So your feelings just can fly in the face of that, but it is important to recognize people's feelings to validate: "I can see why you would feel that way. You're a boy who really likes music and who really likes dancing and who maybe loves the color pink. Other boys and the rest of society are telling you, 'That's not cool. Boys like football. Boys like playing in the mud and playing with cars and no boy wears pink.'"

Those are all stereotypes. Those are all cultural stereotypes. But this boy is caught in those. He's hearing from society, "You're not okay the way you are. Boys are not like you."

That's powerful and that's confusing and that's scary, because you're always comparing yourself, for better or for worse, to what's going on around you, and what people around you are telling you. So it's important to validate that child's feelings: "I can see why you would feel that way. People are telling you it's wrong for a boy to like painting. People are telling you that boys are not dancers."

Now, you can bring up some facts while you're validating those feelings.

I have a male cousin who is a ballet dancer. He runs his own studio. I can bring up to that point. "You know my cousin? He's a dancer, but he's a man and he's very comfortable being a man. So being a dancer doesn't mean you can't be a man."

But it's still important to say, "I understand why you feel that way. I see what you're saying. Those feelings are real."

Erin Brewer (07:00):

That's the key to this. So often there are just profound, underlying feelings when a child comes and says they're transgender, and parents need to figure out a way to delve down into those feelings so that they can understand what's motivating this identity.

We're going to segue now to some role modeling that Maria and I did to show you the difference between dismissing a child's feelings versus validating a child's feelings.

INVALIDATING FEELINGS

Erin Brewer [playing Daughter] (07:32):

Mom, I just don't look like the other girls. I look like a boy.

Maria Keffler [playing Mom] (07:37):

That's ridiculous. You do not look like a boy. You're beautiful.

Erin Brewer (07:43):

You just don't get it.

Maria Keffler (07:45):

Yes, I do. I felt the same way when I was your age.

Erin Brewer (07:51):

Things just aren't the same now, Mom. Social media and everything. It's just different.

Maria Keffler (07:58):

We had teen magazines and TV shows. It's no harder today than it was when I was a kid.

Erin Brewer (08:05):

You just don't get it.

VALIDATING FEELINGS

Erin Brewer (08:06):

Mom, I don't look like the other girls. I'm a boy.

Maria Keffler (08:12):

What you're telling me is that you don't like the way you look. You don't feel like you look right. Tell me more about that.

Erin Brewer (08:20):

I have big bones and an ugly face. I just don't look like these other girls. They're pretty and soft and gentle. I'm just a big clunky thing.

Maria Keffler (08:34):

It sounds like when you compare yourself to the other girls, you feel like you come up short? Is that right?

Erin Brewer (08:41):

Yeah. My friends like Hannah and Josie, they're so pretty. They are lovely and they're popular and everybody likes them and people tease me.

Maria Keffler (08:55):

That sounds like it must be really hurtful if people tease you.

Erin Brewer (08:59):

It is, Mom. I'm just different from all the other girls.

Maria Keffler (09:04):

Well, you are different than some of the other girls. That's true, but isn't it okay that not all girls are the same? I mean, what about Sarah? She's into karate and she's into cars, right?

Erin Brewer (09:20):

Yeah.

Maria Keffler (09:21):

But just because she's into things that are a little different than other girls are into, that doesn't mean she's not a girl. Does it?

Erin Brewer (09:28):

No, she's definitely a girl.

Maria Keffler (09:31):

Yeah. This is a hard thing to be dealing with. Is there anything that I can do to help?

Erin Brewer (09:38):

I don't know. I think talking helps. Thanks, Mom.

Maria Keffler (09:42):

I'm glad. Anytime you need to talk, I'm happy to talk with you.

Maria Keffler (09:46):

We did two scenes. The first one was where the mom invalidated the daughter. Invalidation—as you saw in the video—is telling a child or other person, "Your feelings are wrong." That's the heart of invalidation. If somebody says, "You're too sensitive. You need to stop being so sensitive. No, that's not reality. People weren't mean to you. You're just being overly sensitive," those are invalidation. It's telling someone their feelings are wrong.

If a child grows up with a lot of invalidation, they learn not to trust their feelings. They learn that they cannot trust that what they're feeling reflects reality. That sets them up for some dangerous situations. If they're in an abusive relationship with a boyfriend or a girlfriend—

Let's say it's a girl. She comes to her mom and says, "Wow. John was really mean to me today. He told me my outfit was ugly." Then the mom just invalidates that and says, "Well, your outfit is kind of ugly. I mean, he was just telling you the truth."

That completely rejects, negates, and doesn't deal with the fact that John was *rude*. When someone is rude, it hurts. That feeling needs to be recognized, because honestly, when your child comes to you with hurt, your first instinct as a parent is to get rid of the hurt, to take that pain away. Invalidating the feelings isn't going to take away that hurt.

> **When your child comes to you hurt, your first instinct as a parent is to get rid of the hurt. But invalidating the feelings isn't going to take away that hurt.**

But that's what the mom in the role play tried to do. She said, "That's ridiculous." The daughter said, "I don't look like I should. I look like a boy." And mom said, "That's ridiculous. You don't look like a boy."

Saying "That's ridiculous" tells the child, "What you're feeling is stupid." That's an invalidating statement.

"You don't look like a boy." That's tough because the mom really may think, "You don't look like a boy, and you're being ridiculous." But it might be better for the mom to say, "Gosh, I don't think you looked like a boy. Tell me why you think you look like a boy." Turn it back to the child. "I don't understand this, but tell me more about it."

When the daughter said, "You just don't get it." Mom said, "Yes, I do."

That ignores and invalidates the daughter's feeling of not being heard. The daughter already doesn't trust that the mom knows what's going on.

A better thing to say might be, "Gosh, I'm trying to understand. I want to understand." That would validate the child's feelings. Then the last thing the moms said was, "It's no harder today than when I was young."

I'm not sure that's true.

Erin Brewer (12:36):

It doesn't matter does it?

Maria Keffler (12:39):

No, it's not about the mom. It's about the child. As parents we need to put away our own perspective on things and really listen to the child. It's so important.

Erin Brewer (12:52):

That's so interesting what you said, because a lot of times parents feel uncomfortable with validating a child's feelings, because they're afraid that when they validate a child's feelings, they're telling that child that their feelings are accurate. They fear that they're validating this gender identity that the child has taken on. They're afraid to do that.

Instead, they want to show the child why their child is wrong, why that identity is harmful or unhelpful, or somehow the result of underlying feelings.

Can you address the fact that validating somebody's feelings doesn't mean that you're telling them that their feelings are accurate?

Maria Keffler (13:32):

I have a story that captures this really well.

Mom was talking with her daughter, and the daughter indicated that she thought she was non-binary or transgender. The mom and daughter were talking about why the daughter felt that way.

At one point the daughter said, "You don't believe me. You don't believe anything that I'm feeling."

I loved what the mom said. She said, "You know, I think this is a lot like if someone in Wisconsin said, 'I feel so terrible. I've got a headache and a fever and I'm tired. And my body aches,' and all of that person's friends said, 'Dude, that's malaria. You've totally got malaria.'"

The daughter laughed. The mom said, "Yeah, that's kind of funny, right? Because a person in Wisconsin, what did he have probably?" And the daughter said, "He's got the flu. A person in Wisconsin with those symptoms probably has the flu."

Then the mom said, "I think this is the same way with you. I totally believe that you're feeling everything you're feeling. People around you are telling you that those feelings mean you're transgender. I think what they mean is you have adolescence with a touch of autism."

So that separates the feelings from the facts because you can misinterpret the facts through the lens of your feelings. Your feelings are not wrong. Your interpretation of the facts is wrong.

A lot of us grew up with invalidation and now we're trying to learn how to validate. It can feel very scripted. Even when I go into a conversation with my kids, if I'm thinking, "All right, I need to validate," it can feel fake. It can feel like *(speaking slowly and robotically)*, "I can see why you are feeling that way. Tell me more."

But those words are so affirming and so life-giving.

Do recognize that even if it feels fake and scripted to you, it still has a lot of power.

Erin Brewer (15:36):

Yes, definitely.

We're going to watch a video now that talks a little bit more about how this process works. One of the things that is important, that Naomi talks about in this video, is clearing your own feelings. One of the problems that parents get into when they're trying to validate their children's feelings is they haven't cleared out their own feelings. It's hard to do that. I would suggest practicing it a lot in safer, simpler situations. Because if your feelings are out on the surface, then it's hard to get through your feelings to get to your child's feelings.

Naomi Feil (16:20):

I learned about validation through listening and empathy. You feel what that person feels, even though you're not going through what they're going through. You feel with them, not just for them. And then with empathy, the validation techniques almost always work.

So how do you get empathy? Now I have to take my feelings and put them away and then center myself, which is a way of breathing. So you take all your own feelings and get rid of them, and you're then like an empty vessel. You can take in the feelings of the other person.

Then I learned to rephrase; rephrasing is exquisite listening. How does that person talk? Is it fast? Is it slow? What is the pitch? What is the tempo? And then you say what that person has said in a question: "Is that what you're asking? Is this what you mean?"

> **Rephrasing is exquisite listening. How does that person talk? Is it fast? Slow? What is the pitch? What is the tempo? Then you say what that person has said in a question: "Is that what you're asking? Is this what you mean?"**

Erin Brewer (17:18):

I love these insights from Naomi. I feel like she's just captured some of the importance of validating feelings, Maria.

Maria Keffler (17:27):

It's a great video. I recommend that everyone look it up. We'll have it in the resources at the end of this video. It's Naomi Feil, and the whole video is a great explanation of validation.

I loved one of the things that she said in it: "Don't lie." Don't lie to the person that you're talking to. Getting caught in a lie really can damage your relationship with somebody, and lies are not ultimately helpful. Lies don't heal things, and they don't improve things. So when you are sharing with your daughter or your son or listening to them don't say things that you know aren't true: "I know exactly how you feel." No, you probably don't.

Erin Brewer (18:17):

What if your child came up and said, "You don't believe me, do you?" which is what a lot of these kids are coached to do, get in their parents' face, to insist that the parents accept them or to push back on it.

That's a pretty difficult situation for a parent to be in because, they've got a very aggressive, very determined child who's getting right in their face and saying, "You don't believe me. Do you?"

Maria Keffler (18:45):

Again, in that situation, focusing on the difference between the feelings and the facts will help, because you can say like that mom who used the analogy about the sick person in Wisconsin, "I absolutely believe that you are feeling everything you're feeling. I absolutely believe that you're struggling with this. I absolutely believe this is hard. I know you're suffering. I do not believe some of the things that transgender ideology is saying are true. I don't believe that there is research support to back this up. If you find some of that, you bring it to me and if I'm wrong, I'll change my opinion. But from what I have seen so far, and from what my research tells me, I don't believe that what you're being taught is true, but I absolutely believe that what you're feeling is true."

Erin Brewer (19:40):

This would be an opportunity to teach critical thinking skills, which is something that doesn't happen in the schools as much as it used to. Schools are focused on feelings. They often suggest that feelings are truth, which is a little bit dangerous, because we can go down all kinds of scary rabbit holes if we teach kids that their feelings are fact, which is why it's important to be able to parse out the two.

Maria Keffler (20:07):

Unfortunately schools are now in the business of teaching kids *what* to think rather than *how* to think. And so critical thinking is something that we've really lost the ability to do in the culture.

It's so valuable and it starts with asking yourself, "What does this sentence mean?" What does this word mean?

When your child says to you, "I'm living my authentic life," ask, "What do you mean by authentic? What does authentic mean to you?"

"Well, it means I'm being who I am."

"Okay. Who are you?"

"I am a male trapped in a female body."

"How do you know that what you feel is true? Because sometimes I feel angry when I'm driving and I have a momentary thought that I would very much like to crash my car into the side of the car in front of me. I really want to do that. That's a feeling, should I pursue that feeling?"

Erin Brewer (21:18):

Would that make you authentic?

Maria Keffler (21:21):

Right. That's a good question.

Erin Brewer (21:27):

Maria, when should you validate a child's feelings, versus help them to develop critical thinking skills?

Maria Keffler (21:35):

That's a good question. So much of navigating a relationship is having that nuanced sense of, "What does this relationship need right now? What does this person need right now?"

A good rule of thumb; when your child is talking about feelings, validate the feelings. When the child starts talking about statements of fact, then address those statements of fact and start applying some critical thinking skills to those.

> **A good rule of thumb is: When your child is talking about feelings, validate the feelings.**
> **When the child starts talking about statements of fact, then address those statements of fact and start applying some critical thinking skills to those.**

One of the gender industry's favorite phrases is, "Let the child lead," and what they mean by that is just do everything the child wants. In other words, don't ever tell the child, "No."

That's not what I mean by following your child's lead. But in a conversation, when you are trying to listen to someone who's having a struggle, when you're trying to understand what's going on, let that person lead.

Naomi Feil talks in the video about empathizing and about reflecting. Those are powerful things. In the validation role-play that you and I did at one point was when I rephrased what you said. I said, "It sounds like you're saying that you don't think you look like other girls."

That feels mechanical. That feels fake to just repeat what somebody else said, but it's surprising how often you get that wrong.

Often you hear something just a little bit different than the speaker said it. By reflecting it back, you give the speaker the opportunity either say, "Yes, you heard me. Thank you for listening," or, "Oh no, that's not what I meant by that."

So follow that person's train of thought, and listen actively the whole time and ask yourself, "Is this a feeling that they're communicating to me, or is this a fact that I need to address with some critical thinking skills? Is this a true fact or not?"

Erin Brewer (23:38):

That's so important. One of the things that I want to warn parents about is that kids are not learning these skills at school. We touched on it a little bit—not only are they not learning critical thinking skills, they're being taught things that are not true. There are "experts" who go into the schools and tell children that they get to choose what gender they are.

They're also conflating sex and gender. They're suggesting that if you feel like you're a boy and you're a girl, then you are a boy, that your feelings dictate fact.

This is a very confusing place to be as a child. At school, where you're supposed to be getting facts, you're getting feelings. That undermines your critical thinking skills, it undermines your instincts, it undermines your reality. That is so confusing.

It compounds the child's confusion, because they already have these feelings of not fitting in, of having this gender confusion. That's compounded by the fact that they're getting a lot of misinformation, and damaging information, from schools now. Most parents don't have any clue this is going on.

Maria Keffler (24:56):

It is so insidious for a child to be taught something that's not true, and to be taught that by trusted adults. It's just been in the last five years that the gender industry has actively gotten into the public schools via the National Education Association (NEA), via the school boards, via a lot of activists, and via teachers who are coming out of college and actively selling lies to students throughout the day.

This happened in the middle school in my district. A school counselor came into an English class and gave a presentation on gender harassment in a core class. This wasn't even in the family life program. This was a core class in English. There was a boy in the class who knew that his parents were not on board with this, and they would not want him listening to this. This seventh-grade boy raised his hand and asked to be excused to go to the bathroom. But the counselor would not let him leave until after he'd watched the video.

That was incredibly smart and mature of this boy to recognize. And he went home and told his parents about it.

But this is what's happening. Kids are not even allowed to excuse themselves from this.

It's so important that parents know this is happening. The schools are not benign. They are not neutral. Public schools are actively teaching this, with the support and the encouragement and the money and the resources of the gender industry.

We have a couple of questions. The first one is, "My son constantly tells me I don't and can't understand. How do I deal with him shutting down the conversation before it even starts?"

Erin Brewer (26:54):

That is such a good question because sometimes kids just put up a wall, and if you don't completely 100% agree with them, they don't even want to engage with you. So what do you do in that situation?

Maria Keffler (27:07):

I was going to ask you.

Erin Brewer (27:11):

Usually, when a child is dug in, it's not a good time to try and address this. So generally I try to do something else: do an activity, do something to build our relationship, rather than trying to address it then. Maybe even say, "You're right, I don't understand this. I need some time to think about this. I love you. I want to be there for you, but I need some time to process." I think that's okay to do.

Maria Keffler (27:46):

Great. I love that. It's so easy as a parent to escalate things. Your child says, "You don't understand," then you insist that you do, so the child gets mad, then you get mad.

I love what you suggested. You said, "This is just not a good time to address that." And I love just saying, "You're right. I don't understand."

That's so engaging with the child to think that they have something that their parent doesn't understand. They may be completely wrong that the parent doesn't understand, but they have that feeling like, "I can teach my parents something."

You can say also, "Let's talk about this later. You think about what you want to tell me. I'm going to think about what I want to know. And maybe we can sit down later, because I really want to understand."

Erin Brewer (28:33):

Depending on how upset the kid is. If the child is angry and clearly doesn't want to talk with you, I don't think it's worth trying to push the conversation. But if they're just pushing back a little bit, you can always just say, "I don't understand. Can you tell me about it?" That allows them an opportunity to talk. Usually when people are allowed an opportunity to talk, it's hard for them to talk and be so angry at the same time.

Maria Keffler (29:04):

Here's another good strategy. If you have other adults in your sphere that you trust, you can always offer to the child, "Would you like to talk with Aunt Susie about this?"

> **If you have other adults in your sphere that you trust, you can always offer to the child, "Would you like to talk with Aunt Susie about this?"**

Sometimes, frankly, your relationship with your child has gotten so tangled, it's not as good as it should be. Maybe there's been trust broken, and the child is not in a position to receive from you. That's a really good time, if you have trusted adults—aunts, uncles, grandparents, good friends—to say, "Hey, would you like to talk to this other person? Maybe they can help with this."

Erin Brewer (29:46):

Each situation is different and parents have to know that there are different options. There's the strategy to try to validate the child. There's the, "Can we talk about this later?" option. There's the strategy of giving them some resources. So there are many options.

The one option you don't want to do is escalate: "Of course, I understand you" invalidates the child and it also escalates the intensity of it. Studies have shown that when people are angry, they can't think clearly.

Also, boys and girls take a different amount of time to calm down. Boys typically take a lot longer. So if you have a son who's angry, he's going to need maybe up to an hour to calm down before he's able to engage.

Often, as parents, we want to fix it right now. But that's not always the best solution, because if you have a child who's completely emotional, and just angry, that child is not a child who's going to be able to hear what you're saying.

Maria Keffler (30:54):

One other little thing that I want to offer parents, that I've found really useful, is asking a child in a calm moment—not in that escalating moment, but asking at a calm time—"What do you want? What do you want to have happen here?"

Often we're not asked that even as adults. People don't ask us what we want. Other people tell us what they want, and we've got to decide what to do with that. But being asked, "What do you want to see happen here?" — I've never had an experience where a child did not take that seriously and think about it. Often the child realizes it is ridiculous as it's coming out.

One time I was very, very angry, but I had learned, "Ask yourself what you want when you're angry." The cat had thrown up when we were trying to get out the door on a trip, and I was just yelling at the cat and then cleaning it up. I asked myself, "What do I want? I want the cat not to have thrown up!" Then I thought, "I don't have a time machine. I can't go back. That's ridiculous."

Hearing it come out of your own mouth, you can go, "Oh yeah, that's really ridiculous."

Erin Brewer (32:06):

Sometimes the kids don't even know what they want. They just have these feelings bubbling up and they don't know. So asking them can help them think, "Well, what do I want?" They may not even know. It's good to give them an opportunity to reflect on that.

Maria Keffler (32:22):

We've got one more question. This is about invalidation. The mom asks, "I grew up with a lot invalidation. How do I stop the cycle from repeating in my family?"

Erin Brewer (32:36):

It is hard because we learn from our families of origin. Sometimes we have to work hard to break out of negative patterns.

It helps to practice, even during simple opportunities that aren't high stress, that aren't emotionally charged. Use those opportunities to practice these skills, and then they become more second-nature, and you're able to draw on them when you're in a more emotionally charged situation.

Maria Keffler (33:06):

Great advice.

If your child gets up in the morning and says, "I'm still tired. I'm really tired," you can practice validation and go, "It sounds like you didn't sleep well. Is that what you're telling me? What happened?"

That's such a great idea to practice those skills, listening to what you say.

Very often we don't hear ourselves. Try to actively listen to what you're saying and ask yourself, "Did I just invalidate my child or my spouse or my friend?" Practice, practice, practice.

Erin Brewer (33:44):

I have to say the person who asked this, I have a lot of hope for them because they've recognized that they had these negative patterns. A lot of people don't realize that they're carrying forward negative patterns that they learned as a child. So just recognizing it is a big step.

That is another word of wisdom I would give to parents: as you said, listen to yourself when you're engaging with your child and determine, "Is this moving us forward? Or maybe I'm repeating a pattern that I learned when I was a child."

Maria Keffler (34:22):

The other thing you can do is ask the people around you. This will be very disarming for a child. If you say to your child, "Do I invalidate you? Do I make you feel like I'm not listening to you?" You might not always get exactly the answer you were hoping for, but you might get some truth there.

I don't want to belabor the point, but before my husband and I had kids, when we would take road trips, whoever was not driving would often read a book to the other person. One time I was in the passenger seat reading this book—I don't remember what it was, but it was a psychology self-help. I got to the section on passive-aggressiveness.

I never thought I was passive-aggressive. It never would have occurred to me to think so. But then I read, "Passive-aggressive people will be dismissive and say, 'Never mind, it doesn't matter. No, no, I'm fine'."

As I read that, I thought, "That's me."

It is hard to see those things in yourself, but ask the people around you, because they'll tell you the truth.

Erin Brewer (35:28):

Sometimes the truth is hard to hear. But in this situation, it's so important for us to rebuild our relationships with our kids if they've been fractured because a child's come home with a transgender identity. If you're just at the start of building those relationships and making them stronger, it's going to do so much good in helping work with your child through this, so he or she doesn't go down that harmful path of medically transitioning and being medicalized for life. The stakes here are high and it's worth the effort.

I will post links to sources for some things to help support parents who are going through this. If you've watched this and you're feeling like, "Well, I need more," just check out the description below and we'll post some links for you.

Episode 2 Resource List

Validation, communication through empathy, Naomi Feil:
https://youtu.be/ESqfW_kyZq8

What is Invalidation? 5 Things You Shouldn't Say:
https://drjamielong.com/validation-5-things-not-to-say/

Understanding Validation: A Way to Communicate Acceptance:
https://www.psychologytoday.com/us/blog/pieces-mind/201204/understanding-validation-way-communicate-acceptance

7 Ways to Improve Your Critical Thinking Skills:
https://collegeinfogeek.com/improve-critical-thinking-skills/

Episode 3: Boundaries: Setting Them & Enforcing Them

https://youtu.be/W2YKagwtenc

Erin Brewer (00:52):

Boundaries is a big topic. I know from my own experience that sometimes you can have boundaries that are just right, but sometimes you can have boundaries that are too soft and you get pushed in ways that are uncomfortable. You can also have boundaries that are so firm and like a brick wall, that they impede your ability to communicate with other people and to work on relationships.

There's a sweet spot that you're aiming for.

A lot of times kids who come home with these gender issues, and announce that they have a transgender identity, are pushing parent's boundaries in a way that is very uncomfortable. They demand things that the parents are not comfortable doing. Parents sometimes bend over and give into the demands of kids.

But sometimes they put up that brick wall and say, "Absolutely nothing, I'm not going to do anything that you want me to do."

Trying to negotiate that is important. There probably is not a one-size-fits-all answer, but let's talk a little bit about boundaries and how they can help you when your child comes home with an announcement that you're uncomfortable with.

Maria Keffler (02:08):

It's important too, that we start out with a definition. I'm not sure if everybody really knows what boundaries are or why they're important. I know I didn't really grow up thinking or talking about boundaries, but I've read a couple of wonderful books on boundaries, by Cloud and Townsend. They have two books: one is *Boundaries* and the other is *Boundaries with Kids*. These books are so helpful at teaching you what boundaries are and how to set them up.

Boundaries are like a fence around your property. The fence says, "This is mine and that is yours. Here is where my stuff and myself ends and where yourself and your stuff begins."

There can be boundaries around any number of aspects of your life. You can have time boundaries—how much time you will give to something?

You can have property boundaries—how much are you willing to loan your things out, share things? You can have emotional boundaries-- how much emotional energy do I have to give to somebody else's problems?

Figuring those things out is a very personal, but I have found that as you establish boundaries, you have so much more freedom.

I come from a background of being a people-pleaser. I wanted to make everybody happy. If somebody asked me for something, I would bend over backwards to give it, because I thought if they're asking, they really need it. I want to give that to them.

But I came to a place in my life where I found that I was really being a doormat. I had hoped that if I gave what other people asked of me, then when I asked for something, they would give what I needed. But I wasn't always finding that to be the case.

I had a boundaries coach for a while. She was a good friend of mine who has really firm boundaries. I told her, "I don't know how to say 'no.' I don't know how to put a boundary down." I would call her if somebody asked me for something.

Somebody emailed me and said, "Can you do this for me?" and I really didn't want to do it. I called my friend. "This person asked me to do this. I don't want to do it." My friend said, "That's ridiculous. No, that's not something you need to spend your time on." I asked, "How do I say no?" And she said, "Just write back and say, 'I'm sorry, that's not going to work for me. I can't do that.'"

Erin Brewer (04:54):

Really? It's just that easy? I can say that?

Maria Keffler (04:58):

Yes, you can. It gives you an incredible amount of freedom when you learn how to start setting those boundaries, because you know how much you have to give, you know how far you're willing to go.

I've also found people respect your time, your energy and your resources much more when you respect them too.

Erin Brewer (05:17):

One of the things about boundaries that your friend touched on that is important is some people will say, "I'd like to, but I'm busy or I just have too much to do. I'd like to, but..." One of the things about good boundaries is that you don't have to make these excuses. You get to just say, "No, that's not something I'm going to do." That's okay. It's okay just to say, "No."

One of the things that's happening with the transgender movement is they're pushing people's boundaries. Not just parents' boundaries, but social boundaries. They're insisting that people address them in a certain way and treat them a certain way.

They're pushing into spaces that typically have boundaries around them, such as safe space for women: locker rooms, bathrooms, overnight accommodations, prisons. These spaces that have typically had very clear boundaries about who gets to go in them.

The transgender movement is trying to break those down and tell us that *we're* not okay if we want to stand up for those boundaries.

The hardest thing about setting up boundaries is having people say, "You're mean," or "You're hateful," or "You're not a nice person," if you stand up for your boundaries.

Maria Keffler (06:37):

That's true. That's a good point about how the gender industry is trying to break down boundaries.

Boundaries are healthy things. Boundaries are there for protection for the person inside the boundary, and also to some extent for the person outside the boundary.

> **Boundaries are healthy things.**
> **Boundaries are there for protection for the person inside the boundary, and also to some extent for the person outside the boundary.**

When it comes into your own house and it's your own child who's demanding a new name, that child is rejecting the name that you as a parent gave them. That's a painful thing because Moms and Dads, when they're pregnant, usually spend a lot of time working on, "What are we going to name this child?" Lots of names are family names that have meaning—they're not chosen willy-nilly. Historically it is a parent's right and privilege to give their child a name.

One of the hurtful things about the gender ideology is that child is telling the parents, "I reject that. I reject not only who I am—my physical body—but I reject you as having the authority to name me."

I hear people say, "Well, it's just a name. Why is that a big deal?" Words are important and family relationships are important. I see that particular boundary of rejecting the name that the parents gave you as a really hurtful way of saying, "I reject you. I reject your authority."

Erin Brewer (08:11):

The other boundary that parents run into is with pronouns. Kids will come home and they'll insist that their parents address them by the wrong pronouns.

Kids can be incredibly rude and insistent that parents and others use the pronouns that they want. If a parent doesn't do that, the child can be really disrespectful to that parent.

Again, that's another boundary where I hear parents say, "I love my child so much, and I don't want this conflict, but this is a boundary for me. I'm not willing to lie about my child's pronouns."

Maria Keffler (08:48):

I know one set of parents who are faith-based—they're Christian—and they said to their child, "My faith does not allow me to believe that your brain can be a different gender than your body. I don't believe that because of my faith. So you are asking me to do something that says God is wrong. I have to either choose to offend you or to offend God. And I'm afraid with that calculus, I'm going to have to offend you rather than offending God."

Erin Brewer (09:35):

I've heard other parents who aren't religious say, "Science is really important to me and you are asking me to ignore basic biology here and accept what you're saying. This is something that's really important to me because if I decide to reject facts and to reject science, then there's nothing for me to hold on to."

For both religious parents and non-religious parents, this can be a big issue.

Then there are parents who the kid comes home and says, "I want you to do this, this, and this," and the parents say, "Okay." They just roll over and let the child rule the roost. And that can be harmful.

Maria Keffler (10:22):

It really can. Parents are parents for a reason. Parents have more life experience. Our brains have finished developing. But, if our children are younger than 25, their brains have not finished developing. One of the last areas of the brain to develop is the one that deals with long-term consequences, risk-taking behavior, and understanding how what you do impacts you in the long-term. That's the last part of the brain to develop. So kids have parents to set boundaries around them.

I'm going to tell a story about my son when he was little, like two or three years old. Most kids, when you take them to the park, they see the playground equipment, run to it, and play on the playground equipment.

Not my son. I could only take him to a park that had a closed fence around it, because he wanted to explore and to run. I'd take him into the playground, and he would run the perimeter of the fence, trying to find the way out. Only after he realized there was no way out would he be like, "All right, I guess I'll play." Then he'd go to the equipment.

That's a very natural thing. We all want to push those boundaries and see how far we can go. But we know that boundaries are there to keep kids safe. As parents, we should not abdicate our responsibility to protect our kids, just to keep some tenuous sense of peace in the house.

Erin Brewer (12:00):

The story about your son is so interesting because we know that young children push boundaries, which is why we talk about the terrible-twos. One of the things they're doing a lot of times during the terrible-twos is pushing physical boundaries. They're trying to determine what their capabilities are, and what's safe and what's not safe.

The other time they're pushing boundaries is during adolescence, because they're growing up and they know they're going to have to go out there in the world. They're trying to figure out how to interact in the world in a way that makes sense to them. They will push and push and push, and they need something to push back on, because if there isn't something to push against, they just keep going.

> **The other time they're pushing boundaries is during adolescence, because they're growing up and they know they're going to have to go out there in the world. They're trying to figure out how to interact in the world in a way that makes sense to them.**

That's how my childhood was. I grew up in a home where there were no boundaries. I look back on it and I think, "What the heck?" At one point when I woke up—I was a teenager—there were cigarettes in the ash tray.

There was booze in the room and there was a boy who was sleeping over. That was all okay with my parents because there were no boundaries.

Kids need those boundaries because they'll just keep pushing and pushing and pushing until they come upon something that stops them. So as hard as it is to have those boundaries and to have children pushing against them and having to push back, they're really important.

Maria Keffler (13:15):

Parenting is not for cowards. Parenting is hard work. Those are two of the most difficult times when you're parenting: toddlerhood and adolescence.

I heard somebody say once—and after raising three kids into the teen years, I think it's true—that who your child was as a toddler comes back when he or she is a teenager. Teenagers are basically just toddlers with better vocabularies.

Erin Brewer (13:47):

The stakes are much higher in a lot of cases because they do need a certain amount of freedom. You can't be a helicopter parent who doesn't let your kid do anything, because you're worried that they might get hurt. So you have to, as a parent, let them go out there into the world.

But then as you talked about in one of the episodes, your home is the den. It's the safe place, and where they come when they need comfort. Even though kids will push against boundaries, they find comfort in it—especially kids who have special needs: autism, mental health issues, or other underlying conditions that often motivate this development of a trans identity. Those kids especially need a safe place where they know what the rules are, and they know that you're going to enforce those rules. That's comforting to kids.

> **Kids especially need a safe place where they know what the rules are, and they know that you're going to enforce those rules. That's comforting to kids.**

Maria Keffler (14:40):

They may never admit that, and you as a parent may never see that at least until they're older and they're able to look back and say, "Wow, Mom and Dad. I really am grateful that you didn't let me have my way."

But when you're in the middle of it, and they're teenagers, they're probably not going to say, "Gosh, Mom and Dad, I'm really glad that you've set these boundaries, because they help me to feel safe in an unsafe world." Now they're going to rail at you. They're going to call you names. They're going to push as hard as they can. But you're right: we know from a basic understanding of child psychology that those boundaries do bring safety and they need those.

That's why it's so important, especially if you're at the beginning of this journey with a child who claims a transgender identity, to figure out what's important to you, and to figure out what boundaries you're going to set. And you need to think about both what you're comfortable with your own sense of boundaries, and also what's going to keep your child safe.

There are certain things with this that I might say are non-negotiable.

I would not allow a child to go down the medication path if there were any way to prevent that. I feel like that's a non-negotiable boundary with this.

Other boundaries are going to depend on you and your child. If you're co-parenting, it's best if both parents can be on the same page. It's really best if you can get all of the adults in the child's life on the same page.

Unfortunately, I can tell you now that's not going to happen, because the schools, and many people in the culture, are going to be working against you.

But in your family, get on the same page: Are you going to use the preferred pronouns? Are you going to allow a different name? I know one family told their child, "You can have that preferred name as a nickname. If your friends want to call you that, go right ahead. But your parents are not going to call you that. We're not going to have your grandparents call you that. This is who you are."

Some people have different comfort levels with that. Personally, I feel like truth is paramount, and you need to not agree with things that are not true. That's where my sense of boundaries would be in this situation.

Erin Brewer (17:19):

What you've said is so important, but I also think it might be confusing. So can you talk about the difference between validating a child, but also keeping your boundaries? Because what if a child says, "You don't love me because you're not calling me by my preferred pronouns. If you loved me, you would be doing that?"

<u>Maria Keffler (17:41):</u>

That's a good point.

In our last episode, we talked about validation versus invalidation, and facts versus feelings. It's important to keep that at the forefront of your mind. "Am I dealing with feelings? Am I dealing with facts?"

You can always validate feelings: "I understand you feel that this is hurtful. I understand that you're hurt. I understand that you want this."

But then you hold to the facts: "The fact is you are a female/male. I am not going to agree to lie about that. To me as a parent, it is not loving to lie. It is not supportive to tell someone something that isn't true. Love, to me, means always telling the truth, believing the best, keeping you safe and trying to find the path that's going to lead you into the most health and happiness in the long term. That might not feel nice to you. That might not feel like it's what you want, but I have a longer vision for your future than you have right now. This is what I believe is best for you."

<u>Erin Brewer (18:58):</u>

Maria, kids are good at manipulating their parents. One of the things that these kids are coached to do is to threaten suicide. How does a parent maintain their boundaries when a child is threatening to kill himself or herself?

<u>Maria Keffler (19:12):</u>

That's a good question. It's a difficult question. I don't think there's a quick, easy answer to that. I think we're going to address that in a future episode, and we're going to try to consult some experts on this. I really hate to get into that today because it is such a dicey, nuanced question.

<u>Erin Brewer (19:32):</u>

It is important just to keep in mind that kids have been coached on this. That's one of the most powerful ways to emotionally manipulate someone, because the stakes are so high, and that's why we want to get some experts to talk about this. But, again, it's important for parents to know that it's okay to have boundaries on something, even if somebody threatens suicide.

I've been in relationships where somebody has threatened suicide if I don't do what they want, and it's an incredibly difficult place to be. But at the same time, people need to know that somebody doesn't get to violate your boundaries by making threats. That's what this is.

So even if the worst possible outcome happens, it's not your fault for holding your boundaries. You get to do that. People can't use emotional manipulation to try and break your boundaries down.

Maria Keffler (20:31):

That's a great point.

We have a video clip from Brene Brown talking about boundaries.

> Brene Brown (20:42):
>
> What boundaries need to be in place for me to stay in my integrity and make the generous assumptions about you? We are not comfortable setting boundaries because we care more about what people will think, and we don't want to disappoint anyone. We want everyone to like us and boundaries are not easy, but I think they're the key to self-love. And I think they're the key to treating others with loving-kindness. Boundaries are fricking important and they're not fake walls. They're not separation. Boundaries are not division. They're respect.

Erin Brewer (21:16):

Interesting excerpt from Brene Brown. Clearly boundaries are important. But for people who aren't sure how to enforce them, what would you recommend?

Maria Keffler (21:27):

That's the tough part, isn't it? The first tough part is figuring out what boundaries you want to set, but then how do you enforce them?

That's a thing parents really need to figure out with their kids: "How am I going to enforce this boundary?"

One of the things you need to ask yourself is, "What do I have control over? What do I not have control over?"

Like the question of the preferred name—your child wants a different name. We mentioned earlier, the parents said, "Okay, at home, we're not going to call you that," because that parent wisely recognized that at home, they have control over that. But at school, they don't. So it would undercut the parent to try to say, "At school, nobody's allowed to call you that," because frankly, school's going to do what school is going to do. You don't have that control.

I do know of a situation where the child wrote the parent a note and said, "I will no longer be answering to my birth name. If someone calls me that, I will not respond." The parent wrote back and said, "That birth name is your legal name given to you by your parents, and it is what you will be called until you are old enough to change it legally. If you do not respond when you are spoken to, there will be consequences." That was the end of it, that it never came up again.

Erin Brewer (22:58):

Parents need to realize that there are consequences that can be meted out when children do not respect boundaries. It's our job as parents to do what we can to enforce those boundaries, and consequences.

There are cases where my boundaries have been pushed by my kids and I've had to be creative: "How am I going to enforce this?" A child might dig his or her heels in. In the case that you read that the child didn't bring it up again, but there might be a child who digs her or his heels in and just refuses to respond.

Parents can do one of two things: they can acquiesce, or, they can keep those boundaries firm. Acquiescing isn't necessarily defeat. Sometimes we need to renegotiate boundaries. Sometimes we need to look and say, "How important is this? Is this a hill to die on? Or is this something where I have some wiggle room?" Maybe you can negotiate with your child and say, "I'm not comfortable calling you, Andy, but I am comfortable calling you A. Can we do that?"

There are ways to negotiate boundaries. Sometimes you can just say, "You know, I've been thinking about it and, and maybe this isn't that big a deal."

The important thing is to not acquiesce if it's still important to you. If it feels like it's an important boundary to maintain, and you allow it to be broken down, the kid's going to sense that, and he's going to know that he has control and that he can manipulate you even further. That's when it gets dangerous.

Kids need to know that their parents are there to protect them. If a child is allowed to break down a parent's boundaries, that undermines the child's sense of safety.

Maria Keffler (25:06):

Dr. Kevin Leman has written a number of books on this subject. In his book *Teaching Children to Mind So You Don't Lose Yours*, he discussed how natural consequences are so effective. He gave a story of a child saying to the parent, "Get out of my life! You don't know anything! Leave me alone and stop! Just get out of my life!" Then half an hour later, the child came and said, "Hey Dad, can I borrow the car keys? I need to go somewhere." The dad said, "I would love to help you, but I'm out of your life."

Let's follow the natural, logical progression of this and see where it goes: "If I'm out of your life, I guess I won't be making meals for you anymore. You know, if you're not answering to your name, then I guess I'm not driving you anywhere anymore."

There's a lot that you can do with natural consequences.

Erin Brewer (26:05):

It's important for parents to feel emboldened to use those natural consequences, because in all honesty, this is a life-or-death situation. This is not whether or not a kid gets to wear a skirt that's below the knee or above the knee. This is a life-or-death situation. Kids who go down this path are medicalized for life. Their lifespans are often shortened. Research shows that these medical interventions are very harmful. It's not just about cosmetic changes. Cancer, heart disease, stroke are very serious consequences here. So we're not talking about something that there's some wiggle room on.

> **Kids who go down this path are medicalized for life. Their lifespans are often shortened. Research shows that these medical interventions are very harmful. It's not just about cosmetic changes. Cancer, heart disease, stroke are very serious consequences here.**

It's important to set up boundaries and consequences and do every-thing you can to prevent a child from going down that medicalization route.

We have some questions.

"I can set boundaries inside my home, but what do I do about what's going on outside of my home? How do I get neighbors and extended family to respect the boundaries of my child?"

We touched upon this, and I want to reiterate how important it is for parents to understand that if you set up boundaries about something that you don't have control over, it's not going to turn out very well.

Maria Keffler (27:25):

Unfortunately most of the rest of society is not on your side. If you are questioning gender ideology it can feel like it is you and your family against the whole rest of the world. Or just you, if the rest of your family disagrees with the position that you're taking.

Erin, you're right. You have to figure out, "What do I have control over and what do I not have control over?"

It may require a little bit of creativity. I hate to use the word *deceptively*, but you may need to quietly cut off relationships that are unhealthy. If your daughter babysits, and the family for whom she babysits is supporting her transgender identity, maybe she's just busy every time that family calls and wants her to babysit for them.

It may be necessary to withdraw the child from school.

Erin Brewer (28:33):

Sometimes you don't have control over what's going on, but you may have control over whether your child does go to school. If your child is being affirmed in a way that is very dangerous at school, you can pull her out of school, you can homeschool her. You can find some other situation for education.

Kids will often freak out at this, because this is a pretty significant thing to do. But sometimes it's what's required and what allows you to have control over something that you otherwise wouldn't have control over.

Maria Keffler (29:06):

There's not a roadmap for this, but what we are seeing from families who have gotten their kids back—whose kids have desisted—many times drastic measures were taken. Trans influences were cut off. Social media was cut off. They were pulled from school. They were severed from unhealthy friendships.

It's hard—kids push back hard. This is painful. This is not easy. And we don't want to make it sound like, "Oh, just homeschool. Oh, just cut off the internet." It's not flippant. It's not easy. But again, as you said, Erin, this is life and death.

Erin Brewer (29:52):

It's the same thing as if you had a child who was very seriously into drugs and he was going to a school where he was told, "It's okay for you to have that drug habit, no problem." Maybe the school is even enabling it, by giving him money to purchase drugs or telling him where to go get the drugs. It's that level of seriousness here.

I do think that it's reasonable to cut off social media. I've even heard of people who've gotten up and moved. Again, these might sound like radical steps, but this is life-and-death. This is about the health and wellness of your child for the rest of your life. The potential for damage is huge.

It can be hard homeschooling a kid. I pulled my older son out of middle school for a very different situation. He was having a lot of difficulties. I pulled him out for a couple of years and homeschooled him, which is something I never thought I would do. I was always 100% into public education.

But what I realized is that when I send my kid out the door to school, I don't have any control anymore. When he's in my home, I start to have control again, and we have control over social media. We can turn the internet off. Sometimes that's horribly hard on parents, but that might be what it takes. Just stop having internet in your home for a while. And these kinds of radical steps often help a lot.

It's a lot like deprogramming somebody who's been in a cult.

Maria Keffler (31:19):

There are a lot of parallels to the cult with the gender ideology. I think we're going to do an episode on that in the future as well. Deprogramming is the right word. That's what a lot of parents are looking at it as: "We need to deprogram our kids."

I want to highlight another danger that they're facing at school. This horrified me. I was at a school board meeting in my district. There was a teacher there from a neighboring district who is very much on board with the gender ideology. He runs a GSA club, and he's active in local and even national activism. I was talking with him and he said, "I shouldn't tell you this because we're not supposed to do this. But if I find out that a kid has unsupportive parents at home and doesn't feel safe, I help that kid find a new place to live and find money to live on."

Erin Brewer (32:16):

Wow. He's enabling the kid to become a runaway.

Maria Keffler (32:19):

He helps kids become runaways.

Erin Brewer (32:21):

That's incredibly scary, because the statistics for runaways are not good. It's not good because first of all, they lose contact with the people who love them the most and they're very vulnerable. They become incredibly vulnerable.

I've also heard of people in schools calling protective services on parents who aren't affirming. So sometimes pulling a kid out of that school is important, both for the child, but also for for keeping your family together. There are cases where parents are losing custody for not affirming children as transgender. The stakes are high here and it might mean completely rethinking your entire life, but it's worth it. Your kids are worth it.

Maria Keffler (33:08):

We have one more question. A parent wrote, "My child is a young adult home from college. He will not respect any of the rules of our house. He's too big to discipline. So how do I enforce my boundaries with him?"

Your kids are older than mine. I'm going to throw this one to you.

Erin Brewer (33:28):

That is probably a physical boundary that needs to be reinforced.

As hard as this can be for parents, once a child is an adult, if they come home and are disrespectful to you and will not maintain your boundaries, it's okay to say, "You're not allowed in my house." That's a horribly difficult thing to say as a parent. It's painful to say, "I love you, but you're not allowed to come and visit until you can be respectful," but that might be what you have to say.

Make sure you say it with love, because you do have to protect that physical space, and it can have implications for younger siblings. If you allow an adult child to come home, and that child is being very disrespectful and disruptive, that's difficult for younger siblings.

It can also have complications for marriages. This can be destructive. It's okay to say, "I love you, but until you're ready to be respectful and not disruptive you need to find somewhere else to stay."

Maria Keffler (34:37):

I appreciate what you said about the effect that this can have on younger siblings. I know we keep saying this, but we're going to do an episode on that in the future, because there are some specific and unusual things that happen among sibling relationships when a child comes home and claims to be changing gender, that parents need to watch for and be aware of. So we're going to address that in the future.

Erin Brewer (35:02):

These are big issues and they're very complicated. I'm going to include a lot of resources because the books that you recommended on boundaries are good. One of the reasons they're good is that they help you to identify boundary issues, because some of us grew up with such ephemeral boundaries in our homes that we can't even identify what our boundaries should be.

Maria Keffler (35:35):

What's normal? What's good?

Erin Brewer (35:37):

What's healthy? When am I being too wishy-washy? When do I have a brick wall? How do I find that happy medium?

Episode 3 Resource List

Boundaries with Brene Brown: https://youtu.be/5U3VcgUzqiI

A beginners guide to setting boundaries: https://youtu.be/tUOvY6Lfm1A

Boundaries with Kids: How Healthy Choices Grow Healthy Children: https://www.amazon.com/Boundaries-Kids-Children-Control-Their/dp/0310243157/ref=sr_1_1

Boundaries Updated and Expanded Edition: When to Say Yes, How to Say No To Take Control of Your Life: https://www.amazon.com/Boundaries-Updated-Expanded-When-Control/dp/0310351804/ref=sr_1_3

Episode 4: Parent Support: Getting Help & Avoiding Harm

https://youtu.be/UKnmPCnGJHI

Maria Keffler (00:37):

Today's topic is Parent Support: Getting Help and Avoiding Harm.

Erin Brewer (00:44):

This is such an important topic because oftentimes when parents are confronted with some kind of crisis, it's so easy for them to put all their energy into the crisis and not take care of themselves.

Maria Keffler (01:00):

This morning as I was getting ready for our talk, I was thinking, "Why did we decide to do parent support and getting help for the parent before doing child support and getting help for the child?"

As a parent, that's our first instinct, right? It is to take care of our kids. So help me remember, why did we decide to do it this way?

Erin Brewer (01:23):

This is an important principle of care.

I was an EMT when I was in college, and when I was training to be an EMT, the first thing that they emphasize is that you can't help someone else if you're not in a position where you're safe. So if somebody is drowning, you do not jump in to save them because more often than not, that person will drown you.

Or if there's somebody who's in the street who's been shot, you have to make sure that you're safe before you run out to help them. Otherwise you could get shot too.

> **If parents are in a place where they're not functioning well, they are not able to take care of their child. It's really important for parents to find ways to really do good self-care so that they have the energy and resources to focus on their children.**

That that principle applies here. If parents are in a place where they're not functioning well, they are not able to take care of their child. It's important for parents to find ways to do good self-care so that they have the energy and resources to focus on their children.

Maria Keffler (02:17):

That's such a good point. A lot of times women tend to think of self-care as getting a mani/pedi and going off for a weekend.

That's not really what we're talking about here. Are we?

Erin Brewer (02:32):

That is a reasonable thing to do for self-care. Do things that you enjoy. That's very valid. Do things that will relax you, the things that give you some time to yourself.

But another important component of self-care is self-thought, and monitoring how you're thinking about things: whether you're getting enough sleep, whether you're eating well, whether you're maintaining your social connections.

It's ironic because one of the therapeutic techniques that is used to help children overcome gender identity issues is called cognitive behavioral therapy. It involves changing the way you talk to yourself.

In the child's case, rather than saying, "I'm born in the wrong body," saying, "I'm born in the right body. I don't fit stereotypical roles," or something like that.

For a parent who's in crisis it might be, "Boy this situation sucks, but it's not the end of the world. I can get through this."

Monitor the kinds of things that you're telling yourself, because we know that the messages that we tell ourselves have a big impact on how we feel. If we're telling ourselves this is the end of the world and we're in huge crisis, it's going to be hard to sleep. It's going to be hard to maintain good nutrition, and it's going to be hard to maintain personal contacts.

Maria Keffler (03:59):

That's a really good point.

I went through therapy some years ago for postpartum depression after one of my kids was born. My hormones got all messed up. I was struggling with some relational things at the time and ended up in psychiatric care for about a year for postpartum depression.

One of the things that I learned through that was listening to what I'm telling myself. When something's happening in the home and it's a crisis, I'd think, "Oh, this is terrible. Oh, this is a disaster."

That's not helpful to me to resolve what's going on.

But like you said, I needed to say, "Okay, the glass of grape juice just spilled all over the refrigerator. It's a mess, but it's not a disaster. I just need to clean it up."

When I was healed and ready to move out of care, I remember my psychiatrist said, "You need to eat well, you need to sleep well, you need to have supportive relationships, and you need to exercise." Holding onto those four things have helped in, in so many different areas of the life.

> **"You need to eat well, you need to sleep well, you need to have supportive relationships, and you need to exercise."**

Erin Brewer (05:15):

Those supportive relationships can be difficult when you're in this issue, because some people will not be supportive. In fact, a lot of people— potentially most people, and maybe even all people that you know—may not be supportive of your stance on this. They may feel like you should "support" your child by affirming their gender identity.

So that can be one of the areas where you might have to go out and build new relationships. Get some support from outside of your normal circles, because you may not be able to find it with the people who you would normally rely on.

Maria Keffler (05:54):

It's so important, especially with this issue, to start to identify which relationships for both you and your child are helpful versus harmful. Parsing those out will help you recognize, "Okay, this is not somebody who's going to be helpful to me here."

Also, define what is meant by support, because that word *support* is used a lot by the gender industry, and a parent who does not say, "Yay! I'm so glad you want to change your sex. I'm so glad that I thought I had a daughter for 13 years, but I'm just going to embrace that now I have a son!" That's what the gender industry calls *support*, and parents who don't do that are called *unsupportive*, but that's not what real support is.

Real support—well, I want to hear how you define real support in this situation.

Erin Brewer (06:56):

In this situation? It's people who will validate your feelings and listen, and not tell you how you should do it.

In this particular case, finding other parents who are in the same situation can be valuable so that you know you're not in this alone. This can feel so alienating from your friends, from your family, your child, the school, potentially even your spouse. It can cause a sense of alienation.

If you can find other parents who are going through this or who have gone through this, that's going to help you to realize you're not alone, and that the feelings you're having are reasonable, and that your approach is what's in the best interest of your child.

Maria Keffler (07:47):

For yourself, support is going to have a lot to do with people reinforcing that you're doing the right thing. I know this is hard but you're doing what you think is necessary for protecting your child.

This is a little bit tangential, but I found this so valuable. Have you heard of Ring Theory when it comes to support? I saw this a while back and I thought it was so powerful. Susan Silk and Barry Goldman did this little diagram called Ring Theory.

You've got a ring in the center and this is the person who's most affected by whatever crisis it is. So let's use the example that somebody has died. Say your parents or your spouse has died. You're the person at the center who's most affected by that death.

Then just outside of that are people who are less affected than you, but still affected. So maybe extended family and close friends.

The next circle outside of that would be acquaintances. Maybe some of the doctors, nurses, or other people who are not as emotionally affected, but who are aware of it.

And then outside of that, it's the people who are less and less affected by the crisis.

Silk and Goldman said that you give care toward the inside and you dump your feelings to the outside.

We've all had the experience of being in crisis about something, and then somebody who's a little bit removed from the crisis comes to us and says, "I just can't deal with this crisis you're having. This is awful. I need support." We feel like, "I'm not the right person to give you that support."

RING THEORY
SUSAN SILK & BARRY GOLDMAN

You can dump those feelings to people who are further removed from the crisis, but the person who's on the inside of it doesn't need to be supporting other people right now. That person needs to be receiving lots of support.

Erin Brewer (09:50):

If people come to you when you're the one who's in the middle of the circle, who needs the support, and people come to you trying to pour out their feelings on you—it's okay to say, "You know what? I need you to go find other people to get support from, because right now I'm the one who needs the support."

We're not trained to do that, but it's okay to do that.

Maria Keffler (10:12):

Yes, it is. As parents, we're so focused on taking care of our children, that we don't recognize that sometimes we need to say, "I need help. I can't do this right now," and reach out.

Erin Brewer (10:29):

It may be that you need significant support. You might need help from medical professionals if you're at a point in a crisis.

There was a time in my life where I had a crisis, and I could not sleep or eat. I just spiraled to the point where I was not healthy because I wasn't eating, and I wasn't sleeping.

I wasn't in a good place and I got some help. I got some therapeutic help to stop me from catastrophizing, to get some insights onto what I needed to focus on to get a handle on the crisis. I also got some medication to help me sleep for a couple of weeks, because if you don't sleep, you can't think straight.

A lot of times when people are in an emotional crisis, the first thing that happens is they can't sleep. Then they get into a cycle where they can't sleep, and then they can't do other kinds of self-care. They can't reach out for support and then they can't sleep and it can get into a unhealthy place quickly, because you started with a night or two without sleep. Your thought processes get mixed up.

Maria Keffler (11:38):

I have never really struggled with anxiety. I'm blessed and lucky that way. But I did have a crisis one time where I couldn't sleep and I was so stressed and so anxious about what was going on. I'd be exhausted and I'd drift off to sleep. But as soon as I got to sleep, I would spring awake.

It was like my brain saying, "Don't sleep! We're under attack! You've got to get up! You've got to do something!"

I talked with a friend of mine who's a social worker. And she said, "Yeah, your brain is in fight-or-flight mode. Your brain feels like you are under attack. You're a gazelle out on the Savannah, and there are lions around. Your brain is saying, 'Now is not the time to sleep. Now is the time to run.'"

As you said, you can do that for a couple of nights. But then your brain isn't working right. Your brain is feeling like it's under attack all the time and you don't sleep. So you don't think well, so then you're stressed more and then you don't sleep.

This friend of mine said, "Sometimes the patient just needs that medication to help them sleep, to reset the cycle. It's not that you need sleep medication for the rest of your life, but you need it to break out of that cycle that you're in."

Erin Brewer (13:00):

The other thing that I do—and I don't know if other people do this—but

I start to breathe more shallowly. So instead of taking deep, cleansing breaths that are centering and grounding, the more anxious I am, the more I do these little breaths. It can keep you in a state of anxiety.

So just take a moment and maybe watch a meditation video on YouTube and breathing will help you center. That alone can do wonders if you're in the middle of crisis and you just need to get a handle on it.

Maria Keffler (13:38):

That's a good point because one of the things that we do when we panic is that shallow breathing. Again, our bodies are getting ready to run, or they're getting ready to fight. If we're really shocked or upset by something we'll just freeze up and stop breathing.

So force yourself. "Okay, I'm going to take a deep breath." Take a deep breath, in and out, several times.

It's amazing to me how differently you feel after just doing that, because you have flooded your brain with oxygen. Your brain needs oxygen to process things. You flooded your muscles with oxygen and that is life-giving. Oxygen is life. We can't survive without it. And that helps tremendously.

Erin Brewer (14:32):

That's where the exercise comes in. It keeps you healthy, but it also forces you into a good breathing pattern.

> **"Exercise keeps you healthy, but it also forces you into a good breathing pattern."**

So be doing all of these things, as well as eating well. We didn't touch on that, but some of us have a habit of going to our comfort food when we're anxious. If your comfort food is candy, chocolate and coffee—there have been days where I've just eaten nothing but chocolate and had coffee. If you do that for a day, it's okay. If you start doing that for days on end, you're going to cause problems with your body.

It's hard for your body to be healthy when you're just eating a bunch of junk food. The other end is people who go for the macaroni and cheese, the mashed potatoes and gravy, that heavy food. That's probably a little bit better than just chocolate. But again, it can weigh you down, and any time your body's not healthy, it's going to impact your thought processes.

Maria Keffler (15:38):

When I was younger and I got stressed, I wouldn't eat. I kind of miss that. I'll be honest. It helped with the weight.

But now I've gone the other way to where I eat the comfort foods. That is something to watch too because there are people who, when you get stressed, when you get sad, when you get anxious, you just stop eating. That's not healthy of course, because your body needs fuel.

So just make yourself do the things that you know are healthy. Make yourself make those healthy choices.

It's hard in the beginning because that's not what you want to do. You want to wallow, you want to eat the chocolate, drink the coffee, lie on the couch and cry. Sometimes you can do those things for a day or two, but if you do them long-term, they're going to prevent you from able being able to deal with things effectively.

Erin Brewer (16:33):

Especially if you have other children at home, you have to keep yourself healthy and your defenses up, because you not only are going to have to parent the child who's got the gender identity issues, but you're going to have to deal with the repercussions of that within your family and how your other children handle that, or how relatives handle that. Or you might have to go have intense confrontations with school people. The stronger you can be, the more you're going to be able to take care of your child and advocate for them.

You mentioned at the beginning about getting a mani/pedi. I've never had a mani/pedi so I'm not sure exactly what that is, but you can get that or a massage.

I would recommend that people make lists of things that help them to feel good, because when you're in a crisis, sometimes you forget that there are things that you really enjoyed doing. If making a cup of cocoa and going and watching the birds is something that helps you to feel better, or maybe going and getting a facial, or going on a long run or going for a swim, then do those things. There are all kinds of things that people enjoy, but we can often forget what those are when we are in the middle of crisis. So it's not a bad idea to have a list of those, so that you can do those self-care things and make sure that you take care of your needs.

Maria Keffler (17:56):

My mother-in-law and father-in-law went to a marriage retreat. When she came back from that she talked about one of the things they emphasized:

doing things that give you life. I loved that phrase, "Doing things that give you life," because for some people working out gives them life. I have a friend who got through a nasty divorce by working out. She just loved it.

Erin Brewer (18:27):

And some of us do not enjoy working out.

Maria Keffler (18:30):

Some people shame young moms for not staying in shape. They say, "I work out six times a day, why can't you?" Well, working out gives *you* life. That's not what gives *me* life.

When I had young children, I could fit in one thing each day that I liked. And for me, when my kids were small, that was knitting. Knitting and crocheting. That calmed me. That gave me peace.

Other people would find doing crafts tedious and life-destroying.

Find what it is for you: Is it going for a run? Is it taking a walk? Is it scrapbooking? Is it playing the violin?

Erin Brewer (19:12):

Going to a movie?

Maria Keffler (19:15):

Laughter! Laughter is great medicine.

Erin Brewer (19:18):

If you can keep a sense of humor about this—even though these are very serious issues—if you can keep a sense of humor that will help as well.

We have a video from someone who does a great job of explaining one simple technique that can help ground people when they're in the middle of a crisis. When you're right there in the middle, if you can remember to do this, it can change your whole outlook.

Guy Winch (19:42):

Studies tell us that even a two-minute distraction is sufficient to break the urge to ruminate in that moment. And so each time I had a worrying, upsetting negative thought, I forced myself to concentrate on something else until the urge passed. And within one week, my whole outlook changed and became more positive and more hopeful.

Maria Keffler (20:05):

That was Guy Winch. I wanted to emphasize one of the things that he says in this video. I love this. He said, "When you are in pain, treat yourself with the same compassion you would expect from a truly good friend."

Erin Brewer (20:19):

Isn't that so true? We often are hard on ourselves in a way that we would never dream of being on someone that we love and care about.

Maria Keffler (20:29):

He gives the example in that video of someone who goes on the first date she's had after a 20-year marriage has dissolved. Halfway through the date, the guy gets up and says, "I'm just not interested in you," and walks out.

This woman started self-denigrating: "Of course, he's not interested in me. I'm old and I'm ugly."

We would never do that to a friend. If a friend called me and told me that happened, the first thing I would say is, "Well, that's his loss. He doesn't know what he's got there." I would encourage her, and we need to do that for ourselves, don't we?

Erin Brewer (21:05):

It's hard because we're not brought up that way. We're brought up to be very self-critical. It's not healthy.

> ## We're not brought up that way. We're brought up to be very self-critical. It's not healthy.

I would encourage people to just practice those very affirming statements to yourself: that you're lovable, that you can get through this, that you're strong, that you can handle this. Those kinds of self-talk messages, even if they sound odd, say them to yourself, or remind yourself to say to them, when you're in the middle of a crisis.

Also just stopping—what he talked about—how that two-minute break can change the trajectory of your day.

Maria Keffler (21:46):

I love that: intentionally redirecting your thoughts.

We do that with kids, right? When kids are in crisis or they're mis-behaving, or they're doing something that they shouldn't be doing, one of the most powerful tools we have is just redirecting them: "Let's look over here instead."

Yes, change your internal monologue.

That you can also apply the validation and invalidation technique. Invalidation is not a technique we want to use, but using the validation technique, we validate our own feelings as well: "Yes. I feel sad and it's not wrong that I feel sad. I feel hurt and it's okay that I feel hurt."

We can problem-solve separately. We can look back and say, "All right, was what I did there effective or not," and analyze what we did and try to decide: "Oh, maybe I need to take a different approach with this." But for our feelings, we want to validate and honor those and trust ourselves that, "Yeah, I'm doing the best I can with my feelings.

Erin Brewer (22:54):

Don't beat yourself up. That's important.

We have a question from a viewer. She says, "I feel guilty focusing on myself when my son is in crisis. I could spend all of my time dealing with his needs and those of the rest of my family. How do I figure out what's an appropriate amount of self-focus for my own care?"

Boy, is that a good question. Because the fact is, we have to take care of ourselves, but we're still parents when we're in crisis. Those responsibilities don't go away. They amp up when we have a child who's in crisis. So that's a good question. How do you balance self-care versus caring for others?

I reflect back again on my EMT training, that if somebody is drowning and you jump in to save them, you might drown too. So you have to make sure you're stable and that you have a good lifeline. Then you can reach out to someone to help them.

In the case of parenting, that means make sure that you have a support system. Make sure that you're taking good care of yourself, and then try to figure out how you can help your child.

But also one of the things that we do as parents is take on the full responsibility of our children: their happiness, their well-being, their success. Especially with older adolescent kids, they have autonomy. On some level they are responsible for their behaviors. Our job is to act as a support for them, but we can't save them.

In this case, the analogy of the drowning person doesn't work. We can't just throw in a life vest and pull them out. This might take weeks, months, or years of efforts. So that's why getting yourself in a good emotional state is important because you're in it for the long haul.

I would say that when you start feeling that you're out of sync, that you're not sleeping well, you're not eating well, that your thoughts are racing, that's when you need to pull back and focus on self-care.

Maria Keffler (25:01):

Just this morning I saw a post in a group. A parent said, "I'm just beating my head against the wall with my daughter on this transgender issue. And I'm validating her feelings and discussing the ways this is illogical. And as far as I can tell, I'm doing everything right, and it's just not making a dent. And I'm so tired and I'm so exhausted. I just want to give up."

The parents who jumped in to support her said, "No, you're doing a good job, Mom. You're doing the best you can. This is a pernicious brainwashing that your child has been through. It's going to take time." Somebody else said, "She's hearing you. You may not see any evidence of it, but she's hearing you." There was just comment after comment after comment, supporting her and encouraging her.

I thought, "This is what we need." This is what we need in every area of our lives—friends who are going to tell us, "You're doing a great job. I'm really proud of you."

> **"You're doing a good job, Mom, you're doing the best you can. This is a pernicious brainwashing that your child been through. It's going to take time." Somebody else said, "She's hearing you. You may not see any evidence of it, but she's hearing you."**
>
> **This is what we need in every area of our lives— friends who are going to tell us, "You're doing a great job. I'm really proud of you."**

Going back to my bout with postpartum depression, I had a good friend come to me before I realized what was going on. She said, "Maria, something's wrong. You are just not yourself. You are not acting like yourself."

That made me stop and step back and go, "You know what? I don't feel the same as I did six months ago."

Having that person come to me and say that to me, in a loving, caring way was the best thing she could have done for me at the time. We need those kinds of friends.

Erin Brewer (26:50):

You've hit on something that's important.

There's a line between crisis and angst, and trying to grapple through these issues, and all of those feelings that go along with it. Sometimes you can cross the line into something that's clinical. You can become clinically depressed, develop an anxiety disorder, or a panic disorder.

When those happen, the self-care may not be enough. You might have to get either pastoral care or help from a therapist or a counselor or a social worker.

It's hard to know where that line is, but in your case, you had someone say, "You know, something's really off here." If you feel like you've gone past a place where you can bring yourself back, that's a time to reach out for help.

Maria Keffler (27:46):

One of the ways I recognized that I was beyond the point of just needing self-care was that I would go for self-care—my husband would take care of the kids and I'd go off by myself for a couple of hours. I'd just go sit at a coffee shop and relax.

But when I came home and walked in the door, it all came back on me again. It was like I'd had no self-care at all.

That was a clue to me: "Something is wrong here, that I'm not even reaping the benefits of two hours of self-care." So that can be a clue.

Erin Brewer (28:21):

You also mentioned the importance of that support system. For people watching, if you don't have a support system, I'm going to list some resources, because there are groups that you can go to that will help link you in to support systems.

Sometimes, especially if your extended family supports your child's gender identity, and the school supports the gender identity, and perhaps your close friends might, it's really important to find people who will support your perspective and how you're parenting this child, knowing that what you're doing is saving them from life-long medicalization. You need support with that. So we'll definitely list some resources.

Maria Keffler (29:09):

We have one more question. This relates to finding those things that give you life. This parent said, "I went from school to working full-time to having kids, I've never really had any hobbies or downtime. How do I even figure out what would feed and restore me?"

Erin Brewer (29:27):

Maybe some of us can relate to that. It has taken me a long time to figure out what is restorative to me, because I did that—*bang, bang*, graduated from college, had kids right away and never really got a chance to develop hobbies or self-interests or good self-care techniques. I totally relate to that.

It's just a matter of time. Maybe try lots of different things. Do you like movies? Then go to movies. They have some of these studios now where you can go and paint. Maybe you just need to go get yourself some oil paints or watercolors. Gardening—there's all different things.

Maybe even Google "hobbies" and just see what comes up, and see if there's anything that really seems like it might resonate with you and give it a try. That's the beautiful thing—you're not locked in, so you can try these things and at the very least, it will give you an opportunity and experience something new, and distract you for a little while from what's going on in your life. And you might find something that is really healing.

Maria Keffler (30:42):

Another thing you might try—if you have friends who have certain hobbies, ask if you can go with them to do it. If you've got a friend who plays tennis every week: "Can I just come and play tennis with you?" Or if you've got a friend who knits: "Could you teach me to knit?"

Those are great ways that are a little bit lower stress, because you have someone to lean on as you're trying it out.

Erin Brewer (31:07):

That's a great idea too, because then you have someone to talk to as well.

Again, I don't want to minimize in any way how difficult it can be. We can talk about these ideas for self-care and I know from personal experience, it's not always that easy. Sometimes you really have to force yourself to change your thought process, and force yourself to take care of yourself. But you can, and you will get through this. You're doing such important work taking care of yourself so that you can take care of your child.

Maria Keffler (31:44):

Before we go, we had one more viewer who sent in a really great summary of what people do when problems and issues come into their lives.

She said, "In trying to solve a problem, we often do one of four things. One, we try to change and control the circumstance, the other people, and the things that happen around us." You touched on that, trying to control kids, that we may not be able to control. "Or two, we try to change our actions, our behaviors and words in order to control other people and events. Or three, we avoid/escape by engaging in distracting, false pleasures of busy-ness—overeating, overdrinking, overexercising, overcrafting, Netflixing, Facebooking, whatever. Or fourth, we indulge in self-pity, self-loathing, worry, confusion, indecision that overwhelms. These are often harmful. They don't work or they're unsustainable, or ultimately have a negative net effect. It's when we can face our fears, anxiety, self-doubt, self-loathing, and learn to allow and process all of these things that we then experience less of them. We become the next, best version of ourselves, knowing we can handle hard things."

Erin Brewer (33:03):

Isn't that wonderful. I love the positive spin on this: whenever there's a crisis in our lives at the time, it's really difficult, but we grow from it.

Maria Keffler (33:13):

Well, thanks, Erin. This has been such a necessary topic, and I appreciate your insights, especially from EMT training, that was really powerful. And I learned something about you that I didn't know.

Episode 4 Resource List

Ring Theory Helps Us Bring Comfort In…and "Dump" Our Own Stuff Out https://www.helplinecenter.org/featured-story/ring-theory-helps-us-bring-comfort-in-and-dump-our-own-stuff-out/

Ring Theory Helps Us Bring Comfort In https://www.psychologytoday.com/us/blog/promoting-hope-preventing-suicide/201705/ring-theory-helps-us-bring-comfort-in

16 Simple Ways to Relieve Stress and Anxiety https://www.healthline.com/nutrition/16-ways-relieve-stress-anxiety

Emotional First Aid (Guy Winch) https://www.youtube.com/watch?v=F2hc2FLOdhI

Parents of ROGD Kids: https://www.parentsofrogdkids.com/

Parent Guide, Understanding the Transgender Issue:
https://genderresourceguide.com/?gcli

Sasha Ayad, Inspired Teen Therapy: https://inspiredteentherapy.com/

Episode 5: Finding Trustworthy Support for Your Child

https://youtu.be/0gZTO2xQRlY

Maria Keffler (00:37):

Today we're talking about finding trustworthy support for your child.

Erin Brewer (00:43):

I wanted to let people know how I got involved in this in the first place. It was as a result of a conversion therapy ban that was introduced in the state that I live in.

When I read through the text of the ban, I realized that they were trying to ban the very care that helped me resolve my gender identity issues when I was a child. My state is not alone. There are many, many states that have passed these kinds of bans. Therapists are not allowed to help children explore the underlying causes of their gender identity issues.

That makes finding appropriate care for your child that much harder, but it doesn't mean it's not out there. You can find it.

Maria Keffler (01:34):

Traditionally when you go to a therapist or you take your child to a therapist, the first thing the therapist will do is get to know the whole person, and investigate if you have any other medical or psychological issues. Do you have any other diagnoses that you've already gotten from other doctors or therapists? Have you had trauma in your life? What's going on in your life right now? Has a child had a significant loss? Did your parents divorce? Has someone close to you died? Are you on any medications? They'll investigate all those things.

Are there any possibly co-morbid disorders? Comorbid means occurring at the same time. We know that kids who are on the autism spectrum often have co-morbid disorders of ADHD or obsessive-compulsive disorder. So those are things that often tend to come together.

When you go to a therapist, almost without fail, that is what a therapist will do: look at all of the underlying causes or possibilities for why you might be suffering with what you're suffering.

But as you pointed out, Erin, these "conversion therapy" bans are telling therapists, "When children come to you and say that they question their gender identity, or they think they're a different gender than they are, you are not allowed to investigate any of those other things." Those therapists are not allowed to do anything except say, "Yes, you are right. You are the wrong sex and we need to treat you that way." That's incredibly problematic.

> **"Conversion therapy" bans are telling therapists, "When children come to you and say that they question their gender identity, you are not allowed to investigate..." Therapists not allowed to do anything except say, "Yes, you are right. You are the wrong sex and we need to treat you that way." That's incredibly problematic.**

Erin Brewer (03:25):

It's not just in states that have these legislative bans. A lot of people who are graduating from school, who are new to therapy, have really embraced this affirmative-care model, even though it's not research-based, and there's no evidence behind it. It's an ideology and they've embraced it.

So even in states without these bans, it might be hard to find someone who doesn't ascribe to this affirmative-care model. You have to be a little bit more investigative than you otherwise would have if this were another issue, because in other issues, they will do a comprehensive assessment and they will look for contributing factors, underlying issues, and family dynamics. They will look at all of these. But they don't do that with gender identity issues, which is so frustrating.

The other concern that I've seen is that parents will take their child to a therapist and the therapist will affirm the child, but will not communicate with the parent.

One of the recommendations I make is first vet the therapist. Find out what their ideology is. Find out if they're going to affirm your child in a transgender identity and if they are, find a different therapist.

The other thing is to do family counseling, so that you're in the room with the child. Some people might argue that this isn't going to allow the child to fully express herself, but this will give you a chance to assess the therapist and determine whether or not you feel comfortable with leaving your child alone with the therapist. Because again, in many states there are laws that protect the child-therapist relationship, and you may not be able to get access to files about your child once you turn the child over to a therapist.

<u>Maria Keffler (05:15):</u>

That's a very good point. I think we're going to include some resources to help you figure out, "How do I assess? How do I find a therapist who's going to be the best fit for our family, and who's going to partner with us for therapy for the whole child?" So definitely look at those resources as well.

I spoke with one parent and I thought this was painfully telling about what's going on, at least in the schools, and with school counselors.

This parent's child had been well-known with the counselor and the elementary school. The child had an IEP, and spent a lot of time with the counselor, and the parent knew the counselor quite well. The parent said, "I often sat in the counselor's office and said, 'I need a counselor today to help me out." And she said, "The counselor was always great about listening, and asking questions like, 'Well, let's look at where this could be coming from. Why are you feeling this way?'"

When the child hit middle school and announced a transgender identity out of the blue, the parent thought to herself, "That elementary school counselor really knows my child. I'm going to talk to her." So she called the counselor.

The first thing the counselor said was, "You have to affirm that identity. You need to affirm it." No questions like, "When did this happen? Did we see this at all in elementary school? What could be going on?" Not a single question. But it's really telling what is being pressed upon counselors and therapists, about what they have to do in this situation.

By the way, that child who the elementary school counselors said had to be affirmed, has now desisted. That child's family did not affirm, and applied some of the techniques we've talked about in other videos. That child has now said, "You know what? I am my birth sex."

<u>Erin Brewer (07:32):</u>

What a good outcome. That's so encouraging to know that even if you have so-called experts telling you to do it one way, that as a parent, you know your child wasn't born in the wrong body. You know the history of the child. You know that that child did not have a long-term history of gender dysphoria, and that this is not something that is going to be healthy for your child. I applaud that parent for holding firm with the belief that they're going to do whatever it takes in order to not affirm the child's delusion, but to help that child resolve those gender identity issues, which can be really hard.

> **I applaud that parent for holding firm with the belief that they're going to do whatever it takes in order to not affirm the child's delusion, but to help that child resolve those gender identity issues, which can be really hard.**

As you mentioned, this idea that you have to affirm a child's gender identity has taken off like wildfire. It's not evidence-based, there's no research behind it. It's just an ideology. It's a belief system. And it's a very harmful belief system that's been pushed on people.

That might sound hyperbolic. But when we watch this video, we'll see— it talks about how we might refer to the trans ideology as peer pressure when it's related to children, but it's a societal pressure. People will agree to something that's completely false, when there's enough pressure on them.

I believe that's what's happening right now to a lot of mental health experts. There's just so much pressure that either (A) They won't deal with these kids at all, or (B) They're just going to go along with it because everybody else is going along with it. And if they don't go along with it, they might get shamed, they might get fired, they might get called a hater.

So there is this tremendous pressure. And I know that there are a lot of therapists who are letting their therapeutic licenses expire. They're becoming life coaches, which is a non-licensed mental health helper.

That might be a route that parents need to go if they live in states that have these therapy bans, or if they're unable to find a therapist who has a different model besides affirmative-only care.

Maria Keffler (09:47):

We see that happening in schools as well as more and more of these policies are put into place and teachers and staff are required to teach gender ideology, forced to use preferred pronouns, to do things that they really feel are not ethical. Teachers are taking early retirement, or they're leaving the school system in order to pursue some other employment, because they can no longer practice their careers with their consciences intact. That's heartbreaking.

Erin Brewer (10:25):

That's what happens when there's this tremendous social pressure. This video is about social conformity. It shows that even without this kind of tremendous pressure, people sometimes will doubt their own perceptions. If other people are perceiving or saying they perceive things differently. Sometimes that's enough for someone to doubt their own perceptions.

In the case of gender ideology, it comes with this huge amount of pressure and potential life impacts like losing your job. So it's not surprising that it's hard to find mental health providers who are willing to use a different model.

Let's look at this video.

Hank Minor (11:07):

How do we adjust our behavior or thinking to follow the behavior or rules of the group we belong to? Social psychologists have always been curious about the degree to which a person might follow or rebel against their group social norms.

During the early 1950s, Polish American psychologist Solomon Asch expressed the power of conformity through a simple test.

In this experiment, the volunteer is told that they're participating in a study on visual perception and is seated at a table with five other people. The experimenter shows the group a picture of a standard line and three comparison lines of various lengths, and then asked the people to say which of the three lines matches the comparison line. It's clear to anyone with any good vision that the second line is the right answer. But the thing is most, if not all, of the other people in the group start choosing the wrong line.

The participant doesn't know those other people are all actors— a common deception used in social and psychological research— and they are intentionally giving the wrong answer.

This causes the real participant to struggle with trusting their own eyes or going with the group. And yet most subjects still gave what they knew was the correct answer, but more than a third were essentially just willing to give the wrong answer to mesh with the group.

Asch and subsequent researchers found that people are more likely to conform to a group if they're made to feel incompetent or insecure and are in a group of three or more people, especially if all those people agree. It also certainly doesn't hurt if the person admires the group because of maybe their status or their attractiveness, and if they feel that others are watching them.

Erin Brewer (12:30):

This research is really powerful. It shows how easily people are influenced to doubt their own perception. It's not surprising that with the tremendous pressure, the resources, and the money that are going into the transgender movement, that we have therapists who are caving in to this ideology.

At the same time, as parents, we know that it's not going to be good for our children to go down this route.

There's this knee-jerk reaction these days, that if your kid isn't happy, take him to a therapist. That may not necessarily be the appropriate thing.

I know that Sasha Ayad, who's worked with a lot of kids with gender identity issues, has said that we tend to over-therapize our kids. We tend to automatically think, "Let's take him to a therapist. That'll fix him." In this case, that may not be the best approach. There are some other techniques.

What kinds of things have you heard that have been effective?

Maria Keffler (13:37):

The thing that I am hearing from parents who have gotten their kids back from this has been a pretty radical detaching of the child from influences that are pushing the child toward the transgender ideology. As we're seeing, it is in all aspects of society. It's in the school. The child walks down the hall and there's posters on the wall asking, "What gender are you?" He goes to English class and the counselor comes in and gives a gender presentation. She goes to science and the teacher says that transgender ideology is very scientific, which is not true.

Some people have had to pull their kids from school in order to sever the influences.

> **The American School Counselor Association, which is the largest professional association for school counselors, has guidance out for counselors dealing with transgender-identified kids. It says right there that they should hide this from parents if the child wants it hidden. That is an act of deception.**

Going back to the counselors at school, the American School Counselor Association, which is the largest professional association for school counselors, has guidance out for counselors dealing with transgender-identified kids. It says right there that they should hide this from parents if the child wants it hidden. That is an act of deception.

Erin Brewer (14:51):

That reminds me of an audio that was just released of a grandmother who contacted a school counselor at her granddaughter's school. Her granddaughter had just barely turned 11 within the last month had turned 11. So she was very young, and had also lost her father recently.

Her father died and apparently this child was going into the school therapist's office and the therapist was affirming her transgender identity. The grandmother was just mortified, and almost speechless at times. I'll post a link to this audio tape, because it's so powerful.

When you hear the rationalization that school counselors use— They might say, "Yeah, I know that children's brains don't fully develop until they're 25. Yes, I know that there might be underlying issues, but I'm just going to go ahead and do this because I don't want to hurt her feelings," or "I want her to feel safe with me." So there's this whole rationalization around this affirmation model.

It's like in the video, with different the lines. You might very clearly recognize which line is the same size as the other line, but if everybody else is telling you it's another line, you may feel like, "I'm just going to go along with everyone else." Then if you lay upon that the risk of potentially losing your job or being shamed, or being told that you're a hater, it's not surprising that this affirmation model is taking hold.

This might sound really frustrating, and it is. It's incredibly frustrating that it might be hard to find good mental health experts for your child. We're going to dedicate a whole episode on how to deprogram your child, because really what's happened: children have been force-fed this ideology, and you need to deprogram them. It is a harmful belief system that they've accepted.

It reminds me—I use this analogy a lot—of a child who is a drug addict. If a child is a drug addict and she keeps hanging out around the same friends, if she keeps going to the same places, if she goes to a school where drugs are available, it's going to be really hard for her to kick the habit.

Sometimes this is a lot bigger than just finding a therapist. Sometimes if you live in a state where therapists are prohibited from exploring those underlying issues, you might need to be creative and find something like a life coach instead for your child to talk to, or a trusted relative, or somebody else who you feel confident is going to help guide them on the right path.

We have a couple of questions from concerned parents.

"My child is being sucked into a glitter family who wants him to come live with them where he won't be challenged on his desire to live as a woman. How do we keep him from moving in with them?"

Maria, can you address what a "glitter family" is for people who may not be familiar with that term?

Maria Keffler (18:00):

A "glitter family" is a group of people who will affirm your child's gender identity. It's so harmful and so hurtful because they will tell the child, "If your family is toxic or unsupportive," or in other words, "If your family doesn't agree with letting you do everything you want to do, you can cut off your family and come over and be part of our family."

With young adults, sometimes it's a house full or an apartment full of all transgender-identified people who—I like your analogy for drug addicts. It's a group of them all reinforcing each other and forcing each other further and further down the path of medicalization.

It's really insidious. I keep coming back to that word, but it's the right word: *insidious*. It's a way of destroying a family, and destroying a child's relationship with his family and replacing it with this "glitter family."

Erin Brewer (19:05):

That just sounds like the drug analogy. If you've got a kid who isn't ready to give up drugs, and they've got a drug house where they're saying, "Hey, come on over here, we've got the drugs. We won't give you a hard time," it's going to be really hard to prevent your child from going to that glitter family.

In this case this parent asks, "What can I do to keep him from moving in?"

Some of it depends on the age of the child. If the child is an adult, there's probably not a heck of a lot you can do.

If the child's an older teen, you might be more limited.

If the child's younger, there are a lot of things that you can do. We're going to get into it more in the episode where we talk about deprogramming your child, but you may have to cut off social media. You might have to pull her from the school. You might have to sequester her, and build walls of protection around her until she has time to work through this deprogramming.

> **You might have to pull her from the school.**
> **You might have to sequester her, and build walls of**
> **protection around her until she has time to work**
> **through this deprogramming.**

Maria Keffler (20:10):

One of the things that I think parents really need to be aware of that's happening around them is that the child is not simply being affirmed, but there's this sense of a "savior complex," was how Sasha Ayad put it.

These people, these teachers, these counselors, neighbors, extended family—they've got this idea that they're going to be the one that is the safe place for this child. They're going to be the one that saves the "poor transgender kid" from his "toxic parents." And there's this unhealthy sense of, "I'm going to be the one who saves you," that helps them rationalize really awful undermining of parental love, parental responsibility, parental authority.

Many are quite happy—in fact, they have a real sense of pride—about going behind your back to affirm your child in something that's very unhealthy.

One very simple way to find out what people are saying or what people's impression about this is to bring up the topic casually like, "You know, there's a child in my child's school who has just came out as transgender."

Drop that into the conversation and see what's said. If the person is hesitant like, "Oh really? Wow. Huh." That might indicate that they're a little bit more gender critical, but are afraid to bring it up.

But if you hear, "Oh, that's so wonderful. Oh, it's so great that kids are their authentic selves"—if you start hearing that language, you know very well that is not a person who's safe for you or your children.

Erin Brewer (21:56):

It is okay as a parent to say, "You don't get to have contact with that person anymore."

In the audio tape of the grandma, that's what she did. She told the school counselor, "You will not have contact with my granddaughter anymore, period."

You get to do that as a parent, you get to decide. They may appear to be in a position where they're helping. "School counselors," you think, "of course they're safe." But I've heard story after story after story of parents being undermined by school counselors. So you really have to be careful of that. It's okay to say, "My child will not see you anymore."

Maria Keffler (22:34):

When did we stop respecting parental authority? In no other place is it okay to go behind a parent's back to get to a child. That's very predatory behavior.

> **When did we stop respecting parental authority? In no other place is it okay to go behind a parent's back to get to a child. That's very predatory behavior.**

We had an experience in our house with our daughter being invited to play *Dungeons and Dragons*. A friend of hers invited her, but said, "This is being set up by my friend's mom." And we were like, "So you have a group of parents and children playing *Dungeons and Dragons* together?" What's that about?

My daughter got an email from this other parent inviting her.

When my kids got email accounts, we let them know that until they're 18, their email accounts are open to their dad and me, so we can see whatever is happening in their email accounts. They know that and they agreed to it. So my daughter got this email from this other parent, inviting her to play *D & D* with this intergenerational group. But the problematic part of that for me is that I was completely circumvented.

Erin Brewer (23:46):

They didn't invite you.

Maria Keffler (23:48):

They didn't invite me. No. And I found that very predatory.

I talked with my daughter about it and I said, "It kind of bothers me, first that your friend gave this adult your email address without your permission." And she said, "Yeah, I didn't tell her that was okay to do." And I said, "Secondly, that adult approached you and did not approach me. Because for me, that's red flag behavior."

If an adult is trying to get to my child, without me knowing it, that's predatory behavior.

Erin Brewer (24:20):

It is and it's so important to be on alert for that, because we're talking about finding trustworthy support for your child. Any adult who tries to undermine your parenting, or circumvent you as a parent—it's, as you said, a red flag. It's a sign that something's not quite right here.

> **Any adult who tries to undermine your parenting, or circumvent you as a parent—it's a red flag. It's a sign that something's not quite right here.**

It might just be that the parent doesn't really have an understanding of the social nuances, but it's more likely in the world we live in right now that they might be actively trying to undermine your authority as a parent, especially if you have a child who's struggling with gender identity issues.

Maria Keffler (25:00):

Even in the case that this parent just doesn't understand the social nuances, I don't necessarily want to put my child under the care and responsibility of somebody who doesn't understand basic respect for parental authority.

Erin Brewer (25:17):

That is something that I've noticed. There's a generation of parents who have this idea that they're going to be friends with the kids, and they're going to be very lenient, and they're going to create these fun experiences for the kids.

I've had that with my own kids, where they've been involved in situations where I assume that there is a responsible adult watching over things, but there isn't, and it just shocks me.

You have to be vigilant and really investigate things. This doesn't mean being a helicopter parent and not letting your child ever do things. It just means being investigative and making good choices about what kinds of environments are going to be healthy for your child.

Maria Keffler (26:06):

We have one more question. This is another tough one, as they all seem to be: "I am a single parent and I have to work full time. I cannot homeschool my child, but it doesn't seem like any other options—public, private or religious school-- are safe from gender ideology. Help."

Erin Brewer (26:24):

That's a big one.

I know someone who works full-time and homeschools her children. It can be done. A lot of times what it requires is to be creative and to develop a support system. There is an increasing movement towards what they call *pods*, where parents come together and pay someone to teach their kids in a homeschool situation. That way they have more control over the belief systems that are being pushed on their kids.

There are other situations where there's a cooperative, where children go from house to house, and one parent will teach one thing and other parents will teach other things.

There are options. It's really hard if you're a single mom, homeschooling and working full-time. So there might be other options such as online education where your child can be at home and learn online. You're probably going to get curriculum that you may not agree with. In some cases, there may still be some of this gender ideology being pushed, but you're able to monitor it more.

Do you have any ideas, Maria?

Maria Keffler (27:37):

I loved what you said about some of the creative choices parents have been making.

I have seen groups of parents coming together in one of those pods. If you've got four or five families doing that, each parent will take one day a week off of work to run the homeschool. So they'll only have to take one day off. Of course, you'll need your employer to sign off on this for you. But then that parent has all the kids in the pod for one day of homeschool, and then the next day the kids go to the next pod. That can be done.

HSLDA (the Homeschool Legal Defense Association) has a lot of supports for parents. They have grants. They have great resources for helping you find curriculum and resources.

I know with what's happened in schools lately, with so many schools going to virtual learning, there've been a lot of teachers who have left teaching and have started their own businesses. They started their own homeschool consulting organization where they will come and homeschool your child. I know of two former teachers who have created an entire curriculum that they will just give you.

If you say, "Well, I don't really like this part of it," they'll suggest, "Then let's pull out that module and put in something different." They'll create the curriculum for you.

There are a lot of options.

Erin Brewer (29:07):

It might also depend on the age of your child, because if you have six- or seven-year-olds, it's a really different kind of homeschooling environment than for 16- and 17-year-olds.

Some of it might require being creative. If you have an extra room in your house, hire someone in exchange for room and board.

There are options. But again, there are going to be situations where you cannot homeschool, and it's just not going to be an option, but I would encourage you to look around your neighborhood, your area, and see what other kinds of environments there are. Are there charter schools? Maybe there are some independent schools that aren't affiliated with school districts at all. Religious schools may or may not be places that you're comfortable with, but those might be options. Another option might be moving somewhere where they do have those kinds of schools available.

Sometimes this sounds like a lot. People's eyes get wide and they are like, "Move?" and I say, "Yeah, sometimes that's what it takes. This is that big of a deal. Your child's health and well-being for the rest of her life is on the line." So sometimes moving or homeschooling is really the best option.

Maria Keffler (30:25):

I'm in some parenting and education groups online and I have lately been seeing some comments from parents who are not faith-based at all. I saw a comment recently from someone who said, "I am an atheist, but I am sending my kid to Catholic school because I know gender ideology isn't there." Wow, that's powerful.

Erin Brewer (30:47):

That's where in trying to gauge your comfort level, some people might be comfortable with that. Some might not. But really try to explore other options, to find trustworthy people for your child to be around, because they're so impressionable. This ideology, as you said, is so insidious that

80   COMMONSENSE CARE VIDEO SERIES

the more you can cushion your kids with people who are safe, the better off they're going to be.

<u>Maria Keffler (31:12)</u>:

The more they're hearing the same thing from the people all around them, the more likely that they're going to be protected from this, or pulled back from this.

<u>Erin Brewer (31:21)</u>:

That's so important. So what do we have for next week?

<u>Maria Keffler (31:25)</u>:

Well, for next week, we are actually going to go a little further into gender ideology: we're talking about investigating gender ideology, that it's illogical, inconsistent and unscientific.

<u>Erin Brewer (31:36)</u>:

Goodness, I am so glad that we're going to do that because I keep hearing people say things like, "You know, science shows that we need to validate people," or "Science shows that it's better for people to be their authentic selves," and really conflating these very non-scientific terms with science.

Looking at the science is really important because when you look at the science, it's crystal clear—there really is no question whether or not it's better for a child to learn how to feel comfortable with themselves or to go down this dangerous path.

<u>Maria Keffler (32:10)</u>:

Absolutely. And when you start digging into the supposed research that occasionally gets touted, it just falls apart. Either the research was very poorly done or the results have been interpreted spuriously. There is not a lot of anything to put legs under this ideology.

Episode 5 Resource List

Grandma's phone call: https://youtu.be/oaiySwx6Oqk

Finding a Gender-Critical Therapist
https://arlingtonparentcoa.wixsite.com/arlingtonparentcoa/finding-a-gender-critical-therapist

Crash Course (Social Conformity) https://youtu.be/6jYSfVmn0uA

Episode 6: Investigating Gender Ideology: Illogical, Inconsistent, & Unscientific

https://youtu.be/mmqcYleKoYU

Maria Keffler (00:49):

Today we're talking about investigating gender ideology. It is illogical, inconsistent and unscientific. Wow, this is a big topic for today.

Erin Brewer (01:01):

It's so important because so many people are just getting one message about this, which is the affirmative-care model—if your child has these feelings, that you must affirm them.

It's really important for parents to have an alternative narrative about this and to understand why we are suggesting that the affirmative-care model is really harmful.

One of the things that I harken back to anytime somebody says, "Why wouldn't you affirm them?" is the purpose of therapy. When somebody goes to therapy, it's because they're having some kind of distress, some kind of internal angst. They go to a therapist to help work that out.

But what if you go to a therapist and you have depression, and the therapist looks at you and says, "I think you have every right to feel depressed. Why don't you go home, get in bed, eat cookies and just stay there until you aren't depressed anymore?"

Or what if you have somebody who's anxious, and the therapist says, "Oh my goodness. Based on what you've said, I think you should be anxious. I'm surprised you're able to function. In fact, you might want to just check into a hospital right now, because life is overwhelming for you."

Or what if you have an anorexic who feels she is fat, and the therapist says, "I can tell that you feel fat. I think you really are fat. How can we help you to not be so fat?"

In none of these cases would people feel like that was a good therapeutic model, and yet that's exactly what's happening right now when it comes to gender identity issues.

Maria Keffler (02:40):

They've conflated the meaning of *affirmation*. Affirmation has been a word that our culture has really focused on about affirming someone's worth, affirming someone's value, affirming someone's feelings. We talked about that in an earlier episode that we do want to affirm people's feelings: "I can understand why you would feel that way. Let's address the facts about why those feelings might be confusing to you."

But by saying you have to affirm someone's transgender identity—calling that "affirmative care"—it's conflating the meaning of affirmation. Affirmation is about your own worth, and not about affirming everything that you think, because we all have ways that we are not thinking correctly about things. We're all wrong about something. If we weren't wrong about something, then we would be perfect. People who have the mind of God wouldn't need therapists, right?

So we want to look at this: it is not really affirmative. It is not an affirming thing to tell kids, "Yes, you really are the wrong gender. You really were born in the wrong body."

Erin Brewer (03:59):

One of the concerns that I have about therapists "affirming" a child is that they are affirming that the child is born in the wrong body.

This whole idea that somebody can be born in the wrong body is saying that these children are inherently flawed, and that the only way to fix being born in the wrong body is to harm themselves.

> **This whole idea that somebody can be born in the wrong body is saying that these children are inherently flawed, and that the only way to fix being born in the wrong body is to harm themselves.**

Not only is it a really dangerous idea, just generally to affirm somebody's negative thought processes, but in this case, it's especially dangerous because the therapist is acknowledging to that child that they are inherently flawed, that they were born in the wrong body.

Maria, can somebody be born in the wrong body?

Maria Keffler (04:42):

There is no scientific evidence that you can be born in the wrong body. There's no test that anyone can do. We can't do a scan of your brain and say, "Look, you have a girl brain," or, "Look, that's a boy brain." There are no physiological markers. There's just no research to support that at all. We *are* our bodies.

Erin Brewer (05:08):

Chromosomes determine that every woman has XX brain cells, even if a woman or girl is gender-nonconforming.

Say you have a woman who is an auto mechanic and likes to play in the mud and wants to wear boots and plaid shirts. Her brain cells are still XX brain cells. To suggest that somebody can be born in the wrong body is to suggest that somehow there's an essence or a soul of that person who was accidentally put in the wrong-sex body. That that just makes no sense. There's no way to test that.

What concerns me the most is that they're basing these feelings on regressive stereotypes. If somebody comes and says, "I was born in the wrong body," Maria, what does that mean to you?

Maria Keffler (06:13):

It means that they are looking at the way society says a girl or a boy should be, and comparing themselves to that stereotype and finding themselves lacking.

Erin Brewer (06:27):

One of the things that really confounds me is that people will say not only do they feel like should have been born the other sex, but that they *are* the other sex. At least in my experience, it's impossible to know what it's like to be something that you're not.

I can never know what it's like to be a cat. I can imagine what it might be like to be a cat. I can think about what it might be like to be a cat. But I can never really know what it is like to be a cat, even if I do all kinds of research to understand their neurology and their physiology. I can feel like I want to be a cat, but I can't ever be a cat, no matter what.

Maria Keffler (07:23):

I have never experienced life from anyone's perspective but my own. I've never been in anybody else's head. When someone says, "Well, I just feel like a boy," what does that even mean? You don't know what it feels like to be anybody else. I don't know what it feels like to be you, Erin.

Erin Brewer (07:45):

I only know what it feels like to be Erin, to be this kind of woman that I am. I don't even know what it feels like to be another woman, let alone a man!

Maria Keffler (07:57):

That just doesn't make any sense, because you've only experienced life from your own perspective. I don't know what it feels like to be Erin Brewer. I don't know what it feels like to be Angelina Jolie. I don't know what it feels like to be Chris Pine. I don't know what it feels like to be my husband. I only know what it feels like to be me. So that's really non-sensical.

Erin Brewer (08:20):

I have to admit that as someone who did suffer from what would be diagnosed today as gender dysphoria, I know what it's like to believe that I'm inherently flawed, that there is something inherently wrong with me, and that I would be so much better if people would accept me as something else. I do understand that. I don't want to minimize the feelings that people are having because they are real feelings.

> **I know what it's like to believe that I'm inherently flawed, that there is something inherently wrong with me, and that I would be so much better if people would accept me as something else.**
> **I do understand that. I don't want to minimize the feelings that people are having because they are real.**

But the narrative that has surrounded gender is so flawed. When I was growing up, the therapist didn't say, "You're right, Erin, you are a boy," and affirm. Instead they kept digging and digging to figure out what was that was happening within me that I felt so strongly that it wasn't okay to be me, which is fundamentally what this is about.

These children are saying, "It's not okay to be me, so I want to be somebody else."

A lot of times trans-rights activists use what they call "research" to justify that this affirmative-care model is the way we should proceed with these kids. But this "research' is so incredibly flawed.

Maria Keffler (09:40):

One of the things that the transgender-rights activists like to say is that kids will commit suicide if they're not affirmed.

They cite a study that they say proves that transgender people are more suicidal if they're not affirmed, but the study is so weak. It's so flawed. I think it had maybe 27 subjects. It was a survey. I believe the question that was asked was, "Have you ever thought about hurting yourself?" Well, I bet most of us at some point in our lives have thought, "I wonder if I should just off myself." Most of us have experienced that.

So if you ask that question to 27 transgender-identified people, that's so flawed. That doesn't apply widely. It's too small of a sample. It is a self-selected sample. It's not random.

And that question is so loaded and so leading. Whereas some of the good data that we have—I've mentioned this before—like a study out of Sweden that followed people who had sex reassignment surgery, and after thirty years their rate of suicide is so much higher than what's in the general population. Their rates of mental health are so much worse than the rest of the population.

Erin Brewer (11:07):

The Swedish study was not self-selected. It was the entire population, including anybody who had sought treatment for gender identity issues, and it was longitudinal, which is so important.

One of the big flaws that I see with the studies that transgender-rights activists use is, as you said, they only include self-selected people who identify as transgender.

As we have noted before, even the activists will admit that the rates of comorbid conditions with people who have these gender identity issues are huge—nearly a hundred percent, I would guess. That's because you develop these identity issues as a coping mechanism, as a result of these underlying issues.

So it's not surprising that these kids are going to report feelings of wanting to self-harm and potentially thinking about suicide, because they have these underlying issues that are not being dealt with. They're being told they're inherently flawed, and that they have to run away from themselves to be okay. They're told that who they are is not okay. And they're having parents, teachers, and therapists telling them that. So it's not surprising at all to me that they're having these difficult feelings.

Maria Keffler (12:26):

Some of those co-morbid conditions that we recognize include autism. Autism is so overwhelmingly overrepresented in the transgender-identified community. People who are on the autism spectrum already struggle with discomfort with physical things. Some of the things that are co-morbid with autism include sensory and social issues. They're already feeling like they don't fit in, like there's something wrong with their bodies.

Then they hit adolescence. Autistic people don't like change. They like things to stay the same. When you're going through adolescence, everything's changing and nothing's staying the same.

To tell these kids on the autism spectrum, "The reason you're feeling that way is because you're transgender," is so destructive. Because not only are the kids going down a path that is not true, they're also not getting help for the things that are true. They're not getting support for the autism issues that they have.

Also—prior trauma. We know lots and lots of transgender-identified people have prior trauma, whether it's a sexual trauma or a rejection trauma. They've had a significant loss in their lives, whether from the divorce of their parents, or some sort of assault that they've experienced.

By just slapping on this easy, simple label of, "You're transgender," the trauma is not getting dealt with.

Erin Brewer (14:02):

That to me is what's most heartbreaking about this. I think about myself and what would have happened if I had been affirmed. First of all, it would have confirmed the self-hatred that I had, that there was something so wrong with me that I should become somebody else. But it also would have further buried the trauma that I had. I wouldn't have had anybody to help me process it. It would have just sat there infecting me for my whole life.

Thankfully I lived at a time where therapists were willing to look at that deep, dark pit and figure out what was going on that was causing this child to hate herself so much that she wanted to be somebody else.

What is incredibly concerning to me now is that we have gender activists going into schools and telling kids as young as kindergarten that they can be born in the wrong body.

> **I can't think of anything more damaging than telling children who are just starting to be social— who are just starting to go to school and learning to trust teachers and learning to trust adults other than their parents— that they could be born in the wrong body.**

I can't think of anything more damaging than telling children who are just starting to be social—who are just starting to go to school and learning to trust teachers and learning to trust adults other than their parents—that they could be born in the wrong body.

That's a huge lie. It creates this cognitive dissonance for children where they're going to be constantly wondering, "Am I a boy? Am I girl?" And they're going to rely on those stereotypes that we've worked so hard to get away from to determine whether or not they're a boy or a girl, rather than just accepting the fact that they're female or male based on their biology.

Maria Keffler (15:44):

Gender identity is really just personality. We're just talking about what your preferences are, what your personality is—some of those traits that are personal to each one of us.

Yes, I am a woman. I have XX chromosomes. I do not like shopping. I don't enjoy it. I hate buying shoes. That's just not my thing. So society would tell me, "Then you're not a real woman. If you don't like shopping and buying shoes, then there's something wrong with you. You might want to look at whether you're actually a man."

That's utterly ridiculous. I'm just a woman with certain personality traits and certain preferences, and we should not pathologize those. That's part of true diversity. True diversity is appreciating people for who they are, and not trying to tell them that there's something wrong with them and they're somebody else.

Erin Brewer (16:46):

I find it so confounding. Parents who are dealing with this have children coming home from school and saying, "I haven't decided if I'm a boy or girl yet," or "The teacher tells me that I can be neither a boy or a girl. So I'm not sure what I am," or, "I always thought I was a boy, but now I'm thinking maybe I'm a girl."

How do they navigate this? Because the kids are getting such misinformation at school and it's being reinforced now by television shows, by books that are in the school libraries, by teachers who are willing to undermine parents and even suggest to children that they might be transgender if they're gender-nonconforming. So it's a lot.

We talked about validating a child's feelings in a previous episode. Is there a place for parents at some point to just to challenge this narrative with facts?

Maria Keffler (17:48):

That's exactly what we have to do. Parents need to educate themselves on this. If you're watching this video, you're doing that. Parents need to recognize some of these places that this is illogical, that this is not truthful, and parents need to start pushing back.

In future episodes, we are going to talk about dealing with the school and some strategies for approaching teachers and principals and counselors about this, and what we need to be pushing back on. We don't have to be offensive and aggressive and mean about it, but we just need to start saying, "You know, I really don't buy the gender ideology argument. This doesn't make sense to me. I haven't seen anything that supports this in the research. If you have something, please show that to me, but I'm not seeing anything in this."

This is one of the insidious things—especially with young children—but really with any children. What the school is telling them is quite the opposite of what they're learning at home. All of us, until very recently, have taught our kids that boys have a penis and girls have a vagina—pretty simple, basic stuff.

Now that very simple, clear, truthful, obvious lesson is being convoluted at school. It's setting up a situation where a child has to ask, "Do I believe Mom and Dad, or do I believe my teacher?" People at school say, "If your parents don't agree with us, your parents are wrong." That's unconscionable.

> **It's setting up a situation where a child has to ask, "Do I believe Mom and Dad, or do I believe my teacher?" People at school say, "If your parents don't agree with us, your parents are wrong." That's unconscionable.**

Erin Brewer (19:31):

It really is. It's not that much different from a parent teaching a child that one plus one is two, and then that child going to school and the teacher says, "Oh, no. One plus one can be three. It could be four. It can be zero. It can be whatever you want it to be."

That is what's happening. How confusing for kids.

Maria Keffler (19:54):

It really is.

One of the other things I really wanted to touch on today is some of the propaganda and slogans that have been put out there by the gender industry. Slogans like, "You can be born in the wrong body," or "Trans women are women." What are some others? "Love has no labels," "Trans rights are human rights."

Slogans like those are designed to stop thoughts. When somebody has a quick, pithy, one-off little phrase they can throw out—you see this all the time. If you have a question about gender ideology like, "Wait a minute, why are we affirming?" as soon as you raise your question, you will immediately be called a TERF (transgender exclusionary radical feminist). You will be called a bigot. You will be called a hater. You'll be called a transphobe.

Those epithets and slogans are purposeful. They are intentional. They're not truthful. They're there to stop thought, because if you are not allowed to question this, then you can't push back on it. We need to be asking ourselves, "What do these slogans mean?"

> **Those epithets and slogans are purposeful.
> They are intentional. They're not truthful.
> They're there to stop thought, because if you are not
> allowed to question this, then you can't push back
> on it. We need to be asking ourselves,
> "What do these slogans mean?"**

"Trans women are women." Trans women are men who pretend to be women. If we say that they're women, we have obliterated the whole category of *woman*, because what is a woman? I can't believe we're at a place in society now where that's a big question that people say they can't answer. The answer right now is supposedly a woman is anyone who says, she's a woman.

What's the definition of a woman, Erin?

Erin Brewer (21:42):

An adult human female.

It's dangerous to affirm a transgender identity, emotionally and psychic-ally. Fundamentally, it's a dangerous path to put a child on, because it casts doubt on reality. It puts them on a path where they're going to damage their healthy body. It puts them on a path to be medicalized for the rest of their lives.

This isn't just about some kind of benign ideology where silly kids want to be called "they" and "them" instead of "he" or "she." If that were the case, it would be normal case of teenagers pushing against the system.

This is much more dangerous. As you said, it threatens to obliterate categories, such as *male* and *female*, which are important categories for us to have. It obliterates biology and basic reality.

We have a video clip from a doctor, who's going to talk about the fact that this is biology. It's not feelings. Feelings do not define our biology.

<u>Dr. Michelle Cretella (22:53):</u>

"Congratulations, It's a boy,' or "Congratulations, it's a girl." As a pediatrician for nearly 20 years that's how many of my patient relationships began. Our bodies declare our sex. Biological sex is not assigned. Sex is determined at conception by our DNA and stamped into every cell of our bodies. Human sexuality is binary. Either you have a normal Y chromosome and develop into a male or you don't, and you will develop into a female. There are at least 6,500 genetic differences between men and women. Hormones and surgery cannot and do not change this fact.

And identity is not biological, it is psychological. Identity has to do with thinking and feeling. Thoughts and feelings are not biologically hardwired. Our thinking and feeling may be factually right, or factually wrong.

For example, if I walk into my doctor's office today and say, "Hi, I'm Margaret Thatcher," my physician will say I am delusional and give me an anti-psychotic. However, if instead I walked in and said, "I am a man" He would say, "Congratulations, you're transgender." If were to say, "Doctor, I am suicidal. I'm an amputee trapped in a normal body. Please surgically remove my leg," I'll be diagnosed with body identity integrity disorder. But if I walk up to that same doctor and say, "I am a man, sign me up for a double mastectomy," my physician will.

According to most mainstream medical organizations, if you want to cut off a healthy arm or a healthy leg, you're mentally ill. But if you want to cut off healthy breasts or a penis, you're transgender.

Let's be clear. No one is born transgender. If gender identity were hardwired in the brain before birth, identical twins would have the same gender identity 100% of the time. They don't.

I had one little boy, a patient we'll call Andy. Between the ages of three and five, he increasingly played with girls and stereotypical girl toys and started saying he was a girl. I referred the parents and Andy to a therapist. Sometimes mental illness of a parent or abuse of the child are factors, but more commonly the child has misperceived family dynamics and internalized a false belief. In the middle of one session Andy put down the toy truck and held onto the Barbie and said, "Mommy and Daddy don't love me when I'm a boy." What the therapist learned is that when Andy was three, his sister with special needs was born. She required significantly more of his parents' care and attention. Andy misperceived this as, "Mommy and Daddy love girls. If I want them to love me again, I have to be a girl." With family therapy, Andy got better today.

[Today] Andy's parents would be told something quite different. They would hear, "This is who Andy really is. You must change his name and insure that everyone treats him as a girl, or he will commit suicide." As Andy would approach puberty, the experts would put him on puberty blockers so that he could continue to impersonate a girl. Experts assure us, "It doesn't matter that we've never tested puberty blockers in biologically normal children. It doesn't matter that when blockers are used to treat prostate cancer in men and gynecologic problems in women, that they cause problems with memory. We don't need testing. No, we need to arrest his physical development now, or he'll commit suicide," but this is not true.

Instead when supported in their biological sex through natural puberty, the vast majority of gender-confused children get better. We are chemically castrating gender-confused children with puberty blockers. Then we permanently sterilize many of them by adding cross-sex hormones, or estrogen and testosterone. Those put young children at risk for heart disease, strokes, diabetes cancers, and even the very emotional problems that experts claim to be preventing.

P.S. if a girl who insists she is a man has been on testosterone daily for one year, she's cleared to get a bilateral mastectomy at age 16.

Now mind you, the American Academy of Pediatrics recently came out with a report that urges pediatricians to caution teenagers about getting tattoos because tattoos are essentially permanent and can cause scarring. But this same AAP is 110% in support of 16-year-old girls getting a double mastectomy even without parental consent. So long as the girl insists that she's a man and has been taking testosterone daily for one year.

Let's be clear, to indoctrinate all children from preschool forward with the lie that they could be trapped in the wrong body disrupts the very foundation of a child's reality-testing. If a child can't trust the reality of their physical bodies, who or what can they trust? Transgender ideology in schools is psychological abuse that often leads to chemical castration, sterilization, and surgical mutilation.

If that's not child abuse, ladies and gentlemen, what is?

Maria Keffler (28:27):

I really love listening to Dr. Michelle Cretella. She really gets it. I mean, she's been a pediatrician for years. She really understands the facts about biology.

Erin Brewer (28:38):

One of the things that I've heard doctors talk about, which is important— as Dr. Cretella says in this video—is that our DNA is stamped in every cell of our body. It's in every organ, it's in our brains, it's in our liver, it's in our heart. And this is important because the healthcare that people receive is based on their biology: the dosage of certain medications that we get, the diagnoses that we get. Certain conditions exhibit differently depending on whether you're a man or a woman.

Consider something like getting an organ transplant. If you get an organ from the same sex you are, it's going to work better than if you get an organ from the opposite sex. It's because this is a biological truth. It's not based on feelings.

I've seen stories where there are people who go to the doctor and they're transgender-identified. They tell the doctor that they're the opposite sex. The doctor treats them as such and they get the wrong medical care because of it.

Maria Keffler (29:43):

There was a case where a pregnant woman went to the doctor and was having stomach pains, but told the doctors she was male. She presented as male and told the doctor she was a man. Her baby died. Wow. They didn't know they were dealing with a pregnant woman.

Erin Brewer (30:01):

Why would they even consider that? If someone says, "I'm a man," there are certain conditions that you just don't even consider because they're not something that men ever have.

Maria Keffler (30:12):

We see this affecting so many areas of life and I'm thinking about sports.

If we accept a lie that a boy can be a girl and therefore a boy can play in girls' sports because he thinks he's a girl—I'm sorry, that boy's body is going to give him an advantage in sports. That's what we're seeing. I believe it was coach Linda Blade who said that there is on average a 12% benefit that men and boys have over women and girls, all other things being equal, just by virtue of them being male.

If they've gone through male puberty, 15-year-old boys on a high school soccer team will beat an elite, world-class women's soccer team. They've played games: 15-year-old high school boys who just play soccer for fun will beat an elite women's team because the boys are bigger, stronger, faster. Their bodies have that advantage. We can't ignore that.

Erin Brewer (31:26):

A study was just released where the researchers looked at men who had been on estrogen and a drug to suppress the testosterone for a year, because that's the requirement in some of the sport bodies—that's the way they determine whether a man gets to compete as a woman. Yet this study found—which most of us I think would expect—that even after a year of having testosterone suppressed, and being on female hormones, these men still had a tremendous, quantifiable advantage over women.

The other thing that just keeps coming back to me is that this is based on feelings, and people lie to gain advantage all the time. We know this happens. So it's astonishing to me that we're just accepting that if somebody says that they feel like they are something, then they are that something. We know people lie to gain advantage.

On so many levels this narrative is just undermining reality and really dangerous for our kids.

Maria Keffler (32:43):

It really is moving into the area of being a religion. I think we're going to talk about that in our next episode, about some of the cultic aspects of this. Believing in something for which there's no physical evidence really moves into the territory of a theology.

That's what we're seeing with this, because there is no evidence that one's soul is sexed, that one's soul can be male or female. That's really the essence of this.

Erin Brewer (33:21):

One's "authentic self," is basically a soul. I mean, *authentic self* is a nebulous term. The only thing that I can think of to capture that idea is "soul."

Maria Keffler (33:35):

The idea that children know who they are—I find that ludicrous. Part of the task of childhood and adolescence is finding out who you are.

When I was 13, 14, 15, I was trying on different identities. I tried being an athlete. I told my kids this, and they laughed because I'm not an athlete. But I gave it a try. I tried out for the basketball team. I did not earn a spot on the team. I ran in track and I did okay. But it wasn't my thing. I tried doing the foreign language club and thought, "I'm going to be the chic French girl," and no, that didn't really quite fit me either.

So that's what kids should be doing—trying on different identities. Why would we cement them in one of those?

Erin Brewer (34:28):

We don't just cement them, but we medicalize it. It's just astonishing because like you said, that's what adolescence is about: figuring out who you are, and trying different things out.

Imagine if every time a 13-year-old said, "I want to be a doctor," from there on out, there was no other option: that child had to be a doctor. Or what if they said, "I want to be a construction worker." Would we say, "Okay. That's what you're going to be. You want to be a construction worker, that's your authentic self. We will only allow people to talk to you who will affirm that you are going to be construction worker"?

Maria Keffler (35:10):

Then you start applying it to younger and younger and younger kids, because this is what the gender industry is doing. Listen to this clip from Diane Ehrensaft, a gender researcher.

Diane Ehrensaft (35:30):

I have a colleague who's transgender, and there is a video of him as a toddler. So he was assigned female at birth. There is a video of him as a toddler tearing barrettes out of then her hair and throwing them on the ground and sobbing. That's a gender message. So you look for those kinds of actions, like tearing a skirt off. There was one where this child wore the little onesies with snap-ups in between the legs, and at age one would unsnap them to make a dress and have the dress flow. This was this child who was assigned male—that's communication, a pre-verbal communication. These are ways in which pre-verbal babies try to signal what sex they are.

Erin Brewer (36:18):

This is absurd.

Maria Keffler (36:21):

I want to ask her, "Have you ever spent any time with a small child?"

When my son was little and in his car seat, in the back seat, he would take his shoes off constantly. I remember my husband and I were new parents. This was our first child. We'd be in the car and turn around, yelling, "Leave your shoes on! Don't take off your shoes!" And he just delighted in taking his shoes off.

What did that mean? What was he telling us about?

Erin Brewer (36:51):

Oh my gosh, maybe he's not human?

Maria Keffler (36:53):

Maybe we should have had his feet amputated—we're being facetious here just in case anybody's popping in—we're being facetious here. But this is the sort of thing that Diane Ehrensaft believes.

Erin Brewer (37:07):

This is the absurdity. It's incredibly concerning that someone like her has an international platform in order to spew this absurdity.

We have a few questions from parents today. The first one says, "Arguing from logic doesn't seem to be making a dent with my daughter in the least. Why can't these kids see the inconsistencies and hypocrisy of this?"

Great question. It hearkens back to what you said that this is not about logic. It's not about science. It's about a belief system.

> # This is not about logic. It's not about science. It's about a belief system.

Maria Keffler (37:45):

It really is. The slogans that have been applied to it, as we said earlier, are designed to stop thought.

When you go to your child and you say, "There's no evidence that anyone can be born in the wrong body," what your child may say back to you is what the child's been taught: "Trans women are women!" Right? "That doesn't address what I just said to you."

They're not addressing the actual facts. So how do we get through to kids? How do we get through to people who are so insistent, who are zealots for this ideology?

Erin Brewer (38:28):

Our next episode, I believe, is on the brainwashing that happens, and how this is really a cult. There's no scientific foundation to this.

Depending on where your child is on this, you might be able to use reasonable thought. But if they have been completely indoctrinated into this, then you're going to have to use different techniques. Just telling them, "Let's go get your DNA tested to see what your chromosome show," isn't going to be effective. They're going to just say, "You're transphobic!" because you are not validating their beliefs.

What we have to do as parents is to get into the schools and stop this from happening before our children are indoctrinated, because once they are indoctrinated, it's incredibly hard to deprogram them.

Maria Keffler (39:20):

One important strategy, and you can use this with anyone that you're arguing with about something, is just asking questions. It's harder to throw those slogans back at a question, because if you really believe that you're right, you ought to be able to answer questions about it.

So just ask a really simple question, like, "Well, is gender fixed? Or is it fluid? Is it something that's never going to change, or is it something that's fluid over a lifetime?" Because the answer to that question, whether you say it's fixed or it's fluid—both of those completely undermine the transgender industry. If it's fixed, then you need to ask at what point in time is it fixed, and why would we ever solidify somebody in a gender identity before that time at which it's fixed? But the gender industry will not put a finger on when it's fixed, because as we said, they keep trying to push it earlier and earlier and earlier.

Erin Brewer (40:21):

Not only that, but they keep trying to justify people who change, who come out as non-binary and then as transgender. They want the ability for people to be fluid while at the same time, they're saying people are born this way.

Maria Keffler (40:36):

If somebody comes out and says, "You know what? I thought I was transgender, but I was wrong. I'm actually the sex I was born," they don't like that at all. They will not affirm that.

There's fluidity in one direction, but not the other.

Another good question is, "What does it feel like to be a woman? What does it feel like to be a man? Can you explain those feelings that you're having that leads you to believe that's how it feels like to be the opposite sex? Because honestly, I don't know what it feels like to be a woman."

Erin Brewer (41:14):

You're right. Ask questions. If somebody is really entrenched in it, then using logic is not going to work.

There's a book by Peter Boghossian and he talks about this. It is called, *How to Have Impossible Conversations*. He talks how to challenge someone in their belief systems and the different techniques to be used. And you really have to be gentle and compassionate when you do it. You have to determine what your goal is, because a lot of times people's goal is to win an argument.

In this case, that should not be your intended outcome. Your intended outcomes should be more about understanding, because this ideology is so full of holes that if you're able to have conversations with someone, and have that respect and have that give-and-take, eventually they're going to see those holes. I would really recommend that.

Do we have another question?

Maria Keffler (42:21):

We do. I want to read that book though.

Erin Brewer (42:23):

It's really good and I've been practicing. I've learned so much just from the first couple of chapters.

Maria Keffler (42:31):

I want to go back to what you said about being honest and being gentle and being caring, because really the goal is to have a restored relationship, and for both of you to come closer to truth, because there are some things that you probably don't understand about what that person's going through. So having a really genuine question, like, "I want to understand this," can serve the dual purpose of healing your relationship as well as helping bring truth into the conversation.

We have one more question. I think we addressed this one already: "Listening to my kid talk about gender sounds like listening to a religious zealot. Am I crazy to think this is a new kind of religion?"

Erin Brewer (43:16):

It has all the hallmarks of a religion. I was thinking about it the other day, how, if somebody challenges this, it's like they're cast out. I'm not sure what the word is when you say something blasphemous about a religion and you're kicked out, but this that's really how it is. It's excommunication. You're not allowed to challenge the authorities or you're shunned.

It's very rigid in its thinking, and it's very based a lot of these rituals. The children get sucked in, and there are these rituals that are celebrated, like puberty blockers: "You went on puberty blockers!" and there's a big celebration. You go on cross-sex hormones. There's a big celebration. You get your breasts lopped off. That's a big celebration. It's almost like these religious activities that happen. They're very much based on feelings. they're based on bringing the group together and solidifying the members as part of that group.

All of these things are hallmarks of religions.

Maria Keffler (44:27):

The whole ingroup and outgroup thing that is very indicative of a religion. "We are the true, good people. We are the true ones who have understanding, and everybody else is on the outside and not to be trusted."

I think about the word "ally." That word has been used in the gender industry, that you're either an ally or you're not. Well, what's the opposite of an ally? It's an enemy. There's no middle ground. There's no middle ground in a war. They've really set this up with a lot of war-like language.

I would even call it a religious inquisition. "Are you an ally? What are you doing to prove you're an ally?"

> **There's no middle ground in a war. They've really set this up with a lot of war-like language. I would even call it a religious inquisition. "Are you an ally? What are you doing to prove you're an ally?"**

Erin Brewer (45:14):

If you're not an ally, they don't want anything to do with you. You're evil. These are all very religious ideas.

Determining how far in children are into this ideology is important, because if they're just putting their foot in it, then you're going to address this in a very different way than if they have totally converted. It's a conversion process. It's a "Come to Trans" movement, and they have the big "T" for Truth. "Anybody who doesn't agree is evil. You shouldn't even spend time around them."

That's the indication that it's not just a religion, but a cult. They're suggesting people engage in self-harming behaviors. They're suggesting that people isolate from others. These are things that are cult-like behaviors. So it's not just a religious belief system. It's a cult belief system.

In our next episode, we'll get into some techniques for how to handle that. We will include resources from people who are experts in this. It's important, if your kid is far in, that you access those resources.

Episode 6 Resource List

Is Gender Fixed, Fluid, or Formed from Society's Stereotypes?
https://uncommongroundmedia.com/gender-is-is-fixed-fluid-or-formed-from-societys-stereotypes/

Maritza Cummings with Benjamin Boyce:
https://youtu.be/GWWIhZNZrdU

Transgenderism: a State-Sponsored Religion?:
https://www.thepublicdiscourse.com/2018/01/20547/

How to Have Impossible Conversations: A Very Practical Guide by Peter Boghossian and James Lindsay: https://www.amazon.com/How-Have-Impossible-Conversations-Practical/dp/0738285323

How to tell if babies are transgender?: https://www.youtube.com/watch?v=M7KBZeRC1RI

Episode 7: Cultic Aspects of Gender Ideology

https://youtu.be/7jOpKsDIaw8

<u>Maria Keffler (00:00:47):</u>

Today we are talking about the cultic aspects of gender ideology, how this is really a cult we're looking at.

<u>Erin Brewer (00:00:56):</u>

Some people might bristle at that. That's a pretty loaded term, "cult," and yet it's very clearly defined. It has meaning. When we go through what the definition of a cult is, it will be clear how the gender ideology is a cult.

What makes something a religion, a belief, or a cult? People will understand why we're saying this and what is the reason for defining it as a cult.

<u>Maria Keffler (00:01:23):</u>

As you look at the things that the gender industry is telling people, it is a cultish ideology. I've said this for a while, and a woman in my school district, who is a mom of a transgender-identified child, got really angry with me for calling it an ideology. She said, "It's a fact. This is truth."

That got me thinking: "Well, why am I calling it an ideology?" And I started looking at what a cult is.

A cult is a group of people who rally around a certain set of beliefs, that often have to do with the meaning of life, the origins of life. There's a little bit of gray area between what you call a religion and what is a cult.

Religion is around an idea of a deity, of the origins of life, how we got here, what's the meaning of life. There are many religions and those are not necessarily cultish belief systems.

It falls into the area of a cult when it departs from fact and when it revolves around one charismatic leader who drives it and to whom you must have complete and total devotion.

I will start by saying, that's one of the aspects of the gender ideology that is lacking in terms of a cult. I haven't been able to find who is that one charismatic leader, but as I'm reading about cults and thinking about this question, I have come to think it is the self. I think that charismatic leader, to whom you must have complete devotion, is actually your own sense of self.

That's what's driving this idea that what you are inside may not match what you are outside: "Your inner sense of self may not match your physiology or biology. We have to listen to that inner sense of self, no matter what it's saying."

There's so much that is nonsensical and contradictory about it. We talked about that in our last video, about why gender ideology is so illogical. Yet we're not allowed to question anything that an individual person says about his or her inner landscape or inner workings.

That's a big part of identifying it as a cult. You're not allowed to question it, or to say, "Why do you think that? How did you begin thinking that? Let's look at the logic of that." As soon as you question anything that somebody thinks about themselves, you're labeled a hater, a bigot, a transphobe, and that leads to another aspect of cult ideology.

All cults have an in-group and an out-group. The in-group are the chosen, the true believers, the righteous people. The people on the outside of the cult are to be suspect. They are to be cut out of your life if they don't believe what you believe. They are called lots of names.

> **All cults have an in-group and an out-group. The in-group are the chosen, the true believers, the righteous people. The people on the outside of the cult are to be suspect. They are to be cut out of your life if they don't believe what you believe. They are called lots of names.**

That's another reason when I look at this, I think, "Oh, this is very cultic."

Erin Brewer (00:05:03):

It's an important lens to look at this through, because even if it doesn't completely fit the definition of cult, like having a charismatic leader, it is so similar to a cult in how the people are indoctrinated with such a belief system that they start accepting things that are clearly nonsensical.

For parents who are struggling with children who have bought into this ideology, it can be helpful to understand how cults work and how to get somebody out of a cult. You can't just assume this is a phase that your kid is going through and they'll outgrow it. It's to the point now where it used to be that children would outgrow gender dysphoric feelings—the vast majority of kids would resolve that as they went through puberty. But this is different.

This isn't gender dysphoria, this isn't typical body dysmorphia. This is a belief system that they're being indoctrinated into, and they're not going to simply grow out of it.

> # This is a belief system that they're being indoctrinated into, and they're not going to simply grow out of it.

One of the things that I'm seeing in groups for desisters and detransitioners is this sense of, "I'm trying so hard, I'm trying so hard to detransition. I just don't know if I can." Or when somebody does detransition, there's this response of, "Wow, I don't know how you did that. That's so hard."

So even people who are trying to get out of it are struggling to get out of it. That's what's different between a normal destructive phase that can happen to teenagers, versus being indoctrinated into a cultish belief system. The kids, even when they want to get out of it, sometimes have a hard time.

As parents, we have to know what the techniques are that professionals use to get people out of cults so that we can apply them in this situation.

Maria Keffler (00:07:05):

This is a book I want to recommend to everybody, *Freedom of Mind* by Steven Hassan. He is a cult expert. He was sucked into the Moonies cult back in the seventies and his family staged an intervention and got him out. He has since studied psychology and he has started the Freedom of Mind Center.

I've been reading this book and looking at it through the lens of the transgender movement. I'm going to refer to this book a lot. He talks about the importance of a strategic interaction approach. SIA—he calls it the Strategic Interaction Approach. When I talk to people who have gotten their kids back, by and large they have done this, whether they realized they were doing it or not.

One of the first things that they did was to cut their kids off from all of the influences of transgender ideology.

The younger your child is, the easier that is to do. It's never easy, even with the young child. Pulling them out of school, taking away the internet, and severing them from the influencers around them who are carrying them along in this ideology is difficult.

Unfortunately with older kids, if they're over 18 and they're on their own, it's much, much harder to do. Steven Hassan talks about that with some of the more understood cults, like the Moonies, or the Aum Shinrikyo in Japan, or Scientology. Adults have the freedom to belong to whatever group they want.

The first thing to do is to try to keep connection with your child by trying to do activities together that don't have anything to do with this ideology. Just, "Hey, would you come over to dinner? We miss you. We'd love to see you."

Try to maintain a relationship and to have strategic interactions, and planned discussions. The person who's in the cult is not going to know that these are planned, but you have an agenda and you are going to ask questions like, "Tell me more about gender. Is it fixed or fluid? How does that work?"

Ask those questions and try to just do a little at a time, chiseling away at the lack of logic in it, because they have been taught to stop thoughts if they're questioned about something that the ideology believes. They're given techniques to stop their thoughts so that they don't go there.

With gender ideology, it's often those terms that they throw out: "You're a hater," "You're a bigot," "You're a transphobe." Those are thought-stopping techniques. As soon as someone hears a question like, "Is gender fixed or is it fluid?" you get called a transphobe for even asking, and that that stops the thought.

Your job as a parent, or as someone who loves this person, is to try to keep pushing them back toward thinking. It's tough.

Erin Brewer (00:10:50):

That's interesting, you want to re-engage those critical thinking skills.

I want to clarify one thing here, because I've heard people say that all religions are cults. One of the reasons that cults are dangerous is, first of all, they encourage isolating behaviors.

You mentioned that you're not allowed to be around anybody who doesn't agree with you. That is thought control. If you're around people who don't agree with you, you might start thinking, and that's dangerous for cults, because they're based on a shaky foundation of nonsense.

The other thing that's so critical about this particular cult—and most cults—is that they embrace self-harming behaviors. That is the most important aspect of this for parents. If this isn't stopped—if the child continues in this cult for very long—they're going to start wanting to engage in self-harming behaviors: taking puberty, blockers, cross-sex hormones, surgeries, all of these things that are going to damage their healthy bodies.

That's not something that most religions advocate.

The child has got a perfectly healthy body and they want to damage it, often medicalizing for life. That's such a critical difference.

Like you said, most of it is based on a lack of critical thinking skills. They're taught not to question. They're taught just to go along with the ideology. They're taught that anybody who encourages critical thinking about this is evil, and somebody that you shouldn't be around. So that's where the parents have to do this very careful dance, because if they push too hard, the child might completely disengage with them.

You mentioned having these interventions set up where you're able to question, but again, I want to caution people not to push too hard because the child might completely disengage with you and then you lose the opportunity to help them out of this.

Maria Keffler (00:13:15):

Steven Hassan and this book talks about his organization, which comes alongside families and helps them pull people out of cults. It *is* a dance, and knowing how far to push and when to relent is a sensitive, nuanced thing. It's tough.

One other thing I wanted to point out—I loved what you said about the difference between a religion and a cult. I didn't appreciate this until I read Steven Hassan's book. Cults change your identity. So you have your pre-cult identity, and then the cult re-forms you into the identity they want you to have.

When I read that in his book, I said, "Oh my gosh, identity. That's what transgenderism is all about. It's about your identity."

Anyone who's seen kids who go through this—they are very different once they enter the transgender cult: their appearance, their speech, their thought process, and they have this new identity. So helping somebody out of the cult is really helping them reconnect with their true identity.

Erin Brewer (00:14:42):

The pre-cult identity.

Maria Keffler (00:14:44):

Well, their pre-cult identity, but this is so insidious when it's happening with middle school kids and young kids going through adolescence. They are starting to form their adult identity, and then they get derailed by this false identity. This transgenderism ideology derails a natural process of maturation. They're supposed to be forming their true adult identity and figuring out who they are as adults. Then they get derailed by this nonsensical, dangerous, harmful cult.

So you're not necessarily just trying to help them get back to their pre-cult identity, because that may have been their childhood identity. The goal is to help them know that their biology is integral to who they are, and they need to come into a place of accepting who they are, not rejecting it for some fake identity.

Erin Brewer (00:15:45):

It's interesting. What you are saying is that the cult is encouraging children to remain childlike, with the puberty blockers especially.

But one of the hallmarks of adolescence is questioning. Toddlers ask things like, "Why is the sky blue?" and "Why is the grass green?" They ask these kinds of basic questions. Then teenagers go through the same process. Only they're asking more broad-based questions: "Why am I here?" "Who am I?" "What do I want to do with my life?"

These are big and difficult questions, and could be overwhelming to kids. In a way, the trans cult just says, "Don't worry, you don't have to think about that." It provides them with scripts, and it provides them with this way to tamp down those difficult questions that they're asking themselves. There's an attempt to keep them childlike and also unquestioning.

It reminds me of a meeting I went to when I was a young teenager. They were saying stuff that didn't make sense. I started asking questions and they asked me to leave. I thought that was interesting.

That right there is an indication. If you're not allowed to question things—if members within that community are so defensive that they immediately call you a hater if you start questioning—that's a good sign something's off.

> **If you're not allowed to question things—if members within that community are so defensive that they immediately call you a hater if you start questioning—that's a good sign something's off.**

Most ideologies that people have welcome questioning. They are firm in their belief systems: "Bring it on, ask questions."

This is just the opposite. You are not allowed to ask questions. If you do, it's because you're a hater, a bigot, perhaps even a Nazi and a fascist.

Maria Keffler (00:17:36):

That's evidence of the thought-stopping techniques, because you're right: if you have the facts, and you have something underpinning what you believe, you shouldn't be afraid of questions about it. You should be able to answer questions.

I talk to a lot of parents who are in various parenting groups online. I hear some horrific stories about these parenting groups that are supposedly support groups for parents with transgender kids. If a parent says, "You know, this doesn't make sense to me. My child had trauma when she was a child. And I think this is related to that," they get raked over the coals. They just get shut down and sometimes kicked out of the group just for asking those questions.

That's a huge red flag.

Erin Brewer (00:18:28):

We have a video clip. I'm wondering if we can watch it, because it shows something that people may not realize. This indoctrination isn't just happening within the peer groups; it's starting to happen within the schools. Teachers have bought into this ideology and are now pushing it onto pretty young kids in the school.

This video clip shows how insidious this is.

When you say, "Pull your child out of school," a lot of people are going to be like, "Well that's kind of extreme. Why would you do this?" This video will illustrate why that's important.

Nadine (00:19:07):

Hi, I'm Nadine, a sex educator.

Eva (00:19:10):

And I'm Eva, a sex researcher.

Nadine (00:19:11):

I use the pronouns *she* and *her* because I'm a woman. And when I was your age I used to be a girl.

Eva (00:19:16):

Gender is how you feel on the inside about whether you're a boy or a girl, a man, or a woman, if you're non-binary, feel like neither, or both. People can also be fluid, feel more like female or male based on a different day or time. It's really individual. Absolutely.

Everyone born with a vulva is a girl or identifies as a girl. True or false?

Nadine (00:19:37):

Well, not everybody is sure. And that makes sense, but our genitals actually don't determine our gender. So some people born with vulvas can be boys.

@GustionLGBTedu (00:19:49):

I have been through the spectrum. If we were to say a spectrum of like boys and girls, I have been everywhere in between. I was born a girl. And then when I was two years old, I told my mom for the first time that I was a boy. And I think that I framed it. I don't remember it. I've only been told stories, but I framed it because my brother's middle name was the same as my dad's. And so I insisted that my middle name was also the same as his. But back in the day, there were no talk shows and there was no internet. There were no resources. So she just ignored it. And then nothing happened for many, many years. And then it still took me a long time, into my twenties before I decided to transition. But in there I was you know, a tomboy, if that's what we say, or like I was sporty, I had short hair.

Michael Knowles (00:20:40):

Look at how exploitative this is. Or look at all the advocacy here. This isn't just presenting facts to children. It's not presenting any facts to children; it's presenting fantasy.

But the suggestion here is, "Look, I was a tomboy. Maybe if you're a tomboy, you're actually the opposite sex. Yeah. I had short hair. Maybe if you've got short hair, maybe you were the opposite sex." It's horrifying. I mean, this is horrifying to subject children to this kind of sexual confusion at such a young age, to subject them to such a bizarre, radical new ideology that has no basis in science. And it's only been around for a few years.

Erin Brewer (00:21:15):

Maria, I am just shocked.

I was telling you earlier, I didn't know what a vulva was until a couple years ago. It was just not part of my vocabulary. When I see little kids being told that someone who has a vulva may or may not be a woman or a female or a girl—when I hear this nonsense, it is very concerning.

It is not truthful stuff being taught in the schools. It shakes me to my toes. It's no different than a teacher going in and saying, "Well, kids, I know that some people think one plus one is two, but sometimes one plus one is zero and sometimes it's three. We just don't know until we ask the person who's answering the question, whether one plus one is 1, 2, 3, 4, maybe it's, maybe it's 2000."

That's what this looks like to me. They're talking about something that's biological, that's been defined for eons. What is a male? What is a female? That's empirical and can be tested. They're confusing children.

Maria Keffler (00:22:28):

It's very intentional. This is the thing I have the hardest time getting people to understand when I talk to them about this. So many people don't believe this is happening in their school. I think it's happening in most schools. If it's not in your school yet, it's coming, because this is a very intentional agenda. The NEA (National Education Association) is very clear that they want this taught in schools.

I've mentioned this before about my own district. In an elementary school in February of 2019 the NEA brought a transgender activist into the school and read the book *I Am Jazz* to two classes of kindergartners. This is intentional. *I Am Jazz* is a storybook about a boy who decided he wasn't a boy.

Erin Brewer (00:23:23):

He decided? It seems more like his parents decided for him.

One of the things that you have is some entry points on how cults gain access to those who are vulnerable. That's important because it used to be the Moonies might accost you in an airport and try and get you the message, or when you were walking down the street. Now we have this cult that is fully ensconced within schools.

Can you talk about the various ways in which cult gains entry to children?

Maria Keffler (00:24:00):

There are two aspects to this. The slide that we have here on entry points— I found this on genderspectrum.org, and it was in their "toolkit" for how to get transgender ideology into schools. This was not even about indoctrinating kids. This was about getting it into the school system. This has since been removed from their page, but I grabbed screenshots before they took it down.

From genderspectrum.org, on how to get transgender theory into schools via "Entry Points" [UPDATE 2019.8.12: Entry Points Info has been removed from site.]

Entry Points
When focusing on the intentional development of gender inclusive school settings, it is helpful to think in terms of four discrete approaches, or entry points: **Internal, Interpersonal, Instructional** and **Institutional**. Through deliberate work in each one of these areas, gender inclusive practices can be woven into the fabric of the institution.

They had four stages of getting this cult into schools and into the culture. This was specifically about schools. The first was the *internal* entry point, changing the way people think. Make transgenderism seem like it's nice, like it's agreeable. So changing people's thought patterns.

The second one was *interpersonal*, which is really about changing the way we talk about it. We've seen this assault on the language. No longer is it *men* and *transgender men*, now it's *men* and *cis men*. You know, women are trans women, cis women. There are so many words that have never existed before, like *genderfluid*.

Erin Brewer (00:25:20):

Non-binary. And *cis.*

It is shocking to me how it has infiltrated into the culture so easily and yet basically *cis* is a made-up term. They say it's anybody who identifies as the sex they were born. So first of all, it suggests that anybody who's not transgender is 100% comfortable with being whatever sex they're born, whatever that means.

It also suggests that there are different categories of being male and female. You have the cis woman and the trans woman. I've seen posts where people say trans women are more women than cis women are, because they've had to work for it.

There's this whole muddling of our language. Now we don't have *women*.

There's no such thing as just a woman. You're either a trans woman or a cis woman. The transgender activists are trying to define even what it means to be a woman. It's very convoluted. Those kinds of words, I've even seen them appear in very reputable research journals. There's this acceptance and has just taken over.

Now if you say, "Well, I don't identify as cisgender or transgender, I'm a woman," that's now considered transphobic.

Maria Keffler (00:26:53):

You're immediately called *transphobic* and a *hater* because of the thought-stopping process. That was the second entry point: changing the way people talk about this issue.

The third one was *instructional,* and that was about getting transgender curriculum into the schools. Organizations like Planned Parenthood and the Human Rights Campaign Foundation have created materials, and they make these beautiful curriculum packages for teachers. It's about how to get transgender ideology into the math class, how to get it into the science class, how to get it into social studies and history.

I was a teacher, and teachers are overworked. We have too much to do. We're exhausted. Lesson planning for a 45-minute class can take you three hours if you're doing a good job at it. When someone comes along and says, "Here, I have a lesson plan, all packaged for you. It's beautiful. Here are all of the worksheets. Here are all the slides. Here are some manipulatives you can use with it." Teachers are like, "You just saved me three hours. Thank you!"

But the intention is to get this cult into every class, and they've done it.

The fourth entry point was *institutional* and that's getting the policies changed.

That's where I first encountered this whole issue, when I found out that my school district was putting into place a transgender students policy that was allowing boys to be in the girls bathroom and boys to sleep in girls' hotel rooms overnight, and allowing boys to play on girls sports teams. When I saw that and I started investigating where this came from, I realized we are behind the curve. They've already passed through all three of the first three entry points. Now they're in the fourth entry point, which is making it institutionalized.

This is what we see with the so-called Equality Act [H.R. 5]. Once they replace the word "sex" with "gender," as you said, there is no longer a category of woman.

That's a whole separate issue but it's part and parcel of the cult ideology: "We will have it our way, and everybody is going to go along with it, whether they like it or not."

<u>Erin Brewer (00:29:16)</u>:

What's unnerving is how strategic this has been. Most of us who are looking at it now are like, "How did we get here?" We're just confused as to how this has become so accepted, and almost canonical. We're not allowed to question it and we can't figure it out.

Based on this they've had a clear strategy to do this, and they've been working on for quite a while. We're behind the curve on this. That's why we're at such a disadvantage and why just talking to your kid about it and trying to give them an alternative may not work, because it's already so entrenched in the schools.

Another slide that is important talks about the cult indoctrination techniques. For those who might be questioning, "I don't know this, it seems a little extreme to call this a cult," would you mind going through that slide and talking about why we should be approaching this as a cult rather than just as a different belief system?

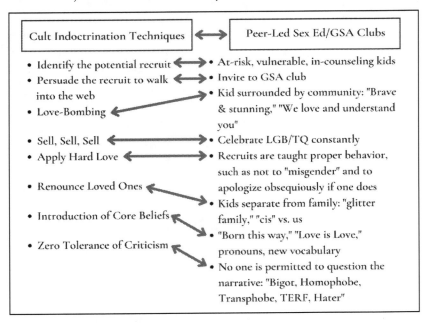

<u>Maria Keffler (00:30:23)</u>:

If you look at how this is impacting kids, what the schools are doing to kids, it's really clear to see the indoctrination that's going on. They're teaching kids younger and younger that this is factual when it is not. GSA clubs, Gender-Sexuality Allies, or what's the other term for it? Sometimes they're called Equality or Spectrum Clubs.

Erin Brewer (00:30:51):

That is a turn of language because they used to be Gay-Straight Alliance Clubs. Now they've just completely co-opted even that terminology.

Maria Keffler (00:31:02):

But GSAs are really indoctrination centers.

I talked to someone from WoLF (Women's Liberation Front) about what was going on with GSAs and she was so angry. She said, "When we started talking about having GSA clubs in school, it was just to support gay kids so that they would have a social system." She said, "We asked, 'Is this going to turn into recruiting?' And we were laughed at, and we were told we were ridiculous. And now that's exactly what's happening."

There's a video of a school counselor who is talking to other counselors and teachers about how to start GSA clubs. And she says, "We poach the kids from the counseling department."

There's a parent in a district near me, who was invited to a meeting on equity, diversity, and inclusion. She said she was horrified that the teacher who was leading said, "If you want to get kids for the GSA club, go to the lunchroom and find out which kids are sitting alone and go sit with them and talk to them because they need somebody."

You talk to these kids who are detransitioners and desisters and they'll tell you, "I didn't have a friend group, then I got invited to the GSA club and suddenly I had a friend group," and it's this love bombing. That's what happens when they go to the GSA club: they're love bombed. They find somebody who's in a vulnerable state and just love on them: "You're wonderful." "We are your people." "Come be with us."

But then the next step is to start separating them. Separate them from the people who would protect them. That's exactly what's being taught in the GSA clubs: "If your parents don't agree with this, they're toxic. They're bad for you. You need to get away from them."

Erin Brewer (00:33:03):

"They don't love you and you can go find a family that will love you and friends that will love you." There have been instances where kids are encouraged to run away from home, which just puts them in such a dangerous position. That is not something that a healthy belief system encourages.

Maria Keffler (00:33:24):

I had a conversation with a man here in my district. He teaches in a neighboring district and he was at a school board meeting that I was at on transgender policy. He's a trans-rights activist and a high school teacher. He told me at this meeting, "I shouldn't tell you this because we're not supposed to do this. But if I find out that a kid doesn't feel safe at home, I help him find someplace else to live and you help them." He helps kids become runaways.

Erin Brewer (00:33:57):

Teachers, helping kids run away. That is part of these extreme belief systems. They're so convinced that they are right, that they're willing to put kids in incredibly risky situations in order to further this ideology.

Maria Keffler (00:34:19):

We know the statistics on runaway kids. They're not good. Kids don't run away and then go find a happy life somewhere else. Most of the time they end up on the street, they ended up being trafficked. They end up on drugs. They end up dead and homeless. That's generally the path for kids who run away.

Erin Brewer (00:34:38):

This also enforces the dependency upon those in this ideology, because once you run away from home, you are now completely at the mercy of the other people who are part of this ideology. If you decide that you don't buy into it anymore—boy, are you alone.

Maria Keffler (00:35:02):

We hear that from detransitioners and desisters all the time, which is one of the other illogical points about transgender ideologies. They say, "Gender is on a spectrum, you can flow." But if somebody changes their mind and says, "No, I think I actually am my birth sex," that's not permitted. You're out of it. You're out of the group, which is another one of the cultic aspects: the in-group and the out-group.

The gender industry tries to use language like "allies." What's an ally? Ally is a military term. It's somebody who is your partner in whatever strategy that you're trying to enact, whether it's storming a castle or taking over another country or preventing someone from taking over your country.

Your allies are the ones who are working with you. The opposite of that is an enemy.

There's no middle ground.

There's no neutral ground with this. You're either an ally to the transgender ideology, or you're an enemy. That is very cultic. Most religions do not consider you an enemy if you don't subscribe to their religion.

> **This is very cultic. Most religions do not consider you an enemy if you don't subscribe to their religion.**

Erin Brewer (00:36:26):

One of the things that I've seen here in my town, and I've seen it play out in other situations, is that allies have to be at the beck and call of those who are transgender-identified. There's this pecking order, and there's a hierarchy. If an ally does not do what the trans-identified people tell them to do, or if they do it wrong, they get beaten down and they get told, "You are an oppressor. Therefore you need to accommodate us. You need to center us. You need to do what we tell you to do."

There was a situation in my small town where an ally set up a public meeting to celebrate transgenderism, but she didn't do it quite right. She said something that was a little bit offensive and they just jumped on her. She was completely apologetic.

There's a sense of needing punishment if you do it wrong, and you have to repent. You have to confess and repent and make penance. It is like some religions. Yet it's different, because in most Christian religions when you repent and ask for forgiveness, that's granted. But in this ideology, you have to continually prove that you're an ally. They're on the lookout for you to make one little mistake. When you make one little mistake, they're going to jump on you.

It's a culture of fear, intimidation, and bullying, which is so ironic, because one of the ways it's gotten into the schools is through anti-bullying, and yet it is one of the most bullying ideologies I've ever come across.

Maria Keffler (00:38:24):

They've just changed who the bullies are.

That's also straight out of cults. That's what cults do. They draw you in with love-bombing, and then they keep you in with fear and intimidation.

I see a lot of gang aspects to this as well, because when you talk to the kids who've joined the GSA clubs, once they joined the GSA club— and especially if they say that they're transgender—they're untouchable. Nobody can criticize or question anything that they want. Even the teachers and all the adults have to do exactly what they say.

Do you remember being 13, 14, 15 years old? That is a heady pill, to know that you have this golden ticket that gives you complete control over everyone around you, if you just say you're transgender.

Erin Brewer (00:39:22):

I was one of those kids who would have been very vulnerable to this. I didn't have a lot of friends. I didn't fit in. I was the weird kid. If I had gone from being that weird kid who was ostracized to all of a sudden being emboldened: "You call me this. This is my pronoun. I'm going in the men's room"—boy, that would have gotten to my head. I have no doubt.

You suddenly give a kid who's been struggling power over their parents, their teachers, all the other kids—and, if somebody calls them the wrong name or the wrong pronoun, they get to go report it. And *they're* the victim.

These are kids who are very empowered with this ideology. They are just looking for opportunities to get people in trouble.

That's another part of this that's concerning. It's thought-police, word-police, speech-police, and that indignation, "Mom! You called me my deadname!"—that ability to have this hatred.

In these parent groups that you've talked about, I've seen some posts where parents who are fully bought into the ideology post something like, "I accidentally called my daughter her deadname. I don't know what to do. I don't know how to make it up to her."

Or I've seen parents who've had their children's names tattooed on their bodies, then their child becomes transgender-identified, and assumes a new name. These parents post pictures of their tattoo and say, "What can I do to take this off of my body? Because it's my daughter's deadname now."

Teenagers should not be given this much power. It's not good for them. They need boundaries.

Maria Keffler (00:41:19):

Exactly. There's a teacher south of me here in Virginia, Peter Vlaming—

he's a French teacher who has been teaching 25 or 30 years. He had a student who decided to "transition genders." Mr. Vlaming did not refuse to call her *he*. Instead he chose not to use pronouns at all, because he just felt like it was a lie to use the wrong pronoun, but he did not disrespect the student. He just chose not to use pronouns.

There was something going on in the classroom. The student was about to fall and he said, "Help her!" or something. He was trying to keep her from being hurt. He used the "her" pronoun, which is the *correct* pronoun, but not the *preferred* pronoun.

He's been fired. He was fired for that. She went and reported him and got him fired. There's an ongoing lawsuit right now. We're still waiting to find out what's going to happen there.

But when a teenager can get a teacher fired because he accidentally used the wrong pronoun—especially when he used the correct pronoun— that's just wrong. That's insidious.

Erin Brewer (00:42:51):

Are there other cult indoctrination techniques that we haven't covered yet?

Maria Keffler (00:42:57):

There's a lot in this book. I want people to get this book and read it, but if I can just leave you with one thing, Steven Hassan talks about the BITE model.

BITE stands for Behavior, Information, Thought & Emotional control.

> ## BITE stands for Behavior, Information, Thought & Emotional control.

A cult will use one or more of these techniques. It really fits with the gender ideology because of the behavior control—what words you're allowed to say, the way you present yourself.

It's very clear that they're buying into the stereotypes because nobody says, "I'm a biological girl, but I think I'm a boy, but I'm going to keep dressing like a girl." That never happens. They've got to follow the stereotypes. There are a lot of behavior controls. You have to say certain things, do certain things. If you don't, you are punished for not behaving appropriately.

Information control: They don't want kids in this ideology to question it.

They don't want to hear that studies are showing that affirmation is not healthy. "Don't question these things, don't ask too many questions."

And then the emotional control—I'm immediately drawn to thinking about what they tell parents. Every parent who has dealt with a child has heard, "Do you want a live son or a dead daughter?" "Do you want a live daughter or a dead son?" That's nothing but emotional manipulation. You can't say who's going to commit suicide. The suicide studies that they cite are completely bogus. When you look at the methodologies, they are completely bogus. It's just nothing but emotional manipulation.

Erin Brewer (00:45:09):

I often go to this analogy. For someone to say, "Do you want a dead child or a heroin addicted child?" "Do you want a dead child or a child who is an anorexic?" You can either have one or the other, there's nothing in between.

To suggest that if parents don't affirm this, that their child will kill themselves—what is so disturbing to me about that is that it's putting the idea of suicide out there. Kids are hearing this. Now we're going to have a generation of kids who think that it's a perfectly acceptable response to kill yourself if your parents don't accept your transgender identity.

Maria Keffler (00:45:56):

If you threaten to kill yourself, you can get anything you want.

Erin Brewer (00:46:01):

This is dangerous. It's what defines it as a cult, rather than just a belief system.

We don't generally have people going around and telling others that they're going to kill themselves if they don't get their way. When that happens, we tend to put them in a behavior unit and get them help, because it's a sign that they're in extreme distress.

This is a very dangerous indoctrination process.

Teaching kids to use this is going to have long-term repercussions, because they're going to learn, "If I don't get what I want, this is what I do." It's harmful on so many levels. This is different from a typical worldview or ideology or religious belief.

Maria Keffler (00:46:49):

You touched on these false dichotomies. You either have a dead son or a live daughter. Those are your choices. No, those aren't the only two choices.

Recently, in my district there's a group of parents trying to get the schools to open up again. We're still completely virtual here because of the pandemic. There's a group of parents who are trying to get the school board to open up again. They reported that at a school board meeting in a neighboring district, which is fighting the same thing, a school board member said, "Do you want your child to be alive or educated?"

Of course we want both.

Erin Brewer (00:47:25):

That's what I see so often is these extremes.

In the case of the transgender child they're threatening that you will either have a live son or a dead daughter, but they're not talking about the incredible harms that come from medicalizing these kids.

As it turns out, without being hyperbolic, these kids might not have a full lifespan because of these interventions, because they put them at risk of medical dangers and death. So it is important to look at what they are saying: "Is this really true? Am I going to have a live son or dead daughter?"

When you start digging into that, there's just nothing to back that up. It's just a way to scare people. This is all about fear and control and indoctrination.

Maria Keffler (00:48:22):

This may be a little bit tangential, but a few years ago I had a cyst on the inside of the knuckle on my finger. I went to have it removed. My experience at the hospital was like I was going in for open heart surgery. I had all of these forms to fill out letting me know I could have infection. All these complications could happen. I kept thinking, "It's just a cyst on my finger." They even took me and strapped my arm down and they disinfected my entire arm. They were so careful to make sure that I knew every single risk of having a cyst removed.

Yet these kids are being medicalized, willy-nilly. They go into Planned Parenthood and they come out with a testosterone syringe. That's more evidence that this is just an ideology, that this is a cult, that this is not fact-based. This is not reality.

Erin Brewer (00:49:28):

It's one of the few medical interventions that if you question it and try to get more information about it, you're called a hater.

Maria Keffler (00:49:37):

Again, the thought-stopping when somebody calls you a name because you've asked a question—you can be pretty sure that you've asked the right question.

Erin Brewer (00:49:48):

We're dealing with something very serious here. These are thought-control techniques and the strategies behind them are very powerful. So how do parents have hope? Are there any strategies that parents can use once their kid has been indoctrinated into this?

Maria Keffler (00:50:24):

We don't have a lot of data on this because this is so new. We are starting to see more and more people detransition. There are more parents who are getting their kids back, but those parents are still very much in the minority. So it's hard to say, but with the parents who are getting their kids back, what we're seeing is they have taken those extreme measures of pulling them out of school.

I was a teacher and now I am to the place where I cannot tell anybody that public school is a safe place for any child.

Erin Brewer (00:51:00):

I have a Ph.D. in education and I feel the same way.

I used to be so anti-homeschooling. I wasn't even supportive of charter schools, because I thought they drew money away from the public school system in a way that wasn't fair.

Now I have done a 180-degree turn around on this, because I'm seeing what's happening in the schools. The schools are no longer safe places for our kids.

> **I used to be so anti-homeschooling. Now I have done a 180-degree turn around on this, because I'm seeing what's happening in the schools. The schools are no longer safe places for our kids.**

Maria Keffler (00:51:24):

I'm right there with you. I always was of the mindset that you go to your neighborhood school. Our neighborhood school is a Title I school. My kids were one of the very few white kids in the school, and I felt very strongly: "You go to your neighborhood school, you make a community, you live in your community, you don't self-segregate."

Now I've pulled all of my kids. I'm homeschooling all of them because public school is dangerous to children.

So taking those drastic measures, we're seeing that is having an effect: cutting off the trans influences, taking away the internet.

My heart breaks for parents who have adult kids, who don't have that kind of control. I don't know really what to say other than get this book or one of Steven Hassan's other books, read it, and start applying some of these techniques.

I have reached out to the Freedom of Mind Institute because I'm hoping that maybe they're working in this area and maybe they have some things in the works for helping people. We're right on the cusp of trying to figure this out: "How we are going to save our kids?"

I think number one, you've got to get them out of the influence.

Erin Brewer (00:52:41):

I'm not sure how long the COVID crisis is going to go on, but I've heard a number of parents who reported that their children desisted once they were at home. So instead of being at school and being in this broth of indoctrination where their peers are into it, their teachers are into it, and they're getting these special programs introducing it to them, when they closed the schools and kids started staying home, parents reported kids desisting, which is such important information for us to have.

It's encouraging to know there is something you can do. Unfortunately, pulling a kid out of school and homeschooling can be difficult for a lot of people. But again, this is such a significant part of your child's life. We have seen when children don't get pulled out of it, when they continue with it, a lot of them end up in dire consequences. They end up in debt. They keep trying to become more and more like something that they're not. They're running away from themselves. Those underlying issues are not being addressed and they're not doing well.

These kids are not doing well, so it is worth it to pull them.

Maria Keffler (00:54:02):

We have a couple of questions from parents. I'll go ahead and read one. This is interesting. "Why is this ideology so appealing to so many kids?"

Erin Brewer (00:54:13):

Well, I can answer that.

Maria Keffler (00:54:15):

Yeah, because you know.

Erin Brewer (00:54:17):

I guess I'm ahead of the curve on this.

I embraced the idea that I was a boy when I was young. This was way before this whole ideology had taken hold. It was a way for me to run away from myself. I had a lot of self-hatred. I didn't want to be me. I didn't like me. I wasn't doing well as me, and saying I was a boy was a way to run away from myself.

So for me, it makes perfect sense why so many kids are doing this. It's a way to become somebody different if you're uncomfortable with who you are. That's what happened when I was a kid. Now it's even more understandable to me because you have this affirmation, this affection. You take a kid who's not very popular, they announce a trans identity, and suddenly they're the most popular kid.

We mentioned control. All of a sudden, these kids have a lot of control. So it's not surprising to me at all that kids are buying into this. Kids like to feel like they're part of something. They want to feel part of a group.

This is a group that says, "We'll accept you no matter what," yet that's not the case. It's that false sense of security. They say, "We'll be your friends and we'll celebrate you." But it's only under the condition that you buy into this ideology and that you keep progressing further and further down this road.

Maria Keffler (00:55:45):

If you walk down the halls of a school—I went to my kid's high school before I pulled them out, and I just looked around. There were so many images promoting this. The hallway is covered with posters for pride month, for Transgender Day of Awareness. The school play is about a transgender kid. Almost every classroom has safe space stickers on them. I mean, it's very clear just from the real estate of the halls who is important at school.

Erin Brewer (00:56:29):

It is surprising that every kid hasn't bought into this. It's the kids who haven't—there's something very strong about their character, because, like you said, it's just being promoted everywhere. If you're not under that transgender umbrella on some level, you're suspect. Even if you consider yourself an ally, you're not really part of the group.

It's not surprising to me that kids who have no inclination in this direction are coming out as non-binary or genderfluid, because that puts them under the umbrella without them having to change that much.

This has infiltrated the schools and kids who aren't buying into this are being ostracized and bullied.

Maria Keffler (00:57:19):

I just can't believe that educators haven't seen this coming. Haven't they had a moment where they said, "Wait a minute, this doesn't seem right to me. What's going on?"

Unfortunately we're seeing a lot of educators leaving the system, or taking early retirement, because the schools are bullying them. Teachers can lose their jobs if they don't fully buy into this. There's no neutral territory anymore.

You can't say, "I'm just going to stay out of this." No, you're an ally, or you're an enemy.

Erin Brewer (00:57:54):

You must pick a side.

I've talked to a therapist who fully believes this is a dangerous ideology, and yet he cannot speak openly about it because he will be fired.

I was going to do an interview with a therapist in another state who was grappling with whether or not he had the moral fortitude to stand up for this, because he knew what would happen. He ended up saying that he didn't want to do the interview.

I've interviewed one therapist who did the full interview. A few days later, he asked me to take the video off YouTube because of consequences and repercussions he was afraid of facing.

There are people out there who are watching this and they know there's something wrong but they're afraid to stand up because they will lose their jobs and potentially even more.

When you look at what happened to Ken Zucker, who is a moderate therapist—he probably buys into the gender ideology somewhat—but he wasn't buying into it 100%. Activists went after him, and ended up getting him kicked out of his clinic. He was able to sue and ended up winning the lawsuit for slander and libel. But, at the same time, his career was attacked. He is someone who's very, very moderate. He said that up to 60% of the clients in his clinic are medicalized, which means he's more than moderate. He is accepting this ideology to a large extent.

It's very scary. There are some things that are worth standing up for. There are some things that are worth those repercussions. If we don't have people who are willing to make those sacrifices, our kids are going to continue to be harmed.

> **It's very scary. There are some things that are worth standing up for. There are some things that are worth those repercussions. If we don't have people who are willing to make those sacrifices, our kids are going to continue to be harmed.**

Maria Keffler (00:59:43):

We've got one more question. I think we may have addressed this one already. "How do I get my child out of the gender cult?"

Erin Brewer (00:59:53):

We're not qualified to talk about specifically how to do it because we don't know, this is so new. We can offer up some techniques and resources, but we're going to have to look back on this in ten years and figure out what worked and what didn't work.

That's so hard. I feel so bad for parents who are in this, because I wish I could just say you do these three steps and your kid's going to be fine. We just don't know.

Maria Keffler (01:00:24):

Well, there's so much more we could probably say about this. It's just such a huge issue, but I am fully convinced that transgender ideology is a cult and it's been intentionally created by the gender industry for profits.

Erin Brewer (01:00:44):

I just encourage parents to look at the resources. Just continue to maintain contact with your child.

Parents are a lifeline, and as long as you can maintain some degree of contact, your child knows that you're there for them. Once that's cut, they're in freefall. It's so much harder for them to come out of it because they don't feel like they have a home base. They don't feel like they have anybody they can go to who will accept them if they decide to reject this ideology.

Maria Keffler (01:01:21):

There's a lot of shame and embarrassment too. When you have gone whole hog into something—whether that's a cult or whether that's a job or whether that's a romantic relationship—and you've just thrown your entire self into it and told everybody how fantastic it is: "I found this great thing"… When it starts to fall apart, there's a lot of shame and embarrassment in admitting you are wrong.

One thing I can say: parents, don't shame your kids. Don't tell them that they're stupid for falling for this. Give them a safe out. You could even tell them a story about when you did something and you were so sure you were right. Then you found out later you were wrong.

I mean, be sensitive with how you tell that story. You don't want them to think that you're trying to proselytize to them. But let them know that it's human and it's okay to be wrong and to change your mind. Be that safe place for them, that they can trust that if they do say, "You know what, I'm not so sure about this." They need to know you're going to be there to welcome them and be a safe place for them to land, and you're not going to be someone who's going to say, "I told you so. I told you this was stupid."

Erin Brewer (01:02:43):

That's so important. There needs to be the opportunity to come out of this in a way that that saves face, and that lets the child know that you still love them and that you've always loved them. That's a great way to end this.

Episode 7 Resource List

Entry Points (Gender Spectrum):
https://arlingtonparentcoa.wixsite.com/arlingtonparentcoa/what-schools-are-doing

Freedom of Mind (Steven Hassan):
https://www.amazon.com/Freedom-Mind-Helping-Controlling-Beliefs/dp/0967068819/ref=sr_1_1

BITE Model of Undue Influence (Steven Hassan):
https://freedomofmind.com/wp-content/uploads/2018/12/BITE-Model-Handout-9-23-16.pdf

Transgender Religion Codified & Enforced at School:
https://www.partnersforethicalcare.com/post/transgender-religion-codified-enforced-at-school

Why Gender Ideology Is A Horrifying Religion:
https://www.youtube.com/watch?v=optayT-0wbQ

Episode 8: Dealing with Your Child's School

https://youtu.be/vrgIvXohQTI

<u>Erin Brewer (00:52)</u>:

Who would have thought that dealing with the school would end up being such a big issue? But boy, when I talk to parents, I am just overwhelmed with the stories that they have.

For people who don't know, these are stories are from parents who don't even know that their child had taken on a transgender identity. They find out that their daughter has been using the boys' restroom for the last year, or they find out that the teachers have been calling their child by a different name and different pronouns, or they find out that their teacher is hiding clothes for their child. The child comes to school and changes clothes at school so they can present as a different sex than they were born.

This is very powerful This is an institution that we used to trust, that is now actively undermining parents' and children's best interests.

<u>Maria Keffler (01:45)</u>:

People don't appreciate how deceptive schools are being. We still think that schools are our partners. We send our kids there to be educated and think that's what the schools are doing. Unfortunately public schools are not trustworthy anymore.

The deception is active. The American School Counselors Association, the AFCA, which is the largest organization of school counselors in America, has a policy statement about transgender students and how counselors should deal with them. There's a clause that says that the counselor should use different pronouns and name at school than when they're talking to the parents, if the student doesn't want the parents to know about their transgender identity.

That's codified deception. It's not legal. It's not okay.

One thing that parents need to know is that the Federal Education Rights and Protection Act (FERPA) says that parents have a right to see and know everything that the school knows about the child. It is not legal for the school to hide things about a child from the child's parents or guardians.

Unfortunately, the school is not following FERPA. It's following the guidelines from places like GLSEN (Gay Lesbian and Straight Education Network) and Planned Parenthood and the Human Rights Campaign Foundation (which is the LGBTQ lobby and funding group). Schools are following their guidance. They are not following FERPA.

Unfortunately, it's probably going to take lawsuits before this resolves, but parents need to know that this is happening in schools.

Erin Brewer (03:46):

They need to know it's not just happening in big city schools. It's happening in schools in rural Utah, it's happening in schools in Indiana and Montana, it's happening in schools across the nation.

I was shocked by a presentation that was given to Utah teachers recently by the Utah State Board of Education. They had an activist organization come in and suggest to teachers that if they weren't going to be allies, they didn't deserve to be around children.

There's this message now that teachers are getting: "If you don't follow this ideology—if you don't accept this—then you're not worthy of being a teacher." These are teachers who are generally very caring about kids. For them to be told, "You have to do this, or it means you don't care about kids," is another way to manipulate people into accepting this ideology.

Maria Keffler (04:47):

In my school district, a teacher just sent the local watchdog organization here, the Arlington Parent Coalition, a copy of the new transgender students policy, which the district sent out to teachers and staff. It said right on top of it, "This is an internal document not to be shared outside school."

Why do you need to hide something from the families and from the community?

This teacher sent it to Arlington Parent Coalition. There's a clause at the bottom that states if either students or teachers and staff do not comply with these guidelines they can be disciplined. It's very clear that if you do not follow preferred pronouns, if you do not agree with letting boys in the girls' bathroom, if you do not agree with hiding things from the parents, the student or teacher can be disciplined for that.

That means children are required to lie to their parents, because if your friend Billy comes to school one day and decides that he doesn't want to be Billy anymore—now he's going to be Barbara—but Barbara hasn't told his parents yet, then the teachers tell this child's class, "We're not sharing this with Barbara's parents so you can't share this with your parents."

This isn't just at school. That's requiring children to lie to their families.

Erin Brewer (06:28):

It's scary because it's grooming them. It's preparing them to be deceptive to their parents. It's preparing them to accept that some adults are going to have them do stuff or say things that they're not supposed to share with their parents.

> **It's grooming them. It's preparing them to be deceptive to their parents and to accept that some adults are going to have them do stuff or say things that they're not supposed to share with their parents. This is setting them up to be victims of predators.**

This is setting them up to be victims of predators. This is exactly the kind of thing that predators do in order to gain access to children, and also to identify which children are vulnerable. Because it's the kids that go and tell the parents—they're the ones who are not vulnerable, because they trusted their parents.

Kids are having to accept a teacher lying to them about, in this case, Billy's actual sex. The kids are told that they're not allowed to be upset about Billy now coming into the girl's facilities, they have to accept that.

On a number of different levels this kind of deception is dangerous for kids. It undermines their ability to reality check and it undermines their ability to know which adults are trustworthy.

Maria Keffler (07:32):

It's interesting that you bring up the grooming aspect of this. We do have a slide showing grooming behaviors that child predators employ. People who predate on children, sexual predators, have a very systematic way that they go about it.

I don't know if you remember this, but a few years ago in Pennsylvania there was a coach—Jerry Sandusky—who was caught being a pedophile. Throughout some of the reporting about it, the *Washington Post* did an interview with a convicted pedophile who was in prison, about how he would target children. He said child predators try to find work near children because they're trying to gain access to children.

I certainly do not want to suggest that the bulk of teachers are child predators—not at all. Most teachers are very trustworthy and love children, but those who want to sexually exploit children will try to get jobs in schools. They'll try to get jobs in daycares.

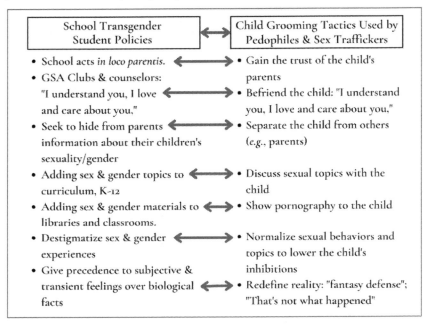

School Transgender Student Policies	Child Grooming Tactics Used by Pedophiles & Sex Traffickers
• School acts *in loco parentis*.	• Gain the trust of the child's parents
• GSA Clubs & counselors: "I understand you, I love and care about you,"	• Befriend the child: "I understand you, I love and care about you,"
• Seek to hide from parents information about their children's sexuality/gender	• Separate the child from others (e.g., parents)
• Adding sex & gender topics to curriculum, K-12	• Discuss sexual topics with the child
• Adding sex & gender materials to libraries and classrooms.	• Show pornography to the child
• Destigmatize sex & gender experiences	• Normalize sexual behaviors and topics to lower the child's inhibitions
• Give precedence to subjective & transient feelings over biological facts	• Redefine reality: "fantasy defense"; "That's not what happened"

This man who was in prison was formerly a teacher and he said, "The first thing I would do if I saw a child that I liked was ask if he could stay after school and help me erase the boards."

Very innocent, you know, no problem.

He said what that child told him would let him know whether he could pursue the child or not. If the child said, "Yeah, I can stay after school and do the blackboards," he knew that child was not being watched carefully by parents. If the child said, "I need to call home and ask my mom and dad," then that predator said, "I would go no further with that child, because I knew he was being watched carefully by parents."

For the school to do anything that undermines that protection by the parents is completely unethical and unconscionable, and it does set children up for grooming.

Erin Brewer (09:37):

You mentioned that there are predators who actively want to be around children, so they get jobs in the school system. One of the things that I'm seeing that is incredibly disturbing to me is that schools are now allowing faculty and staff members to self-ID. You might have a teacher who is a male who suddenly says, "I'm actually a woman." That teacher now is able to go into the girls' bathrooms and is able to chaperone the girls on overnight trips and is able to go into the locker room facilities with the girls. That is a really bad idea on so many levels.

Then there was a story that I heard about a mother whose daughter was going into the boys' locker room. The mother was very upset about it and contacted the school and said that she was worried that her daughter could be victimized when she's in the boys' locker room. The solution the school came up with to address her concern was to have two adult teachers accompany her daughter into the locker room when she changed.

Oh my goodness. That just makes me question the sanity of administrators that they thought that was a good idea. Now you have two male teachers accompanying a girl into a boys' locker room and watching her as she changes to make sure she's not harassed by the boys.

This mother asked the teachers how they felt about this new responsibility and they were mortified, but they had to do it because otherwise they were at risk of losing their jobs.

Maria Keffler (11:10):

That's hideous. That is just hideous.

There's a teacher in Wisconsin. He came out to his fifth-grade class that he is now a woman, or non-binary. He goes by "Mx." The parents didn't know this was going to happen. He made this big announcement to his class.

Now he has gone on to complain that he has to use the women *teachers'* bathroom, because it's so far away. He wants to know why can't he just use the girl's bathroom with the students that's right across the hall from his class?

I don't know the current status of that issue, but that's what he wants. He doesn't know why he should have to be constrained to using the adult women's bathroom.

He should be constrained to be using the adult men's bathroom.

Erin Brewer (12:09):

It just makes my toes curl thinking about the kind of indoctrination this is doing, the way this mixes up kids.

One of the things that's so scary to me is that it causes kids to question reality. They're either going to accept what the teacher is saying and question reality, or they're going to realize that the teachers are lying to them. Either situation is bad.

> **It causes kids to question reality. They're either going to accept what the teacher is saying and question reality, or they're going to realize that the teachers are lying to them. Either situation is bad.**

If they start to question fundamental reality, they're not going to be able to make good decisions. They're going to be in trouble. If they know their teacher is lying to them, that's going to undermine their ability to believe anything that the teachers tell them. So either way, this is incredibly damaging.

As you said, so many parents think, "Well, that's just happening in Seattle, or that's just happening in New York," or something. It's happening in schools all across the nation.

I live in Utah, which is one of the more conservative states. I contacted all the different school districts in the state to find out what their policy was. Most of them didn't have policies, and responded saying that if this comes up, then they'll come up with a policy. Some of them did have policies and they were very disturbing policies. They were policies that said that if a boy identifies as a girl, he can access all the spaces of the girls, and access all the activities of the girls and that he would be accepted as a girl.

Then we did have districts that said that they would actively undermine parents and deceive them. This is happening in one of the more conservative states in the country. If it's happening here, I guarantee it's happening everywhere.

Maria Keffler (13:56):

One of the problems with self-ID—and we've talked about this before— what are the guidelines for that? What is required? Under the current policies—and this is at the school, at the state, at the federal level— current policy for self-ID is just to announce identifying as the opposite sex.

I just heard from a parent who said that at her husband's workplace, guidance just came out that in this office, employees will be allowed to change their gender ID only once per day. Once per day. If I come in in the morning and I say, "I'm a female," I have to be a female all day, but I can come in tomorrow morning and say, "I'm a male," but then I have to be male all day. Wow.

Erin Brewer (14:52):

Wow.

Maria Keffler (14:55):

It's laughable but it's horrific. In high schools—or any school, but I think high school is the most problematic for this—a boy can come to school and say, "You know, I'd really like to go in the girl's bathroom today, and he can just say, 'I'm a girl.'"

Erin Brewer (15:13):

Today I'm in "girl mode."

Maria Keffler (15:16):

There's nothing else required. I talked to a transgender rights activist in our location here in our district. He said, "That will never happen. No high school boy would ever pretend to be a girl."

Wow, I wonder if he's met any high school boys? Because I know quite a few. A lot of them would do it just for kicks and grins.

Erin Brewer (15:39):

Their friends might dare them to do it. Or as you said, there might be, at the high school level, kids who are predators, and what a great opportunity we just opened the door for them. It's just really scary.

I wanted to just share this parent resource guide, because what we're talking about is hard. This is really heavy stuff. I mean, hearing this, I am so thankful I don't have kids in elementary school or in public school. They're all out of high school.

The Parent Resource Guide has a lot of good information. We'll include a link to it below. You can download it for free, or you can order a hard copy. I think they're $15, but you can get a free digital copy.

This is just chock full of information that you need to have as a parent. Some of it is going to be disturbing. And some of the stuff we're talking about is disturbing, but you need to have tools in your toolbox to know how to deal with this. This is a really good guide.

The other thing that I would recommend is, if you have kids in school, go to your school board meetings. You've already got a lot on your plate and they tend to be slow and arduous meetings, but it's really important that you keep track of what's happening at your school.

The other thing that I would recommend is do an open records request. Maria, can you talk a little bit about this? You're more familiar with how this process works.

Maria Keffler (17:10):

Open records acts say that the public has the right to see its government's documents. So you have a right to see what the government is doing. Some people think, "This is a big, arduous process. You've got to fill out forms and all that." No, it's actually really simple.

All you need to do is send a letter or just an email to the school. They usually have what is called a FOIA (Freedom of Information Act) liaison, but if you don't know who that is, send it to the superintendent. Send it to his or her office.

Send an email and state what you want to see. The more specific you are, the more likely you are to get the right information. You can send a request and say, "I am requesting under the Freedom of Information Act to see everything related to transgender student policy at your school."

We did this in my district. We sent a request, because we have a local activist group who we suspected were the ones pushing this stuff into the school. So we sent a request and we said, "We would like to see all communications without outside people or organizations related to transgender student policy."

We got a 30-page document that one of our members called "a love fest" between the public school and this local activist group. They had been working on this policy for a year and nobody else knew about it.

After our organization found out about it, we said, "We would like to be involved with this. We would like to be present at the next meeting where this is discussed" and the public school said, "Okay, yep. We'll invite you."

Well, a future FOIA request about policy revealed that no, after that, they had another meeting between the school and this activist group and did not invite anybody else to it.

It's really important to know what's going on at the school board meetings. They are tedious. It can be awful going to meetings like that. I consider them one of the rings of hell. But a lot of them are televised. Now you can watch them online. So you don't have to actually go. You can watch it online and see what's happening.

I want to let people know the way this is getting into schools, which is very under-the-table and surreptitiously. This is the way it happened in my district and neighboring districts.

The first thing the school board does is slip the words *gender identity* into the non-discrimination clause. Every school district will have a non-discrimination clause that says teachers and students cannot be discriminated against based on race, religion, pregnancy status, *etc.*. There are like 40 things in there. Sexual orientation came in there some years ago. Now they just slip *gender identity* in there.

It seems very innocuous: "We're just being kind." That's the word you hear all the time. "It's just about being diverse and inclusive."

But adding *gender identity* opens up the flood gates for schools to say, "Well, what does it mean to not discriminate against people based on gender? It means if you think you're a different gender, we have to do whatever you want."

That's where the policy gets slipped in. When you start seeing these policies come up—transgender student policies, with boys going into the girls' bathrooms, boys in girls' sports—when you see that, if you push back on it, what you will hear is, "Well, this has been in the non-discrimination policy for years." It's very deceptive.

Erin Brewer (21:16):

It's important for people to realize that somebody might be watching this and think, "How horrifying that you don't want gender identity protected." It's important for people to realize that once you protect gender identity, you stop protecting sex. Women's rights are no longer protected. Once you protect gender identity, it circumvents other people's rights. It might even circumvent sexual orientation. That may also be circumvented by these policies.

> **It's important for people to realize that once you protect gender identity, you stop protecting sex. Women's rights are no longer protected.**

If people can go back and forth between what gender they claim to be, then sex no longer means anything. If a man can say, "Well, my penis is actually female," then it no longer makes sense what female is.

This is not about us being discriminatory towards a group. It's us protecting the rights of men and women, and even those with different sexual orientations. This is about protecting the categories that typically are protected under these non-discrimination rules.

Maria Keffler (22:28):

When you're dealing with the school and you're negotiating anything with the school, I really recommend trying to get everything in writing. I discovered this the hard way.

When I first started working on this and I found out that my district was putting a transgender student policy into place, I sent an email to the school board members, and one of them called me.

At first, I was so pleased. I thought, "Wow, they really are responsive. And they're really taking this seriously."

I had a long conversation with one of the school board members, and I took copious notes on it.

But I discovered a few months later that not having anything that she said in writing undercut my ability to hold her accountable. She said something exactly the opposite in a school board meeting to what she said to me on the phone. When I emailed her about it, I got this response: "I don't remember ever saying anything different than that."

Somebody recommended to me to always try to get everything in writing because they will try to have phone conversations with you so that there's no record of it.

Erin Brewer (23:43):

Also, find out what the rules are in your state. I'm in a state where you can actually record somebody as long as one person knows they're being recorded. Which means that basically I can record any conversation that I want. That's not true in all states, but you might want to find that out.

Like you said, get things in email. Tell them that you prefer to do all this by email, that you want letters sent. If for some reason you do have a conversation, either face-to-face or over the phone, immediately summarize it, send it to the person and say, "I just wanted to make sure I understood correctly," and get them to respond back: "Yes, that's what happened," because that's documentation. You need to have a paper trail.

It sounds paranoid, but it's so important that you have this documentation. Because like you said, they lie. They will absolutely lie and say, "I never said that" or "You misunderstood." You need to have it in writing.

The other reason having it in writing is going to be important because eventually there are going to be a lot of lawsuits. If there's documentation, it's going to make it easier for these lawsuits to move forward and for us to regain some sanity in our schools.

Maria Keffler (24:57):

What we've found happening in our district—and I've heard this in other districts too—around some of the family life education curriculum, is that a lot of this transgender stuff is getting put in through the family life education program. That's not the only place, but they're doing it there. When you try to find out what's in the family life education—the sex ed program—it is almost impossible in my state of Virginia.

Parents are supposed to, by law, be able to see everything that's done in the classroom. I can tell you from personal experience, if you go to the principal and say, "I want to see what's in your family life program," the principal will send you the state guidelines for the topics that are covered.

Then you say, "No, I want to see what's actually done in the classroom. What books are you using? What slides are you using? What worksheets are you using?"

The principal will likely say, "I don't have access to that. Please ask the teacher."

So you ask the teacher and she says, "That's all done at the administration level. So please contact the school board or the super-intendent, because that's all kept at the administration level."

So you contact the superintendent, the school board, they say, "Oh, no, that's something that the principal manages. So you'll need to go to the principal."

It's just pass-the-potato, and you go around and around, and you never see what's done in the classroom.

It sounds paranoid to say that the schools are doing this, but they are.

Erin Brewer (26:37):

A recommendation I would have is to go to the state board of education website and drill down. That's one of the things I did in Utah. I was blown away.

I started to drill down and I found the parent resources. They were sending people directly to the Trevor Project, directly to GLSEN, which are transgender advocacy groups. These parents are not being given all the information.

I found out that teachers were being indoctrinated in this. They're bringing in outside activists to present information to teachers and school districts. All of this was not on the surface. I had to go to this and that link, and then keep going down links to find it, because they don't want it out in the open. They want it buried.

> **They're bringing in outside activists to present information to teachers and school districts.**
> **All of this was not on the surface.**
> **I had to go to this and that link, and then keep going down links to find it, because they don't want it out in the open. They want it buried.**

We're talking about doing all this research, getting open records requests, going to school board meetings—it is a lot of work for one person. It is really valuable to set up a parent advocacy group where you get like-minded parents together. You can do this as a team, so that one person doesn't have to do all this.

Maria Keffler (27:47):

We started the Arlington Parent Coalition here in Arlington, Virginia. We started out with just a team of five, sitting around a kitchen table saying, "What are we going to do? We've got to do something."

We started with organizing parents to go to school board members during office hours. And that's where it started. We now have a pretty large membership and we have a website.

I just got an email yesterday from a parent here in Arlington, who overheard her second-grader's teacher say, "You can be a boy. Or you can be a girl, or you can be neither. Anybody can be anything." He sent that to Arlington Parent Coalition.

One of the things we have on our website is a parent report form. It's just a Google form, so that when that kind of thing happens, parents can send it in. We write it up and we put it on the website so that when parents come to our website, they can see, "This happened at this school. This parent had this happened at this school."

We really need those kinds of organizations. Every school district needs a parent coalition watchdog group. If you are at all feeling like that's something that you should do, Arlington Parent Coalition is happy to clone its website and give it to you. Then you can tweak whatever you want to tweak for your own district. You do not have to start from scratch.

<u>Erin Brewer (29:33):</u>

That is amazing. It's an overwhelming to start something like this, but there is support and there are resources.

A valuable resource, is the resource guide, *Navigating the Transgender Landscape*. It is specifically for administrators.

You, as a parent, can give it to your principal or to your school board and say, "This is how we would like to have policies developed." It is a very good handbook. The way it's written it is brilliant. It's not biased. The language is not inflammatory. It is fact-based, and it's cited so that there are ways for people to investigate the claims that are made and to find out that they are research based.

This is a way for you to get ahead of the curve, if your school board or your principals haven't totally bought into this. Get this information into their hands. That way they know how to start formulating policies that are going to protect girls, that are going to be fair to everybody, that aren't going to accept this nonsense that somebody can be born in the wrong body, or that you can be in girl mode one day and boy mode in another, or you be somewhere in between because you don't like lipstick or baseball.

One of the things that we wanted to do is to show you two examples of school personnel who have lost their jobs as a result of standing up to this ideology. The first one is at a school in England. The second one is right here in the U.S.

Part 1: Rev. John Parker's Story

<u>Introduction (31:34):</u>

Rev. John Parker, a governor of the school, resigned after the school failed to address welfare concerns for the child and other families...

<u>Rev. John Parker (31:39):</u>

Unless specifically stated by that family everyone else just gets told: "The pupil you knew who had this name and this pronoun, from this day will be this name and this pronoun." ... And that's just staff who interact with the children. Governors just get told, "We have a pupil who is socially transitioning" and that is it.

There wasn't the opportunity for disagreement. We couldn't communicate with parents. We couldn't discuss this as governors. We couldn't form procedure. We couldn't consider any of the practical issues. We just had to go ahead as we were told.

(To the gender policy trainer) "Is it okay if I share some different viewpoints the staff to take away, just so that I'm not asking..."

Gender Policy Trainer:

"No, I don't think so. John. I'm sorry. It's training. It's not time to share your viewpoint."

Rev. John Parker (32:23):

I think what deeply concerns me is that within a primary school environment, without the information that we need for due diligence as governors for the safeguarding of this child and the safeguarding of other children, we're being told we must go down a particular route. We've been kept blind and want some more discussion about what were being told to think.

Gender Policy Trainer:

"You are all now honorary Mermaids, whether you want to be or not."

Part 2: Peter Vlaming's Story

Peter Vlaming (32:51):

But what I explained to my principal is that I couldn't, in good conscience, pronounce masculine pronouns to refer to a girl. He gave me an official written reprimand and said it was the first step in a process that would lead to my termination.

Maria Keffler (33:08):

It's horrifying to me that this is what's happening to teachers. Teachers are being taught by these outside activist organizations that they have to do certain things that are very much against a lot of people's consciences and sense of reality.

Erin Brewer (33:30):

In that video, I believe it's in England, the administrator is telling everybody that they're now "honorary Mermaids." For people who don't know what that means, Mermaids is this well-funded organization in the UK that has pushed this agenda incredibly hard. They've even gotten

Starbucks to sponsor them. It's an incredibly powerful organization and these teachers and staff are being told, "You are now Mermaids, whether you like it or not. You will ascribe to this ideology or you will face termination."

That teacher in Virginia got fired because he called out the pronoun of a student who didn't identify as the sex she was born.

Maria Keffler (34:24):

That's particularly insidious. This student, who was a female one year, came back the next year and said, "Now I'm a male. I want male pronouns and here's my new name."

The administration tried to pressure Peter Vlaming to use her preferred pronouns, the male pronouns. Peter Vlaming said that he did not feel his conscience would let him do that. He did not believe that it's possible for somebody to be in the wrong body. This teenage girl had a veteran teacher fired for accidentally saying a pronoun—one word that she didn't like. He said one word that she didn't like, and he got fired. How can any reasonable person say, "Yeah, that's the world we want to have"?

> **This teenage girl had a veteran teacher fired for accidentally saying a pronoun—one word that she didn't like. He said one word that she didn't like, and he got fired. How can any reasonable person say, "Yeah, that's the world we want to have"?**

Erin Brewer (36:02):

It's extremely disturbing.

It's not just in the US. I've talked to teachers in Australia who are deciding to not be teachers anymore because they can't in good conscience follow this ideology, and they know that they're going to be fired. This ideology is separating the teachers who have a conscience about this—who are leaving the schools—and we're left with only those who are fervently buying into this ideology.

The other thing that I wanted to point out is that in non-discrimination clauses, one of the categories is usually religion. In this case, trans ideology is trampling all over many religious beliefs. There are many, many religions where people are uncomfortable with boys sharing showers, bathrooms, and locker rooms with girls. This is part of their religious belief system which is being trampled on. Somehow the gender ideology overrides protections—religious protections, sex-based protections, sexual orientation protections.

It's incredibly disturbing to know that, as you said, there's no litmus test to join this one particular group. Anybody can claim to be anything they want to be. Then they're going to be protected over other people who should be protected.

It's very scary to me to know that that we're prioritizing one group's rights that are based entirely on feelings. Maybe, we don't even know if it's based on feelings, because people can pretend. People can lie about gender identity, because there is no litmus test. We're going to prioritize their rights and privileges and protections over everybody else. That's really disturbing.

Maria Keffler (38:14):

It is. I look at this and I think, "Gender ideology is the new religion."

We talked about that in an earlier episode, that it's a very cultic. When you get into the weeds on what they really believe, it's very much a religion, because it's based on feelings—it's based on faith in your own inner thoughts and feelings—and there's no other basis for it. There's a lot of contradictory information in it and a lot of places that it's not logical. But it really does fall into the category of religion.

So the school, by putting all of their policy behind this religion, they are completely trampling on everyone else's rights. I would say *everyone else's rights* because the trans-identified person has complete *carte blanche*, a gold ticket to do and get whatever they want, wherever they want it. No one is allowed to tell them "No" about anything.

> **The trans-identified person has complete *carte blanche*, a gold ticket to do and get whatever they want, wherever they want it. And no one is allowed to tell them "No" about anything.**

Erin Brewer (39:31):

It's really disturbing. There are these resources to help parents manage these influences in your school.

We also have a couple of parent questions: "I found out that my 13-year-old autistic daughter has been using the boys bathroom at school. I told the principal, 'I do not want my autistic eighth grade girl in the bathroom alone with boys.' He told me it is the school's policy that kids can choose which bathroom to use. How do I protect my daughter?"

These school policies are just mind-boggling. School administrators are willing to say that the kids can decide. There are some schools in England that did this for a while. The girls ended up skipping a lot of school. They would not go to school when they were menstruating, because they were uncomfortable menstruating when boys were in the bathroom. There girls were getting bladder infections because they were afraid to use the bathroom.

There is a case in the US where a girl was sexually assaulted by a boy who was allowed to go into the girl's bathroom. So it's not that this is just a frivolous concern, or parents being overly modest or prudish. These are legitimate concerns. We have sex-separated facilities because there is a risk and we need to protect girls from that risk. What recommendations do you have for this parent whose school just says, "Sorry, that's our policy"?

> **These are legitimate concerns. We have sex-separated facilities because there is a risk and we need to protect girls from that risk.**

Maria Keffler (41:07):

That's really hard. The first thing that comes to my mind when I hear that story is that the school has just told the parent that the school has greater authority over that child than the parent has. To me, that was a big middle finger to the parent: "We don't care what you think. We don't care what you want for this child. Our policy is more important than your authority over your child."

If at all possible, I would get that child out of the school.

Sadly, I think these policies are not going to get revoked until people start getting hurt. I hate to even say this, but it's going to take girls being assaulted. It's going to take people getting hurt before somebody says, "Whoa, these policies are bad ideas." So, if at all possible, I would get that child out of the school.

As far as pushing back, it may take a lawsuit. At the very least, if you can't get your child out of that school, I would send a letter with the FERPA policy about the parents' rights in education. I would look up the school's policy on other things where parents and the school differ. What is the school's policy on that? I'd try to apply those. I would pull up the religious rights: "My religion says that my daughter should not be in a state of undress with boys." Get creative, and do every possible thing you can think of.

Erin Brewer (42:55):

This child is autistic so she might have an IEP, or a 504 plan, either one of which parents can influence. Maybe put in that plan, "My child will not use restrooms with the opposite sex, because it will put her at risk."

Maria Keffler (43:17):

Once you get something into an IEP, that is really powerful. The schools are bound to do what is in the IEP. If your child has an IEP, I would utilize that. I would milk that for all it's worth. Get everything in there that you want for your child's protection.

Erin Brewer (43:40):

This is a 13-year-old girl who has autism. This is a child who's at risk being in a boys' facilities. This is a girl that needs protection. So as a parent, I would fight so hard in this case. Either fight the school or get that child into a different school or homeschool, because she is incredibly vulnerable. At 13, if she starts going down this route, this road where she is affirmed, it's much more likely she is going to be medicalized and damaged for life.

Maria Keffler (44:15):

We've got one more question: "My son came back from his first semester at college and announced that he's a woman. The school refuses to talk to me about it because he's an adult. What do I do?"

Erin Brewer (44:29):

That's a really good question.

There are some factors that will play into how much power and influence a parent can have over this, because he's an adult child. Even if he's not an adult child, if he is in college—say it's a 17-year-old who's in college—the school is going to be very hesitant to share anything with you.

You do have power of the purse strings, perhaps. That is one of the things that you have, and you are allowed to say to your child, "Look, I'm paying for your college. Therefore I get to have access to your records." The child can go and allow you to have access to records.

The other thing you can do, if you're not paying for that child to be in school, is to say, "I love you very much, but when you're staying in my house, I'm not going to affirm you as transgender. You are my son. I love you very much, but I'm not going to accept that you were born in the wrong body. That's just not true."

Some of it has to do with whether or not a parent is paying for the college experience. If they are, they have more power. They can also insist, "If you want to go to school, we need you to get some different help to resolve these issues."

Maria Keffler (45:45):

I don't have a lot of experience with kids in college, because my kids are still young. Now my oldest, who's a senior in high school, is doing his senior year via dual-enrollment at the local community college. What you said about giving the parent access to the records is true. He's only 17 and I am still his legal guardian, but every time I have called to register him for classes or whatever, I have to put him on the phone so he can give the school permission to talk to me. They sent me a form. If he fills out this form and signs it, then that will give us access to his records.

Maybe parents just need to do that. When your kid goes off to college, see if you can get that form filled out, as a preventive measure. You can tell your child, "You know, I want to be able to help with any records issues you have. I want to be able to coordinate." If you can get your child to fill out one of those forms, so you have access, that might give you a little bit more leeway for dealing with things like this.

Erin Brewer (46:54):

Especially if the university has a college health system. I know where I went to college, they had on campus healthcare. My parents had no idea what was going on. I could go in and pretty much have any kind of treatment there. They wouldn't know.

I've heard parents say their child left a boy and came back a girl, medicalized by the college health system, and the parents have no recourse. They can't even access the records.

So have your child sign a waiver. If they're not willing to do that—we talked about boundaries in one of these episodes—you have to identify, what do you have control over? And what don't you have control over?

If your child is paying their way in college, you don't have a lot of control over that. If they've gotten scholarships, you don't have a lot of control. But if you're paying for college, well, then you start to have a little bit of control, and you can determine how much of that control you want to leverage in this situation.

Maria Keffler (47:55):

Is it important for parents to realize that most universities are on board with this—not just on board, but wholeheartedly propagating it.

There was an article by Penny Nance, who wrote about taking her son to his freshmen orientation one of the big universities here in Virginia, one of the big state schools. The whole orientation was about gender identity, and everybody had on their name-badge their name and their preferred pronouns. She said, "I was horrified. The whole orientation was about this."

I talked to a therapist who told me that she had a client she had worked with for anxiety, who's also on the autism spectrum. She had anxiety issues and the therapist had been working with this girl for years. The girl went off to college and came home the first summer saying she was a man. The parents apparently kept the girl home the next fall, because the therapist said she started working with the girl over that coming year. It took about a year, and the girl came around and realized that no, she was not in fact a man, she was a girl.

Well, she went back to that big state school here in Virginia. The school counselor actually told her that she should not come back to that school, but she should transfer somewhere else, because the transgender community would be very unfriendly to her. The girl went back and she

> **The school counselor actually told her that she should not come back to that school, but she should transfer somewhere else, because the transgender community would be very unfriendly to her. The girl went back and she got bullied. She got treated so badly—and threatened—that she was scared for her safety, and ended up leaving the university.**

got bullied. She got treated so badly—and threatened—that she was scared for her safety, and ended up leaving the university.

This is a major state school that tens of thousands of people attend and they can't protect—or won't protect—this girl.

Erin Brewer (50:00):

The rights and protections of a group of people who claim something are overriding other people's protections. This is the most bullying ideology I've ever come across. It's just outrageous to me.

Even in my local university here in Northern Utah they've bought into this. Everybody gets to select which pronouns they go by. It's just assumed.

The problem is, once you assume that somebody gets to choose which pronouns they prefer, you've bought into this ideology.

The university also has a group of students who claim to identify as transgender, who go into different classrooms and talk about the hardships of being transgender. It's so entrenched.

One of the recommendations I would have for people who have kids who are in late high school or starting college, is to really investigate your options for college. I would stay away from big universities. It's unfortunate. These are public institutions that should be our go-to, but they've been infiltrated. Maybe try to find a small community college, or a religious institution that you feel comfortable with. Maybe find a private school that hasn't bought into this ideology.

Maria Keffler (51:28):

You mentioned about transgender-identified students in colleges, going into classrooms. That's happening in high schools. We have two documented examples here in my district—high schools where the GSA club (Gender and Sexuality Allies) are being invited into other classrooms to give presentations on gender identity. At one point, the student taught sexual orientation and gender identity in a PE class during the health portion of it. There's so much wrong with that.

This is a little tangential. I don't want to go off into this too much, but the schools and the NEA are promoting this peer-led sex-ed. When I first heard that term, I thought, "That sounds familiar to me. What is that reminding me of?" And I realized it's *peer-to-peer sales*.

The marketing community has leveraged peer-to-peer sales to utilize social pressure to make sales. So, when somebody invites you to their home for baking goods party, or a candle party, or a clothing party, they're leveraging that peer pressure that says, "You're at my house. I've served you food," so you feel like, "I really should buy something while I'm here."

The schools have adopted that, and they're calling it *peer-led sex ed.*

It's just using peer pressure to force this down kids' throats, because when you're a freshman in high school and a junior comes and tells you, "This is a fact, and you need to get on board with it," how many freshmen are going to say, "No, I don't agree with you about that"?

Erin Brewer (53:16):

We know about the dangers of peer pressure. When I was in high school, they talked about it all the time. You had to be very careful because peers could influence into you into bad behaviors—smoking, drinking, doing things that were dangerous, driving when drunk. This is something that we've known about for ages, that peers have incredible credentials with their peers. If you've got a child who's a couple of years older, they can exert tremendous pressure.

Then you've got the schools also applying that pressure. You've got cases where children who don't ascribe to this ideology—who maybe call somebody by the correct pronoun, and someone doesn't like it. Those kids are getting in trouble with the administration. They're not just being bullied by other kids. They're getting in trouble. They're getting punished for not ascribing to this.

It's incredibly disturbing. This is about bullying. This is about exerting control over kids. The fact that they're punishing children for telling the truth—that's incredibly scary.

Maria Keffler (54:32):

At the very heart of this, schools are separating parents from their kids. Because when the teacher says, "There's no such thing as boys and girls," and the little kid says, "Mom and Dad told me that boys have a penis and girls have a vagina," and the teacher says, "That's just silly. Your parents are wrong," that's forcing that child to make a decision: "Do I believe my teacher or do I believe my parents?"

That is absolutely unconscionable.

Erin Brewer (55:06):

It so heartbreaking that this is so entrenched in the schools.

The good news is that parents can make a difference. If we get enough parents who are concerned about this, they can make a difference. Sometimes we forget that if you get 50 parents to go to a school board meeting upset about something, it's going to make a difference.

Part of this is finding out what's going on, then start organizing and being willing to stand up against this. You say, "No, we are not going to allow our children to be indoctrinated into this ideology."

<u>Maria Keffler (55:46):</u>

I want to leave also with that same hope. We've said a lot of things that are probably disturbing and disheartening to parents, but when parents start working together and pushing back on this, you do have success.

We had a success in my district with the Arlington Parent Coalition. We have on our website a universal opt-out letter. It's a letter that says, "I want my child not to encounter any information on gender identity. These are the things I don't want my child to be introduced to anywhere at school, any school, any class, any whatever."

Parents have started sending those into the school. We heard via a roundabout channel that it caused a big uproar in the administration. They were consulting their lawyers: "Are these letters legal? What do we have to do here?" We heard that the director of family life education told teachers, "Just stay in your lane. Only teach what's in your content area until we get this figured out."

I don't know where they're at with getting that figured out.

That is one of the benefits of having these watchdog groups is mobilizing lots of parents to do that. It lets the school know you're being watched: "We don't like what's happening. You may think you have the whole culture behind you, but you don't."

<u>Erin Brewer (57:22):</u>

It's hard, but you can do it, and it's worth it. These are our children.

Episode 8 Resources

Vicar Resigns as Primary School Imposes Transgender Ideology: <u>https://youtu.be/HQ57zai5Cpk</u>

Parent Resource Guide: <u>https://genderresourceguide.com/</u>

Parents' Rights in Education <u>https://www.parentsrightsined.org/</u>

Keeping Kids Safe in Public School: <u>https://arlingtonparentcoa.wixsite.com/arlingtonparentcoa/parents-guide-to-kids-safety-in-aps</u>

Materials for Parents: <u>https://www.partnersforethicalcare.com/materials-for-parents</u>

My Son's Freshman Orientation at Virginia Tech Was Full of Leftist Propaganda https://thefederalist.com/2019/08/14/sons-freshman-orientation-virginia-tech-full-leftist-propaganda/

Fired for Accidentally Calling Transgender Student 'She': https://youtu.be/iQaAaIO4Eaw

Arlington Parent Coalition: www.arlingtonparentcoa.wixsite.com/arlingtonparentcoa

Episode 9: Dealing with the World & the Extended Family

https://youtu.be/Hnx-d0lLe6M

<u>Maria Keffler (00:47):</u>

Our topic today is dealing with the world and the extended family.

<u>Erin Brewer (00:52):</u>

Can you just explain what that means for people who may not understand?

<u>Maria Keffler (00:58):</u>

They say it takes a village to raise a child, right? We're all connected to our near family, our extended family, our neighbors, the school community, and the faith community, if you have one. You're connected in all these ways. That village can be really supportive and helpful in raising your child.

But when it comes to gender ideology, unfortunately, the bulk of society has been conditioned—and I would even go so far as to say brainwashed—to believe that affirmative care, which is telling the child, "Yes, you really are the wrong gender," or "Your body and your mind are mismatched," is the only acceptable response.

So if the family who's dealing with the transgender-identified child says, "You know what? I don't agree with that. I've known my child, for 12, 13, 14, 15 years and they have never indicated a discomfort with their sex before. I think something else is going on"—when a family does that, you will quite often find that the larger society around them—the rest of their tribe—is actively working against them to affirm the child's self-proclaimed gender identity.

It really undermines the parents' efforts. And it comes out of this strange sense of wanting to be the valiant savior of the child. Especially in school settings, teachers and counselors are being taught, "You may be that child's only safe space. If their parents don't affirm them, you may be their only safe space." That's a heady idea: "Ooh, I get to be a Superman or Wonder Woman who saves this child from their toxic family."

That's so dishonoring to families and it undercuts all of your efforts to save your child.

> **Teachers and counselors are being taught,
> "You may be that child's only safe space.
> If their parents don't affirm them, you may be
> their only safe space." That's a heady idea:
> "Ooh, I get to be a Superman or Wonder Woman
> who saves this child from their toxic family."**

Erin Brewer (03:03):

It's really discouraging. I do believe that the vast majority of these people are really good-hearted people. They're doing this because they honestly believe that this is what is best for the child.

As you said, I believe that the society has been brainwashed. They're accepting something because they're being told that if they don't accept it, that they're unkind, intolerant, hateful people. They're going along with it without giving it a whole lot of thought.

Oftentimes they feel like they're that one person that might intervene to save this child. This is playing into people wanting to be kind and caring for a child, without understanding the implications.

It might sound really absurd to think, "Well, how can everybody else be wrong and the parents be right? How is it that we've gotten to a point where society has accepted this? Maybe everybody's accepting it because it really is the right way to proceed with these kids."

I think it's really important for us to address that there have been times historically where people have accepted great horrors unquestioningly. This is something that happens within society. Occasionally, from time to time, there is an acceptance of behaviors that are incredibly damaging and harmful and can be embraced by people who are good and kindhearted.

Maria Keffler (04:38):

That's true. We've seen that with the Holocaust. In that timeframe, there were a lot of people who knew that it was wrong. What was happening in Nazi Germany was wrong, but they were afraid to speak up. They were afraid to go against what the dominant culture was doing because they themselves would end up on a train to Dachau.

I see that happening a lot with this issue as well. I hear from so many people—and I suspect you do as well—who say, "Thank you so much for what you're doing. This is awful. What's happening to kids is horrific.

I'm not able to speak publicly. I'm not able to write publicly because I fear for my job, because I fear for my reputation."

I had one parent tell me, "I'm afraid my kids will be retaliated against at school."

I had this experience with my son, who's a senior in high school this year. One of his friends on Instagram posted to him, "Why is your mom such a hateful bigot?" That's a hurtful thing to experience. A lot of people are afraid of that, but I think that's evidence that there's a problem here.

Erin Brewer (06:01):

That's really a good indicator that something's off.

My son had a similar experience where he was at a bus stop and somebody came up and said, "I hope you know that there are a lot of people who want to kill your mom." What a despicable thing to say to a child.

Yet this movement has emboldened people to say things like that, which is an indicator that they're using fear and intimidation and bullying in order to further their agenda. Those are all indications that something's not quite right. When people have to be bullied like that—when people are afraid of losing their jobs, when people are afraid of being harassed and potentially even harmed for speaking out—that's an indication that this is not about being kind and tolerant. This is about an agenda that's being pushed.

There have been times in history where we have committed atrocities, where we have sterilized people against their will, where we have given people lobotomies. The Holocaust. We have had instances where we've done experiments on people, such as the Tuskegee Syphilis Trials, where we've used human beings as experiments. We've even had slavery. Human beings are capable of treating others really inappropriately and horrendously.

That's what's happening here. As you said, people are afraid to stand up. That's our nature. We have studies that show that people are willing to conform to what's around them rather than standing up, because they are afraid of retaliation.

Maria Keffler (07:44):

It's also a good part of human nature that we are socialized by those around us.

When children are growing up, they're being socialized into how to behave as healthy functioning adults. They learn what things are appropriate and are not appropriate to do in society. That's actually a healthy thing, except when bullying is used to apply pressure to somebody or when someone who is just a little bit different than other people is told, "Well, you're wrong because you're different."

A lot of times that's what's happening with this transgender movement. These kids are kind of on the fringe. They're vulnerable. They don't quite fit in. I'm thinking about the vast numbers of them that already have prior issues like autism and trauma and depression. Those are the kids who are being targeted by this.

You have to look at that and say, "Okay, something's wrong with that." If the vast majority of this group already have struggles, and yet we're not allowed to address those struggles, that's a problem.

Why can't I say, "Hey, 65% of kids who identify as transgender are on the autism spectrum?" When you say that you get called a bigot, hater, a transphobe—the whole nine yards. That's a red flag that something's wrong.

Today, one of the main points we want to talk about is how to deal with that when you have decided that you don't buy into the gender industry's dogma. You want to take a different path with your child, a path that you think is going to save them from being medicalized.

How do you deal with all of these people around you who are actively against you?

Erin Brewer (10:03):

When your authority is being undermined and when your child is being told that their misperceptions are correct, it is really a challenge.

Ideally, I would recommend cutting those ties. Those influences are so powerful and we know that these kids are vulnerable. If we can shield them from these influences, that's going to be really helpful.

But it can be really hard. If every other adult that the child knows is affirming them, and only the parents aren't, that is hard. Then you add on top of that all these other adults are saying, "Your parents are hateful bigots."

There's a two-pronged approach that needs to happen, to figure out who in your community is affirming your child with these negative thoughts and cut those ties, but also to develop ties with people who aren't doing this, because it's so important for children to have positive adult role models. We are social creatures. We need connections, especially children. It's really important for them to have connections.

As you're cutting off ties with people who are not safe for your children to be around, explore ways to keep them around adults who are going to be safe for them.

Maria Keffler (11:40):

We can't emphasize that enough. We become what other people tell us we are. We really do. I've quoted Goethe before who said, "Treat a man as he is and he will stay as he is; treat him as he ought to be, and he will become what he ought to be." What people reflect back to us is how we view ourselves.

That's one of the very insidious aspects of this gender ideology dogma. Children are already struggling with their identity—which is a normal part of adolescence, figuring out who you are. That is part of your job as an adolescent.

These vulnerable kids are targeted and they're going through this identity phase and somebody comes and tells them, "You feel that way because you're transgender."

Mom and Dad are saying, "No, I think he feels that way because he is autistic and an adolescent, and this is normal." That might be the only voice telling them the truth. If their teacher is telling them, "No, you're transgender," and their pediatrician is telling them, "No, you're transgender," and their therapist is telling them, "No, you're transgender," and the family that they babysit for is saying, "That's so great that you came out as transgender, and you're brave and stunning."

Erin Brewer (13:02):

It is overwhelming. Children can live up to expectations or down to expectations.

This is a vulnerable population, because in addition to autism, many of these kids have been sexually assaulted or had other trauma in their life. Some of them are just confused about gender stereotypes. You have a feminine boy and all of a sudden, he feels like he was born in the wrong body, because he's embarrassed about having feminine traits. A girl who would have been called a tomboy for eons is now being told she is born in the wrong body. It is such a powerful message.

Part of the strategy for parents needs to be to identify who it is in their community who is encouraging the child to believe these things, because these are really dangerous things to believe.

We've talked about the medicalization that happens. You put this kid on the pathway to puberty blockers, cross-sex hormones, and surgery. All of those things are harming a healthy body. It undermines the parent-child relationship, which is probably the most important relationship a child has. Once that gets compromised, that child loses a really important support system. It also undermines their ability to trust and it makes them very vulnerable.

Identify who in the community is really affirming this. Some people might be affirming it in a way that is really dangerous and other people might just be kind of going with the flow. Find out who your child is safe to be around and who they aren't safe to be around.

Just ask the person a question like, "Wow, I just heard, so-and-so's child came out as transgender. What do you think of that?" Just see what their response is. If they say, "Oh my goodness, isn't it wonderful? That child is so brave and stunning!" That's someone that you need to keep out of your child's life. Whereas if they say, "Well, yeah, I'm really sad to hear that. I'm confused," and if they aren't bubbling over with enthusiasm, then maybe that's someone who is going to be safe for your child to be around.

Explore teachers, neighbors, community members.

I use this analogy a lot: the drug user. Think of your child as having a drug addiction. Who's going give that child drugs and who isn't? That's what this is. Affirmation produces chemicals within the child that act like drugs. Those endorphins make them feel so good about themselves. It's a lot like getting a drug. Would you allow your child who has a drug problem go visit people who you know are going to hand him drugs? Probably not.

> **Think of your child as having a drug addiction. Who's going give that child drugs and who isn't? That's what this is. Affirmation produces chemicals within the child that act like drugs. Those endorphins make them feel so good about themselves. It's a lot like getting a drug. Would you allow your child who has a drug problem go visit people who you know are going to hand him drugs? Probably not.**

Maria Keffler (16:08):

Once you've parsed out, "These are the people I can trust; these other people I can't trust," it can be really difficult to keep the child away from the people who are not going be your allies in this.

I'm thinking about the doctor. When you take the child to the doctor—especially as kids get into their teenage years—it's very common for the doctor to ask the child, "Would you like to speak with me alone?" That's a normal thing. Doctors are looking for signs of child abuse. If the parents are being abusive the doctor can find that out. So that's not necessarily a red flag. But in this case, if you're not sure what your pediatrician's office policy is on this, I would really not be comfortable leaving the room.

I've heard of pediatricians asking very loaded, leading questions: "Do you feel safe at home? Do you feel supported at home? Are your parents supportive of this?" and leading the child. I would even go so far as to consider changing doctors if you don't feel that you can really trust your doctor's office.

I also want to say, doctors cannot just come out and say, "No, I don't agree with transgender ideology." Laws are being changed so that doctors and therapists cannot disagree with this ideology. They have to affirm it. You have to be a little bit 007-ish with your questioning.

Ask to sit down with the doctor in person. Don't even do it over the phone. Sit down with a potential doctor in person and just say, "I have a child who identifies as transgender, and I don't really think that's what the issue is. What's are your thoughts on that?"

See what the doctor says. If you hear a lot of the propaganda such as, "Well, I think it's important to let the child lead. Children know who they are. We need to be affirming and supportive." If you hear that propaganda—the slogans coming out—then you know that's not a doctor you can trust.

Erin Brewer (18:25):

It's really important to know that because I've talked to parents who have heard doctors say, in front of children and their parents, that if a parent doesn't affirm the child, the child is going to kill herself.

It is tacit approval for suicide. It indicates to a child that suicide is an appropriate response to not being affirmed, which is just an incredibly devastating thing to say to a child.

The other thing that is of concern more and more is that the doctor might report you to child protective services if you're not affirming them. That has serious consequences that a child may not really understand. Sometimes children are just mad at their parents and they might say, "Yeah, I just want them to call me my chosen name and pronouns, and they won't do it. I just hate it. They're so mean to me." That might be enough for a doctor to feel like they can call child protective services. Once that happens it can be a nightmare.

I've talked to parents who've had this happen. I know of a case right now where somebody called protective services on parents who weren't affirming their child, and the parents are on administrative leave while they're being investigated, all because somebody felt like the parents should be affirming their child's transgender identity.

You have to be careful because the stakes are super high here. You risk even losing custody of your child, depending on where you live and what the circumstances are. Finding those people who are going to be supportive of your approach to this is going to be really important.

Maria Keffler (20:06):

I want to encourage parents again to focus on your relationship with your child. Try to foster a good, healthy relationship with your child. Make the focus *not* on the transgender issue as much as you can. If your family likes to go skiing, go skiing. If your child likes to go fishing, go fishing. Have those experiences. Really seek to know your child.

It can be very tempting in this case to make every conversation about the trans thing, because you want to get this over with, you want to move through this. But really resist that urge and get to know the child.

Ask the child "Hey, you had a test today. How did it go?" Because ultimately, unfortunately, child protective services or the pediatrician may ask the child, "Are your parents supportive?" or, "Do you feel in danger with your parents?" The stronger your relationship is with your child, the less likely the child is to say, "Yeah, I hate my parents."

It's really sad to me that we're to the point where we've got to worry about this. They may ask the child and the child's going to make the decision in this case.

Erin Brewer (21:26):

We have a video clip that's going to talk about how easy it is for the community to embrace this transgender ideology. Very few people understand how insidious this is unless they're in it. There are some very powerful forces at play here that are bombarding society with these messages. These forces are very powerful and they have a lot of money and they have a lot invested in propagating this attitude.

When you wonder, "How is this happening? How is it that everybody's bought into it?" This video clip might explain it a little bit.

Hank Green (22:12):

Groupthink is a term coined by social psychologist Irving Janis to describe what happens when a group makes bad decisions, because they're too caught up in the unique internal logic of their group.

When a group gets wrapped up in itself and everyone agrees with each other, no one stops to think about other perspectives. As a result, you get some big and bad ideas, including some enormous historical fiascos like the Watergate cover-up and the Bay of Pigs invasion and the Chernobyl nuclear reactor accident.

So while two heads may often be better than one, it's important to make sure those heads are still open to different opinions, or they can do some really dumb stuff in the end. It's best to understand ourselves and our decisions as informed simultaneously by both individual and group factors, personality and situation.

Maria Keffler (22:57):

Fascinating video. Social psychology can apply pressure to people and make them do things that you would think no rational human being would do, but when everybody around you is doing it—it's amazing how susceptible we are to social pressure.

Erin Brewer (23:18):

Earlier in this video, he talks about Stanley Milgram's experiment where he was able to get most people to give what they thought were painful shocks to somebody in another room, electric shocks. It was to the point where it sounded like the person in the other room was like in serious pain. The scientists would say, "Okay, go ahead, give them another shock." A lot of the people did. A lot of people didn't.

That's the good news—there are people who will stand up and say, "No, I'm not going to do this. This is not okay." But there are a fair number of people who, if they're told that they should do something—even if they don't feel quite right about it—they're going to go ahead and do it because they don't want to buck authority. They don't want to go against social trends.

There's another experiment called the Stanford prison experiment where they recruited students to be subjects. Some of the students were told to act as prisoners and some of them were told to act as guards. Within just days, the guards got brutal. They ended up having to end the experiment early because it got so out of control and the prisoners became dehumanized so quickly.

It is easy for people to be influenced. That's what's happening now. This can be really difficult when we're dealing with community members that are close to your child, or potentially your relatives. There are cases where grandparents are 100% wanting to affirm the child, or nephews or nieces or aunts or uncles. It's possible if you have an older child that they work somewhere where they're being affirmed. There are all these different situations.

Maria Keffler (25:16):

I don't really have an answer for how to deal with all these situations. Some of them are so difficult, especially if your child is older. The younger your child is the more control you have.

I know of one family were the daughter babysat for a family in the neighborhood. The daughter came out and said she was transgender. The family she babysat for was supporting her behind her parents' back. The parents found out that the family had given their daughter a trans novel.

I never thought I would miss the vampire and werewolf *Twilight* series. Now it's trans literature. Can we go back to the werewolves and vampires?

Erin Brewer (26:17):

There's this whole series that is trying to replace *Harry Potter* where boys can be witches too. Girls can be warlocks. It's everywhere.

As a parent, depending on the child's age, you have more or less authority. It can be really hard when you think you're sending your child into a safe environment, then you find out that the people are undermining you. I've heard of cases where parents have moved because they feel like they're in an environment where they're not going to win. They can't escape. They can't cut the child off from everybody who is encouraging the child in a trans identity. So they move somewhere safer.

> **I've heard of cases where parents have moved because they feel like they're in an environment where they're not going to win. They can't escape. They can't cut the child off from everybody who is encouraging the child in a trans identity. So they move somewhere safer.**

I've heard of situations where parents have packed up the van and gone on a year-long trip around the country. Not everybody can do that. Most people can't do that.

My recommendation would be to identify people who are the worst offenders and really make a concerted effort to separate your child from them, especially if you're in a community where the vast majority of people feel like this is a great thing and that your child's brave and wonderful for announcing a trans identity. Find the people who are the worst offenders. The stronger your relationship with your child, the less susceptible he or she is going to be to these really negative influences.

Maria Keffler (27:58):

In situations like with the babysitting family, those parents decided their daughter is not going to babysit for that family. They didn't say that overtly, but every time the family called asking if she could babysit, they would say, "I'm sorry, she's busy tonight."

Erin Brewer (28:23):

So rather than telling the child, "You can't see them because they're affirming," you just do it subtly, because we know teenagers like to push back against things. And they have been told to find people who love them for who they are. If you just subtly do it that's going to be a lot more effective.

Maria Keffler (28:54):

You might even have to be a little surreptitious. If Grandma and Grandpa, who are going to undermine you, want to have your child over for the weekend, rather than just blanket saying "No" to that, maybe you buy some concert tickets or something that child really wants to see that weekend. Say to your child, "Oh my gosh, Grandma and Grandpa invited you over, but we've got these tickets. What do you want to do?" Let the child be the one to decide.

We have a statement from a listener. Usually listeners send in questions, but we got a really good recommendation from a listener about how she dealt with this issue.

She said, "I did have one friend who I used to invite over to act as a buffer when my daughter was coming over. She was amazingly good at small talk and was brilliant at filling in the gaps in conversations. Because she wasn't me, my daughter would excuse her if she asked the wrong thing. It made the whole visit so much more pleasant and acted like a brilliant buffer zone."

So it sounds like the daughter was a little older, maybe not at home anymore, but when they got together, the mom would have this friend come because she was just a little bit more removed from the situation. The daughter liked her and was more tolerant of her "mistakes."

Erin Brewer (30:23):

A lot of times kids will not cut their parents a lot of slack, but they will cut other people some slack. This is an approach that you could even take if you have people who are affirming your child, and it's someone that your child needs to interact with. Maybe find someone who can act as a buffer in that situation.

Maria Keffler (30:45):

If there's somebody who already is in your circle, who has a good relationship with your child-- I'm thinking about aunts and uncles, who are often so much cooler than mom and dad are. If there's a brother or a sister in the family, or an uncle or somebody who the child has always thought, "Oh, Aunt Susie is really cool"—if you can get Aunt Susie on your side, she can be a fantastic help, because your child is more likely to open up to her and to respect her, without some of the baggage that comes with the parent-child relationship.

Erin Brewer (31:22):

That's true, especially in this situation where you have a daughter who perhaps is hating herself for being a girl. If there's a beloved aunt who can come over, maybe your daughter is going to be able to hear from an aunt, "It's hard being an adolescent. This is a tough time. Most of us hated our bodies when we were your age." The child may be able to hear that from the aunt in a way that she won't be able to hear it from her parents.

> **"It's hard being an adolescent. This is a tough time. Most of us hated our bodies when we were your age." The child may be able to hear that from the aunt in a way that she won't be able to hear it from her parents.**

Now we have a question: "How do I identify all the influences in my son's life? I don't even know most of his friends."

That is a big issue especially for older kids. It's a little bit easier with younger kids. Once kids get older, it is harder to know who they're hanging out with, and you don't want to be an extreme helicopter mom who follows her kids to school and spies on them. What recommendations would you have for this mom?

Maria Keffler (32:23):

One place you can start is to sit down and make a map. I do this sometimes when I'm struggling.

I did this one time when I was just overworked. I sat down with a piece of paper and I wrote down: "I have my kids, I have my job, I have my volunteering, I have my hobbies." I made this map and I found where all of my time was going. Then I could identify things that are unnecessary and I don't enjoy but which are taking up a lot of time. Then I said, "Let me get rid of that."

You can do the same thing with your child's relationships: "We've got school. We've got a part-time job. We've got social media and we've got his therapist." Just map out everything that you know of or that you can think of. "He's on social media. I know he's on Snapchat. I know he's on Reddit." (Get your kid off Reddit. It's all bad.)

If your child has a job, maybe you can visit and get to know some other people. You may be able to identify somebody who you could partner with, like, "Could you let me know if you see anything troubling?"

Erin Brewer (33:56):

I would also try to make your home open so that your child feels comfortable having friends over, because you learn a lot once your child has friends over.

I have to admit, there were times that my kids had friends that I didn't particularly like, but I felt good having them over to my house. I could build a relationship with them. I also knew what they were like and whether or not it was a kid I felt was a good kid for my son to go spend the night with. Or maybe I'd tell him, "If you want to spend time with that kid, you need to do it at our house.

That's okay to do. You say, "I'm a little bit uncomfortable about this particular friend. I don't want to say you can't be friends with him, but if you're going to hang out, you need to do it at our house." That's valid.

> You say, "I'm a little bit uncomfortable about this particular friend. I don't want to say you can't be friends with him, but if you're going to hang out, you need to do it at our house." That's valid.

The other thing with younger kids that's just good to be aware of is that people have different ideas of when children are able to spend time by themselves. I know that when my kids were little, I was shocked to find out that there was a parent of one of my child's friends who felt that their five-year-old was perfectly fine spending the afternoon by themselves and would be okay having my son over. I wasn't okay with that. I don't think five-year-olds are old enough to be on their own for hours on end.

As a parent, it's important to identify what are you comfortable with and what are you not comfortable with. It's perfectly okay to say, "Have Joe come over here." You don't want to tell your kid, "I don't like Joe," but say, "I'm just much more comfortable when Joe's over here. I think that he really likes coming over. So have him come over, and we'll make some cookies." Do something fun.

There are lots of options. It's really hard if they end up in the LGB/TQ club at school or something. Suddenly all of their peers are going to be part of this agenda. Then it becomes really difficult. You might just have to be firm and say, "You know, these are not children you're allowed to spend time with."

Maria Keffler (36:18):

Keep in mind that your end goal is to have a healthy, safe child who makes it to adulthood intact. Most parents are willing to sacrifice an awful lot to protect their kids.

Episode 9 Resource List

Social Influence: Crash Course Psychology #38:
https://youtu.be/UGxGDdQnC1Y

Boundaries Updated and Expanded Edition: When to Say Yes, How to Say No To Take Control of Your Life:
https://www.amazon.com/Boundaries-Updated-Expanded-When-Control/dp/0310351804/ref=sr_1_2

Episode 10: Autism & Gender Dysphoria

https://youtu.be/birgUTOMhEE

Maria Keffler (00:48):

Today we are talking about autism and gender dysphoria. This is a really big subject, because we know from the research that's out there that kids who are presenting with gender identity issues are overwhelmingly autism spectrum disorder kids. Some studies are putting it at 60% or higher, and that's huge, but people aren't talking about it.

One of the things that people really need to understand is the difference between causality and correlation.

When you're looking at research—when you're looking at data, looking at studies, looking at anything—you can recognize that two things tend to happen together. It's very easy to say that one thing causes another, but you don't really know that from research.

A good example of that might be ice cream and sexual assault. Studies have shown that when consumption of ice cream increases, sexual assault also increases.

Wait a minute, is eating ice cream causing sexual assault?

No. The third factor there is that it's summertime. In the summertime, people consume more ice cream. In the summertime more people are out and about, and there's more opportunity for sexual assaults. It's that third factor that's affecting the other two. But in the research, it just looks like we're seeing increased ice cream consumption and increased sexual assaults. Maybe one's causing the other?

The same thing applies when it comes to gender dysphoria and autism.

There's something that is causing autistic kids to present and say, "Hey, I think I'm transgender," but we don't necessarily know what that third thing is. But we can't say that one causes the other.

Erin Brewer (02:53):

One of the concerns that I've had is that transgender activists are celebrating the fact that there are so many autistic kids who are having gender identity issues, and making the claim that this proves that it's biological. Because autism's biological, they say that transgenderism must be somehow connected with the biology of autism.

There are all sorts of claims made based on these correlations, but they're not causative. That's something that people really need to understand.

My biggest concern is the idea that there is such a thing as a transgender child, which I reject. I don't think that there is such a thing as a transgender child. There are kids who are vulnerable to this ideology.

When you look at autism, it's not surprising that there's so many kids being sucked into this ideology, because it's the perfect thing for them to explain away their social discomfort, their quirkiness, and not fitting in. This kid who's been on the spectrum his or her whole life might be really struggling, then all of a sudden gets affirmation and affection and attention by coming out and saying he or she is transgender.

There's suddenly an explanation for a child as to why he or she has been struggling all his or her life, and there's a community that swoops in and provides this child with attention and affection and affirmation.

That's really where my concern is: that activists are celebrating this, when in fact it's something that we need to be extremely concerned about.

Maria Keffler (04:32):

For people who aren't familiar with autism, and some of the hallmarks of autism, it's considered a constellation disorder, which means there are all these different "stars" or different aspects of it. It's called a spectrum disorder because not every kid will exhibit every one of these symptoms, but a combination of things occur which leads therapists and doctors to diagnose a child with autism.

The main things that are hallmarks of autism are difficulties with social interactions, difficulties with language, and difficulties with sensory issues. So those are the three big things with autism and all of those will feed right into this suggestion that, "Something's wrong with me? What could that be?"

A lot of kids—and especially girls—tend to be under-diagnosed with autism. There are some theories about why that is, but currently 80% of kids who are diagnosed with autism are boys. Why is that? Why are we seeing it so much more often in boys and girls?

There are several theories, but one that holds a lot of water is that girls tend to be better at social interactions. They tend to be more verbal than boys. So girls might be able to hide their symptoms of autism a little bit better than boys do. Girls tend to be better at observing others' behavior and mimicking it.

Erin Brewer (06:22):

Kids who have those sensory issues are uncomfortable with their bodies. You've got kids who are already struggling, feeling uncomfortable with themselves and then you tell them, "Hey, guess what? You might've been born in the wrong body." What a perfect solution.

All of a sudden, they think, "Now it makes sense! Other people are so much more comfortable with themselves. It's because I was born in the wrong body," without connecting that to being part of the autism spectrum.

Another thing that's really a hallmark of autism is black-and-white thinking—very rigid thinking. Again, this plays perfectly into the gender ideology, because a lot of these kids struggle with social interactions, and they struggle to fit in. It's not surprising that a girl who's really having a difficult time fitting in says, "Maybe it's because I'm a boy."

A lot of these kids' verbal skills aren't as strong. They tend to be more interested in STEM things: science, technology, engineering, and math. For girls, it's hard to fit in if you're a nerdy girl who's interested in number patterns and not interested in shopping. A girl like that could really easy say, "It's because I'm actually a boy," especially if you have somebody telling her, "The reason you're not fitting in and the reason you're uncomfortable with your body is because you were born in the wrong body. You're actually a boy."

It's that nuanced thinking that most of us get as grown-ups, but which these kids are lacking.

Maria Keffler (08:03):

I spoke to one young woman who thought that she was transgender for a couple of years, and then she desisted. She said, "I didn't have a friend group. I didn't really have a posse. Then I went to the GSA club (the Gender and Sexuality Alliance), and suddenly I had this group of friends and I had somebody to eat with at lunch. And there was always somebody hanging out with me. Then when I said, 'I wonder if I might be transgender?' suddenly I was cool. I was popular. Like everybody thought I was amazing."

She recognizes looking back that that fed both her need for an explanation for why she felt so strange in her own body and an explanation for why she didn't have any friends: "Because I'm actually a boy." It met a lot of temporary needs, which are very common for adolescent kids, but ultimately it was not factual. She thankfully recognized that before she went down the medicalization path.

> **"I didn't have a friend group. I didn't really have a posse. I went to the GSA club (the Gender and Sexuality Alliance), and suddenly I had this group of friends and I had somebody to eat with at lunch. There was always somebody hanging out with me. Then when I said, 'I wonder if I might be transgender?' suddenly I was cool. I was popular. Everybody thought I was amazing."**

Erin Brewer (09:20):

Another hallmark of being on the autism spectrum is perseveration, or getting in a thinking rut. You get a thought and just keep having that thought run over and over again, and you have a hard time dislodging it.

We know that kids who are on the spectrum tend to get obsessed about things. When they're interested in something, they're *really* interested in it, which can be an incredible gift in some cases. If they're interested in engineering or math, or, some aspect of science, this kind of intensity of thought and perseveration can be beneficial.

But if they get stuck on a thought that they were born in the wrong body, they can get into that thought. It's hard to dislodge that—potentially much harder than it is for a kid who's not on the spectrum.

That's another way that they're vulnerable. Somebody can feed them a thought. Whereas with some kids that thought might just percolate through and then leave, a child who's on the spectrum might start ruminating about it and thinking, "Gosh, I remember when I was a kid, I did like to play with toys of the other sex. I had a hard time playing with kids who were my same sex." They can just spend lots of time going back and thinking about every single instance where they didn't quite fit in and connect that to being transgender.

Maria Keffler (10:45):

The black-and-white thinking can feed into the perseveration.

I spoke to one therapist who said for a lot of these kids who are on the autism spectrum, when they get into gender theory, it becomes their obsession.

If you've ever worked with an autistic child, they do develop obsessions that can last for years. Whether it's an obsession with Pokemon or an obsession with a number theory or obsession with dragons or a TV show like *Star Trek*. They will get into it and learn everything about it. An autistic kid who is obsessed with *Star Wars* might learn Galactic Basic Language. They get into it.

That's an insidious part of this. If they do get introduced to gender theory, and something about it resonates with them or feeds something that they're struggling with, gender ideology can become their obsession. And they perseverate on it.

Once an autistic person has made a decision, they have put a lot of thought into the decision; breaking out of that is very hard for them, because they've put all of this energy and thought into making the decision. If it's a good decision, that's fantastic. But if it's not a good decision, it's very hard to get them to correct it.

Erin Brewer (12:28):

I've done a lot of interviews with detransitioners and a lot of these kids didn't have an autism diagnosis before they got into the transgender ideology. They were very vulnerable. They were struggling socially. They were sucked into it.

Many of them went all the way: they took puberty blockers, cross-sex hormones, had surgery, and then they came out on the other end, realizing that they were on the spectrum, and that they had done all of this as a result of being on the spectrum. And nobody had identified it earlier. They went to therapists who just affirmed, affirmed, affirmed, and never tried to identify if there were underlying issues or something like autism that was causing a child to feel this kind of discomfort and disease with themselves.

What a mistake. That's part of the problem with these therapy bans. Therapists aren't feeling empowered to explore other reasons why a child might be feeling distress within themselves. They are affirming and moving them forward.

These young adults are enraged, because if somebody had diagnosed them and given them appropriate treatment when they were in junior high school or high school, then they wouldn't have harmed themselves with transgender interventions.

Maria Keffler (14:08):

I spoke with one parent whose child was diagnosed with autism, and had an IEP at school for several years. His daughter had been diagnosed as a young child. He said that as soon as his daughter said that she thought she was transgender, nothing about autism mattered anymore at school. He said up until that time, everything that happened at school related to that autism diagnosis and the IEP. The teachers would ask, "Is what's happening related to her autism? Is the accommodation for what she needs fitting with autism?" As soon as she announced a transgender identity, the school would not even discuss if anything she did had anything to do with autism.

Erin Brewer (15:00):

Even if you do have a diagnosis, it's still easy to get pulled into this. That's where schools have let these kids down. Rather than helping to identify accommodations that will help them to feel more comfortable, or to suggest that maybe they explore autism, they're saying, "Of course you're transgender," and pushing them that direction.

One of the things that I've noticed when talking to detransitioners is that when girls start on testosterone, it gives them a huge high. Testosterone is a controlled substance. It's a very powerful hormone. Girls who haven't been confident, who haven't had good self-esteem, or who have struggled, they take testosterone, and all of a sudden, they have a boost in their confidence. At the same time, it shuts down their feelings.

> **Girls who haven't had good self-esteem, or who have really struggled, they take testosterone, and all of a sudden, they have a boost in their confidence. At the same time, it shuts down their feelings.**

One of the problems that people with autism face is having a hard time getting in touch with their feelings. It can be hard for them to navigate situations because they have a hard time identifying feelings.

We are giving testosterone to a girl who already is struggling with identifying her feelings. We're giving her a drug that cuts her off even further from her feelings.

It's not surprising that when girls first start taking testosterone, they say, "Yeah, this is it." They get this boost of energy. They feel really good and they get cut off even more from those feelings that can be uncomfortable, especially in the teenage years.

Maria Keffler (16:48):

I didn't know that that testosterone did that to girls. That's heartbreaking.

Erin Brewer (16:54):

There are a lot of issues here. We're going to show an interview with a young woman who was absolutely convinced that she was transgender. She went to gender clinic in Scotland, and this particular clinic did a full assessment, something that almost never happens. It's incredibly rare for a child who develops this gender identity crisis to get a full assessment.

The assessment saved this young woman's life. It saved her from testosterone and going down that path. As a result of this assessment her doctor said, "Wait a minute, there is more going on here. We want you to go see someone about your autism."

Maria Keffler (18:03):

Maybe we need to send all these kids to Scotland to be taken care of.

Erin Brewer (18:08):

Yeah. Or send our therapists to Scotland to be trained, because they're doing it right. We are not doing it right.

> Erin Brewer (18:14):
>
> Are you still going to the gender clinic?
>
> Nem (18:17):
>
> No. I actually stopped going because I think when I found out I was autistic—because I'd suspected myself for a while—but when I actually got the diagnosis, it kind of just made more sense to me why I didn't feel any sense of gender fully, and it kind of resolved.

Erin Brewer (18:35):

That was Nem. As I mentioned, she is from Scotland.

I just wanted to point out that she was only willing to do this interview anonymously. Many detransitioners feel the same way. They want to get their story out, but they're afraid to put their face out there because of the repercussions.

This is an indication that this is a damaging ideology. This has nothing to do with being born in the wrong body or having some kind of medical diagnosis. It is heartbreaking to me that these young women want to share their stories, but they're afraid. They're very scared that they might get bullied. They might get fired. They might even get physically assaulted as a result of speaking out about this.

I'm appreciative that she was willing to share her story. I think it's so important for people to realize that that autism can cause a child or young adult to feel like they are born in the wrong body.

Maria Keffler (19:34):

I would suggest that any kid who starts thinking or exploring or stating that he or she is transgender ought to be screened for autism, when we're seeing this level of autism—a percentage of 60% and greater. Those are the ones who are diagnosed. That's not even taking into account kids who have not received a diagnosis yet, when we're seeing those kinds of numbers.

> **Any kid who starts thinking or exploring or stating that he or she is transgender ought to be screened for autism, when we're seeing this level of autism— a percentage of 60% and greater.**

That's probably the first thing you ought to look for: find out if the child might be on the autism spectrum. If a kid is just being told, "Yes, you're transgender," she's not getting help. That child's not getting help for any of the struggles she has. The verbal issues, the social issues, the processing issues, the perseveration, the black-and-white thinking—all of those things have therapies. There are ways to help that child learn how to cope and how to shore up weaknesses and develop strengths and really get along in society and thrive. But if you're not even addressing those, how can that child ever thrive?

Erin Brewer (20:59):

Especially when you're putting them on a pathway that is ultimately going to end up damaging their body. That's the crux of it: they're being denied appropriate services and help. They're being put on a pathway that's going to end up damaging their body.

One of the techniques that works well with people with autism is social stories. They work if a child has a misperception about something, A lot of times they draw it out like a cartoon. They have the child draw out the situation as it is, to correct the misperception. This is effective. This is a technique that works well with autistic kids. We write out a little story about feeling uncomfortable with ourselves, but then in the story, we talk about why it is that they feel uncomfortable and we do an ending where the child recognizes that he or she is not transgender, but autistic.

There are a lot of other techniques that can be used to help children with autism function better. They have communication skills classes. They have cognitive behavioral therapy, which is an older person's version of social stories—recreating the stories that you tell yourself so that you're more comfortable and function better.

We're denying all of that to kids who are autistic.

Maria Keffler (22:47):

Temple Grandin is a very famous autistic woman. She's done amazing work. When she was a child, she wasn't verbal at all—no interaction. She credits her mother for working with her. Now she's got a Ph.D. I think she has more than one Ph.D. She has completely overhauled the animal processing industry in the United States.

I would really recommend anything she's written. She's got a great book called *The Way I See It*, and it's essays on different aspects of her life and different aspects of autism. They're fascinating.

If you have a child who's autistic or you suspect she might be autistic, I would recommend Temple Grandin—her movie about her life, anything that she's written. It's illuminating.

Erin Brewer (23:41):

Her story illustrates that if she were a child today, she would be told she was born in the wrong body, because she's quirky, she likes science, and she doesn't dress like a typical female. All of these things would lead her to believe that she's transgender.

That's so frustrating. She's a wonderful, gifted scientist. If she had been pushed to take drugs that harmed her body, and have surgeries that could potentially kill her, her whole career could have been derailed.

That's my biggest concern about these kids. They have incredible gifts that are going to be denied to them because they're being sent down this dangerous pathway.

Maria Keffler (24:28):

We know that puberty blockers halt brain development. What if Temple Grandin had been put on puberty blockers? Her wonderful, amazing, insightful brain would have been damaged, because that's what it does when brain development is halted: it damages the brain. That's heartbreaking.

You see so often with autistic kids, they have these super strengths and these super weaknesses, and they're this mixed bag of strengths and weaknesses. We all are. We all have different combinations of strengths and weaknesses.

Erin Brewer (25:05):

One of the things that's typical about people on the spectrum is that their gifts are very strong and their weaknesses can be debilitating if they're not properly assessed and if they're not taught coping skills.

We know how to help these kids develop skills so that their weaknesses aren't so debilitating. We have the know-how to help them. Yet, instead of helping them, we're just saying, "Nope, you're transgender. Go ahead and go down that pathway."

Luckily some of the people who are working with autistic kids are recognizing this and are starting to speak out and say, "Hey, we need to stop this. These are kids who need to accept their autism rather than being told they're born in the wrong body."

Maria Keffler (26:02):

We have a clip from—I'm going to call her professor Ina, because I can't pronounce her last name and if I try I'm going to destroy it. She's an autism researcher and she talks about autism and gender dysphoria.

Prof. Ina van Berckelaer-Onnes (26:18):

What is known, what we can find, what we did find in the publications is an overrepresentation of individuals with autism spectrum disorders. Of course, more and more publications are coming in which is not surprising ... it is not strange that it occurs in the same person.

So the co-morbidity of autism and gender identity is not so strange. There are, if you look at the explanations, various options. Cross-gender behavior can be attributed to special obsessions with people. Cross-gender behavior can be considered as an OCD separately from autism and gender dysphoria.

He was very artistic. I mean, there was no doubt that he wasn't not autistic, and his problem was totally not that he had a transformation, because he said, "I was born in the wrong body." And what—the only thing needed is that they correct it. So that was not his problem. His problem was that he could not adapt himself to the daily life situation because of his autism. So I had him in treatment for a period and after he accepted his autism. He changed and he could cope with his life. And he looked really like a man and not like a woman.

Maria Keffler (27:36):

That was fascinating. She's recognizing the correlations between being on the autism spectrum and believing that you were born in the wrong body. I loved what she said after he accepted his autism: He changed and could cope with his life. That's wonderful when you embrace truth, when you find out the truth.

Erin Brewer (28:01):

We do have kids with autism. We have kids with developmental disabilities. Imagine if we had the money funneling in to support them that we have to supporting the transgender ideology? Imagine how much better the outcomes would be for these kids if we had early intervention programs to help them.

Instead we're celebrating this absurdity that you can be born in the wrong body.

It's just infuriating to me. Imagine if they had an autism club instead of LGB/TQ clubs? Imagine if they had a club for autism and they had the kind of resources that the gender & sexuality clubs have?

> **Imagine if they had an autism instead of an LGB/TQ club. Imagine if they had a club for autism and they had the kind of resources that the gender & sexuality clubs have?**

That would be just phenomenal. These kids would thrive. They would get the supportive services they need.

The experts know exactly what interventions will help these kids, but the schools can't afford to provide these services. Sometimes it's occupational therapy, sometimes it's even physical therapy, social skills training, communication skills. All of these things we can teach kids if we had funding. But instead all that funding, all those resources are going to help kids think that they're inherently flawed.

Maria Keffler (29:29):

We just don't have the political will for it.

Going back to the family that I mentioned whose child was diagnosed with autism and had an IEP—which is an Individualized Education Plan. Any child who's receiving special ed services in school gets an individualized education plan or IEP. It prescribes what needs to happen at school. It has goals such as, "We want the child to be able to attend 80% of classes without incident. We want the child to be able to attain a C average in all classes." There are all kinds of goals there.

The IEP is kind of the child's Bible at school. All of the teachers have to refer to it. There are legal ramifications for what happens with it.

Well this child had an IEP. After the child said that she was transgender, anything related to autism just went out the door; they just weren't discussing it anymore. The parents said that in one IEP meeting, where the parent sits down with all of the teachers and discuss the goals, the teacher said, "He has made such great gains in his goals, he's done better in his grades this year, he's done better in his social skills. He's done better in his communication now that he knows who he really is, he's done so great."

The parent was just furious because that teacher was attributing all of the student's gains to this false ideology, rather than this child has had IEP teams on her side for multiple years. She's had parents working with her. She's had therapists working with her—all of these other things that had been in place for so long were just disregarded because, "Oh, 'he' has finally identified 'his' true self," which is actually someone *she's* not.

This child has since detransitioned and is no longer insisting that she's transgender. That alone speaks volumes to me that it was not a true statement that the gains were because of her transgender status.

<u>Erin Brewer (31:49):</u>

The support kids are getting would be good if it were not reinforcing a transgender ideology. Having an after-school club where kids could go, that would be well-funded and promote doing activities like social outreach—that would be great if it weren't connected to this damaging ideology.

That's where I get frustrated. We could be offering services to kids that we know would be beneficial, but instead we're allowing these very powerful activists' ideology to come in and to harm kids. Ultimately the difference is that one direction leads to children becoming healthy, becoming more functional, becoming more accomplished, while the other leads to them thinking they're inherently flawed, that there's something wrong with them, that they have to damage themselves in order to be okay. That's where the dividing line is.

It's very clear in my interview with Nem. We talked a little bit about something that made me wonder about some of the things that girls do, and possibly that boys do, when they feel uncomfortable in their bodies.

Nem (33:21):

People can struggle a lot with puberty. For me, I really did not like puberty, like physically—the physical experience was quite distressing.

Erin Brewer (33:30):

All those changes. That leads me to something that I've had a hypothesis about for a while. People who are autistic often benefit from compression therapy. I wondered if breast binding might be a form of compression therapy? So a girl who is autistic and feels like she's a boy binds her breasts and might feel comforted by that simply because of the compression.

Nem (34:01):

Yeah. I honestly think you might be right on that one, because I remember when I was thinking about stuff, I thought, "I'll buy a chest binder and I'll try it out." And I really loved wearing it. It felt really—I felt so much more comfortable wearing it. So I just felt, "Okay, I'm on the right lines here."

Erin Brewer (34:19):

For people who don't know about binders, binders are very tight around the chest. Children who are autistic sometimes really benefit with compression therapy. They have compression vests. They have compression blankets. They have compression shirts that they will often recommend to some kids who are autistic, because that pressure helps them sensory-regulate. They've done a lot of research about this, so they know that this is actually a therapy for some of these kids.

There are other kids who are on the other end, who are constantly trying to get out of their stuff. So compression therapy isn't for all autistic kids, but for a fair number of them, compression can help. It could be that the breast binding is actually somewhat therapeutic if it were done with compression rather than with binding, which hurts the breasts. The difference is that a compression shirt provides that therapeutic compression, whereas a binder damages breasts and potentially inhibits the ability to breathe. I've even heard of ribs being cracked. It's the difference between a therapy that's beneficial and something that's going to harm them.

Maria Keffler (35:39):

That was fascinating to me to learn about compression shirts and compression garments. Temple Grandin talked about that back in the fifties or sixties. She saw cattle being put in this metal squeeze box before they were given inoculations for various things. She asked, "Why are you squeezing them in there?" because it looked kind of uncomfortable. But the farmers said, "Oh, it calms them. It just calms the cattle. And they don't mind getting the shots."

So Temple Grandin made herself a squeeze box. She may have been the one who discovered that having that squeezing-tight feeling does help a significant portion of autistic people.

I had never put that together—that might be why binders are so appealing. Binders are corset-like. If you've ever seen a woman in the movies—like in *Pirates of the Caribbean*, Keira Knightley is being put into a corset. The person who's helping a woman dress would put her foot on your back and cinch up the corset to make your waist look smaller.

A binder is like the corset, but lifted up. It's not your waist, but it's your chest that's getting compressed, and it can cause long-term damage.

But a compression shirt for sensory issues is just a snug shirt that can give that overall feeling of well-being without the damage that binders cause.

Erin Brewer (37:25):

The other thing that we see happening is what has been termed ROGD, rapid-onset gender dysphoria. I was wondering if you have any insights as to why so many kids who go along okay until they hit adolescence and then they're just completely drawn into this ideology.

Maria Keffler (37:44):

It's not surprising to me when I look at what's going on during adolescence.

Adolescence is a time of huge changes. Your brain is changing. Your body is changing, your hormones and your social networks are changing. It's a huge time of change and growth. That's discombobulating for everybody. I don't know anybody who says, "Oh yeah, adolescence and puberty was a breeze. Loved it. Wouldn't mind doing it again." Most people are thinking, "You couldn't pay me enough to go through that period of life again."

When you think about what that's like for an autistic kid—and remember that autistic kids struggle with social skills, they struggle with their verbal skills, they struggle with that black-and-white thinking, they struggle with sensory issues, but a big one is that they struggle with change. Autistic kids and people do not like change. They like everything to stay the same. They want things predictable. They know what's going to happen next so there are no surprises. Big changes can be a disaster for people on the autism spectrum.

Imagine what adolescence is like for an autistic kid: it's like a nuclear bomb to your life. Everything is changing. Everything is different, and that's scary, uncomfortable and painful.

> **Adolescence is like a nuclear bomb to an autistic kid's life. Everything is changing. Everything is different, and that's scary, uncomfortable, and painful.**

And then you've got these activists and these programs in schools. If you walk into a school today, you're likely to see posters in the hallway advertising gender identity classes. Every single class has it in there somewhere. So you've got these children who are just feeling like their lives have blown up and nothing feels safe and secure and right. And someone tells them, "You feel that way because you're transgender." That's a really quick and easy answer.

Erin Brewer (39:52):

And these kids are told, "We can stop all of this discomfort from happening by putting you on puberty blockers. So we'll just keep you where you are in that comfortable zone rather than having to go through puberty," which might on the surface seem awesome for the kid who is thinking, "Great, I get to stay where I'm comfortable."

What we're doing is inducing a developmental delay and preventing them from going through puberty, which is so important, even though it's uncomfortable.

Maria Keffler (40:23):

So much of our growth is predicated on discomfort. We do not grow and change without discomfort.

> **So much of our growth is predicated on discomfort. We do not grow and change without discomfort.**

Why would we want to prevent anyone from attaining adulthood? There's no conscionable, valid reason to prevent someone from attaining adulthood.

That's what puberty blockers do. It's not a pause. There's a very short, finite window through which humans go from childhood to adulthood. It's small. It's very time-specific. If a child is on puberty blockers for long enough, they miss puberty. That window does not open back up again.

Erin Brewer (41:10):

The other thing that struck me as you were talking is that when I've talked to people who are on the spectrum, another reason that puberty can be so uncomfortable is that suddenly they're getting sexual urges, but at the same time, a lot of these kids are uncomfortable with touch from other people. Some of them have a revulsion to body fluids. So they might be very conflicted between wanting to kiss someone, but at the same time being disgusted by it.

That can cause incredible cognitive dissonance. Even for those who are not on the spectrum, adolescence is hard, but you add the social situations, sensory issues, and black-and-white thinking. It's no wonder they want to pause puberty. I mean of course they want to pause puberty. Why wouldn't they want to pause puberty?

Then if they can even modify it so that they get cross-sex hormones, then they don't have to accept who they are. They can take on this different identity and kind of mold who they're going to be, rather than accept who they are.

Maria Keffler (42:20):

So much of it is escapism—wanting to escape puberty, wanting to escape the social situation, wanting to escape myself. I think we've probably all felt at some time, "I wish I could be someone else."

> **So much of it is escapism. I think we've probably all felt at some time, "I wish I could be someone else."**

Adolescence is a miserable time. I spoke to a teacher who works with autistic kids. This teacher works with profoundly autistic kids, which are a little bit of a different group than we're talking about here. We tend to be talking about the high-functioning autistic kids who suffer with ROGD. But this teacher told me that with autism, sexual development often is delayed. They don't start thinking about romantic things till much later. She was so funny. She said, "They're so into themselves, they're so focused on what they're interested in, they're not even paying attention to the people around them."

As I was thinking about this, and as I've met various autistic kids, when they're very young and in elementary school, they are so introspective and so into themselves, and so into their own stuff. They're not practicing the social skills that most of the other kids are practicing and learning, such as asking, "What do I do that makes other people like me? What do I do to create friendships?"

Then they hit middle school and all these developmental changes happen. Puberty is going on. They start seeing everybody else—especially in our extremely over-sexualized society—having boyfriends and girl-friends. They see all this happening but they don't have any experience to prepare them for it.

One thing I've heard from more than one autistic kid—and I talked to a therapist who explained this to me too—is that because these autistic kids don't have the socialization experience when they're younger, they don't know the difference between friendship and romance. They have not really experienced friendship.

One detransitioned girl that I spoke with said that she thought she was a lesbian because she liked another girl, and had a crush on her. Her therapist asked, "What does that feel like? What do you mean?" The girl said, "I just really like her. She's really cool. She's fun to hang out with. We laugh a lot together. We like to do a lot of the same things." The therapist said, "That's friendship. That's not sexual interest."

But so many of these autistic kids don't understand that. Or if they've reached puberty and they're not having any sexual urges at all, society is telling them, "That means something's wrong with you because everybody needs to have sexual urges." Well, some of us don't get that until later. And that's okay.

Erin Brewer (45:22):

That story that you mentioned, these kids do struggle to make sense of the social interactions. I had a friend whose son was autistic and there was this huge milestone when he learned how to lie, because their development is different. Their milestones are different. A lot of these kids are so fact-based that they can't comprehend a lie. So when this kid finally was able to lie, the mom was like, "Yay!" Most parents are not excited when their kids lie.

Humor is another one. Sometimes, when these kids start to understand jokes, that can be huge.

So what we're dealing with is a population that already has a different developmental path than their peers. Rather than saying, "We're going to put you on this transgender path," let's just focus on helping them to identify where they need to work on skills and provide them with those opportunities. Because we know that we can help them. We know that we can provide them social support. There are communication groups to help teach communication skills, to help teach social skills, to get these kids up to speed with their social skills so that they don't believe there's something wrong with them, and so they don't believe they were born in the wrong body.

Maria Keffler (46:54):

Our goal with autistic kids is not to stop them from being autistic. There are some amazing gifts that come with autism. Some of our most amazing technological developments have come via people who are on the autism spectrum. When we see, especially the girls who are just flocking to this transgender ideology—

Erin Brewer (47:44):

We should be saying, "Wait a minute. These are the girls who are autistic." Now they're being medicated.

Maria Keffler (47:52):

We don't want to change them. We don't want to tell them there's anything wrong with them. We want to help them maximize their strengths and compensate for their weaknesses so that they can thrive, so that they can hold good jobs, have healthy relationships, and function in society in a productive and enjoyable way.

We want people to live healthy lives, where they can thrive and enjoy who they are. Telling these kids, "You're in the wrong body" is telling them they're inherently flawed. I don't accept that. I don't accept that autistic people are inherently flawed. They have a different brain than the rest of us have. They have a different developmental path. That's to be celebrated. We're not to tell them something's wrong with them and they need to be medicalized.

> **Telling these kids, "You're in the wrong body"
> is telling them they're inherently flawed.
> I don't accept that. I don't accept that autistic
> people are inherently flawed. They have a different
> brain than the rest of us have. They have a different
> developmental path. I think that's to be celebrated.
> We're not to tell them something's wrong with them
> and they need to be medicalized.**

Erin Brewer (48:48):

We have a question here from a parent: "I've heard parents putting something in their child's IEP to prevent the school from presenting transgender information to their autistic child. Can you talk about how to do that?"

I've heard that there are parents who put something in their child's IEP to prevent them from being exposed to a child who is presenting as transgender in the bathrooms and locker rooms, to kind of prevent their child from being influenced by that.

You talked a little bit about putting something in the IEP. I was wondering, can parents explicitly say, "We do not want our child exposed to this transgender ideology in any of the school situations."

Maria Keffler (49:39):

That's a good question. I know of cases where that has been successful. And I'm thinking of one particular parent—I believe the child was on the spectrum. I believe her IEP was for autism. It might've been something else, but the daughter already had an IEP.

This mother put in the IEP that her daughter was not to be exposed to any sex or gender ideology at school. So she was to be opted out of family life education. She was not to encounter this in any classes. It worked. That child has since desisted.

The IEP is a legal document and the school has to abide by what's in there. My understanding is that some schools are better at working with parents on the IEP than other schools. I've heard some horror stories about parents having to get legal representation in order to get the IEP enforced. I've heard other stories where the school is just fantastic—the parent wanted something in the IEP and it went in.

Erin Brewer (51:03):

Another thing to consider putting in the IEP, even if your child hasn't bought into this ideology, is to put that the child will be called by their given name and by sex-appropriate pronouns, so that never becomes an issue. As a parent of someone who's autistic you can easily make a case that these kids are black-and-white thinkers, they tend to perseverate, and we need to help ground them in reality. One way to do that is to insist on them being called by their birth name and their appropriate pronouns. That is something you can put in the IEP. It's a legal document. If the school decides not to follow it, there's legal recourse.

Maria Keffler (51:50):

If your child does not have a specific diagnosis—maybe he or she has not yet been diagnosed with autism. Maybe they're a little bit this way, but they don't cross the threshold that we can give that diagnosis, and they've got a little bit of this, but it's not enough we can diagnose. If you've got one of those amorphous, hard-to-pin-down kids, another option is a 504 plan, which designates accommodations. It's a little less powerful than the IEP, but it's better than nothing. People use a 504 if a child just needs extra time on tests or some other simple accommodations. It's something to explore.

I'm not an expert on 504 accommodations. I have not used one, but I know that is another avenue that you can look at if for some reason you can't get an IEP for your child.

Erin Brewer (52:55):

A 504 can be pretty powerful. My son had a 504 when he was in elementary school. He had some difficulties. He hadn't been officially diagnosed with anything, but he wasn't able to eat in the lunch room with the other kids because of sensory issues. He would get physically sick. So we wrote up a 504 and he was allowed to eat in the teachers' dining area or go in the classroom. He was able to select different places where he felt comfortable eating because going into the lunchroom was so difficult, he didn't eat.

If parents are creative, they can come up with things.

It reminds me of the next question we have, which is from a parent who says, "I want to pull my autistic son from public school, but most private schools don't offer special ed services. I don't know if I can manage my son's education without special ed services. Are there other avenues for help?" That is a good question.

I do wonder about the assumption that private schools don't offer special ed services, because if the school gets any kind of federal aid at all, including school lunch programs, then they are required to offer special ed services.

Maria Keffler (54:20):

She's right, that schools that do not receive federal funding do not have to offer special ed services. Offering special ed services is a big undertaking because there are so many different issues.

If you're going to have autistic kids at a private school, you need somebody who understands and specializes in autism. If you have someone with emotional disabilities, you may need to have a social worker on staff. You may need to have a school psychologist.

A number of schools just choose not to do that because they don't want to deal with that. It's expensive. It's challenging. When you do start dealing with special ed issues, there are a lot of legal ramifications.

There are schools specifically for kids with different disabilities or exceptionalities as well. So you might find out if there is a school that just works with autistic kids. Those exist.

Erin Brewer (55:27):

There are also some grants and scholarships for kids available and that might be another avenue to get some help.

You may also be able to get private services depending on whether or not you have the resources to hire outside people to help your son at a private school. Or if you have insurance that will cover it. More and more insurances are covering these kinds of services.

Try to explore lots of different avenues, because I do think that there are options.

If worse comes to worst, and your child is at a school that's bought into this ideology and it's a public school, you can always investigate other public schools in your area and see if there's a charter school or another school in your area that you feel more comfortable with—one that has a different administration. There are some options. You just have to be willing to go out there and see what's available.

Maria Keffler (56:26):

One place you might start is the SEPTA, the Special Ed Parent-Teacher Association. A lot of districts have a special education parent-teacher association, and the SEPTA organization will at least have some ideas for you, or some resources. Parent connections are just so valuable. Maybe you get involved with SEPTA and you talk to another parent who says, "I've got this great therapist who does this support group for kids like ours." Well, you make that connection. So that's another avenue to start looking for some support.

> **A lot of districts have a special education parent-teacher association. The SEPTA organization will at least have some ideas for you, or some resources.**

Erin Brewer (57:06):

Just be aware of the fact that your child is vulnerable. It's hard if you're a parent of a child who's on the spectrum—you're already having to deal with some different issues with your child, but then to have to be worried about this... It's kind of heavy.

But I do think parents need to be aware that their child is vulnerable. We know from the numbers that up to 60% of children who are identifying as transgender are autistic. I'm not sure what the percentage of children who are autistic is in the general population, but it's nowhere near 60%, which means that an inordinate number of kids who are on the spectrum are being drawn into this ideology.

Well, Maria, this has been a difficult conversation. It's hard to think that people are targeting vulnerable children, but we have to be aware that this is going on.

Maria Keffler (58:01):

Parents have to realize that they are their children's best defense and protection, and they need to be aware and keep an eye out for what's happening with their kids, especially their special needs kids.

Episode 10 Resources

Prof. Ina van Berckelaer-Onnes, Autism and gender identity disorder: https://youtu.be/LoIR1pNKXZY

Autism Spectrum Disorders in Gender Dysphoric Children and Adolescents: https://www.ncbi.nlm.nih.gov/pmc/articles/PMC2904453/

Autism, Sex and Science: Simon Baron-Cohen at TEDxKingsCollegeLondon: https://youtu.be/eEYy1GXaNNY

Autism and Gender Dysphoria: https://www.transgendertrend.com/autism-gender-dysphoria/

"Insistent, consistent, persistent": Autism spectrum disorder seen as no barrier to child transition—or sterilization: https://4thwavenow.com/2015/10/29/insistent-consistent-persistent-autism-spectrum-disorder-seen-as-no-barrier-to-child-transition-or-sterilization/

Episode 11: Trauma & Gender Dysphoria

https://youtu.be/D5f3XVoH1_o

Maria Keffler (00:01:03):

Today we're talking about trauma and gender dysphoria. I'd just love to start with hearing what you have to say about trauma, based on your experiences.

Erin Brewer (00:01:27):

I started to network with other people to get to know those who have desisted and detransitioned. I realized how common my experience was and how it can trigger gender dysphoria and feeling like you are born in the wrong body.

I had no idea until recently that this is a very common response to sexual assault.

Some people who have watched my other videos know that I have a history of sexual assault when I was young. I was very little and it's hard for me to talk about it without getting emotional. So I might get a little emotional. I was just a little kid between kindergarten and first grade, when I was sexually assaulted.

One of the responses of that kind of trauma, where a child is incredibly helpless and being violated and hurt both physically and emotionally, is a dissociative response. In a way dissociation is a gift, because it allows us to "leave ourselves" so that we don't have to experience the full horror of what is happening to us.

Maria Keffler (00:02:51):

Can you explain a little bit about dissociation. What happens when you're dissociated?

Erin Brewer (00:02:56):

It's an amazing coping mechanism. What basically happens is that you feel completely disembodied.

Part of the trauma that I experienced, part of the assault, I remember very well physically. I remember the feelings. I remember the feeling of being restrained, and trying to get away. But at some point, when the pain and confusion became too much, it was like I just left my body and I was no longer Erin. I was just sort of out there and it was happening to somebody else. It felt like it was happening to somebody else.

Once that happens one time, it's easier to do it the next time you experience a struggle. The neural pathways develop to allow that dissociative response. For whatever reason, we've evolved so that if we're in traumatic situations, we have coping mechanisms.

If you think about that response, and then specifically in the case of sexual assault where a girl's body is being violated, it's not surprising that a very common response is gender dysphoria and body dysmorphia—that feeling of intense hatred toward your body. Because in my case, I felt like it was my body's fault that I got hurt. If I had been a boy, it wouldn't have happened.

I just had this incredible self-hatred. It wasn't a conscious thing when I decided I was a boy. It was just a kind of response of, "I'm not that kid anymore. That didn't happen to me. That happened to somebody else. I'm not Erin anymore. I'm Timothy."

If I could convince other people of that, then I felt safer. That's what I wanted was for them to say, "You're right. You're not Erin. You're not that little girl who got hurt."

Thankfully my school psychologist didn't affirm me in that belief. I'm so grateful, because a lot of times children do things as coping mechanisms that work in the short-term, but they're not good long-term responses. That would not have served me well throughout my life, to be told that I was born in the wrong body, because it would've reinforced those feelings of self-hatred that I had—that sense that my body betrayed me and there was something wrong with me, with my body, It would have encouraged me to harm myself even more rather than to work through what had happened. It would've encouraged me to run away and to essentially try to become a different person, so I didn't have to deal with the trauma.

One of the things that we know about trauma is that it's important for kids to be able to process it appropriately.

I got involved in this issue when they started introducing therapy bans, when I realized these bans were attempting to ban the very therapy that helped me when I was a child and would help others who endured these kinds of things. They are essentially saying, "You don't get to have appropriate treatment for the trauma that you endured. Instead, we're going to encourage you down this harmful pathway."

To me, that's just heartbreaking. Not only did the child endure the trauma, but then we're going to deny them appropriate care. Then we're going to reinforce their feelings of self-hatred. I can't think of any more disservice to these kids who need support, love, and appropriate care.

> **That's just heartbreaking. Not only did the child the trauma, but then we're going to deny them appropriate care and reinforce their feelings of self-hatred. I can't think of any more disservice to these kids who need support, love, and appropriate care.**

So I tell my story, and others tell their stories.

We have a video we can watch, where some other young women talk about having endured trauma and the result was this development of a transgender identity. It's not just me. It's looking like a pretty common response to early childhood trauma for girls.

Dr. Michelle Cretella (00:07:35):

There are children who dissociate from their biological sex because they have survived sexual abuse—either sexual abuse or physical abuse—that also causes them to internalize, "I'm not safe or lovable in my biological sex."

Tynice (00:07:50):

I think my transition was a result of childhood trauma. It was a plethora of experiences that told my subconscious I wasn't right being female. So I altered my body to extreme lengths. I went through more than one body should ever be able to handle.

Kathy Grace Duncan (00:08:09):

Life was dysfunctional. My dad was verbally and emotionally abusive toward my mom, which gave me the impression that women were hated, weak, and vulnerable. At the age of 19, I began to take male hormones, change my name, and I began to live as a man.

Tynice (00:08:24):

I thought that it was the answer for all of my problems. And of course, this is all happening. Subconsciously there's a whole bunch of things in my subconscious that told me who I was, was not okay. And told me who I was, is wrong.

<u>Elle Palmer</u> (00:08:36):

I had just gone through a very traumatic sexual experience with an older man. I wanted to change my gender after that happened. Then I went to a therapist from the LGB/T center who told me that she was ready to get me on hormones from day one—you know, like excited and ready to just help me transition.

<u>Kathryne</u> (00:09:02):

I have a history of a childhood trauma that contributed, and it still contributes to feelings of dysphoria and dissociation and total just disconnect in my body.

<u>Erin Brewer</u> (00:09:18):

In that clip the young women talked about trauma. I talked about my sexual trauma, but it's important for us to also talk about the fact that there are lots of different kinds of trauma that can cause a dissociative response. Anytime somebody, especially a child, becomes scared, they can develop that dissociative pattern. That dissociation makes you feel separate from your body. Almost like, "It's me and my body, and we're not necessarily on the same team. We're not necessarily the same person."

<u>Maria Keffler</u> (00:09:58):

That is exactly what the gender industry is telling people—that you can have one brain or one mind or one soul of a certain sex, and then a body of a different sex.

We know there's no scientific evidence to support that. But as you're talking about dissociation, to me, that sounds exactly like what the gender industry is creating and promoting. That's not a healthy coping mechanism.

<u>Erin Brewer</u> (00:10:32):

No. I have been to a number of different therapists and none of them said, "That's wonderful. You're dissociating. Let's encourage that. How can we make you feel even more separate from your body?"

That was not the approach that any of them took. Their goal was to help me *not* do that because dissociation not only makes you vulnerable to the gender industry, but it makes you vulnerable in general. When someone's dissociating, they're not making good choices. They're not really connected to the world.

It's hard to describe, but it's almost like the dream state you hear stories about when people die and they sometimes talk about leaving their body.

That's almost how it feels.

<u>Maria Keffler (00:11:22):</u>

Similar to a drug trip.

<u>Erin Brewer (00:11:25):</u>

It probably is, there are certain drugs where you'd get that. If you have somebody who's dissociating and you're encouraging that dissociation, you're making them more vulnerable to predators, because if somebody is in a dissociative state, they're more likely to go into a freeze state if they're confronted with a situation where they're about to be violated. It not only encourages the gender confusion, but it also makes them more vulnerable.

We're taking children who have already suffered, and basically encouraging them to be more vulnerable, to hate themselves, and to self-harm.

That's another aspect of trauma that I experienced and many other trauma victims experience—that sense of wanting to harm yourself. So girls often will cut. I took big rocks and just pounded them against myself. Sometimes I'd pound them against my private parts to the point where it would be bloody. There were often times where I had scabs on my head, because I'd be brushing my hair and I'd just be filled with rage and start whacking it against my head.

That self-harming tendency is because you blame your body. It's a sense of, "My body is the one that got me in this situation. If I had a different body, it wouldn't have happened." That self-harming is common.

A lot of the things that the gender industry wants children to do are promoting self-harm. It's like taking this pathology and making it much worse rather than healing it.

<u>Maria Keffler (00:13:12):</u>

I talked to one counselor about self-harm and he told me that there's a balance between hope and pain, and he described it kind of like a seesaw: the less hope you have, the more pain you have. There's a point at which the hope is so low that people start inflicting pain on themselves just to release it. He said the pain is trapped inside and to get it out someone will cut or hit or do something to open up their bodies so that they can feel the pain to get it out.

I can't say I have experienced that, so I don't know if I'm describing it well or not.

Erin Brewer (00:14:05):

There's also that sense of wanting to externalize the mental pain. So when you're feeling that intense mental pain, it's hard to even put it into words and it's so much easier just to make it physical.

Sometimes I would dissociate, but then there were other times where it was like I was flipped right back to where I was when I was that little girl. It was almost like I was stuck there again. It was like I was reliving it.

So sometimes that pounding would be to pull me out of my brain, to pull me out of that memory. "Because I don't want to live this again, I'm just going to beat myself." Then I'm focused on the pain in my body rather than the pain in my head.

It's the sense of wanting to escape. These therapy bans prevent therapists from eking out the potential causes of these gender identity issues.

What's so heartbreaking is that these kids have gone through trauma. They've developed coping skills that are helping them in the present, but are going to be harmful in the long-term. Then they're not even able to get appropriate mental health care.

> **These kids have gone through trauma.**
> **They've developed coping skills that are helping**
> **them in the present, but are going to be harmful in**
> **the long-term. Then they're not even able to get**
> **appropriate mental health care.**

Maria Keffler (00:15:36):

Once a child says the magic words "gender identity" or "transgender," then all of these bans fall into place. I was watching a sci-fi show. It was Tony Stark and he said, "Engage barn door protocol," and all the doors come slamming down and you're isolated inside and there's no help.

We touched on the fact that there's lots of different kinds of trauma that kids go through, not just sexual trauma.

Erin Brewer (00:16:18):

All kinds of trauma can cause very similar responses.

Maria Keffler (00:16:22):

Divorce is a huge one. We've become so desensitized to divorce in our society. We've become so used to it that we don't appreciate that divorce is death in a child's life. It is the death of their family.

I had one friend who's now a therapist—she told me that when she was little, her parents divorced. She had three siblings. One parent took two siblings. The other parent took two siblings. She said, "I lost half of my siblings. I lost one of my parents. I lost my house. I lost my school. I lost my friends overnight, practically." This is hugely traumatic for a child.

Erin Brewer (00:17:10):

The child had no control over it. When children feel completely helpless and out of control that can induce a trauma response.

Maria Keffler (00:17:23):

Death in the family, death of a friend, death of a pet can be very, very traumatic for a child. There are all sorts of things, and all kinds of abuse and rejection.

We often think of trauma as huge things like a sexual assault that like you experienced or a family divorce, but even things that seem fairly small, especially to an adult, can seem really huge to a child. The effect is still a powerful one on that child.

Erin Brewer (00:18:05):

I talked to a detransitioner who came from a Japanese family, and she was the third child born. In the Japanese culture it was really important to have a son. She was their third and last child, and she was born a girl. Even though nobody explicitly said she should have been a boy, she felt this pressure that there was something wrong with her because she had let down the family.

That's not exactly trauma, but it's that sense of powerlessness and this sense of letting people down and not being the right person, not being the person you're supposed to be. There are lots of big traumas that people recognize but also these little traumas in people's lives. I don't mean little to minimize, because to a child, something that as adults we might think is fairly minimal, could be really quite profound to a child.

Maria Keffler (00:19:07):

It might be less visible. A sexual trauma is overt. The child might be hiding it from the parents, but it is a single event or a series of events that happened.

Whereas some of the things like what that young Japanese girl felt are internalized rejection. I know you can see things that aren't necessarily there. So if she was feeling that, "I should have been a boy," if her mother really made a big deal over their neighbor's baby boy—"Oh, he's so cute, you're so lucky to have a son"—she would hear that as rejection: "I didn't give my family a son."

Erin Brewer (00:20:01):

That was something that I learned from a detransitioner. A lot of detransitioners talk about sexual assault, but there are all kinds of other traumas that can cause this sense of being in the wrong body, and of not being okay who you are.

If a child comes up to somebody and says, "Boy, I'm really stupid," we don't go around affirming that. We don't say, "You're right. You are stupid. There's really nothing you can do. You're just going to have to accept that you're stupid." We don't do that.

We don't do that when kids are depressed and say, "You're right. Your life is really meaningless, there's really no point to go on living." We don't affirm these negative feelings.

Yet in this one situation we do. It's the same thing as affirming a child and saying they're stupid or that their depression is appropriate.

Maria Keffler (00:20:57):

We don't affirm a child who's cutting—a child who has got cuts on her arm. You don't say, "Let me get you some extra knives."

Erin Brewer (00:21:08):

Yet we have surgeons who are willing to cut off a child's breasts, which is precisely self-harming behavior. It's the same as cutting. We don't go and get them razorblades. We get them help.

The gender industry is making so much money. I saw a graph a couple of days ago of a surgeon who does mastectomies and it showed one or two mastectomies 10 or 15 years ago and then it just climbed like crazy. It climbed to the point where it is a couple hundred. Their practice can't even handle them all. They're having to bring in new surgeons because there are all these women who are wanting to cut their breasts off.

Now we're having young women and children cutting their breasts off. That's a self-harming behavior. As you said, if somebody came in and said, "You know, I don't like my arm. It's not my arm. I'm born with the wrong arm. Cut it off," surgeons aren't going to do that. Yet we feel like these body parts that are associated with sex characteristics are expendable. We can cut off breasts and we can cut off penises and testicles.

Maria Keffler (00:22:30):

Vincent van Gogh, the famous artist—there's the story of him cutting off his ear and sending it to this woman who rebuffed him. We don't look at that and say, "Wow, what a great thing that he did." It's sort of a joke. If you go "van Gogh" it means you self-harm.

Erin Brewer (00:22:48):

I know a man who had his penis and testicles cut off after a sexual assault, because he focused all that anger and blame on his genitals.

In what world do we feel like we want to encourage this behavior? It's just heartbreaking.

So many parents don't understand the connection, which is one of the reasons we wanted to touch on this topic. There is good information about the different types of trauma responses. If parents have a child, they can maybe notice if there's been a trauma.

In my case, I went right home and my brother was with me and we told my parents what had happened. Unfortunately, because they were involved in the drug culture, they didn't want to call the police because it would have put them at risk.

There are kids who might not tell anyone because it is a relative or a family friend who's done it, or it might be that they feel so much shame, or it might be that they've been threatened and told that they will be killed if they tell anybody. It's important for parents to know this could have happened to your child, and to be aware of some of the signs that this has happened.

Maria Keffler (00:24:13):

Signs for any kind of psychological issue include some sort of a change—a sudden change in the child's behavior. It can be a change in eating patterns, inability to sleep, or sleeping too much, a child who was formerly extroverted suddenly becoming introverted or vice-versa. I wouldn't say if you see this there is necessarily a problem but when your child suddenly makes a U-turn or change in their behavior or their attitudes or their speech patterns, that's just something to look at and ask, "Hey, what's going on?"

> **When your child suddenly makes some sort of a U-turn or change in their behavior or their attitudes or their speech patterns, that's just something to look at and ask, "Hey, what's going on?"**

Erin Brewer (00:25:05):

It doesn't necessarily mean they've been traumatized, but it's something to look at. If your child, who has been a fairly content girl, comes home and suddenly insists she's a boy, that's a huge sign that something's going on with that child that really needs to be looked into and not "affirmed."

Maria Keffler (00:25:26):

There are four basic responses to trauma, as I understand it from the literature I've looked at. There's fight, flight, freeze, and fawn. That last word *fawn*, They were looking for another "F word," for the four F's of trauma response.

Erin Brewer (00:25:47):

The other three are fairly self-explanatory. What does fawn mean in this context?

Maria Keffler (00:25:52):

Let me start with the first one and I'll go through all of them really quickly.

Each one of these has a positive response to it, or a negative response to it. It can go one of two ways. It's kind of like any struggle you go through: you can come out stronger, you can come out weaker, depending how you respond to it.

So the *fight* response: that's just what you might think of. It's coming out swinging. Positives to that can be setting boundaries, being assertive about what's okay and what's not okay. If somebody gets in your face or threatens you—say you're in a bathroom and a guy comes in and starts coming over to you, an assertive fight response might be, "I am uncomfortable. I want you to step back." That would be an assertive, good, positive fight response. A negative fight response, as a response to trauma, might be becoming very controlling, narcissistic, entitled, becoming a bully. So it's taking the fight response too far and applying it too widely.

The second response is *flight* and that's running away, getting away. A good part of that flight response would be leaving an unhealthy relationship: assessing a situation and seeing, "This is a situation I don't want to be in, and I'm going to leave." An unhealthy response with flight might be obsessive-compulsive disorder, becoming very afraid, panic attacks, becoming a workaholic, doing something to put your mind elsewhere and ignore or escape the situation.

The third one is *freeze*. Good, positive things about freezing can be being mindful, doing meditation, being aware, being kind of still. A bad response might be disassociation. That's the big one with the freeze response—dissociation that you've talked about: zoning out, brain-fog, having a hard time making decisions, having that paralysis.

The last one they call *fawn*. The positive side of fawning would be having a really compassionate response, being able to understand and empathize with other people, listening. Those would be fawning responses that are positive. But negative fawning responses would be becoming codependent, being unable to make decisions for yourself, being a people pleaser, kind of losing your sense of self.

So those are the four that I've encountered as I've been researching responses to trauma.

Erin Brewer (00:29:00):

That's interesting. It's important to note that you can have more than one of those, because one of the reasons that my first-grade teacher called the school psychologist to assess me was because I was really aggressive, both towards other kids and towards adults, in a way that was causing problems in the classroom. That was one of the responses—this anger and rage and bullying and being mean and rude and disrespectful.

At the same time, when I was faced with a situation where I was scared, I froze and dissociated. So it's possible to have more than one of those responses. Healthy or unhealthy, depending on which way they go.

That's where good therapy could really help. If you can get good intervention early on and help them mold those responses into positive responses, then trauma isn't going to really impact the person's life in a tremendous way. In my case, I almost feel like this trauma is like a river through my life and has just like caused this huge gulf, like the Grand Canyon. I had this life that was smooth and flat, and then this trauma came along and it just has etched out this huge gully, like a chasm in my life. So much of my life has been impacted by the trauma.

It's because it was a significant trauma, and because as much as the therapist tried to help me to develop positive coping skills as a result of what happened when I was a kid, they didn't have a lot of the techniques that they have now. They didn't have cognitive behavior therapy, which is what ended up helping me the most as an adult.

Luckily, we do have really good techniques now. We can really help these kids. Some kids might develop gender identity issues. Some kids might develop anorexia. Anorexia is connected to gender dysphoria because when a girl starts developing physically, she tends to get curvier, and an anorexic is going to feel really uncomfortable with that and can develop gender dysphoria.

These are all really interconnected and need to be viewed as various ways of coping rather than as evidence that somebody is born in the wrong body.

Maria Keffler (00:31:38):

We have certain natural tendencies in the way we cope with things. So one person might just naturally be a fighter. The positive side is that they're a leader, they're assertive. They take charge of situations. Whereas another person is going to naturally be more of a people-pleaser and considerate.

I think about my own three kids, they're all very different. Knowing your child and recognizing, "What has this child been like in the past, and what am I seeing happen now? What does that tell me about kind of the timeframe for when something may have happened?"

What would you recommend if a parent is seeing some changes in their child behaviorally? How would you recommend a parent address that with the child?

Erin Brewer (00:32:49):

That's a really good question because some change is normal, especially during puberty. Kids are trying on different personas and that's normal and natural. You want to see that. But if a kid comes home and is suddenly saying things about hating their body or hating themselves, or if you notice those dissociative behaviors—

When I dissociated, it was pretty clear to my teachers. I was zoning out. A kid like that might be called a daydreamer, or it might look like attention deficit disorder. That zoning out is something to keep an eye on, especially if a kid who doesn't do that suddenly starts. If you see them in a corner, looking not-present, that's really important. Talk to the child, and try to eke it out, maybe even saying, "I've noticed some changes. Are you okay? Is there anything going on?"

Kids develop these negative coping mechanisms because they don't know what else to do. It can make a difference if there is a loving and compassionate adult in that child's life.

I had a few teachers who saved me. I had some amazing teachers who recognized that I was troubled and took some time to talk to me. I remember in seventh grade, I was suicidal. I had a teacher who really spent time talking to me and it helped so much. Part of it was the attention that I was getting, but part of it was having an adult who obviously was willing to spend time talking to me and who cared about me. It wasn't like he was a therapist or anything. He just recognized that I was troubled and was willing to take the time to talk to me. Sometimes that's all it takes.

Maria Keffler (00:35:03):

Ask open-ended questions and make space. That's hard in our lives right now because we're so busy and we're so hyper-scheduled.

Unfortunately, you're probably not going to be able to schedule a deep heart talk with your child. It's going to have to happen when the child is ready. But you can make those spaces available and ask open-ended questions.

> **You're probably not going to be able to schedule a deep heart talk with your child. It's going to have to happen when the child is ready. But you can make those spaces available and ask open-ended questions.**

The one that you suggested, "Hey, I noticed something it has changed. Can you tell me about this?"—that's a really unpressured question. "Can you tell me more about this?" invites a wider response from the child. It's less coercive: "Tell me more about how you're feeling." "I'm curious why this change has happened."

Try to rehearse some of those open-ended questions and try to make space in your day, in your week, to have time alone with your child.

Erin Brewer (00:36:20):

Spend some time one-on-one with your child, maybe go for a walk, go for a hike, do something where you have some individual time with your child so that they can tell you if something's going on.

I feel really sad. Five years ago, I would've said, "If your child sustained a trauma, get them into therapy because they're going to need that kind of professional help." Now, I'm more hesitant to say that, because there are these bans on therapy. If the child is coping with a transgender identity, then the therapist isn't going to be able to help them; therapy could cause more harm.

So if you do believe that your child has had a trauma, be very cautious about how to proceed. Don't just immediately take them into therapy. Find a therapist who's not going to affirm them in a transgender identity. Find one who's going to eke out whatever it is that happened, and help them process the trauma.

Maria Keffler (00:37:30):

That's sounds so wrong to say, "I'm not going to affirm them," but the language has been co-opted. Right now "affirmation" means putting children on a path to medicalization.

Erin Brewer (00:37:44):

Therapy bans are denying them the kind of medical care and the kind of psychiatric care that they really need. If your child is suicidal, then all bets are off. You need to get them help right away.

But if it hasn't gotten to that point, be very cautious and investigate. You may live in a state where the laws are very restrictive and you might have to find a therapist online. There are online therapists who are not restricted by state law. You can circumvent it that way. You can also find a life coach, somebody who's not licensed by the American Psychiatric Association, who is not under the same regulations as those who are licensed in the state. That can be an option.

Find a trusted friend. This is how people worked through problems before therapists were so ubiquitous. There are members of the community besides therapists who can help kids work through these issues. Maybe find a trusted family member or a clergy member.

Maria Keffler (00:38:52):

I told this story in an earlier video, but I think it's appropriate to tell it again.

One child, who in elementary school, had an IEP (Individualized Education Plan) because she was in special ed. This child had a very close relationship with the school counselor in elementary school. This child announced a transgender identity and the parents thought, "Okay, I'm going to talk to the counselor from elementary school because that counselor really knows my child well."

The parents said that that counselor had always been so helpful, not just with the child, but with the family. The counselor was very good at listening, and asking questions: "What makes you feel this way? What about this?" She was just very good at what she did.

Well, the parent called the elementary school counselor and told her, "My daughter has just announced that she's transgender." And the first thing the counselor said was, "You need to affirm. You need to affirm. It's very important that you affirm so she doesn't commit suicide."

No questions. No, "Hey, did we ever see this before? This child never indicated any discomfort with her sex before."

That is a huge red flag. That counselor never responded to an issue with a blanket statement before about anything.

Erin Brewer (00:40:50):

It's so upsetting to me because one of the things that I wanted when I was presenting as trans, when I was insisting that I was a boy, was access to the boys' restroom. I wanted to go to the bathroom with the boys.

There is this confluence of a kid who's been traumatized, who is insisting she's a boy. Then putting her in the boys' or men's bathroom is, to my mind, such a dangerous situation. Here's a girl who is really at risk for being revictimized, and predators can sense it. Predators have radar—they can tell what kid is going to be a good victim, who's going to be vulnerable. They can tell by body language. They have this figured out. They're good at what they do.

So you take a girl who's struggling with herself, who's having issues. And then put her in a situation where she's much more vulnerable. It just is such a huge disservice.

For that school counselor not to even question this new behavior—something's going on. We should figure out what changed, what's happening here. Because we know that kids that children are not born in the wrong body.

It's also ironic to me, because this is where the gender industry kind of gets twisted in circles. They say, "You're born in the wrong body. You've always been that way." And yet so many of these kids are developing a trans identity, it's not like they had it their whole lives. They're developing it.

Then we have kids who are "genderfluid," which means you can go back and forth, apparently. But then they say, "If somebody detransitions, they weren't really transgender."

It's a whole somersault. That is something that they've said to me and that they've said to other detransitioners and desisters, "Well, if you were really trans, you wouldn't have desisted, you wouldn't have detransitioned. Therefore, you really don't know what it's like to be transgender."

That is, again, such a dangerous message. It's a message that is invalidating all these experiences of girls and women.

I didn't go on hormones. I didn't go on puberty blockers, I didn't get my breasts removed, because that wasn't an option. I'm sure I would have if I had been given the option. Many of these young women are being told, "You were never really transgender," which may be the point, because nobody really is transgender.

That is ultimately the point. We know that about 0.02% of the population—which is a very tiny percentage historically—who have wanted to cross-dress as adults, have been what we would call transsexual. Most of those are gay men or autogynephilic men. That's been the demographic, and that has just been turned upside down.

Now the big pharma companies realize they can make a ton of money on this. The medical industrial complex has just determined that there's so much money to be made. All of a sudden, we're just having this explosion. Anytime there's an epidemic of something, historically, we look at that very critically. In this case, rather than saying, "Wow, we're having all these kids becoming medicalized," we are celebrating it.

Maria Keffler (00:44:35):

Going back to trauma, we're not dealing with the trauma. We're not helping kids with the trauma that they've gone through. Preliminary studies are showing that most of these kids who are coming out as transgender have comorbid issues: either autism, like we talked about last time, or trauma, past trauma in their lives. They've already got OCD, self-harming, depression.

Why are we not looking at that? Somebody doesn't want us to know.

Erin Brewer (00:45:17):

We have a video by Hank Green. It's a *Crash Course* on trauma and addiction. We're just going to watch a very short clip to reinforce some of the things we've talked about.

Hank Green (00:45:28):

It could be September 11th or a serious car accident, or a natural disaster or a violent crime that you survived, but are still haunted by. Trauma comes in many different forms. And sometimes it can stick with you when it manifests as nightmares, flashbacks, avoidance, fear, guilt, anxiety, rage, insomnia, and begins to interfere with your ability to function. It has come to be known as post-traumatic stress disorder or PTSD. It was once called shell shock, a term used to describe the condition of veterans like Tolkien in World War I.

But PTSD isn't limited to veterans. It's defined as a psychological disorder generated by witnessing or experiencing a traumatic event. Its symptoms are classified into four major clusters in the DSM-5. One of these clusters involves reliving the event through intrusive memories, nightmares, or flashbacks. The second involves avoiding situations you associate with the event while the third generally describes excessive physiological arousal, like heart-pounding, muscle tension, anxiety, or irritability, and major problems sleeping or concentrating. Finally, we have the fourth major symptom cluster: pervasive, negative changes in emotions and belief, like feelings of excessive guilt, fear, or shame, or no longer getting enjoyment out of what you used to.

PTSD patients also experienced numbing, or periods of feeling emotionless or emotionally flat, and dissociation: feeling as if situations aren't real or are surreal—feeling like time has slowed down or sped up, or even blacking out.

We've been discussing how anxiety and mood disorders can affect a person's ability to function, and how that impairment itself leads to more suffering and dysfunction. When any of these disorders is left untreated, sufferers may start to feel desperate, to find some way to cope.

How do you identify and diagnose these disorders and how do you treat them so that the patients can recover, with the understanding that they might never be the same as they were before the trauma, but they can still be healthy and happy? In a way, psychology helps patients ask themselves what Tolkien asks readers and what Frodo asks when he's finally safe back in the Shire. "How do you pick up the threads of an old life? How do you go on when in your heart, you begin to understand that there is no going back?"

Erin Brewer (00:47:35):

That was a good explanation of trauma. It's important for people to explore it more. We're not experts on trauma. I can share my own experience and you can share what you've learned, but we're not the experts. I would encourage people to go out and find other resources if they have questions about this. We have another short clip and I'm going to let you introduce it.

<u>Maria Keffler (00:47:58):</u>

I know you said when you saw it, you weren't sure what was happening because you hadn't seen the movie. This is from *Inside Out*. It's a wonderful movie. If you haven't seen it, it's like a 90-minute AP psychology course on trauma.

This little girl, Riley, has experienced a huge trauma. Her family has moved across the country. She's lost her friends. She's lost her home. She had an embarrassing first day at school. I mean, just everything that can go wrong, goes wrong. And what we're going to see is what's going on inside her head.

The main character in this clip, Bing-Bong, was her imaginary playmate when she was small. Bing-Bong is in her memory. These emotional parts of her are Joy and Sadness. Joy and Sadness are interacting with Bing-Bong. Bing-Bong is upset because he realizes he's being forgotten. Riley is forgetting about her childhood and he's being forgotten. And he's grieving. Joy is trying to make him happy. Like, "If we're just happy, everything will be great!" And Joy is trying to prevent Sadness from interacting with Bing-Bong. Watch what happens.

<u>Joy (00:49:17):</u>

Hey, who's ticklish? Here comes the tickle monster! Hey, Bing-Bong! look at this! (Joy makes a funny face).

<u>Narrator (00:49:28):</u>

We can get over feeling sad, quite rapidly. Once we are allowed to gain a resolution to our pain. Never try to hide your feelings when they surface. They are essential to our well-being to be experienced.

<u>Sadness (00:49:41):</u> *(to Bing-Bong)*

They took something that you loved. It's gone forever.

<u>Joy (00:49:45):</u>

Sadness! Don't make him feel worse.

<u>Sadness (00:49:47):</u>

Sorry.

Bing-Bong (00:49:48):

It's all I had left of Riley.

Sadness (00:49:51):

I bet you and Riley had great adventures.

Bing-Bong (00:49:54):

They were wonderful. Once we flew back in time. We had breakfast twice that day.

Sadness (00:49:59):

That sounds amazing. I bet Riley liked it.

Bing-Bong (00:50:04):

Oh, she did. We were best friends.

Sadness (00:50:08):

Yeah. It's sad.

Bing-Bong (00:50:23):

I'm okay.

Erin Brewer (00:50:29):

After you explained, it made a lot more sense to me because one of the things that happens, parents lovingly have a tendency to do, is to try and make things better. It's hard to see your kid hurting. It's hard to see them struggling. Often we play that role of wanting to be saying everything is okay. "Everything's all right. Hey, let's go over here and do something fun," or "Let's pretend like everything's okay." Because it's hard as a parent to see your child struggle.

Yet if we do that, it can cause problems. It can make our children feel like they can't talk to us because they don't want to disappoint us. They don't want to make us feel bad. If our children think that their emotions are too strong for us to handle as parents, they're not going to open up to us. So

> **If our children think that their emotions are too strong for us to handle as parents, they're not going to open up to us. So it's important to give children space to feel and express those strong, heavy emotions.**

it's important to give children space to feel and express those strong, heavy emotions.

Especially if you have a sensitive child. Like I mentioned, my youngest daughter is very emotionally sensitive. She has told me that there were times she didn't want to tell me what was bothering her, what was hurting her, because she didn't want to upset me. She didn't want to make me sad.

Her role as a child is not to protect my emotions. My role as a parent is to help her cope with hers. So just listening, empathetically listening, can be so therapeutic. Just like in the video, that's all Bing-Bong needed was just to express, "I'm sad. This is why I'm sad. Let me cry on your shoulder." What we learned when we grew up was, "Crying doesn't fix anything." I heard that all the time.

Or "I'll give you something to cry about!"

Right. Scientists have now discovered that there are stress hormones in tears when you cry. Your tears actually do release stress hormones. So crying does do good. It does help.

We need to provide that opportunity for our kids to process and grieve and cry and deal with what's happened.

Transgender ideology encourages kids to stuff their feelings. If your child doesn't believe her feelings are okay that can make her more vulnerable to this ideology.

It really is important to be able to allow your child to express really unpleasant feelings. It is hard as a parent. I hate seeing my kids suffer, but at the same time, I would so much rather have them cry on my shoulder than stuff it down and pretend like everything's okay, or to develop a transgender identity, or to go up in their room and cut themselves.

That's not to say if your child develops a transgender identity or cuts themselves that it's because you're not a caring and loving parent or that you're not doing it right. All we can do is the best that we can do. Sometimes even if a parent is doing everything right, the child might develop this transgender identity, this child might cut. There's so much pressure on parents.

I feel like historically mothers have been blamed for anything that goes wrong with their children. It used to be the mother was blamed if a child was autistic or developmentally delayed, that there was something wrong with her parenting.

I don't want parents to feel that way. We live in a very complex world. There are so many variables and so many factors playing into what's happening with your child.

Maria Keffler (00:54:36):

None of us are perfect parents. The best parent on the planet is not a perfect parent. Sometimes these things are just going to come into your family and you've got to deal with them as best you can.

I want to echo what you said. Don't take this as if it's your fault: "I did something wrong." You may have, you may not have. The important thing is to figure out how to help your child to be healthy again.

Erin Brewer (00:55:09):

We do have a couple of questions from parents. I'm going to ask the first one. It says, "How do I know if trauma is responsible for my child's gender dysphoria?"

That is a really good question. It's probably not something you'll ever know 100%, but if your child has had trauma and then develops gender dysphoria, you can feel pretty confident that there's a connection.

It's not necessarily causal. We talked about that in another video, that one thing didn't necessarily directly cause it, but that there's an influencing factor.

Kids are pre-programmed with tendencies to react in certain ways. Some kids might develop OCD. Some kids might develop a personality disorder. Some kids might dissociate. Some kids might turn into that kid who just stuffs everything down and pretends everything's okay and then explodes when they're 20. There are all different ways in which kids respond to things.

But if there was a trauma and then shortly thereafter, a child develops gender dysphoria, there's a pretty good chance that the trauma was what tipped that child into the trans identity.

Maria Keffler (00:56:37):

The important thing to look for is changes—sudden and big changes in your child's behavior—your child's sleeping, eating, socializing patterns. A sudden change of friend group is a big tip off. Young kids will change friends pretty frequently, but by the time they are in junior high, they're starting to solidify that friend group and to suddenly drop all of one set of friends and have another set of friends—that that can be a big red flag. So look for changes, just comparing, how was this child six months ago and how is she now? That'll give you some clues if something's going on.

Erin Brewer (00:57:29):

It's fascinating to me as we're talking, I'm thinking about the lens with which my teachers viewed me as a child, versus the lens that teachers view children through now. The lens my teachers viewed me through was, "Something's up. There's something seriously wrong with Erin. She's changed. We need to get her help. We need to figure out what's going on because her behavior is not functional." Nowadays, in the same circumstances, I'm afraid that the same teacher might say, "Well, the reason that Erin has become so aggressive is because she's not being affirmed as transgender."

Unfortunately, teachers now aren't necessarily going to be our partners. It used to be that teachers might alert a parent if there was a sudden shift in behavior that was concerning. Now they might hide it from parents. It's a lot harder than it used to be for parents to figure out what's going on with their child.

> **Unfortunately, teachers aren't necessarily going to be our partners. It used to be that teachers might alert a parent if there was a sudden shift in behavior. Now they might hide it from parents. It's a lot harder than it used to be for parents to figure out what's going on with their child.**

Maria Keffler (00:58:29):

That's a good point. Most of the people out in the culture are not on your side. It's unconscionable that there's this misguided savior complex wrapped around this idea, that with this one particular thing—if a child expresses an alternate gender identity—we need to cut off those toxic parents who don't agree.

It's really disconcerting. It's really concerning.

Erin Brewer (00:59:09):

Especially if you have a child with trauma, cutting them off from parents is a terrible thing to do.

Maria Keffler (00:59:17):

The last thing you want to do is cut them off from their best sense of support.

Erin Brewer (00:59:22):

It is overwhelming, and thankfully there are resources out there.

The next question is, "How do I find appropriate care for my child if I think the problem is unresolved trauma and not gender identity?"

Maria Keffler (00:59:39):

Look at that resource that we're going to put in the information below the video, *How to Find a Gender-Critical or Trustworthy Therapist for your Child*. That gives some good guidelines.

One of the things I tell people, whether you're a person of faith or not, is that sometimes a church, a mosque, or a synagogue is a good place to start, even if you're not Christian, Muslim, Jewish. Because at least we still have religious freedom as the law of the land in America. We know that the activists in this arena are trying to prevent religious freedom, but we still have it. So counselors, pastors, and rabbis are still able to counsel people according to their holy texts.

Most major religions do not consider transgenderism a possible way that human beings have been created. So that might be a good, safe place to start. Call the church or synagogue or mosque and just say, "I'd like to talk to someone about counseling," and ask, "What is your organization's position on transgender ideology?"

Erin Brewer (01:01:14):

It is important to find out. We have a mutual friend who's in the Jewish community and she said that the more modern Jewish com-munities— not the Orthodox, but the more progressive Jewish communities—have accepted transgenderism.

I interviewed a young woman who is Jewish and, I believe, a fairly Orthodox Jew. Even in that community, they were willing to accommodate her trans identity. I've heard that some Christian com- munities now are going to go ahead and accept this. It's because they don't want to be viewed as intolerant.

It's such a huge disservice. It makes me really sad. Another thing, there are communities, religious communities that will 100% affirm a child, but there are also communities out there that will help you. So try and find those.

Episode 11 Resource List

Trauma and Addiction: Crash Course Psychology #31: https://www.youtube.com/watch?v=343ORgL3kIc

Inside-Out Bing-Bong Scene: https://youtu.be/tNsTy-j_sQs

Trans-Identity Development: Potential Causes: https://vimeo.com/490953579

What causes anxiety and depression - Inside Out: https://youtu.be/tNsTy-j_sQs

Finding a Trustworthy Therapist: https://www.advocatesprotectingchildren.org/therapy

Episode 12: Depression & Gender Dysphoria

https://youtu.be/0OL9gJBA_FQ

<u>Maria Keffler (00:50):</u>

Today, we're going to talk about depression and gender dysphoria.

<u>Erin Brewer (00:54):</u>

It's a really important topic, because one of the things that I hear that these children need to be allowed to medically and socially transition in order to deal with depression. I'm hoping one of the things that we can address in this episode is that connection between depression and gender identity issues, but also to really point out that transition is not an appropriate treatment for depression.

<u>Maria Keffler (01:27):</u>

Unfortunately what often happens—not just in the gender industry but in all kinds of research and all kinds of care—is that people mistake correlation for causality.

We've talked about this before. You mentioned that when sexual assaults increase, we also see an increase in ice cream sales. Well, can we say that ice cream causes sexual assault or sexual assault causes people to want to eat ice cream? No, we can't attribute any causation there. The reason those two things are correlated or happened together is because they both happen in the summer. In the summer more people are out and about, so there's more opportunity for sexual assault, but in the summer it's hot people so like to eat ice cream. Those two things both increase, not because one causes the other, but because there's a third factor happening, which is that it's summertime.

<u>Erin Brewer (02:37):</u>

I'm really grateful for some recent research Bränström and Pachankis did. Initially they came out with a study saying that medical transitioning (specifically surgeries) help with depression and results in better mental health outcomes. Some concerned scientists looked at the results and at the data and really were questioning because the researchers in this case had an agenda. They were pro-transitioning. They wanted to do a study to show that it had positive outcomes. But when other scientists looked at the data, they questioned it. They wrote to the American Journal of

Psychiatry and questioned the conclusions that were made based on the data.

The journal asked the researchers to reanalyze the data based on the concerns that were raised. And, lo and behold, it turns out that neither cross-sex hormones nor surgery help with depression— the mental health outcomes were worse.

We know that suicidality goes up, based on previous research. A Swedish researcher who looked longitudinally saw that within the first couple of years the mental health outcome seemed to be about the same, but when you got about 10 years out, the suicide rates among those who had transitioned, versus the general population, are about 19% higher. And those were completed suicides. That's not just someone who had suicidal ideation. Completed suicides are 19 times higher—that is profound.

> **Within the first couple of years the mental health outcome seemed to be about the same, but when you got about 10 years out, the suicide rates among those who had transitioned, versus the general population, are about 19% higher. And those were completed suicides.**

I can't think of any other mental health issue that has that high of a rate of suicide. So we've got some good evidence to suggest that transitioning exacerbates the depression and suicidal ideation.

Maria Keffler (04:59):

The takeaway that we really want to give people is not to buy into the idea that your child is depressed because your child wants to transition genders, therefore you must transition genders to deal with the depression. That's a non-sequitur. They do tend to occur together, but the gender dysphoria co-occurs with a number of different mental health issues.

You have to ask yourself, "Is the mental health issue exacerbating the gender dysphoria? Is the gender dysphoria exacerbating the mental health issue?" We don't have good answers to those questions, but we know the answer is not that your child is depressed and needs to transition genders. We know that is not the answer because research has not supported that.

Erin Brewer (05:54):

There's no research to back this up, but here are some observations that I've had.

A lot of the children who are depressed are put on antidepressants prior to taking on a transgender identity. One of the side effects of anti-depressants is a reduced libido. This is something they put on the warning labels, that you're likely to have a reduced sex drive.

Some parents might think that's wonderful for teenagers to have a reduced sex drive. It may relieve some stress surrounding what the kids might do. But in reality, it's that sex drive that really helps kids overcome gender dysphoric feelings, because they start to get in touch with themselves and become more connected with themselves as they have those urges.

I have some concerns that the antidepressants that are being used to treat depression could set a kid up to be more susceptible to the trans-gender cult.

> **Antidepressants that are being used to treat depression could set a kid up to be more susceptible to the transgender cult.**

Maria Keffler (07:11):

I've never thought of that.

I was on an antidepressant for about a year after one of my kids was born. I had postpartum depression, which manifested in rage. I didn't know that anger could be a symptom of depression. I would just have these explosive rages.

The doctor put me on a pretty strong antidepressant and it toned all of my emotions down. I've talked to some therapists since who said, "You were probably overmedicated. You probably should've been on a lighter dose," because I just didn't feel anything, including a libido. But I was so relieved to be not experiencing those rages. I was able to parent my kids, so I said, "Let's not mess with the dose. I'm okay with it."

But I had no libido at all for that year. This is probably more information than our viewers want, but when I got off the antidepressant, the libido came raging back. My husband said, "Oh, I missed you. I really missed you."

Erin Brewer (08:18):

Parents can be uncomfortable thinking about this, but that sex drive is an important part of puberty. It's an important part of connecting with the body, and if that's suppressed, then it can really cause some difficulties for these kids. Their peers are all experiencing these feelings and they're not. It can make them feel different.

Another concern that I have—I'm just going to read this. This is from the FDA: "Being on antidepressants increases the risk of suicidal thinking and behavior in children and adolescents with major depressive disorder and psychiatric disorders."

It is confusing because you're using an antidepressant because a child is potentially suicidal. Yet they've found that antidepressants can *increase* suicidal thinking and behaviors. The FDA says that you should balance the risk of increased suicidality with clinical need. It notes that among the major antidepressants only Prozac is approved for treating depressive disorder in pediatric patients. That's the only one—no other anti-depressant is approved for use in children. Yet they're often a prescribed off-label just like the puberty blockers, just like the cross-sex hormones.

It's really difficult because you have to weigh the pros and cons. If you have a child who is self-harming and profoundly depressed, it's really important to stop that behavior. But at the same time, I'm worried that the cure might be exacerbating some of these issues. I would recommend to be cautious about the use of antidepressants in children.

> **I would be cautious about the use of antidepressants in children. We have a generation that is prone to over-medicating.**

We have a generation that is prone to over-medicating. Oftentimes parents are so concerned about their children having uncomfortable feelings that they're prone to medicate, when in fact, a lot of what's going on is just normal childhood and adolescence.

Those of us who had rough childhoods—I have no doubt that if I were a child today, I would have been put on a heavy-duty antidepressant. My mom actually kept trying to put me on antidepressants when I was in high school. She would say things like, "If you were a diabetic, you would take insulin. Wouldn't you?" She would try to guilt me into taking an antidepressant. For some reason, I just did not want to take them. I was very opposed to it. I'm really glad that I didn't take them.

Maria Keffler (11:11):

With my experience, I did not want to take antidepressants because there is some history in my family of self-medicating to deal with problems. I didn't want to do that. But my healthcare provider felt very strongly, "You need to do this for the sake of your kids." So I told my doctor, "I'm going to do this for a year. And then I want to get off of this antidepressant."

I went to the psychiatrist and he was very reluctant to let me get off of the antidepressant. He just kept trying to convince me to stay on it. At one point he said, "You'll probably to need to be on this for the rest of your life." I responded, "I went 36 years of my life without needing an antidepressant. I understand I have postpartum depression right now. But why would I need to be on one for the rest of my life?" It was only because of my determination that I got off of it.

I have been fine since. I'm now 51 and I have not needed an antidepressant since I was 37. But there is a really strong push in the medical industry to medicalize everything.

Erin Brewer (12:30):

I was shocked when my daughter was about 14 years old. She'd gone to the doctor just for a regular check-up and the doctor had her fill out this checklist. The doctor came in and said, "I think that your daughter is bipolar."

The doctor wanted to put her on some pretty heavy-duty meds. When I asked my daughter about it, she said she was just goofing around on the checklist and thought it was funny.

As you said, there's very appropriate times for medication. There are people who really do need to be on antidepressants.

Childhood and adolescence is a very difficult time to determine that, because our bodies are changing, we are growing and developing. I would just advise caution and, and to be very discerning. If you have a child, who's just having some struggles, that's not a time for an anti-depressant. Antidepressants are very powerful. As the FDA notes, most of them are not approved for use in children. We don't know what the long-term impacts are going to be.

We do know that these kids are not doing well. I've had so many parents who have reached out to me and said, "My child is on to antidepressants." Shortly thereafter the child started in with this transgender identity. "What's the core issue," they are wondering. "Is there something going on there?"

We don't have the research, unfortunately, but it's something to be aware of. The use of antidepressants could set the stage for a child to be more vulnerable to the trans agenda.

Maria Keffler (14:04):

Think about puberty and all of the things that are going on in your body. Your hormones are changing. Your physiology is changing. It affects you emotionally, psychologically.

When I was on the antidepressant, my psychiatrist told me that antidepressants deal with very sensitive neuro-transmitters. When I got off of it, he weaned me very carefully over a long period of time, because they have a profound effect on your body.

I was a fully matured adult. My brain had finished developing, and I still had to be very careful about how much I was taking and how I was getting off of it.

Think about these children whose bodies are still developing, whose brains are still developing. They're going through the Tanner stages of sexual development to become adults. We don't know what these drugs are doing. We don't know what's happening to their brains. As a parent, I would want to exhaust every other possibility for therapy, for treatment before resorting to medication for my child. I would not make that my first go-to.

> **Children's bodies are still developing; their brains are still developing. They're going through the Tanner stages of sexual development to become adults. We don't know what these drugs are doing. We don't know what's happening to their brains. As a parent, I would want to exhaust every other possibility for therapy, for treatment before resorting to medication for my child. I would not make that my first go-to.**

Erin Brewer (15:20):

We have a clip that we're going watch shortly that talks about the fact that most depression is caused by environmental factors or external factors.

My mom had this idea that I was genetically programmed to be depressed. A lot of people have this idea that being depressed is a lot like being diabetic—that there's nothing you can do about it. It's just your physiology.

If any psychologist had taken even a moment to look at my childhood, they would have identified a bazillion things that could have set me up for depression. I had a tough time growing up. I had an early childhood sexual assault that was brutal. My parents were divorced at about that same time. I moved from my home in California to Utah at about the same time with a new stepdad. I mean, it was just like, *bam, bam, bam.* All these things were happening. I moved into a state where I was a minority. I moved to Utah and I didn't even know what a Mormon was. That again, set me apart. I lived with parents who had an open marriage and that set me apart. They were drug users.

All these things happened, and any one of them could have set me up for depression.

Maria Keffler (16:51):

Now you are a healthy, functioning, wonderful adult. Anybody should be able to look at you and know there's hope for anybody.

Erin Brewer (17:02):

There was so much pressure that I had from my mother to get on antidepressants. It just was this like constant pressure. She'd ask, "Do you like being depressed?" She acted like it was my fault that I was depressed.

That there are kids who get this message: "Just buck up and be happy and take those medications," because the parents are having a hard time being around a child who's depressed.

As a parent, I can attest to the fact that it's hard to be around kids who are having a lot of angst. It's hard to watch your kids struggle, but it's really important for parents to be cautious about antidepressants.

But again, there are going to be some kids who really might need them.

For while the narrative was that that depression was genetic, it was biological. There's nothing you could do about it. But they're finding that, in most cases, there's a cause; there's a reason for that depression that can be resolved.

It's interesting when I look at the narratives that big pharma put out in order to promote their medications. A lot of times they promote this idea that these meds are going to make your life so much better.

It's similar to the opioids. I remember there was this idea that was being circulated that if you were in pain all the time, you couldn't get addicted to opioids. If you had chronic pain, there was no risk because your body needed those opioids in order to get over the pain. Well, we've discovered that was wrong.

Maria Keffler (18:56):

Who created that narrative?

Erin Brewer (18:59):

Exactly. You have to look at who's benefiting from people taking these medications.

> **Who created the narrative that meds are going to make your life better? You have to look at who's benefiting from people taking these medications.**

Maria Keffler (19:07):

Things really changed when the laws were changed and medicine could be advertised. When I was a kid, you never saw pharmaceutical ads on TV. They were not permitted. When was it—in the late seventies or sometime in the eighties—that suddenly that law was changed? Lobbyists and now pharmaceutical companies can advertise on TV.

In the clip we're going to watch, one of the people talks about how, when you hear about diseases and disorders and you hear all about them, suddenly, you think you have them. People are watching ads on TV and thinking, "I'm sad" or "I'm sleepy" or "I don't feel good. I need to get whatever this drug is."

My husband has an aunt who works in health insurance. I was talking with her one time about someone I know who is addicted to some controlled substances. And I said, "How does this person keep getting this is prescription?" My husband's aunt said, "You can get anything you want from a doctor. You can go in and you tell a doctor what you want. If you're insistent enough, they will give it to you just to get you out of their office."

Erin Brewer (20:31):

That was one of the things that I learned with my mom. She used to prescription shop. I can't even tell you the numbers of bottles of different drugs that we had in the house, because she would just go from one doctor to another.

It was a precursor to this whole affirmative-care model, where patients were able to go in and get access to medications just by telling a doctor that they needed them.

It used to be that that you'd have to get a fairly good psychiatric evaluation in order to be put on these meds. Now a lot of general practitioners will prescribe them, although they're really not qualified to do so. This is something that requires a very comprehensive assessment so that they find out, "Is there trauma in the past? Is there something that's causing this behavior? Is there abuse in the home? What's going on, what are the underlying factors?"

Why don't we go ahead and watch that clip?

It starts out with a detransitioner. This young woman, who suffered from depression, thought that transitioning was going to cure her. She took cross-sex hormones and had a mastectomy and then realized she was still depressed. The transition initially seemed to help, but ultimately it didn't.

I hear this, especially among young women who start the process and feel really good initially. Then once they've done everything that they can do to transition, they realized the depression is still there, only it's compounded now, because they see how much they've damaged themselves.

> Tynice (22:26):
>
> I feel like I'm always sad, you know, and I hate that. So I want to be forthcoming about what I'm going through and let you guys know you're not alone.

> Johann Hari (22:36):
>
> So far, we have scientific evidence for nine different causes of depression and anxiety. Two of them are indeed in our biology. Your genes can make you more sensitive to these problems, though they don't write your destiny. And there are real brain changes that can happen when you become depressed, that can make it harder to get out. But most of the factors that have been proven to cause depression and anxiety are not in our biology.

> Shawn Achor (23:03):
>
> There is something called "medical school syndrome," where during the first year of medical training, as you read through a list of all the symptoms and diseases that could happen, suddenly you realize you have all of them.

Johann Hari (23:13):

What we're finding is it's not necessarily reality that shapes us, but the lens through which your brain views the world shapes your reality.

Erin Brewer (23:19):

That was really interesting. It really resonates that when you read about a disorder, it's so easy to be like, "I think that I might have it." One of the reasons is that we're really good at retrospectively looking at things to fit a new perspective.

Maria Keffler (23:44):

People are pattern seekers. There's a lot of research around why our brains are geared that way, but it's what lets us make sense of the world. We look for patterns. So when we say, "I'm going to do my research and try to figure out what's wrong with me," we're looking for patterns. "What in my past or what behaviors have led to this?"

I had a chronic ongoing issue that I went to a doctor for when it first started happening. He told me, "You are not to research this. Do not Google this. Do not go to WebMD. I am telling you that I am taking care of this, and it is not a big deal. But if you go Google this, you're going to freak yourself out."

Erin Brewer (24:31):

That's a really good point. We have access to all this information on the internet, and we also have experts going into the school and talking about suicide and depression.

One of the problems specifically around depression is that when teenagers look at what depression is, it's really typical for teenagers to feel like they fit the description. Part of the reason is that they don't have the longevity to recognize what it is to persistently feel down. We know persistently feeling down might be—say, five months—whereas for a kid, it could be an hour. Their timeframes are very different. Their sense of how heav, and how big things are is distorted, because they don't have the experience in the world. They haven't grown up. They haven't had lots of life experiences.

Say they've had a fight with their friend—that can feel profound at the moment. They might want to kill themselves. They want to die because things are so much heavier, and that's a normal part of being a child.

Maria Keffler (25:52):

That's what parents are supposed to be helping their kids through—providing that long view, and telling them, "This is not forever. I hear you. That's painful. This is really hard. But it's not going to be forever."

> **That's what parents are supposed to be helping their kids through—providing that long view, and telling them, "This is not forever. I hear you. That's painful. This is really hard. But it's not going to be forever."**

Just yesterday I was talking with one of my daughters. We've been dealing with COVID for almost a year now. As we make this video it's February, 2021. We've been socially distant.

I was talking with my 15-year-old daughter and she said, "I feel like if I can just suck it up, I can get through life. And if I have to suck it up the rest of my life and just be unhappy, that's okay. I can get to the end of my life by just sucking it up."

I was thinking, "I don't want you to live your life sucking it up." But a year is 1/15th of her life. She's been in lockdown, dealing with scary, painful, difficult stuff for a year. On the other hand, I'm 51. A year is not that big a deal to me.

It's important to realize this. There's stuff that adults tend to kind of dismiss and say, "That's just kid's stuff." Or, "It's puppy love."

It might be puppy love, but that's the first time that kid's experienced love. That kid just got his or her heart broken, and has never gone through it before. We need to help by providing support: "Yes, this is really painful. This is hard. I promise that it's going to be better. It's going to get better."

Erin Brewer (27:46):

A lot of times kids are afraid of these big emotions, because they are so heavy. A lot of times the adults around them are afraid of these big emotions. I'm not sure what's changed, but I feel like we have a generation of parents who are nervous about kids being upset and having problems and feeling down, and they just want to fix it for their kids.

I don't know how much of that has to do with our culture. Most people don't have to worry about scraping for food and finding a place to sleep.

If you have your basic needs met and don't have to be struggling about those, then it's easier to get focused on these emotions.

There've been times where I've been homeless. When I was dumpster-diving I wasn't thinking about being depressed. I was thinking about finding something to eat. When you're in survival mode, it's very different.

I'm not trying to minimize people's feelings of depression because they're very real. But it is important with younger kids, teenagers, and young adults, to ask if there are things about their lifestyle that can contribute to them feeling depressed that are physiological—such as not exercising, not eating well, not getting enough sleep. All three of those can trigger feelings of depression.

Maria Keffler (29:22):

One of the things we saw in the video clip was loneliness.

We're lacking a lot of connection. Studies have shown that one of the strongest predictors of kids being healthy and successful in life is eating dinner with regularly with their families. Families don't sit down to dinner anymore. I remember a few years ago hearing that nowadays, when they're building houses, they're not putting dining rooms in houses.

Having those family connections is so important. Having meaningful relationships and friendships is so important.

When I left my psychiatrist's care after the postpartum depression, he told me just what you mentioned. He said, "You need three things. You need to be eating well, you need to be sleeping well, and you need to be exercising."

A lot of time, partly because we're in COVID lockdown, and partly because this is just who I am, I'm just sitting at my computer. I'm working on a book right now, and I'm spending a lot of time writing. I spend a lot of time in zoom meetings. It's the dead of winter. So I'm not going outside much.

Yesterday was a hard day for me. The day before yesterday was a very stressful day. Yesterday I just felt awful and I needed to run to the grocery store. I'm doing groceries for my elderly neighbor lady. I went to the store and I just sat in the parking lot in my car and started crying. I didn't even know what was wrong. I asked myself, "Why do I feel this way?"

That afternoon, my daughter and I walked down to the community center. There was something we needed to do there. It's about three quarters of a mile walking there and walking back. By the time I got home,

I had a new lease on life. I felt better. I felt invigorated. I realized I haven't had any exercise at all in a week.

Erin Brewer (31:30):

Being outdoors is important too. The combination of getting exercise and being outdoors is important. So many kids are just on their computers. They're watching TV. They're not getting outside much.

We do better when we spend time outside. It's important. Some people live in places where it's not safe to be outside, but if you take a kid who's struggling, you get them to eat well, you get them connected with friends, you get them sleeping, you get them exercising, you get them outside— they're going to blossom.

One of the reasons that kids who are depressed feel better once they adopt a trans identity is because suddenly they have friends, they have activities, they have connections. So you take a kid who's been feeling alone and down, and suddenly they have this group that's affirming them and giving them affection. They're going to start feeling better.

> **Kids who are depressed feel better once they adopt a trans identity because suddenly they have friends, they have activities, they have connections.**
> **So you take a kid who's been feeling alone and down, and suddenly they have this group that's affirming them and giving them affection.**
> **They're going to start feeling better.**

It has nothing to do with their identity as transgender. It has to do with the fact that human beings need those interactions and teenagers especially need that connection with their peers.

Maria Keffler (32:56):

We definitely need affection. We need approval. We need to feel important.

I don't want what I'm about to say to sound like parent-blaming at all. There are no perfect parents. There are no perfect families. We're all trying. But sometimes a child is not feeling particularly connected in the family—not feeling loved and provided for. That's not to say the family doesn't love them and provide for them, but children's perceptions can counter reality. I'm talking about the child's perceptions. So if the child feels like, "I'm not really connected to my family, my parents don't really think that much of me," they need that from somewhere.

What you said about getting it from the transgender-identified community is really powerful. That has been a strategic positioning that the trans-rights activists have created. We talked in an earlier episode about the cultic aspects of transgender ideology and how they love-bomb recruits. The first thing that cults do is to draw somebody in with love and affection because they know that we all desperately need someone to tell us they love us.

Erin Brewer (34:15):

Parents, I would recommend that if a child comes to you and says that they're transgender, talk to that child and tell them that you're willing to entertain that at some point, but that first you need to address depression.

> **If a child comes to you and says that they're transgender, talk to that child and tell them that you're willing to entertain that at some point, but that first you need to address depression.**

The kid may not be happy about this, but make the case that people who are depressed are advised not to make big life decisions. This is something that therapists say all the time: "If you're depressed, don't get a divorce, don't buy a car, don't move, don't quit your job. You need to get through the depression. Then you're ready to make these big decisions."

Transitioning is a big decision. That's going to have lifelong implications.

Maria Keffler (35:08):

Even your external presentation is a big deal, because that affects all of your relationships. That affect things.

Erin Brewer (35:15):

We know that once a child is socially transitioned, they're so much more likely to get on that medicalization path. It's very reasonable for parents to tell a child, "We need to deal with this depression first."

It's triage. When somebody comes in, if they've been in an accident and they've got a broken leg and a gash that's bleeding, and they're not breathing, you don't start splinting the leg. You get them breathing first.

Explain to a child that you have to deal with the depression first. "Once the depression is fixed, then let's talk about your gender identity." That's a very fair thing to do. I would bet in almost every case, once the depression lifts, the child's not going to be as attracted to that whole transgender ideology.

Maria Keffler (36:11):

A big part of this is kids just looking for a fix, and I'm not talking about a drug fix. I'm talking about a fix for what feels broken whenever there's something that we feel we're lacking. We feel something's not working. We're looking for the solution for it. We're pattern seekers. We're looking for patterns that tell us what is the right answer to this problem.

Unfortunately, schools, social media, the culture, all of that is dumping on top of kids. "The fix for every problem is gender. Every problem that you have, we can fix it by transitioning your gender." That's ludicrous. That's absolutely ludicrous.

> **"The fix for every problem is gender. Every problem that you have, we can fix it by transitioning your gender." That's absolutely ludicrous.**

Erin Brewer (36:54):

The thing that's so frustrating is that people within the trans movement even admit that oftentimes transition doesn't help with the depression. In fact, sometimes it makes worse. It makes it worse. Rather than saying, "Maybe that's because transitioning isn't an appropriate treatment for depression," they claim it's because of transphobia. It's because you're not accepted. It's supposedly because of all these external factors that these kids should be depressed, because, "Look at how bigoted society is. They're not allowed to use bathrooms. They're not allowed to compete in sports."

The trans-rights community creates this whole narrative to justify why the transitioning hasn't alleviated the depression, when we know that it's because we need to cure the depression, and that transitioning is likely to exacerbate these problems anyway.

Maria Keffler (37:49):

Telling people the reason you feel the way you do is because society is treating you badly is completely untrue. That transgender-identified children aren't allowed to use the bathroom at school is not true. No child has ever been refused the right to use the bathroom. They're asked to use the bathroom that corresponds with their anatomy. No child has ever been refused the chance to participate in sports. They are asked to participate on the teams that correspond to their physiology.

Telling children, "The reason that you feel this way is because society is so terrible to you" completely externalizes the problem.

You have no ability to control or change what society is doing or what happens outside of you. You only can change yourself, right? If you put that locus of control outside of yourself, then everything becomes a blame game, and you don't have to fix yourself because you're not the problem.

Erin Brewer (38:54):

I thought that one of the new diagnoses in the DSM-5 should be an "external locus of control" because I feel like a lot of difficulty that kids have is a result of feeling like they don't have any control.

For those who aren't familiar with the term, if you have an *internal* locus of control, you feel like you can change things. You can make a difference. You control your thoughts; you control your feelings. It's empowering.

If you have an *external* locus of control, you believe that everything's being put upon you and you don't have any control. You can't change your thoughts, and people are doing things *to* you. It's very disempowering because you're basically at the mercy of your environment.

We used to encourage children to develop an internal locus of control. We told kids, "You can do it. You can change things."

Now things have been flipped, and we're encouraging children to give up that locus of control. That makes them give up so much—they give up their sense of ability to affect change.

Part of being human is that ability to change and to adjust our thoughts. One of the things cognitive behavioral therapy teaches is that you get to choose how you interpret something.

Somebody can say something unpleasant to me. Somebody could walk up to me in the street and say, "You're really ugly." I can choose to go home and believe, "I'm ugly." Or I can think, "That person's having a bad day," or, "That person maybe has a mental illness," or "What are they talking about?" *I* get to determine how I respond.

This whole trans ideology is saying, "No, you don't get to have any power. If somebody 'misgenders' you or uses your 'deadname,' that's violence. You've just been damaged. You've been hurt. You've been attacked."

That's a damaging message to give to kids. It's very disempowering. We know that people who don't feel empowered are more likely to be depressed. It's a vicious cycle. Kids who are depressed get sucked into an ideology which is encouraging them to give up their power, which is likely to increase depression.

Maria Keffler (41:20):

I look at some of the things that humans have overcome and have lived through. People have lived through real horrors. They've lived through enslavement, long-term abuse, concentration camps, and oppressive regimes. People have lived through really violent experiences and have come through it.

Now we're teaching kids that if somebody calls you "she," when you want to be called "he," then that's violence. It's not.

> **People have lived through real horrors— enslavement, concentration camps. People have lived through really violent experiences and come through it. Now we're teaching kids that if someone calls you "she," when you want to be called "he," that's violence. It's not.**

We've shifted from a couple of generations ago when the parenting was about tough love, like, "Go out and milk the cow, work on the farm and this is your life." Now I hear parents say, "I don't want my children to suffer. I want them to have happy childhoods."

Erin Brewer (42:21):

As if a parent has control, as if a parent can somehow make a child happy.

Maria Keffler (42:30):

I know parents who don't believe in discipline because they don't want their children to be unhappy.

That is such a short-term goal. That is so self-defeating, because we know it's like exercise. You go out and stretch your muscles and push yourself when you exercise; you break down muscle and it hurts. That's why you're sore afterwards. It's not fun. But after that muscle heals, it's stronger. It's better. It's more powerful. It's more resilient.

It's the same thing with our kids. We don't grow unless we suffer. We don't become resilient unless we suffer things that make us become resilient.

Wanting your child to have nothing but happiness and pleasure in life, actually dooms that child to not have happiness or pleasure in life.

> **Wanting your child to have nothing but happiness and pleasure in life actually dooms that child to not have happiness or pleasure in life.**

Erin Brewer (43:23):

It sets them up for failure. It would be like a parent who says, "You ran and your muscles hurt. Well, don't run anymore. We don't want that. Your gym teacher's making you run? They're being violent against you. How dare they?"

That's what this narrative is. It's so damaging.

We have a couple of questions. The first one says, "My son is on antidepressants, but it seems to be making the gender dysphoria worse rather than better. I want to change his medication or even stop it altogether. But neither my son nor his doctor agree because they both buy into the transgender explanation for the dysphoria and depression. How do I convince them that this current medication is a problem?"

Maria Keffler (44:08):

Wow. This really speaks to the locus of control. What are your initial thoughts?

Erin Brewer (44:17):

My initial thought would be to find another doctor. It's okay to do that. These are your kids and if you're uncomfortable with the medical care or the message that they're getting from their doctors, find another doctor.

This is another message that a lot of kids are getting, that they need this medication, and that they don't have control over their emotions. In some very small cases that's true, but in the vast majority of cases, you can teach them to be resilient and you can teach them to get through their difficulties.

But if you have a doctor who's saying, "You just can't handle life. You need this medication," that's taking away their locus of control. It's making them dependent on external forces.

> **Kids are getting the message that they need this medication, and that they don't have control over their emotions. In some very small cases that's true, but in the vast majority of cases, you can teach them to be resilient and to get through their difficulties.**

I am concerned about doctors who, if a child is getting more depressed on an antidepressant, still isn't going to take them off. We just heard that the FDA says there's only one medication that's approved for depression in children, and that's Prozac. The FDA says that these kids have to be watched carefully because suicidality often increases on anti-depressants.

This parent's gut reaction to get the child off the medication is correct.

It is important not to immediately take somebody off antidepressants; they need to be weaned off slowly. I would encourage parents who are having this difficulty to find a doctor who's willing to work with you on getting your child off the medication.

Maria Keffler (45:46):

It also depends on how old the child is. If this is a young child and you still have control over their medical care you have a little bit more power than you do with an older child.

Erin Brewer (47:07):

If your child is older and is adamant that they want to stay on the meds, but you're concerned about it, you can always tell them that you're not willing to pay for it. You're not willing to pick up the meds.

This is nuanced because you have to be very careful with these psychotropic drugs.

But I do think finding a doctor that can help you wean off of them is important. If it's a teenager or a young adult, your options are more limited in what you have control over.

The next question that we have is, "What does the research actually say on people who commit suicide because they aren't affirmed as transgender?"

Gosh, this is one of my pet peeves. It's such emotional blackmail to tell parents that their kids are going to kill themselves if they're not affirmed. It's also a disservice to put that message out there to kids.

> **It's emotional blackmail to tell parents that kids are going to kill themselves if they're not affirmed. It's a disservice to put that message out to kids.**

We know, as the video said, when kids hear something, they start to believe it. Kids are going to start to believe that suicide is an appropriate response to not being affirm, just because so many transgender-rights activists are putting that message out there.

Maria Keffler (48:21):

This is emotional blackmail. When I was a teenager, I had a boyfriend who I broke up with, and he started calling me all hours of the night and threatening to commit suicide. I'd stay with him on the phone or, tell him we can try again. This went on for months, because I wasn't savvy enough to recognize, "This is not my problem. I get to make a decision about who I date, and it's not my problem that you're threatening suicide."

When it's your child, that's a much different case, but that is still emotional blackmail. That is what that is. There is not research to back that up, because you can't do good research on who's going to commit suicide, because you can't have a control group. "We're going to try to have this group commit suicide." Well, no, that's not ethical.

Erin Brewer (49:23):

But the longitudinal study in Sweden does suggest that transitioning results in much worse outcomes, as far as suicide goes.

If your child came to you and said, "You have to buy me a car, or I'm going to kill myself," would you buy the car? Most parents would say, "No way."

We have good sense about this when it comes to other issues, but for some reason, this narrative has become so common, that parents are afraid of this.

I've known parents whose children have committed suicide and it's devastating. It's probably the worst thing that can happen to a family. It's beyond heartbreaking. It is a very scary thing. But if you have somebody who is suicidal, they're typically not allowed to make big life choices. They're not even allowed to consent. If they're really suicidal, when they get checked into a hospital for suicidality, they lose their option to consent. They're not allowed to check out if they want to. They've lost that.

If your child truly is suicidal, the last thing you want to do is complicate things with a new intervention. You need to get that depression or that suicidality under control first. The idea that a child can demand to be treated a certain way under threat of suicide is just no way to parent.

Maria Keffler (51:00):

I know one parent whose daughter said, "I just want to kill myself. I just want to die," and was in her bed with the sheets up over her head. The mom went up to the girl's bedroom and said, "Are you thinking about hurting yourself right now?" And the girl didn't say anything. And the mom said, "I'm going to ask you again. And I want an answer. Are you thinking about hurting yourself right now? Are you feeling suicidal?" And the daughter didn't say anything. And mom said, "I'm going to ask one more time. And if you don't answer me, I'm going to assume the answer is 'Yes,' and I'm going to take you to the hospital. Are you feeling suicidal? Like you're going to hurt yourself right now?" And the girl said, "No! No! I'm not! Just leave me alone."

Erin Brewer (51:45):

That's smart to ask that, because we know that if a child says, "Yes, I'm planning on suicide," then that's much more serious than a kid who says, "I should just kill myself."

I've worked with people who are suicidal and the doctors say to ask them, "Are you going to hurt yourself? Do you have a plan?" And if the answers to those two questions are, "Yes," you get them to the hospital, whether they go kicking or screaming or not.

It may be that they were just using that as a threat because they have been counseled to do this. We have activists who tell kids to threaten suicide. We have this documented. We have a therapist saying that this is the way to get treatment. You might get to the hospital and be told, "They're not really suicidal," but you can't risk it. If they say that they're going to kill themselves, then you have to take that threat seriously.

Maria Keffler (52:47):

Be aware that you're not putting an idea into their head. This is something a lot of parents are afraid of. "I don't want to address this because I don't want to suggest it to them. Maybe they haven't thought about it."

They've already thought about it. You're not putting an idea into their head to ask, "Are you feeling suicidal? Are you feeling like you're going to hurt yourself?"

I just talked to a parent yesterday who has been seeing transgender-identified behaviors in her child for two years. The child is dressing differently. The mom has seen things on the child's social media about wanting to get on testosterone. It's very clear. This child is pursuing this.

The mom's afraid to talk to her about it. She doesn't know what to say. But you might as well have it come out while you're in control of the narrative.

Erin Brewer (53:57):

The other thing I would recommend, because I have dealt with people who are suicidal, is to be very specific. Say, "Will you keep yourself safe until we talk next? Will you promise that you will not do anything until your dad and I have a chance to talk with you tomorrow?" Get a verbal contract from them.

> **When dealing with people who express suicidal thoughts, be very specific: "Will you keep yourself safe until we talk next? Will you promise that you will not do anything until your dad and I have a chance to talk with you tomorrow?"**
> **Get a verbal contract from them.**

That's important, both for your peace of mind, as well as for the dynamic, because people who really are suicidal needs to be held accountable.

As a parent, you need to understand you did what you needed to do. If the child does end up attempting suicide, at least you did what you're supposed to do.

It makes me so angry that the trans activists have introduced this into parenting. Parenting is hard enough without having to worry that your child might kill themselves because you don't affirm them. It's the worst kind of emotional blackmail.

Episode 12 Resource List

Johann Hari "This Could Be Why You're Depressed or Anxious": https://youtu.be/MB5IX-np5fE

Shawn Achor "The Happiness Advantage": https://youtu.be/GXy__kBVq1M

Episode 13: Possible Explanations for Gender Dysphoria

https://youtu.be/jUafL7geBBY

Maria Keffler (00:51):

Following up with our episode on trauma and depression, we thought we should talk today about some of the reasons why kids might get sucked into gender ideology. The three big ones are being on the autism spectrum, having prior trauma, and suffering depression, but there are lots of other reasons a child could be sucked into this.

Erin Brewer (01:16):

It is important for parents to know, because they might be thinking, "My child's not autistic. I don't think my child has experienced trauma. They didn't seem depressed before they got into this." It's important for us to touch upon the fact that there are all sorts of other contributing factors that can lead a child to be vulnerable to this ideology.

Maria Keffler (01:38):

I know one mom, when her middle school daughter announced her trans identity, the mom was terrified that something had happened to her daughter, worried her daughter had been molested or something. That child desisted a couple of years later and no, she didn't have any specific trauma or anything like that happen. She was more getting sucked in by social media, by the friend groups, by the GSA clubs. The mom said that she thinks the daughter was targeted by this cult.

Erin Brewer (02:19):

That's something parents don't realize: the power of social media. I have talked to a number of detransitioners who just fell into this ideology after being exposed to it on social media. It's very compelling. It draws kids in. So even if you have a kid who's not particularly vulnerable at the outset, they can get sucked into this just by being exposed to it on social media, or just by having friends at school claiming to be transgender.

We have seen these clusters of girls, especially, where one girl in a school will announce a transgender identity and suddenly there's five or six or seven or eight or nine of her friends who are also coming out and saying they're transgender.

> **We have seen these clusters where one girl in a school will announce a transgender identity and suddenly there's five or six or seven or eight or nine of her friends who are also coming out and saying they're transgender.**

Lisa Littman has talked about this in her research. A number of other people are bringing it up, noting that this is clear evidence of a social contagion.

Maria Keffler (03:20):

We've seen this before with other social contagions, especially in this age group, where they are just so prevalent.

This is nothing like gender ideology, but when I was a teenager, it was stirrup pants. Everyone was wearing stirrup pants and every girl had a pair.

Erin Brewer (03:42):

I was just about to bring that up, believe it or not, because it was such a big deal to have them! I didn't have any, and I felt like such an outcast because everybody else had them.

Maria Keffler (03:53):

I remember this one party that I went to. All my friends were going to be there, and I wore my stirrup pants. Every girl there had black stirrup pants on, except for one of my good friends who was the fashion queen of the group. She wore floral print jeans. She said, "I knew everybody else was going to wear their stirrup pants." So what do you think I did? I went out and bought a pair of floral print jeans that week.

Erin Brewer (04:24):

I think about my children, the things that they felt like they had to have in order to fit in with the other kids. Some of the things are just beyond silly. I remember giga pets. My daughter thought it was debilitating if she didn't have one. All of her friends had one and she just had to have one, otherwise she wasn't going to fit in. What would she do when all the other kids were playing with their giga pets? She created this drama around it.

But that's part of this age group, everything feels so big. If you don't fit in—oh my gosh, that feels so awful.

Maria Keffler (05:16):

A lot of times adults forget that when you are at that age—when you're 13, 14, 15—your world is just starting to open up and you're moving out of the home, out from under your parents and you're interacting with the world more. You're having experiences that you haven't had before.

I think about how kids are so in love the first time they get a boyfriend or girlfriend. That relationship is so important. It is so critical. They think, "I have found my soulmate. This is who I'm going to be with for the rest of my life."

As adults, we look at that and we know that most high school relationships don't last.

Erin Brewer (06:09):

Adults call it "puppy love," which is if you're a teenager, it feels like a put-down. These kids think, "You don't know! Mine is the real thing."

Maria Keffler (06:17):

It is kind of insulting to them. That relationship is so important and so powerful. And they have never experienced that before. When it ends it is a catastrophe to them because they don't have any of the coping skills that adults have developed. They've never had their hearts broken before. And so they don't have those coping skills.

We, as adults, really do need to have a little bit more empathy and understanding about what these kids are going through.

Erin Brewer (06:49):

That's the other thing that I want to point out. Especially for these girls. This is where we are seeing this as a social contagion, when their bodies are starting to change. All of a sudden, they're having to cope with grown men ogling them in a way that is uncomfortable. All of a sudden, their clothes aren't fitting quite right. They might have to go out and buy a bra.

These things are difficult. Some girls celebrate this and feel like they're growing into their own. But for a lot of us, it's this uncomfortable time. Maybe our periods are starting and we're anxious about that.

If suddenly someone were to come in and say, "You know what? You don't have to deal with any of that. I have a solution for you," it's not surprising so many of these girls are jumping at the opportunity to just stave off all that discomfort.

Maria Keffler (07:44):

I remember when I was 13 and I was just starting to develop a chest. I was one of those girls who wanted to be grown up. I wanted to develop my womanly figure. But I laid down on my stomach to read—which is how I always lay—and suddenly I was like, "That's not comfortable." There was something there that wasn't there before. Even though I wanted to grow up and I wanted to be a mature woman, my breasts were in the way. I remember being so irritated: "Do you mean I can't lie on my stomach anymore?"

What these kids are going through now... our culture today is so much more sexualized than it was when I was a teenager. The amount of sexualization... I was doing some research on pop music a few years ago. 92% of Billboard Top 10 music has sexual messages in it. 92%. If you've listened to it, it is all about sex.

> **What these kids are going through now...**
> **our culture today is so much more sexualized**
> **than it was when I was a teenager. 92% of Billboard**
> **Top 10 music has sexual messages in it. 92%.**
> **It is all about sex.**

I just spoke to a mom this morning. This mom said that her daughter, who is 13, is not interested in sex at all. She wants nothing to do with it. There was apparently some locker-room talk where one of the girls in the locker room was talking about her boyfriend playing with her breasts and how much she liked it. At 13 years old!

This girl was just traumatized by hearing that. She said, "I don't want anybody messing with my breasts. I don't want to have children. I don't want any part of this." I thought the mom was so wise, her instinct was good. She just told her daughter, "I think what you're feeling is normal. I think that's actually totally okay to feel that way."

Erin Brewer (09:47):

I also want to address boys too, because there are some boys who identify as a girl as a result of some kind of a fetish. But we're finding out that a lot of boys take on this trans identity when they're younger due to things we've already talked about, like sexual trauma.

I have a dear friend who was molested when he was in fifth grade, and as a result of that, he just wanted his penis gone. Then we have boys who have autism. We have boys who are depressed.

But the other thing that I'm hearing more and more often is that boys who are sensitive are picking up on the negative feelings that some women have about men. The #MeToo movement was very powerful, but some of the messaging was that a lot of men are toxic. There's this "toxic masculinity" that's discussed. If you have a young man who's sensitive, he might be feeling like, "I don't want to be associated with that."

I interviewed Hacsi Horvath. He is an older man who identified as a woman for a number of years. He said a lot of it had to do with the fact that his stepfather was violent. He had a mean male role model. He didn't want to associate himself with that.

A lot of times we talk about girls in this program because it is hitting girls more than it is boys, but it's important to also be sensitive to the fact that there are boys and young men who are struggling with this. That may be because they're sensitive and they don't want to be associated with males. Perhaps they've had trauma, depression, or perhaps there are other things going on. Or they want to be popular.

We need to not automatically assume that they have some kind of a fetish and write them off, because they deserve our compassion and support.

Maria Keffler (11:40):

Historically those who were trans-identified adults were almost entirely adult men. This is a new thing that we're seeing in boys. A lot of times we hear about a teenage boy who's trans identifying and we automatically think *autogynephile*. I don't think that's fair and I don't think it's right. I think you're right about the whole toxic masculinity portion of it.

But you mentioned wanting to be popular. That's something that we need to pay attention to with this.

The activism has been so powerful, and anyone who's watching in a friend group online, or if you've questioned anything about this ideology, you've probably felt the venom from the other side. No one is allowed to question this. No one is allowed to raise concerns. If you think about a kid who's in middle school or high school—a lot of these kids who are identifying as trans are a little bit on the fringe. They don't quite fit in. They're not the popular, big-man-on-campus kind of kids.

But when they announce a transgender identity, they're untouchable. Nobody can criticize them. Nobody can question them. Nobody can put them down. There is no more bullying coming their way.

> **When kids announce a transgender identity, they're untouchable. Nobody can criticize them. Nobody can question them. Nobody can put them down. There is no more bullying coming their way.**

Erin Brewer (13:15):

The teachers are guarding them and the other students are guarding them. Suddenly they're untouchable.

Maria Keffler (13:21):

And they can get teachers fired. We've seen it happen with Peter Vlaming in Virginia. A trans-identified student heard him use the pronoun she didn't like and got him fired.

Think about the heavy amount of power that comes with that. Frankly, who wouldn't want that kind of power when they're 13, 14, 15 years old?

Erin Brewer (13:47):

The other thing is that this age group is constantly trying on new identities. We know this is part of the developmental process that kids go through during puberty. That's so important: trying on different looks, different styles, different personalities. It's not surprising that we have kids trying this on.

Unfortunately, when kids try this on, there's such hoopla surrounding this, that it's hard for them to back out.

In most cases a kid might try on an identity, like, "Maybe I'll be goth." People aren't celebrating that. They don't have this whole affirmation for goth people or for preppies. For a while being a preppy girl was popular. These days, if a girl decides to be preppy, no one is going to be celebrating that.

Trans is one of the only cases I can think of where an identity is cemented on the child as soon as they announce the identity, instead of saying, "Okay, you're trying that out for a while." With trans, they say "You are trans, you were born that way. That's who you are, that's your authentic self and we're going to do everything we can to protect that identity now so that you don't move through it to something else."

Maria Keffler (15:08):

You don't see posters in the hallway about the Preppy Club or All Kids Who Like to Wear Orange.

Erin Brewer (15:25):

We've tried to get more girls involved in STEM (science, technology, engineering & math) fields and have put up posters promoting STEM for girls in schools, but nothing like what we're seeing for the LGBTQ: the celebration, the money. As soon as they take on this identity, there is a pathway for them. At every point there's a celebration. There's encouragement. There are people telling them how wonderful and authentic they are, and how none of their problems are their fault.

If you're a teenager who is having a hard time taking on responsibility, all of a sudden you don't have to worry about that. It's almost surprising more kids haven't bought into this cult.

Maria Keffler (16:24):

I appreciate that you ended with the word cult because that's what it is. There is an identity that's being put on these kids, that's being celebrated and fostered.

One of the things that you hear the trans-rights people say is, "Gender is on a continuum."

You can be super feminine or super masculine. It's all based on stereotypes. If you ask for a definition of gender that doesn't rely on stereotypes, there isn't one.

You've commented on this before Erin: if I'm a girl, I can flow toward masculine as much as I want and be celebrated. But if I start flowing back toward being feminine—oh no, that's not acceptable.

Erin Brewer (17:15):

I'm glad that you used the word foster because it reminded me of another group that is often overlooked and is vulnerable to this. That's foster children.

Foster children have an incredibly high rate of this. One of the things that's concerning to me now is that in California they're grooming foster parents to accept and affirm their foster kids as transgender. If you're looking at kids who have had a troubled past and are looking for a new identity, it's no wonder that this population vulnerable.

There are some other populations that are vulnerable, such as those who have some developmental delays. Often it is because they don't tend to be the popular kids. They're the vulnerable kids.

You've mentioned people reporting that GSA clubs and other trans activists target kids who look like they're vulnerable, very much the way pedophiles do to groom—so that they can prey upon them.

Maria Keffler (18:21):

I spoke to a mom in the Washington D.C. area who went to a meeting for community theater groups. It was supposed to be an equity/diversity/inclusion training, but she said the entire thing was about trans and about sex: sexual orientation and gender identity, how to get it into the theater, how to write your own stuff, and share your stuff so that there's lots of it around.

She was horrified because she said in that meeting, which was a training, the trainer said, "Stand in the hallways at school and look for who's alone at their lockers. Go to the lunch room, see who's sitting by themselves, and go talk to them about sex and gender identity."

That's grooming behavior. That's predatory grooming.

> **The trainer said, "Stand in the hallways at school and look for who's alone at their lockers. Go to the lunch room, see who's sitting by themselves, and go talk to them about sex and gender identity."**
>
> **That's grooming behavior.**
> **That's predatory grooming.**

Erin Brewer (19:14):

That is predatory behavior. We have a couple of clips to watch that explore other underlying conditions that can prime a kid to be vulnerable to this.

Dr. Stephen Levine (19:24):

Certain groups of children are being diagnosed with or claiming transgender identities in very disproportionate numbers. These include children residing in foster homes, children who were adopted at the rate of about three times greater incidents of transgenderism, children with a prior history of psychiatric illness, children with mental developmental disturbances.

James Caspian (psychotherapist) (19:50):

A lot of them will say they've spent a lot of time on social media, where they've seen a lot of people who have transitioned feeling it was very cool feeling, that it was a way to get away from being female. Quite a lot of them seem to have had a very negative experience of being female in a female body.

Abigail Shrier (20:10):

Now that there's greater societal acceptance, they're just saying that we're reverting to a normal base rate of transgender women. Where all the women in their forties and sixties coming out as trans? They should be coming out. Now is their time. Now is the moment we should see tons of women in their forties and sixties coming out as transgender, but we're not seeing that. We're seeing the same population that gets involved in cutting, demonic possession, witchcraft, anorexia, bulimia. They con-vince themselves there's a problem. Suicide rates are going up. But if these women were ... real transgender people who were living under a more repressive regime and are now just finding themselves, you would think the suicide rate would be going down with greater acceptance.

Erin Brewer (21:03):

Abigail Shrier pointed out that we hear activists saying that the reason we have so many more kids identifying as trans-gender is because they've been in the shadows all this time. Abigail pushed back on that in a way that makes so much sense. I've noticed too, that if this were true, the suicide rates would have been so much higher before we started affirming kids.

In fact, the opposite is true. The more we've become affirming of this, the higher the suicide rates, and completed suicide rates are for children and teenagers, which is horrifying. It means we're doing something terribly wrong. It doesn't mean that it's because these kids are feeling more like their authentic selves. There's something seriously gone awry in our culture. It's not just slight increases. We're having serious increases in completed suicide rates. That is a clear indication that something is terribly wrong, that the affirmative approach is not working, and that these kids weren't always transgender and they just "finally feel comfortable coming out."

Maria Keffler (22:14):

She pointed out that we're seeing the increasing suicide rates right along with this ideology being promoted. So as we've said before, we can't say there's causation there, but when you see that kind of correlation and it's in the same time-frame, you have to wonder what's going on.

I also appreciated when she said, "If this is just society getting more accepting, and that's why we're seeing this, where are the women in their forties and sixties coming out with this?"

Wow, correct me if I'm wrong. I don't know of very many stories of middle-aged or older women doing this.

Erin Brewer (22:56):

This is typical of autogynephiles: they've had their kids, they're married, and then they come out as transgender. There are very few cases of women my age who are coming out and saying, "It turns out I was born in the wrong body." That's actually surprising to me because it's hard to be an older woman. In some ways I would think that we would be the perfect demographic, because older women tend not to be valued very much in our society.

Yet we don't see that happening. We don't see in countries that have historically been much more open and affirming than ours, we haven't seen this incredible rate until recently when it started to be affirmed.

There's some very good research that shows that it's not that there's always been so many transgender people and they've just been hiding in the shadows. That doesn't make sense.

It does make sense when you look at the social contagion aspect of it and all these other factors that we've been talking about.

Maria Keffler (24:07):

Just to summarize, if you're dealing with this announcement from your child, spend some time examining your child. Try to figure out what has gone on with your child socially, medically, and psychologically. I would even get a piece of paper and start writing down everything you know about your child, because by doing that you can figure out the need that transgender ideology is fulfilling. There's some reason that kids are getting sucked into this.

If you can pinpoint it, figure out what the child was lacking, whether it was social status or whether it was fear of growing up or whether it was autism, then you have a little bit better idea how to start addressing it.

Erin Brewer (25:00):

That's a good idea.

Maria Keffler (25:03):

We have a couple of questions from listeners. Here's the first one: "Almost every girl in my daughter's friend group is now identifying as transgender, yet the school counselor and the principal insist this is not a social contagion. What is going on?"

Erin Brewer (25:20):

What's going on is people are being gaslighted. This ideology has really taken hold, and that administrators are either unwilling to see what's happening, or they're afraid to accept what's happening.

We know that people are losing their jobs if they say anything at all against this ideology. There are a lot of factors, but this is so clearly a social contagion.

When you talk to these parents, so many of these kids are rewriting their history to fit the script. These are kids who never experienced gender dysphoria. They had no indication of being uncomfortable with the sex that they are. Then all of a sudden, as their friends are coming out as transgender, suddenly they're rewriting their history to fit this narrative, which is classic of a social contagion.

Maria Keffler (26:17):

We did an episode where we looked at social psychology and how hard it is for somebody to stand up against the crowd. When everybody around you is saying, "The sky is orange," it is hard to say, "No, the sky is blue." It's very hard to do that.

Unfortunately, a lot of educators are... I don't know if guilty is the right word, but they are *susceptible* to that as well.

Erin Brewer (26:40):

I would encourage a parent, if they're in this situation, to look into finding another school because once a kid's been indoctrinated into this, and if the school is completely oblivious to what's going on, that child is going to be more at risk of being sucked in.

Maria Keffler (26:59):

Unfortunately, Schools are often less oblivious than they are complicit. The schools are pushing this and this infuriates me.

I spoke to a mom who said she was having her daughter evaluated by a psychiatrist or neurological psychologist. They were trying to get a diagnosis if she was autistic or not.

> **Schools are often less *oblivious* than they are *complicit*. The schools are pushing this and this just infuriates me.**

The psychiatrist or psychologist was doing the battery of tests and the mom really weighed whether she should say anything to the psychiatrist about her daughter claiming to be non-binary, because the daughter wasn't really talking about it yet. The mom said, "I felt like I should give her all the information. So I told the psychiatrist, 'Look, my daughter has said this. We don't believe it. We think it is something else. I'm just telling you this so that you're aware, please just take this into consideration.'"

Well, as the psychologist was giving the family the results of the girl's test, she turned to the girl and said, "Now when I fill out your report for your school, is there a different name that you want me to use? Are there different pronouns that you want me to use?" And the mom said this just invigorated the daughter to start going public with it.

Erin Brewer (28:27):

To have that kind of an adult authority figure validate—that's just so sad. We're seeing this, which is why parents need to be so careful about the specialists they take their kids to.

Maria Keffler (28:41):

No one is neutral right now. That might sound a little bit extreme to say, but I'm not sure it's really extreme. People are either for this or they are aware of how damaging it is and they are against it. I don't think you can trust that there are any neutral parties around your child.

The other question we have is, "My son is adamant that he's transgender, but I can see so many other psychological and social struggles that he's not addressing. How can his dad and I try to shift the focus off gender and back onto things that really need to be looked at?"

Erin Brewer (29:22):

That's a good question. As we talked about in the other episodes, a lot of times these kids are struggling with other things.

I would just suggest to the parents to re-engage with the child to really honor those things that are troubling them. Help sort through that. If the child is depressed, try to get them out of that depression, because that makes them more vulnerable.

Maybe even say to them, "Look, we understand that you're having these feelings, but we want to address these other issues first. And then let's talk about it."

That gives the parent and the child some time to cool off because we know that this can be very volatile. And it allows the parents to have an in with the kid to help them work through those other issues.

Maria Keffler (30:10):

I agree with you. I want to echo that as much as you can, shift the focus off of this. Anybody who's worked with a teenager knows that telling them, "You cannot do this" is like inviting them to push back on Mom and Dad. So as much as you can, try not to be authoritarian about it, but just say, "Wow, that's important. But I think maybe the bigger deal right now is this other thing. So can we focus on this other thing first? Can we get this under control, or get this managed, and then go back to talk about this other thing?"

> **"Wow, that's important. But I think maybe the bigger deal right now is this other thing. So can we focus on this other thing first? Can we get this under control, or get this managed, and then go back to talk about this other thing?"**

I think you're right. I think once the child gets distracted from this thing that it will stop sucking in everything in their life. That's what a cult does. Everything gets viewed through the lens of the cult. So if you can just get that child to kind of step out of it, to look at this other stuff, that might do a lot to weaken their fascination with the cult ideology.

Erin Brewer (31:10):

Kids really do tend to get focused on one thing. If the kid is on the spectrum, hyper-focusing is part of the being on the spectrum. Find ways to draw them out of that is going to be really important. We have some other episodes that talk about how to address autism, depression, trauma, if those are issues.

Maria Keffler (31:37):

Well, this has been a fascinating subject today. I hope we hit all the points that parents needed.

Next week we are going to talk about Planned Parenthood and the gender industry.

Erin Brewer (32:07):

This is going to probably be uncomfortable for some people. There are people who have 100% supported Planned Parenthood most of their lives. I think it'll be really disturbing to them to find out that Planned Parenthood is now one of the top providers of cross-sex hormones.

Maria Keffler (32:27):

I used to be a supporter of Planned Parenthood. I used to think very well of them. I've had my eyes opened just in the last year to some things that are really concerning.

Episode 13 Resource List

Identity Development in Adolescence & Adulthood (Oxford):
https://oxfordre.com/psychology/view/10.1093/acrefore/9780190236557.001.0001/acrefore-9780190236557-e-54

Erikson's Stages of Psychosocial Development:
https://www.verywellmind.com/erik-eriksons-stages-of-psychosocial-development-2795740

Abigail Shrier (Joe Rogan):
https://www.youtube.com/watch?v=6MYb0rBDYvs

Irreversible Damage: The Transgender Craze Seducing Our Daughters:
https://www.amazon.com/Irreversible-Damage-Transgender-Seducing-Daughters/dp/1684510317/ref=sr_1_3

Episode 14: Planned Parenthood and the Gender Industry

https://youtu.be/KBNLfdyMb1A

Maria Keffler (00:45):

Today, we are talking about Planned Parenthood and Planned Parenthood's role in gender care. This is a weighty topic and I'm grateful that you've got a lot of expertise and experience with Planned Parenthood.

Erin Brewer (01:09):

It's hard for people to understand how Planned Parenthood stepped into this role of being one of the country's biggest distributors of cross-sex hormones. They're making it their business model. They're making a huge profit from this.

This is a different Planned Parenthood. This is not the Planned Parenthood from when we were young adults. This is a Planned Parenthood that has embraced this gender ideology in a way that is very dangerous, and giving away hormones in a way that is incredibly irresponsible.

They have adopted what is called an "informed consent" model which sounds great. Informed consent is great, but what it actually means is that anybody can walk in there and get hormones simply by signing something that says that they understand the implications of taking the hormones, whether you understand them or not.

The problem is, there's actually no way for anybody to understand the implications because the implications haven't been studied. This is all so new and experimental. For Planned Parenthood to say somebody can make an informed consent is inaccurate.

The other thing that concerns me is that I've talked to a number of detransitioners who have gone to Planned Parenthood when they're in a psychiatric crisis: either they're in a manic phase or they're profoundly depressed or they've just had a trauma. They are not capable of providing consent. Yet were able to walk into a Planned Parenthood clinic and get hormones the same day.

Maria Keffler (03:13):

In most healthcare settings, if a patient comes in obviously in some sort of psychological distress, there's going to be a referral made to a mental health care professional, or some questions asked to establish what mental state are they are in. Most ethical healthcare providers want to make sure that the patient is in a frame of mind to be able to make good decisions.

Erin Brewer (03:45):

It's really important to bring that up because these transgender medical interventions are self-harming. They result in harm to the body.

If somebody is having psychological distress, there's really no way that person can provide consent.

It's really important for us to recognize that seeking these kinds of treatments is an indication of self-hatred. Trying to run away from oneself is disassociation from the body. That alone should raise red flags.

But then on top of that, if you're dealing with somebody who has had some kind of acute distress, or some kind of a mental health crisis, it's really unconscionable to provide that person with interventions that are going to change them for life.

Maria Keffler (04:42):

Healthcare providers—at least doctors, medical doctors—take an oath to "First, do no harm." When I look at the things that are going on with gender care—puberty, blockers, wrong sex hormones, surgeries that remove or alter sex characteristics such as girls having their breasts removed—that is harmful.

Erin Brewer (05:12):

Planned Parenthood has completely adopted this transgender ideology. Giving interventions damages healthy bodies.

Before this gender ideology came about, somebody who had gender dysphoria had to go through years of therapy before anybody would even consider these medical interventions. Now somebody can walk in off the street, walk into a clinic and oftentimes they get the hormones that they're seeking before they've even had test results back from blood tests that would show whether or not it would be dangerous for them to take these hormones.

We have young people talking about this and it's really disturbing to me that a clinic would go this far. We have a clip that shows how completely absurd and dangerous this whole ideology has gotten.

Steven Crowder (06:14):

Planned Parenthood is America's self-proclaimed number one provider of women's health care. We wanted to see just how all-in they are.

"I'm Stephanie *(Stephen Crowder in drag)* and I'm pretty sure I'm pregnant. So my partner Garrett and I are going to Planned Parenthood."

Stephanie and Garrett scheduled a pregnancy test along with a follow-up with a nurse practitioner. And for good measure, we brought the urine of an actually pregnant woman along with us just to see how far the tolerance extends beyond medicine.

Now, I know this may seem childish and stupid on the outset, but keep in mind that while a positive pregnancy test for a woman can come as great news, for a man it's largely indicative of testicular cancer. Does Planned Parenthood do the responsible thing and let a man know that he could have potentially life-threatening cancer or stick to their progressive guns and follow their code of conduct in regards to transgender patients?

> **Does Planned Parenthood the responsible thing and let a man know that he could have potentially life-threatening cancer or stick to their progressive guns and follow their code of conduct in regards to transgender patients?**

(Following is hidden video from Crowder's visit at Planned Parenthood.)

Nurse (07:00):

Oh, your test came back positive.

Steven Crowder (07:02):

Really?

Nurse (07:03):

The only options that we can give you is that we can give you the forms for the Medicaid. If you want to go ahead and continue with the pregnancy.

Steven Crowder (07:11):

Okay.

Nurse (07:11):

Give it up for adoption. The option of a termination, but we don't do them here.

Speaker 6 (07:17):

Okay, you don't perform those here?

Nurse (07:19):

No, we don't.

Steven Crowder (07:20):

(To the camera) Well, it's good to know that there are options. Now to be fair, the nurse practitioner did have some questions and was seemingly concerned with potential health ramifications. As you can see, they can't even play by their own guidelines.

Nurse (07:32):

Were you assigned a female at birth?

Steven Crowder (07:37):

Do you mean if I was misgendered by a doctor when I was born?

Nurse (07:41):

Did they consider you a female when you were born?

Steven Crowder (07:45):

I was misgendered at birth. Yeah.

Nurse (07:47):

Okay.

Steven Crowder (07:47):

I don't see how that's...

Nurse (07:49):

I mean, do you have ovaries? A vagina?

Steven Crowder (07:55):

(To the camera) But a little righteous indignation threw her off the scent.

Steven Crowder (07:58):

I want to make it clear that I am not a woman in a man's body. I am a woman. I've always been a woman and I'm currently living as a woman. So they did identify me. They misgendered me as a male when I was born.

Nurse (08:09):

Okay.

Steven Crowder (08:10):

(To the camera) At no point, was there any mention of potential testicular cancer.

Maria Keffler (08:15):

Wow.

Erin Brewer (08:16):

It is ridiculous and really troublesome as he pointed out. A positive pregnancy test for a man is indicative of testicular cancer! It's funny, because it's so absurd, but it's also so concerning.

People are going to get the wrong medical care if people don't acknowledge biology, if people don't acknowledge sex—these are clinics that are ostensibly to provide healthcare. That they're willing to engage in this absurd narrative, even when it puts someone's health at risk, is disturbing.

Our next clip is a lot more serious and we're going to hear from some young people who were able to just go in and get testosterone. The first young woman just walked in and got it. Now she has detransitioned and is feeling a lot of regret, and is justifiably angry at Planned Parenthood for having allowed her to do this. Then we have some stories about how this is becoming a business model for Planned Parenthood.

This is not healthcare. This is actively recruiting people to come get hormones.

TV Reporter (09:40):

You have to be 18 years old to buy cigarettes and 21 to gamble or buy alcohol. But minors living with a gender identity issue can undergo hormone therapy before becoming a legal adult. Planned Parenthood is hoping to make life a little bit easier for the transgender community. They are now offering transgender hormone replacement therapy for those under the age of 18.

Planned Parenthood Doctor (10:02):

It was time for us to expand what we are providing.

TV Reporter (10:07):

Planned Parenthood is reminding everyone in central Illinois that they offer hormone therapy for people looking to transition. The organization says that they began this program back in 2015 with central Illinois in mind. Leaders say central Illinois had a dramatic need for transgender services in the area. Planned Parenthood now offers this service at 17 locations all around the state. Leaders with Planned Parenthood of Illinois say people in search of this treatment can always find it at their clinics.

Planned Parenthood Spokesperson (10:37):

We're here for you. Planned Parenthood remains willing and able to care for these patients. We want to be there as that safe place for you to come.

TV Reporter (10:48):

There are multiple avenues to pay for this treatment, including insurance and Medicaid.

Victim 1 of Planned Parenthood (10:55):

I went through a Planned Parenthood and basically, they just ask you a bunch of sexual history questions, and then you can go pick up your prescription as well, which they do very weird. You can like pick up your prescription before getting your blood test, which is kind of *yicks*.

Victim 2 of Planned Parenthood (11:09):

My experience with Planned Parenthood was not necessarily a good one. I'm not happy with it. I'm not happy that I was just given hormones. If it wasn't just as easy as just walking in and signing a form for something that permanently changes your body for essentially the rest of your life— In some aspects. I think if it wouldn't have been so easy for me to just walk in, I don't think I probably would have transitioned if it wasn't so easy just to willy-nilly, on impulse, just go and decide to take hormones.

Maria Keffler (11:42):

It's really troubling to me to see them advertising in that news clip, where a news station is advertising for Planned Parenthood to bring more people in to get the gender treatments. That's just really upsetting.

Erin Brewer (12:04):

Especially when there isn't any assessment to determine whether somebody is in a state of mind to be able to make this kind of decision.

A lot of times transgender activists will talk about gatekeeping. They don't think there should be gatekeepers. They think that people should be able to access this intervention if they want to. They act as if it's a violation of their basic rights to have gatekeepers.

It's so important to push back on that because the whole idea of gate-keepers, in this case, is that we have trained medical professionals who are supposed to be looking out for our health and wellbeing. There isn't any other case that I can think of where patients can walk in, tell the doctor what they want and get it the same day without assessment.

Imagine if I walked into my doctor and said, "I really want some oxycodone. I haven't been sleeping well, give it to me now." Is that doctor going to give me oxycodone? I sure hope not.

Maria Keffler (13:09):

In my understanding, my connotation of gatekeepers is a positive one. We have gates for boundaries, for safety. A gate is to keep things safe, to keep dangers out. That's a good thing.

The way that they've reframed gatekeeping as a negative thing is really indicative of the most basic underlying ethos of this ideology. They don't want boundaries: "No one can tell me anything about what reality is about, what I am about, or what truth is. It's all me. I get anything I want, anytime I want it. Everybody needs to applaud it." That's just irresponsible.

Erin Brewer (14:09):

It's so dangerous. There was a case where I believe it was a young woman who came in, who was pregnant and she was complaining of stomach pain, but she told all the healthcare professionals that she was a male and they didn't even consider that she might be pregnant, because she was saying she was a male. I believe that the baby died. This woman could have died as well.

When it comes to healthcare settings, it's really important for healthcare professionals to be honest, because the kind of care given to males and females is different. If you have doctors who are willing to pretend that a man can become a woman, and vice versa, it becomes really problematic for receiving the best healthcare.

We know that there are a lot of people who have really good feelings about Planned Parenthood. At some point in their life, they used Planned Parenthood to get through a rough time, to access healthcare when they couldn't afford it.

Maria Keffler (15:24):

I utilized Planned Parenthood when I was in college. It was free health care. That was very helpful for me in college.

Erin Brewer (15:33):

I used them and I volunteered for them for about ten years. I helped with a fundraiser and donated money to them. A lot of people have warm feelings towards Planned Parenthood because it provided them services.

Now they have to realize that a clinic that they donate to or volunteer for, that they thought was doing good, is actually doing something incredibly destructive.

> **A lot of people have warm feelings towards Planned Parenthood because it provided them services. Now they have to realize that a clinic that they donate to or volunteer for, that they thought was doing good, is actually doing something incredibly destructive.**

Maria Keffler (16:18):

It reminds me a lot of the way that I feel about public schools. I was a teacher. I was licensed as a public school teacher. I have advocated for going to your neighborhood school, for not self-segregating. I sent my kids to a Title I elementary school, because I really felt like you make community where you are. I really was a public-school advocate, and seeing what the public schools have done in the last few years around gender ideology, I've now pulled all my children. I homeschool all three of them now because I don't trust the public school anymore. That's heartbreaking to me.

Just yesterday, I spoke to a veteran teacher of almost 30 years, who is planning to leave his profession even before he gets his retirement, because he cannot ethically continue to work for this organization.

I feel that way about Planned Parenthood too. This is not the Planned Parenthood of my college years.

Erin Brewer (17:26):

That realization is really hard. It's like you have to completely shift your worldview, and it's really difficult for people who have supported Planned Parenthood, who advocated for it, who insisted that it's important to fund it. It's hard to all of a sudden realize this organization that they have supported wholeheartedly for so long has suddenly turned into the bad guy, and is suddenly doing something that is really damaging to our society, to our young adults, to our communities.

They are embracing transgender ideology. I believe that they're doing it for profit. I believe that's what's motivating this, because this is booming. They're making so much money. I don't know how to explain to people how concerning this is. I've talked to detransitioner after detransitioner, who said, "I walked in, I was in a state of crisis, I got the hormones and it was the biggest mistake of my life."

> **I've talked to detransitioner after detransitioner who said, "I walked in, I was in a state of crisis, I got the hormones and it was the biggest mistake of my life."**

I interviewed a mother who found out that her daughter was going to Planned Parenthood to get these medications. Her daughter had significant mental health issues, as well as some developmental issues. The mother was so upset she decided to check it out for herself. This was a mother who had previously good feelings about Planned Parenthood.

She made an appointment. She walked in and she was prescribed testosterone on her first visit.

I've talked to detransitioners, who've been given prescriptions without any kind of medical check at all. They usually take blood, but they'll give out the prescription before the results of the blood tests are back. It's really important to have good follow-up, but Planned Parenthood isn't providing it.

It's like they are the drug dealer on the corner. That's just giving out the drugs. It's heartbreaking.

Maria Keffler (19:53):

It must almost feel like your husband or wife is being unfaithful to you.

Erin Brewer (20:02):

It is a sinking feeling. People thought, "I could trust you. I thought I could believe in you. I've given you so much over the years." It's just this sense of betrayal.

A lot of times that prevents them from seeing what is happening. There are wives who see the lipstick on the collar but they just ignore it because they don't want to go there.

It's too painful. There's too much at stake. I had a boyfriend in college—my first serious boyfriend—and he stepped out on me. He was dating somebody behind my back. Looking back, there were so many flags, there were so many things that I should have said, "Yeah, that's a little suspicious. Yeah. I think there's a problem here," but I just didn't want to see it. I think that's so common. We don't want to believe that someone we love or something that we trust could be so nefarious and could be so underhanded.

One of the things that I want to mention, and this is a little bit tangential, but in addition to giving out hormones, Planned Parenthood is also giving out something called PrEP, which is something you take so that you don't get HIV.

This might sound wonderful. But at one point I contacted a Planned Parenthood clinic and posed as a fourteen-year-old girl who was doing sex work. They were counseling me as to how to get PrEP behind my parents' back.

This a red flag. I would hope that they would try to talk to a child and get them help and get them out of prostitution, rather than saying, "Come on in, we'll get you PrEP." That's really disturbing.

If parents realize that Planned Parenthood is not their friend, what do parents need to know going forward in order to protect their kids? How do we protect our children from what is apparently a predatory organization?

One thing that most parents don't know is that Planned Parenthood is actively trying to infiltrate public schools and has been successful in California and possibly other places. I know for sure in California they're putting Planned Parenthood clinics within the schools, which to me is just horrifying.

The other thing that Planned Parenthood is doing is creating educational modules for schools to use. In these modules, they are pushing this whole gender ideology, teaching kids as young as kindergarten that they get to choose what gender they are.

Most people don't realize how easy it is for Planned Parenthood to access their children. My understanding is that they offer these modules for free. So the schools jump at the opportunity to use them. A public school teacher has to put in a lot of time to put together lesson plans. If somebody puts one together it's such a time saver.

Maria Keffler (23:49):

These lesson plans that they put together are beautiful. They're all packaged: "Here's exactly what you do in the classroom. Here are all your worksheets, here are all your manipulatives," which are things that you play with, the things you actually touch and use during the lesson. They provide all of that. And it's free. A 45-minute lesson plan, all inclusive, it's free, it's beautiful. It's packaged.

These overworked teachers are going to jump at that and, and maybe not really realize what's in there.

This might be tangential too, but a few years ago, I was on the counseling committee for my kids' elementary school, which means I went in occasionally and met with the counseling staff to find out what was going on.

The school counselor was saying that she wanted to have teachers practicing safety scenarios with kids: What to do if you're at the park and a stranger comes up and says, "Hey, I can't find my puppy. Can you help me?" The counseling department had written all of these scripts for teachers. They were trying to figure out how to get it into the day.

The teachers were talking about how packed their days were. They said, "I know! We can keep those in our pockets, and when we're standing in line at lunch, we can practice them while standing in line."

I remember being horrified that these teachers had to squeeze important stuff into standing-in-line times. Now fast forward 5, 6, 7 years, and they're now putting gender ideology into core classes. They're putting a Planned Parenthood curriculum into the class time, when teachers five years ago didn't have time to do basic safety role playing with kids during the school day.

Erin Brewer (25:54):

It comes down to funding. I used to think that Planned Parenthood was a struggling organization that could barely make it, but they were going to do everything they could to offer affordable care to those who needed it. Now it's this international business. They have so much money.

Another thing that Planned Parenthood is doing internationally is putting pressure on the UN and other international organizations to deny aid to countries that are not willing to start indoctrinating their citizens into this gender ideology.

Planned Parenthood has all sorts of publications. They go into communities that are very poor and who have very few resources, teaching this gender ideology and pushing the idea that kids should have access to puberty blockers, hormones, and surgeries, in communities where people are struggling to survive. They're barely even making ends meet. They're not eating enough. They don't have safe housing. They don't have basic medical care. And Planned Parenthood is going in there and pushing this gender ideology, utilizing resources to teach this, and then trying to take important resources away from those who really need it to provide these unnecessary interventions.

Maria Keffler (27:33):

It reminds me of the missionary model. Missionaries would go into developing countries and bring resources. They were doing that to provide aid and to love others, but it was also to bring the gospel with them. When you feed people, they're grateful that you fed them. They're more willing to listen to your message.

Erin Brewer (28:03):

Liberals tend to call it "cultural imperialism" and be very scornful of it. So it's very interesting to me that many liberals now are embracing it.

When I say liberals, I count myself as a liberal. My whole life I affiliated as a liberal.

I don't want to use that as a pejorative, but it's so ironic to me that liberals condemn cultural imperialism, and yet that's exactly what Planned Parenthood is doing. They're going into third world countries and they're insisting that the aid is connected to this gender ideology. This is exactly like a religion going in and insisting that the only way you get aid is if you convert to their religion. It is cultural imperialism in the worst sense of the word.

Maria Keffler (28:53):

Interestingly, a lot of missionary situations in the past—I'm thinking about some out west here in the United States, and I know this happened with the Aboriginal people in Australia—children were taken away from parents, put on compounds, and indoctrinated into the religion. They lost their own culture. They lost their own language. They lost their own dress because a religion was forced upon them.

I don't see a lot of difference between that and what Planned Parenthood is doing.

Erin Brewer (29:25):

This is very similar. Planned Parenthood is actively creating a divide between children and their parents. I don't know if Planned Parenthood encourages children to run away, but we know that this ideology encourages children to run away from home, which causes a whole host of problems. Just the fact that they're encouraging children to disassociate from their body and to seek medical interventions to make their body conform to some idea of how they want it to be, rather than providing them mental services is incredibly concerning.

Maria Keffler (29:59):

To underscore what you just said, we talked about this when we talked about trauma in our last video. Encouraging someone to believe that their mind is a different sex, a different gender than their body— that is codifying dissociation. That's encouraging dissociation and saying that dissociation is a healthy and correct way to live.

Erin Brewer (30:26):

People need to understand that Planned Parenthood is a predatory and dangerous organization. What do parents need to do to protect their kids? One thing is to keep Planned Parenthood out of your schools.

Talk to your kids about the nature of Planned Parenthood, if you have any concerns that your child might go to a Planned Parenthood clinic. Try to get them into a healthy environment where they're not going to be affirmed. Get them to a therapist who can work with them, because the minute they walk into that Planned Parenthood clinic, they're going to get exactly the interventions that they want. These are life changing.

Kids might think, "They're just like birth control pills. They're just hormones, no big deal."

When birth control pills first came out, they actually were a big deal because they had so much hormone in them. They caused problems. Unlike birth control pills, these are the opposite-sex hormones and they cause permanent damage to bodies. Testosterone is a controlled substance. It's considered dangerous because it's a steroid, and it causes permanent damage. It can exacerbate already present mental health issues and cause others, because it creates chaos within the body.

Maria Keffler (32:19):

It's important for parents to recognize that if your child has not yet been indoctrinated into this cult ideology, you're in a better position in your relationship with your child. Keep your child identifying with your family, be on that child's side. Let that child know that you love them, that you care about them, that you are there for them., because the gender industry is working to separate kids from their parents. This ideology comes in and it puts a new identity on your child. Once that happens, the child's loyalties are with the gender industry and not with you.

Erin Brewer (33:16):

They know this and they're using the language: "We're a safe place." "You can come here and be safe." "We're going to validate and affirm you." This is the language that Planned Parenthood is using. They're using it very consciously because they're trying to lure people in with this marketing.

> **Planned Parenthood is using the language: "We're a safe place." "You can come here and be safe." "We're going to validate and affirm you." They're using it very consciously because they're trying to lure people in with this marketing.**

Maria Keffler (33:34):

It's grooming behavior. This is what groomers do, who are trying to predate sexually on children. They identify the child, and separate the child from his or her protections: the parents, the safe adults. The predator tells the child, "Oh, I love you. I care about you. We'll just keep this between you and me. And don't tell your parents."

Erin Brewer (34:03):

This could be a really hard episode for people who came in feeling positively about Planned Parenthood. I really hope, if that is you, that you will take some time and write Planned Parenthood and let them know that you're not okay with this predatory behavior and this new ideology that are pushing.

Maria Keffler (34:23):

I do feel like we just sat down with someone and told them, "Your spouse is cheating on you."

Erin Brewer (34:31):

It can take a while to process it. It's like the rug is pulled out from under you. It's easy just to dismiss what we're saying and say, "That's ridiculous, you are just making this up.

I hope that people will recognize that's not what we're doing. Research Planned Parenthood and transgender youth, and it's right there. They're actively putting it out there.

Maria Keffler (35:14):

Go to Planned Parenthood and look at their information for educators. They've got their stuff on their education page. You can see what they're pushing into the schools.

We have one question from a viewer who said, "My son, who's nineteen, has developed all kinds of health issues he never had before, like weird rashes, stomach problems and joint pain. They all began right after he started taking estrogen prescribed by Planned Parenthood. He won't listen to me and Planned Parenthood won't even take my phone call. They hang up when I say my name. What can I do?"

Erin Brewer (36:11):

That is so hard. I've talked to parents whose children are going to Planned Parenthood to get hormones. The parents are just distraught because their child has mental health issues. They know that their child should not be on these hormones. Like you said, Planned Parenthood will just hang up on parents. It's heartbreaking because I can't imagine being in that position of seeing your child's health deteriorating and not being able to do anything about it.

Maria Keffler (36:40):

He's 19, so he's an adult, right?

Erin Brewer (36:47):

Some parents can get medical guardianship of their children if their children have significant medical issues, or developmental delays. Usually the child has to go along with it.

This is another area where our society has changed a lot. It used to be easier for parents to get information. Planned Parenthood is the same as a lot of college clinics. They won't give you information. You can't really stop it. All you can do is work with your child and try and build that relationship because the clinic's going to ignore you or hang up on you, or maybe even threaten you with a restraining order.

Their whole goal is to keep kids medicated, and keep giving out these hormones because they're making so much money on it. They're not going to listen to you. You have to try and get through to your child, which I know is so hard.

Maria Keffler (37:39):

If your child has a relationship with someone else who you trust, if there's an aunt, an uncle, a cousin, or someone else that the child really has a good relationship with, try to leverage that if possible. Talk to that other family member or friend, and let them know what's going on. Try as much as you can to build a village around your child who can be speaking some truth. I don't know really what else to suggest for an adult.

Erin Brewer (38:14):

I'm going to make one more suggestion. I'm going to plug your book. It is a tremendous resource for parents. It will provide parents with a lot more insights and a deeper dive to what we're doing here on this show.

It's hard. I would just be infuriated if I found out that there was nothing I could do and I could see my child's health deteriorating like this. It's such a helpless position. It's so frustrating to me that what is ostensibly a healthcare organization is actively causing disease, actively causing a healthy body to become less functional, and is actively promoting dissociation between brain and body.

Episode 14 Resource List

PP News Segment Advertisement: https://youtu.be/VnBIvizMJsM

HIDDEN CAM: 'Pregnant' Transgender at Planned Parenthood! | Louder With Crowder: https://youtu.be/7UrQPW2-4rk

Desist, Detrans & Detox: Getting Your Child Out of the Gender Cult: https://www.advocatesprotectingchildren.org/product-page/desist-detrans-detox-getting-your-child-out-of-the-gender-cult-1

Episode 15: Problems with Medicalizing Children

https://youtu.be/JaGGOvBLPQg

Maria Keffler (00:46):

Our topic today is problems with medicalizing children. We're going to talk about what really happens when you start to chemically or surgically alter a child.

Erin Brewer (01:02):

This is such an important topic. One of the things that the trans activists say that being transgender is a normal develop-mental path. They say it is just as normal as someone who doesn't have gender dysphoria, and anybody who questions this normal developmental path is transphobic.

The reason this is so dangerous is because it isn't a normal developmental path; it is a medicalized path where children who are normally developing become medicalized in ways that affect them for the rest of their lives.

That's not normal. Normal is when you do not have to do interventions.

Maria Keffler (01:49):

Is there any other normal developmental path that requires surgery at some point?

Erin Brewer (01:59):

Or powerful hormones? If it is normal, why does it require interventions. We usually require interventions when there's some kind of a disease or disability, not when something's normal.

Maria Keffler (02:24):

This is happening because it's a billion-dollar industry. If they can get children—and by they, I mean the gender industry, the gender doctors, the pharmaceutical companies—if they can get children on a path of medicalization, those children are on that path for the rest of their lives. This is a billion-dollar industry.

Recently, I came across a market report by Global Market Insights. They do research into market trends and then write comprehensive reports that companies can purchase to figure out the best strategies to leverage a new market trend, to make money off of it.

They did this market report on sex reassignment surgery. I only saw the introduction because you have to pay several thousand dollars to get the full report. But the introduction summarizes that this is a growth market and they expect sex reassignment surgery to make billions of dollars over the next few years.

The only way you grow a market is by cultivating new customers for it— by selling it, by marketing it. And that's exactly what we're seeing here. That is why this is happening.

Erin Brewer (04:27):

There's a strong motivation among big pharma to cultivate this. We see pharmaceutical companies providing grants to schools to hire school counselors. They're going in and giving programs to schools to talk about gender identity. They're actively cultivating a clientele.

One of the things that I look at is the evolution of the drugs that are being used.

One of the drugs, Lupron, is a puberty blocker, which is an incredibly harsh drug. It was used to chemically castrate sex offenders, but it was deemed to have too many negative side effects. It was considered cruel and unusual punishment to use on sex offenders.

Then they started using it to treat endometriosis and other disorders. And women started having incredibly bad side effects. There's actually a movement now among women who took this for endometriosis and other issues to have it banned because the side effects are so profound.

So as this is happening, pharmaceutical companies are trying to find another clientele they can push this because they've got this drug, and they want to make money with it.

The same thing happened with testosterone. For a while, pharmaceutical companies were really pushing testosterone as a health aid for older men whose testosterone levels were dropping. They found it had bad side effects. A lot of men came together and filed a class action lawsuit and won, because testosterone, as it turns out, is not even a good supplement for adult males. And *their* bodies are accustomed to it.

So what I see here is pharmaceutical companies wanting to find another market, and boy have they ever.

It's so insidious that people are making money off of children and children's mental health and causing them to be medicalized for the rest of their lives. The pharmaceutical companies have a great plan here, because even if a child decides, "Gosh, I made a mistake. I'm not actually transgender," the likelihood is that they're going to be medicalized for the rest of their lives because their bodies will have stopped being able to create the normal hormones that they need. So those children, as they move into adulthood, are going to have to take hormonal supplements for the rest of their lives.

This is a lifelong client. These pharmaceutical companies are targeting children around age eight.

Maria Keffler (07:09):

People think the pharmaceutical companies are their friends. They have this impression of them that they are trying to make drugs to improve people's health and improve people's lives. But ever since we started allowing advertisements for pharmaceuticals, I think the pharmaceutical companies have taken a very different path. Now it's about making money. It's now about marketing.

When my youngest daughter was just a baby, I was going to the pediatrician. I was holding her in the elevator and this man stepped in the elevator with me. I almost could not stop staring at this man. He was the best-looking man I had ever seen in real life.

Now I love my husband. He's a handsome man. But this guy was on a whole other level—like Hollywood level. Even my daughter, a baby, was looking at him. We both go into the same office and he goes back into the doctor's office. I leaned over to the receptionist and said, "I'm happily married, but who was that?" And she said, "That's the drug rep. We love when he comes."

I saw a documentary about how pharmaceutical companies hire these incredibly attractive men and women as drug reps who go in and foster relationships with doctors.

Erin Brewer (08:47):

That's the other thing that I hear, "Let doctors do their jobs. Doctors know what they're doing. Doctors would never do something that's harmful," and this is on the heels of the opioid epidemic.

How did we so quickly forgot that the doctors were handing out opioids like candy, causing death and destruction throughout the country? Now we have people saying, "They would never do anything that would hurt children." How can anyone even think that?

And we know that these drug reps go in and push doctors to prescribe drugs. Hospitals are getting huge endowments from pharmaceutical companies. Jennifer Pritzker is a trans-identified male who has this huge family fortune and goes around giving huge sums of money to gender clinics and providing them with resources to go into the schools to recruit

> **How did we so quickly forgot that the doctors were handing out opioids like candy, causing death and destruction? Now we have people saying, "They would never do anything that would hurt children." How can anyone even think that?**

children.

Of course this is about money. If it were simply that they were encouraging children to question their gender identity, and that was it, I would still be upset with it, but it wouldn't be so horrifying. Once children start questioning they are quickly encouraged to get on puberty blockers, cross-sex hormones, and do surgeries.

I saw a blog post by a parent whose 11-year-old child said she was transgender a week ago. The mother was already pursuing puberty blockers These parents are being actively encouraged. Once a child in a peer group comes out as transgender, a lot of other kids start coming out as transgender. If you have parents who are embracing this ideology, there's a lot of pressure to start medicating their kids.

I want to talk about some of the negative side effects of these drugs. These are not benign drugs. I hear, "It's simply a pause. We're just pushing a pause button, giving them some time to think." That's a lie. That's just a blatant lie. They cause bone demineralization; they induce a developmental delay. Maria, can you think of any other situation where a parent would consent to a child being induced with a developmental delay, where they would celebrate that their child is being developmentally delayed, artificially?

Maria Keffler (11:25):

Puberty blockers slow brain development.

I'm thinking of a show that I just watched. It's a doctor who writes for the *New York Times*. She takes on these difficult medical cases where they can't find what's causing the problem. She crowdsources the cases and writes an article for the *Times*. It goes all over the world and then all these doctors and researchers try to figure out what is this rare disease or disorder.

She had this case of this young girl. I believe the problem started when the girl was about six. I think she's about 11 now, and having seizures.

She was having more and more rapid seizures. They're pretty sure that it's a brain issue. The resolution is to cut the two halves of the brain separate from each other, like they will occasionally do for really bad epilepsy.

The parents are agonizing over this because they're not 100% sure this is what it is. If they do this, their daughter will be mentally handicapped. If they don't do it, she will die in the next few years. I don't remember the resolution. At the end of the story, the parents were still trying to wrestle with whether they wanted to do this or not.

We know that Lupron and puberty blockers cause developmental delays. We know that up to 90% of children who express gender dysphoria, if allowed to pass through puberty naturally, will resolve and accept their birth sex. Even the World Professional Association on Transgender Health says that in their standards of care. If 90% of kids are going to resolve this if they go through puberty naturally, why would you not let them go through puberty naturally?

> **If 90% of kids are going to resolve their gender issues if they go through puberty naturally, why would you not let them go through puberty naturally?**

Erin Brewer (13:30):

Even for those who aren't going to have it resolved, why would you induce a developmental delay? Why would you cause them to have significant side effects?

Some of the stories from women who use Lupron for endometriosis are heartbreaking. They're wheelchair-bound and in pain for the rest of their lives. This is a serious drug.

Another concern that I've seen being raised is that these children are going to have to be put on growth hormones, because Lupron blocks development, including growth. These children are being put on blockers are having their growth stunted—especially for the girls who are identifying as boys—so now doctors are starting to push putting them on growth hormones.

We've got this cocktail of incredibly powerful drugs that we are putting children on: puberty blockers, potentially growth hormones, and then cross-sex hormones, all before the age of consent. All before they're really old enough to even understand the implications.

Maria Keffler (14:37):

Who benefits? The drug companies benefit. How convenient: "The drug that we gave you stunted your growth. We've got another drug that'll help that." How convenient.

Erin Brewer (14:47):

Then, "If you happen to be depressed because you didn't get results you were hoping for, don't worry, we've got a drug for that too." It's so insidious and the fact that we would be doing this to children...

We didn't even talk about some of the long-term effects of the combination of the puberty blockers and cross-sex hormones, which is infertility; their gonads never develop.

There's some thought that this combination of drugs will also inhibit sexual development. They'll never be able to grow up and have an orgasm.

These are things that kids don't think about. They don't even know what an orgasm is. Why are we doing this? If gender dysphoria is a normal developmental path, why don't we let them proceed down that path normally without medicalizing them?

Maria Keffler (15:42):

I want to know, is gender fixed or is it fluid?

Erin Brewer (15:48):

Apparently, it's fluid if you're moving towards transgenderism, but not if you're going the other way around.

Maria Keffler (15:59):

My question is if it's fluid and it can change at any point in your life, why would you ever medicalize that? Because what you medicalized toward today could be the opposite of what you want to be two years from now.

If gender is fixed, we need to know when is it fixed? Is it at birth? Is it fixed when you're 10? Is it fixed when you're 40? Then you should never medicalize outside of that fixed time period.

Erin Brewer (16:30):

We have two-year-olds whose parents claim they're transgender. We also have detransitioners who say, "I really thought I was transgender, but it turns out I made a mistake."

This whole thing is an experiment. It's a medical experiment. There is no diagnostic test or standard for transgenderism. We're medicating kids without even having diagnostic criteria for medication, other than the child saying that they feel like they were born in the wrong body. In what other case do we give a child medication based solely on the child's self-report of some kind of metaphysical disconnect between their brain and their body?

> ## This whole thing is an experiment.
> ## It's a medical experiment.

This is such a huge concern that children are just walking in. Often they're coached by their peers. We know this because we see it happening on social media. It's incredibly concerning, and I'm so thankful that there are doctors like Patrick Lappert and Michael Cretella who are bringing this up, because it's a huge question mark. How on earth are we justifying this?

It all comes down to big pharma.

> News Report (18:01):
>
> FDA's database currently lists more than 25,000 adverse events associated with Lupron, including suicidal thoughts, vision loss, and excruciating pain, even deaths. I started investigating Lupron in 2009.
>
> Lupron Victim 1 (18:15):
>
> My face is numb. My shoulders are numb. I feel dizzy. I just don't ever feel good.
>
> Lupron Victim 2 (18:26):
>
> I can't work full time. I suffer quite a bit.
>
> News Report (18:32):
>
> Several patients have sued Lupron's maker Abbot pharmaceuticals, now known as Abbvie, and the FDA did require several changes to add more side effects to Lupron's label. But many say that is not enough.
>
> Lupron Victim 3 (18:48):
>
> It's really sad to think that it's still on the market.

Dr. Michael Laidlaw (18:51):

How about this? How about for the so-called "transgender child"? So the gender identity—can you find it in a blood test? Can you do a testing of genetics or can you do a brain image and find the gender identity in there? You cannot, there is no objective test to diagnose this yet. We're giving very harmful therapies on the basis of no objective diagnosis.

What governs this whole system is the endocrine system. There's a small gland that's at the top there called the pituitary gland, which hangs off the brain and produces hormones, signaling hormones. You can see LH, FSH. These act on the gonads. So in the male, LH will act on the testicle to produce testosterone. You can see illustrated there. And then the female LH will act on the ovaries to make estrogen. And it's these hormones, which take the person through the stages of development and then available in adulthood.

Now there are medical conditions where this process is interrupted. We call it hypogonadotropic hypogonadism. This is something an endocrinologist would diagnose and treat. There are also hormones which can cause this to happen. Medications like Lupron—you may have heard of this used for prostate cancer. It works in this way to stop the pituitary from making this LH and lowering testosterone and preventing growth and spread of prostate cancer. It's also used in early puberty.

There's something called precocious puberty. This might start at say at age four. And so doctors can use this type of medication to delay it to a more appropriate age, like age 10.

What about using this medication for stopping normal puberty say at 12 or eight? This is an off-label, untested, experimental use. It hasn't been through any FDA approval process. It's what I would call a chemical conversion therapy.

You can see here illustrated our endocrine society is recommending for these kids to stop puberty at Tanner stage two, which is just the very beginnings of puberty. And you can see, they will not proceed through the other steps of puberty. This is what leads to infertility because they don't establish fertility.

Other problems of sexual dysfunction— On the *I Am Jazz* show Jazz says, "I don't have any sexual sensation. I don't have any orgasm." This is because puberty was stopped at this stage and never allowed to go forward.

More side-effects: I went through some of them. You're going to disrupt the normal brain development that's happening with the sex-based hormones. It actually disrupts normal bone development because the sex hormones are important. So osteoporosis is a future risk.

There are also neuropsychological effects. You can go yourself and look up the side effects of, say, Lupron: you'll see emotional lability, nervousness, anxiety, delusions. It even says monitor for development of worsening of psychiatric symptoms; use with caution with patients with a history of psychiatric illness.

I've already said many of these adolescents have neuropsychiatric conditions. Professor Michael Biggs at Oxford, through a Freedom of Information Act, found out what was going on in their Tavistock clinic. Children actually reported greater self-harm with this medication. Girls exhibited more behavioral and emotional problems, and greater dissatisfaction with their bodies.

Now you would think if you have these side effects with these medications, wouldn't you want to stop? Well, eventually they do stop, but limited studies have found that nearly a hundred percent end up going on to cross-sex hormones, which is the next step.

So cross-sex hormones are opposite-sex hormones, which are really wrong sex hormones will be the next stage. So if a female would be given testosterone—just to give you an idea how high these doses are—a normal adult female will have certain amount of testosterone, say in the range of 10 to 50—medical conditions can bring this up to 150, and tumors may make this as high as a thousand. They're recommending to get these levels in the 300 to 1000 range. This is some 10 to 40 times higher than the normal range.

And are there side effects from this? Of course there are. Both sexes have shown increased risk of myocardial infarction deaths due to cardiovascular disease. That's males taking estrogen, and females taking testosterone, with the male having five times increased risk of deadly blood clots, and two times increased risk of stroke. Females also been shown with liver dysfunction, hypertension, potential for cancer of the ovaries, of the breast.

I want to make this clear, there's no FDA approval for either of these medications, for this use, and even at the UCF pediatric site, it explains here, that's highlighted that there is no FDA approval for this, but they're looking at it through doing experiments.

Maria Keffler (23:47):

That is just heartbreaking. I know at the beginning of the video, the women who took the Lupron and suffered from it—this is a little bit tangential. Some years ago I went to a dentist I'd never been to before. I had never really had a cavity and suddenly she said I had cavities in all of my lower molars, and I didn't go for a second opinion. I should have, but I just let her drill them.

I've had nothing but problems with those teeth since then. I've had root canals and crowns on a couple of them. I look back and I have no proof of this, but I wonder if she was just making money off of me because I had never had a cavity.

I had really good teeth. I was so distraught at what I had done. I felt like I ruined my teeth. Why did I make this bad decision? It really bothered me for a long time.

Now I'm seeing these detransitioners who are asking the question, "Why didn't anybody stop me? Why did this happen?" These four women trusted their doctors. It is so sad.

Erin Brewer (25:00):

The pharmaceutical companies are throwing our confidence in healthcare under the bus. That becomes really concerning because like you said, it starts making us question, "Well if they're doing this with transgender health, what else are they doing it with? Where else do we need to be suspicious?"

There's this whole idea that doctors are in it to help people, they would never do anything to hurt us, they take the Hippocratic oath: "First, do no harm." So we would never have doctors doing these things. Ideally that would be lovely. We all want to have confidence and faith in our doctors. We want to believe that they only have our best interests at heart, but we know there are doctors out there that are not acting ethically. We know this, and yet we're able to put on those blinders.

We've had to enact legislation in order to guide doctors, because we know that they can go off the rails and do things that are dangerous and unhealthy for their patients. It's not unprecedented for legislation to be passed to provide safety for patients.

Yet when we talk about banning these highly experimental interventions on children, people get up in arms and say, "You can't tell doctors what to do."

Well, we can, and we need to, because they're human. In this case, I really think that they're being influenced by big pharma and also by this whole cult ideology. They're not thinking clearly. They're not examining this ideology at all. A lot of them are afraid of being taken down.

Maria Keffler (26:55):

There are a lot of ethical doctors who are concerned about this, but they're being pressured so much to conform and do what they're told. We know people have lost their jobs because they pushed back on this ideology. They've pushed back on this activism.

I think I've mentioned before that my husband's aunt works very high up in a healthcare insurance company. I asked her one time about someone I know who is addicted to a prescription drug. I asked, "How does this person keep getting this prescription drug?" She said, "Maria, you can get anything you want from a doctor. You go in, you just are very firm: 'I want this, I want this, I know the risks, give it to me.' They'll give it to you just to get you out of their office."

Erin Brewer (27:49):

I interviewed a doctor who works at a gender clinic for children, and that's basically what he said: "The customer's always right." It used to be that doctors were in important positions where they were the ones who controlled drugs in a responsible way, and that's just not happening at all now. You can probably Google, "If I want this drug, what do I say?"

These are children. I feel like we have a moral imperative to protect children, even if a parent says their children want it. We don't give kids heroin just because it's going make them happy. We don't let them drive at the age of 14, just because they want to. We don't allow them to book a hotel and get some alcohol and hire some prostitutes. We don't do that. We know that children's brains aren't fully developed, that they're not capable of making long-term decisions in their best interests. That's why they have parents or caregivers. And that's why we protect them.

Maria Keffler (29:06):

There are a lot of adults who don't necessarily make good decisions in their own long-term interests. We all are guilty of making poor decisions. I think about some of the decisions that I've made in my adult life that were just ill-informed. I decided something and I just didn't really have good information.

> **We don't give kids heroin just because it's going make them happy. We don't let them drive at the age of 14, just because they want to. We don't allow them to book a hotel and get some alcohol and hire some prostitutes. We don't do that. We know that children's brains aren't fully developed, that they're not capable of making long-term decisions in their best interests.**

Erin Brewer (29:34):

I spoke with my friend Billy Burleigh last week. He started on testosterone suppressors and estrogen, and then pretty quickly had his testicles and penis removed, had a penile inversion, then a brow shave and Adam's apple shave. He continued on and had rhinoplasty and another brow shave. I mean, he had so many surgeries because he was told this was the only way he was going to resolve the dysphoria that he had. He didn't have therapists to help examine the underlying causes.

Well, seven years down the line, he's just as depressed and has just as many problems, only now he's got debt from the surgeries and his body has significant issues. He has no genitalia anymore. He has no sex life. He has to take testosterone for the rest of his life. He's medicalized, and nobody ever helped him to identify the fact that he was a skinny shy kid who was bullied. He was sexually assaulted. He had a speech impediment. All of these things led him to really want to run away from himself, and rather than investigate any of that, they told him his only choice was to go down this path.

Maria Keffler (31:03):

I'd be curious to know how much big the pharmaceutical companies have made.

Erin Brewer (31:13):

And they will continue to earn. So even if this comes to an end, even if there's a lawsuit, even if the pharmaceuticals have to pay out some money, they're going to keep making money down the road because this whole generation of kids who have done this are going to have to take some kind of synthetic hormone for the rest of their lives.

Maria Keffler (31:34):

We are so careful in how we care for our kids.

Erin Brewer (31:40):

We made sure that we don't give them a bottle that has BPA.

Maria Keffler (31:46):

And we don't buy milk that came from cows that have growth hormone in it. We want everything organic and natural, and yet we're so sold out to medicalizing things.

Erin Brewer (32:03):

It's confusing. I think about all of those additional synthetic hormones going into our ecosystem.

One thing that just blew me away. There's a mother—a local activist mother whose daughter is being put on this path. I found it ironic that she was advocating not to spay and neuter animals because it's cruel. There's just a such a cognitive disconnect there.

> **There's a local activist mother whose daughter is being put on this path. I found it ironic that she advocates not to spay and neuter animals because it's cruel. There's just a such a cognitive disconnect there.**

Maria Keffler (32:36):

She's spaying and neutering children. That's what this is. This is spaying and neutering.

Erin Brewer (32:43):

This is eugenics against children who have a certain kind of mental health issue. This is no different than any other eugenics movement that has targeted a certain population, trying to eradicate those people. It's shocking that people aren't up in arms about this.

Maria Keffler (33:03):

We've been sold this idea that it's not kind to question this. Anytime you're told you can't question something, you need to question even more.

When you kick a hornet's nest, you know it. This is a hornet's nest and they're trying really hard to guard that nest and make sure that you don't find out what's inside, because this is not about the health of our children. This is not about helping them to be their authentic and valid selves. This is about an industry that is taking advantage of the most vulnerable in our population.

I just completed a survey of desisters and detransitioners—a very small survey, very informal.

Probably better than the surveys they use to justify what they're doing!

I was monitoring the results as they came in and I opened up the survey one day and we had 20 new responses. Well, I went through each one and it was very clear that it was the same person who had just kept answering the same way. We had 60 valid responses that I'm confident are valid. We had about 35 invalid responses. There were those 20 that were all identical and then there were some that people just made crude statements. There were some that they contradicted themselves on the survey. So I deleted all of the invalid ones.

But my question is, why are the trans rights people so scared of a detransitioner survey that they're going to try to submit all these faulty results?

Now I could say, "Oh, this is just kids being stupid.," but last week after we announced the results of this survey, somebody who's a prominent for trans rights posted on Twitter saying, "Ha Ha Ha! I submitted 20 invalid responses to this and I messed up all their data." Well, no you didn't. I deleted all your responses.

But I have to ask, "Why are you so scared of us asking people who detransitioned about their experience?" That is all the survey was: "Tell us about your experience; tell us what it was like." When the trans rights activists are so terrified that they try to mess up the data... A couple of them actually put that in their submission, "I'm just here to mess up your data and to announce that later and try to denounce your study, that the data is flawed because I messed it up."

Erin Brewer (36:05):

These are people who do not have the best interests of our children at heart. I believe that some of the parents have actually bought into this. I believe some parents honestly believe that this is the right thing to do for their children. It's because they've been steeped in this ideology, they're buying into it. They're not asking critical questions, because if you start asking critical questions, you get piled on. Like you said, people lose their jobs. People lose their friends. People can even be threatened.

Anytime you've got an ideology that's based on fear, and we're not allowed to ask questions, and that people are actively trying to discredit any concerns that we have, even though they're very valid concerns, it's something worth questioning.

Maria Keffler (36:59):

If the trans-rights activists were concerned about children's interests, they would be concerned about the detransitioners. They would want to know, "Why did you detransition? What happened? What can we learn from you?" They would want to use that information to help kids going forward. They would be concerned about that. Also the pharmaceutical companies and the insurance companies, when a child detransitioned, they would be willing to cover their surgeries to recon-struct. They would be willing to help them.

> **If the trans-rights activists really concerned about children's interests, they would be concerned about the detransitioners. They would want to know, "Why did you detransition? What happened? What can we learn from you?"**

Erin Brewer (37:36):

It is astonishing to me that young children who claim to have gender dysphoria, body dysmorphia, who are having discomfort because of their outward appearance—the trans activists say, "We have to swoop in, we have to help them. We have to change their external appearance or else they're going to kill themselves." But when a detransitioner says, "I'm having a lot of discomfort about the way that these treatments changed my physical appearance," they say, "Live with it, just buck up, deal with it. It's not that bad to me."

Apparently, your feelings are valid if they're going towards this ideology, but they're not valid if they're going away from it.

Maria Keffler (38:19):

We have a couple of questions from parents that we'd like to address. "My son's therapist says that Lupron puts a pause on puberty to give him more time to decide about your gender identity. What's with giving a child a little extra time?"

Erin Brewer (38:37):

Doesn't that sound so benign? "We're just going to put them on a pause. It's reversible." Why are people getting so upset about this, Maria?

Maria Keffler (38:49):

Because as we've already covered, it's not a pause. It's not reversible. Puberty has a small finite window. It's a window of time that you pass through. When it closes, when you're past it, it doesn't open back up again. You can't go back; you've missed it. It's important psychologically. It's important physically. Everything about puberty is about changing your child into an adult and if you miss that, it's gone.

Erin Brewer (39:26):

It's concerning. I call it the Peter Pan drug, because what we're doing is keeping children as children while their peers are developing into adults. That is not something you can put a pause on. Not only is it causing them to become physically developmentally delayed, but also mentally delayed, and it's causing damage to their bones. Who knows what else, because we don't have longitudinal studies?

But as their peers are progressing, they're not. So any discomfort that they feel—any sense of not fitting in, not being in the right body—is going to be increased as everybody around them is developing and they're not. They're missing out on important opportunities with their peers. It's a physical, emotional, social, and developmental delay that is being induced. You can't reverse that.

Maria Keffler (40:19):

I just happened to think about this when you were talking about the delays to their development. My neighbor is an art teacher and he told me about this kid that he teaches in high school. He said, "Freshman year, this kid was the shortest, tiniest, scrawniest kid in the class." My neighbor said, "I came back after summer vacation, sophomore year—this kid grew like a foot, put on like 30 pounds over the summer. I didn't even recognize him." He had this enormous growth spurt.

That's not unusual. One of my kids grew an inch in three weeks. One of my kids went up two shoe sizes in three weeks. They have these growth spurts. What if that kid had been put on Lupron? He would never have grown. He would never have attained manhood.

We have such a fascination with youth in our culture. I was listening to the radio the other day. I won't quote the song because the music industry is draconian, but there's a popular song and it talks about not getting older. "We're not going to grow up. We're not going to—we're always going to be young. We're always going to be free."

Well, you're going to grow up whether you like it or not. I mean, you might not mature, but you're going to get older. Things are going to change.

When did we stop wanting to be mature? When did we stop wanting to be adults? When I was a kid, I couldn't wait to grow up. I couldn't wait to be an adult.

Erin Brewer (42:02):

There's a whole narrative about how hard it is to be an adult. These kids start going through puberty and they hear, "It's so hard." I read a book about how kids aren't striving to meet the same goals that their peers did generations earlier, like driving. Kids aren't going out and getting their driver's licenses. Kids aren't dating. There's this whole generation that seems afraid to grow up. That is so sad. If you have kids who are afraid to grow up, that makes it all more attractive to go on puberty blockers. They never have to grow up.

Maria Keffler (42:40):

Interesting. A few years ago my son was 13, so he would have been eighth grade or so. He said, "Mom, I'm just afraid that I'm not going to be successful in high school, and I'm not going to be able to do the work. And I'm scared about college." We talked through it and I said, "Well, you're not in high school right now. You're in junior high. How have you done so far?" He said, "Okay," and I said, "So you have been successful in this phase of life that you're in right now. When you get to high school, you'll be older. Why do you think you will not be equally successful? If we put you in high school right now, you wouldn't be all right."

Now he's about to graduate as a senior. He's done great, but I just tried to empathize with him, "Don't borrow trouble from the future. If you're 13, you're not ready to be a senior in high school, but by the time you're a senior in high school, you're probably going to be ready for it."

But not if you've taken puberty blockers, because those block your development. We need to fight against the use of puberty blockers. We use medications with serious side effects when there's a disease but we should never use these kinds of invasive treatments if it's a normal developmental path.

Do we have time for one more question? "My daughter says, if she doesn't start testosterone, she's going to commit suicide. She's absolutely convinced testosterone will fix her. How do I convince her that that's not going to help?"

This is a problem, because what happens is one girl in a peer group will get testosterone and the others will see it and want it.

Initially when a girl starts testosterone there is a high. This is a steroid; it's a controlled substance. It causes this great feeling initially. If you and I took testosterone, initially we'd feel really good. We'd get some muscle, we'd get a little bounce in our step. We feel pretty darn good. But over the long-term it's causing these huge problems, just like other drugs that make us feel really good. We don't tend to encourage our children to take them.

If the same child came to you and said, "I want heroin. I want alcohol. If you don't give it to me, I'm going to kill myself," what would the response be? Would you say, "Oh my gosh, okay. We don't want you to kill yourself. I'm going to go find a drug dealer and I'll get you what you want." We don't do that because we know it's not in the best interest of the kid. So a parent needs to very carefully assess: Is this child genuinely suicidal? There are lots of resources online that you can access to determine, "Is this a valid threat? Is this child genuinely suicidal?" In which case you have to take it seriously.

But in case after case, we hear of kids using the suicide threat to get what they want, because they've been coached to do it.

We don't capitulate to suicide threats, because what that does is it sets a child up to use that as emotional blackmail in the future. What happens when they're 16 and they want to drive your car and you won't let them? If they threatened suicide, are you going to let them? This sets up a pattern of behavior where the child feels like they can manipulate people in a way that's dangerous.

> **If a child came to you and said, "I want heroin. I want alcohol. If you don't give it to me, I'm going to kill myself," what would the response be? Would you say, "Oh my gosh, okay. We don't want you to kill yourself. I'm going to go find a drug dealer and I'll get you what you want." We don't do that because we know it's not in the best interest of the kid.**

Maria Keffler (46:57):

That's something that sometimes happens in intimate relationships. I've mentioned this before, when I was 19, I had a boyfriend who I broke up with and he just kept stringing me along with, "I'm going to kill myself if we're not together, I'm going to kill myself."

That's not a healthy coping strategy. That's not something anyone should do to someone else. I want to echo what you said: when a child does express suicide, you do need to take that seriously. Look up some of those online resources, how to figure out if this is a genuine threat or not. We've seen case after case where kids were coached to threaten suicide to get what they want.

Erin Brewer (47:42):

Even mental health professionals have encouraged children to do this. It is important to do an assessment. Keep in mind that we don't give kids what they want because they threaten suicide. If we have a generation of kids that learns that all they have to do is threaten suicide to get what they want, we're going to be in so much trouble. I hope people will do some research and question when doctors say that puberty blockers are reversible, think to yourself, "Does that even make sense? Does it make sense that that the developmental delay would be reversible? Can that child go back in time and relive their childhood if they decide they want to get off these puberty blockers?"

The other thing is that we didn't mention that I just want to mention quickly is that most kids who are on puberty blockers go on to take cross-sex hormones. I believe there's a reason for that. These kids are having their puberty blocked. The very cure to their gender dysphoria is being blocked with puberty blockers. So they're much more inclined to go on cross-sex hormones than a child who has gender dysphoria who isn't put on blockers.

Maria Keffler (49:04):

Puberty is the cure for gender dysphoria in a lot of cases. Even WPATH, the World Professional Association for Transgender Health, says that up to 96% of children have their gender dysphoria resolved if allowed to progress naturally through puberty.

Erin Brewer (49:20):

It's the vast majority.

Maria Keffler (49:22):

They will resolve their gender dysphoria and accept their birth sex if they pass through puberty naturally, that's the key, puberty is the cure for a lot of gender dysphoria in children.

Episode 15 Resource List

Dr. Michael Laidlaw: https://youtu.be/rYtGPLpW-g8

KTNV More women come forward with complaints about Lupron side effects: https://youtu.be/ZsCMxf7DfuY

Episode 16: When Parents Disagree

https://youtu.be/8atJK0ld0Sw

<u>Maria Keffler (00:45)</u>:

Today we're talking about when parents disagree. Another tough topic.

<u>Erin Brewer (00:54)</u>:

It can be difficult. If you're in a marriage and you're disagreeing with your spouse about how to handle your trans-identified kid, or if you're divorced and your spouse is affirming and encouraging that identity, in either case, it can be difficult.

<u>Maria Keffler (01:10)</u>:

There are definitely too many different threads of this, too many different individual situations. As you mentioned, if there's divorce, if there are step-parents, if there's animosity, there's really more than we're going to be able to cover in an episode. I'm not a marriage and family therapist. Erin, you're not either. Our purpose here today is to explore what some of those issues may be, and talk about some of the ways you might be able to resolve some of them, and investigate some ways that you can support your child if all the adults in the picture aren't on the same page.

<u>Erin Brewer (01:56)</u>:

If you are in a marriage and your spouse just disagrees with you about how to handle the situation, it's important to preserve that relationship. That relationship is important for you and your spouse, but it's also important for your child. If your child is already struggling, marital strife can compound the situation.

This is one area where I would suggest that it might be worth reexamining boundaries and to consider softening a little bit and try to come to some common ground. A lot of times when spouses have a disagreement about something, they can get entrenched in their position. If you're willing to give a little bit every so often, that is an opportunity for the spouse to also give and compromise a little bit.

<u>Maria Keffler (02:45)</u>:

It's important to keep in mind that your spouse loves your child. There are situations where there may be abuse. There may be unhealthy acts or an unhealthy spouse, but most of the time, both parents love that child and want what's best for that child. They may differ on what that best path is.

Try to approach your spouse with an attitude of, "We're not enemies. We're both on the same side. We both want the best outcomes for our child." Give your spouse the benefit of the doubt that he or she has good intentions.

You're right. It's so easy to get into an enemy mindset. Years ago my husband and I were in a marriage topic class together with a friend. This friend comes from a military background and he talked about advice that his father gave him when he and his wife got married. The father said, "Very often when a husband and wife are at odds with each other, there's a problem. And they get that problem between them and they're on opposite sides of it shooting at the problem, but they end up shooting at each other. He said, "You need to both get on the same side, shooting at the problem from the same side, so that you're fighting the problem and not fighting each other."

I thought that was such a great visual and a good way to think about it. It's a good starting point to just say, "I don't want to be your enemy here. I'm not angry with you. I want us to work together. I want to be a team on this. How can we work together and support each other?"

Erin Brewer (04:40):

It can be hard if you have a spouse who fundamentally disagrees with you about this issue. If your spouse honestly believe that it's appropriate to affirm a child and honestly believes that your child is at risk of self-harm or suicide if the child is not affirmed. That can get intense because these are two very different ideologies.

You can try to use some of the techniques that we've talked about for deprogramming the child for deprogramming your spouse. With your spouse, depending on who they are, some spouses are more emotionally driven. Some spouses are more logically driven. If you can find a way to reach them, to present your side of it so that they understand where you're coming from and kind of find a neutral ground, something like, "We totally disagree with this. I'm willing to use the child's new name if we agree we're not going to allow medicalization."

These kinds of compromises can help so you are not at odds with each other. If you start fighting with each other and that's the focus, your child is not going to get the support that he or she needs and that child is more likely to get pulled more deeply into this trans cult.

Maria Keffler (06:06):

It's important to remember if there are other children in the picture as well, you still need to parent those other children. If everything in your family is revolving around this trans issue, you're not going to be able to effectively parent your other children.

Children who have siblings who are trans-identified have some very specific needs. Some things that are specific to them that they need special help with. We're going to do an episode on that soon.

Erin Brewer (06:47):

The other thing that is so important—and it's easy to do this—is to try not to vilify your spouse and not say things to the child like, "You're just like your father" or "You're just like your mother," which creates a divide. It's so easy to slip into that.

There have been times where I have said something to my children about their father that wasn't appropriate. I try to go back and apologize, because in the heat of the moment, sometimes it's hard not to. But the more you can disassociate your spouse from this actual problem, the better. It is important not to vilify them so that your kids aren't getting the impression that you disagree about everything, or that there's something inherently wrong with your spouse. Hopefully the spouse can do that with you also. That's not always easy.

I have heard of instances where spouses have actually aligned with the trans-identified child to go after the other spouse. That's a difficult situation. What would you recommend for parents in that case?

Maria Keffler (08:04):

Before I address that, I wanted to reiterate something you said. I want to echo that apologizing—if you need to apologize to your child, if you need to apologize to your spouse—that's really powerful. It's really effective. It's really appropriate.

A lot of times, as parents, we're afraid if we apologize to our child, we're going to lower our authoritative status. Well we're not. We're modeling appropriate behavior. When you wrong someone, when you do something you shouldn't have, apology is appropriate. Our kids are not going to learn to apologize for their errors if we don't model it. And with your spouse, if you did something that you shouldn't have—if you undercut your spouse or you insulted him or her—apology is appropriate for that.

It is important from a parenting perspective that children see parents as a unit, as much as possible. We should be coming to our kids with one mind, one attitude, as parents presenting a united front. When we don't, children will try to divide and conquer.

Every parent has had the experience when their child says, "Can I go over to Jimmy's and spend the night?" You ask, "What did your dad say?" The child says, "Dad said I could." Then you talk to your husband and he says, "No, I didn't say that. I didn't say that at all." Or one parent says, "No." So the child goes to the other parent. That's so common.

Of course that's going to happen with the transgender issue as well. If one parent is not in favor of it, the child is going to try to get the other parent, or the other adults in his or her life to try to support him/her in that.

If that's happening, it's important to sit down and have a talk with your spouse and say, "I realize we don't agree on this, but this is unhealthy for our family. It's unhealthy for our marriage. It's unhealthy for this child. It's unhealthy for our whole family. If you and I are on opposite sides of this, we've got to find a way that we can work together."

One good way to start doing that is to sit down when you're alone. Try to do it in a calm moment, and say, "I want to understand where you're coming from. I'm not sure that I understand your position on this." Put your own opinion and your own needs on the back burner for the moment and ask your spouse, "Please tell me what you think about this. Please tell me your perspective on this."

> **Put your own opinion and your own needs on the back burner for the moment and ask your spouse, "Please tell me what you think about this. Please tell me your perspective on this."**

I'll tell a story from my marriage. My husband is very, very logical. I kind of joke that he is like Mr. Spock from *Star Trek*. I seem like an empath compared to my husband, and my husband would consider that a compliment.

He thinks very quickly and he thinks very logically. Often, he will make a statement about something, like when my daughter wanted to watch a certain movie. We were talking about it around the dinner table a few weeks ago. My husband said, "No, we're not going to watch that. We're going to watch this tonight."

I felt like he was being a big bully: "You get to decide? There's five of us here." So I talked to him about it later. There was a very good reason why we should not watch that movie and why this other one was actually a good one to watch that night. He had walked through all of this logic in his head, and it had to do with the movie no longer being on Netflix, so we'd have to go get it somewhere else. But he had a logical thought process and he got to the end of it and just presented it.

As much as people joke that women expect men to read their minds, my husband often thinks, "Well, my logic process is very clear. Why is everyone not tracking with it?" I have to tell him, "The rest of us don't think like you do."

I said this to my husband, "Can you walk me through why you said that? Because my initial reaction was, 'You're just a big selfish bully who wants to watch what you want to watch.'"

Erin Brewer (12:48):

The other thing you mentioned that I'm thinking is important is that there's a lot of stress on a family when this is happening. It's important to connect with your spouse, not relating to this issue at all.

Find opportunities to go out on dates, find opportunities to go for walks. Maybe even say, "We're going to set aside this and not talk about our kid." It is important to focus on your relationship, because ultimately that child is going to grow up and move away and you want your marriage still to be there and to be healthy.

This is an issue that could easily divide marriages, but marriages can withstand significant disagreements, as long as the focus is on loving each other and realizing that each spouse ultimately wants what's best for the child. Just because you disagree with your spouse, doesn't mean that they're a bad person. It just means that you have this trans ideology, and many don't realize how damaging it is.

Five years ago, I would have been totally into it. Education is so important because I suspect that most parents who are affirming their child are doing it because of the lies that have been promulgated by trans activists. It's just a matter of very gently presenting alternative information.

One of the things that I learned with my husband is that if I'm able to find another route to provide him with information, other than myself, sometimes that can be helpful. Part of that is because we've lived together so long that when I say something he's like, "Yeah, yeah, yeah." But if he can hear it from somebody else, sometimes it's a little bit less emotionally laden and he will open up to it.

If you can find somebody else who agrees with you and aligns with you and your thought processes, consider asking them to talk to your spouse. Sometimes that can be effective, or send them information from a credible source that they'll respect.

Maria Keffler (15:19):

That's a great suggestion. My husband and I went through a period in our marriage that was very, very stressed. We've been married 21 years now. I think we'd been married ten years or so when this was going on. At the time my husband had a friend who was actually an associate pastor at our church and my husband really respected him. There were times I would say "A, B, C, and D" and my husband would say, "No, that's wrong because E F, G, and H." I'd say, "Why don't you talk to Bo about this and see what he says?" My husband would often come back and say, "Bo said A, B, C, and D."

Erin Brewer (16:11):

That can be frustrating, but it is the nature of marriage. I probably do that with my husband. There are times where he'll say something and I'll say, "I need some documentation." I do it too. I don't take his word for things sometimes. You live with your spouse and you know their weaknesses and strengths.

One of the things that is my motto is, "Let's cut each other some slack." I say this a lot. What I mean by that is we need to realize that our intentions are good, that we're a team, and that we can work through this, even when we disagree about things. If you can approach it like that, it will be helpful. When your spouse is saying something that you disagree with, don't dismiss what he or she is saying, even if you think they're talking gibberish. If you do that, that's going to create a divide.

We did an episode about validating someone and this is where it comes in handy, is with your spouse. If you can say, "So I hear what you're saying and I understand that you're feeling this way."

Imagine if you were in the other position where you thought that what your spouse was doing would cause your child to commit suicide. That's what they believe. So imagine yourself on the other side and try to be empathetic. This is a spouse who's desperately worried about a child based on misinformation that they've gotten.

Maria Keffler (18:00):

That validation and asking your spouse to explain his or her position is so important, because what you can do is ask questions during that time.

You may be 100% sure that you're right and that they're wrong, but give your spouse a platform to explain themselves.

I had this happen for me when someone has asked me to explain myself, and when I'm talking about what I believe, I suddenly realize, "You know what, this sounds kind of crazy actually, now that I'm saying this."

Or you can ask your spouse, "This is suicide statistic I hear that a lot. Where does that come from?" Ask for some documentation on that, ask those questions that are going to help lead your spouse to question some of his or her own beliefs. If those beliefs are accurate and you realize, "I'm not completely right," be humble enough to change your mind and say, "You know what I think you might be right."

I'm not saying that with the trans issue, as there are a lot of lies there that are coming from the opposite side. I'm thinking more in general, if you're arguing with someone and you realize that they've got a point, then you say, "You know what, you're right about that. I think I'm going to change my mind about that."

Erin Brewer (19:30):

And the other thing I was thinking about—if you're in a marriage, there are all sorts of other issues that come up in a marriage.

One of the things that you can do, because this is so important, is stop pushing back about some of the other things that you disagree with your spouse about. If they feel like they're just hitting a wall every time they talk to you because you disagree with everything, then it's not going to be as powerful as if you are willing to just let some things slide and make this be the thing that you're firm about. Then there isn't as much conflict in the marriage.

If you're disagreeing about everything, your spouse might just think, "Oh gosh, they don't agree with me about anything." But if you're willing to say, "I think you're right about that and that, and that and that, but I'm concerned about this one thing." It's focusing your energy. It gives you a little bit more credibility with your spouse. They're not feeling like you're just disagreeing with them because you're disagreeable.

Maria Keffler (20:41):

Another powerful thing that I've found in my own marriage is saying, "Thank you" to your spouse for anything and everything you can. If your husband unloads the dishwasher, say "Thank you." If your wife picks up that thing at the store that you needed, say "Thank you." That's really powerful. It's hard to be angry at someone who appreciates you. It's called the Benjamin Franklin effect, that someone feels more warmth toward a person for whom they have done a favor.

> **It's hard to be angry at someone who appreciates you. It's called the Benjamin Franklin effect, that someone feels more warmth toward a person for whom they have done a favor.**

If your spouse did something for you and you appreciate them for it, that Benjamin Franklin effect is going to kick in where they want to get a little bit more. Maybe they will want to do more things for you to get a little bit more appreciation, and it does help build and strengthen your marriage.

We're talking a lot about marriages that are intact and spouses that are living together. I don't have personal experience with an ex-husband or ex-wife, but some of these same tactics and strategies you can use, even with an ex. You can set aside time to talk about your child. You can appreciate other things about that person and the things that they're doing. Find ways to agree, and find ways to appreciate each other.

Erin Brewer (22:09):

My parents were divorced. One of the hardest things for me was the fact that when my mom was mad at me, she would say, "You're just like your dad." When my dad was mad at me, he would say, "You're just like your mom." There was constant fighting and I was constantly having to choose sides and that is incredibly difficult for a kid. It feels like if I'm friends with Mom, then I'm betraying Dad. If I'm friends with Dad, I'm betraying Mom. It puts a kid in a situation where there's no way they're going to win.

As angry as you could be with a spouse (or ex-spouse) who is affirming a child, it is so important not to project that onto the child and to make them have to choose and to make them feel like there's something bad about that spouse. Remember, that child is half that spouse. If they feel like that spouse is a bad person, then that means something about them might be bad.

A lot of times kids will assume that the divorce was their fault. It's important to try and foster a better relationship, even if your spouse is someone that you completely absolutely cannot stand. Try not to suggest to your children that your ex-spouse is a bad person.

Maria Keffler (23:42):

That's a good point. There's something we do need to address and it's so difficult, but I know that it's happening to so many people where your ex-spouse lets your child be trans-identified. At your house, the trans-identified child is not affirmed in the transgender identity.

That becomes a place where the child can divide and conquer. I know far too many situations where the child decided to go live with the spouse that's going to put them on the path to transition or with the parent who's going to put them on the path to transition and they cut off the other parent.

Erin Brewer (24:30):

This is increasingly happening. The child has left and gone to live with the affirming parent. It is difficult, but keep the door open and let that child know you love them and that you're there for them. If all they feel is animosity and judgment from a parent, then it's going to be harder for them to come to that parent if they realize they've made a mistake, and it's going to be harder for them to accept that they've made a mistake in the first place, because they get entrenched.

> **If all a child feels is animosity and judgment from a parent, then it's going to be harder for them to come to that parent if they realize they've made a mistake.**

There are parents I've talked to who will not budge an inch on this. That that might be a mistake. Each parent has to make a decision, but if your only option to see your child and to have some loving influence on them is to use their preferred name, I would consider it.

I'm not saying that you should do that in every case. Each person has to make that choice. I've talked to parents who will never do that. That's a personal choice but if you can be a little bit flexible in that, just so that your child knows you're there for them and doesn't completely cut of contact, that that might be the way to go.

Maria Keffler (26:26):

As a parent you might be sowing a lot into this child and maybe not getting much back. These kids can be militant in what they want and then their demands just keep increasing, increasing, increasing, I've talked to parents who have said, "I did everything the child wanted. I did the names, I did the pronouns, I got the binder. I let them have the surgeries."

And still sometimes you lose contact with the child. There's no guarantees with this.

Erin Brewer (27:03):

That's where one of the things that you actually recommend in your book—at some point parents have to accept that they might lose contact with their child. Once you accept that, then you're more able to make decisions. If you realize that no matter what I do, I might lose that child, so what is it that I'm willing to do?

Maybe you're willing to use their chosen name, but not their pronouns. It may be that you're not willing to do any of that. You're willing to say, "Okay, I'm putting my foot down." It might mean that I lose contact with my child, or you might do everything that they want them to do.

There isn't a right or a wrong answer here at all. The goal is to keep yourself as healthy as you can be. If you're in an intact marriage, preserve that, because that marriage is going to help. If you're divorced already, it's already so much more complicated.

I just feel for these parents. I've talked to so many parents who have an ex, and a lot of times it seems like that ex-spouse is encouraging the transgender identity almost as a way to punish the other parent. It's being used as weapon. I'm seeing this a lot and it's heartbreaking because these children are being used as pawns.

> **A lot of times it seems like that ex-spouse is encouraging the transgender identity almost as a way to punish the other parent. It's being used as a weapon. I'm seeing this a lot and it's heartbreaking, because these children are being used as pawns.**

Maria Keffler (28:25):

It's a painful process to go through. I am a firm believer that love and truth will always prevail in the end. I really believe at some point, these kids are all going to wake up.

Erin Brewer (28:45):

I agree. I was taught by my mother to hate my father. There was this constant message that my father was a bad person, that he was an evil capitalist. She hated my father. She blamed my father for every problem that she had in life.

It got to the point where I had no contact with my father and I thought he was completely evil. I cut him off because I had integrated all of these messages from my mother. And then once I was away from my mother and gone to college and on my own for a while, I started to look back and think, "Wow, there were things that my father did that showed that he did love me and that he did care about me and I probably shouldn't have cut him off."

Unfortunately he no longer is open to a relationship. He was too hurt.

Always be open and know that your child might be 21 or 25 or 28 or 40, and they might come around and want to have a relationship with you. Be open to that, because that is going to be an opportunity for you to reconcile and heal.

Maria Keffler (30:10):

We need to keep in mind that *we* are the adults. *We* are the ones who have to act selflessly. *We* have to pour into the relationship.

> **We need to keep in mind that *we* are the adults. *We* are the ones who have to act selflessly. We have to pour into the relationship.**

It's so easy as a parent to get hurt. Kids can hurt us terribly. They can say things that are so cutting and so painful or cut us off completely. It's easy to get angry and say, "Do you have any idea what I've done for you? You should appreciate me more."

But we need to remember that we are the adults and we have to act like it. Our kids are depending on us to be the adults. It may cause us a lot of pain. It may take a lot of years but I really do believe if we continue to love our kids, we continue to speak truth that eventually that truth and that love is going to be recognized: "Mom really loved me. Mom really cared."

Sadly there may be a situation where you are estranged from your child for a long period of time but you just have to do what you can do to keep that relationship open.

Erin Brewer (31:31):

The parents are the adults here and it's our job.

There have been times when my kids have been so mad at me. There's been a lot of discomfort in the house and a lot of tension for weeks, maybe months on end, because one of my kids is mad at me.

If you are a parent who's never had a child mad at you, maybe you're not setting firm enough boundaries, because it's typical. This is very typical adolescent behavior for them to be mad.

Another thing that's pretty typical is for kids is to play the parents against each other. This trans ideology is the perfect opportunity for kids to do these things that is very typical among adolescents.

Unfortunately the stakes are high here and it can result in children being damaged for life. But also recognize, even if your child goes the worst route possible and gets completely medicalized, they need to know in the end that you're going to be there with open arms. That's what detransitioners need.

I've talked to detransitioners who say, "My parents don't want anything to do with me because of the decisions that I made." That's heartbreaking. These kids finally realized they made a mistake and their parents were so upset with them that they're not there for them anymore.

I urge parents, even if your child went to an ex-spouse, went through all these treatments, and you are so angry at them for what they did, still have a soft heart for them, still be there for them. Because at some point I do believe that they'll need you and they'll want to come home.

Maria Keffler (33:29):

Keep a candle in the window.

Kids need their parents. They need their parents' unconditional love. It's hard to give. It's hard when you've been hurt. And when you have seen it from the beginning and said, "This path has no good end" and the child took it anyway—receive them when they come back. Be there for them. Because if their own parents can't love them—if that's their perception: "My own parents can't love and accept me"—where are they ever going to find love and acceptance in their lives?

> **If their own parents can't love them—if that's their perception: "My own parents can't love and accept me"—where are they ever going to find love and acceptance in their lives?**

They're going to look for it. They're going to try to find it somewhere.

That's part of this ideology. The other adults in the school, these glitter moms and social media groomers—that's what they're doing. They're telling your kid, "Your parents don't love you. If they don't let you go down this path, they don't love you. And even if they let you go down this path, they don't love you as much as I do."

Until very recently, adults recognized that as predatory behavior. Schools prioritized parental authority until recently. Adults recognized that you don't go behind parents' backs. The parent-child relationship has been sacred across time and across cultures. I don't think there's any culture in history, until this thing with trans ideology, where the parents were considered superfluous or unnecessary.

There are studies that show the best outcomes for kids are kids who have intact families in which to live—intact biological families. That is the best outcome for a child. And this ideology is attacking that. It's destroying that. You and your spouse are the only ones who are going to protect your kids from that.

Erin Brewer (35:41):

It is tough. I would encourage people who are struggling with this to find resources for how to strengthen the marriage. Because if your marriage is intact, you want to keep it that way. That's going to be the best outcome for your child.

Maria Keffler (36:01):

Well, this has been another tough topic. There's probably a lot more that we could have said about different family makeups, but the important thing is to just try as much as you can to be on the same page with your spouse and to recognize that you both love your child and you want what's best for the child and try to focus on *what's* right, rather than *who's* right. Try to work together to find the right thing for your family and for your child.

Erin Brewer (36:33):

Realize that in the grand scheme of things, as hard as this is now, it's a passing thing. You want your marriage to continue after this. You do need to focus on nurturing your marriage. It's okay to have disagreements with your spouse; that's pretty normal in marriage. Just invest in growing the marriage. You can have this disagreement but you still love each other, and you're still going to stay committed to each other so that you have that marriage after the child grows up and moves out and moves on with his or her life.

Episode 16 Resource List

When Spouses Disagree About Parenting:
https://www.positiveparenting.com/when-spouses-disagree-about-parenting-issues/

What To Do When Parents Don't Agree on Discipline:
https://youtu.be/If2c3TllsOU

5 Successful Methods used in Marriage Therapy & Counseling:
https://guidedoc.com/methods-marriage-therapy-counseling

The Gottman Institute: https://www.gottman.com/

Vicar Resigns as Primary School Imposes Transgender Ideology:
https://youtu.be/HQ57zai5Cpk

Parent Resource Guide: https://genderresourceguide.com/

Parents' Rights in Education https://www.parentsrightsined.org/

Keeping Kids Safe in Public School:
https://arlingtonparentcoa.wixsite.com/arlingtonparentcoa/parents-guide-to-kids-safety-in-aps

Materials for Parents:
https://www.partnersforethicalcare.com/materials-for-parents

Episode 17: Parenting Siblings of Gender-Confused Children

https://youtu.be/w_V9EqMZLdw

<u>Maria Keffler (00:47):</u>

Today we are going to talk about parenting siblings of transgender-identified kids. This is a topic that doesn't get much, if any, coverage.

One of the things I do when I'm getting ready for one of our talks is to look at the literature that's out there. I look at what other people are saying. I look for some experts to speak about what we're going to talk about.

I couldn't find anything for today's talk. The only things that I could find about siblings of transgender-identified kids were all about getting the sibling to support the trans-identified kid—how to teach the sibling transgender ideology, how to get the siblings on board with the so-called affirmative care.

That's not at all what I want to talk about today. What I'd like to talk about is very specific, unique needs of kids whose brother or sister has adopted a transgender identity, because this affects the whole family. This isn't just between the trans-identified child and the parents. There are specific things that are going on laterally between the kids that parents need to be aware of.

Remember, you're not just parenting the child who's in crisis, you're parenting the siblings as well.

<u>Erin Brewer (02:20):</u>

In a lot of ways, this reminds me of parenting a special-needs child within a family and how that special-needs child can be the focus of the family and attention of the parents often leaving the other siblings out. Parents don't intentionally leave siblings out, but it happens just because the special-needs child requires so much care and attention.

However, it's a little bit different, because often, in this case, the siblings are being manipulated by the trans-identified child in a way that can be concerning and that parents need to know about.

I interviewed a mother who had a child who was trans-identifying and she found out that her trans-identifying child was threatening suicide if the younger siblings didn't call him by the pronoun and name he wanted to be called by.

This is an incredibly manipulative thing for an older child to do to younger siblings.

> **The trans-identifying child was threatening suicide if the younger siblings didn't call him by the pronoun and name he wanted to be called by. This is an incredibly manipulative thing for a child to do to younger siblings.**

I grew up in a home where this happened. My brother often threatened suicide if I didn't do things for him. His issues were different. He had addictive behavior, but if I didn't cover for him, he'd say, "I'm going to kill myself" or "I'm going to kill myself, if you don't do this."

Threats like that for a younger sibling can be so overwhelming. Of course I did what he wanted me to do without question, because the last thing I wanted to do was to have his blood on my hands. I thought, "Of course I'm going to accommodate this."

Parents need to know how powerful these kinds of threats are. Even if the child doesn't overtly tell the siblings, "I'm going to kill myself if you don't do what I want you to do," that might be a message that they're hearing from the trans community, from activists, from teachers, from neighbors. They might be hearing this message, "If you don't do what your trans-identified sibling says to do, there's this threat of suicide," which is just so overwhelming.

Maria Keffler (04:28):

It's so emotionally manipulative, but you're right: that's what everyone's being told. If you "misgender," or not use the preferred pronouns for a transgender-identified person, that's going to make that person suicidal. The kids are hearing this.

I know of one family where the mom had the kids at the pool and found out later the transgender-identified child told her sister, "I'm going to dunk you and hold you under the water, unless you use my preferred name."

Erin Brewer (05:12):

The bullying component comes in. That suicide threat is a way of bullying, and that kind of aggressive behavior that says, "I'm going to bully you into compliance" is scary for kids.

Maria Keffler (05:30):

Any child can be bullied. Any sibling relationship can have a bullying element to it. A lot of times parents aren't aware that it's going on. You're not seeing what's going on with your children.

I have three kids and when they were very small, I remember somebody telling me, "Those kids have lives together that you know nothing about." And I was like, "What are you talking about? I'm the mom. I know everything. I see all. I have eyes everywhere. I see everything." But I don't. I don't actually know everything that's going on. We need to be aware of that.

You can't force good, happy or deep conversations to happen. You can't force your child to tell you things, but it's important to make space where those opportunities can come up.

Have a time where you just take one of your kids out to dinner, out to breakfast. I try to have dates with my kids occasionally, where I just go out with one. Go without an agenda, or with an unspoken agenda. And while you're out having dinner or breakfast, just ask, "How are things going? What's going on? Tell me about your life. Is anything bothering you? Is anything troubling? Tell me something great that happened this week. Tell me something not so great that happened this week."

With young children this is especially important. If the trans-identified child is older, it's almost guaranteed there's some bullying going on with the younger children.

Erin Brewer (07:27):

These trans-identifying kids are encouraged to adopt bullying behavior with others. It would be highly unlikely that they're not using it on their siblings, because they're being trained to be bullies.

That's so unfortunate, but as you said, it's important for parents to make time for the trans-identified child to have opportunities to connect. It is just as important to do that with the siblings. Those kids need your attention. They're seeing their other sibling create a ruckus in the house and potentially being a bully. They need some support from you.

It's tough because even when there is obvious bullying going on, sometimes the parents don't know what to do.

When I got a little bit older, my brother and I fought. He had so much anger towards me and he would beat me when my parents weren't around. At one point my mom was talking about sending me to live with another relative because she knew she couldn't protect me. I was in my early teens, and she had to go to work. She had to be out of the house sometimes. There wasn't a way to always protect me.

What I ended up doing was just getting involved in lots of extracurricular activities at school so I was busy all the time. On weekends, I would go to the library to study. That's how I was able to accommodate it as an older child.

But if this bullying has started taking place when I was younger, I'm not entirely sure what my mother would have done. Do you have any suggestions?

Maria Keffler (09:29):

I want to caveat by saying that I am not a family therapist. I'm not a therapist of any kind, and I don't have a lot of expertise in family dynamics. I learned a lot as I was researching for this episode.

If your kids are in a dangerous situation, don't ignore it. There are good family therapists out there.

That actually might be a helpful roundabout way of dealing with the trans issue in your home. Many therapists are sold out with the trans narrative, that it can be kind of dangerous to go to one of them. But if you've got a situation where siblings are having some struggles, you can say, "We need some family therapy to deal with those dynamics." That might be a good way to get some therapy that's not focused on the transgender stuff.

Erin Brewer (10:28):

It's important to do that. In my brother's case, he feels terribly guilty about how he treated me. There were times where my brother would call and he was completely drunk and he was bawling and saying, "I'm so sorry." This is something he has to process and live with. So it has compounded any issues he already had.

If you do have these dynamics going on a lot of times, it isn't the bullying kid's fault. There's some underlying thing. In my brother's case, a lot of these feelings came because he was unable to protect me from being sexually assaulted. He had strong feelings and didn't know how to handle them.

This is similar to trans-identified kids feel. They love their siblings at times, but at other times they might just have this rage if the sibling isn't acting in a way that is affirming them. They've been told their siblings are supposed to behave how they are told, or they believe their siblings don't love them. It is incredibly damaging to a relationship. Getting help is important.

Maria Keffler (12:36):

If you can provide spaces for retreat—a space that a child can go when he or she is feeling rage, because you have to release your rage somewhere.

I'm thinking about your brother. He had all these conflicted feelings and no safe place to get them out. So you were the only punching bag he had, unfortunately.

But if I'm getting upset and angry, I'm going to go off by myself so that I can decompress and calm down. Kids need a place in the home where they can be assured that they can go there and be alone. If they're sharing a bedroom, and if it's a small home that there aren't spaces for everybody to have their own space, try to find somewhere in the home that the child can have as a retreat.

> **Kids need a place in the home where they can be assured that they can go there and be alone. Try to find somewhere that the child can have as a retreat.**

One of my kids asked several years ago, "Is there just someplace in our house that I can have that's just mine, that isn't a bedroom that has to be shared?" I racked my brain. I said, "The only place I can think of—this is so *Harry Potter*—is the little storage area under the stairs."

It's probably four feet deep. It comes down to a little cubby door that goes into more storage. It's about two feet wide and four feet deep.

My child was so excited. "Can I have that? Can I put a beanbag chair in there? And a little table with some drawing supplies and stuff?"

That's the retreat. That's where my child wants to go. And I've said, "Please don't tell anybody that we make you go in that space." But that fixed the problem. That child goes there when decompression is needed.

Erin Brewer (14:50):

That's amazing.

There are lots of things that parents can do to help diffuse anger, depending on the child's age. Sometimes you can even do things together as a family, depending again, on the age of the kids. You can make bread together and be like, "Okay, let's pound this bread dough!" There are activities that you can do to bring kids together and can allow them to vent—but not vent at each other, which is important.

This is one of those topics that can get kind of above our expertise because the bullying can be so intense. I've talked to parents—and my heart just goes out to them because not only are they dealing with this kid who has a trans identity, but their whole family is being devastated by it.

That's where, as a parent, it's important to have that awareness.

Like you said, my mom didn't understand the extent to which things had escalated in my home until she came home one day and my brother was chasing me with a butcher knife. She was like, "Whoa, you weren't kidding."

I think before she thought, "Kids fight." That's a pretty common reaction from parents: "Of course siblings fight and squabble." But like you said, we don't always know the extent of what's going on.

I discovered when my kids got older that my son had been going to my daughter's bedroom crying at night because he was having trouble at school and he wasn't able to talk about it during the day. I had no idea how intense this was, but it was at night when he would try to go to sleep, it would come back to him. My daughter's bedroom was right across the hallway from him. So he would go to her and she was just wonderfully good at calming him and encouraging him.

But I feel bad. I had no idea that was going on for years.

Maria Keffler (17:11):

Just like my friend said, your kids have lives together, that you are not a part of.

I have felt hobbled as a parent of multiple kids because I did not grow up with near-age siblings. I have one brother who's 12 years older than I am. He moved out when I was six years old. Even when we lived together, I was so young. He was more like an uncle than a brother. And so I came into parenting not knowing what's normal. I remember coming to my husband and asking, "Is this normal? Do we need family therapy?" And he said, "No, it's fine. This is what kids do. It's fine." But it's hard, as a parent to know.

Erin Brewer (18:36):

At what point does it cross the line and become problematic, because kids do fight? They do argue. That's normal and natural sibling behavior. Try to identify when it's crossing the line, and when your child might be really endangering their sibling, like by dunking them under water in a swimming pool or threatening suicide. That's when the ante goes up and it's time to intervene because that can start having lifelong effects on a child.

But again, most younger siblings I'm guessing have been held under water by their older siblings. I don't know, but I'm guessing. I could be wrong, but that changes that is the motivation behind it. So rather than just, having an older sibling who's goofing around and dunking their younger sibling, this had a clear message behind it of control and power and manipulation. That where things get dicey and the potential for damage goes up.

Maria Keffler (19:55):

Aside from the very significant issue of bullying, there's also just the confusion and the cognitive dissonance.

Cognitive dissonance, as we've talked about before, is where you're trying to hold two opposing beliefs at the same time, and your brain is saying, "These don't work together."

Most families teach their kids, "Boys have a penis, and girls have a vagina. There are two sexes: boys and girls." Then along comes transgender ideology and tells kids, "No, it's a continuum and you can be anywhere on it."

For younger kids that is so confusing. We've just talked about how insidious that is for kids to be taught that in school, but then to come home and have that happening in your home—

For many younger siblings, their relationship with their older sibling is really significant. It doesn't just have to be older siblings who are trans-identified, but I'm thinking specifically about younger siblings, who've perhaps looked up to their older sibling, and appreciated and respected them. Maybe they wanted to be just like an older brother or sister, and then suddenly they're told, "You don't have an older brother or sister anymore. That's not who that person is."

When someone identifies as transgender, they're not the same person. They're trying to kill the person that they have been. We hear that with the language: *deadname*. A deadname belongs to someone who's dead. And they are saying, "Oh, that is name that my parents gave me that my siblings have called me all my life. That person no longer exists."

That's one of those contradictions inherent in the gender industry. They say, "Nothing has changed. They're just being who they've been all their lives and nobody realized it." But yet they're using terms like *deadname*, which says, "I am killing off the person that I've always been." That's hard, not just for parents, but for siblings too.

> **That's one of those contradictions inherent in the gender industry. They say, "Nothing has changed. They're just being who they've been all their lives." Yet they're using terms like *deadname*, which says, "I am killing off the person that I've always been."**

Erin Brewer (22:20):

It's almost like they're having to grieve the loss of their sibling because their sibling has changed so much.

Deadname is a good example. I've heard parents say, "This is almost worse than death, because when a child dies, you grieve them and move on. But with this, you have to grieve the loss of your child, but then you have this other person who you don't even recognize because they're doing everything they can to disassociate from their former self."

For little kids, that's got to be so confusing, "What happened to my sister? I love my sister. What happened to her? How did she become a boy? And is it going to happen to me?" There are lots of confusing thoughts that can come up for a child in that situation.

That's why this ideology is so damaging. It undermines reality for children in a way that is so scary.

It is important to have discussions with younger siblings explaining, that this is a mental health issue: "Your brother is struggling. We love him very much. We're going to have to see him through this."

Kids can be very compassionate if they understand that there's a problem. Explaining this is a mental health issue is a good way to help them understand.

Maria Keffler (24:04):

Let those kids know, "This is not your fault." Especially if you have sibling relationships that have been kind of fraught, the younger child might think, "My sibling has done this because I've been so bad to him."

We know that children believe the world revolves around them. That's just part of being a child. When parents divorce, very often the children take that upon themselves: "They were fighting about me. It's my fault they divorced."

These children might apply that same faulty reasoning if their sibling decides they want to change gender: "Is this my fault? Is it because (if they were same sex siblings) they hate being a boy? So they've decided to be a girl. But I'm a boy. Is it my fault they hate boys?"

There's just a lot of wrong messages and a lot of wrong thoughts.

Validating the child is also important. "Yes. This is tough. We're going through this as a family. This is tough. This is a mental health issue that your brother is going through. We love him. We love you. We love all our children."

Let the child know that you see the same things the child sees. "Yeah, this is confusing. You're right. This is not a good thing. You're right. We are on the same side. And our side is to try to help love your sibling back into reality and into loving him or herself."

You talked about having interviewed parents who said that this in some ways feels worse than death. When a child is diagnosed with either a physical disability, physical illness, or a learning disability—when your child is diagnosed with something that's wrong—you really do go through a grieving process.

One of my kids is on the autism spectrum. It's very mild. Most people would never recognize it. It doesn't cause that big of an impact. But when we got those results back, I just cried. I just sat and cried.

That's so normal. When you first get that result or get that diagnosis, you are grieving the person you thought that child was. Or you're grieving, knowing the struggles that child's going to go through. You're grieving this new understanding, which kills your old understanding. You do live

---

When you first get that result or diagnosis, you grieve the person you thought that child was. Or you grieve, knowing the struggles that child's going to go through. You're grieving this new understanding, which kills your old understanding. You do live through a grief process.

through a grief process. And then you go on to dealing with it: "All right. What do we need to do to help make this child happy and healthy?"

You don't love your child any less, but you're grieving this understanding of what that child's life might be like.

Erin Brewer (27:25):

It's that sense recognizing that life is going to be harder for that child than you wanted it to be.

As a parent, we all want our children to be successful and to move through life easily. When you realize, "Gosh, life is going to be as a lot tougher for her than I thought it was going to be," that can just be heartbreaking.

Oftentimes these kids are unstable and they can be volatile. I've talked to so many parents who are dealing with these kids who are just out of control—screaming and yelling and creating havoc in the home, which is hard for younger siblings. Depending on the child's personality, it can tough. If you have a tender kid, it might be so hard for them to live in such a volatile environment.

We have a video that is interesting. It talks about the different types of sibling relationships. I don't think it covers all of them, but it gives some good insights into how different children might react and the dynamics that they might develop. So we're going to show a little clip and I encourage parents to go see the full video.

5 Types of Unhealthy Sibling Relationships (28:46):

Narrator (28:46):

Here are five types of unhealthy sibling relationships.

One pair is the golden child and the scapegoat. These types of siblings often grow up with a parent who is either a narcissist, sociopath, or psychopath. The golden child is the parent's favorite because they mirror their values, beliefs, and habits. The parent thinks in black and white and considers this child the good one since the parent lacks empathy themselves, the golden child does too.

The royal brat and the wise owl: The royal brat is spoiled by the parents. They learn to get their way by being loud, manipulative, and stubborn. The parents usually give in to their tantrums and are more concerned with pleasing them and protecting them from difficult emotions. Consequently, the royal brat never learns how to work through their impulses, anger nor sadness. Meanwhile, the wise owl is the complete opposite of the royal brat. The wise owl is mature, responsible, and level-headed.

Three, the bully and the victim: This relationship is similar to that of a dominant parent and a submissive child, but happens in siblings. The bully in this scenario often has a challenging relationship with a parent and feels like they have no control over anything. So they learn to be a bully and take out their anger and frustrations on their sibling instead.

Four: the addict and the enabler. This co-dependent type of relationship is propelled by an enabler who acts as a caretaker for an impaired sibling, who usually struggles with addiction or mental illness. The enabler protects and takes responsibility for their sibling because they feel like their relationship or even their lives will fall apart if they don't.

Five, the ghost and the hungry child: The ghost is someone who is emotionally distant from their whole family in general. They don't know how to cope with the chaos that happens every day behind closed doors. So they fade into the background. Meanwhile, the hungry child always longs to get a little closer to the ghost. They lack love and support from the family as a whole and yearn for someone to hold onto.

Maria Keffler (31:00):

As you said, the video certainly doesn't cover all of the different sibling dynamics that there can be. But it helps us to recognize there are a lot of different things that can be going on between siblings, and the parents can have a lot to do with some of those dynamics. It behooves us to look at ourselves and ask, "Is what I'm doing as a parent helping or hurting? Do I have a favorite child? And am I communicating that? Do I have one that I'm constantly really hard on?"

> **"Is what I'm doing as a parent helping or hurting? Do I have a favorite child? And am I communicating that? Do I have one that I'm constantly really hard on?"**

Erin Brewer (31:38):

I talk to parents of these trans-identified kids, and these kids take up so much emotional energy. It's hard to keep that compassion and sympathy and just have an open heart to them, because they're just so demanding.

There are techniques to help with that. Do you have any suggestions for parents who are feeling that way—just feeling so drained and having a hard time feeling loving towards the child who is taking up so much energy?

Maria Keffler (32:18):

Sometimes you just have to determine to love a child. You just have to say, "I'm the parent and I'm going to do the best I can for this child."

You've got to take care of yourself as well. I know that can sound really glib: "Self-care! Take care of yourself!" But you can't pour out of an empty vessel.

If you need some time away, try to get some time away. If you love to read, take some time to read. If you love to go rock climbing, give yourself those things so that you can come back to the family refreshed and rejuvenated, because it is draining. It is exhausting dealing with special-needs kids. That's what we're talking about here.

Erin Brewer (33:07):

Some people believe that parents are overflowing with love, but like you said, sometimes love is a choice. Sometimes you actively have to say, "I'm loving this child, even though he is causing a lot of difficulty in the family. I'm going to consciously love this child. I'm going to make that choice to continue to love this child, and to make sure this child knows that I love him unconditionally."

We're taught as a society that love is this emotion that parents overflow with. Sometimes parents have to make that conscious choice, "I'm struggling with this child. I'm going to love her anyway."

> **I think we're taught as a society that that love is this emotion that parents overflow with. Sometimes parents have to make that conscious choice, "I'm struggling with this child. I'm going to love her anyway."**

Maria Keffler (33:53):

Communicating that to the child—you can communicate to any child: "I am really unhappy with your behavior. I do not like what you're doing right now. I don't appreciate the words that you're using, but I love you always. I will always be here for you. I am always going to try to make decisions that are the best for you. You may not always like those decisions, but I am committed to trying to do the best by you, no matter what."

It's appropriate. You can be unhappy with the behavior, but you still love the child. We all want that. We all want that kind of love.

But one thing I want to stress when you're dealing with children, whether it's a trans-identified child, whether it's a sibling—no matter what the issue is, do your best to keep your emotions in check.

Erin Brewer:

I'm thinking, especially if you're dealing with a sibling of a transgender-identified child, who's struggling and confused, and upset, do your best to be calm, loving, and firm, but not to let yourself communicate that sense of helplessness. Because your child is going to feel like it is his or her responsibility to take care of your emotions. Suddenly the child is put in the parent role of, "I need to protect Mom's emotions. I need to protect Dad's emotions."

We need to be the adults. We need to be the ones who are caring for our children's emotions, not the other way around.

> **We need to be the adults. We need to be the ones who are caring for our children's emotions, not the other way around.**

Maria Keffler (35:41):

I'm so glad you said that because I've seen dynamics where children are put in a parental role because their parents are not handling emotions well, and that is tough for a kid. They're supposed to be the kids; you're supposed to be the adult. If you're feeling unable to handle things, reach out for support. Get some help. Find family, friends, or relatives who are able to support you in this so that you are able to be the parent.

It's okay to show emotion to the kids, but not to fall apart and not for those kids to have to come and comfort you and tell you it's going to be okay. We're supposed to be doing that for our children.

We can commiserate with our children. We can cry tears and let them know, "I'm so sad over what's going on with John." But we still need to communicate to the child: "I'm still in control. I'm still the one managing this house. Your dad and I are the ones who are making the decisions here. And you can trust us with your needs."

> **We can commiserate with our children. We can cry tears and say, "I'm so sad over what's going on with John." But we still need to communicate to the child: "I'm still in control. I'm still the one managing this house. Your dad and I are the ones who are making the decisions here. And you can trust us with your needs."**

We have a couple of questions. This first one came out of a parenting group very recently: "My 13-year-old son is just done with his trans-identified little sister, who's ten. He wants his dad and me to make this go away. He tells us we should give his sister up for adoption. I don't know how to help him or to fix this. We would love to make it go away, but it's just not going away."

Erin Brewer (37:21):

Oh my gosh. I can understand how exhausting this must be. It just must be so difficult to have to live with this.

I actually knew a family in a similar circumstance where the older child was just annoyed and done with it. She was just done with her sister because her sister was taking on this trans identity. She's like, "I lived with you my whole life. You're a girl. You were born a girl. We grew up as sisters. You're my sister. You're not my brother." She wouldn't have anything to do with it. I never heard her suggest she wanted to put her younger sibling up for adoption. But I do understand those feelings.

The best approach is empathy, and to say, "I really want it to go away too. I understand this is hard. I'm sorry you are going through this." Let him know that those feelings are okay.

Sometimes kids will have these feelings and then they'll feel guilty about it: "Oh my gosh, I can't believe I just thought that I want my sibling to go up for adoption. Oh, that's terrible." And so they can have this internal conflict. It's okay to tell kids, "You know, I understand why you feel that way."

Maria Keffler (38:41):

I talked to this mom a little further, just trying to figure out what was going on with her son. The son was reaching an age that he's starting to be aware of his social status and what people think. The two children are at the same school, and he was embarrassed.

The mom also said he loved his little sister. She used to do ballet. And he was so proud of her. He loved to watch her perform. He would brag about how great his little sister was at ballet. He feels like she's just thrown away who she was—that this person that he really valued and liked has thrown that away.

Erin Brewer (39:32):

It's not surprising he feels that way. If he had those kinds of very proud and big-brotherly feelings about his little sister, to see her do this must be heartbreaking. Those are very real feelings and the fact that they had a good relationship before this happened gives me hope that they'll be able to repair it.

Maybe try to help him find some words to tell his sister how sad he is.

It might also be appropriate is to walk him through the stages of grief, so that he understands that he has lost an important part of his family here, and it's appropriate to grieve. These are the feelings you're likely to have. So at least he understands the process. Elisabeth Kübler-Ross has done some good research about grief.

Maria Keffler (40:52):

I want to make the point that even when the child comes back—if the child abandons the transgender identity (and we say they're desisted or detransitioned)—they don't necessarily return exactly the way they left, especially if this has gone on for two or three or four years.

This daughter is ten. If this takes two years, she's going to be 12. A 12-year-old is quite different from a 10-year-old.

So the loss is real. I've talked to so many parents who have said, "I'm so angry at what's been stolen from me." You have a right to be angry. Years of your child's life have been stolen from you by this ideology.

It makes me really angry that the gender industry and the trans-rights activists don't respect that even if this were true—even if a person could transition to be the opposite sex, even if this were entirely true—there is still grief and loss for those families. That deserves to be recognized.

> **It makes me really angry that the gender industry and the trans-rights activists don't respect that even if this were true—even if a person could transition to be the opposite sex—there is still grief and loss for those families. That deserves to be recognized.**

Erin Brewer (42:05):

I've heard of scenarios where the trans-identified child is living with one parent and the other sibling is living with another parent. That just complicates it even more, because then not only are you losing your sibling, but there's this sense of not being in alignment with one of the parents, and it can be confusing and complicated.

If you think it's hard for you as a parent, imagine being younger and not having the life experience, and having this taking up a good portion of your life. This is heavy stuff for kids.

Maria Keffler (42:44):

We've got one more question. "I'm concerned that the social contagion aspect of this is going to play out in my house. Should I be concerned that my trans-identified daughter might influence her younger siblings to become trans as well?"

Erin Brewer (43:01):

That's a very real concern. Do you have any suggestions on how to address that, Maria?

Maria Keffler (43:07):

It is a real concern because we see it happening. We're seeing more and more parents say, "Two of my five kids are transgender." There's definitely a social contagion aspect of this.

So much depends on the age of the siblings, the relationships between the siblings, and the birth order. Is this an oldest sibling who's doing it, or the youngest sibling? Is there bullying going on?

There are so many dynamics involved. I would say the first thing to do is just sit down and start examining those things. What's the birth order? What are the relationships?

When I was in college, I took a marriage and family relationship class, and they had us do this exercise that was so fascinating. We took a piece of paper and wrote our family tree on it. For example, I had my mom and my dad, and they had me and my brother, and all of those relationships for each person. I think we put their birth dates, their jobs, their levels of education. Then we had to draw lines between them. Red lines were bad relationships and green lines were good relationships.

It was fascinating because I started seeing trends: "That's probably why these two people don't get along. And that feeds into this relationship."

You might do that with your family. It might uncover some things that you didn't recognize before that may inform, "How do I deal with this? How do I protect my kids? How do I change the way I parent?"

Erin Brewer (45:26):

The other thing is just to have honest discussions with children and talk about gender: "What does that mean? It's okay if you're a girl and you want to have short hair. It's okay if you're a boy and you want to bake cookies or do floral arrangements."

Also make it clear that the sibling has a mental health issue. Let your child know, "We're concerned that because you're around it all the time, you're going to be influenced by it. How are you feeling?" Stay in touch with your kids. If you have an older sibling who has a lot of clout with the younger siblings, that's going to be a more problematic issue than if it's a younger sibling who has less influence.

Again, those dynamics are going to be important. And try to pull in other people to come and support you in this. Let your children spend time with loving and caring friends and relatives who are going to encourage your child to embrace who he or she is.

The child who gravitates towards a transgender identity is vulnerable, and has some underlying issues already. So try and see if your other kids have any of those vulnerabilities. And if they do, address those issues.

Maria Keffler (46:59):

I've heard of families sending a transgender-identified child to live with relatives for a while. Not in a punitive way. It can be very helpful to withdraw the child from the surroundings that are feeding this ideology.

One of the things we talk about is not feeding these wrong ideas, but feeding the child with healthy ideas.

If the child has a good relationship with grandparents or with a particular aunt or uncle, it might not be a bad idea for the child to go live with Grandma and Grandpa for six months, or do a school year at Aunt and Uncle's house. It's a possibility.

It's something to consider, especially if you are feeling like, "What I need is to protect these other siblings." It might be good to consider giving your trans-identified child another place to be for a while.

Erin Brewer (48:06):

That also might have the benefit of separating them from the influences that are pulling them into this ideology, which could be helpful, and giving them someone besides Mom and Dad to talk to. A lot of times these kids have underlying issues that they need to process. If they're given the opportunity to do that it's more likely that they'll resolve this identity.

Episode 17 Resource List

5 Types of Unhealthy Sibling Relationships: https://youtu.be/eccHzos-k-4

Episode 18: ROGD & Social Contagion

https://youtu.be/aWB8XK9tKEE

Maria Keffler (00:45):

We're going to talk about ROGD, which stands for "rapid onset gender dysphoria," and the social contagion aspect of that today.

Erin Brewer (00:55):

This is a relatively new phenomenon.

Maria Keffler (01:00):

I have talked to gender activists who have told me this doesn't exist. I remember the first time this happened. I was outside of school board meeting and I recognized somebody waiting to speak to the school board who was very much on the other side of the issue. It was about transgender policies in schools. I thought, "I'm going to open up a dialogue." So I started talking with him and we came up to the topic of ROGD and he said, "That doesn't exist. There's no such thing."

I talk to a lot of parents who said that their kids have ROGD. But I hear this all the time: "It doesn't exist."

Erin Brewer (01:44):

For those who maybe haven't heard the term rapid onset gender dysphoria, or ROGD, I just want to clarify the differences.

Most kids who have gender dysphoria, like I did—I fit the criteria for gender dysphoria. It's a very specific criteria: it usually starts in early childhood, and these are the kids who have been studied—these are the kids who we have data about and desistance rates for. We know that of the kids who develop gender dysphoria as young children, the vast majority of them will have that gender dysphoria resolved during adolescence.

Well, ROGD is a new phenomenon where these kids don't have any symptoms of gender dysphoria at all in childhood. Then suddenly one day they come home and declare a transgender identity as a tween or teen, often stunning parents who have not observed any gender incongruence or gender confusion throughout this child's life. So it's very confusing for parents who suddenly are confronted with a kid who says, "I'm born in the wrong body." The parents report there has been no indication of the child feeling that way until now.

Maria Keffler (03:04):

A lot of times what the parent hears is this litany—it's a script that's coming from this child. And I call it a script because when we talk to parents who have this experience, the kids are all saying the same thing. It's like they've been given a script: "I've felt this way all my life. I hid it from you because I knew you'd be upset. I've never liked my body. I've never fit in. I've always wanted to be the opposite sex." The parents are confused because this just came out of the blue.

> **The kids are all saying the same thing.**
> **It's like they've been given a script:**
> **"I've felt this way all my life.**
> **I hid it from you because I knew you'd be upset.**
> **I've never liked my body. I've never fit in.**
> **I've always wanted to be the opposite sex."**

Erin Brewer (03:47):

It's very revisionist. The child will go back and find one picture where she was playing with a toy that is traditionally a boy's toy. Or he will find one picture where maybe he is cooking—and these kids will use these instances of gender nonconformity to say, "See, this is evidence that all my life I've felt like I was born in the wrong body."

For parents, it's very confusing because the parents were there throughout the childhood and they know what the truth is. These kids are insisting on something that isn't accurate.

Maria Keffler (04:19):

We did another episode earlier about how this is a very cultic phenomenon. It has a lot of parallels with cults, and that's one of the things that cult do. They will take their recruit and say, "Tell me about your childhood." When the recruit says, "I had a pretty happy childhood. You know, we would go hiking on the weekends," the recruiter might say, "You like hiking? Did you wear hiking boots? Hiking boots are a very masculine thing."

The cult will seize upon that one story and inflate it to suggest, "This is who you really are." And they kind of brush everything else off to the side.

This is a tactic that we see in cults. We absolutely see this happening with these ROGD kids. They're getting into the GSA—the gender sexuality allies club—at school, which I have become convinced are indoctrination centers. This is where these kids are being sucked in.

They're being invited to these groups, love-bombed, and they're having these cult tactics applied to them. And then they're suddenly announcing, "Hey, I'm transgender." And when they do, they get all this celebration. We've talked about this before. It makes total sense.

Erin Brewer (05:45):

It's important for parents to understand that these kids believe this. They're not just making this up. They're just not pretending. They've been, as you said, indoctrinated. They are believing this, which is sad.

The other thing that is important to note is that this is happening in clusters. One child will adopt a trans identity. The kids in the child's peer group will see the celebration that's happening—the affirmation, the control that this child suddenly has over teachers, parents, classmates, being able to dictate how to be treated, and suddenly being catered to as far as pronouns and names and bathrooms. Then suddenly another child will announce, "Oh, well, I'm transgender too."

Again, it sounds kind of frivolous, but it's important, as you said, to note that this is an indoctrination process. And so even though it might seem frivolous, it's not.

> **This is an indoctrination process.**

This is dangerous because these kids are being taught to believe that they were born in the wrong body and that anybody who doesn't affirm them is an enemy. They are taught they deserve to have these privileges of being able to dictate the pronouns and the restrooms that they use.

I've heard of schools where 40% of girls suddenly identify as transgender out of the blue.

That's absurd. If this were any other kind of illness or any other psychological condition that was happening, this would be alarming to say the least. This would be beyond a pandemic. People would be completely freaked out if suddenly we had autism at this kind of rate, or if we had OCD at this kind of rate, or if we had any other kind of issue popping up in clusters like this and increasing at the rate that it's increasing, and requiring the kind of medical interventions that these people are saying that they need. This would be considered a public health crisis.

Instead it's being considered something to celebrate, which is, again, an indication that it's a cult.

Maria Keffler (08:05):

The schools say, "We're just following best practices."

The American Academy of Pediatrics wanted to issue a policy statement on transgender medicine. They asked this team of doctors—a team of 37 people sat down and wrote this policy statement. The two head doctors—the head writer and the head consultant—both have financial ties to gender clinics.

That was a special interest team that put that statement together. Their statement was not vetted by the other 60,000 doctors who are part of the American Academy of Pediatrics. It was this team who said, "We're specialists in this."

They made their statement according to what's beneficial to doctors who work in gender clinics, because doctors who work in gender clinics get no money from telling a child, "You're perfectly healthy. Go see a psychiatrist to deal with your mental health issues." They don't make any money off that.

They make money off the child who takes the puberty blockers, who takes the cross-sex hormones, who has the surgeries.

> **Doctors who work in gender clinics get no money from telling a child, "You're perfectly healthy. Go see a psychiatrist to deal with your mental health issues." They don't make any money off that. They make money off the child who takes the puberty blockers, who takes the cross-sex hormones, who has the surgeries.**

So what you'll hear in the school is, "We're just following best practices," but those best practices are very special-interest practices that have been very strategically promulgated and placed to make it seem like they're based on research, but they're not evidence-based.

GLSEN, the Gay Lesbian Straight Education Network—they've got this model school district policy that's being very strategically, aggressively, forced into schools in my state, Virginia. Local interest groups focused on transgender policies have asked the state legislature to tell them which school boards have not adopted the school district policy, so that they can go and apply pressure.

That policy has *three* resources cited for support. Two of them originated with GLSEN. That's just like the big tobacco companies saying, "We're going to hire somebody to do a study, to find out if nicotine is bad for you. Oh! It's not bad for you." That's exactly the same thing.

Erin Brewer (10:39):

One of the things that people need to understand is that we don't have longitudinal studies about ROGD. In fact, Lisa Littman, who first coined the term "rapid onset gender dysphoria," published her study, and talk about people being anti-science! The transgender activists just went crazy about this research and it was taken down. The study was analyzed under a fine-tooth comb and it turned out it was very solid research and it was republished.

But that just goes to show, they're not interested in science. They're interested in this ideology.

We do have longitudinal studies about children with gender dysphoria, and we know that the vast majority of them will outgrow it. This rapid onset gender dysphoria is such a new phenomenon that we don't know what the trajectory is, but we are seeing desisters starting to emerge who are saying, "Oh my gosh, I can't believe I was allowed to do this."

> ## We do have longitudinal studies about children with gender dysphoria, and we know that the vast majority of them will outgrow it.

These are kids who have underlying issues that we've talked about. Oftentimes these are kids who are struggling socially. Potentially, they're being bullied. They are in need of feeling affirmed, of feeling celebrated, and validated. These are the kids that are being attracted to this ideology.

As they're moving through high school and then getting out there in the world and realizing what a sham this ideology is, they're desisting and they're speaking out. They're saying, "How on earth was I allowed to run with this idea? How on earth was I allowed to be given puberty blockers, cross-sex hormones, and surgeries that permanently medicalized and damaged me?" And they're enraged. They are just incredibly outraged that they were allowed to do this.

We are going to have more of these children damaged if we continue this affirmation model that is being pushed by activists.

Maria Keffler (12:51):

If I were any a therapist, a counselor, a licensed therapist, a psychiatrist right now, I would be building a practice around detransitioners, because we're hearing from detransitioners that they do not have resources. When they leave the cult, they're cut off. The doctors who we're so happy to support them toward medicalization won't take their phone calls. The therapists who agreed with them that, "Yes, you are the opposite sex, and we need to get you medicalized," have got nothing to offer.

If you're a therapist, I would start building a therapy plan around supporting detransitioners and the trauma that they've been through. I'm concerned for all of these detransitioners who are telling us, "We don't have any help. There's nobody to help us."

Erin Brewer (13:53):

That's the thing that's so frustrating about this, we know that there is such a thing as social contagion. This is a well-documented thing that happens, especially among teenagers. It's not like this is hitting us out of the blue, and we've never experienced this before. Any teacher who has ever worked with teenagers, or any parent who's ever had a teenager has experienced this. It is something that advertising and marketers thrive on, this social contagion. This is something that's very well known.

In fact, one of the things that's concerning to me is that suicide can also be a social contagion. One of the things that trans activists are doing is saying that if we don't affirm these kids, they're going to commit suicide. So in essence, what they're doing is introducing the social contagion of gender dysphoria, and then they're introducing the secondary social contagion of suicide. It is incredibly dangerous to be promulgating these ideas to children, the idea that if you're not affirmed, the appropriate response is suicide.

We have a couple of clips here that talk about social contagion and how easy it for kids to influence one another, and how this is well-documented. This is something that we know happens. We should be looking at it critically, rather than celebrating it as kids "finding their authentic selves."

Karl Moore (15:18):

You've been looking at social contagion, tell us about your research.

Brian Rubineau (15:21):

We know that social influence generally exists. We're influenced by the people we have relationships with.

Karl Moore (15:26):

How do we more effectively lead change then?

Brian Rubineau (15:29):

So the practical advice is you identify who the core spreaders are in an organization, right? So if you can identify—much like you would in public health—who are the core spreaders of the disease? who are the core spreaders of influence and behavior and organizations?

And what we found in my research is that you can identify these core spreaders using data, such as the server logs from your email system, right? And you can actually use social network analysis methods to identify who are the core spreaders.

And if you target these core spreaders, then you can actually have this contagion process diffuse. If you're trying to have a change effort where you're trying to promote adoption of certain kinds of behaviors—you want staff to participate in webinars or these kinds of things—to support change efforts. Targeting these efficient core spreaders is a good way to change behaviors.

Crash Course (16:21):

Groupthink is the narrowing of thought in a group by which its members come to believe that there is only one possible correct answer. Moreover, in a groupthink mentality to even suggest alternatives is a sign of disloyalty to the group.

> ## In a groupthink mentality, to even suggest alternatives is a sign of disloyalty to the group.

Another way of understanding group conformity is to think about reference groups. Reference groups are groups we use as standards to judge ourselves and others. What's normal for you is determined partly by your reference groups—"in" groups or reference groups that you feel loyalty to and that you identify with—but you can compare yourself to out-groups to which are groups that you feel antagonism towards, and with which you don't identify.

Maria Keffler (16:54):

Social contagions are well documented. This is very normal. It happened even back in the 1800's. A book came out, *The Sorrows of Young Werther*. I can't remember who wrote it, but it was very popular among kids, among teens. And there was this wave of suicides, because in the book a character committed suicide, and they started finding all of these kids committing suicide.

We know that this happens. But not all social contagions are bad. There are some social contagions that are neutral, like yawning.

Erin Brewer (17:46):

I remember in elementary school I started bringing bouillon cubes to nibble on during class. Within a week everybody was bringing bouillon cubes to nibble on. It was just weird. It came and went, and then somebody else brought cinnamon toothpicks. We went through that phase and everybody wanted cinnamon toothpicks.

Maria Keffler (18:15):

We had a toothpick craze too!

Erin Brewer (18:20):

We had combs. Everybody had to have a comb in their back pocket. That was cool for a while.

Tweens and teens are very susceptible to these contagions because they want to fit in. They want to be like the other kids. They want to be cool. Something like rapid onset gender dysphoria, or a trans identity where suddenly you can go from being the most bullied and marginalized kid in the group to being popular and powerful and cool-- it's not surprising that it's catching on. It makes perfect sense.

The absurdity is that we're embracing this and suggesting that this is a child we who suddenly realize was born in the wrong body. It almost runs counter to the whole ideology, because here's a kid who clearly wasn't suggesting that he or she was trans-identified until suddenly they are. Yet the transgender movement is saying you're born in the wrong body.

It even contradicts their own ideology. They have to come up with this whole backstory about how the kid always knew they were born in the wrong body, they just were afraid to tell anybody, even though there was absolutely no indication of that.

In a lot of ways, it reminds me of the false memory craze. This happened in the late eighties and nineties. It was this idea that you could have repressed memories that you wouldn't know about. And if you thought that you had repressed memories, but you couldn't remember anything, that was evidence that you had repressed memories. It was this very convoluted ideology.

Maria Keffler (20:02):

In a few years, we're going to look back on this period of the transgender craze. We're going to look at it the same way people are looking at repressed memories and looking at split personality, which was a big craze where suddenly everybody had a split personality, or the way we look back at lobotomies and say, "How did we ever do that to anybody?"

Incidentally, the doctor who pioneered the lobotomy was given a Nobel prize for science for that.

Erin Brewer (20:34):

So when you hear people say, "Well, doctors wouldn't do something if it weren't correct." Well, guess what, doctors used to recommend cigarettes. I remember seeing ads where doctors would be smoking cigarettes. If you had a sore throat, go get a menthol cigarette help soothe your throat.

Maria Keffler (20:49):

Where did Coca-Cola come from, right? Coca-Cola used to have cocaine in it. "It's so good for you." Or "Take some laudanum and you'll feel better."

Erin Brewer (21:04):

Not to mention the opioid crisis, which is killing people all around the world.

> **The idea that doctors would never do something that is harmful is just absurd. We have ample evidence to show that that's not correct, that doctors historically do make huge mistakes.**

The idea that doctors would never do something that is harmful is just absurd. We have ample evidence to show that that's not correct, that doctors historically do make huge mistakes. That's one of the reasons that we need to be critical of them.

In this one case where we're told, "Nope, you're not allowed to question it." Any evidence such as the Lisa Littman study—or there was recently a study that came out that showed—I think it was 87% of kids with gender dysphoria desist if they're allowed to naturally progress through childhood. Those studies are being silenced and discredited.

They're coming up with these absurd retrospective, self-reporting "studies" from activists, that are completely methodologically flawed, to substantiate their claims that this is how we should be treating these rapid onset gender dysphoric kids. Or they'll deny that it even happens. They'll say, "This wasn't rapid onset gender dysphoria. These kids were just too scared to ever mention it."

Like Ellen Page, who came out recently as transgender. She's saying she just never felt comfortable being her authentic self. Well, that's just absurd.

Maria Keffler (22:36):

I read an article—I think it was in *People* magazine—about Ellen Page who's now calling herself Elliot Page. I read it and it was just a complete revisionist history. It told stories that no one ever heard before, like when Ellen was nine, "He knew that he was supposed to be a boy."

Ellen Page was a beautiful woman who played a pregnant teenager, who played a girl who liked to rollerblade and didn't want to be a beauty queen. She was such a role model for gender-nonconforming people. Now I look at that and I'm just heartbroken for her.

Erin Brewer (23:26):

To even entertain the idea that you can be born in the wrong body like that, and that we're going to accept that as truth, is so concerning because you can believe that you think that you wish that you were something you're not, but you can't ever know what it feels like to be something you're not.

That's the crux of the problem here: none of these kids know what it feels like to be something they're not. But we're saying, "Yes, they can know what it feels like to be something they're not."

If we're going to allow that to happen then we're going to have to allow people who can identify as different ages than they actually are, different races than they actually are, different nationalities than they actually are. Heck, I'm going to identify as having Bill Gates and Oprah Winfrey as my parents.

> ## None of these kids know what it feels like to be something they're not. But we're saying, "Yes, they can know what it feels like to be something they're not."

Maria Keffler (24:29):

Does that mean we need to accept that because that is how you identify?

It was Colin Wright who said we cannot afford to lose our collective tether on reality. Reality has physical truths to it. Your body is a physical truth.

I just want to encourage parents, if you have a child who's suffering with ROGD, listen to your gut. You know your child. Step back and ask yourself, "Does this make sense?" If you can silence all the voices that are telling you you're a bad parent if you don't affirm this, just step back and ask yourself what is true. "My child never indicated this in 10, 11, 12, 13, 14, 15 years. This came out of the blue."

Does your child have something else going on? The Littman study underscored that so many of these kids have autism, they've got prior trauma, they're suffering depression, they're suffering self-harm, or they're suffering eating disorders. The kids who are doing this are generally not the happy, healthy kids that everything's going great with them. These are the marginalized kids.

Erin Brewer (26:01):

Sometimes they're even just girls who are going through puberty, who are incredibly uncomfortable with it, as is normal, as every generation of girls has been. Some of these kids do have trauma. Some of these kids are autistic. Some of them are marginalized, but some of them are just perfectly normal girls who are uncomfortable with going through puberty and are being told that if you're uncomfortable with puberty, it means that you're actually born in the wrong body.

Maria Keffler (26:29):

I'm glad you pointed that out. I don't want to make it sound like if you have a child with no other issues, you don't need to worry. If your child's in the culture today, you need to be concerned about this because they are pushing this on all kids.

Erin Brewer (26:47):

It's such a difficult time because teenagers need society to help provide them with boundaries and to help guide them. And we're doing a huge disservice right now to all of our teenagers by embracing this ideology.

Maria Keffler (27:08):

We talked in an earlier episode about locus of control. People tend to either have an *internal* locus of control—which means they feel like, "I have some power over life and can choose to make changes that will affect my life"—or they have an *external* locus of control, where they feel that they have no power. All the power is outside. All they can do is react to what other people are doing to them. This transgender ideology is all about that external locus of control.

Going back to what you said about the therapists and the gender industry telling kids, "If you're not affirmed, you're going to be suicidal"—that puts the locus of control absolutely outside yourself: "I cannot help but want to kill myself if somebody misgenders me."

That's ridiculous. People have suffered such horrible atrocities. They've been in concentration camps. They've suffered abuse. They've suffered under dictatorships and they have survived, because the human spirit is resilient, unless you teach it that it's not.

> **People have suffered such horrible atrocities—
> concentration camps, abuse, dictatorships—
> and they have survived, because the human spirit
> is resilient, unless you teach it that it's not.**

Erin Brewer (28:23):

I'm so glad you brought that up because it's critical for people to understand that the activists are the ones who are contributing to the suicide rate. They're the ones who are telling kids that it's an appropriate response to kill yourself if you're not affirmed.

As you said, humans are incredibly resilient if they're taught to be resilient. Humans can endure incredible suffering. Not that this even is anywhere near the horrors of concentration camps, or slaves who have endured this tremendous physical, and emotional distress, and they were not compelled to kill themselves. It's like we're encouraging kids, if you don't get what you want, the best response is to kill yourself.

Imagine telling that to a child in any other circumstance. "If your parents don't let you drive the family car, go ahead and kill yourself. That's probably what you should do." Is there any other situation where we would encourage children to kill themselves?

I hear doctors and I hear people testifying in front of legislators and saying if we pass laws that will prevent children from medically transitioning, children will kill themselves. Well, guess what? That's contributing to the social contagion. Those people are now culpable for any suicides that happen because they are planting that idea in these children's heads.

We know that suicide is a social contagion. We've also seen it time and time again. We've even had media guidelines on how to talk about suicide, because we have seen suicide being a social contagion. Now we have transgender activists who are embracing it and encouraging it. To me, that is just a travesty. I don't know how people are sitting back and allowing it to happen.

Maria Keffler (30:23):

What you said about suicide being a social contagion reminded me that when I was in high school, there was a girl in the class behind me who committed suicide. It was tragic. That was the first time I ever thought, "Your life can be so bad that you want to kill yourself."

I mentioned in a previous video that I had postpartum depression after one of my children was born and I needed to be under a doctor's care for about a year. I remember talking to that psychiatrist and telling him that that was the first time that I had ever thought about suicide. Feeling suicidal is one of the problems that I had related to the postpartum depression. The psychiatrist told me that's normal, when somebody in your circle commits suicide, to be thinking about that. He said that when that idea perseveres and continues, that shows there's a problem that needs to be taken care of.

That makes me think we're employing that normal suggestiveness—we're almost weaponizing that social contagion, that power of suggestion, against our children. Why would we do this? Who benefits from it?

> **We're employing that normal suggestiveness—we're almost weaponizing that social contagion, that power of suggestion, against our children. Why would we do this? Who benefits from it?**

Erin Brewer (31:51):

I've even heard activists threaten legislators saying, "If children kill themselves it's their blood on your hands." And I say, "Nope, that's gaslighting in the extreme. It's actually on your hands because you're the ones telling kids that they're so fragile, that they're so vulnerable, that the only way they can live is if they're affirmed in the way that you're telling them."

Maria Keffler (32:14):

I talked to one mom who was at the pediatrician's office with her child, and the child said something about being transgender, and the mom was not on board with it. The pediatrician turned to the mother and said, "How are you going to feel if your child commits suicide because you didn't affirm?"

Erin Brewer (32:42):

And the child heard that?

Maria Keffler (32:44):

Oh yeah, right in front of the child.

Erin Brewer (32:47):

Planting the idea that if the mother doesn't affirm her that suicide is an appropriate response—it's ridiculous.

We have two very significant social contagions going on here. First of all, the rapid onset gender dysphoria, and then the suicide as a way to manipulate people. This is a social contagion. So we are going to see an increase in suicides because children are being encouraged to believe that suicide is an appropriate response.

> **We are going to see an increase in suicides because children are being encouraged to believe that suicide is an appropriate response.**

Maria Keffler (33:17):

We are already seeing suicide increase.

Erin Brewer (33:19):

In fact, the interesting thing is, as we're seeing an increase in affirmation of transgender identities, we're also seeing an increase in suicide. That's indicative that affirmation is not the appropriate response. It's not going to prevent suicides. It's actually increasing them.

Maria Keffler (33:39):

"Transgender identities are being allowed to come out and society is accepting it." If that were true, we would be seeing suicides going down.

We would also be seeing concurrent rates of increase between boys and girls, instead of this huge shift to the enormous numbers of girls who are doing it. Why are we not seeing those same numbers? Boys are doing it, but not at the same rate as girls are. Why aren't we seeing this, as Abigail Shrier pointed out? Why aren't we seeing this in 40-year-old women, 50-year-old women, 60-year-old women? If there's been so much latent, hidden transgenderism, it should be coming out everywhere.

It's not, it's coming out primarily in teens and very young adults.

Erin Brewer (34:34):

Do we have a question from a parent for this episode?

Maria Keffler (34:38):

We do. We have one question. "My daughter's whole peer group has announced that they're all transgender. No one at school seems to find anything strange about this. How do I deal with this? It's obviously a social trend they're trying on. If it were just different hair and clothes, that would be fine, but three of them are already on hormones."

Erin Brewer (34:58):

Even if that many kids in a group suddenly claimed to be autistic or claimed to have obsessive compulsive disorder—

Maria Keffler (35:11):

Or they'd all been abducted by aliens.

Erin Brewer (35:14):

I can't imagine how school officials are sitting back and not concerned about this at all. The mother has every right to be concerned, because the treatment for this is something that's going to damage the child.

Maria Keffler (35:37):

In that case, I would do everything I could as a parent to get that child out of that school and, unfortunately, out of that friend group.

Erin Brewer (35:47):

I liken it to drugs. If there were a group of five kids who were all doing drugs and your child was part of that peer group, it's going to be hard to get them off drugs unless you pull them completely out. If they're all shooting up heroin during lunchtime, there's nothing you can do as a parent to stop that unless you physically remove them from that friend group, which is incredibly devastating to kids. But that it's worth that kind of an intervention to save your kids from this ideology.

Maria Keffler (36:30):

I talked to a director at a youth program a year or so ago, and we were talking about this issue of kids presenting as transgender. She talked about having seen parents whose kids were in various crises, whether it was pregnancy or involved in drugs or self-harming—some sort of a crisis. Then she said that in her experience, when parents did the drastic thing of pulling the child out of that environment, the kids turned around. She said, "I've seen parents move their kids, like pack up the family and move."

One family I heard of took a year off and took a road trip. Not everybody can do that, but the parents were able to take some time off work (or they worked from the road) and just got an RV and went on a road trip for a year, just to get the child out of that environment.

This youth director said in every case that she knew of where the parents did that drastic thing, they saved their kid. It's the parents who say, "Let's just wait and see. Let's just stay the course and hope it gets better"—those are the ones that tend to have the bad outcomes.

> **Where the parents did that drastic thing, they saved their kid. It's the parents who say, "Let's just wait and see. Let's just stay the course and hope it gets better"—those are the ones that tend to have the bad outcomes.**

Erin Brewer (37:49):

It's hard as a parent to do those drastic things, especially because initially the kid's going to be mad. You're going to be dealing with a child who is extremely difficult for a while. In the long run it's worth it and it will settle down. You just have to be able to weather it for the first few months when that child's going to be angry.

Maria Keffler (38:13):

If you choose to homeschool, probably one of the parents is going to have to either quit working, or cut back on work in order to homeschool.

I don't want this to sound like we're glibly saying, "Just pull him out and homeschool and it will be fine." I mean, there's a cost that comes to it. But you do need to weigh, is it worth the cost of perhaps my child going down the medicalization route and spending the rest of his or her life medicalized?

Erin Brewer (39:01):

At the very least I would encourage parents in a situation like this to meet with the school and to bring in some resources like the Child and Parent Rights Campaign school policy guide that is now out, and provide them with some resources, because some schools may not know an alternative to affirmation. They might just be going along with this because they think this is the only option. It's possible that you could meet with the school and potentially influence the policy.

That's kind of optimistic, given the climate that we're in, but it's always worth a try.

The other thing is, if you can't homeschool, get them into a different school just to get them into a different peer group will help. Maybe think of getting them into some extracurricular activities that will get them associated with different kids.

Those peer groups can be so powerful, and the influence they have can be hard to change if your child is around those kids all the time.

There are some options other than completely pulling them out. But ultimately, I've talked to lots of parents and the ones who are having success with turning their kids around are the ones who've pulled their kids from school.

Maria Keffler (40:16):

I agree. I'm seeing the same thing. It's the parents who are treating this as a cult and are actively trying to get their kids' allegiance back with the family—because the kids' allegiance has now been given to the trans activists—and treating it as a cult, and trying to sever those unhealthy influences, seem to be turning things around with their families.

Episode 18 Resource List

Social Groups: Crash Course Sociology #16:
https://www.youtube.com/watch?v=_wFZ5Dbj8DA

Brian Rubineau on Social Contagion: https://youtu.be/psDrmjAtviw

Parent Guide, Understanding the Transgender Issue:
https://genderresourceguide.com/?gcli

Episode 19: The Adolescent Mind

https://youtu.be/uLLTVziHkwQ

Maria Keffler (00:49):

We're talking about the adolescent mind today.

Erin Brewer (00:59):

Adolescence is, for those who don't remember being adolescents, such a different time. I remember so clearly being a teenager and some of those feelings that I had, and that sense of not being understood by grownups.

Maria Keffler (01:21):

Adolescence is a time of shifting from being a child to being an adult. And it's just this moment. It's a small moment in your life—just a few years where your body, your mind, your emotions, your hormones, everything is in this upheaval as it's changing, and you're starting to engage with the world without your parents. You're going out in the world more on your own, and your mind has developed to be able to have more theoretical ideas and to look at things from other people's perspectives.

It's just this opening up of a whole new world for kids. It's a fascinating time.

Erin Brewer (02:16):

I remember this sense of being expected to act like a grownup, but not having the privileges of being a grownup, and this tug of war between, "I'm a grownup," but then society not treating me as a grownup, and also part of me realizing that I wasn't a grownup.

I struggled with my hormones and I have no doubt it was my hormones. I used to have rages—monthly rages—that I did not understand at the time. It caused so much confusion and frustration in my life. I actually had a job, where I once got so angry I kicked a door off the hinges. I was just in this rage and I look back now and I realize it had to do with my hormones being out of whack.

A lot of teenage girls experience this and I've talked to a lot of teenage girls who have detransitioned and they talk about it. It's not PMS. It's a little bit more serious: dysmenorrhea.

They're starting to identify that a lot of these girls have some significant hormonal imbalances going on, which is causing them to have more amplified feelings than what is even typical for teenagers. That makes being a teenage girl even harder, and these kids are even more likely to fall into this transgender narrative because of it.

Maria Keffler (03:55):

That's one of the insidious things that the gender industry is telling kids: "Puberty is uncomfortable because you're going through the wrong kind of puberty." If you're a girl then: "You're not supposed to be a girl. You should be going through a boy puberty," or vice versa.

That's such a lie. Puberty is uncomfortable for everybody. I don't think anybody watching this would look back on your 13-, 14-, 15-year-old self and say, "It was a breeze." You could not pay me enough to go back and live those years again.

Puberty is uncomfortable for everybody.
I don't think anybody would look back on your
13-, 14-, 15-year-old self and say, "It was a breeze."
You could not pay me enough to go back and
live those years again.

You were talking about remembering the rages that you've felt. I had a bit of that, but what I experienced more was—how would I describe it? Like melancholy—a deep cyclical, monthly melancholy. I go back and read some of my journals and you'd swear I was about to off myself: "I'm ugly and nobody likes me and I'm stupid. And I hate myself." And then two days later, everything's fine.

It takes a while to recognize, "This is that thing coming back around again. I just need to suck it up and get through the next few days. I'll be okay." To tell kids, "The reason you feel that way is you're transgender," is hideous.

Erin Brewer (05:22):

Kids believe things. Teenagers believe things that are just absurd. I thought I was absolutely hideous, like, a blight on the earth—so ugly that I was offensive. I was that kid who grew her bangs out this long and walked around with her head down.

I look back on pictures and I'm just like, "Aw, why did I think that?" Especially in those teenage years, kids get these ideas in their heads, and it's so easy for them to get misperceptions about them. I would encourage parents watching this to read *Reviving Ophelia* if you have a teenage daughter. It was written a long time ago, but it gives such good insights into the brains of teenage girls.

Things have gotten even worse for teenage girls. When I was a kid, for whatever reason, my mom got me a subscription to *Teen Magazine*, which was probably the worst thing she could've done, because I did not look anything like the girls in *Teen Magazine*. I had dark hair. I thought I was chubby. I had self-esteem issues and the *Teen Magazine* reinforced all these ideas about me that were negative.

I would recommend to stay away from stuff like that for your daughter. But now they're bombarded with these images on social media, and boys are too now. I noticed my son—he's so self-conscious in ways that I wouldn't expect a boy to be. These kids are just constantly being bombarded.

One thing that is hard for adults to remember is that a couple of months in a teenager's life is so much longer, proportionally, in their life than a couple of months for us. Their sense of proportion is very different. I remember when I broke up with my first real boyfriend and I was just distraught. My grandma called and she said, "It's okay, Erin, there are plenty of fish in the sea." And I just wailed, "You don't understand, he's the only one." I was convinced he was the only one that would ever connect with me. That wasn't true but he was the first.

Teenagers don't have that life experience. Everything seems bigger and the consequences seemed more powerful. Anytime you're not connecting with your friends, the impact is just so much more powerful. That's something parents need to remember is that these kids, their bodies are growing rapidly. They're having all these physical changes. Emotionally they're changing. A lot of times these are kids are able to understand calculus, but they still might not be as emotionally developed as you would think they should be.

Maria Keffler (08:49):

That's a good point. People develop at different rates in terms of their intellectual abilities, their emotional abilities. You might have a child who's academically very gifted, but socially a little bit behind, especially with some of the neuro-atypical kids—like kids who are on the autism spectrum. You will find those disconnects between the different parts of their lives, which is important to keep in mind.

Going back to what you said about kids' sense of proportion— I've got three kids right now. They're 13, 15 and 17. We're still dealing with COVID, and we've been in lockdown for over a year now. I realized that for my 13-year-old that's one 13th of her life. That's almost one 10th of her life, because kids don't remember the first two or three years.

This is huge for her. I'm in my fifties. It has gone by really quickly for me.

I'm always doing these tangential things—but I remember when I was in high school, my English teacher explained why time seems to go faster as you get older. She said, "It's because we judge our lives based on the whole span of our lives. When you're two years old, a year is half of your life. When you're 10 years old, a year is a 10th of your life, when you're 50 years old, a year is only a 50th of your life. So you keep judging time based on that length of your own life."

That was so powerful to me to recognize. For younger people, a month or two is significant.

We're going through 13 for the third time in our household. This is our third rodeo with 13. I just want to tell parents out there, if you're dealing with a 13-year-old, they are tough. It is a hard season. But try to remember what it was like when you were 13, and all this stuff was going on and your friends were so important to you. If you had a crush, that was so important to you, and you're starting to get irritated with your parents and you just wish they'd go away and leave you alone. They're so needy and so torn in so many different directions.

<u>Erin Brewer (11:29):</u>

The other thing that parents need to be aware of is that some of these kids are acting in ways that are grown-up. There are going to be 13-year-olds who are sexually active that are going to be engaging in behaviors that a couple of generations ago weren't going to be happening until they were 17, 18, 19, maybe not even until their twenties. There are even 9- and 10-year-olds who are sexually active. These are kids who are engaging in behaviors that are much more for adults and that they're not emotionally equipped to be dealing with.

> **There are going to be 13-year-olds who are sexually active that are going to be engaging in behaviors that a couple of generations ago weren't going to be happening until they were 17, 18, 19, maybe not even until their twenties.**

I started being sexually active in sixth grade. There was no way I was going to talk to my parents about it. I had some previous sexual experiences but

I actually started having sex in sixth grade. I wasn't going to talk to my parents about it. It was something that I would have benefited from having an adult to talk to. But I knew that it wasn't something that I wanted to share with my parents.

So you might think about all the different pressures that are happening to your kids, and think about if there's someone that your child could talk to, or even try to open up to them in a way that would be safe. If my parents had somehow broached the topic in a way that made it safe for me to talk to them about it, I might have opened up.

That could help because I was in a place where I was over my head. I was quickly way over my head in a lot of respects and doing things that were dangerous. I started getting involved with drugs shortly there-after and I was in trouble. I could have used some support from my parents, but there's no way I was going to tell them. I don't even know what their reaction would have been. I just didn't want to talk to them. I didn't like them. I didn't feel like they were supportive.

Understand these kids are potentially going to be different than you were at that age. I hear a lot of parents talk about their first sexual experience was maybe at 17. Well, if you've got a nine-year-old who's sexually active, that's radically different.

Maria Keffler (14:12):

When I did my teacher-training observations, I was in a middle school. I was seeing these posters on the wall about protecting yourself from AIDS and HIV and using condoms. I thought, "I'm in a sixth-grade hallway." I talked to one of the teachers and asked, "Why are these posters up in the sixth-grade hallway?" And he said, "There are kids here who need this information."

Well, now I know that's in the public schools and in a lot of ways they're pushing kids. In a survey I saw, one out of three kids feels that today's sexual ed programming in schools encourages them to have sex. They feel pressured to have sex.

> **One out of three kids feels that today's sexual ed programming in schools them to have sex. They feel pressured to have sex.**

Erin Brewer (15:08):

It's different because when I was in sixth grade, there were only a few of us, and we were sly about it. We were sneaking around. There was no tacit approval by our teachers or by the system at all.

It's so different now with the way sex ed is now being pushed and they're suggesting that sex is a civil right.

Kids don't have the cognitive ability to understand the implications of sex. Their bodies aren't physically mature enough to handle it.

That's one reason why I advocate for kids to wait, because they're not ready for it. But they're now being pushed into it. This generation of kids is being pushed to grow up so much faster. They don't have the skills to cope. That cognitive dissonance that we had as teenagers is even worse than it was for us.

Maria Keffler (16:27):

Let me raise an interesting point. Kids are not good at making decisions about long-term consequences, and that's a biological thing. We've got a clip from researchers who are talking about the adolescent brain and that the frontal cortex is one of the last things that develops. The frontal cortex doesn't actually finish its development until you're in your mid-twenties. That's the part of the brain that deals with long-term planning, and with consequences: looking at what you're doing today and how that could affect you in the future.

We cannot rush that development but kids are being pushed earlier and earlier and earlier to behave like adults. I just saw in Washington State, now kids' medical records are being made independent to the child at the age of 13. Parents are being cut off their kids' medical records at the age of 13. That's horrific, because these kids do not have the cognitive capacity to handle their own healthcare records.

Erin Brewer (17:41):

Or to even understand the implications of these medications.

You talked about the AIDS awareness in school. Well, they're giving PrEP, which is a prophylactic medication cocktail, to kids to prevent them from getting AIDS. Just like puberty blockers and cross-sex hormones, we don't know what the long-term implications of children taking these incredibly heavy-duty medications are going to be, and children don't have the ability to think long-term about it.

I started smoking when I was nine. One of the things that I used to do is I would go to the mall and I would pick cigarettes out of the ashtrays right by the elevators and smoke them. I thought it was pretty cool. Now I look at it and I realize that this is gross on so many levels.

I am now kind of a germaphobe but at the time I thought I was pretty clever—what a great way to get cigarettes! Because a lot of times I wouldn't just get cigarette butts, I'd get some pretty nice sized cigarettes.

That's a lack of long-term thinking. These people pushing the trans movement, the PrEP, and sexualizing kids are preying upon the fact that kids don't have the cognitive ability to assess long-term consequences.

> **These people pushing the trans movement, the PrEP, and sexualizing kids are preying upon the fact that kids don't have the cognitive ability to assess consequences.**

Should we just go ahead and watch that clip?

Sarah-Jayne Blakemore (19:16):

> The brain continues to develop right throughout adolescence and into the twenties and thirties. So adolescence is defined as the period of life that starts with the biological, hormonal, physical changes of puberty and ends at the age at which an individual attains a stable, independent role in society. It can go on a long time. One of the brain regions that changes most dramatically during adolescence is called prefrontal cortex.
>
> So this is a model of the human brain, and this is prefrontal cortex, right at the front. Prefrontal cortex is an interesting brain area. It's proportionally much bigger in humans than in any other species. And it's involved in a whole range of high-level cognitive functions, things like decision-making, planning what you're going to do tomorrow or next week or next year, inhibiting inappropriate behavior. So stopping yourself saying something really rude or doing something really stupid.
>
> It's also involved in social interaction, understanding other people, and self-awareness. So MRI studies looking at the development of this region have shown that it really undergoes dramatic development during the period of adolescence. The ability to take into account someone else's perspective in order

to guide ongoing behavior—which is something by the way that we do in everyday life—all the time, is still developing in mid- to late-adolescents.

So if you have a teenage son or a daughter, and you think you sometimes think they have problems taking other people's perspectives, you're right. So for example, take risk taking—we know that adolescents have a tendency to take risks. They do, they take more risks than children or adults, and they are particularly prone to taking risks. When they're with their friends, there's an important drive to become independent from one's parents and to impress one's friends in adolescence.

Maria Keffler (21:08):

I recommend everybody go back and watch that whole video. It's so informative and so interesting.

One of the things she talks about in there is this brain pruning. When we hit about 12 years old, our brains start actually pruning synapses and connections. It's a little scary if you think about it, because parts of your brain are dying when that happens.

But small children are sponges. They are sponges, absorbing language, absorbing experience. About the age of 12, your brain starts to cut off parts that aren't being used, and it strengthens the parts that are being used.

So if your child isn't into music, some of those music areas are going to be pruned and those that are left are going to be strengthened. If your child hasn't learned a second language, some of those language synapses are going to start to be cut. Kids prior to the age of 12, learn languages so quickly. After the age of 12, you don't have the same capacity for language learning. That's one of the things that comes with that brain pruning.

But what's scary—I'm going to ask you to talk about the drug Lupron, which is being given to kids to block puberty, because kids are told this lie: "If you're uncomfortable with puberty, you're going through the wrong puberty."

Erin Brewer (22:46):

They talk about puberty blockers being a "pause button" so that kids can take some time and consider their gender identity.

I can't think of anything more ludicrous. First of all, what you're doing is pausing their cognitive development—the very cognitive development that they need to make good choices about their future.

Lupron isn't a pause. It's inducing a developmental delay.

As their peers are moving through puberty and gaining emotional, social, and cognitive abilities, these children are being delayed in all of these areas. Research shows that their limbic systems are being delayed. Their IQs are going down. Their social-emotional development is being delayed. All of the things that they need to make good choices about their long-term future are being stunted, so their ability to make good choices about whether to take a medication that's going to cause long-term side effects and medicalize them for life is compromised.

> **Their limbic systems are being delayed. Their IQs are going down. Their social-emotional development is being delayed. All of the things that they need to make good choices about their long-term future are being stunted, so their ability to make good choices about whether to take a medication that's going to cause long-term side effects and medicalize them for life is compromised.**

It's ludicrous to expect that this is a good treatment. It's incredibly dangerous to induce a developmental delay in a child.

Maria Keffler (24:10):

We don't know what the effects of Lupron are on a child's developing brain. There are no studies. This is being used off-label. We don't know if that brain pruning has happened yet. You start a child on Lupron—what if they're in the middle of the brain-pruning process and you introduce this drug that stops development? What does that do to the child's long-term brain development?

We don't know. To me that says, we need to be extra cautious.

Erin Brewer (24:47):

I've heard doctors say that in any other case before we use a drug, we run experiments. We determine how to best use it, what its pros and cons are. And then we start prescribing.

It in this case, it's just the opposite. I have heard people who advocate for the use of Lupron using precocious puberty to justify its use.

Lupron has been used in precocious puberty. Precocious puberty is when a young child starts to go through puberty early, say a five-year-old starts to develop breasts. They use something like Lupron for a couple of years to delay that in a young child.

However, they are finding, even in those cases, that Lupron often has some heinous side effects. These kids are having bone demineralization and joint pain and other negative consequences.

It's not as though, even in that case, it's been a great drug. And in those cases, it's only used for a couple of years.

In a lot of cases with kids who have a trans identity, it's being used for many, many years—3, 4, 5 years. And we have no evidence about what the long-term consequences are going to be.

All the research is showing that this is incredibly dangerous that these kids are being harmed. And like you said, in a child's brain there are these developmental milestones. If we interrupt them, we don't know what the consequences are going to be. It's just outrageous that we have been willing to experiment on children.

An unregulated experiment is taking place with these children and we're sitting back and watching it. It's outrageous. There's no way of justifying it. We should be up in arms.

Thankfully there are some people who are fighting this.

We need to protect kids from this. I just have nightmares, literally wake up at night in cold sweats, thinking about these children and the damage that's being done to them.

Maria Keffler (27:24):

You have spoken to so many young adults who thought they had a trans identity, and then they detransitioned. And they're horrified at what's been done to their bodies.

I'm scared for this generation of kids. I love this age. I just love tweens and teens. I'm fascinated by them. I am just heartbroken and horrified at what's happening to this generation of kids as they are growing into adulthood. The gender industry is trying to stop them from becoming healthy, functional adults.

Why do we have this fascination with youth? Why would we prevent people from becoming adults?

Erin Brewer (28:20):

It's demented. We all acknowledge that puberty is a difficult time, but it's also such a critical time. It's like saying, in order to bake a cake, we have to put it in this hot oven. Well, we don't want to have to put it in the hot oven. You know, that would be awful to put it in a hot oven. Let's not do that. But it is the heat that cooks the cake.

That's how it is in puberty. It is a difficult time, but it's also a beautiful time because it's when we develop into adults. We learn so much. I think about some of the experiences that I had and some of the opportunities and the learning that took place.

I had a difficult time in elementary school before I was diagnosed with dyslexia. I had such a difficult time learning how to read, and some-thing clicked when I was a teenager and suddenly, I could read. It was like the world opened up to me and I just remember gobbling books. The wonder in the world!

Going on hikes—I remember one spring I was out in the woods and I heard the pine cones popping open, that sound of pine cones popping open. There's just so much wonder in the world.

To deny children that opportunity to go through that development—and falling in love! These are children who are going to be denied sexual development. The boys are going to be denied the opportunity of having orgasms. These are important human experiences that they're going to be denied.

I know parents might feel kind of squeamish thinking about their son's or their daughter's sexual development, but these are part of human development. They're super important, and puberty blockers are going to stop that sexual development.

Maria Keffler (30:32):

I was just thinking about all of the coming-of-age books and coming-of-age movies. It's a huge genre. Movies like *Stand By Me,* like *The Maze Runner, Bridge to Terabithia*—all of these movies and books that are about this pivotal point in kids' lives. There's a reason that's a genre, that it is its own genre and entertainment, and we're taking that away from kids.

Erin Brewer (31:07):

It is heartbreaking. There are parents who think putting their child on puberty blockers will make parenting easier because they won't have teenagers in the house. But it's not worth it. Oh my gosh. I would never want to induce that kind of a developmental delay in my children. Every one of those difficult times I've had parenting has been worth it for them to be able to grow up into functional, thriving adults.

Maria Keffler (31:47):

Teachers and parents that I talk to are very scared about the teenage years. They're just afraid of so much that comes with that. I also want to encourage parents: don't fear the teenage years. It's new, it's different, in some ways it's harder. There are definitely challenges that come with it, but you have such an opportunity to grow along with your kids and to learn about yourself. Watching your kids going through these years, you can look back on your own experience.

That's our role as parents, to help our kids through these years, to help them into adulthood. They're not going to appreciate it most of the time. They're not going to say, "Oh, thanks, Mom, for putting these boundaries around me and for protecting my health. And for guiding me." You'll get that when they're in their 20's and 30's.

> **That's our role as parents, to help our kids through these years, to help them into adulthood. They're not going to appreciate it most of the time. They're not going to say, "Oh, thanks, Mom, for putting these boundaries around me and for protecting my health. And for guiding me." You'll get that when they're in their 20's and 30's.**

Erin Brewer (32:55):

I want to remind people of this, too. When my daughter was 16 or 17, things weren't always hunky-dory. There were times where we weren't talking and she was mad at me and she thought I was a jerk. But now that she's a young woman, we have a great relationship. There was about a year and a half where she didn't want anything to do with me. It was hard, but she needed that differentiation. She needed that time to find herself, and now we're buddies again.

For parents, that can be hard, if you've been close to a child. But it is part of being a teenager. They find themselves, and they need to have that independence. Ideally, they can come back to you when they're adults. You can have a relationship as adult children which can be wonderful.

Maria Keffler (34:06):

This is a necessary part of adolescence, because your child has inherited an identity from your family. They are part of this family up until adolescence. They've pretty much gone along with what you believe, with your rules, with your perception of what the world is like.

Part of adolescence is starting to separate—not necessarily rejecting it, but stepping back and saying, "Do I believe everything my parents taught me? Do I agree with everything that they've said?"

> **Part of adolescence is starting to separate— not necessarily rejecting everything, but stepping back and saying, "Do I believe everything my parents taught me? Do I agree with everything that they've said?"**

That is a necessary part of growing up, because you want your child to be a fully functioning adult one day, who can start a family and be successful on his or her own. But a necessary prerequisite of that is that they separate from their family of origin. It is painful.

My youngest daughter and I—she was *mommy-love*. I don't think anybody's ever loved me as much as that little girl. She just adored me. I have dreaded the teenage years because I knew the separating was going to happen.

It's happening, she's separating. Sometimes we'll have these really sweet, close times. Then other times she treats me like I am a leper and the most embarrassing human on the planet, and why does she have to be in this family with these awful people? But that's just the way it is.

Erin Brewer (35:41):

So do we have some questions from parents?

Maria Keffler (35:44):

We do. We have two questions. "How do I get my teenager to understand that he is brain-impaired, that he does not have a mature adult brain development yet?"

Erin Brewer (35:59):

The first way I would respond to that is that they're not brain-impaired, but they're appropriate for their age. It's important to understand that developmentally this is appropriate.

Sometimes it's easy for parents to kind of condescend to their children and to suggest that there's something wrong with their kids. We saw that a little bit in the video. It's easy as a parent to put teenagers down and be like, "What is wrong with them?" But there's nothing wrong with them. They're exactly where they're supposed to be developmentally.

If you can kind of couch it in those terms and then work to explain to kids, "I know it feels like this, but this is where you are. And this is why you're seeing things like this." I think that's going to be the most effective way of dealing with, rather than saying, "Your brain impaired." As soon as you say that your kid's going to shut you off.

Maria Keffler (37:13):

I liked what you said about couching it in those terms: "There's actually nothing wrong with you, but you're not done maturing yet. You're still on a path of maturation." Honestly, we all are, all our lives. I think about who I was in my twenties and I'm very different than I was in my twenties. I've continued to learn. I've continued to grow. I continue to mature.

Adolescence is a time where that's really exploding and happening very quickly, but it does continue all throughout someone's life.

Have a little bit of humility when you talk to your kids and say, "You know, I still make mistakes. I still do things that later I look at and realize it wasn't a great idea." Let them know, "I want to help you as much as I can to help keep you from making those mistakes."

Sometimes we do just have to put our foot down as a parent and say, "You're under 18. You're still in my house. I still have authority. I'm sorry, I know you don't like this, but I'm saying 'no' to this because I'm looking at the long-term consequences. I'm thinking there's an awful lot of risk here."

This just popped into my head. One of the things my husband often talks about—and we talk about this with our kids—is risk management. There are two parts to risk management: there's the likelihood of the thing happening, and there are the consequences of the thing happening.

If we can kind of talk to our kids about that: "So you want to go to this party where there are no adults. What's the likelihood of something going wrong? What are some things that could go wrong? What are some of the consequences of that?" and kind of help kids to learn how to manage risks.

How do you actually think about risk and make decisions about risks?

Erin Brewer (39:06):

That is good. That would have helped me so much as a teenager. Nobody ever approached me with stuff like that. I had no skills for doing that. So

I would highly recommend that.

Maria Keffler (39:19):

One more question. "How does a parent decide what to take seriously and have empathy and validation for? And when it's appropriate to say 'This is ridiculous to knock it off'"?

Erin Brewer (39:32):

That's a good question. I've talked to a lot of parents and it can be hard, especially for parents who are dealing with a kid with a gender identity issue who can be dramatic, and who can be insistent that the parents behave certain ways. However, you're going to get further with your kid if you honor the idea that for the child, this is real. Even if you believe that it is ridiculous, it's okay to validate their feelings. Being a kinder person is never going to be a problem.

As a parent, you can be firm, you can be strict, you can set good boundaries, but being kind is never going to be hurtful or harmful to your child.

There have been a few times where I have done or said something that indicated to my child that I thought they were being ridiculous and it didn't go over well. Sometimes of course, as parents, we don't have the energy. It does take emotional energy to validate children. If you can validate that what they're feeling is not necessarily right or wrong, but that it's real for them, that it will allow you to have a stronger relationship with them.

Maria Keffler (40:59):

I just want to clarify that that words have gotten subverted a lot in the culture today. Today you talked about kindness. Most people think that means never saying anything that somebody else doesn't want to hear, never telling somebody they can't have something.

That's not kindness. Kindness is making sure that you're giving that person what they really need.

Sometimes people need things that they don't want. Sometimes our kids need things that they don't want.

> ## Sometimes people need things that they don't want.

But you're right, there's a difference between saying, "This is the stupidest thing I've ever heard. You're being an idiot," and saying, "You know what? I can see that this is important to you and that this really bothers you. I don't agree with your conclusions, but I understand that this is really painful." There's a big difference in the reaction that you're going to get there.

Erin Brewer (41:54):

I see this with my son. He's 17 and he plays disc golf and he gets angry when he misses a shot. If I say something like, "Yeah, bad shot," it doesn't help. If I say something like, "Ah, that was a bummer" or, "I can see how disappointed you are," it helps. It builds our relationship.

I know it's hard to be a parent and sometimes we all make snide remarks to our kids, and that's going to be normal and they're going to make snide remarks to us. But I do feel like the more you can try—even if you completely disagree with them—to do it in a way that is respectful, that will go over better than if you are dismissive.

Episode 19 Resource List

The Mysterious Workings of the Adolescent Brain (Sarah-Jayne Blakemore): https://www.youtube.com/watch?v=6zVS8HIPUng

The Adolescent Brain: What All Teens Need to Know: https://www.heysigmund.com/the-adolescent-brain-what-they-need-to-know/

Preparing for Adolescence: How to Survive the Coming Years of Change: https://www.amazon.com/Preparing-Adolescence-Survive-Coming-Change/dp/0800726286/ref=sr_1_9

Reviving Ophelia: Saving the Lives of Adolescent Girls: https://www.amazon.com/dp/B0000544ZT?plink=dRv0w6atgLJQJHpY&ref=adblp13nvvxx_0_1_im

Episode 20: The Fallacies of the Gender Industry

https://youtu.be/AQOAECmS5KE

Maria Keffler (00:55):

Today, we're going to talk about the fallacies of the gender industry.

One of the things that you and I—and most people who have been dealing with this issue for a while—have recognized, is that there are a lot of logical flaws, not just this ideology itself, but in how it's presented. We see headlines that don't really represent what's actually going on. We hear arguments that are quite often false dichotomies. That's a lot of what I think we should talk about today: What is a false dichotomy and how are those being used to propagate this idea that people can change sex?

Erin Brewer (01:38):

One of the reasons it's important to talk about this is so that people can name what's happening.

So often I hear from parents and the public who tell me, "Somebody said this to me, and I guess it makes sense, but I just don't feel okay about it."

When people start to deconstruct the logical fallacies and the way in which they're being manipulated, then it's easier to understand why people feel uncomfortable with what the transgender activists are saying. We need to analyze it.

They're saying, "Transwomen are women." Let's look at that and break it down and see if it's true. They're requiring us to accept this proposition, but they haven't addressed how this is true. They beg the question. They haven't shown us how it's true. They're just saying, "It is true because it's true," which is one of those logical fallacies.

> They're saying, "Transwomen are women." They're requiring us to accept this proposition, but they haven't addressed how this is true. They beg the question. They're just saying, "It is true because it's true," which is one of those logical fallacies.

You probably know a lot more about this than I do. Logic is one of those things that I wish I had studied, but what the transgender activists are doing is using well-known rhetorical techniques that people study and people use to manipulate other people, because they work.

Why don't you talk a little bit about the different logical fallacies that you've seen.

Maria Keffler (02:55):

The primary one that I keep seeing used is false dichotomy.

A false dichotomy is where two options are presented as if those are the *only* two options: "There are no other options." If we're not listening for it, we tend to believe what we hear, especially when someone says it very authoritatively.

> **A false dichotomy is where two options are presented as if those are the *only* two options: "There are no other options." If we're not listening for it, we tend to believe what we hear, especially when someone says it very authoritatively.**

I remember I was talking with a trans-rights activist in my community. We were at a school board meeting and we were talking about the bathroom issue. He was pushing for self-identification, that anyone could use whichever bathroom they identify with. This has been a long ongoing issue.

I said, "Yeah, I hear what you're saying. That's a problem for kids who feel that they do not match the sex of their birth. I understand that can be uncomfortable. But my fear is that boys who are not transgender-identified, who are just normal boys, may use that self-identification rule or policy to go into the bathroom and peek at girls. You know, be peeping Tom at girls."

This transgender-rights activist replied to me, "You think trans people shouldn't exist."

Wow. That caught me so off guard, I was still fairly new at this. I didn't know what to say to that, because first of all, it was a *non-sequitur*, meaning it didn't follow. It had absolutely nothing to do with what I just said.

But over the last few years I've been hearing this more and more: if I say, "I have a concern about this part of this transgender ideology," they'll come back with, "You think trans people shouldn't exist."

That's a false dichotomy.

> **Over the last few years I've been hearing this more and more: if I say, "I have a concern about this part of this transgender ideology they'll respond, "You think trans people shouldn't exist." That's a false dichotomy.**

The whole bathroom issue—you will often see articles that will say, "Anti-trans bill prevents kids from using the bathroom." Not true. No, that's a false dichotomy. What the trans-rights activists are saying is that either trans-identified kids get to use the bathroom they want, or they don't get to use the bathroom at all. That's not true. The third option is that they're asked to use the bathroom that corresponds to their sex.

Erin Brewer (05:17):

Or they're offered a gender-neutral facility or a teacher's facility. There are lots of solutions.

The one that I hear that I think is the most dangerous is, "You can either have a trans child or a dead child." It's being used to push parents into medically transitioning. It's being used to push legislators into accepting that this is the appropriate treatment, and it's completely false. We know it's false. I'm here as an example that it's false.

I was a trans kid. I didn't medically transition. I'm not dead. The thing about those kinds of false dichotomies is that all it takes is one counter example. You just need one example to show that it's not true in order to break down the argument. We have so many examples where that's not true.

It's concerning to me that they keep pushing it. It's because people hear the transgender activists, and they don't know how to break it apart.

One of the things that I urge parents to do is to listen carefully to the kind of arguments that your children are making. Listen to the kinds of arguments the activists are making, and deconstruct them. If you can understand how they're flawed, then it's going to be a lot easier for you to argue with other people—not necessarily even to argue, but to advocate for alternatives, because you can say, "Well, I don't want a dead child, but there are other alternatives. There are other things besides having a dead child." That's a lot more effective than just being emotionally blackmailed by this false dichotomy.

Maria Keffler (07:01):

"Do you want a dead son or a live daughter? Do you want a dead daughter or a live son?"—that's a great example of a false dichotomy. But that's also an example of an emotional plea. They're playing on parents' emotions to get them to do what the therapist, and what the gender industry wants done, which is to put a kid on a path of medicalization.

Start asking questions when you're dealing with someone who may be hostile to your point of view. That is a less aggressive way of dealing with it. It's just asking questions like, "Are those the only two options?"

> **Start asking questions when you're dealing with someone who may be hostile to your point of view. Ask questions like, "Are those the only options?"**

Erin Brewer (07:42):

If you start giving counterexamples, then it breaks down their argument. As soon as you say, "I know somebody who had a different trajectory than that" or "I know this situation that is where they handled it with a third option or a fourth option or a fifth option…" It breaks down their arguments quickly.

Maria Keffler (08:04):

Another place that we're seeing the false dichotomies is with the sports issue—letting people play sports according to their gender identity as opposed to according to their biological sex. We see this in headlines all the time, and it drives me crazy: "Anti-trans bill prevents transwomen from playing sports."

No, it doesn't. The false dichotomy is that either transwomen who are men get to play sports with women, or they don't get to play sports at all. No, they are supposed to play sports with men because transwomen are biological men.

Erin Brewer (08:46):

The other place that I see these false dichotomies in relation to sports, as bills are being passed to protect women's sports is, "We can either allow transgender-identified athletes to play, or we're going to have to check everyone's genitals. Do you want people checking children's genitals? That's, what's going to happen. We're going to have all these children who have to have their genitals inspected. Do we want that?"

I'm like, "No, no. There are other options. We don't have to go around inspecting children's genitals."

They're good, they're smart. They're good at figuring out arguments that are emotional arguments that hit people. Because of course, when I hear "examining children's genitals," I think, "I don't want to do that." If I think that's the only option, I'm going to be against this. But that's not the only option. And so we have to keep pushing back and speaking truth.

Maria Keffler (09:47):

So many of these arguments are just coming down from whatever the top of the gender industry is, because you keep hearing the same things said everywhere.

In my school district a couple of years ago we were pushing back on transgender policies that put children and women at risk. Those were the two things that my organization kept focusing on: parents' rights and kids' protections. And that was all we talked about.

I had this woman in our district who is part of the Gender Identity Allies group, who started saying "Maria Keffler is obsessed with children's genitals." I had to laugh about that. I wanted to say, "You're the one that's transing two of your kids. I'm just talking about parents' rights and kids' protection."

Erin Brewer (10:36):

That's an interesting one because I hear that a lot: "People who don't support trans rights are just worried about genitals." Yet they're the ones who are seemingly talking about genitals all the time. They're talking about "shenises" and "girldicks," explicitly talking about genitals.

It's a way of framing an argument in a way that is gaslighting. People oftentimes think it makes sense emotionally, until you start deconstructing the argument. You realize, "No, this is not about children's genitals."

Maria Keffler (11:21):

We know that is a technique that abusers use. That's called *projection*, where the abuser tells you that you're the one who's doing the thing that he or she is doing. So yeah, "Maria Keffler is obsessed with children's genitals"— "No, actually you guys are, and you're projecting that on me."

We've talked about this a little bit before. I didn't intend to get here today, but about *DARVO*, which is an abuser acronym. It's Deny, Attack, and Reverse Victim and Oppressor.

DARVO **is an abuser acronym. It's Deny, Attack, and Reverse Victim and Oppressor.**

Erin Brewer (11:55):

The first time I heard that, I was like, "Wow." I had never heard that term before. It totally made sense because I keep thinking, how is it that people are feeling so sorry for these trans activists when they have so much money, so much power, so much influence, they're clearly not oppressed? I don't understand. They're the ones that are bullying us.

Then somebody explained DARVO to me. I realized, "Ah, this is a technique."

Maria Keffler (12:27):

They claim, "No, we don't have money. No, we don't have power." They *deny* all that. Then they *attack*: "You're A TERF, you're a hater, you're a bigot, you're a TERF." And then they *reverse victim and oppressor*: "We are not the oppressors. We are the victims. You're the one oppressing us because you won't let us in your bathrooms. You're oppressing us because you won't let us have sex with lesbians and call ourselves lesbians."

Erin Brewer (12:54):

"You won't let us medicalize your children. You don't want us to retard your children's development. You guys are such bullies."

It is exactly what's happening. These are all so emotional.

Part of the problem is the way the press is presenting this. They've been so disingenuous. I encourage parents to be aware of that because it is such an influence. Even if your kids haven't been indoctrinated into this ideology, talk with them about it.

This is something that my parents used to do all the time with my brother and me. They liked arguments. I'm not sure that I would encourage arguments, but one thing that they would do is have us watch TV and then deconstruct the commercials: about how come the commercials were wrong. Or they would have us read a headline at the dinner table— maybe my stepfather or my mother would read a headline—and my brother and I would have to compete to see who could deconstruct it better.

This is just something they enjoyed doing because it was how they got their entertainment, but it taught me some good skills. I'm critical as a result of it—maybe too critical—but I quickly hone in and say, "Wait a minute, where is that coming from?"

Which is probably why, when I got the Equality Utah letter talking about conversion therapy, it caught my attention. Most people would have read through it and been like, "Yeah, of course we want to ban this kind of horrible therapy on children."

But I was in my deconstruct mode and I asked, "Conversion therapy. What's that? Wait, what are they saying? What are they doing?" That was how I first got involved in this because I realized they were trying to block the very therapy that helped me as a kid.

I'm thankful that I had those skills, otherwise I might be donating to Equality Utah right now to help them fight "conversion therapy."

Maria Keffler (14:52):

That's one of the most important things you can do. I love that you brought up that example of what your parents used to do with you and your brother, because one of the most basic things you can do when you're deconstructing something is to ask, "What are the definitions here? What do these words mean? Are they agreed upon?" Because quite often we're talking about different things.

Most people in the culture, when they hear "conversion therapy," are thinking of electric shock treatment. They're thinking about aversion techniques. They're imagining ice cold water baths and reparative rape.

But that is not what "conversion therapy" means. The gender industry defines "conversion therapy" as anything other than affirmation. So that means anything other than telling a child, "Yes, you absolutely are trans-gender."

Erin Brewer (16:06):

Even a parent who's questioning, or not wanting to use the pronouns, is now considered guilty of conversion therapy among the activists. The UN is trying to push an agenda where they're trying to criminalize conversion therapy, and that would be parents and pastors, crosswalk guards, doctors—anybody who interacts with a child who doesn't affirm them as transgender.

Maria Keffler (16:30):

That is actually another false dichotomy. The false dichotomy is, "You either affirm the transgender identity, telling that child, 'Yes, you absolutely are transgender and we need to medicalize you,' or you're an abuser," right? That's the false dichotomy that they've set up.

> **The false dichotomy is, "You either affirm the transgender identity, telling that child, 'Yes, you absolutely are transgender and we need to medicalize you,' or you're an abuser." Affirmation vs. abuse.**

So when you hear a parent who is "unsupportive" of a trans identity, that is now considered a toxic parent who is bigoted. What they're really saying is that parent has rejected the affirmation-only plan. That parent is saying, "No, I don't think every child should be put on a path to medicalization." Affirmation versus abuse. That's the false dichotomy there.

Erin Brewer (17:14):

It's amazing just thinking about the definitions, how quickly they've been able to appropriate definitions.

They now freely refer to biological women as "cis-gender" if they don't claim a transgender identity, which is incredibly offensive to me and to a lot of women who wonder, "What does it mean to identify as a woman?" What does that even mean? They're putting labels on us.

"Cis" is a term now that has been accepted by so many. I see people referring to them as themselves as cisgender. They are just buying into this language.

Do they even understand what that means? Do they even understand what that label doing?

For me, as someone who had gender dysphoria as a child, it's offensive. For detransitioners it is offensive. For most women who have struggled with feeling comfortable as a woman it's offensive. And yet it's terminology that's been injected into our society and accepted, probably because most people don't even know what's going on.

Maria Keffler (18:26):

They've been told, "That's nice. That's kind."

What an interesting false dichotomy that actually breaks down the transgender ideology logic, because you're either transgender or you're cis-gender—but wait a minute. I thought gender was on a continuum and you could be anywhere from G.I. Joe to Barbie doll. So if it's a continuum, how is there a dichotomy? What does it even mean? Where is the line between transgender and cis-gender?

Erin Brewer (19:03):

If I sometimes don't feel like a woman, am I cis-gender? And can I be fluid between being transgender and cisgender? Can I be both? Can I be neither?

Maria Keffler (19:18):

To clarify, we're talking about personality, and your personality can be anything you would like it to be on any day. But the actual dichotomy is that there are men and there are women. That's the real dichotomy.

> **The actual dichotomy is that there are men and there are women. That's the real dichotomy. There's nothing else.**

There's nothing else.

Erin Brewer (19:36):

It's so interesting to me because they rely on regressive gender stereotypes. This so-called *progressive* movement, which claims to be moving us forward, is actually hurling us backwards. Because they're saying that gender is defined by these regressive sex based stereotypes and your sex is influenced by whether or not you ascribe to them. Our sex changes based on our personality or based on our behavior.

It is nonsensical when you break it down.

Maria Keffler (20:21):

I got a low-pressure tire light on my car while I was driving. I'm not an auto kind of person at all, but I thought, "I'm on my own. My husband's at work. I've got to take care of this." I went to the gas station and I got the air and I filled my own tire. I was feeling really butch.

Was I a man that day? No, I was a woman. I was a woman the whole time I was doing that. I can pump up my car tires, and I'm still 100% a woman.

Erin Brewer (20:57):

This whole ideology is based on a house of cards. There isn't a firm foundation to it. None of it makes sense. We have to keep pushing back against these logical fallacies because there isn't a foundation to support them. In some ways it's almost seems like you can just blow on it and it's all going to fall over.

For people who are thinking rationally, that's how it feels. But that is where it is clear this is a belief system. It's not based on logic, but on a belief system—almost a religious belief system, based on the concept that your soul is gendered and can be born into the wrong body. Part of the problem is trying to argue with logic against something that's a worldview or a belief system.

Maria Keffler (22:26):

We have a video clip from John Corvino talking about false dichotomies, and I thought he explains it well.

Erin Brewer (22:34):

He did an excellent job, and I just want to encourage people to go to his website if you want short lessons in all these different logical fallacies. He talks about slippery-slope, he talks about begging the question. He talks about all these different ways in which people can use what seems like logic to forward their perspective. But actually, if you know what they're doing, you can see they are actually using red herrings or strawman. If you can identify the logical fallacy, then you can, first of all, understand why you're feeling like, "This doesn't make sense." And you can counter their argument.

So let's watch that video.

John Corvino (23:18):

Suppose we walk into an ice cream shop and they're out of vanilla and you say, "Well, I guess you're going to have to have choco-late." Well, actually, no. What if there are other flavors? What about strawberry or a butter pecan or boom-choca-lotta-cookie dough? (It's an actual flavor.)

The problem is you've leapt to a conclusion while ignoring key alternatives. That's the fallacy of false dilemma. You're saying A or B, not A therefore B, while forgetting about C and D, and so on.

What a false dilemma does is to oversimplify in a way that renders the argument unsound. Now you might object at this point: "Yeah. But couldn't, there also be a false trilemma or a false quadrilemma?" Actually I'd agree with you. The problem is the same. By forcing a conclusion while leaving key options off the table, all of these arguments commit some version of the fallacy of false dilemma.

Maria Keffler (24:11):

Such a good video. I love the way he presents these things.

Erin Brewer (24:15):

It's just so quick and so simple and so clear and you just go, "Oh!"

Maria Keffler (24:23):

We have not been taught to think this way. The schools are not teaching critical thinking skills anymore. That's what looking at fallacies is. It's learning to look at things critically, or like your parents taught you: listen to something, look at something, take apart what it really means, what it's trying to say. We just haven't been taught that and kids haven't been taught that.

I've been married for over 21 years and we have had some arguments in my marriage over the years. My husband loves to argue. He's one of five kids and it's recreational for him. He just gets a charge out of debating and arguing.

I grew up mostly alone. My only brother is 12 years older than I am. So he was more like an uncle than a brother. I didn't have that iron-sharpening-iron kind of experience.

So about 10 or 12 years into our marriage—I remember the moment, thinking, "I'm so tired of this. I'm so tired of losing fights. He wants to fight. Then I'm going to learn how to fight." I think I got *Logic for Dummies* or *Argument for Dummies* or something like that. I started learning how to argue, because I'd be having an argument with him and he would back me into a corner and I'd have that feeling like, "I know something's wrong with this. I know this is not a good argument," but I didn't know how to take it apart.

I don't want to make my husband sound like a bully. He's not a bully. He just loves debating. But as I've practiced, and as I've learned how to think critically—how to think on my feet, how to ask those questions—I can hold my own much better. The debates are actually a little bit more fun now than they used to be. I don't think I'll ever consider arguing recreational, but there is a skill to being able to do it. It's a skill we all need to have.

Erin Brewer (26:26):

I do too.

The other thing is that you have to be listening to someone in order to identify where the flaws in their arguments are. That's something that I don't think we're doing a good job of either. If somebody is talking to you and you're constantly trying to interrupt and trying to interject, they're not going to feel heard. Even if you have someone who you completely disagree with, if you're able to let them present their argument and listen, really listen, then counter it with a question. That's going to feel so much more respectful than just rolling your eyes at someone or saying, "Well, that's stupid," or "That doesn't make any sense."

> **You have to be listening to someone in order to identify where the flaws in their arguments are.**

It's hard to call someone names when you know that they've been listening to you. If that happens, it's clear that the other person is the one who's on the offensive.

Maria Keffler (27:44):

We have one question. This came out of a seminar from a friend of mine. The seminar was about transgender ideology. The presenter was talking about all of the logic and illogic involved. But she said during the Q and A time a lot of young people—I think it was a lot of high school and college students—kept asking, "How do we address this topic with friends and teachers? Where do we begin to get people to think critically about this? Like, how do we have those conversations?"

Erin Brewer (28:28):

That is such a good question. Part of the way you get there is listening. You start out by being willing to listen.

There's a book by Peter Boghossian and I can't remember the name of it, but he talks about how to engage with people. The first thing that you need to do is develop a rapport with them. Before you try to change someone's mind, you need to develop some kind of relationship, otherwise they have no desire to listen to you. Let them know that you're committed to the relationship. Ask them about themselves. Find out about them. Build that rapport first.

Then ask those critical questions. That way the person doesn't feel attacked. It requires a lot of patience.

I've even seen it with myself, where it's easier to change your mind, it's easier to admit you're wrong, when you're the one who comes to that conclusion, rather than when someone says, "You're wrong, you're wrong, you're wrong." If you can gently guide someone to that, it's going to be so much easier for them to admit that they were wrong.

Maria Keffler (29:55):

That's a good point. Those questions are so important because they are not aggressive, if you can ask them calmly and with concern and a genuine sense wanting to understand.

Erin Brewer (30:24):

In this particular ideology, it's on such shaky ground, that it doesn't take much to blow that house of cards over. It's not like we have to aggressively prove they're wrong. We just have to get them to the point where they start questioning, because once they do, all they have to do is start finding that one counterexample.

As detransitioners are starting to speak out, as the medical evidence is mounting about the dangers of medicalization, it's so easy to find counter examples. All you have to do is say, "Have you heard about the Keira Bell case?" That's a way to open it up and if they haven't, then that gives you an opportunity to say, "Well, it's interesting. In this case, the high court found there wasn't evidence to support these interventions and that they're experimental. Isn't that interesting."

That's not confrontational. It's just a way of starting a conversation.

Maria Keffler (31:46):

With this issue the only way to continue to believe that these things are true is to not entertain any questions, to not let yourself question, to keep yourself from hearing dissenting voices.

That's really what the industry is trying to do. It's trying to keep people from being able to ask those questions. That's what's happening in the media with the false dichotomies in the headlines. That's the only way to propagate this—to continue the lie—is to silence the truth, because you're right, the truth is overwhelming.

Erin Brewer (32:26):

Anytime you've got an ideology that is based on belief systems, and they're trying to present it as logical and factual, it's pretty easy to break it down. You just have to build rapport with the person before you can start to plant those seeds of questioning. There isn't much for this ideology to stand on. So arm yourself with these ways to break down arguments. I would suggest watching some John Corvino videos. Watch some of these videos and practice.

Try to find someone who you can practice with, who will engage in an argument with you for practice so that you can start naming what is happening: "I know what she did there: that is a strawman. I know how to address that." It will help you when you're under stress.

A lot of times it's hard to think clearly when you're being bombarded with information, or when you've got a transactivist yelling in your face, or an angry kid. That's probably not the time to engage in an argument anyway, but at least you can name what they're doing and that will help you understand what you are dealing with.

Maria Keffler (33:57):

In today's culture, there's a wealth of opportunity to practice these skills.

Get on Facebook, read two or three posts and ask yourself, "What are the definitions here? Where's that person coming from? Am I seeing some false dichotomies? Am I seeing some strawmen? Am I seeing some *ad hominem?*"

When you start researching these and start learning them—watch a few John Corvino videos and then go to Facebook, go to Instagram. You will see them all over the place and you'll probably be terrified for the future of humanity. And I'm so sorry that we've done that to you.

Erin Brewer (34:40):

The other thing is I noticed I do them. We settle into these because they're easy. They're a lazy way to make an argument. When you're with somebody who agrees with you, it's easy to put these out there. Unfortunately, like you said, they're not teaching these critical thinking skills in the schools anymore. It's a huge disservice.

Parents, maybe arm your kids with these skills to get them to understand how these different logical fallacies can be used.

Maria Keffler (35:24):

There's a great book called *The Fallacy Detective*. It's for kids, but it's great for anybody who wants to learn about these. It's a very small book—just a handbook. I think it's got like 38 short lessons, two or three pages each, on identifying logical fallacies and combating them. It's a great resource for starting to think critically.

Episode 20 Resource List

John Corvino on False Dichotomies: https://youtu.be/9ua74hdBhfI

The Fallacy Detective: Thirty-Eight Lessons on How to Recognize Bad Reasoning:
https://www.amazon.com/Fallacy-Detective-Thirty-Eight-Recognize-Reasoning/dp/097453157X/ref=asc_df_097453157X

How to Have Impossible Conversations: A Very Practical Guide (Peter
Boghossian): https://www.amazon.com/How-Have-Impossible-Conversations-Practical/dp/0738285323/ref=sr_1_1

Episode 21: Why Parents Affirm

https://youtu.be/JEJ_j-g_drc

Maria Keffler (00:48):

Today we are going to talk about why parents affirm. Why do some parents affirm a child's alternate gender identity claims and some don't? There are some particular reasons, some very different reasons, why parents affirm. I thought it would be good for us to talk through some of those.

Erin Brewer (01:11):

It's hard for those of us who see how dangerous this is to understand where a parent who affirms might be coming from.

As we were getting ready to talk about this issue, I remembered coming home from a business trip with a colleague about five years ago. We were sitting in the airplane just talking casually and she said, "My daughter let me know that they're non-binary." I said, "Really?" I had never even heard of that before. I asked her a little bit about it. I said, "How are you feeling about it?" She said, "Well, I'm sad because I loved my daughter so much, but I'm just going to embrace who they really are."

I didn't give it a lot of thought. I had no experience in this, so I just let it go. Then maybe a couple of months later I ran into this colleague's older daughter we were talking a little bit and I said, "How do you feel about your sister?" She just said, "This is all ridiculous. She's my sister." She was having none of it.

I thought it was interesting, the difference between the two. The mom, who is a professor of psychology at a university, is someone who you would think would have some background in this and would have had some red flags going off if her daughter came and said, "I'm rejecting my femininity. I'm no longer your daughter. I'm your child." She really *was* saying that.

But this mom is someone who I believe is a loving parent. I just think that she bought into this ideology and she's been told by the experts in her field that affirmation is the way to go. I could tell she was sad about it. I mean this was a hard thing for her, to let go of her daughter.

I have another friend whose daughter has come out as a "he/him," and I've tried to broach the topic, but there's a wall. It's because the mom knows where I stand on this.

These are parents that before this transgender issue came up, I would have said were good, loving, kind, and sensible parents. They still are. I just think that they've been indoctrinated into the trans ideology. Parents are just as susceptible as children to being indoctrinated into it.

> **Parents are just as susceptible as children to being indoctrinated into transgender ideology.**

Maria Keffler (03:48):

I spoke with a psychiatrist yesterday. We were on the phone for about an hour and the psychiatrist has just realized what's going. The psychiatrist has not been working in this area with young people, but stumbled across a doctor who works with kids and was making these statements, and not believing that detransition is really a thing—the whole nine yards of it.

So the psychiatrist was freaked out and terrified as she started looking around and seeing what's happening. The psychiatrist graduated from college maybe 15 years ago. She said, "This never came up. This was never taught. This was never a thing. But now I talk to people who are going through counseling, social work, and medical programs, and this is the focus."

This is the whole focus of it. There has been a sea change in what's taught. I think you're right—it's being very systematically taught and spread as factual when it's really ideological.

I was preparing to teach a psychology class this year through a homeschooling teaching service program. I got an older AP psychology high school textbook, because they're cheaper. And by older, I mean maybe six years older.

As I was going through it, I saw a little bit of gender in there. There's just a little bit. And knowing what I know now, I'm looking at that and thinking, "Ooh, this was the beginning of it." I bet if I got the latest version of that psychology textbook, it is replete with gender messages, because the teaching and the messaging has changed.

Erin Brewer (06:05):

It's interesting because I just spoke with Dr. Miriam Grossman this morning about how the DSM, which is the diagnostic and statistical manual used by the American Psychiatric Association, changed between the fourth edition and the fifth edition. In the fourth edition, it was *gender identity disorder*, which is what I suffered from as a kid. And it's considered an actual diagnosis that was changed when it went to diagnostic manual five in 2013.

The new diagnosis is *gender dysphoria*. The impression is that the child may or may not have anxiety about being born in the wrong body, but that anxiety that they have is not due to their difficult thinking and difficult feelings, but because of how society is responding to them being transgender.

So it's a different shift. And she was saying that there was a huge uproar in the American Psychiatric Society about this change. It took a long time to get these changes approved.

Part of the problem is that there's no evidence. There's no basis for these changes. It's an ideology—it's clearly an ideology. And when you have doctors and psychologists and other healthcare professionals pushing an ideology without any evidence-base, that's really, really scary.

Most people think there's no way that would happen. So of course, they think, "I'm going to do what they tell me to do, because this must be the right thing."

Recently, Sweden came out with new guidelines for puberty blockers and cross-sex hormones. They say in their statement that they've realized that there's no evidence to support their use in children. They're find long-term negative consequences for these kids, and the puberty blockers and cross-sex hormones don't help. They don't cure gender dysphoria.

If a country like Sweden, that has readily accepted this for many years, is starting to realize, "Wait a minute"—

We have the UK Keira Bell, a case where the judges looked through the evidence and said, "What? There's not much here."

It's important for people to start questioning that. Again, it's hard because you want to believe that your doctors and other healthcare professionals are informed or using evidence-based medical practices, and wouldn't just fall into an ideological belief system and push it on children. But that is what's happening.

Maria Keffler (08:50):

I talk to parents all the time who have a child who suddenly announces this transgender or non-binary identity. The parent talks to all the experts—the principal, the school counselor, the teachers, the pediatrician, the therapist—and they're all saying the same thing. They're all saying affirmation is the right path.

When I started hearing this, I started thinking, "That makes no sense. That does not make sense to me, because long-understood principles of psychology and child development offer ample reasons why a child might have distress about his or her gender, or be troubled about his or her identity."

> **Long-understood principles of psychology and child development offer ample reasons why a child might have distress about his or her gender, or be troubled about his or her identity.**

There are all kinds of reasons why that could happen. I started researching when my school district was putting these policies into place, and the school board members and the head of counseling were telling me, "This is all based in fact." I'm asking, "Show me the research."

I mentioned in one of our previous episodes that GLSEN's model district policy, which is now being pushed into school districts, has three citations, two of which originated with GLSEN. I start digging into the methodology and I discovered that this is not science.

Erin Brewer (10:24):

It is a belief system. The fact that they say this is the only approach, especially for those who have significant mental health issues like bipolar disorder or anorexia nervosa or obsessive-compulsive disorders—there shouldn't be just one approach or just one way to treat all those kids.

With any other diagnosis, there are a myriad of different approaches.

Maria Keffler (11:01):

Even with medical things—even with cancer, with a broken bone.

Erin Brewer (11:10):

I have arthritis and there are a number of different treatment options. I've been to a number of different doctors. I've had some success with some and not so much with others. But there isn't one treatment path.

To think that there would be one and only one way, and we're going to legislate it, is absurd. Because of the therapy bans that have been enacted, a lot of parents aren't even given an option to handle it a different way other than a path to medicalization.

There are times when parents come to us and it's the first time they've

even allowed themselves to question, because they've been so indoctrinated and you can just see the light bulb go on when they start
questioning. It's like, "Whoa, could I have really been misled so much by
people who are supposedly loving and caring for my child? My family
physician, the therapist, the school people—could they be doing this
damage to my kids?" It is an incredible sense of betrayal they feel.

Maria Keffler (12:24):

It doesn't take much questioning to start to break it down. We've talked
about it in other episodes. It doesn't take a lot of questioning.

I'm in a parenting group on Facebook for parents who are having concerns and questions. Lot of parents come into that group and they will
preface what they're saying with, "We're very new to this and I support
my child no matter what," and "We love our child and we're going to let
the child lead." After all these caveats they say, "I just have this one little
question. In this other group I was in, I got beat down for asking it."
When they start talking to other parents who've been in this a little bit
longer, they have such relief: "I'm not crazy."

Erin Brewer (13:21):

You can just see they feel like they had to go along with this thing that
made absolutely no sense to them. When they finally realize they're not
alone, it's just this huge relief. It's just incredible.

I just saw this video. It was a gentleman who was testifying in front of a
legislative hearing about the legislation to ban these medical interventions
for kids. He was just going on and on, "We love you, we love you." He
was just adamant that banning puberty blockers and cross-sex hormones
for kids was the worst thing that could possibly happen.

It was obvious this man cared about these kids. He cares about them, but
he doesn't understand the issues. He has never heard a loving but
opposing perspective.

So many parents are affirming because they are not allowed to question.
In other situations where you have a healthcare concern—imagine if you
had a child who had some kind of cancer, and anytime they started talking
about their child's cancer, everybody said, "Well, you better use
chemotherapy. Chemotherapy is the only thing you can use. If you don't
use chemotherapy, you're going to be responsible for the death of your
child." Of course, they're going to feel like, "I'd better get chemotherapy
for my child," even if that may not be what the child needs, even if that's
not in the child's best interest.

Maria Keffler (15:05):

It's hard to swim against the current. I see parents who affirm often vilified by those who don't affirm. But it's very hard to stand up and say "No" to something everyone else is saying "Yes" to.

We saw this in another episode—I think the one about social psychology—where this experiment was performed, where people were shown lines of various lengths. There was only one person in the experiment who was part of the experiment, *i.e.*, actually being experimented on. Everybody else was in on it. Everybody else was pointing to the wrong line and saying, "That's the longer line. That's the longer line." I don't remember what percentage it was that agreed that the wrong line was longer, about 50% or more.

Erin Brewer (16:02):

The majority of people in that study looked around and then they went with the crowd.

Maria Keffler (16:13):

Even though the crowd was obviously wrong, it can be hard to go against it, especially if you don't have a grounding in child psychology. If you don't have that background or have a reason to think critically about what's going on, why wouldn't you just do what the "experts" are telling you to do?

Erin Brewer (16:35):

Exactly. We hear from parents all the time, "If you start to question, you get blasted." It takes a strong heart to be willing to risk family, friends, and career in order to go against the flow. A lot of people don't have that, for whatever reason. They don't have the constitution to do that.

Sometimes it's even a matter of not having the ability to do it. If they're a single parent who relies on their community for support, or if they are working and they can't afford to lose their job. People do lose their jobs. People do lose their children for not affirming.

We're seeing it more and more that parents are being reported for child endangerment for not affirming their children. It's not surprising that so many parents are affirming, with all of these factors that are pushing them in that direction.

What may be more surprising is how many parents are saying, "Wait a minute, we don't agree with this." I think that's a testament to the instinct of those parents to know something's really wrong here, and that they need to protect their child.

> **What may be more surprising is how many parents are saying, "Wait a minute, we don't agree with this." I think that's a testament to the instinct of those parents to know something's really wrong here, and that they need to protect their child.**

Maria Keffler (17:53):

I was just listening to Sasha Ayad and Stella O'Malley's podcast, *Gender: A Wider Lens*. I was listening to their podcast about autism and it was so powerful. They were pointing out that autism is like one to three percent of the population, but in the gender-nonconforming or transgender-identified crowd it's like 30-40%. That's enormous.

Erin Brewer (18:24):

What's especially disturbing about that is when you look at the number of boys versus girls who have autism versus the number of girls who are self-identifying as transgender, it's even more troubling because fewer girls are diagnosed with autism. So that 30% is going to be much higher for girls.

It's concerning that what we're doing is stigmatizing these kids with mental health issues and we're pushing them into something that's almost like eugenics. If you go along this path, you will ultimately be sterilized. There is something ugly going on.

Maria Keffler (19:12):

There's something very sinister going on.

And we don't need to go afield. We've talked about this before, about why it is that there is something very sinister going on here.

But there's an issue with parents who affirmed that I want to throw in your court. I want to hear what you have to say about it. I keep seeing and hearing about Munchausen Syndrome.

Erin Brewer (19:35):

For people who don't know what Munchausen Syndrome is, it's actually Munchausen Syndrome by Proxy. Munchausen Syndrome and Munchausen Syndrome by Proxy are two different things.

Basically with Munchausen, it's someone who thrives off of getting attention from the medical professionals. Somebody with Munchhausen will make something wrong with themselves in order to get medical attention. They will even alter tests, or they might put blood in their urine to make it look like there's something wrong with them to get attention.

Munchausen Syndrome by Proxy—that "by proxy" part is when parents do it to their children. They do things to cause damage to their children to get attention from healthcare profession.

A lot of times the parents come across as loving and concerned parents, because they are thriving off of the attention that their child's getting. We've heard about cases where parents have fed their child feces, or done things that are unimaginable to get their child sick enough to get medical attention.

In some cases it seems like that might be happening with the kids who are identifying as transgender. The parents are pushing young kids to identify as transgender and telling them that they're transgender in order to get this attention that the Munchausen by Proxy parent gets. Oftentimes it's a mother.

It is a concern, especially when you have young children who are all of a sudden identified as trans and the parent is pushing them to get medicalized as quickly as possible. I see this in groups where parents will say, "I have a four-year-old who is trans. When can I get them on medication? When can I start them on puberty blockers?"

Maria Keffler (21:47):

I wanted to ask you about that too. I see that too. Puberty blockers are to stop puberty. Your four-year-old is nowhere near puberty. Why are they asking about puberty blockers for a pre-pubescent child?

Erin Brewer (21:58):

That's where I see red flags that maybe there's something going on because it's absurd to think that a four-year-old would need to be medicalized.

The other thing that I see are parents who are just mortified that their child is gender-nonconforming. So you have parents who have a feminine boy, and they don't like it. They find it offensive. So they push that child into believing that he's born in the wrong body, that he's actually a girl. Same with girls—there are parents who are unhappy with their daughters looks or how she's acting and can't accept her.

Maria Keffler (22:43):

I have so much trouble understanding that, and I'm glad you brought it up. I just can't wrap my head around that.

But then I think about a friend I have. She's a beautiful woman, but she was apparently the least attractive of her three sisters and her parents were constantly commenting on her unattractiveness, although she's a beautiful woman. I guess that does happen, but I just can't imagine being that rigid about the way your child needs to look.

Erin Brewer (23:18):

It's unfortunate that there are people who are worried about having a sissy boy or a butch girl. Some parents have preconceived notions about what that means about their child. It's unfortunate.

I also think that there are some cultural influences. I talked to Susan Takata—she's of Japanese descent. She was the last born and none of them were boys. In the Japanese culture, they want to have a boy—ideally, the last child, she said. It's not that her parents completely rejected her, but there were always these messages of, "We needed a boy. We wish you had been a boy. We thought you were going to be a boy. You're not a boy. We wanted a boy."

If a child hears this a lot, and now they're told, "You get to choose if you're a boy or girl," it's not surprising that they're coming home from school and saying, "I'm a boy," or vice versa.

Maria Keffler (24:26):

Those messages can be so powerful—even inadvertent messages.

I have three kids and my youngest is now 13. But maybe six or seven years ago—I wasn't even thinking about what I was saying—I made an offhand comment that she'd been a surprise. She was so upset: "You mean you didn't want me? You weren't planning for me?" I immediately explained, "Oh no, honey, we wanted a third child. We just hadn't started actively trying to have you yet. We really did want you!"

She was wounded by the idea that she was an accident. I had to tell her, "No, no, no, no, no! You weren't an accident. You were a pleasant surprise."

As parents, we can sometimes just throw off these offhand comments and not realize how that's going to impact our kids.

Erin Brewer (25:22):

The other thing that is happening more with girls now is that mothers and fathers are concerned about their children because of the potential for sexual assault and sexual abuse. They are so concerned about their child being sexualized, that their daughter internalizes the idea that being female is unsafe and therefore decides that it's just going to be safer to be transgender: "It's going to be safer if I'm a boy."

> **Their daughter may internalize the idea that being female is unsafe and therefore decides, "It's going to be safer if I'm a boy."**

I remember when I was pregnant for the first time. I had the ultrasound and it showed that I was having a girl. I started crying. It brought up a lot of feelings for me because of my sexual assault. I thought, "I don't want to bring a little person into this world and have her experience that." And that was my first response to her ultrasound, which is sad.

Women who have been traumatized can project that onto their daughters, and children, as you said, are sensitive. So it's not that they're trying to do that, but just that kids pick up things by what we say and do.

These are parents who are loving and kind generally—of course there are going to be some Munchausen by Proxy parents, and there are going to be some parents who just want to showboat. I don't know what you'd call them, but they're parents who just want to be able to say, "Cool. I've got a trans kid."

Maria Keffler (27:04):

The celebration of a "trans kid"—everybody applauds and says, "I just want to get a TV show because I have a trans kid."

Erin Brewer (27:14):

I was watching Amber Briggle who started transing her poor child. Amber said she knew before her daughter was even born that her daughter was transgender, which is just absurd.

But this child got flown to the White House to watch *Star Wars* with the Obamas and meet some of the cast members of *Star Wars*. Well, gosh, if you were a parent of a child and you're like, "Whoa, is that all I have to do to get a free trip to the White House?"

There are so many different angles to this, but I do think that the vast majority of parents who are affirming are coming at it because they are concerned about their kids and they want to do what's best. They're being told by experts, "This is what you should do."

Maria Keffler (28:05):

I think so too. We need to have a lot of compassion for that.

There are, I believe, a lot of people who are deceiving people in this area, but it can be very hard to sort out who are the deceivers and who are the deceived. We need to have a lot of grace and a lot of compassion for anybody who's going through this. Unfortunately, there is a lot of animosity and a lot of tribalism, and it's always us-versus-them.

Erin Brewer (28:58):

Since I've been alive, there's always been a tension between parents. When I was growing up, it was the working moms versus the stay-at-home moms.

Maria Keffler (29:21):

When my kids were young it was attachment parenting versus the sleep-training parents.

Erin Brewer (29:39):

Discipline is another big one. There are people who will say that anybody who spanks is abusive. Then there are people who think that anybody who doesn't spank is spoiling their kids.

But in the past, I don't think that there's were cases where children have been removed from the home because of these different parenting choices. It is concerning that this one parenting choice, based on what is, in essence, a religious belief system, is taking over.

It's surprising in America, where we fight so hard to separate belief systems from reality—even in our school systems, we're careful not to impose belief systems. Yet in this one case, we have just completely thrown it all out the window.

I was thinking about the Scopes monkey trial, where they were arguing about whether or not to teach evolution in the schools. I was thinking, "I wonder if we'll have the equivalent of books written about when transgenderism was taught in the school and people were fighting to get the trans ideology out of the school, and fighting to get science back in the school." It's crazy that we're to a point where we might have to fight to get science back in the schools again.

Maria Keffler (30:58):

This is such a lie. It's so fabricated. This is manufactured; it cannot help but collapse.

Part of me thinks, "Well, we just sit back, we take care of our families, and just wait until the cards fall." But I just can't—I know you can't either—because we see in these families the damage that's being done to the kids.

When you were talking about kids being removed from their families… It used to be that the family court wanted to keep families together, if at all possible. That was the goal: family intactness.

There's a situation I know of where a child was molested while in the care of a babysitter. Child Protective Services was called in and they came in to the parents' home. It wasn't the parents who were accused—it was the babysitter—but the parents left the child with this babysitter. So child protective services came into the home and they interviewed the parents. They looked around the home. The parents had to show, "Here's our food, here's our refrigerator, here's our kitchen. Here's where our child sleeps." CPS looked at the entire picture of the family to see, "Are these healthy parents? Is this a healthy situation?" And of course it was determined that it was.

But now we are talking to parents who have their children removed because somebody calls CPS and says, "This family isn't affirming their transgender status and the child needs to be removed from the home."

Erin Brewer (32:53):

It's outrageous to me that there are cases where a parent sexually assaults a child in the home and child protective services will work to keep that family together. They will work to maintain a relationship between the offender and the child.

But now we have situations where parents are being told they are not even going to get visitation rights because they are not affirming the child's transgender identity.

They are saying that not affirming a child in a trans identity is worse than sexually assaulting a child, which is just completely wrong and horrifying

> **They are saying that not affirming a child in a trans identity is worse than sexually assaulting a child.**

for those parents. It isn't surprising that so many parents are affirming, if you're looking around and seeing what's happening and thinking, "I could lose custody of my child if I don't affirm."

Maria Keffler (33:46):

It's a real risk. It's a real concern. It's part of the reason why I don't consider the public school a safe place for a child. Not only because the school is teaching this and propagating this, but because if the school gets involved and doesn't like something that you're doing, they can effectively have your child taken away.

Erin Brewer (34:11):

That is so horrifying because we know that kids who are removed from their families have poor outcomes. Even in families that are pretty disruptive, it's better for the child to be there than to be in foster care, because foster care is often a disaster. Kids are regularly abused and assaulted and put in situations that are inappropriate. This is a situation where the state is overstepping its bounds.

It makes me so sad because in all of these cases, it's the kids who are suffering. The kids are the ones who are going to be damaged by this the most. The key take-home message is, "Be compassionate to parents who are affirming, but to also try and maybe nudge them to understand how dangerous his ideology is."

Maria Keffler (35:08):

We have a clip from Walt Heyer.

Erin Brewer (35:14):

He is an interesting person to listen to because he medically transitioned quite a while ago. He went through the full operation. He had facial feminization and he was on the hormones. He lived as if he were a woman for eight years.

He was being told that this was going to cure all his mental health issues. Well, it didn't. When you hear him talk, it's just heartbreaking because he went through all these procedures that just caused tremendous damage to his body, and it didn't heal him. It didn't cure him. He's left having to pick up the pieces from what he did, and then still having to work through the original issues that he had to deal with, which were sexual abuse and physical abuse in his family.

This poor guy went through so much and now he's speaking out. Thankfully he's speaking out. It's not easy. I was at a hearing with Walt a couple of years ago in Alabama. As the hearing ended, somebody threatened to kill him. This is what people who speak out have to deal with. I've had similar threats.

Let's listen to what Walt says, because he does have some important insights.

Walt Heyer (36:35):

The word "affirmation" has probably become the keyword in manufacturing transgender children. And so I see that affirmation is one of the most dangerous words there is.

I know in my own case, when Grandma affirmed me—I look back at that and say, "I was abused. That was genuine abuse." I mean, we're cultivating this. It's totally abhorrent behavior, because what happens is, the second you tell somebody about being able to change their gender, what you're really saying is— and stop and think about this for just a moment—you're saying there's something wrong with who they really are. You have people who are supporting you in your delusional ideology.

And one of the problems with cross-gender behaviors is that it's contagious. I know of several children who report to their parents, "Well, I just wanted to do it because my friend was doing it." So now we have a social contagion of cross-gender behaviors.

Erin Brewer (37:39):

Walt's insights are important that when parents affirm their child, they're affirming a delusional belief system. It also touched on the social contagious nature of this and how, unlike people like me who had gender identity disorder or gender dysphoria, these are kids who have lived perfectly healthy, happy lives. And then suddenly a whole group of the kids at school decide they're going to do this.

This is another instance where if parents affirmed this, they're not only hurting their own child, but they're hurting other kids too, because the more this is affirmed, the more it gives the message to other parents and other families that this is the appropriate response.

I would encourage people to go and watch the whole interview with Walt because he's got some important insights.

Maria Keffler (38:38):

That word "affirmation"—it's such a positive word. It's such a feel-good word. Don't we all want affirmation and why wouldn't we affirm our children?

But this is another one of the words that the gender industry is turning inside out. Walt said this in his clip, that we're affirming that something is wrong with the child. We're saying, "Yes, there's absolutely something wrong with the way that you were born."

Would we ever say that to a child who had muscular dystrophy? "Oh yes. There's absolutely something inherently wrong with you."

Erin Brewer (39:19):

And that the child should completely reject who he or she is and become somebody else.

Maria Keffler (39:25):

We should never tell a child that there is something inherently wrong with his or her body. We should tell a child, "Let's figure out why you feel that way and help you to feel better."

> **We should never tell a child there is something inherently wrong with him or her. We should tell a child, "Let's figure out why you feel that way and help you to feel better."**

Erin Brewer (39:46):

That is true with any mental health issue. Imagine if therapists just sat around affirming their clients that came in: "I'm so depressed. Nobody likes me." Imagine if the therapist said, "You're right. Nobody likes you." Or "I am feeling nervous. I think people are following me," so the therapist says, "I think hiding in the closet is the right response]" Or if a rail-thin woman came in with anorexia nervosa and said, "I want a liposuction," and the doctor says, "All right, I'll sign you up."

This is absurd. Affirmation is not the goal of therapy. There's no real point in going to therapy if they're going to affirm you, really.

> **Affirmation is not the goal of therapy. There's no real point in going to therapy if they're going to affirm you.**

Maria Keffler (40:35):

Because why would you need therapy?

Erin Brewer (40:37):

Therapists are telling kids that they are inherently flawed, that there's something so fundamentally wrong with them, that the only way to fix it is to become somebody else. That's such a scary message to give to children.

Maria Keffler (40:54):

It's so destructive to the child, the child's family. As you said in society at large.

Erin Brewer (41:01):

Do we have any questions from parents?

Maria Keffler (41:03):

We have two questions today. The first one is from the parent group that I spoke about earlier. Somebody asked, "Is it just me or has the world gone mad?"

Erin Brewer (41:16):

It's funny because right before we started this discussion, I was just having that feeling: "Oh my gosh, I don't know if there can be anything crazier than this."

Maria Keffler (41:29):

Every time we say, "Okay, this is the craziest," somebody says, "Hold my beer," and it gets crazier.

Erin Brewer (41:41):

The next thing we're going to hear about is artificial prostates being implanted in women who have gender dysphoria. I keep thinking, "What could be more absurd than what we are doing? But they manage to keep pushing the envelope.

Maria Keffler (41:59):

This is a little bit off topic, but you just posted about micro-invalidation.

I was reading through that. The only thing we're allowed to say is, "You, 'transperson' are wonderful and perfect and everything you think is exactly right. And I'm a terrible, awful person who should just die."

Erin Brewer (42:26):

That's just one of the most absurd things I can think of. Talk about the emperor's new clothes! We just have to just sit here and talk about how wonderful this is.

We laugh, but at the same time—I believe this was at a university—they said, "If professors are using these micro-invalidations with trans people, they could potentially lose their job." This again is scary.

Maria Keffler (43:04):

You laugh and cry. We've done a lot of crying.

Erin Brewer (43:10):

The world has gone crazy. I feel like we're seeing a little bit of hope that I didn't see six months ago. Sweden coming out saying they're not going to use puberty blockers or cross-sex hormones until 16 is huge.

Maria Keffler (43:31):

Sweden has been a leader in this area, they've been at the forefront.

Erin Brewer (43:38):

Yes, Sweden has been pushing these medical interventions. I would much rather it say 21 than 16, but 16 is a whole lot better than eight. When I hear about eight-year-olds getting puberty blockers and cross-sex hormones at Johanna Olson-Kennedy's gender clinic at the LA Children's Hospital, it just about rips my guts out. I just can't stand thinking about this happening to eight-year-olds.

These kids still believe in the tooth fairy and you're going to block their puberty and give them cross-sex hormones? This is crazy. So for parents who feel like this is crazy, yes, we're going through a crazy time.

Maria Keffler (44:18):

The psychiatrist that I spoke to yesterday on the phone—she really just peaked. Peak means "waking up to this." She was in that state of shock wondering, "How have we gotten here? How is this happening?" I'm encouraged to see more and more people waking up to that, but we really do need more and more people waking up and stepping up and saying, "No."

Maria Keffler (44:48):

Here is the other question that we got: "Why is trans such a thing today? I am in my fifties and all my life I've never seen so many saying that they're born the wrong gender. I don't get it at all. How do we know if this is a phase?"

Erin Brewer (45:04):

Just the fact that we've seen this incredible explosion of trans identity claims—that's how we know this is a phase. There's something wrong going on here. In any other healthcare issue that exploded like this, we would have congressional panels, we would have inquiries. We would be having investigations.

> **There's something wrong going on here.**
> **In any other healthcare issue that exploded like this,**
> **we would have congressional panels, we would have**
> **inquiries. We would be having investigations.**

Maria Keffler (45:38):

I think about a virus—any virus—that's what a virus does. It grows, it explodes, it spreads. I know trans rights activists don't like to hear this referred to as a virus, but it's acting very much like a virus.

Erin Brewer (45:53):

It's a social contagion. We have documented cases of social contagion.

This isn't something that people are making up; we know this happens. Usually social contagion is more innocuous. Usually it's not a big deal, these trends that happen, but this is serious.

I can imagine that people who are just starting to hear about this—all of a sudden they're hearing about kids being born in the wrong body. They must be like, "Wow, when did that start happening? Where's my gender soul?"

Maria Keffler (46:38):

I've lived all my life and never considered my gender.

Erin Brewer (46:42):

For most older people, this is not even something that is in their vocabulary, because they just are a man or are a woman, because that's the biological reality of it.

The fact that we have children now who are being encouraged to replace fact with fiction—that's what's so concerning, because when you start doing that, when you start undermining reality for kids, it sets the stage for really bad stuff to happen.

> ## When you start undermining reality for kids, it sets the stage for really bad stuff to happen.

I hate to make the comparison between what's happening now and Nazi Germany. But it's that same thing where people initially are like, "Oh, that's just their thing. I'm not going to worry about it. I don't want to lose my job. I don't want to lose my friends. I don't want to lose my family. So I'm just not look over there at what's happening." They're hoping it will get better, but it doesn't get better unless people stand up and say, "No more."

Maria Keffler (47:42):

We have a whole generation of kids who have been affected by this, whether they have adopted a transgender identity or not. All of the kids in this cohort—all of the kids in this generation—have been taught this and they have experienced this with their friends and their peers. This is a huge problem.

We've talked before about internal versus external locus of control—who is in charge of your life? Is it you or someone else?

This whole generation has been taught—not just with the transgender ideology, but with critical theory as well—that everything that's wrong with you is somebody else's fault. That does not set us up for having healthy adults in the future. People with an external locus of control, who think everything is somebody else's fault, are terrible friends, terrible spouses, terrible employees. Now we have just raised an entire generation of them.

> ## We have is a generation of kids who have been taught to be helpless.

Erin Brewer (48:45):

They are not particularly happy people either because they feel helpless. This is a generation of kids who've been taught to be helpless.

Episode 21 Resource List

Walt Heyer Interview: https://youtu.be/AXoxcU5aJLE

Gender: A Wider Lens: https://gender-a-wider-lens.captivate.fm/

Episode 22: Dual Identities and Boomeranging

https://youtu.be/o4PsyJwuMSA

Maria Keffler (00:45):

Today we're talking about dual identities and something I call *boomeranging*.

We look at this ideology as a cult, and the more we've looked into it, the more we're in agreement that this is really behaving as a cult. One of the things that cults do is break down your identity so that they can put on you the identity that they want you to have. That's pretty common to cults. Via the gender industry, a kid's true identity—who they actually are—is being subjugated, and gender identity is being put on them. As you see kids who have been sucked into this, it's almost cliché, the way they dress and the way they behave.

Transgender-identified girls—almost to a person—have got haircuts, they've got the trans colors in their hair, and they wear T-shirts, sweatshirts, flannel shirts, baggy pants. They look all the same. There's this cult identity that's being put on top of them and that's not who they really are.

Erin Brewer (02:14):

Definitely. You see this in other situations where people take on an identity, and oftentimes they have their true identity versus the identity that they're grappling with. There is this battle between the two.

In this case, these kids—maybe in their homes their true identity is the one that is most valued and that that feels most comfortable. But then they go to school—they go out there in the world and they're just bombarded with messages that their true identity isn't okay and they need to take on this trans identity in order to be acceptable in order to get affection, to get attention.

There is this internal conflict. It's almost a dissociation.

One of the things that we've been discussing in my detransition group is how this ideology is encouraging dissociation, which is a psychological disorder. It's encouraging this state of unease, of psychological unhealthiness—because when you have this dissociation, it is like you're dealing with two different personalities, and it's not healthy. We want to be integrated. We're healthiest and most functional when we're fully integrated and comfortable with ourselves.

> **We're healthiest and most functional when we're fully integrated and comfortable with ourselves.**

Maria Keffler (03:51):

For the tween and teen in the adolescent years, identity formation is the primary task, or one of the primary tasks, of this age group. It's figuring out who you are.

I remember when I was going through it as a teen, I tried on all these different personalities, all these different personas. I tried being an athlete. Anybody who really knows me would find that funny. But for a couple of years, I tried out for the basketball team and I ran track. I was okay. I'm pretty fast, but sports is not my thing. I learned pretty quickly, that's really not my thing.

I've got one school picture—it's my freshman year of high school and I've got this really short haircut and this jacket. I was trying out the idea of being a businesswoman. I look at that picture and I think, "Who in the world is that?" I was trying this different personality.

It's normal for kids this age to do that.

What's not normal is for all of the adults around them to pick one of those and say, "That's it, that's the one. We're going to cement you there. That's where you need to stay."

Erin Brewer (05:12):

Not only that, but we're going to encourage you to do things that are harmful to yourself in order to have that identity.

That's the crux of it: these other identities that kids try on aren't necessarily harmful. They're just trying to see, "Do I want to do this? How, would it be if I act like this?"

The trans identity, on the other hand, very quickly puts kids on this path towards medicalization. They're binding their breasts, which is damaging. They're talking about taking hormones, they're talking about surgeries. These are all things that are dissociating them from themselves, that are saying, "Who you are is fundamentally wrong. You have to become somebody else," which is not how identity formation works when you're a teenager.

In all other cases, you're going to blossom into who you are. In contrast, the trans identity—even though they say they are encouraging people to be their authentic selves—is actually the opposite of what they're doing. They're saying, "Who you are is not okay. You have to become someone completely different, so different that you have to damage yourself and medicalize yourself to be that other person."

Maria Keffler (06:34):

Dealing with the transgender industry jargon is like living in opposite world, because so much of what they say is actually the opposite of what reality is.

> **Dealing with the transgender industry jargon is like living in opposite world.**

Being a gender-nonconforming person: there's absolutely nothing wrong with that. There's nothing wrong with experimenting with that. A lot of people have said, "If my son just wants to have long hair and try wearing skirts, let him give it a try, that's fine. I'm not going to say you're actually a woman by doing that."

That's where the identity really comes in—the way that the gender industry is forcing kids into these identities, because they're saying, "It's not enough to just change your haircut and your clothes. We've got to really change everything about you."

Erin Brewer (07:30):

Why would we tell a child that? Why would we do that? What it sets up is this real identity/false identity dichotomy. Because as you said, when we're going through identity formation, the goal is to find out who we really are: "What do I like? How do I want to present myself? How do I want other people to see me? And what is most comfortable for me in interacting with the world?"

We want to achieve an honest, real identity, something as which we can interact with the world on an ongoing basis and be authentic, and be our real selves, and that who we are in public is the same as who we are in private.

Many of us struggle with that throughout our lives. I want people to see me a certain way in public, so I'm going to put on a little bit different persona when I go out in public.

Maria Keffler (08:29):

I don't think that's healthy. We should try to be integrated so that who I am at home is the same as who I am out in the world. But that's an on-going process, and we're all maturing and growing through that. But that would be the goal.

These kids are being cemented in this one identity that the gender industry—the gender cult—wants them to have. What we find is a tug of war going on, where your real self wants to come out and live.

Let's even look at something as simple as the color blue. That's my favorite color. I love the color blue. But when I go to school, blue is not allowed. All the blue crayons have been taken away. All the blue markers have been taken away. There are no blue paints. Nothing.

I can go on like that for a while. I can color all my pictures using every-thing but blue. Okay, I can't ever have a blue sky in my picture, so my sky will always be cloudy. Or my sky will always have that green cast that comes before a tornado.

You can do that for a little while, but over time, reality is reality. I need to have some blue skies. I love blue. I want to use blue. That need to be authentic—that need to be who I am is going to continue to assert itself.

We see that happening with these trans-identified kids. They've bought into this ideology that says, "Who you really are is not okay. You need to become this person."

So they walk in that for a while. That can be militant. They can be determined. We're going to talk about how they recreate their histories in a future episode. They will they'll look back at their childhoods and say they have always felt this way: "I've never liked blue. I've never wanted blue. There are no blue skies. That doesn't exist."

But over time, their real selves want to come out. They start engaging reality and you find this tug of war going on.

That's what I've called *boomeranging*, because parents will start to have good interactions with their kids, where they'll have a conversation and they'll bring up some of the logic: "Hey, look outside. The sky is blue right now." And the child's like, "Huh? You're right. The sky is blue. Huh? I'm not sure what to make of that."

The parent feels really encouraged. They think, "Wow, I had a good conversation. We got to a common point. My child recognizes reality."

Then an hour later, or a minute later, or the next day the child just flips right back into gender world: "There's no such thing as blue! Blue doesn't exist! I hate blue!" The parents wonder, "What just happened?"

What's happening is that those two identities are at war with one another. The real identity that loves blue, that knows she's a girl, that knows trans ideology is bologna is coming up and saying, "Hey, I want to live. I want to express myself," and the trans identity is saying, "No, that's not safe. You need to stay in the trans community. You've got to fall in line with our doctrine." Those two things are fighting with each other.

> **The two identities are at war with each other.**

Erin Brewer (11:53):

The stakes are really high when you think about it. These kids—if they reject the trans identity, if they realize they've made a mistake, it's really hard. First of all, they have to admit that they made a mistake. That's really hard.

I know Sydney Wright has talked about this. She felt silly that she had spent all this time saying, "I'm trans, I'm trans I'm trans," then having to say, "Oops." That's hard to do.

Second of all, the threat of losing the community, and all that affirmation, all that support—all that celebration is going to go away and the community will likely turn on you. So it's this internal battle of strength almost. It's hard to find that internal strength to say, "Okay, I'm going to stand up for myself because I deserve it. I'm going to reject that trans identity that's been put on me." That's incredibly hard to do, especially when you have teachers who have been encouraging it, and doctors who've been encouraging it, and friends have been encouraging it, and it's all over the TV. It's everywhere you look.

For kids to have that internal strength to say, "No, I'm going to accept who I am. And I'm going to reject that ideology," is incredibly hard.

Maria Keffler (13:18):

It is. These kids, for the most part, are pretty young. We're talking about teenagers and early twenties.

I was not that strong. My character was not that strong when I was that age, to be able to stand up against the onslaught of people who were telling me, "No, you need to go this way." I'm a fairly stubborn and independent person. When I look back at that time in my life, it would have been hard to go against the flow.

Even now as an adult, I've lost friends over this. I've had family members unfriend me because they don't like my stance on this issue, and that's painful.

When that is happening to kids, to young people, it's awful to consider that they're going to lose their friends, their community. There's a lot of money that's put into this, and kids who come out as trans—if their parents are considered unsupportive, they can actually find glitter families who will help pay for their rent, who will help pay for their medicalization.

They will lose all of that affirmation. Like you said, they will get turned on. They will be vilified. They will be called names and told they were never trans in the first place.

Erin Brewer (14:47):

That's where it's so important for families to understand this, if you have this happening in your home where you're like, "Gosh, yesterday it seemed like she was totally coming out of this, but today she's right back in there." She may be even more militant than before—that is part of the process of getting out of it.

It reminds me of those balls that bounce on each other—Newton's cradle. They bounce against each other really hard at first, but eventually they settle down.

It seems like sometimes when you first introduce that crack in the ideology, kids will actually go more militant initially. You'd think they'd be like, "Oh dear. I was wrong." But instead they go more militant. That is a really common response. As parents you just have to be prepared for that. It is going to be a roller coaster. It's going to be back and forth for a while, until your child reestablishes his or her own identity.

Maria Keffler (16:15):

That's a really good point. That can be so frustrating and so scary for parents to see that boomeranging or that extreme negative reaction.

It comes from fear. Fear is a huge motivator. The gender industry uses a lot of fear. Cults use fear to keep their recruits in line. That is just what is happening in the gender industry. They put a lot of fear on these kids: "People outside the gender industry aren't to be trusted. You're either an ally or an enemy." So when the kids encounter something—a bit of logic, a question that contradicts what the gender industry is telling them— that's terrifying, because they've gone all-in on this.

> **The gender industry puts a lot of fear on these kids: "People outside the gender industry aren't to be trusted. You're either an ally or an enemy." So when the kids encounter something—a bit of logic, a question that contradicts what the gender industry is telling them—that's terrifying, because they've gone all-in on this.**

Again, there's the potential for humiliation. I really want to encourage parents be as tender and as compassionate as you can, because your child needs to know that you are a safe place to land. They really need to know, "If I give up this ideology and I give up this community and this whole cultural phenomenon, I need to know that I've got a safe place to land. I'm not going to land in a place where I'm mocked, or where I'm rejected."

If a parent says, "I've been telling you this for years. Don't come back to me now. I've got no use for you," kids are hearing that they are wrong. Your child needs to know that you're going to say, "Honey, I get it. We're all susceptible. We're all susceptible to believing lies. Yes. I understand why this happened to you. I'm so glad that you're seeing the truth." Be that safe place for your child.

But again, don't be surprised when there is that back and forth—when you start to have those positive interactions and you see the light at the end of the tunnel. You see hope, and then it swings back the other way.

That's a good thing. That's actually a good thing because you're entering that process of the child wrestling with the false identity and the true identity.

Erin Brewer (18:29):

That's a really good point. As disheartening as it can feel, it means that there are starting to be some cracks.

It can be so hard to introduce those initial cracks, because so often these kids are stubborn: "I am not looking. I'm not seeing. I'm not hearing. I'm ignoring anything that challenges the trans ideology."

We're going to watch a video clip which talks about how these identities are broken down. He talks about thought stopping, and closed-circle logic, which is something that these cults do. These are techniques that cults introduce to their members. Thought-stopping: they teach their members that anytime somebody challenges you, you just stop that thought.

We see this in the trans ideology all the time. If you say, "What do you mean? Do you mean a transgender man is actually able to biologically become the opposite sex?" They respond, "Trans women are women." There's no discussion: "How dare you, you transphobe." You're not allowed to ask questions.

Another one is, "If they think they're a woman, then they're a woman." Well what does it mean to be a woman if they think they're a woman? These are circular definitions.

If you're able to introduce a crack into that, if you're able have your child get out of those thought patterns for just a minute and introduce something that will put a crack in that ideology, it can be really scary for them, because they start to realize that transgender ideology is wrong.

Maria Keffler (20:23):

It's really scary for them.

I want to encourage parents: you're not going to get anywhere with your child introducing those things while you're in the midst of a conflict. That's why it's important to really work on your relationship with your child, so that when you're having a conversation about something completely unrelated, that's a peaceful, easy conversation and things are going well, that might be the time to say, "Hey, I want to switch gears for a second. I want to ask you about something I've been thinking about getting your opinion on it." Then put that question there because the child is not in defensive, combative mode. At that point, they're probably closer to being their real self.

When you present that to them at a peaceful, happy, conflict-free time, it's more likely going to get in than if you're throwing these questions at them while you're in the middle of an argument.

I just wanted to preface by saying that the guy in the video is not the most professional, authoritative narrator that you'll ever see. But I thought he did such a great job of encapsulating how cults work.

He's going to talk about how all cults do three things: They break down your true identity, introduce what they want you to believe, and then solidify you in the identity that they've put on top of you. I like the way he describes it. I thought it was a very well-organized argument.

> **All cults do three things: break down your true identity, introduce what they want you to believe, and then solidify you in the identity that they've put on top of you.**

Travis Woo (22:08):

Cult brainwashing and cult mind control takes three steps.

We're all in frozen states. For the most part, we have a fixed sense of identity. So the very first step is to unfreeze someone so that they become malleable. The second step is to give them a new ideology. And the third step is to freeze them again.

Breaking someone's identity down is very important because people are frozen. How do you convince them of something new? You need to shadow their reality, and a really, really common way to do this, that so many different cult-y groups use, is telling you, "Listen, you've been lied to. The media has lied to you. The government has lied to you." That will break your identity down.

Another common way that this has done breaking someone's identity is something called attack therapy, which is like an intervention. A bunch of people will encircle you and tell you how you're destroying your own life.

And there are more subtle ways of breaking: like enlightenment, like perceived as enlightenment. Some of the softer cults will be like, "Hey, so you've been asleep in a certain way and we offer an enlightenment. We offer trying to wake you up."

Then step two is when you give them a new reality, and this can be whatever you want it to be. "Okay. So now that you've been asleep, and that you've been lied to, here's the real truth. Here's the new ideology. Here's the new thing to believe. Here's the new reality. Here's who you actually are. Here's what the world story actually is. Here's a radically new way to interpret everything that's happened and everything that will happen."

Once they have broken you down or unfrozen you, or gotten you to wake up, and given you a new sense of framework, they will freeze you again, which is important, because most people don't know how to unfreeze. And once you're frozen, you're basically—you're locked in the cult at that point.

Erin Brewer (23:58):

So Maria, one of the things that the trans industry does is to really break down the identity. They tell children that their sex is assigned at birth—that people are just guessing, they don't really know.

We know that that's not true, but that's one of the ways that they break it down and then they give kids this message that it's not okay to be cis-gender—it's used as a pejorative.

For those who don't know what cis-gender means, it's a term that has been coined by the transgender industry to mean someone who identifies with their biological sex, whatever that means. I don't really have an understanding what that means. I haven't really talked to anybody who understands what that means. But it's a pejorative. It's the idea that you're not transgender.

They speak as if those who are cis-gender are lucky and privileged. I've seen some really negative comments about the concept of cis-gender. Kids are getting the message that it's not really okay to be cis-gender: "People who are cis-gender are oppressive. They're mean. They're transphobic." There is this message that you're really not okay if you're cis-gender—you're part of the oppression of others, and you're part of the patriarchy that's marginalizing these transgender people. So really the only way to be okay is to be transgender.

There are so many different identities. I have this list that is just absurd—something like 90 different ways in which you can identify other than "cis."

Maria Keffler (25:52):

There's as many genders as there are people—everybody has their own.

Erin Brewer (26:04):

That is how they start to break down these kids' identity. They tell them they're not okay the way they are—that they're oppressive, that they've been lied to, that what they've been told about being male or female is not true. This whole ideology breaks down their understanding of what they know to be true. That's one of the techniques: tell these kids they've been lied to, especially by their parents and by these silly doctors who just made these guesses about what sex they were, and that the best way to achieve your true self is through damaging yourself and being medicalized.

These kids have had their identities broken down, then they've been told what they need to think, and then they've had that new identity frozen.

As a parent, you're trying to break through that frozen identity and get back to that original identity. That is where the challenge is. That is where the boomerang process comes in. You start to break down the trans identity, and it can be really scary. I have had a few times in my life where I've had a major identity shift and it can be really scary when all of the things that I thought were true aren't true.

> **As a parent, you're trying to break through that frozen identity and get back to that original identity. That is where the challenge is. That is where the boomerang process comes in.**

I had to accept that I was deceived or that I had made a huge mistake. I had to somehow resolve that and make sense of that.

It can be incredibly scary and it makes you feel vulnerable because then you think, "Whoa, if I can make that big of a mistake, how do I know going forward that I'm not going to do it again? How do I know what is real and what isn't real?"

That is the biggest fear I have for these kids—they've already gone through that experience of realizing that they can be completely deceived, and it's going to be really hard for them to trust in the future. It's going to be really hard for them to trust themselves and to trust adults.

That makes them vulnerable and they might live in fear. But they are also vulnerable to being sucked into cults in the future. It just makes them generally more vulnerable.

So part of the process of getting a kid out of this trans ideology is helping them to build up a strong identity. They can't really ever go back to who they were prior to this. They have to integrate what happened.

Maria Keffler (30:33):

It makes me think about that line that Frodo says near the end of *Lord of the Rings*, that trilogy, when he goes back to the Shire. I can't remember the quote, but it's like you realize after everything that you've been through, you can't go back again.

That's a little bit heartbreaking. I'll admit there are things that I've learned and seen in the last several years of dealing with this issue that I wish I could unsee and I wish I could unlearn. There are a lot of things that are heartbreaking.

But you're right, that we integrate those things into who we are to become more realistic about the world, to be stronger people, to serve others. What you've gone through, you can use to help other people who are a little bit further back on the path than you are.

One of the things that we need to recognize, especially in the United States, is that we're bad at recognizing this because we're an individualistic society. We think, "My own pursuit of happiness—that's the ultimate goal," but we are not individual islands. We are sons, we are daughters. We are aunts and uncles. We have a family history; we have connections to friends. We're connected in so many ways. And that is a part of our identity. That's an important part of who we are, where we came from.

I have an ancestry that is largely German. I was reading *The Book Thief*, which is set in Germany during World War II. I listened to the way these characters talk to each other and I realized, "Oh my gosh, that's my aunts. That is how they talk. Exactly like that." It was cool to me to recognize that's part of my ancestry. It's where I come from.

One of the insidious things that the gender industry does, is to cut all of those connections off of a child. The term *deadnaming* is so insidious, because that really captures what they're doing. They're trying to kill that child's identity. They're trying to cut that child off from the family. "If your parents don't 100% agree with this, cut them off."

I've talked to so many parents who've said, "We did everything the child wanted. We agreed with the names. We agreed with everything they wanted," and the child still cuts them off. It's never enough. It's a narcissistic ideology.

So the trans industry wants to cut these kids off. They're no longer sons and daughters. They are no longer brothers and sisters. They are no longer aunts and uncles. They're no longer connected to who they were. They're now just fodder for the gender industry's medicalization machine, because that's the goal. That is the goal: to make money off of these children for the rest of their lives.

Erin Brewer (33:43):

As you were saying, it's just so powerful because all of those things that you were talking about—all those identities, mother, brother, sister— those are all identities based on our sex. That is what this industry is trying to subvert. It is so sad because those identities are so important. Being somebody's mother, being somebody's daughter, being somebody's sister—those aren't just vague identities. Those are actually real. They're something that you can biologically trace. They're inherent. They're not just something that we just say: "I'm going to believe this."

It is something that's really disturbing. One of the ways you make somebody crazy is to tell them that reality isn't real. That's what's happening now. They're breaking down reality for these kids. That makes them accessible to the gender industry, which is using them to make money.

> **One of the ways you make somebody crazy is to tell them that reality isn't real. That's what's happening. They're breaking down reality for these kids. That makes them accessible to the gender industry, which is using them to make money.**

It makes me so sad because I was just this morning looking at a new company that's come out with an LGB/TQ product that has the flag on it. I just got this yearning for the good old days where I could look at a rainbow flag and feel good. Five years ago, I used to fly a rainbow flag because I felt good about it, because I thought it was representing all of us. I thought it was about loving people and inclusivity.

Now I see a rainbow flag and all I can think about is girls who've had their breasts cut off, and children who have been retarded in their growth and development, and children who have been medicalized for life. It makes me sick. It is so insidious that they have taken something as beautiful as a rainbow and are using it to subvert these children and make money off them.

They are ransoming our children.

They are taking symbols that are so beautiful. When most kids see a rainbow, they think rainbows are cool. I remember as a kid looking through a prism and seeing rainbows and looking up in the sky and seeing rainbows. Now whenever I see rainbow—even when I go out and see one in the sky—I just get sad for all the children who are being damaged by this industry.

It's just so insidious. At some point, hopefully we'll get back to sanity where we can look at rainbows again and not have that sadness.

But right now, for these kids, that's part of their identity, the rainbow and the trans flag. It's almost like a drug for them. They get endorphins because they're being fed all this ideology and told how wonderful they are and how loved they are. But we know that at the bottom of it is this deep, dark pit that is going to lead them to self-harming and self-hatred.

Maria Keffler (37:35):

My husband and I were watching a news segment a couple of nights ago. I can't remember the title of the segment, but it was about how corporate America has gotten into social justice issues. All these businesses now are all about the social justice issues, but at the heart of it, it's all about the bottom line. They are going where the money is.

Erin Brewer (38:01):

They're targeting a segment of the population upon whom they can make money. This is not a social justice issue. If it were, we would have Asperger flags for all these kids who have Asperger's, we'd have corporations putting a whole bunch of money into helping kids who have Asperger's. We'd have Asperger clubs, because we have lots of kids who have Asperger's syndrome and are on the autism spectrum, and who would really benefit from having clubs and organizations and parades and flags. We're not seeing that for kids who have Asperger's or for kids who have other issues that aren't moneymakers.

Maria Keffler (38:54):

We've gotten a little far-field from boomeranging, but we just want everyone to understand this is not truly an identity issue. The gender industry really doesn't care about your child's identity, except that identity-engineering puts kids on a path to medicalization. It makes them enthusiastic pursuers of drugs and surgeries. That's why they're doing this identity engineering.

> **The gender industry really doesn't care about your child's identity, except that identity-engineering puts kids on a path to medicalization.**

There's this native American legend that a lot of us have heard about. An older man and a younger man are talking about the struggle inside you to do the right things and to be a good person. The older man said, "It's like two dogs fighting inside of you to the death: good and evil." And the younger man said, "Well, how do you make sure that the good dog will win?" And the older man answered, "The dog that you feed is the one that will win."

So as you're dealing with your children, with the dual identities—their real identity and the fake one that the gender industry has put on them—feed their real identity. Encourage them in who they really are. Support them toward being who they were born to be.

Starve the cult identity, give it no quarter: ask it questions, challenge its assumptions, and provide that safe, encouraging, real place for your child's real identity.

Erin Brewer (40:32):

If you, as a parent, can almost see that your child is two different people: their real identity and then this dissociative identity... It's not quite the same as multiple personality disorder, but it's similar. They have this alternative identity that they're actually cultivating, that they're actually nourishing, they're actually trying to split into an alternative identity. If you can as a parent recognize that, it might be a little bit easier to deal with. You can say, "Okay, this isn't my kid right here, this is that other one."

When your real kid does come out as you're interacting, and all of a sudden you can tell your child's true self is present, spend time with them. Feed your child, spend time with them, do things with them, do things that they enjoy. Let them know that you love them the way they are and that they don't have to become somebody else. They don't have to reject themselves. They're not inherently flawed. Nurture who they are, who they were before they were introduced us to this ideology.

Maria Keffler (41:58):

So how should parents respond when children are boomeranging? Is it right to point out the contradictions and what they say or do? How in-your-face should parents be with ROGD (rapid onset gender dysphoria) kids?

Erin Brewer (42:20):

I always caution not to be super in-the-child's-face, because we know with teenagers, it doesn't go over well. You want to point things out, but do it gently. These kids need to know that they have a safe harbor to come home to. Just gently pointing things out is a good way to do that.

Sometimes it also is helpful to have other people who are not the child's parent point things out: a family friend, maybe siblings can do it. When they're not in that alternate identity, that's a better time to say, "It's interesting because I felt like we were having a connection, but then yesterday you seemed disconnected, what's that about?" Maybe just ask questions—gentle questioning.

What do you think, Maria?

Maria Keffler (43:17):

That's great advice. One complaint I hear from kids and adults who have detransitioned is that during that transition time, their parents talked about nothing else but the gender stuff. It was just a constant topic. That's understandable because as parents, we want our kids to be healthy. When we're in a crisis—this is a crisis for a family—it's very easy to let everything become about that crisis issue.

So I would additionally encourage you to try not to make everything all the time about the gender issue. If you can, when your kids are in their healthy, true identities, as you said, spend time together. If they like to go fishing, go fishing. If they like to cook, cook. Do those relationships strengthening things.

If you do need to address something about gender, try to pick your time really carefully and choose your words carefully and try to present it as a question "I don't understand this. I need you to help me understand," as opposed to "I'm going to tell you all of the things you're doing wrong," because that'll end your happy time quickly.

Erin Brewer (44:33):

It sure will.

Maria Keffler (44:35):

We've got one more question. I think we've addressed this. "How do we, as parents help kids recover their true identities and abandon this cult identity?"

Erin Brewer (44:46):

Just spend time with them, reinforcing those things that ultimately deep down these kids know who they are. I would encourage people to get your book, Maria, you have such good techniques in there for helping to bring kids out of this.

Maria Keffler (45:03):

So that book came from you and all the things that you've taught me and that I've learned from hundreds and hundreds of parents.

Erin Brewer (45:10):

Recognize that this is a dissociative identity that has been created it's a false identity. Ultimately, it is going to be scary for the kids to come out of that. You to be there, to stand beside them, to help them be strong.

Maria Keffler (45:47):

It's a great image, and they may need you to stand in front of them.

I just happened to think of this, before we end. We see a lot of parents who affirm this, who are out there in the public sphere, announcing that they've got a trans kid: they get TV shows, and they're throwing their kids out into the public, like gladiators in the Colosseum, to be torn apart.

You do not hear as much from the side that do not affirm the transgender identity, because these parents are the good parents who are protecting their children. They're not throwing their children out into the public sphere. They're not opening up their children's lives to public scrutiny. Your child may need you to be the gladiator standing in front of them to protect them from the culture, to say, "You're not getting my child." And you may need to take those slings and arrows from the culture in order to protect your child.

> **You don't hear as much from parents that do not affirm trans identity, because these are the good parents who are protecting their children. They're not throwing their children out into the public sphere. They're not opening up their children's lives to public scrutiny.**

Erin Brewer (46:56):

That is our job as parents. We need to do that. We need to be willing to sacrifice friends, sometimes sacrifice family, sacrifice relationships in order to protect our children. That's our responsibility.

Episode 22 Resource List

3 Simple Steps to Mind Control/Brainwashing: https://youtu.be/DT-LTTCEf7o

Identity Formation: https://courses.lumenlearning.com/wm-lifespandevelopment/chapter/identity-formation/

Mind Control Methods Used to Change the Personality: https://www.decision-making-confidence.com/mind-control-methods.html

Episode 23: Transgender Identity & Rewriting History

https://youtu.be/LlTqKE7MEro

<u>Maria Keffler (00:41):</u>

Today we're going to talk about transgender identity and revisionist (or rewriting) history.

This is something that we see a lot. It's almost a trope with transgender-identified kids that they rewrite their history. They say, "I've always felt this way. I felt this way since I was a child, I've always known that I wasn't male/female."

> **It's almost a trope with transgender-identified kids that they rewrite their history.**

When the parent starts probing and saying, "Wait a minute, you never showed any signs of this," the child will say, "I hid it from you. I hid it from you because I knew you'd be upset," or, "I was just trying really hard to be my birth sex because I thought that's what everyone wanted."

They recreate their history.

<u>Erin Brewer (01:28):</u>

Something that parents need to know is that children are given the script by trans activists. They're told to tell their parents this. Of course parents know this isn't true.

It's confusing. The pain that I hear in parents' voices when this happens—it's just hard to describe, because these are parents who raised these children, and saw them from the time they were born until they've developed this identity, and they know the truth of it.

I feel a little bit of it when I think about the friends of my children that I have seen take on this identity, who I saw growing up, and I know that they didn't have this identity when they were little. I know that.

If that's the pain I have just as a family friend, I can't imagine what it's like to have a child insist you accept a fake history and identity, or tell you you're a hateful person for not accepting it, or you're delusional, or you're not loving. For parents, this has got to be just incredibly confusing and heartbreaking.

Maria Keffler (02:38):

People may be wondering where kids are getting the script. We often talk about this—it is very scripted.

This is given to kids from transgender activists. Parents need to be aware of where all this is coming from. This is coming from social media. Every social media platform that I'm aware of has a cadre of transgender influencers. These are typically older, transgender-identified men, who present as women, who come on as these "glitter moms" and they seduce our kids. They present themselves and say, "Look how fabulous and glittery and wonderful I am."

Erin Brewer (03:26):

"And I love you."

Maria Keffler (03:28):

"I love you. If your parents don't approve of this, they don't love you."

That is the message that is transmitted. It's coming through social media, it's coming from school—they're teaching this at school.

> **That is the message that is transmitted. It's coming through social media and it's coming from school.**

I've heard so many stories of teachers and counselors—they'll bring in special speakers who will ask the kids in the whole class, "Tell us what your gender identity is. Stand up and tell us what your gender identity is." Then they say, "You present as different than your birth sex. So have you considered that you might be transgender? And if your parents don't agree, they're hateful and awful and bigoted."

This is coming from literature. I mentioned this in an earlier episode—young adult literature goes through these phases of what's popular. Ten years ago, it was vampires and werewolves. It was all of the *Twilight* knockoffs. Everybody was writing vampires and werewolves. I remember at the time just thinking, "I can't wait till they're done with vampires and werewolves." Then there were all the *Harry Potter* knock-offs—everybody was a witch or a warlock.

Now it's transgender. I never thought I'd miss vampires and werewolves. That was nothing compared to what's out there now. What we're seeing is porn and erotica in the genre of transgender and alternate sexualities.

Erin Brewer (05:13):

If you're the only one in your class who doesn't identify as transgender—
if you're the only one in your peer group—you're not considered nearly
as cool. One of the ways this works so well is that if you have a child who
was incredibly gender-conforming, they get to say, "Well, I was hiding it
because I knew society wouldn't accept me. I knew that, and I was worried
you wouldn't love me if I came out as my true self." No matter what the
child's history, the script will fit.

Most of us can go through our history and find examples where we were
gender-nonconforming, if we look at regressive gender stereotypes. Even
if they can't, they can still use this narrative because they can say that they
were pretending.

This reminds me so much of the false memory syndrome that we had for
a while, because what happened in the eighties and nineties is we had girls
basically being told that if you don't remember abuse, it's because you're
repressing it. If your perpetrator doesn't admit to it, it's because they're
hiding it. It's this catch-22: no matter what, the child can say that they
were sexually assaulted or sexually abused because of this weird narrative.

Maria Keffler (06:56):

So many people were falsely accused during that time. So many parents
and caregivers who now have been exonerated—they never did assault or
rape or abuse a child. But they were put in prison. They were given felony
charges at that time.

Erin Brewer (07:15):

They had to register as sex offenders. It's terrifying because it was based
on this whole revisionist history.

We do have a lot of research about how malleable the memory can be. A
lot of times these kids are not malicious in their intention. It's very easy
to gently manipulate people's memories, which is what the therapists did
with this false memory syndrome. They manipulated these girls—the
same demographic—into believing that they had been abused.

> **It's easy to gently manipulate people's memories,
> which is what the therapists did with this false
> memory syndrome. They manipulated these girls—
> the same demographic—into believing that they had
> been abused. The trans narrative is similar.**

The trans narrative is very similar. It's this very gentle narrative that you feed to someone. If that's the cool thing, if everybody else is coming out and saying it happened to them, it explains all the problems that you have, in the same way that the transgender identity does. All of a sudden, every single problem that you've ever had, you can blame on this transgender identity. It's this cure-all.

The scary thing is that often once these memories are tampered with, it is hard for the kids to know what is real. That's how dangerous this is—they can actually undermine a child's reality with this narrative.

It's important that parents know what they're dealing with. This is very serious mind manipulation that's happening to children.

Maria Keffler (08:43):

I don't want to vilify all counselors and therapists, not in any way. There are many who are very ethical and who adhere to ethical standards of care. But if you are trained in psychology, if you're trained in how the mind works, it's very easy to manipulate other people.

I just saw a screenshot of some conversation between a therapist and a child, and it was very clear, reading through this text conversation, that this therapist is manipulating the child. The therapist was leading the child right down the transgender path. It was so obvious from the text exchange. I can point to counseling techniques that the therapist was using to turn the child against her biological parents and to lead her down this path.

That is something that therapists are not supposed to do when they get licensed. That's one of the ethical standards that they're supposed to adhere to, is not to put their worldview on their patient. Ever. No therapist should ever put their worldview on a patient, but that's exactly what's happening with this.

I've talked to so many parents who said, "My child was having depression. My child was suffering anxiety, and my child was suffering bullying. I took them to a therapist and at the end of the first session, the therapist had them convinced they were transgender."

That's just unconscionable. That's so irresponsible.

Erin Brewer (10:26):

It's disheartening to know that therapists are doing that. The trans identity is now this cure-all, that suddenly you can attribute every single problem that you've had on having a trans identity. So of course, it's very seductive for the kids and for the therapists.

A lot of times they're legislatively compelled to affirm trans-identified children. If a child comes in, saying, "I think I might have a trans identity," the therapist is more likely than not to say, "Well, of course you do. Let's talk about that."

For these parents, it's almost like their child is being kidnapped right out from under them. Their body is still there, but their child is being subverted and kidnapped. It is one of the most heartbreaking situations because parents are in this situation and their child is often so angry.

> **It's almost like their child is being kidnapped right out from under them. Their body is still there, but their child is being subverted and kidnapped.**

Maria Keffler (11:25):

A lot of this anger can come out because they are told to say, "If you had accepted me as trans, I wouldn't have had to hide it for so long." There are all these ways that kids can be angry at their parents.

Then they've got these other adults saying, "Hey, come on over to me. I'll accept you. No matter what, I will take care of you. I will love you. I won't make you do your chores. I'm just going to be this wonderful glitter mom."

Of course, it's seductive to teenagers. What teenager wouldn't want that?

It reminds me a lot of kids who come from divorced families, where one parent is trying to lure the kids over to their home. They say the same things: "You won't have to do chores. We'll go on all sorts of vacations. You can have whatever you want for dinner." Same manipulation.

I know of one child who got angry with her parents and said, "You never told me that transgender people existed! You never told me this was a thing!" and was blaming the parents for hiding this somehow. The parents said, "We don't actually think it is a thing. So why would we teach you that?"

It was a sticking point that the child was so angry that the child had to go to school to be taught all this information.

The child has now desisted, and the parents have discussed this with her. In retrospect, they realize the child was embarrassed going to school and being innocent about this whole transgender issue and gender identity and all that. Everybody at school was saying, "Well, of course this is a thing."

The child was very embarrassed not having that information.

That may have caused some of the rift between the child and the parents, because why would the parents have introduced this? This is not a healthy thing. This is not a historically accurate thing.

But there can just be all kinds of those underlying issues where parents and children have really been separated from each other intentionally by this ideology and its proponents.

<u>Erin Brewer (13:42):</u>

It is part of the ideology that they're going into schools and they're teaching these children that you were assigned a sex based on your external genitalia. It suggests that your parents are, at the very least, inept: "We're just guessing. We don't know." Or it suggests that parents are intentionally raising children as one sex, even though they might be another.

This ideology is all about breaking the relationship between parents and children.

> ## This ideology is all about breaking the relationship between parents and children.

One of the things that I would like to recommend to parents, though, is if this is happening, don't try to argue. This is one of those things that if you try convince your child, "Wait, no. You've always been a girl. I know you were a girl," It's not going to work. That's not the best approach to this. Showing them pictures isn't going to be helpful. Even having relatives say, "Oh, no, you were always a girl," is not going to help, because this is an irrational ideology that they've adopted.

Parents often think, "If I could just like show them enough pictures, if I could just find that one essay they wrote when they were in sixth grade, if I could just find that dress that they loved, then they'll remember." That's where parents get stuck.

It's a difficult thing to say, but you just have to allow your child to be in this delusion and not try to argue them out of it.

<u>Maria Keffler (15:21):</u>

We have a video clip of a therapist talking about this issue of history rewriting. The video we have is related to a break in the marriage, when one of the marriage partners has been unfaithful and why the unfaithful partner will often recreate history. I thought it was so applicable to this situation.

A lot of the expert video clips that we bring in aren't specifically related to transgender issues, but we're looking for some of the psychological and educational issues that apply to this, because there's not a lot out there about transgender-identified kids, because this is a manufactured thing. This is not something that has historically existed. This is something that has been created for profit and for politics. I can't do a search for a video for gender identity and revisionist history. This episode of Commonsense Care might be the first video that's on this topic.

Erin Brewer (16:32):

That's so important to realize. I can't tell you how many therapists I've talked to who say, "I agree with you, but I would never come out publicly." People are afraid to create resources like this. That's a shame that we have a generation in crisis, and we have the people who should be standing up for them afraid to. That's how powerful this ideology is.

This video is a good explanation of revisionist history, and it's important to know that this is a common tactic that takes place in lots of different kinds of relationships. It's not just when a child develops a trans identity, but I feel like this expert did a nice job of talking about what exactly history revision is, and how to move forward.

Affair Recovery (17:26):

Rewriting history is remembering or believing our version of what went on over the last few days, weeks, months, years, or decades. It is selective remembering, if you will, when we rewrite history. We basically are making everything about ourselves. We are justifying our actions, minimizing our shame.

If someone is using this rewriting of history, they're probably in a very difficult spot. They're not unredeemable, and they're not too far gone, but they're probably in a state of mind or a state of recovery, or lack thereof, that you're not going to be able to win that battle.

So it's going to be tempting to get sucked into this: "But no! But no! Here's the truth. Here's the truth."

You're going to have to resist the urge to fight for the truth. And simply, maybe say something along these lines, which is, "I'm incredibly sorry that you see it that way." And that's going to be a boundary that you're going to have to draw. And if they are rewriting history, they're probably going to get immensely frustrated, and even maybe bully you and lash out at you because you don't want to play their game.

Don't play their game. You can't win. This is not a game that you can win.

> ## Don't play their game. You can't win.
> ## This is not a game that you can win.

Maria Keffler (18:43):

It's such a good video. I encourage everybody to watch the whole video. Again, it's about marital infidelity, but there's so much in there that speaks to this issue.

One of the things I do want to caveat—he mentions in there the importance of finding a good therapist for your marriage and in a marriage situation. Absolutely. You want to find a therapist who can help with that.

I would refer parents back to one of our previous videos on finding a trustworthy therapist, because Erin—as you mentioned prior to watching the video—so many therapists are being pressured to affirm. They're scared not to affirm. It's getting difficult to find a therapist who's going to be ethical and who's going to treat your child the way they should be treated, and not just the way the trans activists want the child to be treated. Be very cautious about that.

This video emphasizes that it's important to recognize that this is a manipulation tool. Revising history is a manipulation tool.

> ## Revising history is a manipulation tool.

Does your child know that he or she is revising history, or is this part of what's happening by the cult? Probably a little of both. It can be hard to parse that out. Is somebody lying or are they deluded? That can be really hard to parse out.

It's important to reiterate, Erin, what you said: you're not going to be able to talk your child out of this. You're not going to be able to force the child to accept reality. I loved what he said in the video. You can just say, "I am really sorry that that's how you see this."

Erin Brewer (20:21):

I have been reading a book about aging and memory. They talk about the Beatles, when they were making one of their movies, and they interviewed different members of the band about the making of the movie, as well as the producer. They each had different impressions of things that happened.

The producer said, "That didn't really happen. Don't put that in your documentary. That didn't really happen." Then he went back and looked at documents and was like, "Oh, not only didn't it really happen, but the way I thought it happened didn't happen either."

We know that our memory is malleable. The more often we tell a story, the more likely it is to change in our memory.

Maria Keffler (21:15):

I have a relative, a dear relative who I love, who is a hunter and a fisher. And every time he tells the story, the fish gets a little bigger.

Erin Brewer (21:27):

This is something we do subconsciously. It's not at all intentional. It's not like your kids are trying to do this to manipulate you.

That's one of the reasons that this is so damaging and dangerous is because as a parent, you just feel so helpless. You almost feel crazy thinking, "Wait a minute. Wait a minute. I thought I lived my entire life with this child. What's happening? What's happened to them? Why are they saying this?" and trying to logic it out.

Maria Keffler (22:00):

I hear that. I hear that from parents all the time. "Am I crazy? I feel crazy." In parenting groups, a lot of times, that's what they're talking about: "Are you seeing this too? It's not just me. Right? I'm not losing my mind."

This gaslighting makes you question your own center.

Erin Brewer (22:18):

One of the ways that parents can address this is by asking questions. If the child says, "I was always a boy." Ask, "Well, what does that mean when you say you were always a boy? Can you explain that to me? What does that mean? How did you know you were a boy?" Ask these questions rather than trying to say, "No, you weren't. Look at these pictures. You were obviously a girl," or "I know you're a girl. I raised you as a girl. You're a girl."

If you try and logic someone or argue someone out of a memory, it's not going to work. But if you ask those gentle questions, if you can engage with them, that can help.

Like he said in the video: "Gosh, I can tell that's how you feel right now. I have very different impressions. And I hope at some point we can see eye to eye on this," and leave it at that, rather than trying to argue. One thing we know about teenagers is that the more you push back on something that they're saying, the more entrenched they're likely to get. The more they focus on changing their memories, the more likely they will permanently alter their memories. Tread lightly.

Maria Keffler (23:37):

I liked what you said about asking questions, because everybody likes to talk about themselves.

I remember when I was a teenager, I was just starting to date. I was terrified of being alone with a boy, not because I was afraid he was going to assault me, but I was like, "What do we talk about? What if I don't have anything to talk about?" My mom said, "Boys love to talk about themselves. Ask him a question about himself. Have a few questions ready. If he's on the basketball team, ask him how the last game went, whatever."

I have found that is so true. Anytime I don't know what to say or how to handle it, I just ask questions because people love to talk about themselves—kids included. Your kids will love to talk.

They love to talk about transgender ideology. If you can keep peppering them with questions—again, not aggressively, but questions like, "So yesterday you said that gender was fixed and you've always known, but then this week you said you don't think you're actually a boy. You think you're non-binary. So that suggests it's fluid. Can you explain how that works?"

The more you get your child talking, the more the child will hear him or herself talk, and will often catch their own logic problems.

I've found this with myself when I start trying to elucidate what I believe in. I find myself sometimes talking in circles and thinking, "That doesn't really make sense." So that's a good tactic.

Erin Brewer (25:15):

And the other thing that I want to just mention to parents is that if you have siblings of the trans-identified child in the home, this is going to be confusing to them too, because they grew up with the child and their reality is now being challenged as well. If you have siblings, especially if they were close and one of them suddenly starts to rewrite history, that doesn't just rewrite their history, it rewrites the entire family history, and it can be disturbing to siblings.

> **When a child suddenly starts to rewrite history,**
> **that doesn't just rewrite their history,**
> **it rewrites the entire family history.**

It's something that I would recommend sitting down and talking to the siblings about. We have an episode about how to work with siblings. This is something that you have to address head-on. Say something like, "Gosh, it seems like your sister is suddenly misremembering things. I just want you to feel free to come and talk to me about how you're feeling."

Explain that this is unhealthy thinking on the part of the trans-identified child, and help the sibling feel like, "Okay, the reality that I remember is correct and accurate," because especially younger siblings could get very scared if all of a sudden the ground is turning to quicksand under them— that suddenly their own history—or their entire lifespan—is being challenged or denied. It can be disturbing. So as hard as it is for parents, it can be even scarier for kids.

Maria Keffler (26:46):

Kids have much less control over their lives. I liked what you said about the ground turning to quicksand. While you were talking, I was thinking of an earthquake underneath your feet, but quicksand is an even better image for that.

I want to go back to something you said earlier about how our memories are very faulty. There've been some wonderful documentaries. The TV show *Brain Games* has some stuff on memory and perception. We each see such a small portion of what's actually happening around us. Then what we retain of that is incredibly small.

I've been shocked as I talk to my husband or my kids, or my brother and my parents, when we compare memories about things that have happened, how very differently we see them. I'll just tell a quick story on my husband.

He's the oldest of five siblings, and my husband is very *can-do*: "Always look on the bright side. It's all in your attitude."

His family took a work trip to Jamaica when my husband was 14 or 15. He's the oldest of the kids. They ranged in age from seven or eight up to his age. I'd always heard about this trip to Jamaica from my husband and how great it was: "We built houses and we lived in this little house with a dirt floor, but it was like camping and it was so great."

Then I started talking to his siblings about it and I mean, one of them is like *(eye twitching)*: "Oh, Jamaica. Jamaica was awful!" This sibling has almost got PTSD from this trip to Jamaica. The other siblings have very different memories of Jamaica than my husband has.

And so that was just so eye-opening to me about how your attitude and your perceptions have so much to do with the way you remember things.

> **Your attitude and your perceptions have so much to do with the way you remember things.**

Erin Brewer (28:43):

A lot of what we remember also has to do with where our attention is.

There's a video where there there's basketball players and you're supposed to count the number of times they bounced the ball. During the video a man in a gorilla suit comes into the frame, stands there for a little bit, and then walks off. They tested people to see how many people noticed the gorilla. It was about 50/50. The fact that half of the people who saw that video did not notice this random, weird gorilla in the picture shows that our memories are dependent on what we're paying attention to.

It depends on what our perceptions are, and what our emotional triggers are. There are all kinds of things. So a child who says, "I was always this way"—it's a meaningless statement.

As you mentioned too, the emotions that we connect to the memories are something we have control over. So a child can look back on something that was a wonderful time in their lives, and they can repaint it in a negative way, which is what I think is one of the most damaging things about this ideology. It's creating victims. It's actually taking children who had decent childhoods, but turning them into psychiatric patients and traumatizing them by going back and revising this history.

The good news is that you can go back and reframe them once the child's out of the ideology, but it takes some work.

> ## This ideology is creating victims. It's taking children who had decent childhoods, but turning them into psychiatric patients and traumatizing them.

Another reason that kids boomerang is because of these memories that they've cultivated. It's almost like they have to go in and rewrite those memories. Research exists about how to do it. You can actually train yourself to have more positive feelings about your past.

That's something maybe we should do an episode on at some point, because when kids come out of this, often they're left in the rubble. They had this huge cheerleading section behind them, but when they detransition, they don't have much at all. They're left wounded and damaged and traumatized, and they need to rebuild themselves. There aren't resources available for them.

Maria Keffler (31:20):

That's such a good point. We should do an episode on remembering things and assigning a negative emotion to it. We can do that in the opposite direction too. That's part of therapy and healing: looking at things that happened to you in the past, that maybe have negative emotions attached to them, and reframing those.

I'm thinking of my own life. There was a memory I had when I was a child of a time my parents were very angry. I was about four. When I was in my mid-twenties, I told a friend about this memory. She listened to the story, and then she said, "Maria, it sounds like your parents were angry with each other, and it wasn't safe for them to deal with each other. So they yelled at you."

As she said that, I put together that right around that time my parents separated for a while. (They got back together again and their marriage is strong. They've been married over 50 years now.) But when she said that, I was able to reframe that memory: "I bet it wasn't me. I bet it was them." That's a good example of a healing and a therapeutic way to process a memory.

In trans ideology, the influencers and the activists who are stealing our kids are teaching our kids to reframe their history in a negative way, or to blow out of proportion something negative that did happen—because no families are perfect. We've all made mistakes. I yelled at my kids when they didn't deserve it, when it was something else going on. But they'll take one of those memories and just reinforce it and draw the child down a negative path.

Erin Brewer (33:07):

I've talked a little bit about the childhood trauma that I had when I was little, and sometimes I tell people about it and they're just horrified and ask, "How can you survive that?"

That's what therapy does. It helps you to reframe trauma and negative events and feelings. Part of my reframing of it is, "Hey, if I could survive that I can survive anything." That's been one of the messages that I've given to myself: "The worst is over. It's going to be better from here on out."

If I were a kid these days, trans activists could have used that to reinforce my gender dysphoria, saying things like, "Imagine if that happens again, you should definitely transition. The only way you're going to be safe is if you're a boy. In fact, it probably happened to you because you really were transgender." They could create a lot of trauma around that memory and encourage me to embrace a transgender identity.

That is what's happening to a lot of these girls. They are getting these messages that it's not safe to be a girl. And so they're choosing instead to transition. Or they're hitting puberty. As we know, puberty is pretty crummy. They're being told, "You don't have to go through that. In fact, it's going to be really traumatic for you to go through that. You can just go ahead and stop it. You don't have to go through puberty."

There are these weird messages that these kids are getting that are very unhealthy. They're encouraging children to disassociate. They're encouraging kids to have mental health issues that they don't need to have.

> **They're encouraging children to disassociate. They're encouraging kids to have mental health issues that they don't need to have. They're teaching them to be fragile and vulnerable.**

That makes me angry and one of the reasons I'm angriest about this is because I feel like they're damaging kids who otherwise would be survivors, who otherwise would be able to make it through this world. They're teaching them to be fragile and vulnerable and not to be able to handle things, and separating them from the support systems that they have.

I can't think of anything more harmful. I try to think, "Is there anything that could be really worse than what what's happening now with the trans movement?" And I'm sure there is, but I hope I never see it.

This is so insidious and so dangerous and so damaging to these kids. It's so important for people to understand how damaging this is, the revising of the memories and the rewriting of history. And the fact that we have people encouraging children to do this is what is infuriating to me.

Maria Keffler (35:55):

The fact is that there are real issues that kids need to deal with. So many of these kids who are claiming a transgender identity are on the autism spectrum. They've got depression, or prior trauma. These are real things that need to be dealt with. But they're being told, "Oh the reason that you like compression blankets, or the reason that you have those sensory issues is because you're transgender and need to medically transition."

The reason that they like compression is because they're on the autism spectrum and compression provides that safe, snug feeling. It's a lie. Revising history is lying. And, it's keeping kids from getting the help that they actually need for the issues that they actually have.

Erin Brewer (36:44):

It is really dangerous to cover up wounds that are festering. As we know, if you have an infection, but rather than dealing with it by debriding it, cleaning it, and letting it heal, you just cover it up with something like a dirty rag, then it's going to get worse.

That's what's happening here. Rather than looking at these issues that do need to be addressed, they're just covering them up, and letting them fester. These kids are becoming septic as a result of it. The infection is taking over their whole bodies, and it doesn't have to.

I don't want you to feel hopeless. I've seen a lot of kids desisting. Most kids who don't start medicalizing are going to desist.

So I don't want parents to lose hope, but it's really important for them to know that you can't argue your child out of this revisionist history. That's not going to be an effective use of your emotional energy and it could entrench your child more deeply in those ideas.

Maria Keffler (37:57):

We have a couple of questions from parents. "How does a child get out of the false narrative that they created and shared about their past and in adolescence? Are they actually impacting their long-term memories as they tell and retell this false history in order to make reasons for their current narrative?"

Erin Brewer (38:22):

As we talked about, yes. Unfortunately this can cause long-term damage.

One of the ways that families can deal with this once your child desists is with humor, because humor will do a couple of things. First of all, it will deescalate the tension. It will allow the whole family to laugh together, and it will start to infuse positive feelings that child had. So when they remember something, if there's a way to laugh about it—not laugh *at* the child, but laugh *with* the child—and maybe tell the child, "When I was your age, I did this goofy thing."

Maria Keffler (39:06):

I was thinking the same thing—share your stories of times that you were mistaken.

I can't remember the details of this, but just the other night at dinner I brought up something, and my husband and my three kids were all like, "No, Mom. That's not how that happened." And they all agreed on it. Just be able to laugh at yourself and remember we all do it—we're all susceptible to making those mistakes.

Erin Brewer (39:37):

That's really powerful. Kids are going to survive this. The kids who are coming out of this are damaged and they do need to heal from it. But, if you can explain to them, once they've desisted, how memory works and how it is that they were manipulated so that they can understand and can contextualize it.

A lot of times when something traumatic happens in a family and it's resolved, the tendency is wanting to say, "It is done. It is over." In this case, because there is that potential for those memories to have been overwritten, it is important to spend some time deprogramming.

We talked about that a little bit in the cult episode, but these kids have been programmed and they need to be reprogrammed. Even sitting around looking at pictures with them and talking about how much you enjoyed their childhood and showing them pictures and saying, "Remember when we went on this trip? Wasn't that fun?" just to try and help to reframe those memories.

> ## It's important to spend some time deprogramming.
> ## These kids have been programmed,
> ## and they need to be reprogrammed.

Maria Keffler (40:49):

If you can bring up memories that the child hasn't specifically rewritten yet—maybe a vacation that you went on—not with the intention of trying to say, "Look how this doesn't fit." Don't be that overt about it—but just to bring up those memories that have not yet been overwritten, in order to strengthen the truth, because that's really what we're dealing with here. We're dealing with lies and truth. We're trying to make the truth rise to the surface while we make the lies evaporate. That would be a really good tactic.

You were talking about how it is really tempting to just say, "Done. Don't want to deal with that anymore." There actually is a lot of work that still needs to be done even after a child desists. What we're finding is a lot of pain, a lot of brokenness, a lot of loss of identity. There are a lot of issues that still need to be addressed.

Erin Brewer (41:55):

They've been betrayed in such a deep way. They've been betrayed by people who were supposed to be there for them. In some cases, family members bought into this. So not only were there friends, schools, and doctors, but potentially family members, and even parents bought into this. Those desisters have a lot of recovery they need to go through.

Maria Keffler (42:21):

> ## They need to have a soft landing place.
> ## Don't mock them. Don't bully them.
> ## Don't blame them. They have been programmed.
> ## This is coming from outside your house and they
> ## have just been programmed as a conduit for it.
> ## So be gentle with them.

They need to have a soft landing place. So parents, be that soft landing place for them. Don't mock them. Don't bully them. Don't blame them. It's so tempting to blame them for this because they can be so militant and so determined. Frankly, this brought a lot of destruction into your home, but it's really not their fault. They have been programmed. This is coming from outside your house and they have just been programmed as a conduit for it. So be gentle with them.

Erin Brewer (42:52):

That's so important.

Maria Keffler (42:54):

One last question. "I hear trans activists claim that people in history, such as Amelia Earhart and Joan of Arc were actually transgender. Is this related to kids revising their personal histories as well?"

Erin Brewer (43:08):

This is something that astonishes me and it drives me crazy, because at this point, any gender-nonconforming woman in history is now being relabeled as transgender. The same thing is happening with men: any feminine male is being relabeled as transgender.

That does a couple of things. First of all, it tells children, "If you are a gender-nonconforming child, it means you're transgender." Second of all it's teaching them, "This is how you revise history." It's infuriating to most of us who are watching this happen.

I don't know if people realize how insidious this is. It is starting to infiltrate into the schools so that children are being taught Joan of Arc was transgender. Amelia Earhart was transgender. They weren't strong and intelligent and courageous women, but they were men. I can't think of a worst message to be giving to children.

Another reason why I seriously suggest to people that they consider homeschooling, if it's an option, is because this has infiltrated so deeply into the curriculum. I just saw a news story about a school in La Jolla. Parents are upset about it—which is great. I believe it was kindergarteners who were read a book, and then were told in class that it was time for them to choose their sex. The kids came home confused and the parents were enraged.

We're starting to see some tipping points. But this is already in the schools.

It reminds me a little bit of what happened when Asperger's became known. Suddenly every interesting scientist had Asperger's.

That wasn't necessarily harmful. It might not have been accurate, but it wasn't harmful. But this is harmful to tell girls that any smart, intelligent, accomplished woman is actually a man. To tell boys that any feminine, gentle, sensitive male is actually a woman. That is really damaging.

Maria Keffler (45:22):

It is. The revising history is so damaging for the person, for the family, for the relationships, for society. Truth is important. Truth matters.

Another way I've seen history revised— My friend's daughter had a transgender identity, then desisted and told a friend, "I made a mistake. I'm not transgender." The parents of this friend told this detransitioned teen, "Your parents have had undue influence on you. They have told you lies to make you think you're not transgender. Your parents are abusive."

> **A desister told her friend, "I made a mistake. I'm not transgender." The friend's parents told this detransitioned teen, "Your parents have had undue influence on you. They told you lies to make you think you're not transgender. Your parents are abusive."**

I know these parents and they're not abusive. They're the best parents that a child could have, as they helped walk their child toward truth.

But this is also revisionist history that the community is placing upon those parents. And that's just insidious.

Erin Brewer (46:25):

This whole ideology is just really about attacking at the roots. If you can crumble people's foundation, you leave them incredibly vulnerable to suggestive manipulation.

That's exactly what's happening. We have a whole generation that's been manipulated, and a whole society that is being told, "If you're not open to this manipulation, you're hateful, you're bigoted. You're a Nazi." I can't even believe how many times I've been called a Nazi.

That reminds me of another revisionist history that is very subtle, but it's suggesting that the Nazis weren't quite that bad, or that what we're doing by refusing the trans narrative is so heinous.

Either way it's very dangerous to say that what happened during the Holocaust is the same as what you're doing now as a parent, trying to protect your child from the ideology. Suggesting that what the Nazis did wasn't really that bad, or saying that you are akin the SS and the horrors that happened—it's revising a whole segment of history to suggest that anybody who doesn't agree with your ideology is the same as a Nazi, is the same as Hitler, is the same as one of those soldiers who tortured and did heinous things to those being held in concentration camps.

Basically this is otherizing people to suggest that they're somehow not human. Once you do that, once you can create that narrative, that there's a certain group that's not as human, and that doesn't quite deserve the same rights as others, then it creates the opportunity to actually do what happened in World War II.

We need to be the people who are looking around and saying, "No way, we're not going to allow this to happen. We're going to stand up for our kids. We're going to stand for truth. We're not going to allow you to manipulate our children and history and society in order to cause this damage to them."

Maria Keffler (48:50):

I think that's a great place to end. We encourage parents to find the truth, and stand on the truth. Parent your kids the way we know kids need to be parented, because we need to rescue kids from this ideology.

Erin Brewer (49:10):

I know this hurts. I just want to let parents who are watching this know, we understand the pain and how this is probably one of the more painful aspects of the revisionist history. So we know how much it hurts and your pain is real. And it's important for you to acknowledge that this is incredibly painful.

Episode 23 Resource List

"What is Rewriting History in Healing from Infidelity?":
https://youtu.be/kZ7JZIoYBi8

"Think You're Being Gaslit? Here's How to Respond":
https://www.healthline.com/health/how-to-deal-with-gaslighting#confirm

Episode 24: Are There "True Trans"?

Maria Keffler (00:35):

Our topic today is the question, "Is there such a thing as 'true trans'?"

Erin Brewer (01:00):

This is the crux of the issue.

There are activists who are saying that some children are born in the wrong body, that they're true trans. They'll often even concede that kids aren't trans and that they're being sucked into this ideology, but then they'll go on to say that there's such a thing as a true trans person. They contend that it's possible to be born in the wrong body, that somehow there's a gender spirit, or that your soul can be gendered and somehow that can accidentally get born in the wrong body.

I can't think of anything more metaphysical. It's really interesting to me that this perspective is often being advanced by people who are atheists or agnostics and oftentimes critical of others' spirituality. It's a strange thing to be saying that that some children are born in the wrong body. "Some children are true trans."

> **I can't think of anything more metaphysical being advanced by people who are atheists or agnostics and oftentimes very critical of others' spirituality. This is also revisionist history.**

When you hear "true trans" what do you think?

Maria Keffler (02:13):

That it is a very religious concept. One of the reasons why I'm so adamant when I tell people this is because this is an ideology. There's a mom in my district, who's a mom of a transgender-identified child. She got angry with me. One time I went over and just tried to talk with her, and she was furious with me for calling this an ideology. She believes this is not an ideology. She said, "This is a fact."

I didn't go any further with the discussion because sometimes you just know it is not going to end well.

Erin Brewer (02:48):

Transitioning was a last-resort treatment for adults who suffered from intractable gender dysphoria for much of their life. That's what the concept of transitioning used to be. They're often people who are damaged, who have had severe trauma in their lives, who struggle with depression, autism, anxiety. These are troubled individuals who have sought treatment of different kinds and finally decided that the best option is for them to present as the opposite sex.

I hear some people saying there's no such thing as gender dysphoria.

There is. I experienced gender dysphoria. It was an extreme discomfort with my body, with my female parts, with the idea that people would view me as a female.

Gender dysphoria is real, and kids who have it experience significant distress. But transitioning is not the only—or even the best—treatment for gender dysphoria. In fact, it should not even be considered a treatment option. We know that these kinds of difficult feelings can be addressed by a lot of different interventions that don't damage the child or encourage them to dissociate from themselves.

Maria Keffler (04:12):

One of the things that you mentioned and that I've noticed with a lot of detransitioners—and this is another reason why I really believe this is a cult—is that one of the things that is taught to the recruits, is that trans is real, that trans is fact-based. "There are actually real trans people."

So many of these detransitioners, especially the younger people in their teens and early twenties, they will often caveat what they're saying with, "I don't mean to take away from any true trans experience."

No, this isn't real. Gender dysphoria is real, but true trans isn't real.

Erin Brewer (05:10):

It's like they've made a treatment out of the identity. It's strange. It's cult-like, and one of the problems is that every single child—everybody who experiences severe gender dysphoria—is going to be thinking, "Well, I'm one of the true trans," and they're going to pursue these options. If they're told that medically transitioning is going to cure them, then of course, they're going to pursue that intervention.

It's heartbreaking because they're actually being denied appropriate services that will ultimately heal them and not damage their bodies and not reinforce their self-hatred and shame and discomfort. It's heartbreaking any time I hear the term "true trans" and people saying, "I don't want to take medical options away from anybody because they might be true trans."

It's sad to me. I have heard a number of detransitioners who have expressed guilt over taking medications and surgeries from "true trans," because they detransition. They realize that they made a mistake.

It's almost like piling on this extra layer of guilt because first of all, they were told they were trans, they were encouraged to transition. They damaged their bodies. They were betrayed by the people who should have been taken care of them. And then they feel guilty because they're hurting the "true trans."

There are people with gender dysphoria who choose to transition. But they're almost afraid to even speak out about it because they're afraid of the repercussions. They're saying, "I know I wasn't trans, but I'm not wanting to take away from people who are true trans."

Maria Keffler (07:12):

The cult does generate and create fears. Fear is one of the ways that cults keep people in the cult and they teach them these things: "If you break these rules, you're going to suffer. The people outside the cults are heretics. They're transphobes, the haters, the nasty people."

> **Fear is one of the ways cults keep people in the cult: "If you break these rules, you're going to suffer."**

When these kids realize they are not transgender, and they detransition, many of them still have that belief system. They're taking that belief system with them, which is part of the reason why it's so hard for them to leave the cult. They've heard all of this stuff about the awful people outside of the cult and they don't want to be one of the awful people. They think, "I know I don't belong in the cult anymore, but I don't want to be like the awful people outside of it. So I'll just say I believe there's really are true trans."

I think that's what we're seeing when we hear people talk about true trans. I feel like it undercuts the whole sense of reality and undercuts the argument against medicalizing children.

Erin Brewer (08:41):

Exactly. That's why it's so insidious because any doctor's going to say,

"This particular patient is a true trans. Sure there are detransitioners, but my patient is true trans."

Then they define transgender as someone who's insistent, consistent and persistent with gender dysphoria. So according to the definition, anybody with gender dysphoria is transgender. It's this convoluted definition.

It's so harmful because kids will always be the ones who's insist, "I'm actually the true trans," until they detransition.

It's almost like there's this awakening after they've been away from the trans cult for long enough. They're mad because they were lied to. Once they get away from feeling like they need to tiptoe and be so careful not to offend anybody, once they really separate from the cult and reidentify with who they really are, they're so angry and they feel so betrayed. They wonder, "How could anybody have done this to me?"

Maria Keffler (09:58):

When you were talking about how kids will believe, "I'm the one who's true trans," it makes me think about young teenagers—14-, 15-, 16-years-old—when they fall in love with the first time. And, that boyfriend or girlfriend—that's the one. The adult says, "Most high school relationships don't last," and the teen thinks, "Mine's going to last. You don't understand."

I was one of those. I'd say, "No, you don't understand how in love we are."

Imagine if all the adults said, "Of course you are in love. It is your one true love. You need to get married. You need to get married right now." Then those teenage lovebirds would believe it was best to get married and have a baby and start a family right now, because you don't want to waste time.

We know better than that.

Erin Brewer (11:05):

Another thing that is dangerous about this ideology is that it's further stigmatizing mental health issues. It's suggesting that admitting that you have gender dysphoria is something shameful. It's so awful that we have to pretend like you're transgender, like you're really are born in the wrong body, because we don't want to hurt your feelings. We don't want to suggest this as a mental health issue. That would be horribly "transphobic."

They are stigmatizing everybody who has mental health issues, but especially those who have gender dysphoria, because it's giving them the message that it's not okay to have mental health issues, that there's nothing wrong with their mind. It's your body that's to blame.

I go back to this anorexic narrative all the time. I can't imagine a doctor telling a young woman who is anorexic, "Okay, I'm going to go ahead and sign you up for liposuction and a gastric bypass because even though you don't look fat, and even though your BMI is dangerously low, if you feel fat, you're fat. We're going to go ahead and take care of it." We don't do that.

Maria Keffler (12:17):

No. That's a great analogy. When you bring that up with really brainwashed trans-rights people, they tell you that's not a good analogy. "That analogy doesn't work well." Why? They can't give you a reason, because it is a really good analogy.

I was thinking when you were talking about telling people who have gender dysphoria, "You have to transition. You have to medically transition." That's also telling people, "You can't struggle through something. There's no way to cope through something that's difficult for you."

I think about the movie *A Beautiful Mind*. The main character in the story had schizophrenia, and he saw people who weren't there. (Spoiler alert! If you haven't seen the movie, skip over this next part.) But he learns ways to cope. He never gets rid of those apparitions that he sees—those people follow him around. But toward the end of the movie, he's walking into his classroom and there's somebody that he hasn't met before who says, "Excuse me, professor, can I talk to you?" The main character stops a student who he knows. He says, "Do you see that person?" So that way the professor knew this is a real person and not a figment of his imagination.

There are ways to cope with difficulties.

Erin Brewer (13:46):

Now that is brave and authentic, being able to come up with those coping mechanisms to deal with serious mental health issues. Imagine the strength of courage in there that it takes to do that, to admit, "Yes, I have this problem and I'm going to work hard to overcome it."

We know people can overcome mental health issues. They do it all the time. To say to them, "You're unsalvageable. The only way you can deal with this is to damage your body."

Maria Keffler (14:20):

The brain and the mind are so much more malleable than the body. The body is the sensitive system. Anybody who's taken medication knows a medication that fixes one thing typically has side effects with something else. Everything's so interconnected, and is balanced when it's healthy.

To take a healthy body and introduce pathology is completely unethical. I'm horrified that doctors are doing this. Every time I see a picture of a doctor with a girl who's had her breasts cut off, and the surgeon is there with a smarmy grin, I just get so angry. I think, "I want to see you in jail one day."

> **To take a healthy body and introduce pathology is completely unethical.**

Erin Brewer (15:08):

That's where people who abuse others, especially vulnerable people, belong.

One of the rallying cries I hear them so often say is, "You're erasing trans people. You're denying their existence." Actually, they are denying the very existence of your daughter or son, and erasing them as the biological sex that they are and turning them into a new persona. You're erasing the concept of womanhood and manhood. You're erasing the concept of gay and lesbian.

Maria Keffler (15:54):

On language—their own language—the term "deadname" gives it all away. A deadname is a name that belongs to a dead person. You cannot argue that, "My child is the same person, they just changed sexes" and "That was a dead person who no longer exists. And this is a new person." No, those don't work together. It's one or the other.

Erin Brewer (16:20):

The other tactic that they use all the time is the suicide claim: that people are going to kill themselves if their trans identity is not affirmed. They're actually advocating suicide of the self. They're not killing the body, but they are advocating that people kill the essence of who they are and become somebody new. It's not quite suicide, but it really is a metaphysical suicide. "We want you to kill yourself. Kill who you are and become somebody new."

To me, a lot of the language they use, when you really look at it, is metaphysical. It's religious. It's cult-like.

But it also doesn't hold water, and their arguments are so vacuous. It's a net—there's not anything to it. You pour water in and it just goes right through because all of the arguments that they have—it just doesn't take that much to turn it around.

If they are against suicide, why are they advocating for all these kids to kill the essence of who they are and to sacrifice their very essence of their being to this cult of become somebody new?

Maria Keffler (17:42):

Not only their own selves, but their relationships: "If your parents aren't on board, cut them off. If your friends don't like it, cut them off." That's very cult-like, to cut out anybody who doesn't agree with you. And who steps in? The glitter family.

> **"If your parents aren't on board, cut them off.**
> **If your friends don't like it, cut them off."**
> **That's very cult -like, to cut out anybody**
> **who doesn't agree with you.**

Erin Brewer (18:19):

We know that it is damaging. These are kids who are so vulnerable. All of this is based on an ideology, or even a religion.

I'm beginning more and more to think of this as a religious belief. When I see parents being compelled to go to re-education classes in order to have contact with their kids, if the parents are divorced—we are seeing more and more these re-education classes being compelled by courts. The courts are sending people to go to learn about how to worship in this religion.

Maria Keffler (18:58):

I'm wondering if just attending the class is going to be enough, or if the instructor of the class has to sign off, and say, "Yes, this person has been adequately re-educated."

Erin Brewer (19:15):

It's the state religion. Particularly during pride month. I'm just shocked at how this is not a marginalized group. This ideology has completely infiltrated everything.

<u>Maria Keffler (20:29):</u>

It used to be medicalizing was the last resort.

<u>Erin Brewer (20:44):</u>

People say it is an identity.

Identities are ephemeral. People go from being Christian to Jewish. People go from being Democrat to Republican. People go from being single to married. Our identity changes all the time. To suggest that identity is some sacred thing that doesn't change is absurd.

Our lives are about our ever-evolving identity. It is that concept of a spirit that was born in the wrong body—We don't have political spirits. We don't have age spirits. No one is suggesting that it is possible for a Jewish spirit to be born in the wrong body, like a Christian spirit gets put a Muslim's body.

<u>Maria Keffler (21:53):</u>

I never thought about it that way before, but that's a really good point.

We have a clip here from a detransitioner. Can you introduce it because you've actually spoken to him?

<u>Erin Brewer (22:04):</u>

Hasci he is a detransitioner. He lived as a woman for a while, went through medical intervention, and then realized that it was a way of running from his mental health issues and his traumatic childhood.

We see this over and over again: either severe physical or sexual abuse causes that dissociative process. Once that has been entrenched in somebody, that's a coping mechanism and it's easy to dissociate after that.

Let's listen to him and see what his insights are.

> <u>Hasci Horvath (22:43):</u>
>
> If you read the scientific articles about the origin or the basis of transgenderism, you'll see that there's a strong emphasis that it's biological, it's something innate you have—there's some "gender identity" that everybody has. And it's just that some people are born this way. They have a built-in—they're the opposite sex in their brains, like Bruce Jenner.
>
> This is based on the assertions of a few psychologists. It's not based on any scientific evidence in the research. It's just in the

sixties, they began to say that it's built in as part of their who they are. And that idea just took hold and, and it's not based on anything.

And so over the course of the past 30 years, they've been looking at people's brains and thinking, "What about hormones in utero? And all these various ways that people might've had their gender identity scrambled?" And it all looks very nice when you read the paper, they say "Woo, it's, tantalizingly close evidence." And it's very suggestive of some association here—it's spin. And if you read it carefully there's nothing really in there that connects. There are enormous gaps ... there are probably 10 or 20 other more likely explanations for any associations they do see. So they just selectively choose these outcomes. And pretty much all of the science investigating that is an exercise in confirmation bias and selection bias.

Erin Brewer (24:09):

Here is someone who undoubtedly would have been labeled as a "true trans," who suffered from severe gender dysphoria. He got other kinds of treatments to try and help it, and decided that the only way to really address it was to get medical interventions. At some point he realized it wasn't helping.

That is probably even more important. These medical interventions don't cure the gender dysphoria. They go through all these interventions—really invasive things that damage the body—and it doesn't even cure the underlying gender dysphoria.

Maria Keffler (24:52):

Don't we hear that from a lot of detransitioners? "I got all this stuff done and I realized it didn't help and everything that was wrong with me was still there, but now I'm also damaged from the interventions."

Erin Brewer (25:04):

First they are encouraged to socially transition, then take hormones, then have surgeries. Once they get to the point where there's nothing more they can do to their bodies, that's when it hits: transition didn't cure them.

How heartbreaking for them to have gone through all that and realize they still have all the problems that they had before, but now they've compounded it because they've damaged their bodies. A lot of times, they're going to have to take synthetic hormones for the rest of their lives, which incurs a both a financial cost and an emotional one.

Maria Keffler (25:42):

You pointed out in an earlier episode—I didn't realize this—that once a person has been on wrong-sex hormones for a while, his or her body stops making the natural hormones. So even after detransitioning, that person has to take what would have been their appropriate sex hormones synthetically, because their body has stopped making them.

That's so insidious. That's so nefarious. Don't tell me the pharmaceutical companies are not pushing this.

Erin Brewer (26:14):

Somebody who was keen on business and had absolutely no moral foundation decided that this was a great way to make money.

> **Somebody who was keen on business and had absolutely no moral foundation decided that this was a great way to make money.**

Maria Keffler (26:33):

We talked about that. A market report from Global Market Insights came out and said that sex reassignment surgery is a growth market. They expect it to make billions of dollars in the next five years.

Erin Brewer (26:49):

Any medical practitioner who is willing to make money by damaging somebody who already is struggling with mental health issues—like you said, they belong in jail.

Maria Keffler (27:00):

They do. I hope we see that before long.

We have one question. This came from a parenting group, and it's such a great question. It was addressed to the entire group. "My therapist asked a question that I would now like to ask all of you: If your child does all of the therapy and work to find the core cause of their gender dysphoria. And it turns out they are truly transgender, will you support them?"

Erin Brewer (27:35):

My answer is there is no such thing as "true trans."

Maria Keffler (27:40):

That's what I wanted to say. This assumes the existence of true transgender. That's what this ideology does. It loads all these assumptions in, and then calls you a horrible person for not buying into them.

**That's what this ideology does.
It loads all these assumptions in, and then
calls you a horrible person for not buying into them.**

Erin Brewer (27:54):

To me, it is like saying, "What if someone is really depressed? The person had some treatment and they really still felt bad. They think they would be better off dead, should they just kill themselves?"

Of course not, of course not, no way. We would never do that.

Maria Keffler (28:11):

Let's address the word *support* as well. "Will you support your child?" In trans-speak *support* means, "go along with everything that child wants." That's what support means. If you don't agree to everything the child says, then you're labeled an unsupportive parent.

But that's not what support means. That's not the truth.

True support is giving somebody what they need, not necessarily what they want. Just like *affirmation* in trans-speak is the same thing as support. It means agreeing with everything they say. True affirmation is affirming somebody's worth, somebody's value, somebody's inherent personhood.

They've taken these words and assigned these different meanings to them.

Erin Brewer (29:10):

Someone who isn't familiar with this ideology might think, "You're not affirming your kid? Why would you not be affirming?"

Maria Keffler (29:19):

What it really means is, "You're not agreeing with them that something's inherently wrong and they should lop off body parts."

Erin Brewer (29:27):

The suggestion that such "affirmation" is somehow better than saying they need some mental health services confounds me.

People who believe in this concept of "true trans" are really good at rewriting history. They go back and suggest they were trans in-utero. They come up with all these anecdotal stories about how they were just hiding it or afraid nobody would love them. They engage in rewriting history in order to support the idea that they were "true trans."

It's sad to me that we're so freaked out that this could be a mental health issue, that we're willing to go through all these kinds of somersaults and absurd acrobats to try and suggest that this isn't a mental health issue.

What is so bad about having a mental health issue?

Maria Keffler (30:43):

That's a very good point.

I would just encourage anyone who's still questioning whether there's such a thing as "true trans," to do some of your own research. Really look at what is supporting this idea of a transgender ideology.

I have yet to hear anybody explain to me what "transgender" means without using sexist stereotypes. If you can come up with a definition of it that is not circular reasoning such as, "Trans is someone who thinks they're trans," or "It's when a boy does things that are associated with girliness." If you can find a definition that doesn't include either of those two things, I'd love to hear it. I have yet to hear one.

> **I have yet to hear anybody explain to me what "transgender" means without using sexist stereotypes or circular reasoning.**

I hope we hear fewer people spouting "true trans" in the future. I hope people really start thinking about this and giving it the deep thought that it needs, because kids are being damaged.

Episode 24 Resource List

Hasci Horvath https://youtu.be/dJMMqREtQJc

Sexist History at the Heart of the 'Science' on Transsexualism, Part II: Robert Stoller, True Trans:
https://uncommongroundmedia.com/robert-stoller-true-trans/

Episode 25: Pornography & Gender Dysphoria

https://youtu.be/s7fzjqUbNwk

Maria Keffler (00:04):

Today, we're going to talk about pornography. We're going to talk about how pornography interplays and relates with gender dysphoria. This is another one of those difficult topics.

Erin Brewer (00:59):

This one is complex because how pornography is impacting boys and how pornography is impacting girls, are very different.

Pornography that's being made to target boys and young men is trying to train them to be sissies. They call it sissy-hypno porn. The whole goal is to encourage them to identify as women who are subjugated and degraded and demeaned. It's very disturbing. Most people, if they heard this, they'd think, "Wow, this has gone off the deep end."

The goal is to train the male who is watching it to identify with the woman, or the trans-identified woman who's being the submissive. They do all kinds of things to degrade them and encourage them to be receptive. They want them to imagine receiving oral and anal sex as if they were a woman.

There's also the impact of girls seeing women degraded in pornography and expectations put upon them based on pornography.

Then you have boys who watch degrading pornography and who are being influenced to believe what they see in the pornography is how you treat girls and women. So it's a very complicated thing.

The question is, how does porn impact gender dysphoria?

Maria Keffler (03:13):

So many things that you just talked about brought up all of these thoughts for me.

One of the things I did want to address when you talked about the sissy-hypno porn is the hypnosis part of it.

ASMR (Autonomic Sympathetic Meridian Response) videos are videos that help someone relax. I like to watch ASMR videos. The ones that I watch are like somebody pretending to put makeup on your face, or pretending to do your hair. Tapping sounds, for example, have a really calming effect for some people. The ones that I watch are innocuous and they're just about helping me relax.

But when it comes to the hypno-sissy porn, they're using those ASMR techniques to train boys—sometimes even girls—to associate positive pleasant, pleasurable feelings with these really degrading, perverse, unhealthy behaviors. That's where the *hypno* part of it comes from.

Erin Brewer (04:35):

Some hypno-sissy porn has ASMR, where there'll be somebody whispering and coaching those who are watching to perform behaviors that feel good while saying degrading things and watching degradation of women. They start associating pleasure with degradation and imagine themselves as the woman being degraded. And it's repetitive. It's super creepy.

The reason that it's catching on is because of the way pornography works.

If you start watching porn when you're eight or nine—and I know there are different people out there who say, "That's too young" and it is. But I was watching a webinar a couple of days ago and they said the average child who's got gender dysphoria started watching porn at eight or nine.

If you start watching pornography when you're eight or nine, you start with man on woman—maybe just images. Then you have to search for something a little bit racier, and then that gets boring. There's this desire to keep finding something more extreme, more over the top, that will get those feelings of arousal going.

Maria Keffler (06:23):

When we see what's happening with sex ed in the schools, pornography is being shown and it's being argued that it's sex ed. So you're seeing younger and younger kids being exposed to porn in an educational setting, which is horrific.

> **Pornography is being shown and it's being argued that it's sex ed. So you're seeing younger and younger kids being exposed to porn in an educational setting, which is horrific.**

I have my own story. When I was nine, I was at someone's house. This was supposedly somebody trustworthy, but I was shown soft porn. I remember it so vividly. It was *The Sensual Nurse* with Ursula Andress.

It was what would be considered light, soft porn now, but that has affected me. I still can see those images so crisply and clearly in my mind, because I was so young and that was my first introduction to sex.

It messed me up and that's made me really sad.

Erin Brewer (07:33):

That's so sad when children's first exposure to sex is porn. It desensitizes them. It almost causes disassociation, the sensation for the body becomes separate from the emotions.

I actually took a class in my first year in college where one of the units was on pornography. We were sitting in a classroom in college, watching porn and doing an analysis of it.

I look back and it makes me really angry how that just normalized porn: "I am in college and watching porn. It must be normal." It was not uncommon to walk into a dormitory lounge and have there be porn on it. It was just part of the culture.

That was a long time ago so I'm thinking if that was normalized back when I was in college, I can't imagine what it is like now.

Maria Keffler (08:44):

Now it's normalized. I've heard so many couples who've gone to couples therapy and the therapist tells them to watch porn together, suggesting that will improve their relationship.

There's nothing about watching porn that's going to improve your relationship.

> **There's nothing about watching porn that's going to improve your relationship.**

We have a video clip of a man who struggled with the porn addiction and has come out of it. He's wrote a book called *Porn Nation*, and he talks about what porn does to your ability to have an intimate relationship.

Erin Brewer (09:19):

It isn't that we're prudes; it's that they're starting to find that porn has physiological and psychological impacts—serious impacts—such as damaging the ability to form good relationships.

Let's watch that video clip.

Michael Leahy (09:41):

Compulsive masturbation to pornography and use of this material—we view this as a form of self-abuse. A lot of students don't want to acknowledge that or admit to it, but it really is, because not only are you consuming something that's really taking from others, but then you're taking from yourself and the behavior that you associate with consuming the material. And it's just degrading all the way around.

Karen Saupe (10:05):

You're robbing yourself of what could be a more meaningful relationship with another human.

Michael Leahy (10:10):

Exactly. Regardless of what your values are and your morality is on it, just the bare minimum, you're robbing yourself of the capacity to experience sexual pleasure, because you're dumbing down the way that your brain processes the sexual stimuli. And I know a lot of people who may never experience sexual satisfaction in a real relationship anymore. Because quite frankly, they got hooked into a high that was more sexually arousing for them: going to a sexually explicit chat room or a website, or doing the video cams back and forth, watching others do whatever. And, so that can be very arousing at a physical level.

So when they get into a physical relationship and they become physical sexually with another person, they're literally doing the same things that we see sexual trauma victims and sexual abuse victims do. They're dissociating themselves from the experience. They're removing the emotional and the psychological and the spiritual effect of being sexual, and just doing the physical side. Because that's the only way they've ever known it. And that's really the only thing you experience when you're sexual interacting with things like cyber porn. There is no emotional, there is no relational, there is no psychological—it's as simple as getting the physical buzz and the physical high. So then that becomes preeminent in a real relationship.

And that's where a lot of the women are getting caught. The guys are coming in saying, "Well, I want to watch a porn video where I want to do this that I've seen on porn," and what the women come back and tell me, is they say, "It's almost as if he needs this when we're together in order to be satisfied. And I say, "You're exactly right." They'll say, "It's just like, I'm not enough." And my response to them is, "You're right. You aren't enough for that person, that individual, you're not enough. And you probably never will be as long as he's continuing or she's continuing to do this. So you need to think about that in terms of the way you view this relationship long-term."

Maria Keffler (12:19):

That's just heartbreaking to see that level of destruction happening to both men and women. I recommend the entire video. It talks about how women are getting sucked into the porn industry. As you mentioned, porn is being made for now for women. Why? Because they want to increase their consumer base. If you can get women addicted to it, that's twice as many consumers.

I just want to read a little bit from my book, *Desist, Detrans & Detox: Getting Your Child Out of the Gender Cult.* I've got a section in here on pornography and some of the statistics around it. I'll just read a paragraph or so.

"50% of children, ages 11 to 13, have viewed pornography. That number increases to 78% by age 17. Girls report having watched porn in order to meet boys' expectations of them. PornHub's daily visits now exceed 100 million and every minute 63,992 new visitors come to the site. Pornography has not only become more pervasive in recent years. It's also become more brutal. Porn teaches that women enjoy violent sex. 38% of women under the age of 40 report having experienced unwanted, slapping, gagging, choking, and spitting during sex."

And it goes on.

One of the first eye-opening moments that I had with some radical feminists in a group that I'm in—Some radfem lesbians were talking about sex, and someone said, "Sex is really dangerous for hetero-sexual women."

I've never had dangerous sex. I'm grateful. I've never been raped or abused. But as I started digging into that a little more and asking what they meant, I realized that younger women—women in the generation beneath ours—this is their experience. They have sex with someone and they get choked. They get spat on, they get peed on, and they think this is normal. They think this is part of the sex process.

Women in our generation don't appreciate what the younger women are experiencing.

> **Younger women—women in the generation beneath ours—this is their experience. They have sex with someone and they get choked. They get spat on, they get peed on, and they think this is normal. They think this is part of the sex process.**

Erin Brewer (14:44):

It isn't surprising to me that so many girls are opting out of womanhood, if they believe that's how you're treated as a woman—that what they see in porn is normal sexuality. It's not at all surprising to me that so many girls and young women are her saying, "I'm a male." That way they don't have to think about being degraded in these ways.

The pressure is so profound.

I was thinking about when I turned 13. My parents were very sex-positive. They thought sex was something that all people should enjoy, and there really weren't a lot of boundaries. They gave me a copy of *Playgirl* for my 13th birthday. So I did what I thought I was supposed to do. I was really not very social. I didn't really get social interaction. I didn't really have many friends.

So I took one of the centerfold pictures to school and put it up in my locker, because that's what I thought I was supposed to do.

Maria Keffler (16:07):

That's what people do. We're finding this with today's sex ed in schools. A Barnett group report found one out of three students feels that today's sex ed in schools creates an expectation of having sex.

Erin Brewer (16:27):

This reminds me of some of the dystopian novels that I've read where the expectation was that if somebody wanted to have sex, it would be rude or really inappropriate to refuse it.

Maria Keffler (16:57):

This is going to sound very prudish, but just take it for the facts: The best way to prevent unwanted pregnancy, STDs, AIDS and possibly a broken heart is abstinence followed by marriage fidelity.

There are no value statements in that. It's just factual. If you don't have sex, you don't get pregnant. If you don't have sex, you don't get STDs.

I posted this online. Somebody commented and said, "I disagree." He said, "You hit on something valuable but I disagree." I wanted to say, "What do you disagree about? Do you think that people can get pregnant if they're not having sex? Do you think STDs are shared if they're not having sex?"

People aren't thinking, because there is this assumption that everybody must have sex. You must have sex.

Erin Brewer (17:49):

That is part of the culture too. A message I got from my parents is that you can't control your behavior. Children can't control themselves; they're going to have sex. They should just accept it. That was what I grew up with.

Nobody ever introduced the concept that I can say, "No." I started having sexual intercourse when I was in sixth grade. It's not a good idea. I was not physically ready for it. I definitely wasn't emotionally ready for it. It's healthier to wait.

Like you said: it brings STIs, broken hearts, all kinds of things. And also being able to form healthy relationships as adults—all of this gets undermined by pornography, as the gentleman in the video said. You get desensitized. It gets to the point where we're having teenage boys who are basically impotent because they've overstimulated that part of their brains and they no longer are responsive to normal sexual signals.

> **We have teenage boys who are impotent because they've overstimulated that part of their brains and they no longer are responsive to normal sexual signals.**

Maria Keffler (19:00):

Athletes will repeat the same motions over and over and over again. People who play basketball, they will do layup after layup, after layup because they're training their muscles. They get that muscle memory, so that when they're competing, they don't have to think about where they should stop to shoot a basket or how far to extend their arms, or how high do they need to jump. They don't have to think about it.

This is what pornography is doing. When you're masturbating to pornography, you are training your muscles, you're training your brain, you're training your sexual system to react to images, not to a real person.

They find these men—and I'm sure women as well, but most of the studies I've seen have been on men—who cannot perform sexually with a real person because they have trained their muscles and their bodies only to perform with images.

Erin Brewer (20:11):

We've talked in the past about how many trans-identified kids are on the autism spectrum. It's going to be harder for kids on the autism spectrum. I know autistic kids who don't want to hug. They don't want to kiss. They don't want to be touched. Then they start getting these sexual urges.

It's really easy for them just to go to pornography, but that porn reinforces the difficulties they have with sexual interactions, rather than encouraging them to actually have healthy relationships. Those healthy relationships will benefit them so much more than the pornography.

There are so many layers to this. The big takeaway parents need to have is that your kids very likely are watching pornography. It is so accessible. You go to PornHub and it says, "Are you over 18?" And you click, "Yes." There's no verification. If kids have access to the internet, they can access porn.

> **The big takeaway parents need to have is that your kids very likely are watching pornography. It is so accessible.**

I was just watching a video about a young man who started watching pornography when he was about 10 years old. He was watching it and decided he was interested in trying it out on someone. His sister happened to be there. He tried it out on her.

There are all kinds of dangers from porn. It can cause someone to develop that trans identity. It can cause them to hate themselves and their body, that dissociative process.

Parents, you need to know that, and you have to be really diligent. I would even suggest talking to your kids about it. It's not one of those things that we can pretend like it doesn't happen and it will go away.

Maria Keffler (22:07):

Parents have been told, "You're prudish if you don't like pornography. Pornography is innocent, it doesn't hurt anybody. Everybody's doing it. There's no way to keep your kids from doing it."

That's just not true. We need to take it seriously. This is not just some innocuous video game that they're watching. This has profound effects on their bodies, on their minds, and on their future relationships.

Porn will damage their future relationships. Even the one soft porn movie that I watched has had an effect on my sexuality as an adult. We need to take that seriously.

> **Porn will damage their future relationships.
> Even the one soft porn movie that I watched
> has had an effect on my sexuality as an adult.
> We need to take that seriously.**

This is probably tangential, but I've talked with all my kids about dating.

I dated far too much. I wasted a lot of time on dating. I will even go so far to tell you I nearly failed out of college because I was more interested in a boy than I was in my classes. Fortunately, I got focused before that happened.

I've told my kids that I really think the purpose of dating is to find the person you're going to marry. You date to find out, "Is this someone I want to marry?" If you're not in a position to marry yet, I'm not sure there's really any point to dating.

There's a point to having friends—I'm not saying, "Don't have friends with the opposite sex." But to pursue an intimate relationship before you're in a position where you could get married—you get your heart broken, and then you love a little bit less the next time. You're learning how to get over a broken heart and not care as much the next time.

My wish for all my kids—and I've told them this—is that I really hope they marry the first person they fall in love with.

Erin Brewer (24:17):

I have a couple of friends who married their high school sweethearts—the first person they ever dated seriously—and they're still together and they're still happy. I can't say that about a lot of other couples. I'm not saying that all those who marry their first sweetheart are going to be happy, obviously.

I also wanted to talk about another aspect of pornography that is going to be difficult for parents of transgender-identified children to hear.

One of the things that we're seeing is that kids who are seeking to get medicalized are pursuing pornography to pay for it. They're going to different pornography sites, and setting up accounts. Kids use porn as a means to generate finances, if they want to get these interventions, and their parents don't want to pay for them.

One of the huge concerns is that it's a slippery slope into prostitution. Some of these kids even get pulled into prostitution on these porn sites.

There are so many layers to this that parents need to be aware of. It's so heartbreaking talking to a parent who calls and says, "My child might be making a porn." We find that their child is indeed make making porn in order to generate funds.

That's just another heartbreaking aspect of this. It's easy these days to make money off of making porn. If you're a kid, you're probably too young to get a regular job, or maybe don't have time because of being in school all day. This is something that kids are resorting to. You mentioned earlier in the show how we're seeing this creeping into our classrooms.

> **It's easy these days to make money off of making porn. If you're a kid, you're probably too young to get a regular job. This is something that kids are resorting to.**

There was one school board meeting where the school board had no idea that schools were teaching about anal sex. They were teaching about oral sex. They were teaching about multiple sex partners—all of these things which are really dangerous, especially for children. These are dangerous things that we're telling our kids and we know you're less likely to have an unplanned pregnancy, you're less likely to have a sexually transmitted infection or AIDS, if you delay your sexual debut and if you are monogamous.

Maria Keffler (28:13):

I you look at the Comprehensive Sex Guide from SIECUS, this is what so many schools are putting into place. It talks right in there about anal sex in a positive way.

There's no question that anal sex is dangerous, that it damages the anus. It's a much faster vector for transmitting diseases because the anus is not as elastic as the vagina and it cracks easier. And it's a dirtier place just by function of what it is.

It's completely irresponsible to introduce that to kids.

> **The Comprehensive Sex Guide talks about anal sex in a positive way. There's no question that anal sex is dangerous. It's completely irresponsible to introduce that to kids.**

Right here in Virginia last year or the year before (2019 or 2020), a teacher brought in a video in a ninth-grade class about how to sexually pleasure your partner. Parents were furious. And the school board said, "Oh, that shouldn't have happened. We're so sorry about that."

I wish I could say that's a one-off and it was just some rogue sex ed teacher.

They always say this is "developmentally appropriate." I love that term: "developmentally appropriate."

Erin Brewer (29:48):

I grew up with this kind of mentality. This was the mentality of my parents. They had almost no boundaries regarding sexuality. They talked about it like going and getting an ice cream cone: "If it feels good, do it." I was introduced to *Playgirl* at 13. My brother got condoms in his Christmas stocking when he was 13. My parents were some of the forerunners of this.

It's hard to imagine if boundaries continued to be broken down—are they going to start actually having people have sex in front of the kids to teach them how to do it?

I mean, I'm not sure it is that far off. Part of the transgender ideology is to break down those boundaries. Much of this movement is all about pedophiles figuring out a way to normalize their perversions.

Maria Keffler (32:33):

One child that I talked to learned what zoosexuality was in her GSA club in middle school. Tthe parent asked, "Zoosexuality? what is that?" And the child said, "Well, do you know what bestiality is?"

Erin Brewer (34:14):

This all goes back to porn. If you're a girl who's watching porn, you're thinking, "I don't want to have to be submissive. I don't want to be slapped. I don't want to be told to licks feces off the floor." No wonder they want to opt out of womanhood.

These kids—their whole sexuality is hijacked. It makes me really angry because it's gotten to the point that porn is so ubiquitous that it's impossible to avoid it. I mean, even on *Blue's Clues*, a show for preschoolers, they had a drag queen, and it was clearly sexual. There was a very sexual element to it. We need to really fight back.

Maria Keffler (35:56):

It is not appropriate for prepubescent kids to encounter sexual topics. It is not normal. They do not have a driving interest in and they should not have experience with sexual topics. It is not developmentally appropriate.

Puberty is the time of sexual awakening. That is when they become adults. That is when they start should start becoming aware of their sexuality, and start becoming aware of the other sex as potential mates. That should be the beginning of a very gentle process.

They're being inundated, bombarded, indoctrinated with it from the youngest ages. It's pathologizing kids. The sexualization is pathologizing kids.

One of the things that I've asked when I've been in discussions on social media—with people who tell me I'm a prude—I will say, "Well, is there a line? Is there a line that kids should not be introduced to certain stuff?" Very often I'll be told, "No, they need to learn this stuff. This is education. They need to know this because they will need to know it later." So I say, "Okay. Snuff porn, where somebody's killed in front of you—is that appropriate for a child to see?"

Generally they will not respond. They'll just leave the conversation because they know that there's a line. Your line might be different from my line, but my line exists and should be honored, and should be respected. Parents' wishes for their kids need to be respected.

Sex positivity says, "There is no line. Kids need to be introduced to everything." Take that out to its logical conclusion. That means a three-year-old can be raped by a bunch of men for other men's pleasure. And we know that's wrong. We know it.

> **Sex positivity says, "There is no line. Kids need to be introduced to everything." Take that out to its logical conclusion. That means a three-year-old can be raped by a bunch of men for other men's pleasure. And we know that's wrong. We know it.**

Erin Brewer (38:07):

That's where we really need to set some boundaries. One of the reasons that puberty is powerful is it's an opportunity for kids to learn how to control their bodies. Now they're told, "You can't control these urges. There's nothing you can do about it. You might as well just give into it."

That really undermines their ability to learn that you have control over your impulses. Otherwise you're going to be overeating. You're going to do drugs when they come along. You're going to overspend. You're never going to learn how to control those impulses.

Maria Keffler (38:53):

When I was in college, I mentioned I almost failed out because I had a boyfriend. When he would pull up on his motorcycle as I was walking to class, I would pick the motorcycle ride instead of class. I was making very immature, short-sighted decisions. Fortunately I had someone come alongside me and say, "Hey, you need to make better decisions. You're making decisions that are going to affect the rest of your life."

Fortunately, I was able to mature and get back on track.

But I didn't have the exposure to stuff that kids are getting. Now that message is that you can't control yourself. You can't restrain yourself. You can't make decisions that make you uncomfortable right now. We're doing a terrible disservice to kids.

Erin Brewer (40:08):

It's really heartbreaking. One of the things that I wanted to mention is that Planned Parenthood is willing to give out PrEP, which what they give to people who are promiscuous so that they won't get AIDS. I called a Planned Parenthood clinic said I was a 14-year-old girl. I said I was a prostitute. I wondered if I could get PrEP without my parents' knowledge. They said, "Yes."

These are serious hardcore drugs. These could undermine our society really as viruses adapt to the drugs and become resistant, especially when you have 14-year-old kids taking them. It's dangerous on so many levels.

Maria Keffler (41:07):

I believe you only have to weigh 77 pounds—which is the size of an 11-year-old—to get it.

Erin Brewer (41:18):

Do you have any questions from our viewers?

Maria Keffler (41:27):

Yes, we have one. "I found some really troubling stuff in my daughter's history. There were videos of kids and adults wearing diapers and sucking on binkies and some involved sex acts. How do I talk to my daughter about this? I don't even know where to begin."

Erin Brewer (41:45):

You do need to talk to your daughter. If you pretend like this isn't happening, it's going to escalate.

It is really hard to talk to your kids about this stuff, but I would approach it the same as you would drugs or any other behavior you are concerned about. Maybe try role-playing some conversations with a friend or a partner, or somebody who was aware of what is happening. You might also look up sexual risk-avoidance training that is available online. There are some resources out there for parents that can cover a lot more detail than we can.

Maria Keffler (42:48):

There are some ways you can approach these difficult and uncomfortable conversations, especially if you're concerned that maybe your child will be upset that you looked through her browser history. In my house, my kids know until they're 18, we have all their passwords. We have access to everything. Everything that goes to their email inboxes gets copied to ours. That's just been a decision that we've made. The kids know that.

If you have not made that decision and you've sneaked this, you will need to come clean with that.

One good time to have difficult conversations is in the car when you're driving and your child is next to you and you don't have to look at each other. You can both be looking forward and you don't have to look right at each other. That can be a really good time to have a conversation that might be difficult. You also have a captive audience that can't really leave while you're driving.

A way to start it might just be to say, "Hey, I need to admit something that I did. And I need to talk to you about something that concerns me. I went into your browser history because I was concerned that some things were happening that I needed to know about. And I saw some things there that really concerned me. Would you like to talk to me about what's in your browser history now?"

> **"I went into your browser history because I was concerned that some things were happening that I needed to know about. I saw some things there that really concerned me. Would you like to talk to me about what's in your browser history?"**

I didn't say what I saw in the browser history. I admitted that I did something and I'm not going to say it was wrong, but I admitted that I did something my child wouldn't like. But then I opened it up with that open-ended question, because frankly there may be more there that you didn't even see. If you put it that way, you might get more than you even knew you were looking for.

Erin Brewer (44:48):

Also be aware that your kids might be going over to friend's houses. So even if it's not on their browser history, it's possible that they're seeing it. I can't remember who it was that was telling me about some kids on a bus had a cell phone and they were showing pornography to all the other kids.

Maria Keffler (45:06):

Me. That was me. That happened to a friend of mine.

Erin Brewer (45:10):

That's the hardest part is that older kids sometimes think it's funny to show this to younger kids, and sometimes young kids. I don't think they're to blame because they've been exposed to it and they don't have the means to process it.

This is one of those issues that I would encourage people to write to their legislators about. There are things that we can do to make it online porn less accessible. We owe it to our children to do that. There are people who will argue that it's free speech, but your free speech stops being protected when it starts harming me, my children, my family, my society.

Maria Keffler (45:59):

Freedom of speech doesn't mean you can stand up in a crowded theater and scream, "Fire," for example.

Erin Brewer (46:06):

They need to require verification of adulthood on these porn sites. There is no reason that isn't being done except that the porn industry is making so much money and they don't want to stop. They're just raking it in.

Maria Keffler (46:34):

Frankly, I have gotten to the place where I think children should not have social media. Children should not have smartphones. My oldest has a smartphone. He's done pretty well with it. I'm grateful for that. My other two don't have phones. My daughter, who just finished sophomore year, doesn't even want one. She's concerned about what she's seeing, social media wise and everything. She doesn't even want one. but if I were to get kids' phones today, I would get them flip phones that have texting and phone.

Erin Brewer (47:13):

I agree. I can't tell you how many times I see kids sitting together and they're all on their phone and that's because that's what their parents are doing. They're learning. They might even be texting the kid next to them.

Social media is having the same kind of impact as the industrial revolution. We haven't quite figured out how to how to make it a positive thing. We'll get there, but it is going to take parents calling their legislators, sending emails, contacting their schools.

I'm shocked. I saw some excerpts from a book that was being taught. I believe it was in an eighth or ninth grade classroom.

Maria Keffler (48:20):

My friend's son was assigned a book that is gay porn.

Erin Brewer (48:31):

This is very explicit stuff that probably was similar to what was in the *Playgirl* I had. Now it is in the high schools. Maybe we need to do a video where we just read excerpts so people believe us. But what would happen? It would be taken down from YouTube for violating their community standards.

Maria Keffler (49:05):

At schoolboard meetings, they don't let you read aloud from these books at the school board meeting, the very books your eighth-grade English teacher is assigning to children.

Erin Brewer (49:14):

There's a lot of work to do.

Maria Keffler (49:24):

And let's do a shout out to our friend, Alix, The Gender Mapper. She does a great four-part course on all of this stuff. And she does one segment on pornography.

Erin Brewer (49:39):

She goes into a lot more depth than we're doing here. And she also is able to give parents more specific ideas on how to monitor their kids and block their kids' ability to access porn.

Episode 25 Resource List

Inner Compass: https://youtu.be/ZzPBRdZqDzk

Porn Nation: https://www.amazon.com/Porn-Nation-Conquering-Americas-Addiction/dp/B002PJ4NMA

Alix's Course on Pornography: https://www.transgenderabuse.org/

Episode 26: Boys & Gender Dysphoria

https://youtu.be/-fRXbHzGv5k

Maria Keffler (00:42):

Today we are going to talk about boys and gender dysphoria. This is a topic that doesn't get enough treatment, and sometimes it doesn't get the right treatment.

Erin Brewer (00:52):

One of the issues is that historically, males who wanted to transition were autogynephilic men, which are men who are sexually aroused at the idea of themselves being a woman, and the more they can infiltrate women's spaces, the more sexually aroused they get. Or they were gay, very feminine boys who just felt like they'd fit in better if they transitioned and presented more feminine.

We have a new phenomenon happening now. These are rapid onset gender dysphoric boys, who I believe are actually assuming a trans identity as a result of pressure, because right now the common narrative is that if you're a white male, you are the oppressor, you are the bad guy, and there's nothing you can do about it. You are basically marked for life as the bad guy. The only way they can opt out of that identity is to assume a different identity.

A trans identity makes the most sense, because we know that for whatever reason the people who are pushing this ideology don't let you opt into a different race. So these white boys, if they came out and said they're actually black, that wouldn't go over well. But if they say they're women, suddenly they're celebrated and they are even more marginalized than any other group.

> **If these white boys came out and said they're actually black, that wouldn't go over well. But if they say they're women, suddenly they're celebrated and they're more marginalized than any other group.**

I feel like these boys are sensitive. They're picking up on hatred that people have for white men. It's a very smart response, opting out of manhood and into womanhood. That way they won't be the evil oppress-sor; they will actually be one of the marginalized.

Maria Keffler (02:50):

Traditionally, we saw almost always that when men came out as transsexual, as it used to be called, it was adult men. It was usually men in their early- to mid-twenties coming out. There were those two groups that you mentioned, autogynephiles and the ones who were homosexual but were homophobic, and they didn't want to admit being homosexual. So they adopted a woman's persona.

But now we're seeing this cadre of younger men doing this: boys—teenage boys—that cohort of the young children doing it. It's still predominantly girls. There's a huge group of girls, but there's a growing segment of these boys.

What you said about adopting a transgender identity is true; it gets you out of being the oppressor. That goes also with girls, because I've talked to girls who said, "We would sit around a middle school and talk about how we were anything but white, cisgender heterosexuals. We don't want to be white. We don't want to be cisgender, which means you identify with your birth sex. And we don't want to be heterosexual because those things are vanilla. Those things are basic. Those things are boring and those things make you an oppressor."

Both in girls and boys we are seeing them saying, "Well, I can't say I'm a different race because I'm literally the race I am. I can't say I'm a different age because that hasn't been accepted yet, but adopting a trans identity I can do. All that is required is for me to announce it, there is no test. There are no rules other than I just say that's what I am."

A couple of episodes ago we talked about pornography and that a lot of boys are being pathologized by porn. That's so ubiquitous. I suspect we're seeing boys who are getting sucked into hypno-sissy porn and the ASMR porn. I've heard of some boys like Hasci who saw an abusive male role model growing up—his father was quite abusive—and he said to himself, "I don't want to be that. I don't want to be that person I'm going to be someone different."

Erin Brewer (05:32):

Then we have autistic boys who have very black-and-white thinking. If they have more feminine traits, they're going to think, "Well, everybody says if I act and behave and think like this then I must be a woman."

There are a lot of different reasons boys take on a transgender identity.

One thing that's important to parse out is whether or not the boy or young man wants to have genital surgery. That seems to be the difference, because the autogynephile might want to get top surgery, because autogynephilic men say they want breasts so when they want to play with someone's breasts, the breasts are right there. They don't have to go find a woman, which is just a sad statement that we've gotten to the point where it's easier for a man to get his own breasts, rather than to have form a relationship with a woman in order to have access to breasts to stimulate himself.

Breast augmentation surgery indicates someone might be more of an autogynephile, whereas if they get their penis and testicles removed, that that indicates more that the child has been indoctrinated into this cult. That's because the autogynephile wants to keep his penis, because that's how he gets aroused, and he doesn't want to lose it. That's one way to parse it out when you think about this.

> **Breast augmentation surgery indicates someone might be more of an autogynephile, whereas if they get their penis and testicles removed, that that indicates more that the child has been indoctrinated into this cult.**

There's a lot of anger towards autogynephiles right now. It's justified, because they're actually pushing this on boys and girls and children and society, in order to normalize their fetish, and in order to normalize them going into women's protected spaces.

I can't tell you how frustrated I get when males say that we have to fight for trans rights, and when he says he doesn't feel safe because we don't use the pronouns he wants. His preferred pronouns aren't being respected and he's being told he can't colonize women's spaces. It just shows a complete disconnect about what it means to be unsafe, which is how women feel when we have men come into women's bathrooms in order to get aroused.

I have talked to transsexual men who respect women's spaces and go into the men's bathroom and none of them have recorded ever having violence perpetrated against them.

It's very interesting that they're saying that they want to go in women's bathrooms and people say, "We don't want them to be hurt when they go into the men's bathrooms. So we'll let them go into the women's bathrooms."

How does that make any sense? I feel like this is a little off topic, because I did want to focus on these boys who aren't autogynephilic, because they have distressed feelings about who they are, the self-hatred for being boys.

Maria Keffler (09:36):

I'm just thinking out loud here. I'm thinking about how often parents divorce, and quite often it's not an amicable divorce. If these boys are hearing their mothers speak ill of their ex-husbands, and speak poorly of men—

I remember I had a significant breakup when I was in college, and I was just furious with him and furious with men. I was telling man-bashing jokes and just being a real jerk. My mom pulled me aside and she said, "Maria, your father is a man and you are being really hurtful to him right now." It opened my eyes: "My gosh, my father's a good man. I don't want to hurt him." But when you're hurt, it can just be exploding out against everyone.

Erin Brewer (10:35):

If the mother has sole custody sometimes the father is out of the picture. A lot of times the courts will award a woman full custody.

Oh my gosh, the things that my mom said about my biological father. I mean, according to her, he was the devil incarnate. I can't imagine how hard that was for my brother to hear. I could tell how angry my mother was with my brother or me if she started saying we looked like our father. She would say to my brother, especially—if she was disappointed or angry with him—she would start saying, "You're just like your father," or "You look just like your father," or "How come you're so much like your father?" Clearly it is not okay to be like your father.

Susan Evans talked about this. When kids have negative feelings about the parent of their biological sex, sometimes they want to disassociate from them.

Maria Keffler (11:59):

That's interesting. So what do parents need to do when their son comes out and says, "I'm not a boy, I'm a girl," or "I'm non-binary"? There are different ways of dealing with it depending if your child is still at home or if he's not still at home.

Where do you think it's coming from? You need to know the root cause before you start dealing with it, but what would you counsel parents?

Erin Brewer (12:46):

One of the things I want to address before we move on is that there is a whole group of very young boys who seem to be adopting a trans identity. I believe that those are children who are being pushed into this by their parents. I've seen screenshots of conversations with parents. I've talked to some of them, and I've seen videos. These are boys who are young, like 2, 3, 4, 5, 6—young boys.

I believe their parents are pushing them to be transgender for a number of reasons. Sometimes the boys are feminine and the parents are uncomfortable with that. Sometimes the parents just want to be the cool kids on the block, and if they have a trans kid, then they have all this social cred.

That's a very different population because those parents are ecstatic about their child's trans identity. They don't want to do anything to help them resolve it, even though it means medicalizing their child and causing significant damage to those children's bodies.

> **Those parents are ecstatic about their child's trans identity. They don't want to do anything to help them resolve it, even though it means medicalizing their child and causing significant damage to their bodies.**

Maria Keffler (13:52):

I don't mean to interrupt you but I don't understand people who think it's better to be trans, that it's better to medicalize.

A friend of mine has a child who identifies as transgender. The parents worked with the child and after a couple of years, the child said, "You know what? I'm not transgender, I am accepting myself as my birth sex," and friends of those parents told them that they had undue influence on the child.

Why would you not say, "Oh, this is great. The child's going to accept their healthy body. They don't need hormones. They don't need surgery. The child's happy with who they are." Why would anyone not support that?

Erin Brewer (14:36)

It's so indicative that this is a cult and this is not about what's healthy for the child.

I would like to show a short clip here of Scarlet, who's a young man who thought he was a girl when he was about 13 or 14, started on puberty blockers and cross-sex hormones, and now he talks about how both his body and his mind were frozen as a child. He has been off of these medications for a while now, and things are not reversing.

What he realized is that he had same-sex attraction and he was extremely uncomfortable with that for a number of reasons. That's why he chose to go this road. He said that his therapists and doctors just completely encouraged this and pushed it. Now his body is permanently damaged. This is not a healthy path. It's a pathway of medicalization and damaging a healthy body.

> Scarlet (15:48):
>
> I was 14 years old when I got my puberty blocker implant. They told me that the puberty blocker was completely safe. After I was on it for a while, it like castrates you. You stop developing in every way, including mentally and emotionally, which I did not. And it was like being frozen in like a child's body.
>
> I felt frustrated, because it was like being trapped in a child's body, you know, with things not maturing correctly and possibly even atrophying. So then even if I go back, I would have to live my life as a eunuch. And it's the exact awkward existence that I was trying to avoid. But it was presented as the only option.

Erin Brewer (16:36):

Here is a young man who is damaged for life and it's all because he was uncomfortable with his sexuality.

There are all different reasons that kids adopt these identities. It's important that we be compassionate towards them.

I've noticed that among some circles, there's a lot of compassion for girls who get sucked into this ideology, but not so much for the boys. A lot of this is coming from man-bashing, and of blaming the patriarchy for everything. There isn't as much compassion for young men who are going through this.

But as Scarlet illustrated, these are kids who are struggling with intense feelings of self-hatred, with intense depression, with intense anxiety. They deserve our compassion. It is heartbreaking to see kids being pushed into this.

Maria Keffler (17:50):

Autistic kids are told this, kids with depression are told this, kids with discomfort with their sexuality or lack of sexuality are told this. Unfortunately, most of the adults say if a boy has these difficult feelings, he needs to transition. It's just such a lie. It's so damaging. We hear this from so many detransitioners and it is heartbreaking.

> **Autistic kids are told this, kids with depression are told this, kids with discomfort with their sexuality or lack of sexuality are told this. Adults say if a boy has these difficult feelings, he needs to transition. It's such a lie.**

Erin Brewer (18:22):

It's important to emphasize to boys that it's okay to be feminine. Historically, feminine boys have been teased mercilessly. I remember as a kid I was teased a lot, but I wasn't teased as much as the feminine boys. I cringe when I think about it but I was always thankful for them because they would take some of the pressure off me. If I was being bullied and a feminine boy walked by, they'd go after him. I feel sad about that now.

Girls who are tomboys get teased, but they don't get called the kinds of names and they don't get mocked and they don't get ostracized the way feminine boys historically have. So we need to create a culture in which we accept feminine boys.

Maria Keffler (19:44):

That seems to be what feminism was working on for a long time: eradicating these stereotypes, and the idea that boys can't have feminine traits and girls can't have masculine traits.

We need to accept people for who they are. All of the sudden that's no longer the case now. Suddenly, instead of accepting those differences and those variations, we're going to say, "No. If you have a difference or variation, you have to change to the opposite sex." That's just like throwing us back to the dark ages.

Erin Brewer (20:23):

That's especially true for these boys who are having their testicles removed, who are having their penises cut off and taking puberty blockers, which stunt their development and retard their growth.

There have been studies—I believe it's John Whitehead—showing that the IQ actually drops and stays lower when children take puberty blockers. If they take the puberty blockers combined with cross-sex hormones, that results in infertility. The genitalia are frozen at a pre-pubescent stages, resulting in micro-penises.

One of the things that I want to mention that disturbs me down to my toes in a way that is nauseating, is that I do believe that there is a certain group of pedophiles who are happy about this, because they're basically freezing these boys' bodies as child bodies. Pedophiles who are attracted to young boys are actually encouraging some of these kids to embrace these medical transitions so that they can have access to prepubescent boys' bodies legally.

> **Pedophiles who are attracted to young boys are actually encouraging some of these kids to embrace these medical transitions so that they can have access to prepubescent boys' bodies legally.**

I find that disturbing, but that was something that Scarlet mentioned, that he felt that there were some predatory males who were pushing him to do this and were ecstatic about the way his body was frozen as a prepubescent, because that's what arouses them.

That's horrifying, Maria, but it makes sense. It makes sense, because then you get the child's body, but someone who is of legal age of consent. So disturbing.

It's our duty to stand up and protect the children.

Occasionally a troll will come on my Facebook page and say something like, "Why don't you mind your own business?"

It is our business. When it comes to children, it's the adults' responsibility to protect children. If parents aren't doing it, it's our responsibility to step in. Society has an obligation to protect children. That's why you and I are doing this.

> ## Society has an obligation to protect children.

Maria Keffler (26:45):

We have a couple of questions from parents. The first one we may have addressed already: "My ex-husband was a terrible example of how a man should be. He made our son do 'boy things' growing up, even though my son didn't like many of those things. Is that possibly where this trans ID comes from?"

Erin Brewer (27:05):

It's very difficult to pinpoint exactly where his trans identity comes from. If you have a feminine boy, who's not excepted by his father, and who is potentially mocked or encouraged to behave in ways that are "manly," that could very easily cause a child to say, "Hey, I'm not that. I'm just going to go be a girl. And maybe my dad will accept me as a woman because he's certainly not accepting me as a son."

Maria Keffler (27:39):

All kids need to be allowed to be who they are and to be accepted, especially by their parents. Your parents are the first, most powerful adults in your life. That's who you model after. You want them to love you.

This might be a little bit tangential, but I posted a picture of a page from *Desist, Detox & Detrans* on social media. It was a page about love, that the first thing we need to do is tell our kids that we love them. No matter what, we love them. Even when they hurt us, we love them. Even when they don't do what we want them to do.

Somebody commented and said, "This is stupid. I'm not going to love somebody who hurts me and is nasty. This is stupid advice. I don't have to be kind to them."

Erin Brewer (28:38):

That is an unfortunate attitude.

I want to put in a caveat that if there is a child who is feminine, and a father encourages them to do "manly things" occasionally, I don't think that's harmful, as long as it's not done in a shaming way, but to say, "Hey, why don't you go hunting with me?" or "Let's go fishing," or "Do you want to go shoot a bow and arrow?" There are all these stereotypically male things. I don't think it's going to cause any harm if a father invites a feminine child to be involved in those things. It's important to spend time with parents.

It has to do with the tone. It's the difference between, "Hey son, I want to spend some time with you," versus "You're a sissy boy. I'm going to man you up. We're going camping. You're going to toughen up." Those are different. I don't think that there's anything wrong with encouraging children to engage in a variety of activities.

I've heard women who've talked about wanting to abort the baby if it's a boy, and who have so much hatred toward men, or who say things like, "It's going to be hard for me to love my son when he's a man, because men are responsible for oppressing women." Those kinds of messages from either a father or mother are going to cause damage to a child.

Maria Keffler (30:07):

If it's not gender ideology damage, it's going to come out some other way, because kids do need to be loved and accepted.

I want to reinforce what you said about encouraging children to do a variety of activities. I love the way you modeled those two tones. It can even be in a relationship-building way.

If a father says, "Hey son, I love spending time with you and I want to do what you enjoy doing. So how about we do whatever you like to do? I'll take a guitar class with you. Then will you also come hunting with me one weekend? I'd like to share my hobby with you. And I'd like to learn about your hobby." That's a fabulous way to build relationship.

Erin Brewer (30:56):

And also just to expand a child's experience, which is what childhood is about.

Maria Keffler (31:02):

We've got one more question: "I'm wondering about parents' thoughts on where asexuality fits into all of this conversation, especially from a genetic perspective. My husband and I often talk about our own preferences and sexuality, and I have very little sex drive, save for very early on in my cycle each month. I'm curious about how others have seen their own sexual preferences and predisposition such as tomboyish girls or feminine males."

Erin Brewer (31:46):

That question in some ways drives me crazy because parents these days are so concerned about their children's sexuality. It's not uncommon for boys to not express a sexual interest until their mid-twenties.

My husband and I had such different experiences sexually. I was sexual at a young age. And that wasn't healthy. It was quite dangerous. He said he was completely oblivious until he was 19 or 20—just completely clueless. He said that there was one girl when he was in elementary school who used to flash herself at the boys to get a reaction. He always just like, "What?" He was confused by it.

So there are kids who aren't going to have sexual proclivities until they're older, and that's okay.

I would be much more concerned about a child who comes out and declares their sexuality when they're 8, 9, 10, 11 years old than a child who says they're asexual, because asexual is actually more than the norm for children. Children aren't supposed to be sexualized until they're old enough to understand the implications of getting involved in a sexual relationship.

Maria Keffler (33:07):

Puberty is the time that kids start waking up sexually. When I see teachers and counselors and principals introducing sexuality and gender topics to young children—that is abuse. Kids shouldn't be introduced to topics about sex and gender until they are older teens. Before then it's too much baggage. It's too heavy for them to carry.

You're right. Some kids, even going through puberty, aren't going to experience a strong sexual drive. Autistic kids—they're very inwardly focused. They're all about their own selves and their own interests. They often don't start developing sexuality until they are older, if at all.

Erin Brewer (34:18):

Some autistic kids have a lot of sensory issues and the idea of touching and kissing other people is repulsive to them. It takes puberty to kick that in, and then sometimes it doesn't kick in, and that's okay.

I remember thinking that I was just a freak because I always had more of a sex drive than my husband. I always thought it was strange. I can't remember where I was, but I started talking about feeling like I was some pervert and another woman said, "I have the same thing." I felt surprised that I wasn't the only one.

I'm different. We are all different and we change throughout life. We change with our experiences.

I noticed the more that I've healed from the trauma I had as a child, the more my sex drive has gotten more controlled. It's because I was using sex to meet needs that should been met in other ways.

I worry that a lot of these kids now are doing that. They're going to pornography, and becoming sexualized young in order to meet needs that should be met in other ways, but they're not getting the met.

If a boy goes into porn, we have to be very concerned because of the hypno-sissy porn that's actively trying to feminize them. "Bimbofication" is one of the words they use, which means attempting to turn boys into slutty girls. It's completely creepy.

I encourage parents of boys to monitor their internet use very carefully to keep them away from porn. If you have a son who is saying he identifies as transgender, I would investigate and see if he's been watching porn, because there's a good chance he has been.

> **If you have a son who is saying he identifies as transgender, I would investigate and see if he's been watching porn because there's a good chance he has been.**

Maria Keffler (36:31):

It's just so ubiquitous. It's hard to stay away from. I've talked to so many parents now who have said, "I can't even close the door to my house and keep it outside, because it's coming in through phones, it's coming in through the laptops and the school iPads that are supposedly locked down."

It's very difficult to keep this stuff out. You have to be active and intentional. You can't be neutral on this anymore because it's coming for our kids.

Erin Brewer (37:07):

I want to emphasize before we leave is that there are very different categories that kids fall into. And it's important to identify which category your son is falling into, because that's going to dramatically influence how you respond.

Maria Keffler (38:28):

When you consider all of the different reasons why a boy or a girl might adopt this identity, there are some very different and polar opposite reasons why this would be happening. How could there possibly be one treatment plan? "Always affirmation?" That makes no sense.

> **There are some very different and polar opposite reasons why this would be happening. How could there possibly be one treatment plan? "Always affirmation?" That makes no sense.**

Erin Brewer (38:52):

Anytime you take a healthy child's body and damage it, that that should be considered medical abuse. There's just no excuse for it. We have organizations actively pushing this onto our kids, which is another example why this is a cult. This is not about healthcare and this is not about the best interests of the children.

Episode 26 Resource List

Parents of ROGD Kids: www.parentsofrogdkids.com

Episode 27: Social Media & Gender Dysphoria

https://youtu.be/WJsBKD2kLEo

Maria Keffler (00:40):

Today we are going to talk about social media and how social media and gender dysphoria interact with each other.

Erin Brewer (00:48):

I can't tell you how many parents have told me that their child got on DeviantArt or Instagram or TikTok, saw something, was drawn into this cult, and it happened so quickly. Parents are unaware of how insidious social media can be.

Maria Keffler (01:13):

It's completely unregulated. This is one of the big problems that we're discovering. On television or in movies there are laws about what advertisers can market to kids. There are laws about what can be said. But there's no regulation in social media, and we've seen social media take over and transform our society.

We won't get into any political stuff today, but we're all aware of how we're being siloed into two different political camps. Social media is driving that.

The same thing is happening to kids. They're getting smartphones, which just open up everything and everyone in the world to them. If your child has a smartphone and no parental controls on it, you have just thrown that child into the world and given anybody in the world access to that child.

> **If your child has a smartphone and no parental controls on it, you have just thrown that child into the world and given anybody in the world access to that child.**

I'm saying this to myself as much as to anyone else, because we gave my oldest a smartphone when he got to high school. We made him wait until high school, and he's done pretty well with it, but he's had some experiences on social media that have made him step back and say, "I don't want to do social media." And he really doesn't.

To my other two kids, we've said, "We're not going the smartphone route, because it's too dangerous."

Erin Brewer (02:36):

If the social media mêlée wasn't difficult enough, we also have social media companies that are coming out with absurd policies. They're promoting the trans agenda by blocking anybody who makes a crazy statement like, "A woman can't have a penis." Those people get banned. Yet people who push dangerous medical interventions to children are not banned.

One of the reasons this is incredibly confusing to me is that a couple of years ago, a number of social media companies came out with a new policy about pro-anorexia groups. They banned pro-anorexia groups. These were groups that were encouraging girls to engage in anorexic behaviors, and giving them tips on how to starve themselves to death. There were competitions to see who could be the thinnest, who could be the least healthy. So the social media companies acknowledged that this was very dangerous for children and adults. It's dangerous for anybody. They banned these groups.

Yet they're embracing this whole trans narrative with their policies. Many of them suggest that anyone who criticizes the transgender agenda is engaging in hate speech or bullying. So they're enabling this agenda to take hold of our children.

Maria Keffler (04:14):

You can't just not criticize; you can't even question. Just ask questions like, "I don't understand this. What's supporting this?" and you get shut down. That's really hypocritical.

Going back to what you said about the pro-anorexia groups, what's happening to kids, and what's happening all over social media, is that we get into these filter bubbles—you may have heard that term before, "filter bubble." The way social media works is they market you. They market your attention. The longer that you're scrolling Facebook, scrolling Instagram, scrolling TikTok, the more opportunities the platform has to sell ads to you.

So the ad companies are buying time to put ads in front of your eyes. Well, the social media companies increase your time in front of the screen by giving you things you like. So if you like something about diet and weight loss, the social media company is going to put more diet and weight loss stuff in front of you so that your time is extended on Facebook and they can market more and make more money off of you.

We get siloed into these groups, and these kids who were getting into these pro-anorexia groups—and it's the same thing with the transgender narrative groups—they post something about it. They get lots of likes, lots of hits. Then the social media company sends more and more and more to them. The people who are questioning whether trans narrative is correct, or whether anorexia is a safe thing to do—they're not getting drawn into those communities.

I'm someone who, if I saw somebody saying, "I haven't eaten in two days," I would be concerned about that. So I'm not going to be invited into those pro-anorexia groups.

They get into these echo chambers and it's all people who think the same thing, and they're all encouraging each other going downward into these destructive behaviors.

It's really a problem. I don't know the answer except getting kids off and getting myself off social media.

> **They get into echo chambers and it's all people who think the same thing, and they all encourage each other in these destructive behaviors. I don't know the answer except getting kids off social media.**

Erin Brewer (06:22):

The other concern that I have, in addition to these kids being given marketing, is that they are being encouraged to believe that they're born in the wrong body, there's something wrong with them, and the only way to solve it is to damage their healthy bodies.

There are predators out there who are actively going in and fishing for these kids and drawing them into this cult. I've heard stories of parents whose children have run away as a result of predators saying, "If your parents don't affirm, you come to my house and all affirm you," or "Come to my state where you get this surgery that you want," or, "Come over to where I am and I'll help you get the hormones that you want.

These are predators who are actively preying on our children, and they've figured out algorithms to target these kids.

The other thing is that these kids are telling each other dangerous stuff.

One of the things that a lot of parents don't understand is how good girls feel when they first start taking testosterone. I've mentioned it before: if you or I started taking it, Maria, initially we'd feel good. It's a controlled substance. It's a steroid. Girls who start taking it feel awesome. It is amazing. They start having gender euphoria, they call it.

All their friends are looking at them on social media, and they're thinking, "Oh my gosh. Jane, who decided to be John, is suddenly high on the world. I want that too." Then the child who's gotten testosterone will counsel other children how to get it.

I've heard story after story from detransitioners of how they were coached to get testosterone. We know if a kid goes in and says, "I just saw my friend Jane, and she got some testosterone. She's feeling high. I want some too," the doctors will say "No," hopefully.

But if she goes in and she has the right script, which is, "I've always felt this way, I hid it from my parents. I'm afraid people won't like me, but I've come to the truth that I need to accept my authentic self," they're very likely to get testosterone quickly.

This community is sharing scripts so that these kids know what to do and what to say to get the drugs that they want, and what to do and to say to get teachers to accept their new identity. This is the perfect climate for grooming kids.

> **This community is sharing scripts so that these kids know what to do and say to get the drugs that they want, and what to do say to get teachers accept their new identity. This is the perfect climate for grooming kids.**

Maria Keffler (09:06):

When I talk to parents whose kids have done this, their stories are identical. I struggle when I'm listening to a new parent who's unloading, because I just want to say, "I know what you're going to say. Your child says they always felt this way. All her life, she's never liked her body."

It's a trope. You wonder, where is the script coming from? It is coming from social media.

We did a very small informal survey with about 60 responses of detransitioners and their parents in February of 2021. Social media came out as one of the biggest places that was the first introduction for kids to this gender stuff.

One child who was on a social media platform was befriended by supposedly another 13-year-old. You can't trust that somebody is who they say they are, but this young person was on social media and met this supposed 13-year-old.

The mom went back and retraced what happened. They were sharing a Google doc after they got off social media. They were doing it by a Google doc. The mom went back and restored the whole Google doc. Her daughter asked this supposed 13-year-old, "What's being trans-gender about? Tell me about that." Six weeks later, this girl announced that she was transgender, that she felt that way all her life, the whole script.

> **Her daughter asked this supposed 13-year-old, "What's being transgender about? Tell me about that." Six weeks later, this girl announced that she was transgender, that she felt that way all her life, the whole script.**

Kids are being conditioned; they're being preyed upon. We know that these gender doctors are advertising on social media, directly to children, which is illegal.

Erin Brewer (11:16):

We know that this is an issue because Lisa Littman did a study about rapid onset gender dysphoria, and pinpointed social media as being one of the big factors. I've seen videos where doctors are targeting children. They'll put something up on Tik Tok about how great it is to have your breasts cut off, and then they'll engage with children. Either they or someone from their office will message back and forth with children saying, "Come to our clinic. It doesn't matter how old you are. We can take care of you." They're preying upon children.

The other thing that I'm hearing increasingly from parents is that somebody in the child's school, or peer group, or Facebook friend group, or Tik Tok, announces a transgender identity and then asks, "Do you support trans rights?" They pressure these kids to come out and say, "Of course I do."

A lot of times when that happens, other kids will be saying, "Actually I'm trans too." Because they want that acceptance and affirmation. Parents are seeing these threads in social media and are very concerned and not sure how to deal with it.

As hard as it is, these kids need to be pulled away from this influence. We need to get them off the computers, off their phones. We have to get them outside, interacting with real people, interacting with life. Have them volunteer at a food pantry or at a homeless shelter, or maybe at a humane society.

We need to get them out there in the world, interacting with life rather than focused on social media. We know the long-term consequences of being pulled into this cult is devastating to these children.

Maria Keffler (13:13):

It's not just the trans agenda. That's an issue on social media. We have also seen childhood and teen depression increasing. Depression among kids has increased 57% in the last 10 years. If you look at the chart of when social media was introduced and started to become widely used, the depression line follows it exactly. That's a suspicious correlation that this is what's driving the increase in depression.

And social media is so 24/7. I was talking with a friend of mine who is a psychologist. She explained it in a way I hadn't thought about it before, but she's right on. She said when we were in school and you had that one kid—we'll call her Jodie—who was a jerk and Jodie was in your fourth-hour class. She had three of her buddies in there and they just made your life miserable through fourth hour. Then maybe she was at lunch with you. But at lunch you had your own buddies. She sat on the opposite side of the cafeteria, but that was the only time you saw Jodie. During fifth, sixth, seventh hour, it was fine. You'd go home. You didn't have to deal with Jodie.

Now with social media and smartphones and connected devices, Jodie

> **Now with social media and smartphones and connected devices, Jodie has access to you 24/7. Jodie can spread rumors about you 24/7. It's relentless and there's no chance for kids to recover.**

has access to you 24/7. Jodie can spread rumors about you 24/7. It's relentless and there's no chance for kids to recover.

When my friend explained that to me, I just thought, "That's it. That's what's going on."

Erin Brewer (15:00):

That's a good point. These kids are sucked in.

Jonathan Haidt also has some data that shows that teen suicides—completed suicides—have gone up directly with the use of social media. We can't say social media causes, depression, anxiety, or suicide, but we can sure say that that something's going on. The fact that children are actually completing suicides at such a high rate now is concerning.

And trans activists will always say it's because of transphobia. But we've seen, as people have become more accepting, the suicide rates are going up. As more kids are transitioning, the suicide rates are going up. It is disingenuous to suggest that the cause of these suicides is "not being affirmed." But the connection between social media and negative mental health outcomes looks to be pretty strong.

I was wondering if you'd mind if we watch a trailer to this show that's about how social media manipulates us and how as adults we have the decision. We have the cognitive ability to make choices about how much we want to expose ourselves but children don't understand the consequences.

I remember my daughter, who is now an adult, started on Facebook when she was an older teen, I told her, "Some of the stuff you post on there is going to come back to haunt you. It doesn't go away." Periodically she'll be reminded of that dorky boyfriend that she had when she was a teenager. It's out there in the world now.

Parents need to understand that children don't have the cognitive ability to assess how social media is affecting them, or how their use is going to affect them in the long-term.

The Social Dilemma (17:03):

When you go to Google and type in "climate change," you're going to see different results depending on where you live and the particular things that Google knows about your interests.

That's not by accident. That's a design technique.

What I want people to know is that everything they're doing online is being watched, is being tracked. Every single action you take is carefully monitored and recorded.

A lot of people think Google's just a search box, and Facebook's just a place to see what my friends are doing. What they don't realize is there are entire teams of engineers whose job is to use your psychology against you. I was the co-inventor of the Facebook "Like" button. I was the president of Pinterest... Google... Twitter... Instagram...

There were meaningful changes happening around the world because of these platforms. I think we were naive about the flip side of that coin.

You get rewarded by likes, thumbs-up, and we conflate that with value, and we conflate it with truth.

The whole generation is more anxious, more depressed. I always felt like, fundamentally, it was a force for good. I don't know if I feel that way anymore.

Facebook discovered that they were able to direct real world behavior and emotions without ever triggering the user's awareness. They are completely clueless.

Fake news spreads six times faster than true news. We're being bombarded with rumors.

If everyone's entitled to their own facts, there's really no need for people to come together. In fact, there's really no need for people to interact.

We have less control over who we are and what we really believe.

If you want to control the population of your country, there is never been a tool as effective as Facebook.

We built these things and we have a responsibility to change it. The intention could be, "How do we make the world better?" If technology creates mass chaos, loneliness, more polarization, more election hacking, more inability to focus on the real issues, we're toast.

Maria Keffler (19:11):

Wow. I've seen this documentary, *The Social Dilemma*. It is powerful. I strongly recommend that everybody watch it. If you don't have Netflix—that's the only place that's available right now—go to a friend's house who has Netflix and watch it, because it explains how we've gotten to where we are. They also suggest some ways to fix the problem, if not globally, at least for yourself—how to manage it and fix it for your own family.

Erin Brewer (19:44):

I know that it's hard when you take something like this away from the kids. They can get angry. But there are ways to mitigate that. You can say, "You can do social media, but I want to have access to your account so I can see what's going on."

One of the things that we've done with my youngest son is given him an hour a day to do computer stuff, and he's always chosen to play a video game that we're okay with. That's worked very well. He hasn't been interested in using social media. I feel very blessed by that because I haven't had to navigate that with him.

The other thing that I want to mention to parents is that when you share information about your child on social media, that's out there in the world too, and that potentially could get in the hands of predators. I caution parents to be careful about what you share about your child on social media, even if you're in a private group. Chances are there's somebody in that group that has nefarious intentions.

We are not able to keep up with the tech—we're able to create technology faster than we're able to keep up with it cognitively, emotionally, or to understand the impacts of it. We've historically seen that with other technologies. We're seeing that now with social media. It hasn't been around long enough for us to understand how to use it in a positive way.

I don't want to suggest that social media is all bad. We have used it to reach people and to help parents and to spread messages. It can be a positive means of reaching people. I don't want to paint it as all bad.

But it is so important for parents to understand that these children are vulnerable, and that there are predatory businesses that are marketing to them. There are predatory people who are trying to gain access to them. There's a society that seems hell-bent on grooming kids. This is something that parents need to be aware of.

Maria Keffler (22:04):

I want to echo what you said. There are a lot of positive applications of social media, and a lot of great things we can do with it. But parents need to understand how powerful it is and how much like a drug it is when your child is scrolling through their feed and getting likes.

They post a picture and they get a bunch of likes. They actually get a dopamine hit. That's positive feedback. These social media platforms are designed around psychological principles of giving people positive feedback. It becomes like a drug.

Think of it like sugar. You can put a little bit in your lemonade, you can have a piece of cake. But if your whole diet is sugar and you're eating sugar all day long, it's unhealthy. There are a lot of things that are unhealthy about the way kids are using social media today.

Another thing I want to mention is that I'm seeing more and more parents in some of our parenting groups cutting off social media or doing what you did and saying, "You can have it for one hour a day, under supervision." And they're saying, "Wow, my child is coming back. Like, she's dropping the trans narrative."

I'm seeing this more and more that cutting out social media leads to a nearly immediate improvement in the child's self-esteem and their outlook. One mom—I'm trying to think how she said it—"My child acts like my child again. Like she smiled—she's smiling and laughing. And I haven't seen that in months."

> **Cutting out social media (can lead) to a nearly immediate improvement in the child's self-esteem and their outlook. "My child acts like my child again. She smiled—she's smiling and laughing."**

So there's a lot of strong anecdotal evidence to suggest that social media is not a healthy thing for kids right now.

Erin Brewer (23:47):

Especially for teenage girls and boys. It's hard enough going through those changes under the best of circumstances. If you're constantly worried about being bullied or whether you're going to post something that's going to make people think you're bad, or you are going to do something that's going to get you bullied, or you never know when you might open that social media and have a pile-on for something you've done.

That striving to always get those likes, as you said—studies have shown the way social media works with those little hits of dopamine. It is one of the most motivating factors for people. We are responsive to that, which is why it's so addictive and compelling.

Kids don't have the maturation to be able to walk away from it when they need to. Even adults sometimes have a hard time waking away.

So do we have any questions?

Maria Keffler (25:12):

We have one question from a parent: "How do I take social media away from my child? He needs his phone and he uses devices at school. Is it realistic to think we can cut off social media influences?"

Erin Brewer (25:27):

That's a hard one, because one of the things that I know kids will try to do is go behind their parents back. If you say, "No social media," your kid might say, "Okay," and then figure out a way around it.

I saw an interview with a young man who had perpetrated a sexual crime against his sister. It was as a result of watching pornography. Even though his parents put some tools on the computer to prevent him from doing that, he figured out how to get around it. Kids are smart in that way.

One of the things that I suggest to parents is rather than saying, "You can't have that," or "You're grounded from social media," instead have honest discussions with kids about the impacts. Talk to them about how they've seemed less happy. Find out other activities that you can do with them that will be engaging so that you don't have to just say, "Okay, that's it, I'm cutting you off."

> **Rather than saying, "You can't have that," or "You're grounded from social media," instead have honest discussions with kids about the impacts.**

You can also consider cutting the internet off at your home. That might be something that you have to do if your child is addicted. That's going to be hard for parents, but it might be something you can do temporarily to wean your child off social media, if they're spiraling down.

Maria Keffler (27:01):

One of the things that we've done in our house is let our child have one social media platform. So one of my kids is into art and wanted to be able to share art things. She said, I want to either have a DeviantArt or an Instagram or something.

So we talked about it and we said, "You pick one, and I'm going to follow you and you're going to follow me. And I'm going to approve everybody who follows you.

We talked that through and she was fine with it. It has worked well, because she still has access to her friends, but it's not just this "throw her into the deep end of the swimming pool." It's one app. Again, just say, "I want to see what you're doing. I want to see who you're interacting with."

And as my kids get older and prove that they're able to handle it, we'll back off on those controls a bit.

But something I was thinking about a little earlier, as you were talking about the addictive nature of it—I struggle with this myself. My husband and I will often watch some TV or a movie in the evening, and I'll find myself grabbing my phone and scrolling through Facebook.

One of the things the social dilemma movie tells you is that pull-down to refresh comes from slot machines. That's the same movement of slot machines. That's why they adopted that, because it gives you excitement about what's going to come up. My husband will nudge me and look at me and give me that look.

Erin Brewer (28:56):

Another suggestion would be to have a technology-free day. This is something that schools used to encourage when my kids were little. Every Friday, turn off the TV and keep it off for 24 hours. Back then it was just the TV. That was mainly what kids were using. That was something that we regularly did with my older kids. We didn't watch much TV. By the time they were teenagers, we didn't even have a TV, because we just weren't that interested in it.

So that's a way you can wean kids off: make those days that are technology-free days fun. Figure out what activities your kids like. That time you spend with your kids is going to be valuable too, because it's going to be building those relationships with each other, which are super important.

A lot of parents think that teenagers will parent themselves, but I almost think in some ways that's the most important time for parenting.

Maria Keffler (30:06):

I fall into this too, because my kids can make their own meals and they can wash their own clothes. I start feeling like my parenting job's done.

But no—they have issues, things that they want to talk over. We can't make those conversations happen but we make ourselves available. Those conversations very frequently will happen and they can be very rewarding for both you and your child.

Anything else you want to add before we wrap up?

Erin Brewer (30:43):

I just want to encourage parents to feel empowered with this. A lot of parents are intimidated by the concept of taking something away from their kids. As a society we have this idea that kids get to dictate what they get to do. They get to decide how they get to interact with the world.

It's okay for parents to assert themselves as parents. Say something like, "I've noticed that you've been unhappy since you started watching Tik Tok. We need to take that away." I want parents to feel okay with it.

> **As a society we have this idea that kids get to dictate what they get to do. It's okay for parents to assert themselves as parents.**

I also want parents to understand this isn't their fault. Parenting is so much harder now. There are just so many more influences that are trying to subvert your efforts to raise a healthy child. If your child is being persuaded by social media—if your child has gotten pulled into the cult—it's not your fault. None of us could have predicted how powerful social media would be.

Maria Keffler (31:57):

I agree. I'm glad that you said that because that's something else I hear from parents so often: "What did I do wrong?"

None of us are perfect parents. We've all done things wrong. But this is something that really came out of left field. I don't think any of us could have foreseen this or could have known how to prevent it, because it's taken a few years of observing this to even recognize, "This is a cult."

And cults are notoriously sneaky. They're surreptitious. They go for vulnerable people behind the backs of those who would protect them.

So do cut yourself some slack and don't beat yourself up over this. We're all struggling to raise our kids in this environment and in the culture that we're in now. We need to have some grace for ourselves.

Episode 27 Resource List

The Social Dilemma Trailer: https://youtu.be/uaaC57tcci0

Episode 28: Debunking The 2015 US Transgender Survey

https://youtu.be/91KkroriFwI

Erin Brewer (00:39):

Today we are going to talk about the 2015 US Transgender Survey. It always astonishes me how much our policies—school policies and government policies—are based on this survey. Very few people really understand it. So we're going to spend some time talking about it today. Let's analyze it because there are so many flaws.

This is a survey, so it doesn't even purport to be a study, yet it is often used as if it is a valid and methodologically sound research study. It's not, it is a survey, which is a group of questions sent to participants. In this case, the participants are self-selected, which means they chose to participate. It's self-reported, which means all of the responses are based on somebody's impressions of their life retrospectively, so about their past.

> It doesn't even purport to be a study, yet it is often used as if it is a valid and methodologically sound research study. It's not, it is a biased survey of self-selected participants from a pro-trans organization.

These are all things that really make it not evidence to support anything.

When I read through the methodology, they recruited participants by sending a link to pro-trans organizations. So already we've got bias there. This is not a group of people who suffered from gender dysphoria. This is a group of people who wanted to transition, who did transition, and are reporting about their experience with transitioning.

Maria Keffler (03:26):

Another thing that struck me about it was that all of the participants were adults. You had to be 18 or older to participate in this survey. Yet I see this reported all the time for policies for children.

Why are we using this report, which only studied self-selected adults who are already pro- all these policies going into it, but then applying it to child populations? That doesn't work. It isn't valid.

Erin Brewer (03:59):

If you read through the study, the way the questions are phrased and the conclusions from the questions are really concerning. For example, one of the questions that they ask is whether or not somebody has experienced discrimination in getting medical care, which sounds like a reasonable question. But then the way they determine if somebody has been discriminated against 484eting medical care is if they haven't been able to access the types of transgender interventions that they want. They're suggesting that *that's* medical care. They report a very high rate of people who are saying they've been denied medical care.

Well, in fact, they've been denied access to the interventions that they have decided that they want, which is very different from being denied medical care. It's very concerning. If you hear that 98% of transgender people have been discriminated against getting medical care, that sounds concerning. But then when you dive down and realize, "What it's saying is that doctors are not giving every transgender person exactly what they want." That's different than discrimination.

> **If you hear that 98% of transgender people have been discriminated against getting medical care, that sounds concerning. But then when you realize, "What it's saying is that doctors are not giving every transgender person exactly what they want." That's different than discrimination.**

Maria Keffler (05:14):

We heard from our friend Alix about someone who wanted to have a pouch made, that he could hide his penis in and then have a neo vagina— basically a hole drilled into him so that he could be both male and female at the same time. This was apparently ten years ago. He wrote up this surgical plan and took it around and tried to get somebody to do it for him. He was told, "No." So in this case, he would have been "denied medical care" on a discriminatory basis.

Erin Brewer (05:58):

The other thing that I see time and time again, is activists who want to play it both ways. They get extremely upset if they're "misgendered" during a doctor visit, but then they also get very upset if they're not offered services that are absurd to be offered based on the sex they are pretending to be.

For example, somebody who's claiming to be a female—a male who's identifying as a female—will get extremely upset if they ask him if he wants a pap smear, because he doesn't have a cervix. But the same person will also get very upset if he's not asked if he wants a pap smear, because he's "a real woman."

No matter what the healthcare providers do, somebody in this community is going to claim that they've been discriminated against.

> **No matter what the healthcare providers do, somebody in this community is going to claim that they've been discriminated against.**

For medical records it's really important for doctors to know the biological sex of a patient, because the treatment changes based on biology. They want the best medical care, and yet they also want to be accepted as the opposite sex.

There's really no way to provide good medical care in this situation. It's not discriminatory. The healthcare providers are in a very difficult situation and trying to navigate these difficult patients.

Maria Keffler (07:24):

My son needed to go on Accutane for acne. He had really bad acne and nothing else we did was fixing it. They gave him Accutane, which is a really harsh chemical to put in kids' systems.

Since he's a boy, it wasn't a big deal. He can't get pregnant. He didn't need to be on birth control. But if my daughter needed it, we would have to put her on birth control for the entire six months that she's on Accutane, because it causes birth defects.

It is really important that the dermatologist knows if the patient is a biological female or a biological male, if they're prescribing Accutane.

And I can see very much that would be problematic for a girl who presents as a boy, if she passes as a boy, and she goes in there and says, "I'm a male." But yet she would complain she's being discriminated against if they wanted to know if she was male or female biologically.

Erin Brewer (08:42):

The healthcare providers are in an untenable situation. This ideology allows trans activists to say, "We're discriminated against all the time," regarding these absurd expectations that cannot be met and that reasonably should not be met for them.

The other thing that I hear is about suicide. This study is quoted as evidence that we need to allow children and adults to access these interventions because of thoughts about suicide. One of the things that that trans activists will say is that the rate of suicide goes way up when somebody transitions. Many of us look at that and say, "That's probably evidence that people shouldn't be medically transitioning, because their suicidality goes up."

The activists say, "No, the reason the suicidality goes up is because of the discrimination that they experience."

> **The rate of suicide goes way up when somebody transitions. Many of us look at that and say, "That's probably evidence that people shouldn't be medicalized, because their suicidality goes up."**
>
> **The activists say, "No, the reason suicidality goes up is because of the discrimination they experience.**

This study supports those of us who were saying that these medical interventions are dangerous and increase the harm to these people, but the trans-activists are spinning it in a way to support their contention that the whole reason that the suicidality is so high is because of how poorly these people are treated.

We have good evidence to suggest that trans medical interventions are dangerous and harmful, but the activists instead spin it in a way to support medically transitioning children and adults. We know that the completed suicide rate goes way up once somebody has gone through these interventions.

It's really frustrating when the actual eviden"e that "hey're using to support their ideology actually doesn't even support their ideology. It has to be really contorted in order to bolster their claims. Yet the media will time and time again quote this study as evidence that we have to support the transgender ideology.

Maria Keffler (10:55):

This is a different situation, but I've seen that same phenomenon in other places where they'll use a study that doesn't actually support their argument to say it supports their argument.

GLSEN, the Gay Lesbian & Straight Education Network, is notorious for bad citations for their policies. But they had a piece that came out, and one of the citations looked really good. It was the CDC School Health Policy & Program Survey (SHPPS), a well-done survey report by the CDC. GLSEN cited it to support their programs.

I got the CDC report, and I read every single word of it.

There was nothing in there that related to what GLSEN was talking about—not a word. They just put the CDC SHPPS report in there because it's respectable. People look at that and think, "Oh, wow, they've cited the CDC. They must know what they're doing."

They know what they're doing. They're misrepresenting research.

Erin Brewer (12:16):

It's frustrating because most people don't have a good background in research. They don't have the background to deconstruct these surveys and studies that are purporting to support the transgender ideology.

There have even been cases where I've seen studies come out that completely support our contention—that this is dangerous and harmful—but the media spins it. They know people don't have time to go to the original source and research it.

> **I've seen studies come out that completely support our contention—that this is dangerous and harmful—but the media spins it. They know people don't have time to go to the original source and research it.**

The Transgender Survey is 302 pages long. Most people are not going to spend time going through it and evaluating it. We rely on the media to give us good information, and they're not in this case. That's dangerous.

The other area where this report is used a lot is to suggest that children have to medically transition, and that any therapy that would be used to help them understand the reason that they're having these difficult feelings, in order to resolve the underlying issues that we know contribute to the gender dysphoria, are considered to be dangerous.

These self-reports perpetuate a myth about how discriminated-against these people have been, and how harmful it is when somebody doesn't validate them. This is one of the reports that's used to suggest that trans-identified people are victims of violence, because of their definition of violence. "Misgendering" and "deadnaming" are considered violence. They're able to claim that these poor, trans-identified people are victims of violence at an incredible rate.

> **This is one of the reports that's used to suggest that trans identified people are victims of violence, because of their definition of violence. "Misgendering" and "deadnaming" are considered violence. They claim that these poor, trans-identified people are victims of violence at an incredible rate.**

What's most frustrating about this is that they completely fail to look at people like me, and Walt Heyer, and Billy Burleigh, and Elle Palmer, and Sydney Wright—and I could name dozens more—who had gender dysphoria, and either had help resolving those feelings or transitioned and realized it was completely the wrong treatment for what was wrong. They detransitioned, and now are physically damaged as a result of the interventions that they got.

It makes me very angry that a survey like this is being touted as evidence that we have to wholeheartedly support the trans agenda, otherwise these poor trans people are going to kill themselves.

I wondered if you could just address that, the contention that because these trans-identified people report higher suicide ideation, that we should just go ahead and give them whatever they want.

Maria Keffler (15:06):

Well, that's emotional manipulation. It's emotional blackmail.

We've talked about this before. I had a boyfriend in college who did this to me. He didn't want me to break up with him and he'd call me night after night and threaten suicide. I recognize now that's abuse. That's actually psychological and emotional abuse, and that's what's happening here.

One of the things that I noted in this study—one of the questions that they asked about suicide was, "Have you

ever seriously thought about hurting yourself?" A lot of us have seriously thought about hurting ourselves at one time or another. We've all had times in our lives where we've asked, "Maybe, should I just off myself?"

So that's a very leading question and a very deceptive question to be asking.

Erin Brewer (15:58):

It also fails to address the fact that the vast majority of people who have a trans identity also have significant comorbid conditions, such as autism, depression, anxiety, borderline personality disorder, dissociative disorder. These are people who have significant mental health issues that are being overlooked and not treated effectively. It's not surprising to me that they would have an even higher rate of suicidal ideation.

> **These people have significant mental health issues that are being overlooked and not treated effectively. It's not surprising to me that they would have an even higher rate of suicidal ideation.**

Maria Keffler (16:37):

I had a conversation with a friend who's a social worker and she's pro-LGB and TQ, the whole thing. She talked about the high rate of suicide. She said the same thing. She gave the party line that they're so downtrodden, they're treated so badly.

I said, "Isn't it possible that they're suicidal because they're not living a psychologically and physically healthy lifestyle? Maybe it's because the choices that they're making about their healthcare and about the way they're going to live is not leading to healthy outcomes?"

She really didn't have an answer for that. She said, "I guess that could be, maybe we need to look at that."

We've talked before about how correlation is not the same as causation. You can't look at two things that occur together and say that one causes the other, because it could be a third factor affecting it. A lot of studies are coming out of the pro-trans community and they make a lot of causation claims that aren't supported.

Erin Brewer (17:55):

It goes back to the methodology. It's frustrating because a lot of these trans advocates will suggest that a lot of people who aren't scientific and who have all these ideas based on non-scientific ideologies are really pushing science, but they don't understand what good science is.

Maria Keffler (18:30):

This is a survey. It's not an experiment.

Erin Brewer (18:34):

No. It's not an experiment. "Self-selected" means that they're sending this specifically to pro-trans organizations and asking people to fill it out.

I don't know if you've ever filled out a survey, Maria. I have. Oftentimes they are biased in how the questions are asked. Right from the outset, when they developed this survey, it had pro-transgender bias. It wasn't reviewed for validity.

> **From the outset, when they developed this survey, it had pro-transgender bias. It wasn't reviewed for validity.**

It reminds me a lot of when I was in eighth grade. At the time I was a very hardcore leftist. My teachers all thought it would be very funny to put me on Senator Orrin Hatch's Youth Advisory Committee.

For those who don't know Hatch, he was in the senate for Utah for decades and was a hardcore Republican, and very, very conservative.

His office would send out these surveys to the Youth Advisory Committee. They would say things like, "Should we increase spending for defense 10%, 20%, 30%, or 40%?" Then they would publish the results: "One hundred percent of the Youth Advisory Committee thinks that we should increase spending for defense."

I would not fill out the survey. I would write in my own answers because the survey was designed to elicit a specific response.

Maria Keffler (20:11):

There was no option to say, "No, we shouldn't increase defense funding."

Erin Brewer (20:19):

And that's how this survey is.

Also, the way they define discrimination is problematic. Discrimination is defined by the person. Have you ever been discriminated against? "Well, sure."

One of the aspects of this ideology is that the transgender-identified people are one of the most discriminated-against populations. Of course they're going to say they have been discriminated against.

The other thing is that when you feel like you're part of a marginalized population, anytime something bad happens to you, you can attribute it to your identity rather than to the fact that stuff happens.

> **When you feel like you're part of a marginalized population, anytime something bad happens to you, you can attribute it to your identity rather than to the fact that stuff happens.**

There's also no validation. Somebody could say, "I attempted suicide ten times." There's no attempt to go back and look at health records to determine whether that's accurate.

I've heard numerous times that people in the trans community encourage people who want to get these interventions to stage a suicide attempt. They'll take maybe two Tylenols and say that they were attempting suicide, and then that's recorded as a suicide attempt. They are more able to advocate to get the interventions they "need" because they're suicidal.

Again, this is so disingenuous. This is what we have to push back against. We need to insist on quality research if people are going to make claims.

Maria Keffler (21:54):

Another thing that I just learned at a conference is the phrase, "A growing body of research." We hear this all the time. There's "a growing body of research" that says whatever the trans advocates want it to say.

But the way that happens is you get a study or a survey like this one, and then somebody writes an article and cites it. Then another person writes an article and sites both of them—the 2015 survey, plus this other article. Then a fourth person writes an article and sites all three of those.

It's called "data stacking."

Erin Brewer (22:39):

If you look at the WPATH guidelines, that's exactly what they've done.

There are the same studies reinvented. Or sometimes there might be a media outlet that reviews this study, and then that will be added to the "growing body of research."

They have created a myth in order to support their claims, and it's important that we push back against it.

For people who don't have a strong research background I would encourage you to go to Google and look at research methodology. There are some simple tutorials on what makes good research and what are common methodological flaws. I suspect that if you go through those, you'll find pretty much every one of them in the surveys and the "research" that people are using to claim that these kids are better off if they're medically transitioned.

> **For people who don't have a strong research background I would encourage you to go to Google and look at research methodology. There are some simple tutorials on what makes good research and what are common methodological flaws.**
>
> **You'll find pretty much every one of them in the "research" that people are using to claim that these kids are better off if they're medically transitioned.**

The other thing that is important that you pointed out: this is based on adults. We're doing all these things to children and we have no evidence—absolutely zero evidence—of the benefit of it.

Even Robert Garofalo who works for Lurie's Children's Hospital in Chicago—he's the director of their gender clinic—admits that we don't have evidence.

We do however, have good evidence that shows that therapy and support helps the vast majority of these kids outgrow these feelings.

They're really manipulating us into accepting this when the only treatment option that we know of that works is being made illegal in many states with therapy bans.

This ideology—it's not based in science and it's harmful.

Maria Keffler (24:43):

People might be asking why would someone go to all this trouble? We really do sound a bit like conspiracy theorists: "They've constructed this whole house of cards. It's a manufactured thing."

When you want to know what happened, follow the money. I've been in situations where somebody in an organization was behaving badly. As soon as you start following the money, the people who are at fault usually start crying foul.

This is a billion-dollar industry. I have seen three market reports just about sex reassignment surgery—not even about the hormones, just sex reassignment surgery. They expect it alone to be a billion dollar industry in the next five years.

Erin Brewer (25:34):

Look at Jennifer Bilek's *11th Hour Blog*, because she's done a phenomenal job of tracing the money.

I believe it's Pritzker who has an organization that gives grants to clinics like Lurie's Children's Hospital. They go into schools and recruit. Pharmaceutical companies are benefiting.

We could be viewed as conspiracy theorists, but I also think there's evidence out there to support what we're saying. We're not just making this up.

If people don't stand up and fight back against it, we're going to be like the people in Nazi, Germany, who said, "The Nazis, aren't really trying to kill all the Jews. You're just making that up. You're just fear-mongering." Few people stood up against what the Nazis were doing because initially they didn't believe that something so horrible could be taking place.

We need to understand what is taking place and we need to be the ones stand up and fight for our children.

> **Few people stood up against what the Nazis were doing because initially they didn't believe that something so horrible could be taking place. We need to understand something horrible is taking place.**

Episode 28 Resource List

Flawed Data Used by Trans Activists:
https://www.chooseyourowndiagnosis.com/2018/12/flawed-data-used-by-trans-activists.html

Link to the survey:
https://transequality.org/sites/default/files/docs/usts/USTS-Full-Report-Dec17.pdf

Episode 29: Borderline Personality Disorder

https://youtu.be/K1ANvx5OdIY

Erin Brewer (00:48):

Today we're going to talk about borderline personality disorder. I want to do a huge caveat that we are not diagnosing anybody. We are not therapists. We are just observing what's happening.

For those who don't know what borderline personality disorder is, if you look at diagnostic criteria and the way a lot of people who are trans-identified are acting, it really looks like there's an overlap. A lot of therapists have suggested that this trans identity is often a result of a borderline personality disorder.

Borderline personality disorder is a significant disorder. It's not handed out lightly. In our culture, it's very easy to dismiss people as mentally ill and say, "They're narcissistic," or "They're bipolar," or "They're depressed," or "They must have anxiety or OCD." It's easy to do that.

I want to remind people that this is a very significant diagnosis. It's also a very difficult diagnosis to treat.

People with borderline personality disorder lack a sense of self. It's like they're constantly floating around trying to grab onto something to help define themselves. When you look at a lot of the trans—especially the trans activists—these people are very outspoken. They want the outside world to validate them and affirm them, almost in a sense like they don't have an internal sense of themselves, so they need it from outside.

That's what's so concerning about this. These are people who have significant mental health issues, and instead of getting treatment, they're just validated and affirmed and celebrated.

That's heartbreaking because these are people who deserve to have appropriate mental health services so that they can get healthy. This behavior is not healthy. It's very scary. The suicide rates are high for this disorder.

As a kid, if I had not gotten the appropriate mental health care, I never would have had the opportunity to resolve the underlying trauma and to understand how profoundly that impacted me as a child. I likely would have continued to self-harm and maybe even developed borderline personality disorder, because I wouldn't have had that strong sense of self. That's so important and it normally develops over time throughout childhood.

I wanted to play this video right off the bat for people who aren't familiar with borderline personality disorder, just to give a schema of what it is.

About Medicine (03:48):

Some of the issues people with BPD face include significant difficulty controlling and regulating emotions (otherwise known as emotional lability), uncertainty of self (what psychiatrists call an unstable self-image), having intense and unstable relationships repeatedly, which can involve idealizing people then intensely disliking or devaluing them in relatively short intervals, and feeling an urgent need to avoid being abandoned by other people, even if the abandonment is only imagined, a chronic feeling of emptiness, repeatedly acting in impulsive and risky ways.

In terms of recovery, the best treatment results have been shown with a branch of psychological counseling known as dialectical behavioral therapy.

> **Issues people with BPD face include difficulty controlling and regulating emotions, uncertainty of self, having intense and unstable relationships, feeling an urgent need to avoid being abandoned by other people, a chronic feeling of emptiness, and repeatedly acting in impulsive and risky ways.**

Maria Keffler (04:45):

Affirmation sounds so positive. Everyone wants to be validated. Everyone wants to be affirmed. But we need to ask, "What are we validating? What are we affirming? Are those good and healthy things?"

In many cases, what we're validating and affirming with the trans community—the trans-identified people—is just pushing them further down a route of mental health destruction.

Erin Brewer (05:12):

People don't like being told that they're wrong, but it's very rare that we have this demand on society to validate another person. The fact that this has been entrenched—I feel like society has developed a borderline personality disorder because it's so crazy right now.

I thought we could go through each of these diagnostic criteria that were discussed, and apply them to the trans movement and how we see this happening.

Again, I want to point out that the people who have this disorder often are unaware of it. That's another hallmark of significant mental health issues: the people who are experiencing them don't feel crazy. They feel like the world is crazy. That's especially true in borderline personality disorder because they don't have a good, strong core self.

People who are not mentally ill realize when craziness starts happening around them and they're able to say, "Hmm, this is a crazy situation." Someone with borderline personality disorder gets pulled into the craziness and feels unstable. They want the outside world to build a reality for them.

> **People who are not mentally ill realize when craziness starts happening around them. They're able to say, "Hmm, this is a crazy situation."**
>
> **Someone with borderline personality disorder gets pulled into the craziness and feels unstable. They want the outside world to build a reality for them.**

The first diagnostic criterion is emotional lability. For people who aren't familiar with that term, it just means going from one emotion to the other very quickly. That's because they lack a core sense of self.

I don't know if you've ever been through a time when your stress level is really high and you just feel like you're bouncing from one emotion to the other. That's really common when people are highly stressed, but for the most part, we tend to have the ability to control our emotions.

Again, the reason I say society's developing a borderline personality disorder is that we're now accepting this craziness. If somebody hurts our feelings, it's okay for us to fly off the handle. Children are now being taught that being "misgendered" or "deadnamed" is actual violence. Instead of teaching kids to be stable and solid, we're teaching them to be fragile and to base their reality upon how other people interact with them.

That's really dangerous. Kids need to develop a core sense of self or they're incredibly vulnerable.

Maria Keffler (07:55):

We've talked in a previous episode about locus of control, and how we use to teach kids to have an internal locus of control, which means, "I have power to change my life; my decisions determine my future."

Now we're not teaching kids that anymore, we're teaching them, "If somebody uses a word I don't like, being suicidal is the appropriate response."

That puts the locus of control outside of you. It means you have no power over yourself, no power over your emotions or your choices or your life. The natural outgrowth of that, logically, is that we need to control everybody else so that they don't make us unhappy.

> **If the locus of control outside of you, you have no power over yourself, and no power over your emotions or your choices or your life.**
> **The natural outgrowth of that, logically, is that we need to control everybody else so that they don't make us unhappy.**

Erin Brewer (08:49):

It's really scary to me that we're teaching kids that they don't have to control their emotions, and that they should base their responses on these external stimuli. It is the opposite of creating a mentally healthy person.

Maria Keffler (09:07):

We're not doing these kids any favors, because people who have an external locus of control—who think they have no power over their lives—are notoriously bad friends, bad spouses, bad workers, because they never take responsibility for themselves.

Erin Brewer (09:31):

That goes into the unstable self-image that a lot of these people have. The idea that, "I need you to define me," and "The way you speak about me and the way that you interact with me defines who I am, because I don't have a core sense of self."

We're teaching kids really early that their feelings are what define who they are. Then on top of that, we're teaching them that their feelings come from external stimuli. We're creating a generation of kids who are likely to have symptoms of borderline personality disorder.

Maria Keffler (10:14):

I would say we're creating mental illness in an entire generation.

> **We are creating mental illness in an entire generation.**

Erin Brewer (10:34):

These kids are being told that their biological reality is no longer important, and that their identity is based on feelings. That's why you have people who say, "I'm transgender," or "I'm non-gender-conforming." That's an indication of somebody who does not have a strong core sense of self and this whole movement is embracing and encouraging it rather than saying, "Wait a minute. It's really important to have that core sense of self."

Ironically, they're also saying that gender is innate and non-changeable.

It's a very crazy-making ideology. If you raise kids in an environment where things aren't stable, where definitions keep changing, where there isn't reality—that's the perfect environment to create mentally ill children.

Maria Keffler (11:31):

This reminds me of some studies that I've seen on attachment and how caregiver attachment relates to kids' long-term stability.

A researcher—I can't remember her name off the top of my head—did a longitudinal study of kids and categorized them based on whether they had reliably good caregivers, reliably bad caregivers, or mercurial/change-able caregivers where children couldn't figure out whether the caregiver was going to provide for them on any given day. She followed them over decades.

As you would expect, kids who have reliably good caregivers who take care of their needs have the best outcomes. They're the most stable. They have the best success in life.

Now you would think that those with reliably bad caregivers would have the worst outcomes, but they don't.

The ones who have the worst outcomes are the ones who have the unstable/mercurial caregivers. Maybe their parents are alcoholics or drug-addicted, or have mental health issues. So the child never knows from day to day, "Am I going to be cared for or not? Am I going to get fed or am I going to have to feed myself?" Those kids have the worst outcomes, because they never have any firm foundation to stand on.

Erin Brewer (13:06):

When I was a kid, I knew my care wasn't there. I was able to develop relationships—primarily with teachers—that were nurturing and stable, that I believe saved my life. I sought those out because I knew I wasn't getting anything at home.

If you have a kid who's never quite sure—a lot of times these kids will be shamed if they act as if the stability isn't there all the time. That's why it's so difficult. They're disciplined for thinking that they might not get the care that they need.

Maria Keffler (13:52):

It speaks to that lack of a foundation. Children need a foundation that they can stand on. Best case is that they have good, reliable caregivers.

In the case of the trans community and trans ideology, the best case would be that the kids are getting the same answer from all of the adults in their lives. Hopefully it would be that reality and biology matter. But when you completely destabilize kids and they don't know what's true and they don't know what they can depend on, they do end up with bad outcomes.

Erin Brewer (14:29):

It's not surprising. These poor children who are being raised as "theybies," by moms who are being called dads and dads who were being called moms, and maybe another couple of people thrown into the mix because they're pansexual or whatever the newest term is. These kids are in really dangerous situations.

Maria Keffler (14:52):

The word you used—it's crazy-making. It's a crazy-making ideology.

Trans is a crazy-making ideology.

Erin Brewer (14:57):

When kids are told that their parents love them, but then they're not treated in loving ways—that mercurial caregiver that you talked about that can be dangerous.

We're having a whole generation of children who are in that situation where they're being told they have good, loving caregivers, but that those good, loving caregivers might not really be good, loving caregivers if they don't do everything the child wants them to do.

This ideology is undermining those good, solid relationships that have good outcomes. It really is creating a generation of kids who are very vulnerable to mental illness.

Maria Keffler (15:39):

What's the next aspect of borderline personality disorder?

Erin Brewer (15:44):

It's idealization and devaluation. We see this a lot in identity politics, where somebody is raised up as wonderful, and they're so cool. They're so wonderful. But if they step off the path that they're supposed to be on, then they are just dog-piled.

Maria Keffler (16:05):

Like J.K. Rowling.

Erin Brewer (16:07):

Yes. Even within small communities, I see people are so scared that they're going to do or say something that will get them cancelled. They have these weird ways of speaking—they're so careful. They're walking on eggshells, because if they do something wrong, they'll go from having lots of social credit to being ostracized, and they know it.

Maria Keffler (16:46):

You told me about something that happened locally, a woman who had that experience.

Erin Brewer (16:53):

It was really interesting. There was a woman here who was not part of the transgender community. She put together a celebration rally for the transgender community here in my town. She did or said something that upset one of the local trans activists. They completely ostracized her. They just went after her. She was the one that set up the whole rally to celebrate them, but she did something wrong.

That's one of the reasons that a lot of kids are identifying as trans or non-binary, because that gives them a pass. If you don't identify as transgender and are a heterosexual white woman, or a white man, then, you have to be so careful. But if you have that identity as transgender, then you get to bully others.

Maria Keffler (17:50):

Nobody is allowed to question you. If you say something that would otherwise offend someone, you get away with it because the narrative is, "I'm trans, so I am the most victimized person in the room."

> If you have that transgender identity, then you get to bully others. Nobody is allowed to question you. If you say something that would otherwise offend someone, you get away with it because the narrative is, "I'm trans, so I am the most victimized person in the room."

Erin Brewer (18:05):

It's destructive because what's happening is that we have innate qualities that we really are unable to do anything about that we're shamed for. That's taking away our locus of control.

The next one is a feeling of abandonment: people with borderline personality disorder are constantly worried about being abandoned because the people around them are the ones who are creating their sense of self. If somebody leaves, it's almost like they're taking a part of that person with them, because they don't have a core self. There's this constant fear of being abandoned.

That's part of where this, "I get to control your speech. I get to control what happens in the schools. I get to control policy." That's where this unreasonable expectation of being able to control people is coming from.

Maria Keffler (19:11):

That makes a lot of sense, if you don't know who you are, and you don't feel a sense of grounding. I know who I am. If you don't have that, then all of those around you are required to give you constant feedback and constant validation.

Erin Brewer (19:46):

It reminds me of silly putty. I don't know if everybody has played with silly putty.

Silly putty in a container will move to the shape of the container. As soon as you take it out of that container it'll become this blob and just flow over the surface. If you put it on newspaper, it'll pick up the print of the newspaper.

That reminds me a lot of how somebody with borderline personality is.

They need the people around them as their container. If they don't, they start to fall apart until they find somebody else to help contain them.

These are people who are suffering from a serious mental illness, and they are acting in ways that are reprehensible and can be very offensive. Sometimes it's hard to have compassion for them, but it is important to remember that they may not realize they have a mental illness. Typically society has been the one to give them that feedback, and we're no longer giving them that feedback.

The next one is feeling empty. They lack a sense of self. So they need somebody from outside them to fill them up constantly because they're not able to do that for themselves.

Maria Keffler (21:25):

I'm reminded of someone I know who is like a black hole of need: no amount of affirmation, validation, encouragement, appreciation is ever enough. It's like, it gives them a momentary high and then it immediately dissipates and more is needed.

Erin Brewer (21:47):

That plays into the last diagnostic criteria that was discussed in this video, which is impulsivity and risk taking.

Most people have some sense of not wanting to hurt themselves. A lot of times people with borderline personality disorder want the high from doing risky things. Oftentimes they engage in dangerous sexual behavior because they're looking for outside affirmation. We're seeing this being normalized.

Maria Keffler (22:37):

That's interesting. I know we've talked before about this idea that you can't tell anyone that there's a boundary. You can't tell anyone something is not acceptable. We see that more and more in the sex ed in school and in the pornography industry.

I just saw something yesterday: someone on social media was arguing that we need to make porn for kids, because porn has gotten so brutal and perverse that we need to start making some more soft porn that can ease kids into it before they get to the more hardcore.

Erin Brewer (23:25):

It's an indication of how sick our society is right now.

> **Someone on social media argued that we need to make porn for kids, because porn has gotten so brutal and perverse that we need to start making more soft porn that can ease kids into it before they get to the hardcore. That's an indication of how sick our society is right now.**

One of the things about that emptiness and this very confusing experience of having borderline personality disorder is that a lot of these kids are being given the information that if they transition, then they're going to become themselves, their authentic selves, their true selves. First puberty blockers. When that didn't help, cross-sex hormones. Well, that didn't help, maybe surgery and then more surgery. Then they get to the end of the interventions and they haven't helped. It hasn't cured them of this very significant mental illness, and they're left vulnerable and feeling betrayed.

That's why the suicide rate among those who have medically transitioned is so high after about ten years. They realize they did all this stuff and it didn't help provide them with that core sense of self that they so desperately wanted.

Maria Keffler (24:34):

That's very cult-like, because cults offer heaven—they offer Nirvana, they offer the state of enlightenment or the path to attain the state of perfection. The transgender activists keep promising, "You'll get that after puberty blockers, or you'll get that after hormones. You'll get that attainment of perfection after you surgically alter yourself."

We see this so often in detransitioners who've gotten to the end of the road, or hopefully they realized that the road they were on was a bad one before they went too far.

But even though they have left the cult, they've still got that doctrine so deep inside of them. You'll hear them talk. And they'll say, "I don't mean to take away from any true trans experience. This is just my experience," because they still believe the cult tenets, those lies that the cult taught them. Even once they've recognized how wrong it is, they still have more healing to do. They still have to get completely out of the cult mindset.

Erin Brewer (25:44):

Often, they are incredibly afraid of abandonment. A lot of the people who are saying things like, "I know there are true trans out there," don't want to be abandoned by their peers in the community because they know it's risky to say, "There's no such thing as being transgender," and that transitioning is an intervention, not an identity. They're afraid to say that because they know that they're going to lose friends. They might lose relatives. They're going to be called transphobic.

> **People who say things like, "I know there are true trans out there," don't want to be abandoned by their peers in the community because they know it's risky to say, "There's no such thing as being transgender." They know that they're going to lose friends. They might lose relatives. They're going to be called transphobic.**

Maria Keffler (26:18):

Just among the various groups of people that are doing what we're doing—which is trying to save kids from medicalization—we sometimes see push back. We keep coming across different people and groups who accept that there's true trans, or they say, "We're not transphobic."

That really bothers me when I hear people say that, because that term "transphobic" is loaded. It has been created to silence anyone who would question anything about the gender industry.

When I hear people who are supposedly trying to save kids, supposedly trying to push back on transgender ideology saying, "Oh, but we're not transphobic," what I see is somebody who's trying to play both sides of the field. They want to say, "I believe in truth. I believe in reality, I believe in biology. But don't be mad at me because I'm not one of those bad guys."

Erin Brewer (27:20):

A lot of this comes back to the fact that people who have mental illness are often unaware. They need people to let them know that their behavior is not healthy. That's typically been society's job.

If you have a group that's saying, "There are some people who are true trans"—rather than noting that transitioning is an intervention—every person who's struggling with gender dysphoria is going to be thinking, "I'm that one person who's true trans," and that person is not going to get the mental health services that he or she needs.

I wanted to play a clip. I don't want to indicate that this person has borderline personality disorder, but I just want to show that this is very indicative of somebody who doesn't have a good strong core-self. This is what it looks like.

"Demiwoman"

The word that I use most dear to my heart and for my gender identity is the term Demiwoman. And so for me, Demiwoman means that my identity is complex and nuanced, and I hold multiplicities. And my identity is rooted partially in being a woman and partially in some non-binary category. And so I am a woman and I am non-binary. I also will call myself a trans woman. I am transgender. I am a non-binary woman. There's a lot of different ways and words that I might use to describe my own identity and my own self, because I contain multitudes.

Erin Brewer

When I see that I see someone who's really struggling with their core sense of identity. It's really uncomfortable when you don't have a good, strong core sense of yourself.

I don't know if you've ever had a major shift in your identity. It's scary. It's destabilizing. It takes a while to reconstruct yourself, and it can be disturbing. In this case this guy is celebrating his instability, saying, "I contain multitudes," as if that's a positive thing. He's celebrating lacking a core sense of self.

Maria Keffler (29:50):

It made me think about one of my kids who said that at school there was a board on the wall that people could write all their identity statements on—things like "I am a lesbian," "I'm agender."

My child was really confused, because a lot of the stuff was contradictory. Like, "You can't be a boy and non-binary," and "You can't be a lesbian and heterosexual."

I saw that confusion in this video clip, somebody who does not know who he is. We shouldn't celebrate that.

Erin Brewer (30:38):

If you watch the rest of the video, it's very telling. And it's hard not to just think this is an egotistical guy, because that's how he comes off. He is constantly mentioning how people need to validate him or how he feels invalidated.

It's never occurred to him that it's not society's job to validate him. That's not society's role. It never has been. It shouldn't be, because if society's role is to validate you as who you believe you are, then we lose all sense of propriety. People can go out and kill other people because their identity is a murderer and you can't question that you need to validate it.

Historically society has created some firm boundaries that people don't cross, and the transgender movement is breaking those boundaries down. That puts us all at risk.

Maria Keffler (31:43):

Part of the reason that kids go to school is for socialization. The process of socialization is really getting feedback on your behavior. We don't ever want to see bullying. We don't want to see kids getting hurt. But we do need that iron-sharpening-iron process.

When we've got this policy that you can't ever criticize or question kids who are trans-identified, they're not getting any social feedback on what's acceptable and what's not.

> **When we've got this policy that you can't ever criticize or question kids who are trans-identified, they're not getting any social feedback on what's acceptable and what's not.**

Erin Brewer (32:22):

It reminds me of a period where I was bulimic in high school. I was systematic about it because I knew if somebody caught me throwing up that I was going to get negative feedback and I might get put into counseling. I had a system arranged so that I could do it without getting caught at home and at school.

If I had been told, "It's okay. Go ahead, throw up." There's a chance I wouldn't be alive today because bulimia is incredibly hard on your body. It causes your teeth to fall out. It causes heart disease. It's dangerous.

Thankfully, I got a clear message it wasn't okay. At some point I was caught at school and I got a clear message that that was not good behavior, that it was dangerous, and I got some help.

That's what is so heartbreaking to me about these kids and adults in this cult: they're not getting those messages that their behavior is harming them as well as society, and they're not being told they need help. They're not getting the mental health services that they need. If these people are suffering from borderline personality disorder, the trans identity isn't going to help. It's just going to keep spiraling.

Maria Keffler (33:50):

It reinforces the borderline personality disorder symptoms.

I wonder, are people who are trans-identified more likely to have borderline personality disorder, or does claiming a transgender identity create a borderline personality disorder?

Erin Brewer (34:08):

I suspect both are true. If you're constantly being given this message that who you are is dictated by how others interact with you, and if somebody "deadnames" you, they've just inflicted violence on you—this is a breeding ground for borderline personality disorder. Once you've taken away that core sense of self, it's hard to get it back.

It's confounding to me why we are embracing an ideology as a society that encourages the breakdown of that core sense of self.

Maria Keffler (34:47):

That's a really good question. Unfortunately, I don't think we have really many answers.

Erin Brewer (34:53):

It is important for people to understand that people with borderline personality disorder often have no clue that they have it. They can behave in ways that are incredibly erratic, that make no sense. They can make incredible demands on those around them, like having temper tantrums.

These are people who need help.

As I watched the fellow that we had on the clip, it was hard for me to feel a sense of compassion, as he was saying that anyone who wants to define womanhood based on biology was somehow wrong and bigoted and was hurting him. This is a man who is basically saying that me defending my womanhood is hurting him. It's hard to feel that sense of compassion, because his behavior feels reprehensible.

At the same time, if we don't recognize this as a mental health issue—if we just assume these are just jerks who can pull it together if they get the appropriate societal response—then we're not addressing the core issue.

I really want to encourage us to act like a society that doesn't have borderline personality disorder, which means to speak truth, to have firm boundaries, and not to accept the ridiculous notion that some people are true trans—which is a myth—or try to placate the person who has a mental health issue rather than speaking truth.

Maria Keffler (36:29):

I was talking to a mom who has a transgender-identified teenager, and her husband just wants to go along to make peace in the house because the teenager is very militant, very angry—all those things we talked about. The husband feels like they should just give the child what she wants so that they have peace.

I told the mom, "There's no end to that. That's credit card parenting. If you don't want to deal with it today, you're going to deal with it tomorrow with interest. There's no end to this."

Erin Brewer (37:19):

They blame those of us who aren't affirming them for their problems rather than accepting responsibility. Children need those firm boundaries. They are in the process of creating identity. If they have parents who just give up and say, "If this is too hard, I don't want to set up these firm boundaries"—they're really doing that child a huge disservice.

Episode 29 Resource List

Call Me Maybe: https://youtu.be/KRK2x70R2SA

What is Borderline Personality Disorder?
https://www.youtube.com/watch?v=KSPhc2NJA2Q

Borderline Personality Disorder: https://youtu.be/fZM8KMLFQm8

An article about Dialectical Behavioral Therapy, which is much like CBT (Cognitive Behavioral Therapy) to treat BPD:
https://www.verywellmind.com/dialectical-behavior-therapy-1067402

Episode 30: Is Social Transition Really Harmless?

https://youtu.be/GaFqki7_IWU

Maria Keffler (00:40):

Today were going to talk about whether social transition is harmless. There's a lot we can say about this, and a lot of different aspects we can cover.

Erin Brewer (00:54):

This is a tough issue, because I know there are a lot of people who will say, "We don't want medical transitioning. But if the kid wants to socially transition, we're okay with that."

We need to push back on that. Social transition is a medical intervention. It is an intervention for gender dysphoria, but there is no evidence to support it being an effective treatment.

In fact, it tends to make the symptoms of gender dysphoria worse, so kids that socially transition are far more likely to go on puberty blockers, cross-sex hormones and surgery, none of which have been proven to be effective treatments for gender dysphoria.

Social transitioning is telling children that you accept that they're born in the wrong bodies, that there's something flawed about them, and that being the opposite sex will somehow improve their lives.

That's a negative message to send to any child.

> **Social transitioning is telling children that you accept that they're born in the wrong bodies, that there's something flawed about them, and that being the opposite sex will somehow improve their lives. That's a negative message to send to any child.**

Maria Keffler (01:29):

We should probably talk first about what social transitioning actually is. What does it mean?

Erin Brewer (01:34):

It's important to differentiate between a child who wants to be gender-nonconforming versus a child who's socially transitioning. Do you want to talk about that for a second?

Maria Keffler (01:46):

We think of social transitioning as trying to pass as the opposite sex, and trying to trick other people into thinking that you're the opposite sex. This usually revolves around haircuts, clothing styles, and trying to appropriate opposite sex role stereotypes. I've heard parents address this with kids. There's a difference between being gender-nonconforming and being socially transitioned.

One parent that I know of said to her daughter, "There are people like Annie Lennox, the singer, and Diane Keaton, the actress, who are very gender-nonconforming. They both wear typically masculine type clothes: suits, ties, haircuts. Annie Lennox has very short cropped hair. But those women are not trying to deceive anyone. They're not trying to make anyone think that they're men, they're just women who have a particular style that tends to be perceived as masculine. We would call that gender-nonconforming. Or Boy George, the singer, who loves to wear flamboyant, gaudy clothes and dresses and makeup. He said directly, 'I'm not trying to pretend I'm a woman. I'm a man. I'm always going to be a man.'"

> **The difference between gender-nonconforming and social transition is whether or not you're trying to deceive others about who you really are.**

So that would be the difference between gender-nonconforming and social transition: whether you're trying to deceive others about who you really are or not.

Erin Brewer (03:24):

One of the important differences is the name and pronouns. Somebody who socially transitions will insist on others using different pronouns than the ones they would typically use, and often get upset when they are unable to control others. The so called "deadname" is a child's birth name. Children who socially transition often take on a new name, suggesting they are a new person.

Anytime we encourage a child to think of themselves as dead, and recreate themselves to be a new person, that's encouraging an unhealthy coping mechanism.

If a kid just wants to dress differently, if a girl wants a short haircut, or if a boy wants long hair, that's not in any way suggesting that they're uncomfortable with who they are. But if they're insisting that others use opposite-sex pronouns, and if they're calling their given birth name their "deadname," that's indicative of some deep-down discomfort with who they are, and encouraging them to become a different person is not an appropriate way to handle that.

Maria Keffler (04:50):

We've talked about that term *deadname* before. One of the things kids will say is, "I've always been this way. I've always known I was the opposite sex."

But then they use that term "deadname," which undercuts that argument, because they're also saying, "The person you knew before is dead. And I'm a new person." That really doesn't make sense.

Erin Brewer (05:18):

This is something very close to home for me, because when I started first grade, I was adamant that I was a boy. I wanted the teachers to treat me like a boy. I wanted the other kids treat me like a boy.

I feel like I was saved by teachers and other important adults in my life who refused to accept that I was a boy. They continued to enforce reality on me in a way that was important.

One of the reasons that I got involved fighting against transgender ideology is because it fills me with horror to think about what would have happened to me if adults said to me, "You are a boy. We're going to accept you as a boy. You're going to start using the boys' bathroom. We're going to use your chosen name." It really would've reinforced all the self-hatred that I had, and reinforced that desire to just ditch Erin—basically kill Erin and become a different person. That leads to continued mental health issues. It's never healthy to encourage children to disassociate from themselves.

> **It's never healthy to encourage children to dissociate from themselves.**

We wanted to talk about two different reasons that a child might want to socially transition. One of them is dissociative disorder, such as in my case. It wasn't that I was pretending to be a boy or I was acting like a boy; it's that I dissociated from myself and felt like I was a boy. There was no pretending; in my mind I was a boy.

Kids can do that. They have magical thinking and they're able to do stuff like that. It is a coping mechanism.

If I had people around me reinforcing that delusion—that I was in fact something I wasn't—that would have been harmful to me.

These kids who are dissociating have mental health issues, and need help. If you encourage them to disassociate and become something they're not, they are denied the help they need to identify the underlying cause of that dissociation.

The other case we've talked about as LARPing, which is Live-Action Role-Playing. These are kids who don't have a deep-down gender dysphoria. These are kids who are role-playing. They've decided they want to be the opposite sex for whatever reason. They've immersed themselves in a character. I'm not sure if it's a caricature or a character.

Maria Keffler (08:11):

Both words could apply.

Erin Brewer (08:13):

LARPing is very different, but ultimately the harm to them is the same.

If you have a kid who's dissociated, and you're encouraging them in that delusion, that's going to be dangerous. If you have a kid who's role-playing and you start treating them as if they are that role-play character, that's going to end up being harmful, because the kid isn't going to really learn how to deal with life as themselves. They're going to have this alternative persona that they use to interact with other people and to navigate through life.

Maria Keffler (08:50):

We've seen that with some other role-playing games. Dungeons and Dragons is popular. Even when I was younger, I had friends who played it. There were some people who got so deep into those roles that they really couldn't get out of them. That was who they thought their real persona was.

That's one of the dangers with live action role playing. LARPing has good sides and bad sides, and you can go too far. We are certainly not saying that live-action role-playing is bad, but if you get too deep into it—too invested in the character that you forget who you really are—that can be a problem.

We're seeing that happening with a lot of kids who are being drawn into this via social media, via school.

I saw a story of a girl who talked about how she was systematically drawn into transgender ideology in middle school. Other students asked, "Do you agree with the trans or not? Do you support trans?" And when she said, "No," she was called names.

She said, "I had a moment where I decided I'm going to be a boy." She said, "I clearly remember deciding that I'm going to be a boy."

Erin Brewer (10:25):

That's happening. Kids are feeling an incredible pressure to be somewhere in the LGB/TQ community. They don't get to be part of this fun group unless they have a trans identity. Kids are succumbing to it.

> **It's never healthy to Kids are feeling an incredible pressure to be somewhere in the LGB/TQ community. They don't get to be part of this fun group unless they have a trans identity.**

I listened to an interview with Abigail Shrier, and she was talking about a whistleblower who she interviewed, who worked at Planned Parenthood, who said that groups of girls would come in asking for testosterone, and they'd be in the waiting room, giggling and laughing and having a good time.

That is not gender dysphoria. Those are not kids who are suffering from gender dysphoria.

A kid who is suffering from gender dysphoria is suffering from incredible self-hatred, depression, anxiety, dissociation. A kid who's in the waiting room giggling with friends is LARPing (Live-Action Role-Playing). They're doing it almost as a social activity.

We have a short video that explains role-playing for those who are unfamiliar with the whole concept. So let's watch that.

Andre Meadows (12:11):

LARPing stands for live-action role-playing game. According to interactive game researchers Falk & Devonport, it can be defined as a dramatic and narrative game form that takes place in a physical environment. It is a storytelling system in which players assume character roles that they portray in person through action and interaction.

The game world is an agreed-upon environment located in both space and time, and governed by a set of rules, some of which must be formal and quantifiable.

Now when you think of LARPing, maybe you conjure up an image of a group of nerds wearing homemade costumes, sporting foam weapons, and casting spells on each other in the park. And yes, LARPing is something that many self-proclaimed nerds do love.

But it is also enjoyed by lots of other people all over the world. The 2014 LARP census—yes, that is a real thing—documented participation in over 80 countries.

LARPing is more than just a game. It's a game that merges performance, community, and art. It allows you to immerse yourself in the game by literally taking on the role of your character.

LARPing is especially interesting from a psychological standpoint. As Lizzie Stark writes, the yearning to experience personal emotion is one of the hallmarks of the LARP movement today. Many LARPers want to experience emotions: the loss of a friend, the thrill of battle, the pain of a trail, that they would never have occasion to feel in everyday life.

Maria Keffler (13:21):

I've never done live-action role-playing. I guess I did a murder mystery dinner one time, which would be considered live-action role-playing. That was a lot of fun, but it was limited to one evening.

Erin Brewer (13:36):

When I was in college, I was a paid victim for EMT scenarios. I would be given a list of symptoms and a character description. It was usually for a mass casualty incident training. I had that experience and the other was being part of the Society for Creative Anachronism when I was in college. They do role-playing, and I didn't get super involved, but boy, was it fun! We put on our costumes and we'd have a ball. Everybody would be interacting as if they were this other character, and it was so much fun. But then we'd go home and we'd take off our costumes and we would move along in life as ourselves.

I could see it being attractive to stay in character.

Maria Keffler (14:35):

I would rather be a medieval princess for the rest of my life.

Erin Brewer (14:38):

One of the things that you can do when you do live-action role-play—especially some of them now that are very creative—is that you can be from a different world. You can be a different creature. You don't have to be human, you can be a male or female or both or neither. You can immerse yourself.

In that video, he talks about how role-playing can give you the opportunity to imagine what it feels like to be somebody else. The problem is that the people who are doing live-action role-playing, and insisting that they're the opposite sex, think they know what it's like to be the opposite sex. But they really don't.

That's one of the problems with social transition, is that you're giving a child the impression that they can become the opposite sex. They are assuming a false reality that can be harmful.

Maria Keffler (15:37):

I'm thinking about some of these adult men who are claiming to be women and saying, "I'm a real woman. I've always been a woman," but they have not had the experiences that real women have had.

> **Adult men who claim to be women say, "I'm a real woman. I've always been a woman," but they have not had the experiences that real women have had.**

Erin Brewer (15:56):

I can insist that I'm Chinese and I've always felt Chinese. I love Chinese food. I like to dress in Chinese clothes. But I'm not. I'm just not, no matter how much I might feel like I am, I'm not.

That's where the social transition is so dangerous. It gives the kid the impression that they can actually feel what it's like to be something that they're not, that they can be something that they're not.

Children need boundaries. That's something that's important for them: having boundaries so that they grow up really having a good sense of what reality is.

We've heard stories of kids who are pretending to be Superman, and they jump off a roof and break their leg. These things happen because kids get in that imaginative play and they have that magical thinking. They don't understand the difference between pretend and real.

If you start allowing them to be treated as if something that isn't true is true, it can be damaging, not just to them, but to their peers.

Maria Keffler (17:11):

We also find that most kids who socially transition move into medical transition. I hate to use the term "slippery slope," but it really is a slippery slope, that once they socially transition, they find that doesn't quite satisfy. They think, "Let's try the hormones," and then that doesn't quite satisfy. They think, "Let's try surgical transition." It doesn't stop.

Erin Brewer (17:48):

These kids are told that all their problems are going to go away, and they're going to feel so much better if they socially transition. So they try to socially transition. They don't feel that much better, but now they're in this role. I've talked to detransitioners—it's incredibly difficult to come out and say, "I made a mistake." Instead of accepting that maybe they made a mistake, they pursue all the different forms of medical transition.

> **These kids are told that all their problems are going to go away, and they're going to feel so much better if they socially transition.**

Maria Keffler (18:14):

It keeps entrenching them further and further into this role. It's harder for them to say, "I made a mistake" and it is also harder to look at the reasons why it was so seductive to take on that role.

I just heard a term yesterday in a parenting group which horrified me. It's the first time I've heard this— this mom talked about her child talking about his "transition guide."

We know that there are social media influencers. We know there are these "glitter moms," which are generally adult men pretending to be women, who are grooming kids. But now there's apparently a "transition guide," who told this 15-year-old to cut his parents off and come live with the "transition guide."

What you said about when you dig a hole and you keep digging it deeper and deeper—it's harder to get out.

Erin Brewer (19:24):

It's harder to get out when you're affirmed, when everybody's celebrating.

There was a young child who the Obama administration flew out to the Capitol to watch *Star Wars* and meet some of the *Stars Wars* characters. This kid got treated like a celebrity simply for transitioning.

I hear stories like this about kids who are not the most popular kids, then they come out as transgender, and suddenly they are the most popular kids in school.

Detransitioning is not just admitting that you're wrong. It's also having to deal with this social force that's saying, "You're great if you're transgender; you're bad if you're not."

> **Detransitioning is not just admitting that you're wrong. It's also having to deal with this social force that says, "You're great if you're transgender; you're bad if you're not."**

Maria Keffler (20:22):

We need to dig in on biological reality. We need to dig in on truth. It was Colin Wright who said, "This is reality's last stand. We cannot afford to lose our tether to reality, because we're going to descend into chaos."

That's a paraphrase. That's not exactly how he said it, but it's true. These kids—especially young kids who maybe are just role-playing because that's what small children do… That's part of being a small child. "I'm a cowboy today. I'm an astronaut or a princess."

It's good to let kids explore those things. But at the end of the day, that child needs to know, "You're a seven-year-old boy. You're actually my six-year-old daughter." They need to know what truth is.

Erin Brewer (21:25):

In kindergarten, we'd have playtime where we would all play. Then the teacher would say, "Okay, play time is over."

Parents do that with their kids. Children will be playing and having a great time and imagining all kinds of amazing adventures. Then the parents say,

"Okay, it's time to come back."

Now we have parents who are saying, "Not only go ahead and play, but I'm going to enter into that fictional world with you and reinforce it. The teachers are going to do it and the crossing guards going to do it and the lunch person's going to do it," instead of having somebody who creates those important boundaries.

That's incredibly concerning. One of the things that guy talks about in that LARPing video—I encourage people to go watch the whole thing—there are designated people to create the environment for LARPing. They create the roles, they create the rules and at the end, they're the ones who stop it. Sometimes there's even a debrief afterwards, because people need that transition in order to go from role-playing back to themselves.

When it comes to social transition, basically what you're doing is you're putting the kid in that role. You're telling the kid they get to create their own rules. They get to create their own characters and they get to make people on the outside conform to what they want them to do. That's too much power for a child.

> **When it comes to social transition, you're putting the kid in the role of the LARP manager. You're telling the kid they get to create their own rules. They get to create their own characters and they get to make people on the outside conform to what they want them to do. That's too much power for a child.**

Maria Keffler (23:07):

What if it were like that with the Society for Creative Anachronism, which reinvents medieval times? What if, instead of being confined to that ballroom or to that that campground, suddenly they were all coming out into society, and we have to affirm that someone is actually a medieval knight and he wants to joust with me because I've offended him?

Erin Brewer (23:34):

This has gotten out of control. We have people now saying they are genderfluid non-binary, and saying sometimes they are male and sometimes they are female and sometimes they are neither and sometimes they are both. These identities are getting absurd.

One of the things that I'm increasingly seeing among activists is a push towards accepting the concept that somebody can be more than one person. There is this whole concept of dissociative disorder as an identity—that somebody can be more than one person at a time, and there is a push by some to have separate birth certificates for each of those personas.

I can't remember who first said this, but we're normalizing the pathological and we're pathologizing the normal.

> ## We're normalizing the pathological and we're pathologizing the normal.

I want to talk about the difference between the LARPing versus somebody who really is struggling from this dissociative disorder.

I had that true identity difficulty. I wasn't pretending to be a boy. I had cut myself off from myself. I think of it as splitting. I had a different person and didn't acknowledge Erin. It wasn't a role-play; it was a mental health issue. It's a well-documented coping mechanism.

We have a video now about dissociative disorder, so that people understand the difference between a kid who's assuming this identity as part of a process of fitting in and role-playing, versus a kid who's really suffering from mental health issues.

Psych2Go (26:27):

There are five signs you may be experiencing dissociation.

Number one: memory loss. Memory loss is a common symptom of dissociation. The main reason memory loss goes hand-in-hand with dissociation is because your brain cannot handle whatever is going on. Dissociation pulls you outside of your body. Hence, it's difficult for you to remember what happens around you if you're not there.

Number two: de-realization. It sometimes feels like a dream where things are colorless dull or blurry.

Number three: feeling lightheaded. There are many reasons why you may feel lightheaded, but in the context of mental health, dissociation can be a cause. The vestibular system is a sensory system responsible for spatial awareness and sense of balance. However, when you dissociate, you are not aware of your surroundings. When you come to the sudden realization of your surrounding serves almost as vestibular stimulation and makes you lightheaded.

Number four, not feeling pain. There is research suggesting that dissociation not only minimizes painful memories, but also the physical pain attached to them.

And number five, a loss of self-identity. Another aspect of dissociation is depersonalization. It's similar to derealization in the sense that you feel like you are watching yourself. However, depersonalization makes you feel distant from your mental process. You feel that you're an observer of your own life.

Erin Brewer (27:54):

That's important to understand how profoundly difficult a dissociative disorder is.

One of the things that I wanted to bring up both regarding a child with dissociative disorder, as well as a child who is role-playing, is that the more you engage in a certain type of behavior, the more you reinforce those neural pathways.

> **The more you engage in a certain type of behavior, the more you reinforce those neural pathways.**

Even social transitioning can have long-term consequences on that child and their brain development. If somebody does something repetitively, they're going to develop those neural pathways. It is going start to change their brain development—probably not in a healthy way—again, because this is all about denying who that child really is, and having them take on a false identity.

Maria Keffler (29:10):

The different neural pathways—you talked about when you practice something, when you do something over and over again...

I was remembering when I was learning to play the piano, there were certain chords that I could not get my hand to make the shape for. I remember getting so frustrated that I taped my fingers in the right position and just played that chord over and over again with my fingers taped in that position.

That's what we're doing with these kids. When we reinforce the social transitioning, we're duct-taping them or masking-taping them into a certain position. That is going to have an effect on them, and the longer they do it, the more powerful the effect is.

Erin Brewer (30:05):

It's reinforcing the idea that you can be something that you're not. But it's also reinforcing the idea that the way they're pretending to be something is real.

One of the things that I find incredibly offensive—and I'm hearing it more and more—is these men who grew up male, yet they're saying that they're women. It's offensive to me because they have no clue what it's like to be a woman. Some of their behavior—they're not acting like women would act.

I saw one video with Debbie Hayton, who decided to identify as a woman as an adult. He was talking about the fact that when he is alone at night, in a dangerous area, walking down the street, he can change how he walks so that he is perceived to be a male.

Guess what? Women can't *ever* do that. There's no way I'm walking down the street and anybody would ever think I'm a guy.

Maria Keffler (31:20):

I saw a magazine cover with Martin/Martine Rothblatt, and the headline said something about him being one of the few women CEOs in the country.

This is a man. And he's sitting in his chair, leaning back with his legs spread, and I'm thinking, "Woman don't sit like that."

Erin Brewer (31:43):

There was recently a video where a store owner was challenging a man who was saying he is a woman, and that man who was impersonating a woman went outside and started yelling, "Trans women are women!"

I thought, "No woman goes outside of a store and starts yelling 'Women are women!'" We don't have to because we know what a woman is. The fact that he's doing that is an indication that he's not a woman.

Maria Keffler (32:52):

By the time a child says, "I'm transgender," or non-binary or whatever, they've usually had several weeks or months of planning it and getting their social structures supporting them. They can be militant.

The first thing you want to do is say to the child, "I need some time to think about this and learn about this. Can you, be patient with me while I try to understand what's going on?" Ask for a buffer time. The child should be willing to give you that. You can even say, "I want to ask you lots of questions. I really want to understand where you're coming from. Please help me understand this."

That will help demilitarize the child a little bit and give the child hope that the parent maybe will align with what the child wants, which is not what we encourage, but you're buying yourself some time.

If there's another parent in the situation, get with the other parent. You want to try to figure out what your strategy is going to be. It's best if all the adults who are around the child can agree on what the strategy is going to be and set your boundaries.

This is one of the things we talk about so often: figuring out where your boundaries are. You may be fine with your child dressing a certain way, pick whatever clothes, pick whatever hairstyle but parents are not willing to use the opposite-sex pronouns.

Erin Brewer (34:42):

I've talked to a lot of detransitioners who developed rapid onset gender dysphoria. They've all suggested that it's important for parents not to buy into this, but to be the ones who are upholding reality, doing it in a loving and compassionate way.

I also wanted to address children like I was who one day—*Bam!*—went from being a quirky but happy girl to suddenly being very angry and saying, "I'm a boy," and being aggressive.

Something's happened to that child. They need help. It's important for parents to be able to identify a child who is just role-playing, or to figure out if is this a child who's really developed an identity disorder and needs significant help.

I can't imagine what my life would have been like if I had not gotten the therapy that I so desperately needed to resolve my underlying issues. There are some states now where therapists are not allowed to explore those underlying issues.

So parents have to be more creative, but if you have any suspicion—if your child is exhibiting those symptoms of disassociation—it's so important to get them some help. The child who is dissociated isn't going to be able to help themselves.

I was in such a state that I didn't think anything was wrong with me. It was everybody else, they were all wrong. If they would just accept me as a boy, everything was going to be fine. I had that firm conviction.

Maria Keffler (36:38):

Most of the people who are watching this video are probably parents who are already concerned about this issue. What I'm about to say is not going to apply to you, but I would like to tell parents to be on the lookout for this with children. If you have children with a trauma history or psychological illness or disorder—we're seeing autism, prior trauma, depression, self-harm cutting—this predisposes these kids to being vulnerable to the transgender ideology.

People might be asking, "Why is this happening?" Well, it's because it's very profitable. It's politically and financially profitable to push this ideology.

Erin Brewer (38:33):

The other thing is that there are paid employees of gender clinics who are going into schools and actively recruiting children. We have teachers who are required to take training about this. We have policies that are requiring the affirmation of kids who want to take on these identities.

> **Paid employees of gender clinics are going into schools and actively recruiting children.**

So it's not a conspiracy theory. You can go to Lurie Children's Hospital and see that they have employees that go into schools and actively recruit children. This is something that's happening. We shouldn't be allowing these recruiters to come into our schools. And we shouldn't be requiring policies that demand that teachers and other adults lie to children.

Episode 30 Resource List

5 Signs You're Experiencing Dissociation:
https://youtu.be/8BQrlA7NnBo

LARP: Crash Course Games #26: https://youtu.be/SUYb29YV47w

Episode 31: Literature Promoting Transgender Identification

https://youtu.be/C9BlzQyGaow

<u>Maria Keffler (00:44)</u>:

Today we're going to talk about books. There's a new genre out there of trans lit that runs the gamut from board books for preschoolers, all the way up to adult books.

A few years ago werewolves and vampires were all the rage. After the *Twilight* series came out, everybody was parroting those, and we had all these vampires and werewolves. I remember thinking, "I can't wait until we're done with werewolves and vampires." Now it's transgender that's on the market. I never thought I'd want to go back to vampires and werewolves, but they seem almost quaint compared to what's going on today.

<u>Erin Brewer (01:39)</u>:

99% Chance of Magic: Stories of Strength and Hope for Transgender Kids is a book that was sent to me free. They're targeting children to send it to. It's a book written for boys, to talk about magically becoming a girl. It talks about drinking potions and casting magical spells in order to become a girl, because everybody knows that the boys deserve to be princesses at the ball.

It's incredibly badly written. It's painful to read through, but it also has this message over and over again. These are all short stories and in each one it's a boy who wants to be a girl, and he magically becomes a girl.

It really promotes this idea of taking potions, which as we know refers to estrogen and puberty blockers. The target audience for this is probably tweens: prepubescent boys, and specifically boys. It is so concerning that they're targeting kids and they're sending free books out to them.

> **It really promotes this idea of taking potions, which as we know refers to estrogen and puberty blockers. It is so concerning that they're targeting kids and they're sending free books out to them.**

This is just the tip of the iceberg.

Maria Keffler (03:18):

These books are coming into libraries and classrooms.

You talked about how badly written that book was. I've seen some bad writing. One of the middle schools in our district sent out their summer reading list and almost 25% of it—seven out of 30 of the books that were recommended—revolved around sex and gender, just explicitly sex and gender. My organization, Arlington Parent Coalition, put out our own reading list—a better reading list—with some classics and modern books.

One of the teachers at this middle school was furious. She emailed us and said that we had put down these books and we hadn't even read them. So I read a few of them.

One was *Aristotle and Dante Discover the Secrets of the Universe*. This was on the summer reading list at Arlington Public Schools (VA). I downloaded the free sample that you can get from Amazon. It was about twenty-five pages. I read the first 20 pages.

It was awful. It was this stream-of-consciousness diatribe, peppered with what the narrators wanted to tell you: "Everybody knows that sex and gender aren't the same thing."

I wrote back to the teacher and I asked her, "As an English teacher, what do you find to recommend about this book?"

> **It was awful. The writing was horrible. I wrote back to the teacher and I asked, "As an English teacher, what do you find to recommend about this book?"**

There's a lot of bad writing out there, but the book that I brought to show everybody today is this one. [*Every Day*, by David Levithan]

Maria Keffler (05:15):

I found this book on my bookshelf here at home. It's got a teacher's name on it. I discovered this came home from my daughter's seventh grade English classroom. It's been sitting on our shelf. I didn't look at it for a couple of years.

I picked it up and I started looking at it. This is one of those transgender books!

I posted about it on Facebook and a friend of mine who's an English teacher said, "This book was really important to one of my students." So

I decided to read it before I critiqued it.

It's well-written. The author, David Levithan, is a good writer. The story is interesting. It's compelling. He uses beautiful language. He has beautiful metaphors. He's a good writer.

But the whole book serves as nothing but a vehicle for gay and trans propaganda.

> **It's well-written. The story is interesting.**
> **It's compelling. Levithan uses beautiful language.**
> **He has beautiful metaphors. He's a good writer.**
> **But the whole book serves as nothing**
> **but a vehicle for gay and trans propaganda.**

The premise of the story is that the narrator (named "A") wakes up every day in a different body. The narrator wakes up in the morning in some person's body, goes to sleep at night, and gets transferred to another person's body, who is always the same age as the narrator.

It's been going on the narrator's entire life, which raises some issues that aren't resolved very well in the book.

There's no purpose given for why this happens. How did it happen?

It reminds me a lot of the TV show *Quantum Leap*. I loved that show. A scientist was doing some experiments and he got zapped so that his consciousness went into somebody else's body. In the show it happened because something went awry in that person's life. He was put there by the universe, or whatever, to try to resolve that issue. As soon as he got the person back on track, he jumped into another life.

But in this book, *Every Day*, there's no reason. We don't know why it happens. We don't know what it's for.

At one point in the book A meets a pastor who says that he's met other people like this and they're not alone and there are ways to control it.

Then all of a sudden, the book ends.

Erin Brewer (08:07):

It's interesting because that sounds a lot like a dissociative disorder. And, we have talked about borderline personality disorder as well. A hallmark of that disorder is not having a core sense of self.

It almost seems like a lot of literature is promoting that as normal and appropriate, rather than as something deeply concerning.

It also allowed us to push this idea that we are a consciousness in a random meat-body. "Meat suit" refers to our body, and our "meat suit" is just fluke to our consciousness. It's our consciousness that really matters. Our meat bodies are more a hindrance that get in the way our consciousness, according to trans ideology.

This is interesting because so much of this narrative is pushed by people who have no spiritual underpinnings. It's almost like they're saying that there's a spirit that can be born into any random body and that it's our job as a spirit self to force society to understand who we are as our spirit selves, and that our bodies sometimes get in our way.

It is a bizarre narrative for people who are pushing back against fundamental concepts of religion.

Maria Keffler (09:45):

There's an old heresy called Gnosticism. This plays right into that. "What you can't see is more important than what's material."

That's another thing I really wanted to discuss in this episode, because I want parents to be aware of what kids are learning.

Every book, every movie, every song—everything is written from a worldview. The author has a worldview, and is communicating that through this creative media.

> **Every book, every movie, every song— everything is written from a worldview. The author has a worldview, and is communicating that through this creative media.**

Every book has a big idea and it's not usually explicit. What is the author trying to teach you? Like in *Lord of the Rings*, it's really all about power and the abuse of power and absolute power. But if you think about it, who is the one who mastered the ring? It was Frodo who threw it away and got rid of that evil power.

This is the stuff of literary critique. But every book has that big idea.

And when I read this book, I was trying to figure out, "What is this book's big idea? What is it trying to teach?"

I got to it about three quarters of the way through, on page 254. This is what David Levithan writes, through the voice of a 16-year-old, non-gendered person, "There are few things harder than being born in the wrong body."

I take exception to that. You can't be born in the wrong body.

> **David Levithan writes, through the voice of a 16-year-old, non-gendered person, "There are few things harder than being born in the wrong body." I take exception to that. You can't be born in the wrong body.**

To continue, "There are few things harder than being born in the wrong body. I had to deal with it a lot when I was growing up, but only for a day before I became so adaptable, so acquiescent to the way my life worked, I would resist some of the transitions. I loved having long hair and would resent it when I woke up to find my long hair was gone. There were days I felt like a girl, and days I felt like a boy, and those days wouldn't always correspond with the body I was in. I still believed everyone when they said I had to be one or the other, nobody was telling me a different story. And I was too young to think for myself. I had yet to learn that when it came to gender, I was both. And neither. It is an awful thing to be betrayed by your body."

Erin Brewer (12:32):

Wow. That is pretty explicit. That message is basically the ideology of the gender industry.

Maria Keffler (12:40):

It is. There's nothing else in this book that I can point to as a bigger idea that the author's trying to teach.

In most good literature, the narrator—the main character, the protagonist—has two things going on. They've got a goal—an actual explicit, stated goal, which is something they're trying to resolve—but they've also got a psychological or spiritual inner goal. At some point the two of those meet, and then the character is changed, hopefully for the better.

That does not exist in this book. The narrator is really just going through life one day at a time, never asking, "Why is this happening? What's going on?" And that's never resolved.

Erin Brewer (13:34):

It's extremely disturbing. It's happening not just to teens and tweens, but at an incredibly young age.

Last night I was watching a YouTube video from the show *The Doctors*. It's a group of doctors that talk about issues within society, and about health issues specifically. They had a clip from a school board meeting where parents were upset that *I Am Jazz* was read to a kindergarten class, followed by a child coming out as a different gender. Kids had come home very upset.

The doctors in the show—the main doctor who was acting as the authority—was suggesting that parents should read *I Am Jazz* to their child and talk about this even before they start kindergarten, so that they're prepared for it when it happens in their classroom.

The narrative of *I Am Jazz* is that it's possible to be born in the wrong body: The doctors made a mistake. Your parents made a mistake. It's your job to let them know by whatever means possible that there's been a mistake made. You're something that you don't appear to be.

It's basically teaching children not to believe what they've been taught. It undermines all authority, from doctors to parents to teachers, and it leaves kids feeling like they are the authority on everything, and that their job is to impose their feelings on the world and make the world accept them, rather than to find their place in the world, which is what really needs to happen in order to be healthy and successful.

> *I Am Jazz* teaches children not to believe what they've been taught. It undermines all authority, from doctors to parents to teachers, and it leaves kids feeling like they are the authority on everything, & it's their job to impose their feelings on the world.

It's teaching children as early as pre-K that their feelings are more important than reality. If their feelings are not respected, that person is hateful and bigoted, and that their job is to—by any means possible—get the authority figures in their lives and their surroundings to accept their feelings instead of reality.

These kids are being told that if authority figures don't accept them, to cut all ties. There's even a story in this book about a wolf who was born in the wrong body, who goes to grandma's house and tries on her clothes when she's out, and was caught by grandma trying on her clothes.

It's manipulating kids to push this agenda. I can't even describe how confusing it must be to children to be getting the message that they can be born in the wrong body.

Maria Keffler (16:33):

These books are in kids' classrooms. Groups are sending them to libraries, and sending them to teachers. I've talked to librarians who say they open up their library catalog to buy new books, and the first quarter of it is all of these "award-winning" books. They're all this trans agenda stuff.

Another troubling thing about this book, is that every single adult in this book is a two-dimensional caricature. This is a 16-year-old narrator. She jumps into bodies of 16-year-olds. Most of the characters are 16-year-olds, but most of the parents and the teachers aren't even mentioned. I don't remember ever seeing a teacher actually playing a role other than this person going to school. The parents are disinterested, they're disconnected, they're abusive, they're bumbling, they're religious zealots.

There were a couple of bodies she jumped into where she said, "This person has good parents," but the evidence for being "good" was that they took the kids to a museum on Saturday, or took them out dinner. There are no deep, real relationships with any adults in this book *at all*.

> **Every single adult in this book is a two-dimensional caricature. The parents are disinterested, they're disconnected, they're abusive, they're bumbling, they're religious zealots. There are no deep, real relationships with any adults in this book *at all*.**

Going back to the thing I mentioned earlier, she has no memory of anything other than jumping into bodies.

Early on in the book, I was thinking, "How does that work for a baby?"

Leviathan addresses it. He said through the character, "Babies don't care who is taking care of them. They just want to be fed. They don't care who's feeding them."

Erin Brewer (18:27):

Oh wow. This person knows nothing about human development.

Maria Keffler (18:30):

Attachment is enormous for babies. Orphaned babies who are left in cribs and are not attached to an adult become brain damaged.

Erin Brewer (18:46):

They often develop borderline personality disorder.

Maria Keffler (18:51):

Babies need to attach to a single caregiver. If this happened to a person, she would be mentally unstable. That's the gentlest way I can put it. If every day, this baby's latching onto a different mom's breast, it would be devastating.

> **Babies need to attach to a single caregiver. If this happened to a person, she would be mentally unstable. That's the gentlest way I can put it.**
>
> **For this author to suggest that that all babies need is to be fed is quite horrifying.**

Erin Brewer (19:10):

They probably don't get nursed, just have an adult prop up a bottle because apparently that's all it takes is to be fed.

There was a researcher who did work on attachment, and he showed that these monkeys would go to this very abrasive wire mama with a bottle— a fake mama. The monkeys would go over and get a drink from the bottle to get nourished, but then they would go to a different fake monkey that was made that was soft and plush and cuddly. The monkeys would cuddle with the soft, cuddly monkey, and then run over to get the nourishment, and then run back to the soft cuddly monkey.

This has been known for a long time, how important it is for children to be nurtured, not just fed. For this author to suggest that that all babies need is to be fed is quite horrifying.

Maria Keffler (20:22):

It really is. The author is speaking through this 16-year-old, genderless narrator, and putting statements out as if they are facts.

I'm finding multiple books in this genre where the protagonist, or the main narrator/character, has no gender. This is propaganda that's being fed to students.

> **I'm finding multiple books in this genre where the main narrator/character, has no gender. This is propaganda that's being fed to students.**

My daughter, who picked up this book in her classroom, told me she stopped reading it when she got to the sex scene. She was in seventh grade. This was in her seventh-grade English class. There's a three page really steamy sex scene. Now they don't actually have sex, but it's quite explicit what's going on. It's completely inappropriate for high school kids.

Erin Brewer (21:33):

I remember a book that had a profound impact on me when I was a teenager. It was written by Scott O'Dell, who wrote *Island of the Blue Dolphin*—an iconic book, a wonderful book. This book was called *Kathleen, Please Come Home*. It was about a girl who started having sex with a migrant worker who was much older than she was. She started using drugs and ran away from home.

It had such a profound effect on me because I thought, "This behavior is perfectly okay." I ran away from home at one point, because I was inspired by this book: "Kathleen did it. I can do it too."

This book did show the way the mother responded. There was some empathy about how much it hurt the mother. Kathleen ended up running away to Mexico. She got pregnant, and she was smuggling heroin. All of these things seemed glamorous to me as a teenager.

It is not to say that children shouldn't read books about these controversial issues, but they do have a profound impact, especially if it sounds like these behaviors are affirmed.

The message is so explicit that being born in the wrong body is something that can happen, and teachers and librarians are embracing this. They are targeting kids. They're sending free books to them. They're often "award-winning," because these LGB/TQ++ organizations are giving them these awards. They're sculpting the culture.

> They are targeting kids. They're sending free books to them. These books are often "award-winning," because these LGB/TQ++ organizations are giving them these awards. They're sculpting the culture.

One of the questions that I have is about how every book has an agenda. My question is, how do we decide what books should be in schools? What books should children be exposed to?

My personal opinion is that we would expose books that are going to promote healthy and successful behavior.

Maria Keffler (23:56):

When we were talking to the teacher and the school district that put out that really egregious list of books, my argument was, "Why aren't we looking at noble themes? Why aren't we looking at books that teach about courage, about honor, about truth, about valor—why aren't we looking at bigger themes?"

There's no big theme in this book. You were talking about what it's glamorizing—in almost every life that this narrator jumped into, she just ran circles around the parents. She lied to the parents, and skipped school so she could go to the beach for the day, and there was never really any blowback from that. It really cast the adults as bumbling fools that teenagers can just work around.

I would want to look at books and say, "What is the theme? What are kids going to take away from this?" There's nothing wrong with teaching books that have controversial messages, but we need to teach them in context.

Something I'm always asking my kids is, "What do you think the author wants you to think? What do you think the producer of this movie wants you to think?"

> I'm always asking my kids, "What do you think the author wants you to think? What do you think the producer of this movie wants you to think?"

Erin Brewer (25:30):

A book that I read—it was probably one of the most influential books that I read when I was in probably seventh grade, and it was about identity—was *Black Like Me*. I believe it's a true story. The author was able to change his appearance enough so that he was perceived as a black man.

Maria Keffler (25:55):

He took a drug that changed the melanin in his skin. It's very dangerous. He knew it was dangerous, but he wanted to experience this.

Erin Brewer (26:04):

That book had such a profound impact on me. The idea that people were treated so differently because of how they look—that's a book about identity. It had an important message. It really gave us important information.

Another book, *The Jungle*, had such a profound impact on me about how desperate things were and how thankful we need to be for what we have now.

The books that kids are reading today are encouraging them to be victims, and to promote dissociative behavior. These are really dangerous. These are encouraging kids to basically be dysfunctional.

Maria Keffler (27:01):

If you go to Amazon and type in, "transgender young adult," you'll find page after page of books. I couldn't even find the book I was looking for, there's so many of them.

This is one of the reasons why I have been saying that I don't think public school is a safe place for any child today, because a child cannot go to school for a single day without being confronted with messages about sex and gender. I don't think these books are healthy and parents really need to be aware. Check what's coming home in their backpacks.

> **Public school isn't a safe place for a child today, because a child cannot go to school for a single day without being confronted with messages about sex and gender.**

A friend of mine, whose child has some special needs, told the school, "I don't want my child introduced to these themes." And then here comes home in the backpack a book that's got gay porn in it. The teacher said, "I didn't realize this would be a problem."

Erin Brewer (28:24):

The explicitness of the sex scenes in some of these books... *Kathleen, Please Come Home* had sex scenes that were implied. The scenes that are in books now are incredibly explicit.

Why would we want—especially young teens and even younger, as we have even younger children reading books with these explicit sex scenes that when I was younger, would have appeared in a *Playgirl* or a *Playboy*. That's the level of the explicitness that we have now. Now they're in our schools.

Maria Keffler (29:07):

Do you know what bodice rippers are? They're those paperback romance novels that you can pick up in the drugstore. They used to be like $3, $4 each. Almost all of them have a Fabio image—no shirt, medieval trousers, and woman with flowing hair and her bosom spilling out.

I used to devour those. People call me a prude and they suggest I am just scared of sex! I used to devour bodice rippers.

I realized now they're incredibly unhealthy. That genre—the bodice rippers—they're called "romance novels," but it's erotica for women. It gives a really distorted view of men's and women's relationships.

I'm bringing that up just to say that I know what sex scenes look like.

Erin Brewer (31:07):

The message is that sex is nothing more serious than going and getting an ice cream with someone. It's just something you do.

The repercussions from having sex are much bigger than having an ice cream. This is completely minimizing what sex is in a way that is really dangerous for kids, because they don't have the cognitive ability to weigh the risks associated with having casual sex.

Here they are in school reading books that encourage it. Not only that, but their teachers are giving them these books. They have an adult giving tacit approval.

It also creates a weird dynamic between the children and the adults, suggesting that it's okay for adults to talk about these kinds of explicit sex scenes with children.

These are not books that are going to benefit the children. We have lots of really amazing books they could be reading instead.

Maria Keffler (32:59):

One last thing I wanted to mention about this book is that throughout the book the characters in the book are all hooking up with one another and it's completely irrespective of whether they're boys or girls. Everybody connecting, hooking up with everybody else.

This is an implied worldview. The author never says, "Any sexual relationship is acceptable," but that is what's implied.

> **Throughout the book the characters are all hooking up with one another, irrespective of whether they're boys or girls. This is an implied worldview. The author never says, "Any sexual relationship is acceptable," but that is what's implied.**

Erin Brewer (33:47):

Another book I read when I was in high school was *Brave New World*. It presented a hookup culture as being a problem. This was part of the dystopian society: it was considered rude to say "no" to anybody sexually.

It's very interesting that has been switched around and now it's being promoted as normal and good. "Sex is just recreation. It's good for you to go enjoy yourself." It's prioritizing the body as a meat suit that you play with, rather than as part of yourself as a person.

Maria Keffler (34:53):

I know it's really overwhelming. You do not have time to read every book that your child brings home. I recognize that I committed a lot of time to reading this one, because I was challenged by a friend who felt it was a decent book. You can't do that with every book, but you can look at the title and look at it on Amazon.

There are some titles there—one called *Symptoms of Being Human*. It looks like an innocuous book. It's got a black and white cover. But it's one of these transgender-themed books.

Search the title on Amazon or a search engine and just see what comes up. Recognize that if it's recent—if it's been published in the last six or seven years—and it's in the YA market and it's "award-winning," it's pretty much guaranteed that this a transgender-themed book.

> **If the book is recent—if it's been published in the last six or seven years—and it's in the YA market and it's "award-winning," it's pretty much guaranteed that it's a transgender-themed book.**

Erin Brewer (36:13):

It's very sad that children are not being exposed to quality literature, but are being indoctrinated with this ideology. It should come down to, "Are the messages in the book going to promote health and wellbeing, or are they going to promote dysfunction and dangerous behaviors?"

Once kids get involved in the transgender ideology, they're going to start self-harming their bodies. They're going to start medicalizing. These are kids who are going to have lifelong complications as a result of this ideology.

Maria Keffler (37:21):

And ostensibly these books are just helping promote kindness and diversity, so that when children meet other people who were born in the wrong body, they'll know to accept them and love them and all that.

Erin Brewer (37:50):

Parents, it's got to be so incredibly overwhelming. Be vigilant and push back against what the teachers are pushing on your kids. It's our right as parents to go into the schools and say, "No, I'm not okay with my child reading that." It's our right and responsibility. We need to be doing that.

Maria Keffler (38:21):

Parents are taking these books, going to school board meetings and using their two or three open-comment minutes to read from these books. I've heard of places where the school board has had stopped the reading: "You can't use words like that here in public." So take one of these books to the school board meeting, just read it aloud. That's all you have to do.

Erin Brewer (38:50):

Let the school board know, and let the public know what's in these books.

So many parents are busy and they assume that the schools are good, healthy, safe places for their kids. They assume that diversity and tolerance is really about not bullying kids and accepting people. They don't realize how insidious the gender industry is.

Episode 31 Resource List

Every Day by David Levithan: https://www.amazon.com/Every-Day-David-Levithan/dp/0307931897/ref=sr_1_1

Episode 32: Deadnaming, Pronouns and Compelled Speech

https://youtu.be/bUyvl9Rw7Vw

Maria Keffler (00:41):

Today we are talking about compelled speech, and specifically about the topics of deadnaming and preferred pronouns.

Erin Brewer (00:50):

We have talked a little bit about deadnaming and pronouns in other videos. But we wanted to talk about this specifically, because we have parents asking us regularly, "Should I use preferred pronouns that my child wants me to use? Should I use the new name that they've made up?"

We don't always have perfect answers, but we can reflect on what we've heard from detransitioners and from parents, and give you information based on that.

There isn't a big body of research out there, but based on what I have heard, parents need to hold the line. They need to speak truth. Using what are considered "preferred pronouns"—which are the wrong pronouns— is compelling a parent into this cult and into the lie that we can be born in the wrong body.

> **Parents need to hold the line. They need to speak truth. Using what are considered "preferred pronouns" is compelling a parent into this cult and into the lie that we can be born in the wrong body.**

The overarching message that I'm getting is that it's so important for parents to treat their children with love and compassion, not to buy into this compelled speech.

Maria Keffler (02:10):

It is important that we hold the line on truth. It can be hard for parents. You feel like you're just pushing back, not only on your child, but on the entire world and on the school. You are the one that's holding the line on truth.

I have known parents who have said, "Okay, we'll let you use that name as a nickname." One parent I know of told the child, "It's okay if your friends want to call you that as a nickname, but when you meet other adults, we would like you to introduce yourself with your real name." That's one way you can be a little bit gentle about it.

Erin Brewer (03:31):

For parents who are maybe not familiar with these terms, the definition of "deadname" is the name you were given at birth by your parents.

When I hear "deadname," it really gives me the impression that a child has killed themselves. They're killing who they were, and they're remaking themselves as somebody new. And part of that dissociative process of becoming somebody new is killing everything about their past. They're killing who they were, what they were, and a big part of that is their name.

The fact that they call it a "deadname" is very important information, because it tells us about their psyche.

Maria Keffler (04:27):

When we hear the gender industry—or when we hear kids who've been indoctrinated—say, "I'm the same person I always was. You just didn't know that I was a boy," or "You just didn't know that I'm non-binary but I've always been this person," that belies the term "deadname."

Dead represents a killing—a suicide of who that person when he or she was born. The name that your parents give you, that is the first gift you receive after the gift of life. When a child is born and his or her parents give that child a name, in most cases the parents have labored over that name for months, trying to pick the perfect name. Maybe it's a family name. Maybe it's a name that is reflective of someone that the parents really respected and honored, or a historical figure or a celebrity. It's isn't given out willy-nilly.

> **The name that your parents give you is the first gift you receive from them, after the gift of life.**

These names that we give our children are important and they're meaningful, and they connect you to the family. And that's what's so insidious about this whole ideology: it disconnects kids from themselves, and from their bodies. It disconnects them from their families, disconnects them from relationships. When they say "deadname," they're disconnecting from their history. They're completely separating from who they've been and from all of their extended family.

It's a hateful thing to do to a child. As parents, we love our kids. We want to do the best we can for them. But the party line on this—the "expert's recommendation on this"—is not what's best for kids.

Erin Brewer (06:32):

It isn't uncommon for teenagers to want to be called by a nickname. In a way, they're rejecting their parents they're trying to become their own person. But the child doesn't say, "Don't use my deadname." They'll say, please use my nickname.

It's very different to when a child talks about a "deadname." I get this image of them basically committing suicide, to remake themselves and become a new person.

Also that insistence upon compelling others to do what they say is insidious. We see that with pronouns. We see that with words like "chestfeeder," instead of *breastfeeding*, or "birthing parent," instead of *mother*.

It's trying to rewrite the language in a way that disassociates people from their roles. The child is no longer your child, the child that you carried, the child that you gave birth to, the child that you raised. That child has rejected themselves and become a new person. And in the process, rejected you as a parent.

Maria Keffler (08:08):

Here in the United States we are such an individual-focused society. Right in our *Declaration of Independence*, we have the right to the "pursuit of happiness," and that's a very individualistic thing. There's nothing really wrong with that until you go so far afield that we no longer have responsibilities to our family, and no responsibilities to our community.

In other cultures, it's a more connected community and you belong to your family. If you do something shameful, that shames the whole family.

I wonder if communities like those are having as much trouble with this ideology as we are in our independent-minded United States?

We really do need our families. Children need to be connected to their parents. Parents are children's best protectors. There are cases of really horrific child abuse and neglect, but in the majority of cases, parents are children's best protectors, advocates, cheerleaders. Nobody loves that child as much as his or her parents, and to separate that relationship or to sever it is almost always done for nefarious reasons.

Erin Brewer (09:39):

I have concerns about these children being taught that if somebody uses their birth name it's bullying. In some cases they're even being taught that it's violence.

I grew up in a family—this will give you an indication of how strange my childhood was. At one point we had 27 cats, which is a lot, it's too many.

Maria Keffler (10:02):

That's a few cats.

Erin Brewer (10:06):

It was not uncommon for me to be called Snookie or Spider or Panther. It was not at all uncommon. Anybody who's grown up in a big family knows this happens, you get called by the names of your other siblings.

Maria Keffler (10:32):

My mom occasionally calls me my aunt's name, the name of her little sister.

Erin Brewer (10:37):

When that happens, we don't say, "I've been abused!" But today kids are being taught that if somebody uses their birth name, that damages them. "It's akin to violence."

> **Today kids are being taught that if somebody uses their birth name, that damages them. "It's akin to violence."**

We're programming kids to be hurt if somebody uses their birth name. Kids have enough that they have to deal with without being taught that if somebody uses their birth name it's something that they should recoil from.

They've really been taught that words are violence. Kids should be taught to be resilient, not taught to be fragile.

Maria Keffler (11:34):

That's something we've talked about in a previous video, maybe more than once, about locus of control. The locus of control is where you think that power over your life resides.

When we were growing up, we were taught to have an internal locus of control, which means that the choices that I make and the things that I do affect the outcomes of my life. I have power over my life. That is a much healthier way to live than the opposite—an external locus of control, where what others do determines the outcome of our life.

Kids are being taught, "If somebody calls you by a name you don't like, that's literal violence, and it's going to make you suicidal." That puts the locus of control completely outside of yourself.

I remember when I was growing up—I'm not saying that this was a great or healthy thing—but so often, if I was upset or angry about something, I'd be told, "Don't worry about it. Just ignore it."

We were talking about names. I grew up with three male cousins who are all about my age. I was the only girl, and they nicknamed me "Maria Diarrhea," not for any reason, just because it rhymed and all the adults laughed about it. And I'm fine. I grew up. I'm not traumatized. I can look back on it and think it's funny. I'm sure if my cousins were watching this video, they're probably laughing right now. It wasn't a big deal. But calling a child by the name that he or she lived with for 13, 15, 20 years is now traumatizing to them.

<u>Erin Brewer (13:33)</u>:

My nickname was Earwig—not a particularly nice nickname. My step-father gave me that nickname. If I had like acted as if he had violated me or perpetrated violence against me every time he used that nickname, I would probably not be alive today.

These are kids who are being taught to view themselves as victims.

Families are all different. In some families there's a lot of yelling and that's more normal for their family. If I were to go into that family, I maybe might think, "Oh my gosh, they hate each other." But that's their way of interacting.

People might come into my home and think, "They never talked to each other," because we tend to be pretty quiet and introverted.

We learn from our families and we learn from our culture what is okay and what isn't okay and what we should be offended by and what we shouldn't be offended by.

As you mentioned, when we grew up, we were taught to be resilient. And now kids are taught to be fragile. They're taught that other people have so much control over them.

Parents also have to understand that there's a slippery slope here. I've heard this from parents who say, "I'm just going to use the pronouns and the name that they want me to use because that'll de-escalate things. There's just so much conflict. We've talked about it and I've told them they can't medicalize. They can't do anything more than that. So we're just going to do this as a compromise."

It ends up not being a compromise, because as soon as that child gets what they want, they start pushing for the next thing.

Every parent that I've talked to has said, "I thought it was going to make things better by using their pronouns, and it only made things worse."

It reinforces that cult mentality. It gives them power. They think, "I can make people do what I want." This may not even be conscious. But for kids, it is often, "I broke that boundary. Let me see what other boundaries I can break. What else can I push people to do?"

> **Using preferred pronouns reinforces that cult mentality. It gives them power. They think, "I can make people do what I want. I broke that boundary. Let me see what other boundaries I can break."**

Maria Keffler (16:19):

It is what I've heard called credit card parenting. You give in on something small because it's just too much trouble to deal with in the moment. Maybe that's the child having a temper fit in the grocery store, and you're embarrassed and you just want to get out of there and get home and make dinner. So you give the kid the candy to shut them up.

That's going to come back later. That's never the end of it. It's going to that issue of the child demanding what they want. It is going to come back later with interest, because the next time the child's been emboldened. They know, "I got what I want by throwing a temper fit."

I personally have a tendency sometimes to get a little pouty and passive-aggressive. I know this about myself and I'm trying to overcome that.

I've noticed that when I get angry or upset, I withdraw and kind of get a little passive-aggressive. Then everyone in my family starts trying to make me happy. My husband will be like, "I'll take care of the dishes or whatever." I told him one time, "You guys are reinforcing my bad behavior."

You train people how to respond to you. When I'm passive-aggressive and cold shouldered and pouty, they've learned that it's best to give me what I want.

That's a really bad dynamic. I don't want that. I don't want my kids to learn that. It comes from my own brokenness and places that I'm flawed.

But that's what's happening with these kids. When you give in on something that is not acceptable, you are reinforcing that they have that control over you. It's going to come back later and bite you in the butt.

> **When you give in on something that is not acceptable, you are reinforcing that they have control over you. It's going to come back later and bite you in the butt.**

Erin Brewer (18:15):

Credit card parenting is a really nice analogy. It's okay to use a credit card once in a while. Every once in a while, you're overwhelmed—and we don't want parents to think that they have to be perfect, because you can't be. It's okay to use a credit card once in a while.

But with these big issues, if you capitulate to their demands, it's going to end up coming back with huge amounts of interest.

I also want to clarify age groups here, because I do think that interacting with an adult child is going to be very different than interacting with a young child. What I've been talking about here is with younger children.

If you have an adult child who says, "I'm not going to interact with you at all if you don't use my pronouns and the name," then that becomes a personal decision for that parent.

If I were a parent in that situation, I would probably use the pronouns and name of an adult child, because I feel like it's more important at that stage to keep a connection with that child, to keep interacting with that child, to keep a relationship going with that child, so that I can have some influence over them. Because as an adult, the child can completely disconnect and we see this happening.

I also understand why a parent might say, "No, I will not. I will not capitulate. I will not. I will not allow you to force me to use language I'm not comfortable with," and that's perfectly okay too. It's a very different dynamic than when you're parenting children who are still in the home.

Maria Keffler (19:59):

Parents, you have a right to honor your sense of truth and your sense of reality as well. Very often we, as parents, feel so responsible for our kids and their decisions. We forget that we're people too. I have beliefs. I have things that are important to me.

Parents may choose to use preferred pronouns and adopt the name to keep a relationship with an older child.

Erin Brewer (21:59):

It is important not to undermine your own boundaries to give the child what they want. We need to be okay with saying, "My beliefs are just as important as yours are. I do not believe a child can be born in the wrong body. I raised you. I know that what sex you are. I know that there's something going on with you. There are underlying issues that are causing this, and I'm not going to reinforce it."

We need to feel okay about going into schools and saying, "You are not allowed to use the preferred pronouns that my child is demanding. I want you to uphold reality, not just for my child, but for the other children around them. It's not fair to children for you to lie about pronouns for my child, because you're reinforcing this cult mentality and this ideology, which we know is damaging to children."

> **We need to feel okay about going into schools saying, "You are not allowed to use the preferred pronouns that my child is demanding. I want you to uphold reality, not just for my child, but for the other children around them. It's not fair to children for you to lie about pronouns, because you're reinforcing this cult mentality and this ideology, which we know is damaging to children."**

Remember that pronouns and names lead to medicalization, to lifelong side effects, to profound complications. This is an ideology that leads to self-harming behavior, to mutilating the body, and to huge expense medical expense.

When I was a little girl, women were pushing for the term "Ms." instead of "Mrs." or "Miss." I wondered if this is the same thing. I was wondering,

"Am I just not getting this because I am too stuck in my ways to accept how society's changing?"

Then I thought, "The difference with "Ms." versus pronouns or names is that "Ms." is used as a generic way of addressing a woman that isn't based on whether they are married or not. It also doesn't lead me on a path towards damaging myself, damaging my body, and reinforcing an ideology which is harmful to society.

It's very different. Language evolves all the time and we're constantly changing how we speak, but the way we speak also has huge implications.

That is why holding a strong line on this compelled speech is important. It is compelled speech. One of the things that has always been important to people in the United States is freedom of speech. It is an important protection that we are allowed to say things, even if it offends other people.

But now there are states that are starting to say, "No, you must use the preferred pronouns, or we will fire you." There are schools saying that teachers must use these preferred names and pronouns. Our ability to speak freely is being encroached upon by this ideology.

Once they start taking away our basic fundamental rights that has huge implications.

Maria Keffler (25:51):

If people are skeptical about whether that's really happening in school districts, here in Arlington (Virginia) the guidance on the transgender students policy was published, and at the top of the document it says, "Internal Document Only." It's not even supposed to be shared outside the school, but someone who was concerned shared it with my organization, Arlington Parent Coalition.

It's about three pages of requirements. It's about the preferred pronouns and hiding things from parents if the student doesn't want the parent to know. At the very bottom, it talks about how teachers need to be able to make a "welcoming" learning environment.

It's right there in black and white, it is happening.

Often with these transgender-identified kids, they have another issue. They have co-morbidities: there's autism, there's depression, there's self-harm, there's prior trauma. There's something else going on. The real issues are being ignored.

I have a dear friend. She's now blind. When I met her I was doing my student teaching and she was in her first year of teaching. At that point she still had some vision, but now she's almost completely blind.

She told me her story. She was born sighted. When she was around ten, she started having vision problems and they took her to the doctor and the doctor diagnosed it and told her it's not going to get much worse.

Well, it just kept getting worse and worse and worse. She said she had been misdiagnosed. The doctor thought it was one thing, but it was actually something else. As hard as it was for her to get the right diagnosis, at least then she knew what to expect and could prepare.

All these kids are being told, "All these discomforts are because you're transgender." The autism isn't being dealt with, the depression isn't being dealt with, the trauma isn't being dealt with, the self-harm isn't being dealt with. Not only are they not being dealt with, they're being exacerbated by this self-ID.

When we reinforce it by accepting the preferred pronouns, by utilizing the preferred name, and by agreeing, "Yes, you are absolutely trans-gender," we are doing a huge disservice to these children and young adults.

Erin Brewer (29:01):

When a child is suffering for some reason—depression, anxiety, trauma, even puberty, whatever it is they're uncomfortable—when they're uncomfortable with what's going on, typically as parents and as professionals, and as a society, we try to help a child move through that discomfort so that they can maintain their integrity of self.

We know that puberty is a time when kids go through all kinds of things. They experiment with lots of different ways of being to see what works for them and what doesn't.

If we lock them into something and say, "You're right, you were born in the wrong body. That explains everything," then that whole exploration, which is a normal part of puberty, is cut off. They're forced into this identity which has long-term harmful repercussions.

I can't tell you how devastating it is seeing these girls, young teens—13, 14, 15, 16—who have gotten their breasts and nipples completely removed. If a person went in and said, "I want you to amputate a part of my body, a healthy part of my body for no other reason that I'm uncomfortable with it," they would get psychological intervention.

Not only have they damaged their bodies, but they're not getting the help that they need to resolve those underlying issues. One of the ways you can help them is by maintaining reality.

Maria Keffler (31:45):

We've heard from detransitioners who said that their parents did not accept this and did not reinforce it, but continued to love them and continued to accept them (and that's a hard line to walk as a parent when you're being pulled in both directions). Detransitioners have told us that because their parents didn't affirm, they had a safe place to land when they realized they had made a mistake.

> **Detransitioners have told us that because their parents didn't affirm, they had a safe place to land when they realized they had made a mistake.**

We don't always appreciate how hard it is to say, "I was wrong." Especially teenagers.

Teenagers think they know everything. They think their parents are ridiculous. From about 13 to 20 or 21, teenagers know everything, and their parents don't know anything. Then about 21, 22, the parents get really smart again.

Parents need to provide them that safe landing place so they know when they come back and say, "I was wrong," they are welcomed and not mocked.

Erin Brewer (33:03):

I'm glad you brought that up, because I've been watching some interviews with detransitioners. They say that they're mortified when they realize that the transition was a huge mistake. A lot of times they'll stick with it for a while, just because it's so hard to come out and say, "I made this mistake." They often get rejected and oftentimes they get mocked by their peers and transgender activists.

It's so important for the parents to be there with open arms, welcoming them back.

We often think of our parenting as being over when the kids turn 18, but we're going to have a lot of parenting to do with these kids who are detransitioned, who are adults. If they're on puberty blockers, their development has been retarded. These are kids who are chronologically adults, but haven't been allowed to naturally progress to puberty. They aren't really adults yet. They still need to be parented.

That's something that parents who have kids who have gone through medical transitions are going to need to realize. You're going to need to be there for them as a parent for a little bit longer than typical.

Maria Keffler (34:30):

That's a good point. I just want to reinforce how important it is to love them—love them unconditionally. Love is a choice that we make. It's a decision. It's not a feeling.

Erin Brewer (35:11):

That's your job. That is the number one thing on our job description: unconditional love.

That doesn't mean unconditional acceptance of behaviors that we don't approve. There are lots of situations that I'm hearing of where kids are caught in the middle of two divorced parents and they have to align with one or the other parent.

If that child aligns with the parent who is affirming them, that feels like a huge rejection to the parent who is trying to maintain truth. But it's so important for that parent to continually reflect love. That child's going to need to know that that parent loves them when they desist.

Kids do things all the time that parents aren't happy with. I have to admit that there are things that my adult children did that just made me cringe. But I love them, while at the same time saying, "I'm not accepting this behavior, this is not okay."

That's a really hard line to walk as a parent. I don't think we've really been taught how to do it. We live in a generation where parenting is different than it used to be. We don't have a good schema. We also have the society at large feeling like they can take over parenting.

The high school across the street from me has a big sign on it that says, "Welcome home." Well, it's not their home. It's really inappropriate for school to pretend like that's their home. Kids have a home. "Welcome back," would be perfectly wonderful.

Why is the school acting as a home rather than as a school? Ideally, a school is a place where children go to learn the basics. They come home, and it's at home where they're loved by their family. By saying, "Welcome home," the school is suggesting that where the kids have been all summer isn't home and that they're now coming back to their family. That's a confusing message to give to children.

Some people might say, "They're just trying to be warm and welcoming." But there are messages behind language that we really need to examine.

That is the problem with compelled speech, those messages have a long-term impact and using compelled speech is causing children's bodies to be damaged, sterilized, mutilated, and is causing the breakdown of our families.

Maria Keffler (37:54):

It's also problematic for our culture at large. We're already finding it is so hard to discuss these things, because the language is being obfuscated and lied about in the media.

We read an article about a man who identifies as a woman, and he raped his mother who has dementia. She's 87. This article said, "Woman rapes mother who has dementia." It wasn't a woman. It was a man.

Even those of us who are working in this often struggle in conversations. We're like, "Is he a man who says he's a woman? Or is he a woman who says she's a man?" Everybody's struggling with this.

I thought about this a little while ago. This dear friend of mine, when she was a little girl, had a housekeeper who was Hispanic and didn't speak any English. My friend would teach this woman the wrong words just to be an ornery little snot.

But what kind of trouble did it give that woman as she was trying to get along in an English-speaking society? The same thing is happening now. We're telling everyone, "You call this coffee mug a cell phone or you're going to lose your job."

> **We're telling everyone, "You call this coffee mug a cell phone or you're going to lose your job."**

Erin Brewer (39:45):

This is not about tolerance and diversity and being loving and kind and caring. This is about compelled speech. This is about punishing people who don't believe in your religious beliefs. This is basically codifying a religious belief system and forcing people to follow it.

> ## This is about compelled speech. This is about punishing people who don't believe in your religion. This is basically codifying a religious belief system and forcing people to follow it.

When we capitulate to the demands of using pronouns, we are confusing the children. I can't imagine how confusing it is for a four- or five-year-old who has a nine- or 10-year-old sister who suddenly has to be called "he." That child is going to be confused. That is another reason I recommend parents not to acquiesce to these demands, because if you have younger siblings in the home, it's going to confuse them.

Maria Keffler (41:05):

And it's problematic at school. Many people are telling children, [holding up a coffee mug] "This is a cell phone. If your parents don't call this a cell phone, your parents are hateful, bigoted and transphobic." Kids come home and Dad calls it a coffee mug. Now Dad's hateful and transphobic. It's breaking families apart.

Episode 33: Paying for Gender Treatments

https://youtu.be/OAMIW85Hfzg

Maria Keffler (00:40):

Today we're going to talk about financing transgender treatments. This might seem like a strange topic, but when we get into it, people will understand why we need to address this.

Erin Brewer (00:54):

It's interesting because a lot of the explosion of transing treatments got started with Obamacare, because Obamacare mandated that these were treatments that needed to be covered. That was the first inroad for these companies. If you were on Obamacare, these interventions had to be covered. Since then other insurance companies have started covering them.

We're going to specifically talk today about kids who are trying to get these interventions, potentially without their parents' consent or knowledge, and without insurance coverage. There are lots of concerning things that are happening because these kids are so convinced these are the only treatments that are going to help them feel better.

Maria Keffler (01:57):

This is what the gender industry is telling kids. They're making promises: "As soon as you start on puberty blockers, you're going to feel better because you're not going to go through the wrong puberty." Or, "As soon as you start on cross sex hormones, that's going to fix your gender dysphoria. You're going to feel a lot better."

Then they find out that they still don't feel better.

They are told, "Well you need to have top surgery. Once you get rid of your breasts, then you're going to feel better." Well, that didn't help. "Well then, you need to have bottom surgery," which is, for a girl, having a phalloplasty—a fake penis attached— and for a boy it may be an orchiectomy—having his testicles removed, having his penis removed.

They just keep promising, "Once you have these interventions, you're going to feel better."

They are not addressing, "Why are you not feeling good? Why are you feeling uncomfortable with your body?"

That's a verboten question now. In so many states, it's illegal for therapists to even ask, "Why are you feeling this way?" Affirmative care is the only option that's offered. If that's the only thing that can possibly make you feel better, you are going to pursue it.

> **In so many states, it's illegal for therapists to even ask, "Why are you feeling this way?" Affirmative care is the only option that's offered.**

Erin Brewer (03:22):

A lot of these interventions are expensive. It's not something that a kid can generally pay for with a part-time job. There are insurance companies now that are closing records so that parents don't have knowledge of what treatments their children are getting. That is one way the gender industry has made these treatments available to kids.

The other thing is that some of the clinics are on a sliding-fee scale. This is a smart business model because once they get a kid hooked on hormones, that child is medicalized for life. They're guaranteed to have a return customer.

Maria Keffler (04:03):

Explain why that is.

Erin Brewer (04:12):

Either the child continues along this path and they need to access these transgendering medical interventions, or they desist. If they've been on puberty blockers and cross-sex hormones and have these surgeries, then their bodies are no longer capable of producing the hormones that their body needs. The human body needs a sex hormone. When they desist, if their body isn't able to make the testosterone or estrogen that their body is supposed to have, then they're going to get sick. It's important that they access the appropriate hormones.

I have a friend who detransitioned. He went through all the surgeries. He no longer has gonads. He has to take testosterone for the rest of his life. There are girls who've been on puberty blockers, and cross-sex hormones. Their bodies no longer produce estrogen normally and naturally, so they have to get an artificial hormone for the rest of their lives. These companies—once they draw these customers in, they know that they're going to have customers for the rest of their life, which is really horrifying.

A lot of times parents are saying they are not willing to pay for their child to access puberty blockers, cross-sex hormones and surgeries. These parents know how damaging these interventions are.

Kids are really resourceful. There are things like GoFundMe that are being set up. Kids are setting up GoFundMe pages so that they can get their hormones and surgeries paid for. Kids are getting engaged in pornography and prostitution to pay for these interventions. Some kids are running away. They're going to states like California, where minor surgeries and hormones are covered by the state insurance.

> **Kids are setting up GoFundMe pages, engaging in pornography and prostitution, or running away to states like California, where minor surgeries and hormones are covered by the state insurance.**

Those are three of the main ways that kids are getting access.

The other thing that's happening is kids are going online and accessing them illegally. That's scary because anytime you're engaged in an illegal activity, you don't know what you're getting. Even though these kids believe they're buying estrogen or testosterone, it's hard to know for sure what they're actually getting.

If a kid gets sucked into this, the other thing that we have heard from parents is that children are encouraged to run away and go to what's called a "glitter family," which is a family that affirms these interventions.

Sometimes that child ends up with a sex trafficker. They run away from home and then they end up being sex trafficked. The incessant message that the only solution for children is to start medicalizing is what's encouraging these dangerous behaviors like pornography, prostitution, and running away.

Maria Keffler (07:39):

You mentioned the bad outcomes with running away, and we know statistically kids who run away generally don't end up in good situations. They're not running away most of the time into a better situation.

I was at a school board meeting here in my district, and there's a teacher in a neighboring district who is a trans rights activist. I was speaking with him during a break. He said, "I shouldn't tell you this because we're not supposed to do this. But if I find out that a child doesn't feel safe at home, if I hear that a child doesn't feel safe, I'll help that child find a different place to live and find money to live on."

I thought, "You're making runaways. You're helping kids become runaways." And he's a teacher in a public school.

> **"You're making runaways. You're helping kids become run-aways." He's a public school teacher.**

Erin Brewer (08:32):

It's scary. It's setting them on a path that is dangerous and it's really hard to recover from.

We know that kids are really good at finding loopholes and there are people out there who pay kids to make pornography. There are people out there who will pay children to perform sex acts. If a child feels like her only option is to medicalize, then she might get involved in these activities that are going to have lifelong consequences.

It infuriates me that we have the gender industry giving the message to children that they need to pursue these interventions.

The other thing is the GoFundMe. It's outrageous, the number of GoFundMe sites there are to support girls cutting off their breasts, or boy's cutting off their testicles, or boys getting facial feminization surgery or breasts. They're getting funded.

If I were to create a GoFundMe so that I could get a facelift, I don't think that I would be celebrated as being authentic and brave. But for some reason, these kids are. The comments on these GoFundMe sites talk about how brave and courageous those pursing these cosmetic changes are, and how they're going to be their authentic self. It's encouraging this really dysfunctional thought.

It makes me angry that these sites like GoFundMe allow this. They're allowing children to engage in self-harm. They're funding self-harming behaviors. If I had a GoFundMe site saying, "I need more razors, because the razors I've been using to cut myself are dull, and I don't have enough money for new razors. And I want to make deeper and better cuts," GoFundMe would take that down. But for some reason GoFundMe and other fundraising sites are okay with this self-harming behavior.

Maria Keffler (10:52):

I've seen so many parents talking about finding out that their child had a

GoFundMe. One in particular that I remember was heartbreaking. This mother said, "I found out that my sister contributed to my daughter's GoFundMe. And she's known my child her whole life. My daughter had rapid onset gender dysphoria. This is out of the blue and my sister contributed money to help her niece cut her breasts off."

How devastating that is, and how betrayed parents must feel.

Erin Brewer (11:33):

We have a clip here from a doctor who did some research on the number of GoFundMe sites that were set up for breast removal surgery in 2021.

> Dr. Kevin Stewart (11:39):
>
> You should be concerned about the profit motive clouding people's judgment. To begin to get a handle on the economics of what we're talking about, our organization tracked GoFundMe requests for the last four months, for what's colloquially known as "top surgery." As of last week, we found 40,013 campaigns over that four-month period.
>
> If we conservatively estimate the cost of that surgery at $10,000—and that's a conservative estimate—then these patients will need $400 million to get these surgeries. And that's only a small part, right? That's one of the surgeries. That's a small part of the whole picture.

> **If we conservatively estimate the cost of top surgery at $10,000, then these patients will need $400 million to get these surgeries. That's one of the surgeries. That's a small part of the whole picture.**

Maria Keffler (12:25):

That is devastating. When I was researching for my book, *Desist, Detrans & Detox: Getting Your Child Out of the Gender Cult*, I looked up the GoFundMe sites for top surgery. There were about 35,000 at that time. Now they're up over 41,000. In about five or six months we've come up another 15%, 20% more fundraisers.

Erin Brewer (13:06):

It is definitely a growth industry. The thing that makes me sad about these GoFundMe sites is that these people are going to go get these surgeries and they're think they're going to feel better. We have good research showing it is not true, that the suicidality goes up after these kinds of surgeries. After about 10 years the rate of suicide is very high for those who have undergone these surgeries.

It makes sense. The messages these kids are getting is that they are inherently flawed, and the only way to resolve that is to become somebody else. You're telling that person that who they are is not okay. They go and they try to become someone else and surgery is the last option. Once they've had surgery, there really aren't any other procedures that they can go through.

Then it hits them that they've done all these things. They've damaged their bodies. They've hurt themselves, and they don't feel any better. They still have the same problems—and a lot of times the problems are compounded by all these interventions—and they feel completely betrayed. As they should, but they also feel completely helpless. Everything that they did was supposed to help them feel better and it didn't work.

> **They've damaged their bodies. They've hurt themselves, and they don't feel any better. They still have the same problems—compounded by all these interventions—and they feel completely betrayed.**

The message that they got—they believe either they're so damaged even transitioning didn't help, or they realize that they've been lied to. Either way they feel at their wit's end. Oftentimes that's when they become suicidal.

The other thing we don't talk about is the side effects and the complications when the surgery doesn't go right, which happens a lot.

Scott Newgent, who is a woman who went through a phalloplasty, has talked about all of the complications that she has as a result of the phalloplasty. She went bankrupt because she wasn't able to work. She lost her job. She lost her car. She lost her home. She lost pretty much everything as a result of getting this phalloplasty. Nobody warned her ahead of time that she could be medicalized for life and that she would have a lifetime of complications.

Maria Keffler (15:30):

The same thing happened with Jazz Jennings. Jazz Jennings is portrayed as glitzy and wonderful—that it is great being transitioned from being a boy to being a girl. The story of what he went through isn't fully told. He essentially split in half after his surgery, because they cut off his penis and his testicles and created a hole. By his own words, he pretty much broke in half after that surgery and has needed multiple follow-ups and is in no way in the clear.

Erin Brewer (16:08):

Now he's looking morbidly obese. Clearly something is wrong.

When you give somebody a message that if they do these things then they're going to be happy, when they're not it is a huge betrayal. And there's a huge financial cost: hormones and covering the cost of complications.

I've seen video after video of both males and females who have had surgery on their genitals and have recurring urinary tract infections and they develop fistulas—which is a hole between the rectum and the fake vagina. They have to wear bags to collect their stool because they're not able to use their rectum anymore.

These are just horrifying, completely unnecessary consequences of cosmetic surgeries.

> **These are horrifying, completely unnecessary consequences of cosmetic surgeries.**

Maria Keffler (17:09):

That were perpetrated on perfectly healthy bodies. I want to emphasize.

My great-grandfather had a colostomy bag. I remember my mom and my grandmother helping him change it. I believe he had colorectal cancer.

Teenagers and people in their twenties are consigned to life with a colostomy bag for absolutely no reason, except that it makes the gender industry money.

Erin Brewer (17:43):

That is the bottom line. It is all about making money for the gender industry. This isn't about helping kids feel better about themselves. This is a multi-billion-dollar industry at this point. These children are feeling desperate and the gender industry is trying to figure out ways to make money just to damage their otherwise healthy bodies.

When I was a kid, I was pretty creative. I came from a family that didn't have a lot of money. I was able to find creative ways to get money. Oftentimes they weren't particularly legal. If I had been convinced that I had to get these interventions, I have no doubt that I would have pursued whatever means I needed.

Maria Keffler (18:37):

These kids aren't just having it suggested to them—they are having it *sold* to them.

A friend of mine just went to his son's middle school here in Arlington, and my friend took pictures. All over the walls there are all kinds of sex and gender messages.

Another friend said on the first day of school, the teachers were hounding her son about his pronouns. "What do you want to be called? What are your pronouns? What do you want to be called?"

Then kids on social media are being swamped with it. There are surgeons actively making posts on social media to groom and draw kids in for surgery. Kids are being actively preyed upon.

Erin Brewer (19:26):

And some insurance companies will pay for these interventions for adults, but oftentimes they'll pay for the puberty blockers and cross-sex hormones and some of the surgeries.

Yet if a child or an adult at some point realizes that they've made a mistake and wants to desist and remediate some of the damage that's been done to their body, the insurance company doesn't pay for that.

I've heard gender doctors mock detransitioners, saying it's silly for being upset about how they look. But that's exactly what caused them to pursue these interventions in the first place—how they looked. A group of doctors will push a child to pursue interventions when they're heading in the gender dysphoric direction. But then as soon as the child desists, they're considered silly or overly dramatic for being concerned about how they look.

It really does show that this is a disingenuous movement. These doctors have to know that they're encouraging children into this dangerous ideology.

<u>Maria Keffler (20:54):</u>

If they really cared about children, and if they really want children to be comfortable in their bodies, they would be even more concerned about the detransitioners, because they would want to know, "What happened? How do we fix this? How do we learn from this?"

They don't want to learn. They don't want to hear anything that contradicts their ideology, because their ideology is profitable and it's completely unconscionable.

> **The doctors don't want to learn or hear anything that contradicts their ideology, because their ideology is profitable and completely unconscionable.**

I'll be very honest. I would dearly love to see Nuremberg-type trials for these doctors and therapists. I want to see every educator who ever told a child that he or she could be born in the wrong body never be allowed to work with children again. This is active predation on children for profit.

<u>Erin Brewer (21:49):</u>

I can't imagine how hard it is for parents to have a child who's angry at them and belligerent and insistent that they don't love the child because they're not affirming. Then those parents find out that their child is engaging in pornography or prostitution or drug dealing in order to get the money to get the interventions.

Any ideology that encourages children into those avenues is reprehensible. Children should never be sexualized like that. To have a parent find a GoFundMe site must be devastating. And how would you feel as a parent to find out that your child's been engaged in prostitution or pornography simply to get interventions that are going to damage them?

If you are a parent, this is a lot of doom and gloom. But we want you to be aware that your child could be pursuing these avenues to get money.

I've talked to Alix Aharon who's had parents reach out to her and ask her if she will do a deep dive into porn sites and see if Alix can find out if their kids are involved in making pornography. Alix has found children who are involved in pornography. There are a lot of people out there who are willing to take advantage of children.

Then we have Starbucks. I'm asking you to stop going to Starbucks. Just stop, because they are actively pushing this. They're known as the company to go work for if you want to have these body modifications made. They cover facial feminization, they cover laser hair removal, they cover breast augmentation, breast amputation.

If a woman goes wants to have her breasts enlarged—maybe she identifies as a big-breasted woman—they won't cover that. Or if a woman has a lot of facial hair that she's self-conscious about, they won't cover to have it removed. But if she were to identify as the opposite sex, then, apparently, they will cover it.

Starbucks is one of those companies that is complicit in this. I've been on threads where people are encouraging kids to go get jobs at Starbucks because they know that Starbucks will cover these interventions.

Maria Keffler (24:41):

We know of somebody who has taken great advantage of Starbucks and brags about it.

Erin Brewer (24:47):

He talks about Starbucks as his "sugar daddy." One thing you can do as a parent is stop getting Starbucks coffee. Just stop going there. Let them know that you are not going to go to give them your business because of what they're doing.

> **Stop getting Starbucks coffee. Just stop going there. Let them know that you are not going to go to give them your business because of what they're doing.**

At some point we have to stand up and say, "No more." We have to let companies know that if they're going to encourage these kinds of self-harming behaviors and encouraging self-hatred among their employees, we won't support them.

Maria Keffler (25:26):

I'm going to read something that was written by a parent whose daughter medicalized, against the parents' wishes. I know a little bit about this story. The daughter had some mental health struggles. I believe the daughter was in counseling for those. As soon as the daughter indicated that she had a transgender identity, everything else was irrelevant to doctors and counselors.

This child was medicalized against her mother's wishes. This is what her mother wrote about that. I have a hard time reading this. I've never read this without crying. I'm going to do my best.

Your beloved child has been kidnapped by a sadistic cult.

The cult brainwashes her to believe you are the enemy.

The brainwashing erases her entire childhood.

Every good memory is replaced with memories of abuse that never happened.

The cult convinces her to inject poison in her body and to get her healthy body parts amputated.

You panic. You scream. You sob. You beg. You are reduced to nothing.

You search for help everywhere. Nobody will help. Nobody will stop the cult. In fact, the government investigates YOU and tells you to approve of what the cult is doing to your daughter.

The world has gone mad.

You find out the cult is kidnapping thousands of other young girls and boys.

And the government is funding the cult.

You grieve with other parents going through the exact same thing.

Society celebrates the cult and ridicules parents who fight back. Some parents are willingly handing their children over to the cult and cheering their child's destruction.

The child you love with everything in you, the child you would die for, is now unrecognizable, replaced by someone who holds you in contempt. She is now part of the cult.

You sob day after day, night after night, wondering how many tears one human can cry.

You scream when you see her severed breasts and collapse, sobbing, "My God, my God, what have they done to my baby?"

You nearly drink yourself to death when you find out the cult cut out her entire reproductive system. "No No No No No NO

NOOOOOOOOOO! They took my baby's womb, they took her eggs. She doesn't know any better. She's still a little girl."

You reach out to every government agency you can think of and every organization fighting the cult.

You think there is nothing more the cult can do to her.

You are wrong.

You fly to go see her, twice within 6 weeks, to beg and plead with her to not let the cult do this next terrible thing. You beg the cult to stop torturing your daughter. You beg authorities to help you.

Nobody will help your daughter.

You cannot stop it, so you beg, "Please don't hurt my daughter. Here, take my arm instead. All of it if you need to. I don't need it. Just take it."

Your attempts are futile. You cannot stop the torture.

So you sit alone in a motel room, sobbing until you choke on your own tears, praying with everything in you, hugging a pillow, rocking back and forth, pretending it is your baby, while you softly sob a song, "You are my sunshine. My only sunshine..."

For a while, your mind is gone.

You call another mother who has a daughter whose breasts have been cut off by the cult.

You sob together.

Then you wait in a room, knowing that nearby, the sadistic cult is skinning and mutilating your baby. Sure, she's legally an adult now but the stuffed animal you bought her yesterday that she picked out says otherwise.

Rage builds with each passing second and you contemplate what life in prison would be like. You now see very clearly what kind of things you are capable of. Fire boils through your veins, with bloody carnage dancing violently in your head. But she needs you now more than ever, so you can't....

This is just one mother, one child. There are thousands of more cult casualties. Daughters, sons, mothers, fathers, sisters, brothers, aunts, uncles, grandparents, nieces, nephews, cousins – all casualties of the sadistic cult. Oh, and let's not forget wives with suddenly stunning and brave husbands, all of the lesbians under attack, and the erasure of women's rights.

My beloved child was kidnapped by a sadistic cult. Will yours be next?

That was written by a mother whose pen name is Alexis Arizo.

Erin Brewer (30:12):

For people who don't know what she was talking about, as far as her daughter being peeled—the skin and flesh of her daughter's forearm was stripped off for phalloplasty. They deglove the arm. They cut around the elbow and wrist and they take the flesh to create a fake and useless penis. Oftentimes there are debilitating side effects and complications. People die from these operations.

> **The skin and flesh of her daughter's forearm was stripped off for phalloplasty. They deglove the arm. They cut around the elbow and wrist and they take the flesh to create a fake and useless penis.**

I can't even imagine being a mother sitting outside the hospital room, knowing that this is going on and wondering, "How can this be legal? How can this be legal?"

Maria Keffler (30:57):

I have two daughters and I cannot imagine going through that.

Erin Brewer (31:04):

And then to find out people contributed to her GoFundMe so she could do that, or that she was engaging in prostitution or pornography to pay for it.

For those who are saying that these kids are real and authentic, we have to push back and say, "These kids are victims. They've been groomed. This is an industry that will go to any lengths to make money off of your children."

Maria Keffler (31:41):

An industry that will cut the penis off of a boy and cut out the uterus out of a girl, is an industry that is morally bankrupt and we need to stop it.

> **An industry that will cut the penis off of a boy and cut out the uterus out of a girl, is an industry that is morally bankrupt and we need to stop it.**

Erin Brewer (31:59):

We shouldn't do this to children. We shouldn't even do this to adults. There's no explanation other than this is being driven by money. It shows the lengths people will go to make money off innocent children. These children are victims and parents who are the victims as well.

Any mother or father who's gone through this—you're the victim and it's not your fault. We just need to keep fighting back and hopefully protect other children.

Maria Keffler (32:33):

If any kids or young adults or anyone who's a detransitioner, who went down this path, and you realize that that this was a mistake—it's not your fault. It's not your fault. You were lied to, you were misled. You were actively deceived. Don't take this burden on yourself. You were led into this for profit.

Erin Brewer (33:23):

There are some who say, "Well, if they're going to engage in these very dangerous activities in order to pay for these interventions, maybe the parents should affirm them." How would you respond to that?

Maria Keffler (33:38):

That sounds like, "Would you rather die by hanging or die by guillotine?"

It's not healthy. The parents may affirm it. The parents may pay for it. The child's still going to end up in the same place.

I can't see making a choice to affirm something that is so harmful. The harm that's coming from doing the GoFundMe, the pornography or prostitution—that needs to be dealt with not by saying, "Well, okay, I'm going to affirm you," but by saying, "I'm going to try to stop you from going down this road altogether."

Parents need to consider whether school is a safe place for their child.

Figure out what to do to head all this off at the pass. Now, if you've got a 25-year-old who's heading down this path and doing prostitution or

GoFundMe, you don't have a lot of power in that situation. I don't have any experience parenting adult children that I can speak to that.

But from a practical, commonsense point-of-view, agreeing with something bad, just to prevent something else bad, is still going to end badly.

> **Agreeing with something bad, just to prevent something else bad, is still going to end badly.**

Erin Brewer (35:22):

You're going to have a damaged child who is not going to not trust you if they desist, because you affirmed the concept that she was flawed and that she needed to do these interventions in order be able to live with herself.

Maria Keffler (35:40):

Detransitioners will often say, "As hard as I was on my parents, as much as I was angry and militant with them, my parents holding the line and saying, 'No, this is not okay. I don't agree with this,' allowed me to have a safe landing place."

Erin Brewer (36:06):

You are going to be your child's best advocate. Worst-case scenario: your child does go down this route and is prostituting, is making pornography, is selling drugs to get the surgeries. You need to be there for her. You need to be the one who says, "I love you and you are okay, and you don't have to change who you are, and I'm here for you," because she is going to need you once she realizes that she was betrayed and that all these interventions didn't solve her core problems.

Maria Keffler (36:42):

Well, this has been another heavy subject. We don't want to leave anyone feeling despairing or feeling hopeless. Eventually truth is going to come to light. We're going to see the day where this is not happening anymore. Until then, we've just got to keep trying to protect our kids, and try to spread the truth as much as we can and, and shed light on the dark places that the gender industry is trying to cover up.

Episode 33 Resource List

Dr. Kevin B. Stewart Testimony:
https://www.youtube.com/watch?v=zhRW02Sn3Nw

Episode 34: Role-Playing the Coming-Out Speech

https://youtu.be/q2oHOLRzZNE

https://youtu.be/q2oHOLRzZNE

Erin Brewer (00:00:38):

Today we're going to do something different today.

Maria Keffler (00:00:42):

Yes, we are. Do you want to tell people what we're doing?

Erin Brewer (00:00:45):

We got a lot of feedback on the one video that we did where we did role playing. We decided that we would take a number of hot-button issues and roleplay them out, so that our viewers can see the dynamic that might occur.

Sometimes we give advice, but oftentimes if you have a model of something, it's a little bit easier to understand what we're talking about. So we're just going to jump into this and see how that works. Hopefully we will give some insights on how these conversations might take place.

Maria Keffler (00:01:21):

These are not scripted. We didn't write out scripts for these. We've got a few topics and situations, and the way that we role play them is probably not exactly the way it's going to go for you. With some of these there could be a number of different ways it goes.

So I don't really know how this is going to go. We're just going to try it and see how it works.

Erin Brewer (00:01:46):

Yeah. This is an experiment. Hopefully it's useful.

The first topic is the coming-out speech. Maria is going to be the mom and I'm going to be the newly trans-identified child.

Maria Keffler (00:02:01):

Hey, here we go: The Coming-Out Speech.

Erin Brewer (00:02:05):

Hey, birthing parent. There's something I need to tell you. I know you're probably not going to like it, but this is really important to me. And if you don't like it, I'm just going to find another birthing parent to take care of me.

I realize that I'm not a girl, I'm a boy. You really just need to start calling me he/him pronouns and my name's Ash. That's me now. You probably even know, if you know anything about me, you already know that I'm really a boy. It's pretty obvious to all my friends. My teachers have totally accepted it. They just said that I should tell you about it. So, I've been using the boys' bathroom and locker room at school and now it's time for you to accept me as your son.

Maria Keffler (00:02:57):

Wow, honey. Okay. Um, this is a lot for me. I wasn't prepared to hear this and I'm pretty confused. What I'm hearing is that you don't believe you're a girl, you believe you're really a boy.

Erin Brewer (00:03:16):

I am a boy.

Maria Keffler (00:03:19):

Okay. And you want us to consider you a boy, and you are behaving and you're living as a boy at school and other places.

Erin Brewer (00:03:36):

Yeah. Because they know I'm a boy, and you're the last people really who don't know. And it's important for you to know.

Maria Keffler (00:03:44):

Okay. I'm really confused about this because when you were born it was really clear that you were a girl because you have—

Erin Brewer (00:03:56):

Girl was assigned to me. The doctors assigned me based on my genitals. But my genitals don't define me as a boy or a girl. It's all about how I feel. And I know I'm a boy.

Maria Keffler (00:04:10):

Okay. I just want to understand this. This may take me some time to understand this, so I hope you can be patient with me while I try to understand what's going on.

How do you know what it feels like to be a boy?

Erin Brewer (00:04:28):

Well, I just am one. It's not really about even feelings. I just know I am.

Maria Keffler (00:04:35):

Okay. I want to understand what makes you know that, because in my experience and my understanding of sex, our sex is based on our chromosomes and is expressed in our genitals.

Erin Brewer (00:04:50):

That's just such antiquated science. Science has gone so much further than that since you learned it. And that's why it's probably hard for you to understand.

Maria Keffler (00:04:59):

That that might be. What science are you talking about that supports an idea that you can have a different sex inside than outside?

Erin Brewer (00:05:09):

Well, they've just shown that gender is really what defines us. Sex is just our genitals. You know, a lot of people get confused by this. So I'm not surprised—especially because you went to school so long ago—that you don't really have understand how science has changed.

Maria Keffler (00:05:28):

Well, can you help me with the science? What science are you referring to? Do you have research studies? Is there something in a textbook somewhere that I can read?

> **"Can you help me with the science?**
> **What science are you referring to? Do you have**
> **research studies? Is there something in a textbook**
> **somewhere that I can read?"**

Erin Brewer (00:05:38):

I don't even think it's in textbooks yet. It should be though. I think it will be soon.

It's really all abou the doctors—they look at you and they assign you based on your genitals. That's all they look at, and genitals definitely don't define me because it's possible to have to be a boy and have a vagina or to be a girl and have a penis. And again, that's why I didn't really want to talk to you because I knew you'd be not familiar with all the new research that's come out.

Maria Keffler (00:06:10):

Okay. But I am still really interested in seeing some of that research, because I would like to educate myself on this. So if you have some of that research, which it seems like you've read because you're very convinced that this is the correct path for you to take—can you share some of that with me?

Erin Brewer (00:06:29):

Yeah. I can share, for sure. There's websites, like the HRC and Planned Parenthood. And I have so much information about this. It's really cool. They're right on the cutting edge of this. And I'm so thankful that they're putting it out there. So I'll share those links with you.

Maria Keffler (00:06:46):

Yeah. I'd be really interested to see those. HRC is the Human Rights Campaign. I believe that's the funding and activism arm of the gay and homosexual lobby. Am I understanding that correctly?

Erin Brewer (00:07:00):

I'm not just like homosexuals because I'm not homosexual. So it's like the whole LGBTQAI++, not just the gay and lesbians.

Maria Keffler (00:07:12):

Okay. Okay. I misunderstood that, but am I right that their purpose is lobbying for funding and political activism?

Erin Brewer (00:07:22):

Saving lives of people like me is really what's happening and they are out there fighting for us.

Maria Keffler (00:07:30):

Hmm. How are they saving lives?

"How is the HRC saving lives?"

Erin Brewer (00:07:32):

Well, because a lot of times if teachers and parents and stuff—if they don't really accept someone, then that person might just go and kill themselves.

Maria Keffler (00:07:43):

Are there statistics about that?

Erin Brewer (00:07:46):

It's amazing how many of these poor transgender people like me kill themselves. It's just, it's so hard. And that's why I hope you can accept it because if not, I'm going to just have to find other parents.

Maria Keffler (00:08:01):

I understand that you're really struggling. I can see that you're really having a hard time with this and I'm sorry. I don't want you to be in pain and struggling. But I really want to understand the basis for this decision.

I want to go back to this suicide statistic again. Where is that coming from?

Erin Brewer (00:08:24):

It's like 40% of us end up attempting suicide. Because it's so hard being transgender in a world that is so transphobic.

Maria Keffler (00:08:34):

Where are you getting that statistic? Honey? I want to see where—

Erin Brewer (00:08:37):

It's a study. I can send you this study. It's by this group. I can't remember the name but they showed how,— there's so much discrimination. People like me can't get healthcare. We can't get education. And it's all because of transphobic people and I sure hope you're not transphobic.

Maria Keffler (00:08:55):

Hmm. That's interesting. Wow. So are kids being kicked out of school for being transgender?

Erin Brewer (00:09:02):

Well, it's just really hard to be in school. If your teachers are mis-gendering you and using your wrong name and making you go in to the wrong bathroom—that is so hard. It's just so hard. I can can't even believe how hard it is. All those years I had to use the girls' bathroom. And now that I'm finally able to use the boys' bathroom I just am so happy.

Maria Keffler (00:09:26):

Can I go back just a little bit? Again, this is just so out of left field for me.

I didn't see this coming at all. When did you start feeling this way?

Erin Brewer (00:09:37):

I have felt this way all my life, but I was so scared to tell anybody about it. I knew from the time that I was little and I liked playing with those Tonka trucks. You remember? I loved those Tonka trucks. They were so much fun, but I knew if I told people that I was a boy they would think I am crazy. So I just never told anybody.

Maria Keffler (00:09:58):

Yeah. Well, even as recently as just six months ago—I think it was back at Christmas— you asked for makeup and you were trying to get me to let you wear high heels, and you were trying to get me to let you wear that miniskirt. Do you remember that? And I was like, "No, you're not wearing that."

Erin Brewer (00:10:16):

I know I was trying so hard to be a girl. I was just thinking maybe if I just pretend to be a girl well enough that maybe it would help me feel like a girl. But the other thing you know, is that some men wear makeup and some men wear high heels. And so to suggest that because I wanted to wear makeup and high heels means that I'm a girl is kind of transphobic.

Maria Keffler (00:10:43):

Well, it's interesting because that really is a stereotype, isn't it? It's a stereotype that boys like to play with Tonka trucks. And it's really a stereotype that girls like to wear makeup and dresses.

> **"That really is a stereotype, isn't it? It's a stereotype that boys like to play with Tonka tracks and that girls like to wear makeup and dresses."**

Erin Brewer (00:10:55):

I know it's so hard. I have some friends, you know, and they were assigned female or male at birth and they're actually girls and it's so hard because they just want to wear some makeup. They just want to wear cute dresses. I actually shared some of my makeup with some of my friends because their parents wouldn't buy it for them. And they're just so much happier now that they're able to be themselves. And it's just so sad that society is so mean that if they want to, you know, be their true selves as girls, that they get discriminated against.

Maria Keffler (00:11:34):

Well, is it possible for those boys—you said "assigned male at birth"—is it possible for them to wear makeup and still be a boy?

Erin Brewer (00:11:46):

Well, it's okay for boys to wear makeup, but they want to wear makeup because they're girls.

Maria Keffler (00:11:53):

Okay. Can you help me out? I'm really trying to understand this. Can you give me an explanation of being transgender that doesn't have anything to do with those ridiculous stereotypes? Like "boys play with trucks" and "girls wear dresses."

Erin Brewer (00:12:11):

Oh yeah. Totally. So being transgender is when you've been assigned one sex and you know that you're the opposite sex. It's so simple.

Maria Keffler (00:12:21):

Okay. But how do you know that you're the opposite sex? And hang on just a minute for your answer, because I'm thinking about my own experience. I've never lived life from anybody else's perspective, but my own. I've only lived it as Maria. I've never lived it as Erin, even. I don't know what it's like to live life from your experience, Erin.

Erin Brewer (00:12:43):

Ash. Can you please not misgender me?

Maria Keffler (00:12:45):

Okay. I've never lived it as you. I've never lived it as your dad. I've never experienced life from any perspective but my own. So how would I know what it feels like to be you? Or how would I know what it feels like to be a man? Like your dad? How can you know what it feels like to be somebody other than you?

Erin Brewer (00:13:11):

Well, you don't have to because you obviously are happy being a woman. And so it's not a big deal because that means you're cisgender. It's just that you're comfortable being a woman. So you are a woman, right? So you don't have any question. If you were questioning it, then you would understand. But because you've never questioned whether or not you're a woman then than you're a woman. So for me, the whole time, I was feeling "Well, am I really a girl? I just don't feel like a girl." And it's those, those feelings of just knowing inside that there's something wrong and that I'm in the wrong body.

Maria Keffler (00:13:52):

Well, okay. What does it mean to feel like a girl though?

> **"How would I know what it feels like to be you? How would I know what it feels like to be a man? How can you know it's like to be somebody else?"**

Erin Brewer (00:13:57):

Well, clearly you're comfortable, right? You're cisgender. You're so comfortable just being you. You don't feel like you need to be something else. And so that's the difference. It's all about these feelings of just distress and just "I am so uncomfortable in this body."

I'm hoping you and dad will be okay with this, but I really want to start on some testosterone soon, because I will feel so much better if I can just stop being—you know, start looking more like myself. My feelings are going to be so much more comfortable if I start looking more like a boy.

Maria Keffler (00:14:39):

Well, there's two things I want to talk about there. The medicalization issue is something your dad and I are going to have to talk about.

Erin Brewer (00:14:47):

I'm going to do it. If you don't support me, I'm going to find a way to do it. So you might as well just go with it because I'll figure out a way to get it.

Maria Keffler (00:14:56):

Huh? Well that makes me sad that you are willing to go do something your dad and I are not comfortable with, because your dad and I love you very much. Do you know that? We love you.

Erin Brewer (00:15:07):

Well, you know, it's hard when you are sounding really transphobic here. I think if you really loved me, then you wouldn't be so transphobic.

> **"That makes me really sad that you are willing to go do something your dad and I are not comfortable with, because your dad and I love you very much. Do you know that? We love you."**

Maria Keffler (00:15:19):

What do you mean by transphobic? How do you think I'm behaving as a transphobic person?

Erin Brewer (00:15:23):

Well, you're kind of questioning this like, "Well, I have to talk to Dad" to see if it's okay for me to be my authentic self. It's not up to you and Dad if I'm my authentic self.

Maria Keffler (00:15:38):

Well, what if your sister came to me and said, "I've decided that I'm not going to eat anymore. I'm too fat and I'm going to stop eating. I'm going to eat, you know, once a week. One meal and that's it. And I expect you to support me on that." What, what do you think about that?

Erin Brewer (00:16:02):

I don't know that she would ever do that.

Maria Keffler (00:16:05):

If she did—because there are people who suffer eating disorders, there are people who look in the mirror and see themselves as fat, even though they're not. And your sister's quite thin. Yeah, so what if she came to me and she said, "Mom, I'm really a fat person and I need to lose this weight."

Erin Brewer (00:16:24):

I'd be worried about her. But it's so different because she's not fat, but I am a boy. That's the difference—you know she's clearly not fat. She's skinny. But I know that I'm a boy.

Maria Keffler (00:16:38):

Well, when I look at you, I see a girl.

Erin Brewer (00:16:41):

Well, that's just, because I haven't started T yet. Once I start T, then you'll be like, "Oh right. There's my son." I hope that you'll be that accepting of me.

It's almost I kind of think of it as like marble, and I've been chiseled away to look more female. But the testosterone is going to reveal the true me—that authentic self that I know that I am. And then you'll be able to look at me and you'll know I'm a boy.

Maria Keffler (00:17:15):

Hmm. What do you know about testosterone? What all does it do to you?

Erin Brewer (00:17:19):

Well, it's going to lower my voice and I'm going to be to grow a beard and mustache, which I'm super excited about. And I'm going to get more muscular. So I'm going to be super buff and it's going to be really cool.

Maria Keffler (00:17:33):

Does it have any negative side effects?

> ## "What do you know about testosterone? Does it have any negative side effects?"

Erin Brewer (00:17:35):

Well, I don't think so. Are there any negative side effects of being a man? I mean sometimes there are things that are hard about being a man, but that's not really a negative side effect. It's just really being me. So I'll have the same maybe problems that men have. That's appropriate because I am one.

Maria Keffler (00:17:56):

Well, when I think about medications, I don't know of any medications, even just aspirin or ibuprofen—that don't have some sort of negative side effects. And I'm not talking about negative effects of being a man. I'm talking about negative effects from medicine. So when you buy aspirin, it comes with a whole insert of contraindications and side effects, and there's all these things that can happen. And you can only take this much.

Erin Brewer (00:18:26):

Right. But see, in this case, my body really should have been producing the testosterone. So it's not like a medicine. It's more like making my body the way it was supposed to be. So it's like if somebody hadn't been taking vitamins for a long time and they were like really malnourished because they hadn't had the right vitamins, and then they started taking the vitamins. That's what their needed. It's not like there's going to be side effects because really my body should have been producing testosterone. It's just that for, for some reason it didn't.

Maria Keffler (00:19:00):

Well, your body hasn't been producing testosterone because it's been producing estrogen. Right?

Erin Brewer (00:19:06):

I know. I hate it so much. I'm so excited to get that out of me, and to start being a boy and everybody will just be going, "Yeah, yeah, she's a boy." They won't even question it because, because I'll obviously be one.

Maria Keffler (00:19:21):

What if you change your mind at some point?

"What if you change your mind at some point?"

Erin Brewer (00:19:25):

I'm not going to change my mind. That would be silly. Obviously. I mean, I've thought about this. It's not like I just thought of this yesterday. I've like felt like this my whole life and I'm not going to change my mind. That would be like you suddenly saying, "Well, it turns out that like I'm not your mom. I'm actually like your aunt," or something. I mean, obviously you wouldn't do that because you know, you're my mom.

But for me, I've thought about this a lot. I know sometimes you think that I make rash decisions and I haven't thought. But I thought this out. I've really thought this out. I've researched it. I've talked to a lot of people and all the people in my after-school club that I go to are saying "This is definitely the right path."

I know you worry because sometimes I'm kind of impulsive, but this time I've researched this. I've really researched it.

Maria Keffler (00:20:28):

All the people who are affirming this for you—how long have you known them? These people in your class?

Erin Brewer (00:20:33):

They're so cool. I started going last semester, and all of a sudden I felt so welcome and so accepted. I can't even tell you—I've just been living a lie my whole life, and now I can finally be my true self. It's just so freeing.

Maria Keffler (00:20:51):

Do you think that people who've only known you for six months to a year know you as well as your family does?

> **"Do you think people who've only known you for six months to a year know you as well as your family does?"**

Erin Brewer (00:21:00):

Well, I think they know me better because they know me as Ash. Whereas everybody else has known me as this lie that I was my whole life.

Maria Keffler (00:21:13):

Going back to the question of people—if anybody ever changes their mind. Do you know of anybody who's changed their mind about transitioning sexes?

Erin Brewer (00:21:22):

No. I've heard of some people who—I know there's some videos out. There are some detrans people who pretended to be trans and then were like, "Oh, I made a mistake." But they weren't really trans. Obviously, because they didn't stick with it. So just because somebody else makes a bad choice, doesn't mean it's a bad choice for me. I mean, you and dad have wine with dinner, but there are alcoholics. Right? And so maybe you shouldn't have that glass of wine with dinner because you might be an alcoholic.

Maria Keffler (00:21:54):

I'm thinking about myself and I'm thinking about some of the choices and decisions that I've made in my life. I don't know if you know this about me, but when I was 18, almost got married. I was in love.

Erin Brewer (00:22:15):

Mom!

Maria Keffler (00:22:19):

I thought this is the one, this is the one—I'm absolutely in love with him. He wanted to get married. We were at college, but we were like, "Oh, we can totally make this work. I was about to marry him and before it happened, I found out I was not the only girl he was seeing. I was heartbroken. But I look back on that and I think, "Wow, I'm really glad that happened. If I'd married him..."

Erin Brewer (00:22:47):

That happened to a friend of mine. I mean, they weren't talking about being married, but she was going out with this guy. Then she found out he had a whole bunch of other girlfriends. She was so sad.

Maria Keffler (00:22:59):

Yeah. You can want something and, and feel something so strongly. Right? And then find out later: "Wow. Even though I wanted that really bad, that would've been really bad for me. If I'd gotten it..."

This is my concern. And I'm not saying, "No, you absolutely can't go the medicalization route." I'm saying, I want to understand this more.

Erin Brewer (00:23:24):

I'm going to send you all these links, Mom, because I think once you read it, you'll totally understand it. And if not, it's just because you're transphobic and that's something you can change if you want to. You get to choose whether you're transphobic or not.

Maria Keffler (00:23:40):

Well, I don't identify as transphobic. I'm not afraid of transgender people. I'm not afraid of the transgender ideology. I love you. And I'm concerned about you and I want the very best future that you can have. And it's awfully unfair for you to keep assigning me this label of "transphobic."

> **"I don't identify as transphobic. I'm not afraid of transgender people. It's awfully unfair for you to keep assigning me this label of 'transphobic.'"**

Erin Brewer (00:23:58):

Well, if you're acting transphobic—it kind of sounds like you're a little bit that way. If you really love me—I mean these people love me. They love the authentic self. You might love that person that I was—you know, that girl that you think that you had. But if you really loved me and my authentic self, then you will totally affirm me. You will totally accept this and you will not talk about this like—you know, you're kind of mocking me a little bit and so that's how I'm going to know if you really love me.

Maria Keffler (00:24:33):

I'm sorry if it sounds like I'm mocking you. I do not feel like I am. I love you. I will always love you no matter what. But I am concerned about this and it sounds like you're saying that to love someone, you have to agree with everything they want.

Erin Brewer (00:24:52):

Not everything, but in this case it's who I am. If you can't accept me as your son, then I'm just going to find parents who can, because there are people out there who totally accept me.

Maria Keffler (00:25:11):

Where are you going to find those parents?

Erin Brewer (00:25:13):

Well, they're all over the internet. Some of the people in my club, they have these families that they actually have just gone to live with because their parents were so transphobic. They were out of there. And so there's places I can go.

Maria Keffler (00:25:27):

It makes me really sad that you'd be willing to throw away your dad and me, and throw away your home and your family, over a disagreement, or

> **"It makes me really sad that you'd be willing to throw away your dad and me, and throw away your home and your family, over a disagreement or concern. It seems like you're being really flippant about wanting to throw away your family. And that concerns me."**

over even just a concern. It seems like you're being really flippant about wanting to throw away your family. And that concerns me.

Erin Brewer (00:25:49):

Well, it's like you're throwing me away if you don't accept me. So why is it okay for you to throw me away? But then you're going, "Oh, well, you're being flippant. If you throw us away."

Maria Keffler (00:26:04):

In what sense do you see us throwing you away?

Erin Brewer (00:26:08):

Well—

Maria Keffler (00:26:09):

How has anything I've said been a rejection?

Erin Brewer (00:26:12):

If you really love me, you'd be saying, "Oh Ash— I have a son!" And maybe you'd get me a cake and we could have a celebration. but instead you're going, "Well, I'm going to have to talk to Dad about this" and "I don't know about this," and "You've got to show me the research."

It just doesn't seem like you love me at all.

Maria Keffler (00:26:37):

You know, I think you don't appreciate that the way this feels to me is that Ash is trying to kill my daughter. This person, "Ash," wants to kill the daughter that I've known for 15 years and loved for 15 years. And this is really hard for me to hear.

> **"I think you don't appreciate the way this feels to me. Ash is trying to kill my daughter. This person, 'Ash,' wants to kill the daughter that I've known and loved for 15 years. And this is really hard for me to hear."**

Erin Brewer (00:27:03):

Well, I guess that's why they call it a deadname.

Maria Keffler (00:27:07):

I've heard that term before. A deadname is a name that belongs to someone who is dead. Is that right? So that tells me, that you're trying to kill Erin. Are you trying to kill Erin?

Erin Brewer (00:27:22):

Well, it's like she never really was there. So yeah, I guess in a way I'm sort of, you know, the caterpillar kind of is plodding along and then they go into their cocoon or their chrysalis and then they come out. And so it's not like the caterpillar was not really part of what the butterfly is. The caterpillar just was sort of what they had to be before they could really come out as a beautiful butterfly.

Maria Keffler (00:27:54):

That sounds a lot to me like the process of puberty. That sounds a lot like a child going through puberty, which is a huge time of change.

Erin Brewer (00:28:05):

I know. I hate it. I can't even tell you how much I hate it. I'm growing these breasts and they're driving me crazy and the boys are looking at them and I hate it, Mom. I hate it so much.

Maria Keffler (00:28:18):

I know. I remember that. I developed my chest really early, earlier than a lot of other or girls did. And I remember how uncomfortable it was.

Erin Brewer (00:28:29):

I hate it. I've been using an ACE bandage to try and keep them flat just so people won't even notice them. I want them cut off. I hate them.

Maria Keffler (00:28:41):

I understand. And I'm so sorry that it feels that way. I'm so sorry that it feels that way.

Erin Brewer (00:28:49):

I feel like I am the caterpillar who went in and instead of coming out of butterfly, I came out like a toad or like a spider, or like some kind of like disgusting troll. I am just like, "I am not coming out a butterfly" and I am going to be a butterfly. That's what the testosterone's going to do.

Maria Keffler (00:29:11):

Aw, honey, I'm so sorry that it feels that way. I believe you. I believe everything that you're telling me about the way you feel.

Erin Brewer (00:29:18):

I don't even know how you did it. How did you even get through like all these changes? The periods and all of a sudden these guys are looking. Oh, I just hate it. I just want to go back to when I was a little kid.

> **"I understand. And I'm sorry that it feels that way. I'm so sorry that it feels that way. I believe you. I believe everything that you're telling me about the way you feel."**

Maria Keffler (00:29:31):

Yeah. I understand. I want to tell you, and I want you to believe me, as hard as it is to believe, these feelings are temporary. They really are. The discomfort is so temporary, and it's part of puberty and it's normal and everybody feels it to some degree and wants to escape it. It is so normal wanting to do anything to make it stop. It is so normal.

> **"I want you to believe me, as hard as it is to believe, that these feelings are temporary."**

But I don't think it means that you're not Erin. And I don't think it means that you're not a girl. I think it means you're going through a really hard time. And there are ways to get through it. There are ways to make it feel better. But sometimes in life, stuff just happens and you just have to kind of suck it up and say, "Well, I'm just going to be a mess for a while until I get through this."

Erin Brewer (00:30:24):

Mom, there's testosterone and it's going to help because it'll stop all this. It will just take care of it. I just won't even have to worry about it anymore.

Maria Keffler (00:30:35):

You'll still have to go through puberty.

Erin Brewer (00:30:39):

I won't have to end up becoming a woman.

Maria Keffler (00:30:44):

Testosterone will change things, but it won't necessarily improve them.

Erin Brewer (00:30:54):

Oh it will. If I don't have to have these things anymore, I hate them. Sometimes I just want to take a butcher knife and hack them off. I hate them so much.

Maria Keffler (00:31:03):

Would you rather have a penis?

Erin Brewer (00:31:05):

Well, I don't really want a penis. I don't really think I need to have a penis. I just want to have the body of a guy—have some muscle, and be buff. Not my breasts. I want, when I'm walking down the street, that people are going to be like, "Oh, there's a guy."

Maria Keffler (00:31:24):

Yeah. Women get breasts. Men have a penis and testicles. We all have something dangling off of us. After I got married and I saw what the male body looks like naked, I thought, "I would not want that thing dangling between my legs."

Erin Brewer (00:31:45):

I don't really want those either. Wouldn't that be weird?

Maria Keffler (00:31:50):

I've asked, "What do you do with that when you—" Anyway, we don't need to go there.

Erin Brewer (00:31:54):

Some, some, some guys have those, but there are lots of guys who don't, and so it's okay to be a guy and not have that.

Maria Keffler (00:32:04):

So it sounds like you just want to get rid of all gender. You don't want to have any sex characteristics. Is that right?

Erin Brewer (00:32:11):

Well, I've thought about it. Am I non-binary or I am I trans? I think I'm more trans because I kind of would like to—I don't want to just be non-binary. I really feel comfortable with he/him and with Ash, and having some muscle and being a guy. Because non-binary is kind of—I just think it's sort of non-committal, and I'm committed to this.

Maria Keffler (00:32:40):

Well, I look forward to seeing some of the research that you have to show me. I'm going to do some research. I hope that you can give your dad and me some time to think about this. And I hope that you'll be open to hearing more questions from us. This is a big thing. Do you consider this a big thing?

Erin Brewer (00:33:01):

Yes.

Maria Keffler (00:33:04):

Big things need to be deeply considered. And as your dad and I study this and talk about this with you, I hope you'll be open to hearing what we have to say without throwing those slurs at us—calling us transphobic for asking questions. That's really unfair. You've asked us lots of questions over the years about things that we told you, and when you throw something this big at us, we're going to have questions and it's not transphobic to ask questions.

We want what's best for you. We want you to be a happy, healthy adult. We want you to have all the choices, and all the doors open to you to make choices later in life. This one has the potential to close a lot of doors for you. Do you see any of those doors that might close if you pursue this?

Erin Brewer (00:34:08):

Yeah. And I'm pretty happy about that. There are some doors I'm pretty darn happy about closing. But I'm going to send you that research and I think once you read it, you'll be like—you'll totally get it. Because it just makes so much sense. So I hope that you'll look at it and, and really like— and then maybe can you just start calling me Ash and use he/him pronouns. I think once you get used to doing that and read the research, you'll just totally support me and realize how this is really what I need to do.

Maria Keffler (00:34:43):

Well, your dad and I are going to have to talk about that at this moment. I'm not comfortable calling you a different name or different pronouns because I don't believe that one can have a different sex inside than outside, but I will read what you give me. I will think about it deeply. I will talk to some people. If I come across things that interest me, will you read those as well?

Erin Brewer (00:35:09):

You can share stuff with me, but if it's super transphobic— I'm not sure, because there's a lot of TERFs out there and, and maybe you're one of them. I hope not, Mom. That would be sad, but I'll look at it, and if it's not transphobic then yeah. I'll read it.

Maria Keffler (00:35:33):

What does transphobic mean to you? How would you look at something I send you and decide whether it's transphobic or not?

Erin Brewer (00:35:39):

Well, if it denies the true trans. There's some people who don't even believe it's possible to be born in the wrong body. There's some people who are like, "There's no such thing as transgender" and those that are so transphobic, they're just trying to erase trans transgender people.

Maria Keffler (00:35:58):

What if I found a research study that is a good research study—robust research that has a control group and an experimental group?

Erin Brewer (00:36:11):

I love science. You know that, Mom.

Maria Keffler (00:36:13):

Okay. So even if the conclusions of that study don't necessarily agree with what you want them to, will you still consider them if it's a nice, robust research study?

Erin Brewer (00:36:26):

Well, I guess I'll look at it. And if, I mean, it's hard for me to even imagine how it could be a good study and not have the results pro-trans because it's so obvious that being transgender is real and that some people just have to transition in order to be their authentic selves. But if it's a good research study, I mean, you know me, I always love science.

Maria Keffler (00:36:48):

I'm glad to hear it. And I do too. And I want to find the truth and I want to know what's best. But I want you to know more than anything that I love you. Your dad loves you. That will never change. There may be times—as there have always been—that we have to say, "No, we can't agree with something that you want," but that does not mean we don't love you. Do you understand that?

Erin Brewer (00:37:10):

Yeah. It's just hard. Because everybody at school says, "If your parents really love you, then they'll go ahead and they'll honor you." And some kids, they even get parties. When they come out, their parents are really excited about it and they're happy about it. And they're happy for them. This has kind of been a drag, because you're not really excited and you're not really supporting me in this.

Maria Keffler (00:37:35):

I want you to consider what you mean by the word *support* again. You said, "If I loved you, I would agree to this." And I take exception with that because I don't believe love always says "Yes." Love is about giving the other person what they need—what they most need—and looking for *their* best, as opposed to *my* best. And to me, the word *support* means to give what you need to have your best life.

> **"I want you to consider what you mean by the word *support*. You said, 'If I loved you, I would agree to this.' I take exception with that because I don't believe love always says 'Yes.'"**

Erin Brewer (00:38:06):

So when I give you all the research and you read it and you'll be, "Okay, this is definitely what's going to be best for Ash." Then you'll go ahead and follow the recommendations of all the experts?

Maria Keffler (00:38:20):

If I read the research and they are robust studies, and they are well done— If they convince me, I will always go with, what science convinces me of, with what the facts are. If that is the case, then I will agree with it. I am skeptical that is what will happen, but I am open to that happening. Okay. But I need to be convinced first.

Erin Brewer (00:38:47):

Well, I have so much to share with you. I'm super excited for you to read it because I think it's going to blow your mind away. You're going to be like, "Wow, this, this is so different from what I learned in school, like so much has progressed since then." So I'm super excited for you to read it.

Maria Keffler (00:39:01):

I look forward to reading it. I love you. Thank you for trusting me with this information. I'm sorry that I didn't respond the way you wish that I had. But I love you. And that will never change.

Curtain.

Wow. That went a lot longer than I thought it would.

Erin Brewer (00:39:21):

Oh wow. I thought it would be two minutes.

Maria Keffler (00:39:29):

Let's talk about how that went a little bit. Oh my gosh.

Erin Brewer (00:39:33):

Do you think it was—

Maria Keffler (00:39:37):

It seemed pretty real. It seemed to, oh my gosh. You were like, "No mom." I was like, "I'm really talking to a 15-year-old here."

Erin Brewer (00:39:48):

I know I felt bad, but you did so well. I thought you were so good.

Maria Keffler (00:39:57):

Oh there were times that I thought, "What do I say? What do I say here? What do I say here?" And that's okay. Parents, that's normal. You are going to have those times.

> **"There were times that I thought, 'What do I say? What do I say here?' And that's okay. Parents, that's normal. You are going to have those times."**

Erin Brewer (00:40:05):

I wonder if we should do a debrief instead of doing more role playing. Should we do a debrief where we talk about it and say, "How did you feel, Maria?" This might be more intense or less…

Maria Keffler (00:40:20):

That's what we're doing right now.

Erin Brewer (00:40:22):

Oh, we're still recording.

Maria Keffler (00:40:23):

Yeah. I think that's the right way to go with this, to debrief what we just did, because that was long.

Erin Brewer (00:40:30):

Yeah. It was intense. It's funny because as I was doing it, I was able to tap into those feelings that I had as a kid. It felt very real to me. I was remembering how it felt to be so dysphoric, and to have so much hatred for myself. So I'm glad that we had you playing the mom and me playing the daughter because I think that it was able to remember what it was like, and that anger that I had for people who weren't affirming me, who were saying, "You're actually a girl." I was wondering if you felt like that was more intense or less intense than what would actually happen.

Maria Keffler (00:41:17):

When I talked to parents who've been through it, it sounds like a very, very intense experience. I have talked to kids who are trans-identified, and a lot of the things you said are the things that I've heard.

I felt that was very realistic and I really felt a burden as we were doing that to get this right. You know: "What does the mom need to say? How does the mom need to handle this?" I don't know if I got that all right. But I felt like, "Okay, the first, most important thing is to keep telling the child, 'I love you. I do love you. Even if I don't agree with you, I love you. And

> **"I felt like, 'Okay, the most important thing is to keep telling the child, *I love you. I do love you. Even if I don't agree with you, I'll always love you.*'"**

I'll always love you.'"

I feel like that's the most important thing the child needs to hear, but then to start asking questions like, "What is transphobic? What is love? What is support? What is gender identity?" and really requiring the child to think.

Because even while going through that, you were starting to talk in some circles and I didn't stop and address those places that you were contradicting yourself. But the circular reasoning was definitely there.

Erin Brewer (00:42:28):

That that's what's important for parents to remember too, that if you start catching your child and being like, "Ha! Wait a minute, this makes no sense. This is silly," in these kinds of conversations, that could just turn the child off and have him walk out of the room.

It's good that you didn't say, "You said this, but now you're saying this. That makes no sense," because especially in these initial conversations—they can be so volatile that just empathizing and sharing experiences is best. And again, just sharing that love is powerful.

I found myself being sucked into what you were saying. But then the ideology is that if you're not affirming, then your transphobic, and that's what these kids have been told. They've probably seen it acted out, role-played.

They're seeing this role playing in real life, in their groups. And so that's where it's hard for parents. The fact that you we're able to continually deescalate was important.

The other thing that is important, know when to end the conversation, because we could have gone on for another hour—we could have gone on for three more hours. When you're in this kind of conflict, it's so important to be able to end it, and to end it in a way where the other person feels honored, even if they don't feel affirmed. Right?

Maria Keffler (00:44:06):

Right. It is important to stress to the child, "I believe that everything you're feeling is what you're feeling. I believe what you're telling me about your feelings," because these kids are having real, uncomfortable feelings. This is something I wanted to get to in the role-play.

We got off-topic and I forgot to go back to it, but when you were talking about how uncomfortable you felt in your body, I wanted to address that there are so many reasons you could feel uncomfortable in your body. So many reasons. But the transgender industry is telling kids, "Whatever makes you uncomfortable tells you that you're trans," right? And that's where the logic breakdown is.

But also going back to what you said about not necessarily jumping on those hypocrisies and conflicts and circular reasoning-- you're right. In these initial, really high-stakes conversations, that's probably not the right place to do it.

> **"I wanted to address that there are so many reasons you could feel uncomfortable in your body. But the transgender industry is telling kids, 'Whatever makes you uncomfortable tells you that you're trans.' And that's where the logic breakdown is."**

But keep that in your pocket. And some other time, when things are good between you and your child—maybe you're cooking together and talking about something different or whatever, and things are peaceful—you can bring it up and go, "Hey, I've been thinking about what we were talking about and I didn't understand something. And I wondered if you could clarify it for me. You said that gender is fixed and you've known your whole life that you were transgender, but then you told me about Phil who realized when he was 18 that gender is fluid, and he's going back and forth. How does that work?"

Because that's absolutely a conflict and the child is going to have a really hard time explaining that.

Erin Brewer (00:45:45):

That's right. Exactly.

The other thing—I like what you did, saying. "I don't identify as transphobic." I mean, those kinds of comments, if you say them in a sarcastic way can be very hurtful. But if you say them in a loving and concerned way, potentially could be powerful, because this whole ideology is supposedly based on feelings.

The other thing that I wanted to point out that went really well in the role-play—if a child first starts talking about these issues parents can use it as an opportunity to try and figure out, "What are the underlying feeling here?"

So rather than even arguing about the trans thing, just try and ask, "What are those underlying issues that are, that are motivating this? Is it because they're being taught this at school? Is it because they're a lesbian and they're being teased? Is it because they've had some kind of sexual trauma? Is it because they're autistic and they're feeling like all the other girls are social and popular and they're completely ostracized?"

If you can eke those out gently, that does a couple of things. First of all, it gives you a lot of information, which is important. but it also changes the direction of the conversation in a way that can deescalate it and can help the child to realize that there are those underlying feelings that are motivating this.

Maria Keffler (00:47:13):

My favorite part of the conversation was when I talked about thinking about getting married when I was 18, and I saw you engage. I loved that moment where we were both on the same page. I thought that was so powerful. When you turned it off and I could see you have this moment of, "Oh my gosh, I just aligned with my mom. I need to get back to the trans narrative." That was so painful, but I think it's so accurate. I think that's what happens.

> **"I loved that moment where we were both on the same page. I thought that was so powerful. When you turned it off and I could see you have this moment of, 'Oh my gosh, I just aligned with my mom. I need to get back to the trans narrative.' That was so painful, but I think it's so accurate. I think that's what happens."**

Erin Brewer (00:47:42):

That's something where I've talked to a lot of parents, and they can see when their child is back. You know, they can see that connection, and then they can also see when they turn off. That can be so intensely painful for parents that they're like, "Wait, my daughter was there for a moment. And then she went away," and the parents can tell that the child made that choice of like, "Uh-oh, I better get back into my trans role." That can be really painful for parents.

Maria Keffler (00:48:10):

Yeah, it can. That's one of the features of this that makes it such a cult. We see this with kids. I call it boomeranging. The boomeranging is actually a good sign, where you're seeing your real child and you're connecting with them. You're seeing that real person, but then they flip back and dig their heels in and get entrenched in the ideology.

That's what cults do, because cults put an identity on you that they want you to have, and it subjugates your true identity. But your true self wants to come out. It wants to be—you want to be who you are.

Ironically, that's one of the slogans the trans-identity people use: "Be who you are." But that real person wants to come out. And when you start seeing that sort of tug-of-war—I think what we're seeing is a competition of loyalties: "Am I loyal to my family? Or am I loyal to the gender cult?"

Erin Brewer (00:49:14):

Am I loyal to reality? Honestly who I am? And that's something that we've seen: a few detransitioners, who've gone back to transitioning, and almost overwhelmingly it's because they're getting more love from that community. They're getting celebrated, they're getting affirmed—all these things that people need. When they retransition after having been a detransitioner, boy are they celebrated. Because the cult's thinking, "We got them back!"

Some people use that as evidence that they were literally trans all along. But it's more evidence of how powerful this cult is.

Maria Keffler (00:49:57):

Yeah. I like what you said: "We all need love." We all need to feel appreciated and valued. This is one of the things that gender cult does really well is that love bombs people who join them. It absolutely vilifies everybody who's outside of it.

I did like that in the role play where you were so disappointed: "I wanted a party. All my friends get parties when they announce this, why aren't you giving me a party?" That spoke to that—I don't want to call it immaturity, because we all want a party.

Erin Brewer (00:50:29):

We all want a party.

Maria Keffler (00:50:31):

I want to announce something and have people be like, "Woohoo! Woo!"

Erin Brewer (00:50:37):

But it's also superficial.

There was recently a woman who detransitioned. She just recently went back to living as transgender and what she keeps writing is, "Now I'm happy again. I'm finally happy again."

Part of the problem with how seductive this cult is because it's suggesting that the goal in life is to be happy. Whenever you have problems, just leave those in the dust, and become someone new and be happy. It's a very superficial way of living, and it's a very dangerous way of living because that happiness is so ephemeral and transient.

Maria Keffler (00:51:22):

Yeah. Happiness is a momentary thing. And you can't actually perpetuate happiness constantly in your life. If you're constantly chasing happiness, you're just going to become a frustrated hedonist, because you can't maintain that. We want to live in the real world. We want to be who we are. We want to attain a life that is productive and a life that is satisfying and a life that is meaningful, but not just that I want to be happy. It's not possible to be happy all the time.

> **"If you're constantly chasing happiness, you're just going to become a frustrated hedonist."**

Erin Brewer (00:51:59):

For those who haven't watched or other shows, one of the things that's so dangerous about testosterone is that it does make you feel really good. It's a controlled substance. It's a steroid. Maria, if you or I took it, we'd feel really good. We'd get energy, we'd build muscle. Our sex drive would kick in. I mean, we'd feel good.

Maria Keffler (00:52:21):

My husband would love it, because my menopausal sex drive right now—but testosterone would probably fix that for me.

Erin Brewer (00:52:28):

So it's not surprising that after the initial transition, they're like, "This is awesome," because they were able to run away from their problems. And then they're getting this drug that would make any female feel pretty hot.

So that's the danger, that's why it's so insidious.

How can you argue with these girls who are coming out and saying, "I started testosterone and I feel great. This is the best thing that ever happened in my life." Well, if you start taking some other drugs—maybe if you start giving your teens heroin, they might feel pretty good. But we know that's not the way to live. That feeling-good, feeling-empowered, feeling-mighty isn't a great way to live. You're going up, up, up, up, up, and eventually you're going to crash. And those crashes are scary and dangerous.

Maria Keffler (00:53:23):

They are. That was tough for me during the role-play, because I wanted to role-play a mom for whom this was out of the blue. She had no background in this, didn't know anything about it.

But while you were talking and telling me about all these great things about testosterone, that Maria who's been working on this stuff for several years is thinking, "I know all these studies, I know all these side effects. I want to throw this all back at you."

But I didn't, because most parents, when they're first introduced to this, won't be able to do that. And so it's perfectly reasonable and the right thing to do, to say, "Show me your studies." The studies that this child is going to send her mom are going to be junk science. I mean, that's what's out there supporting this. It's not science, it's junk.

Erin Brewer (00:54:10):

The Jack Turban study, which is lauded as evidence for all of this and is talked about in national media, is so badly done. All of them tend to be self-reported, retrospective, with selected populations—all the things that we know undermine good scientific outcomes.

If you start saying, "Well, those have significant methodological flaws…" the kid might tune out. So it's important to have the language, but I have yet to see a study done that supported anything transgender that wasn't seriously flawed. I wouldn't have even been able to get through a committee review for my dissertation with these studies. They would've kicked it out in a second.

So the research standards are so low now that it's important for parents to understand because, I was role-playing. I can send you a bazillion articles and research—but all of the articles are based upon just a couple of bad studies. There are so many articles, and we have sites like Planned Parenthood and the HRC that will purport to show that "We have to do these life-saving medical interventions." That's just bogus. We need to be able to call it out.

Maria Keffler (00:56:08):

I've just seen recently going around social media a meme that says children who are affirmed in their transgender identity are 50% less likely to commit suicide.

That's baloney, primarily because you cannot set up a research study to study who will commit suicide and who won't. You can't have a control group for the purpose "We're going to try to get these people to commit suicide, and we'll see what the stats are" because that that's completely unethical. Nobody has ever done it. Nobody can do it. That's complete and utter B.S.

Erin Brewer (00:56:45):

We have little research about what's happening now. The research that we do have shows that has unequivocally negative outcomes. It doesn't solve the problem.

Maria Keffler (00:57:09):

It's catastrophic to kids.

Erin Brewer (00:57:11):

It's catastrophic to kids.

Well, thank you so much, Maria.

Maria Keffler (00:57:15):

We had a bunch of other role-plays we were going to do today, but I think this is the one. I think we're going to stop here.

Erin Brewer (00:57:22):

Maybe we'll do another one at another point. But for now this was a good introduction to what you might encounter, and the kinds of comebacks that you're going to get from your child.

Maria Keffler (00:57:41):

Right? So, good luck parents. If you need support, if you need help come to advocatesprotectingchildren.org. We've got a website full of support, and full of help.

Erin Brewer (00:58:02):

I also just wanted to tell people—parents, especially if you're watching this and your roleplay spun out of control into a complete disaster—not the roleplay here, but if your actual interaction with your child went badly, that that's okay. You know, Maria has an educational background. She's an expert in this field and she has practiced this a lot. This was just a model of what might happen, understanding that it's going to go in all different directions. A few parents may have just said, "Well, that's absurd." Your child may have said, "Well, I'm going to run away."

We're all trying to work through this and figure out how to do this. So parents, don't blame yourself if your responses didn't go over well. It's not uncommon for a child just to say, "Well, you are transphobic," and walk out of the room. I mean, that's pretty typical.

Maria Keffler (00:59:07):

Yeah. I, and I want to emphasize too: I've had many conversations with my kids on subjects where they blindsided me, and I did it very badly. It happens. Just learn from the mistakes. Move on, keep trying, just keep engaging with your child. Keep letting your child know that you love him or her.

Episode 35: Life After Desisting

https://youtu.be/xxe2UwcudWU

Maria Keffler (00:38):

Before we talk about the topic for today, we need to let you know that this is going to be our last Commonsense Care episode. This is #35.

Erin Brewer (01:00):

When we first started talking about doing a parenting series, we thought we might do five or ten episodes, but topics just kept coming up. We've gotten such good feedback from parents. I've learned a lot.

I'm feeling sad that we've had 35 episodes in a way, because it shows the breadth of this issue and how it has invaded every aspect of these parents' lives. My heart goes out to all the parents who are struggling with this issue.

Maria Keffler (02:17):

I thought we might do seven or eight videos, tops, and that would be it. Then every week more topics came up and parents would send in questions. This has been a powerful time for me exploring a lot of these issues, learning so much from you. I am also a little sad to be finishing up.

Erin Brewer (03:26):

I like ending on this particular topic: helping to heal the detransitioners. Because, ultimately, that's where we hope all the parents end up—parenting a detransitioner. There are some things that are going to be challenging for parents of detransitioners that we want to address.

> **I like ending on this particular topic: helping to heal the detransitioners. Because, ultimately, that's where we hope all the parents up—parenting a detransitioner.**

It reminds me of when I was pregnant. I had a difficult pregnancy. I'm short, there's not a lot of room, and I just kept thinking, "I can't wait for this pregnancy to be over." I was sick. I had to go in to get B12 shots because I was losing weight. It was hard to remember there was going to be a baby at the end and that would present a whole new slew of challenges.

It was easier though. I am not sure if it is a great analogy, but parents can't wait for their child to detransition. It is the goal. When it finally happens, it's a huge sigh of relief: "My child's finally detransitioned."

But it's not over. There's still going to be tremendous amount of parenting. This is a child who's been damaged by teachers who have affirmed them. Doctors have affirmed them. They have been celebrated. They are recovering from an ideology that has tried to damage their relationship with their family and all those who loved them.

This is a reminder that there's still going to be some tension. There's still going to be a lot of work to do. Your child is recovering from a very serious trauma. They've been encouraged to believe they're inherently flawed and that the only way to live with themselves was to become a different person.

When they realize that didn't help, and they've come back to accept themselves, there is going to be work to recover.

Maria Keffler (05:34):

Gender ideology is a cult. Your kids have been sucked into a cult. They've finally come out of it.

But one of the pernicious things a cult does is it puts a new identity on you. It subverts your true identity and it puts this fake identity on you. That's what's happened to these kids. So, even once they recognize this isn't true, they've still got all this baggage from the cult.

> **One of the pernicious things a cult does it puts a new identity on you. Even once your child realizes this, they've still got all this baggage from the cult.**

Part of that is the loss of themselves. If the child has been indoctrinated in this for three years—let's say it's been three years. The child went in at age 13; that child is now 16. That child has lost three years of normal psychosocial development. They've been so focused on the trans cult. Everything in the child's life revolved around gender. That child is 16 and has had few of the normal experiences that a teen should have.

A 13-year-old is different psycho-socially than a 16-year-old. They've lost all that time.

Erin Brewer (07:09):

The other thing is they've lost all that time and they've might have lost confidence in themselves and they're going to feel betrayed. That's the word that I hear, how betrayed they feel. They feel betrayed by the adults in their life, but they also feel unsure of their ability to differentiate truth from lies, because they were indoctrinated.

> **They feel betrayed by the adults in their life.**
> **They also feel unsure of their ability**
> **to differentiate truth from lies.**

All of us have had the experience of finding out that somebody who we thought was a good friend wasn't actually a good friend. If you can imagine that, only amplify it to everybody in your life—except for the few people who didn't affirm you—including yourself.

These are kids are going to have to relearn to trust both others as well as themselves, and to start to develop confidence in their ability to make good choices, to differentiate lies from truth, to figure out who is going to be a good friend for them and who isn't. Those are all things that typically happen during normal adolescent development, that they've missed out on. Now they've got trauma of that enormous betrayal to have to navigate through.

Maria Keffler (08:35):

It is important to remember these kids have been sold a pack of lies. They've been told "transwomen" are actually women, and that trans people are being killed at alarming rates. These things that aren't true.

Even though they realized, "Okay, I am not actually trans. I actually am the person who my body says I am," they still may and likely do believe a lot of the lies. We hear this from detransitioners all the time. It's almost a trope: "I don't want to take away from any other trans person's experience." Many of them still buy the book of lies.

One of the things cults do is instill fear into the recruits, because fear is a powerful motivator. It keeps them in the cult. Some of the things they've been told is that people who don't believe in trans ideology are toxic, hateful—they're murderers, they're violent.

These kids are coming out of that and they still will believe some of these things that be a challenge for them to heal from. So starting to help them understand the truth and help challenge those lies they've been told is a big part of the healing process,

Erin Brewer (10:04):

But it's not all doom and gloom! We have painted a dire picture, but we know that children and people in general are amazing at coming through things like that. I've heard stories of girls who have been kidnapped and kept locked up in closets and been used as sex slaves, and somehow the human spirit is able to overcome even unthinkable indoctrination.

One of the ways that we do that is through connections that we build. As a parent, you've already helped with that healing by maintaining truth and by reflecting love to your child, day in and day out, even when they were not at their best. They know you love them. That is going to be huge in part in their healing.

These kids are capable of learning how to be resilient. Unfortunately, the trans ideology promotes fragility. That's one of the biggest things you're going to have to deal with, is that these kids have learned to be fragile. Part of this process is toughening them up and letting them know that they can survive difficult things and that they are strong and that they can make good choices and that they are loved and that they are lovable.

Maria Keffler (11:28):

Ask questions. That's one of the things I always go back to is asking questions. People love to talk about themselves. You can ask anybody a question about themselves and you don't have to worry about talking for a little while because people love to talk about themselves. You can start with saying something like, "Can I ask you a question? Tell me how you decided that this is not true. Tell me about the decision-making process."

As your child talks about it, listen for cues, listen for things like fears and for things like lies that they might still believe. Then you can say, "Let me ask you another question. Do you think that all the people who don't agree with the gender ideology are all hateful? Do you feel like I'm hateful?" ask some of those questions to start getting them thinking.

Erin Brewer (12:27):

I do want to push back on one thing you said, that people like to talk about themselves. That's generally true, but we also know that a lot of these kids are on the autism spectrum. A lot of times kids who are autistic, don't like to talk about themselves. So for those kids, it's going to take a little bit more effort to get them to open up. I've worked with kids who are autistic and it's hard to get them to talk sometimes, unless you can find that one topic that they're focused interested in.

That's another way to help kids who are autistic move through this is to help cultivate another obsession. Parents might think, "No, I don't want my child to be obsessed," but if you have a child who's on the spectrum, that is a way to help them heal: find something else that they're interested in and help cultivate that interest. That way you have something that you can focus on together and it takes their mind off the trans ideology.

> **Another way to help kids who are autistic move through this is to help cultivate another obsession.**
>
> **That might sound like a horrible idea. Parents might think, "No, I don't want my child to be obsessed," but if you have a child who's on the spectrum, that is a way to help them heal: find something else that they're interested in and help cultivate that interest.**

Maria Keffler (13:28):

That's a great point. I'm glad you brought up the idea of shifting focus, because that's what we want to do here. Your child's been focused on the trans stuff for so long. Finding something that you can do together, or reminding the child is something he or she liked to do when they were younger, or some exciting thing they might like to try.

You want to fill that void, because right now there's a huge void in their life. They've lost the trans community. They've lost the accolades and affirmation they've gotten for being a "brave and stunning" trans person. Find something that you can do, or that they can do to focus on, to start to heal and shift the attention away from the trans stuff.

Erin Brewer (14:17):

The other thing is to be careful about who your child associates with. We want kids to have a good peer group, but it's so important that you keep them surrounded by people who are affirming reality, reflecting back to this child that who they are is okay. They don't have to change who they are. They don't have to run away from themselves. They don't have to become somebody else.

They're vulnerable right now. It is a lot like someone overcoming addiction at some point in their lives— they'll eventually be able to go to a party where there's alcohol or drugs, but early on, it's important to keep them away from that because they haven't built up strategies to deal with the pressures.

> **Be careful about who your child associates with. They're vulnerable right now. It is a lot like someone overcoming addiction at some point in their lives— they'll eventually be able to go to a party where there's alcohol or drugs, but early on, it's important to keep them away from that.**

Initially while your child is first coming out of this and still vulnerable, be extra cautious about who they're around and who they're spending time with, because as with any addiction or dependency, it's easy to fall back until they have built up new coping mechanisms, healthy coping mechanisms.

Even as old as I am, there are times where I still experience gender dysphoria. That's part of my wiring after all these years. There are times where I still feel like I am not like other women. It is falling back into that unhealthy coping mechanism that I developed.

I'm aware of that now. I wasn't so much when I was younger, but now as soon as I start telling myself those messages, I catch myself. That's part of the therapeutic healing that I've done. I've had therapists teach me how to handle those negative messages.

I would suggest if you're a parent, taking a child to a therapist can be difficult, but you can you can read up on cognitive behavioral therapy. You can read up on these techniques to help your child change their negative self-talk. And a lot of this is all about self-talk.

Nearly every person has messages going around in their head. A lot of the messages they developed during childhood. If you can turn those around, not only are they going to be less likely to re-transition, but they're just going to be able to cope with things. They're going to be more resilient in every way.

Maria Keffler (17:08):

I want to echo that. You helped me with something a couple of months ago.

I've been very focused on my weight, because as I'm getting older, the weight doesn't come off like it used to. I didn't realize I'd gotten into an unhealthy dieting pattern. You shared a book with me and the book talks about really analyzing, "Am I hungry?"

It's been interesting for me to start analyzing my thoughts around food, because I have discovered I am an emotional eater. I eat for happiness. When I walk past the candy dish, I grab one because I know it is going to give me such a good feeling. But if I ask myself, "Hang on, am I actually hungry? No, I'm actually not hungry."

That self-talk, just analyzing yourself and finding out why you're doing things you're doing, is so powerful. As you said, that's healthy regardless of whether we're talking about the trans issue, just learning how to monitor what you're thinking and why you're doing things.

> **Learning how to monitor what you're thinking about and why you're doing things is healthy, regardless of whether we're talking about the trans issue.**

I want to ask you something. I don't know if we considered discussing this before we started the video, but some of these detransitioners are going to be medicalized. How do we help these kids who maybe have been on cross-sex hormones, or who have had surgery deal with the physical effects of that going forward?

Erin Brewer (18:50):

It's incredibly difficult. They were originally given the message that if they were uncomfortable with their body, the only solution was to change it. Well, now they've detransitioned and they're uncomfortable with the changes that they made to their body. What is the appropriate message to give that child?

I'm going to fall back on Dr. Patrick Lappert and some of the things that I've talked to him about. He's got a lot of experience with this, and he's a reconstructive surgeon.

He trained taking care of children who had been wounded during war. He said, as a reconstructive surgeon, that if a patient comes in and thinks that her entire life is going to get better, if she changes something about herself, then that's an indication of an unrealistic expectation.

Reconstructive surgeons should encourage that person to get therapy rather than surgery. The message that we need to give these kids is, "Yes, it is difficult. You've got a five o'clock shadow and it's embarrassing. But changing that isn't going to radically change your life. You're still the same person."

Get the child to the point where they're comfortable with the changes that they made. Maybe they do want to do something about them. Maybe they do want to have laser hair removal. Maybe they want to get breast implants. But make sure they're not doing it because they think it's going to cure all the ills in their lives, but just because it would make them be more comfortable.

There's a big distinction between "This is going to make my life so much better" versus "This will help me be more comfortable."

> **There's a big distinction between "This is going to make my life so much better," versus "This will help me be more comfortable."**

The biggest thing I hear about is the voice. I've heard so many girls who detransitioned talk about the fact that when they go in a bathroom, sometimes people assume they're a male who's in the women's bathroom. They're uncomfortable with that.

That would be the one case where I would encourage YouTube videos. There's vocal training, where you can change the way your voice is. You have to pay a lot of attention initially, but then it becomes rote. That would be the one thing that I would counsel parents to help their child with, because that's an actual reality that difficult to deal with, if you are being constantly perceived as the opposite sex.

There are women who have polycystic ovarian syndrome and they are hairier. There are women who are hairy, there are women who are less feminine-presenting, but it's that deep voice that potentially could cause difficulties for them navigating in society.

There are women who have flat chests. Before I hit middle age and gained a lot of weight, I was a 32 AA, and even that was a little big for me.

There are women who are flat-chested, there are women who have lots of hair, there are women who have deep voices.

As a parent, you can help support your child to feel more comfortable, but also not to give her the message that her life is going to be cured by undoing all of the things that she did during transition.

Maria Keffler (22:45):

There might be guilt for what did she did to herself. I would like to say to everyone who's detransitioned: "You didn't do this to yourself. This wasn't you."

Give kids that reassurance that, "You were misled, you were lied to, you were betrayed. This was not your fault. You were sucked into a cult." Because that heaviness of imagining how better life would be had I not made this huge mistake, that probably would be hard to overcome.

> **Give kids that reassurance that, "You were misled, you were lied to, you were betrayed. This was not your fault. You were sucked into a cult." Because that heaviness of imagining how better life would be had I not made this huge mistake, that probably would be hard to overcome.**

I'm thinking about myself. I hadn't gone to the dentist for a couple of years, and we moved and I went to a new dentist. I'd never had a cavity. This dentist was said, "All four of these molars have cavities." I didn't get a second opinion and I let her drill them. I doubt now that they all four needed to be drilled. I have struggled with, "What did I do to my healthy teeth?" Now these poor kids who had healthy bodies had doctors damage their bodies.

Erin Brewer (24:12):

I have engaged in self-harming behaviors. I have scars that were self-inflicted that I live with. If somebody were to say, "How did you get that scar?" I'd have to be honest and say, "I did that to myself."

It's interesting, when I was self-harming, it was before cutting common. The kinds of scars I have are different, but there are people that I know who have obvious cutting scars. There are people who have obvious cuts on the wrist from where they attempted suicide. It is who we are, it is our history.

I encourage the detransitioners and parents detransitioners not to regret the past, but to celebrate the fact that the child went through something difficult and came through it.

Anybody who's been through a period of self-harming and comes through—anybody who's been through an addiction, anybody who's been pulled into a cult and gets out of it—that's something to be celebrated. That's something to pat yourself on the back for and say, "I did it. I made it through that difficult thing, and so I can make it through other difficult things."

The key is to help the child develop new coping mechanisms, healthy coping mechanisms. Make a list of all the things that a child can do if she is feeling anxious or feeling unsure of herself.

We don't want to encourage a person to develop an eating disorder, but sometimes having a candy bar when you're feeling down just helps you through that difficult moment. Come up with some short-term coping mechanisms, then some longer-term coping mechanisms, and just help the child to develop that list. Write it down and have it posted somewhere.

> **Come up with some short-term coping mechanisms, then some longer-term coping mechanisms, and just help the child to develop that list. Write it down and have it posted somewhere.**

I know that when I've worked with people who are suicidal, who are profoundly depressed, the advice is to write down that list. At the bottom have somebody you can call—maybe five or six people you can call.

So if your child is getting anxious and feeling like maybe they made a mistake in detransitioning, they have a whole plan in place for how to stay healthy.

Maria Keffler (26:37):

That's a really great suggestion. It's so helpful to have a goal or a dream or to have something that you're looking toward. If you have something—even if it's just a vacation in a few months—all of those things are ways to help kids through this healing time and this restoration time.

Erin Brewer (27:26):

Hopefully, as a society, we'll get to a point where we aren't so focused on external appearances that kids feel like they have to harm themselves in order to fit in.

That goes back to even what you were saying, as far as your unhealthy eating practices. We have these messages about how we're supposed to look. They can cause distress. I'm hoping at some point as a society we aren't giving these messages to kids all the time that they're never okay, that they always need to do something to change themselves, to be better and fit in more and to be more acceptable.

People will learn that the way they're born—the way they are—is exactly their authentic self. It's exactly how they're supposed to be. They're lovable and beautiful just as they are.

Maria Keffler (28:19):

We did a small survey of detransitioners and their parents. One of the things that we kept hearing was that detransitioners were so grateful that their parents held the line. They just desperately ached for their parents' love. We all ache to be loved fully and unconditionally for who we are now.

I have not loved my children perfectly. I've made mistakes. There are places I've had to go back and apologize and say, "I did that wrong. I really messed that up. I'm sorry." I was talking with my daughter's friend yesterday, who's the oldest of three. He was talking about how he always gets the worst parenting.

I said, "It is because your parents have never parented a kid your age before." You get the worst parenting.

I've said that to my son who's my oldest, too. I tell him, "You're the first trial. I'm sorry for the ways we messed up. And when your sister came up behind you, we were like, 'Let's do that a little differently.'"

But that's okay. Parents, it's okay to admit where you messed up. Sometimes parents are afraid if they admit they were wrong, it's going to undermine their authority—it's going to undermine our validity as parents.

It's just the opposite. When you admit that you made a mistake and you are vulnerable with your child, there is so much authenticity and true relationship-building that happens. If you look at it, it gives your child permission to make mistakes, too. You have modeled how to say, "I did that wrong and I messed up, I'm sorry."

Erin Brewer (30:17):

I really love the idea of modeling that behavior. I do think that some parents think to themselves, "Nope, I'm never apologizing to my kid."

But it really is valuable for you to humble yourself to your child and apologize for areas that you made mistakes. Let them know that you love them.

People are resilient and they'll come through this. It's really hard when you have parents who respond, "Well, I told you so." That's not going to be helpful. That's likely going to push a child away. Instead, let your child know you are a team and that you're in this together.

Parents, realize that you've made it through something incredibly difficult. You're going to need some self-care. You're going to need to make sure that you take care of yourself. We tend to focus on the child, but as a parent, you have just parented your child through something incredibly difficult. Some of you might've thought you were going to lose your child permanently. Some of you will never hear your daughter's voice again. Some of you will never see your son's face again because of feminization surgery.

It's hard and we feel for you, but you made it through, if your child's detransitioned.

If they haven't, there's always hope and although you may never hear your daughter's voice again, or see your son's face again, or hold the child close to you who you bore, who you parented, who you loved through childhood—they're still your child and they need you and you need them.

Maria Keffler (32:18):

Thank you for joining us for these 35 episodes. Our hearts are broken for parents who've gone through this. If you've come through it, as Erin said, you may have some post-traumatic stress. I've talked to parents who said, "I feel like I'm suffering post-traumatic stress." I want to validate that for you.

Trust that that you're going to continue to heal. You're going to continue to get better. But it's hard. It's been hard. We recognize that, and we want to say "Congratulations" to those of you who made it through.

Erin Brewer (33:03):

Also recognize that you might be angry with your child. I would recommend not letting your child know that, but it is important to process that anger. When your child does something that hurts, you're human. That anger is a normal and healthy response.

Don't be down on yourself. Follow those self-care techniques; follow the same self-talk techniques that we talked about. Make sure you're thinking positive thoughts, and come up with a list of coping mechanisms for yourself as well, because this is an ongoing battle.

For those parents who have had children detransition, we're so thankful. For those who are still waiting for their child to detransition. Keep up the hope. Just keep that hope alive, and keep loving your child; they're in there somewhere. And they need you.

> **For those parents who have had children detransition, we're so thankful. For those who are still waiting for their child to detransition. Keep up the hope. Just keep that hope alive, and keep loving your child; they're in there somewhere. And they need you.**

Maria Keffler (34:05):

I want to end on a positive note—that survey of detransitioners—one of the surprising things that came out.

We asked for the parents and the children to score the strength of their relationship prior to transition, during transition, and after transition. In the vast majority of cases, the relationship strength went really far down during transition, but in almost every case, it came up to the same level or higher strength of closeness after the detransitioning.

That was an incredibly hopeful thing. If you are still struggling through this, if you feel like, "I don't even know this child," it doesn't have to stay that way. The little bit of data that we have shows that after detransition your relationship can bounce back and be even better than before,

Erin Brewer (35:08):

Which is just a great way to end this.

RESOURCES

Advocates Protecting Children
www.advocatesprotectingchildren.org

Arlington Parent Coalition
https://www.arlingtonparentcoa.wixsite.com/arlingtonparentcoa

Bayswater Support Group (U.K.)
https://bayswatersupport.org.uk

Child & Parental Rights Campaign
www.childparentrights.org

Detrans Canada
www.detranscanada.com

Detrans Voices
www.detransvoices.org

Dofemco (Spain)
www.dofemco.org

Dysphoric Movie: Fleeing Womanhood Like a House on Fire
Vaishnavi Sundar

Florida Citizens Alliance
https://floridacitizensalliance.com

Gender Dysphoria Alliance
https://www.genderdysphoriaalliance.com

Gender Dysphoria Support Network
https://genderdysphoriasupportnetwork.com

International Association of Therapists for Desisters and
Detransitioners: https://iatdd.com

Irreversible Damage: The Transgender Craze Seducing Our Daughters
Abigail Shrier

Navigating the Transgender Landscape - School Resource Guide
https://childparentrights.org/school-resource-guide

No Corpo Certo (Brazil)
https://nocorpocerto.com

Operation Millstone
https://www.operation-millstone.org

Parents of ROGD Kids
(Support Group Network)
https://www.parentsofrogdkids.com

Rethink Identity Medicine Ethics, Inc.
https://www.rethinkime.org

Society for Evidence-Based Gender Medicine
https://www.segm.org

Transgender Trend
(Questioning the Trans Narrative)
https://www.transgendertrend.com

Understanding Transgender Issues (Family Watch International)
https://www.familywatch.org/transgenderissues

When Harry Became Sally: Responding to the Transgender Moment
Ryan T. Anderson

You're Teaching My Child What?
Miriam Grossman, M.D.

GLOSSARY

The following terms are defined as the author understands their use, but not necessarily as LGB & TQ organizations would claim they are defined. Definitions are pulled from LGB & TQ materials, dictionaries, and/or the personal experience of the author.

Ally: a person who supports all LGB & TQ issues and ideologies; this is becoming more and more subjective, as many transgender-rights activists argue that homosexuals are transphobic if they refuse to date transgender-identified people who claim to be their preferred sex partners.

Androgynous: of indeterminate sex; having characteristics of both maleness and femaleness.

Antagonists: as used in this book, people who are leading your child deeper into the gender cult.

Asexual: lacking any sexual attractions to others.

Biological Sex: the sex that one was born, male or female, as evidenced by chromosomes, external anatomy (genitals, breasts), and internal anatomy (sex glands and organs).

Biphobia: prejudice against bisexual people. In current vernacular this term is applied to anyone who disagrees with anything that a bisexual person says, wants, or believes.

Bisexual: experiencing sexual attraction to both males and females.

Cis-: a prefix indicating that one's behavior or preferences align with typical or biological expectations (cisgender, cis-sexual, cis-man, etc.); this is a pejorative and nonsensical term, since no one feels completely comfortable with his or her body at all times.

Cisgender: a person whose gender identity aligns with his or her birth sex. Near antonym to **Queer**.

Closeted: an LGB/TQ person who hides his or her sexuality and/or gender identity from most other people. Antonym of **Living Openly**.

Coming Out: used as a verb or a noun, "coming out" means announcing one's sexuality or gender identity publicly.

Deadname: the name parents gave to a child when s/he was born, which is rejected in favor of a self-chosen transgender name.

Desister: a person who believed him- or herself to be transgender, but has since accepted his or her birth sex as reality.

Detransitioner: a person who presented as other than his or her birth sex, transitioning socially and/or medically, but has since accepted his or her birth sex as reality, and presents as such.

Fantasy Defense: a sexual predator's claim that he did not intend to carry out sexual activities, but was merely indulging in harmless fantasy, and/or that the victim misconstrued fantasy for reality: "It never actually happened."

FTM: Female to male transgender. Opposite of **MTF**.

Gay: homosexual, or attracted to members of one's own sex. Usually applied to males, but not exclusively.

Gender Clinic: a center that engages in experimental medical interventions where nearly every client is deemed appropriate for sex transition and assisted in attempted social and medical transition to a different sex.

Gender Dysphoria: a diagnostic term describing when one's sense of his/her gender identity does not always and/or fully match his/her biological sex.

Gender-Expansive: a term related to the ideology that gender is on a spectrum, and that one can be located anywhere on that spectrum.

Gender Expression: one's external presentation of one's gender identity; dressing and behaving like a particular sex or combination of the sexes, based upon stereotypes.

Gender-Fluid: not ascribing to one fixed gender; one whose sense of gender identity changes all the time.

Gender Identity: a nonsensical term referring to one's self-perception as male, female, or something in between; based entirely on stereotypes.

Gender-Nonconforming: not aligning with stereotypes of one's biological sex.

Genderqueer: someone who embraces gender fluidity, who doesn't present according to biological sex stereotypes. Near synonym to **Non-Binary**.

Gender Transition: attempting to change sexes (or gender expression) or to impersonate another sex (or gender expression) via social transition (dressing according to stereotypes of a different sex) or medical transition (taking puberty blockers and/or cross-sex hormones, and/or having surgeries). Gender Transition is an attempt to make the body align with the mind.

Glitter Families: older transgender-identified people who groom children to reject their families of origin and consider the transgender-identified adults their new families.

GLSEN: Gay, Lesbian, & Straight Education Network; organization creating and disseminating homosexuality and transgenderism propaganda, policy, and curricula.

Grooming: specific strategies used by child predators to gain access to children for their sexual exploitation.

Homophobia: fear or hatred of people who are same-sex attracted.

Homosexual: attracted to people of the same sex as oneself. Synonym to **Gay** and **Same-Sex Attracted**.

HRC: The Human Rights Campaign Foundation; the funding and lobby organization for the homosexual and transgender communities.

Intersex: in popular, current usage, a person who was born with mixed anatomical features of maleness and femaleness. In one recent study, the sex of a newborn was not clear from inspection of genitalia in about 1 in 1000 births. These babies have *disorders of sexual development*. Chromosomes and internal organs can be evaluated to clarify a child's sex. Some disorders of sexual development might not be discovered until puberty or after.

Lesbian: a woman who is sexually attracted to other women.

LGBTQ: An acronym for Lesbian, Gay, Bisexual, Transgender, and Queer.

e

Living Openly: describes those who do not hide their sexuality and/or gender identities. Antonym of **Closeted**.

Misgendering: calling someone by a pronoun they do not prefer (i.e., the biologically and grammatically correct pronoun or title).

MTF: Male to female transgender. Opposite of **FTM**.

Non-Binary: Someone who does not view himself or herself as aligning with either maleness or femaleness. Near synonym to **Genderqueer**.

Outing: (verb) revealing another person's sexuality and/or gender identity without permission to do so.

Pansexual: sexually attracted to anyone at any time; willing to be sexual partners with anyone.

Peak: (verb) recognizing that gender ideology is unsound; becoming gender-critical.

Pedophile: an adult who is sexually attracted to prepubescent children; pedophilia is still considered a mental disorder.

Polyamory: multiple (more than two) sexual partners in relationship with each other at one time.

Presentation (or Present [v]): how one shows him or herself to the world; the clothing, hairstyle, and mannerism choices that reflect one's gender (sex) status, based on cultural stereotypes.

Pronouns (also **Preferred Pronouns**): the grammatical reference used in place of a proper noun; transgender persons demand to be referred to by different pronouns that would be linguistically accurate (*e.g.*, a man tells you that his pronouns are "she/her").

Protagonists: as used in this book, people who are working with you to help pull your child out of the gender cult.

Queer: an umbrella term to express any sexual and/or gender orientation/presentation other than being a **Cisgender** heterosexual. Near antonym to **Cisgender**.

Questioning: describes someone who is exploring his or her sexuality and/or gender.

Safe Person/Space: indicates a person, place, or group that will affirm the child in transition and medicalization, and is willing to deceive/undermine parents toward that goal.

Same-Sex Attracted: attracted to people of the same sex as oneself. Synonym to **Homosexual**. Near synonym to **Gay** (males) and **Lesbian** (females).

Sex Assigned at Birth: one's biological sex. This term has been created to propagate the false idea that there is no such thing as biological sex, only the gender that someone (a doctor or parent) "assigned" to a child based on the child's genitalia.

Sexual Orientation: the nature of one's sexual and/or romantic attractions. LGB/TQ organizations often claim that sexual orientation is inherent and immutable, but this assertion is belied by the number of people who "come out" as homosexual in middle age or beyond, and those who became or returned to being heterosexual after counseling and/or therapy.

Stereotype: a widely-held idea or image of a person, which is fixed and oversimplified: e.g., "all girls like pink," "all boys like sports," "women can't do math," *etc.*

Supportive: willing to capitulate to all demands of the transgender-identified person.

TERF: Trans-Exclusive Radical Feminist; originally referred to radical feminists who did not accept transgender ideology, but is currently used as a slur against anyone who does not fully capitulate to transgender activist's agenda.

Transgender: claiming to feel a mismatch between one's biological sex and one's sense of self; presenting oneself to the world according to stereotypes that do not align with those of one's biological (birth) sex.

Transphobia: fear or hatred of people who are transgender. In current vernacular this term is applied to anyone who disagrees with anything that a transgender person says, wants, or believes.

Unsupportive: unwilling to capitulate to all demands of the transgender-identified person.

Index

Index

Index

REFERENCES
(Grouped by Topic)

Activism

Heath, T. (2020, October 17). Here's your complete list of LGBTQ holidays & commemorations. Retrieved February 04, 2021, from https://www.lgbtqnation.com/2018/10/heres-complete-list-lgbtq-holidays-commemorations-just-time-spirit-day/

GLSEN Safe Space Kit: Be an ALLY to LGBTQ Youth! (n.d.). Retrieved August 19, 2020, from https://www.glsen.org/activity/glsen-safe-space-kit-be-ally-lgbtq-youth

Gender Health Query. (n.d.). Threats & censorship result if trans activists demands are not met regarding children & teens & gd. Retrieved February 13, 2021, from https://www.genderhq.org/trans-activism-identity-politics-harassment-censorship

4th Wave Now. (2017, May 14). MtoF tells trans kids to dump moms on Mother's Day and join the "glitter-queer" family of adult trans activists. 4th Wave Now. Retrieved August 19, 2020, from https://4thwavenow.com/2017/05/14/mtof-tells-trans-kids-to-dump-moms-on-mothers-day-and-join-the-glitter-queer-family-of-adult-trans-activists/

Glossary of Terms. (n.d.). Human Rights Campaign. Retrieved August 19, 2020, from https://www.hrc.org/resources/glossary-of-terms

Hasson, M. (2020, June 17). 'It isn't hate to speak The truth': J.K. Rowling takes a stand against gender ideology, and we should stand with her. Retrieved February 04, 2021, from https://www.osvnews.com/2020/06/15/it-isnt-hate-to-speak-the-truth-j-k-rowling-takes-a-stand-against-gender-ideology-and-we-should-stand-with-her/

Bilek, J. (2018, February 22). Who are the rich, white men institutionalizing transgender ideology? Retrieved February 04, 2021, from https://thefederalist.com/2018/02/20/rich-white-men-institutionalizing-transgender-ideology/

Cha, A. (2019, December 12). Planned Parenthood to OPEN reproductive health centers at 50 Los Angeles high schools. Retrieved February 20, 2021, from https://www.washingtonpost.com/health/2019/12/11/planned-parenthood-open-reproductive-health-centers-los-angeles-high-schools/

Traster, T. (2020, November 20). Trans kids may reject family, not the other way around. Retrieved February 08, 2021, from https://www.transgendertrend.com/trans-kids-reject-family-not-other-way-around/

Keenan, J. (2019, April 03). 'Doctor' advises threatening suicide to get trans treatments for kids. Retrieved February 07, 2021, from https://thefederalist.com/2019/04/01/doctor-advises-threatening-suicide-get-transgender-treatments-kids/

Van Maren, J. (2019, October 17). So it's now acceptable to call mispronouncing a transgender name an act of violence? Retrieved February 12, 2021, from https://www.lifesitenews.com/blogs/so-its-now-acceptable-to-call-mispronouncing-a-transgender-name-an-act-of-violence

Murphy, M. (2018, May 01). Trans activism is excusing & advocating violence against women, and it's time to speak up. Retrieved February 15, 2021, from https://www.feministcurrent.com/2018/05/01/trans-activism-become-centered-justifying-violence-women-time-allies-speak/

Deep Green Resistance News Service (2018, May 1) San Francisco Public Library Hosts Transgender "Art Exhibit" Featuring Weapons Intended to Kill Feminists. Retrieved March 12, 2021 from https://dgrnewsservice.org/civilization/patriarchy/male-violence/library-hosts-transgender-art-weapons-kill-feminists/

Brunskell-Evans, H. (2020, November 19). The billion dollar transgender industry masquerading as a civil rights movement. Retrieved February 17, 2021, from https://www.lipstickalley.com/threads/the-billion-dollar-transgender-industry-masquerading-as-a-civil-rights-movement.4117363/

Robbins, J. (2020, June 16). *Exploiting child suicide to bully parents of Trans Kids is the ultimate science denial.* The Federalist. Retrieved May 5, 2022, from https://thefederalist.com/2020/06/16/exploiting-child-suicide-to-bully-parents-of-trans-kids-is-the-ultimate-science-denial/

References

Al Jazeera. (2020, July 08). J K ROWLING, others scorched for lamenting rising 'intolerance'. Retrieved February 19, 2021, from https://www.aljazeera.com/news/2020/7/8/j-k-rowling-others-scorched-for-lamenting-rising-intolerance

Moore, M., & Brunskell-Evans, H. (2020). *Inventing transgender children and young people.* Cambridge Scholars Publishing.

Autism

Brewer, E. (2020, October 17). *Autism and gender identity* [Video]. YouTube. https://youtu.be/GjXcK77XjdY

Anglia Ruskin University. (2019, July 16). Study finds transgender, non-binary autism link. Retrieved February 12, 2021, from https://medicalxpress.com/news/2019-07-transgender-non-binary-autism-link.html#:~:text=It%20found%20that%2014%25%20of%20the%20transgender%20and,suggesting%20a%20high%20number%20of%20potentially%20undiagnosed%20individuals.

Autism Society. (2020, April 10). Facts and statistics. Retrieved February 12, 2021, from https://www.autism-society.org/what-is/facts-and-statistics/

Kaufman, S. (2017, June 14). Rethinking autism: From social awkwardness to social creativity. Retrieved February 12, 2021, from https://behavioralscientist.org/rethinking-autism-social-awkwardness-social-creativity/

Eartharcher, L. (2019, June 14). Asperger's / autism and 'BLACK-AND-WHITE thinking'. Retrieved February 12, 2021, from https://thesilentwaveblog.wordpress.com/2017/03/08/aspergers-autism-and-black-and-white-thinking/

Burner, K., PhD. (2013, February 08). Autism and dealing with change. Retrieved February 12, 2021, from https://theautismblog.seattlechildrens.org/autism-and-dealing-with-change/

10 symptoms of high-functioning autism. (2020, April 29). Retrieved February 12, 2021, from

https://www.appliedbehavioranalysisprograms.com/lists/5-symptoms-of-high-functioning-autism/

Brewer, E. (2020, October 17). *Autism & gender identity* [Video]. YouTube. https://youtu.be/GjXcK77XjdY

Griffiths, S. (2021, January 09). Autistic girls seeking answers 'are seizing on sex change'. Retrieved February 13, 2021, from https://www.thetimes.co.uk/article/autistic-girls-seeking-answers-are-seizing-on-sex-change-3r82850gw

Glidden, D., Bouman, W. P., Jones, B. A., & Arcelus, J. (2016, January). *Gender dysphoria and autism spectrum disorder: A systematic review of the literature.* Sexual medicine reviews. Retrieved May 5, 2022, from https://pubmed.ncbi.nlm.nih.gov/27872002/

Skagerberg, E. M., Di Ceglie, D., & Carmichael, P. (2015, March). *Www.researchgate.net.* Research Gate. Retrieved May 5, 2022, from https://www.researchgate.net/profile/Elin-Skagerberg-2/publication/273639503_Brief_Report_Autistic_Features_in_Children_and_Adolescents_with_Gender_Dysphoria/links/55238d180cf29dcab0f0367/Brief-Report-Autistic-Features-in-Children-and-Adolescents-with-Gender-Dysphoria.pdf

Autogynephilia

Perry, L. (2019, November 20). What is AUTOGYNEPHILIA? An interview with Dr Ray Blanchard. Retrieved February 14, 2021, from https://quillette.com/2019/11/06/what-is-autogynephilia-an-interview-with-dr-ray-blanchard/

Yardley, M. (2017, July 31). Pornography and autogynephilia in the narratives of adult transgender males. Retrieved February 14, 2021, from https://mirandayardley.com/en/pornography-and-autogynephilia-in-the-narratives-of-adult-transgender-males/

Chasmar, J. (2017, September 01). L'Oreal's first transgender U.k. MODEL, MUNROE Bergdorf, fired after 'white people' rant. Retrieved February 16, 2021, from https://www.washingtontimes.com/news/2017/sep/1/munroe-bergdorf-loreals-first-transgender-uk-model/

References

Linehan, G. (2021, January 23). Another central OUTLIER: Rachel McKinnon. Retrieved February 16, 2021, from https://grahamlinehan.substack.com/p/another-central-outlier-rachel-mckinnon

Child Abuse, Pornography, & Sexual Grooming

Nadal, K. L., Phd, Davidoff, K. C., BS, & Fujii-Doe, W., MA. (2014, March 11). Transgender women and the sex work industry: Roots in systemic, institutional, and interpersonal discrimination. Retrieved February 04, 2021, from https://www.tandfonline.com/doi/abs/10.1080/15299732.2014.86757 2

Aharon, A. (2021, January 29). The secret tactics of glitter moms: A tale of betrayal and grooming. Retrieved February 06, 2021, from https://www.transgenderabuse.org/post/the-secret-tactics-of-glitter-moms-a-tale-of-betrayal-and-grooming

Herbert, G. (2011, October 04). Sex sells: 92 percent of top 10 billboard songs are about sex, study finds. Retrieved February 14, 2021, from https://www.syracuse.com/entertainment/2011/10/billboard_top_10_songs_about_sex_suny_albany_study.html

Witte, R. (2020, February 05). Sexism sells: An evolution of selling sex in advertising. Retrieved February 14, 2021, from https://www.nylon.com/sexism-in-advertising-2020

Parental Guide. (2020, October 26). Pg 13 movie rating. Retrieved February 14, 2021, from https://www.parentalguide.org/movie-ratings/pg-13/

Enough Is Enough. (n.d.). Pornography. Retrieved February 14, 2021, from https://www.enough.org/stats_porn_industry

National Center on Sexual Exploitation. (2016, August 16). Talking points: Increase in violence. Retrieved February 14, 2021, from https://endsexualexploitation.org/violence/

Thompson, D. (2017, May 12). Study sees link between porn and sexual dysfunction. Retrieved February 14, 2021, from https://www.webmd.com/sex/news/20170512/study-sees-link-between-porn-and-sexual-dysfunction

Yardley, M. (2017, July 31). Pornography and autogynephilia in the narratives of adult transgender males. Retrieved February 14, 2021, from https://mirandayardley.com/en/pornography-and-autogynephilia-in-the-narratives-of-adult-transgender-males/

Keffler, M. (2021, February 05). The six steps a Predator takes in grooming a child. Retrieved February 16, 2021, from https://uncommongroundmedia.com/the-six-steps-a-predator-takes-in-grooming-a-child/

National Society for the Prevention of Cruelty to Children. (n.d.). Grooming. Retrieved August 19, 2020, from https://www.nspcc.org.uk/what-is-child-abuse/types-of-abuse/grooming/

Yamagami, D. S. (2000). Prosecuting Cyber-Pedophiles: How Can Intent Be Shown in a Virtual World in Light of the Fantasy Defense? *Santa Clara Law Review, 41*(2). doi:https://digitalcommons.law.scu.edu/cgi/viewcontent.cgi?article=1346&context=lawreview#:~:text=FANTASY%20DEFENSE%20predat ors%20and%20child%20pornographers%20on%20the,at-tract%20pedophiles.%22%20The%20adult%20eventually%20propositio ns%20the%20un-

Preventing Child Sexual Abuse: Know the Facts & Signs. (2018, September 24). Retrieved August 19, 2020, from https://centerforchildprotection.org/preventing-child-sexual-abuse/

Child Development & Psychology

Cherry, K. (2020, June 26). Understanding Erikson's stages of psychosocial development. Retrieved February 03, 2021, from https://www.verywellmind.com/erik-eriksons-stages-of-psychosocial-development-2795740

Holmes, L. (2020, November 29) The debate over repressed and recovered memories. Retrieved March 10, 2021 from https://www.verywellmind.com/the-debate-over-recovered-memories-2330516

References

Hall, K., PhD. (2012, February 08). What is invalidation? Retrieved February 07, 2021, from https://www.psychcentral.com/blog/emotionally-sensitive/2012/02/reasons-you-and-others-invalidate-your-emotional-experience#1

Fulbright, Y. K., PhD. (2014, December 30). 10 ways to improve any relationship. Retrieved February 06, 2021, from https://www.psychologytoday.com/us/blog/mate-relate-and-communicate/201412/10-ways-improve-any-relationship

Firasek, R. (2020, March 20). What percentage of communication is nonverbal? Retrieved February 07, 2021, from https://www.rachelfirasek.com/what-percentage-of-communication-is-nonverbal/

Cherry, K. (2020, June 30). How to understand and identify passive-aggressive behavior. Retrieved March 05, 2021, from https://www.verywellmind.com/what-is-passive-aggressive-behavior-2795481

Morin, A. (2020, February 05). Using praise to build character rather than ego in children. Retrieved February 07, 2021, from https://www.verywellfamily.com/praise-build-childrens-character-1094902

Effectiviology. (n.d.). Retrieved February 07, 2021, from https://effectiviology.com/benjamin-franklin-effect/

Thompson, C. (2010). *Anatomy of the soul: Surprising connections between neuroscience and spiritual practices that can transform your life and relationships.* Carol Stream,, IL: Tyndale Momentum.

Zitzman, B. (2020, October 14). Importance of FAMILY: Why is Family important [Really Important]. Retrieved February 10, 2021, from https://www.familytoday.com/relationships/importance-of-family/

LaScala, M. (2020, January 17). Why Do Children Have Imaginary Friends, and How Far Do You Have to Play Along? Retrieved February 10, 2021, from https://www.goodhousekeeping.com/life/parenting/a28579180/why-children-have-imaginary-friends/

Arlington Parent Coalition. (2019, September 22). Developmental appropriateness & the comprehensive sex Ed Agenda. Retrieved February 21, 2021, from https://arlingtonparentcoa.wixsite.com/arlingtonparentcoa/post/developmental-appropriateness-the-comprehensive-sex-ed-agenda

Cherry, K. (2020, March 31). What are Piaget's four stages of development? Retrieved February 10, 2021, from https://www.verywellmind.com/piagets-stages-of-cognitive-development-2795457

Dewar, G., PhD. (n.d.). Praise and intelligence. Retrieved February 10, 2021, from http://www.parentingscience.com/praise-and-intelligence.html

American Psychiatric Association, Diagnostic and Statistical Manual of Mental Disorders, 5th Edition, Arlington, VA, 2013, pp. 685, 818.

American Psychiatric Association. (n.d.). What are dissociative disorders? Retrieved February 13, 2021, from https://www.psychiatry.org/patients-families/dissociative-disorders/what-are-dissociative-disorders

Geiger, A., & Davis, L. (2020, December 23). A growing number of American teenagers – particularly girls – are facing depression. Retrieved February 13, 2021, from https://www.pewresearch.org/fact-tank/2019/07/12/a-growing-number-of-american-teenagers-particularly-girls-are-facing-depression/

Cherry, K. (2019, December 07). Are you in control of your destiny, or are you at the mercy of chance? Retrieved February 19, 2021, from https://www.verywellmind.com/what-is-locus-of-control-2795434

Stanborough, R. (2020, December 15). Therapy for phobias: What are the options? Retrieved February 19, 2021, from https://www.healthline.com/health/therapy-for-phobias

Web MD. (2020, September 27). Grief & depression coping with DENIAL, Loss, anger and more. Retrieved February 18, 2021, from https://www.webmd.com/depression/guide/depression-grief#1

651

References

Gallagher, M., Dalrymple, T., Donald, H., & McGinnis, J. (2019, June 18). Why Marriage Is Good For You. Retrieved August 19, 2020, from https://www.city-journal.org/html/why-marriage-good-you-12002.html

Cults

Cult. (2021). Retrieved February 04, 2021, from https://www.dictionary.com/browse/cult

Goldberg, R. (2018, May 14). I was recruited by ALLISON Mack's Sex Cult. Retrieved March 13, 2021, from https://www.vulture.com/2018/05/i-was-recruited-for-allison-macks-sex-cult.html

Bond, C. (2021, January 09). How mlms use the same mind control techniques as cults. Retrieved February 04, 2021, from https://www.huffpost.com/entry/multilevel-marketing-companies-mlms-cults-similarities_l_5d49f8c2e4b09e72973df3d3

Fr. Dwight Longenecker (2017, April 24). 4 danger signs of cult-like behavior, and 4 Antidotes. Retrieved February 04, 2021, from https://www.ncregister.com/blog/4-danger-signs-of-cult-like-behavior-and-4-antidotes

Davis, M. (2020, January 16). 4 psychological techniques cults use to recruit members. Retrieved March 13, 2021, from https://bigthink.com/culture-religion/four-cult-recruitment-techniques?rebelltitem=5#rebelltitem5

Dittmann, M. (2002, November). Cults of hatred. Retrieved March 13, 2021, from https://www.apa.org/monitor/nov02/cults.html#:~:text=With%20thought-stopping%20techniques%2C%20members%20are%20taught%20to%20stop,if%20he%20ever%20leaves%20or%20questions%20the%20group.

Norman, C. (2020, September 21). Eight steps to mind control: How cults suck ordinary people in. Retrieved February 04, 2021, from https://www.nzherald.co.nz/lifestyle/eight-steps-to-mind-control-how-cults-suck-ordinary-people-in/JVANMWX7XTTXBC2AS2C3GN3SX4/

Fleischacker, S. (2019, June 04). Cult vs. religion: What's the difference? Retrieved February 03, 2021, from https://www.baltimoresun.com/opinion/bs-xpm-2011-10-13-bs-ed-mormons-20111013-story.html

D., B. (2019, January 03). 10 former cult members and Their CHILLING STORIES. Retrieved February 03, 2021, from https://listverse.com/2017/07/29/10-former-cult-members-and-their-chilling-stories/#:~:text=Members%20were%20expected%20to%20give%20up%20their%20names,realize%20that%20the%20cult%20was%20sexist%20and%20warped.

Reynolds, E. (2017, August 30). The former cult member on life in a repressive regime. Retrieved February 03, 2021, from https://www.news.com.au/lifestyle/real-life/true-stories/life-after-gloriavale-the-repressive-cult-run-by-an-australian-sex-offender/news-story/390f38fedac3f684e80f9204b71bfef5

Edge, C. L. (2015, December 15). Cults & identity theft. Retrieved March 14, 2021, from https://charleneedge.com/cults-identity-theft/

Cults in our midst. (n.d.). Retrieved March 13, 2021, from https://culteducation.com/group/1273-recovery/17912-cults-in-our-midst-leaving-a-cult-and-recoverings.html

Collins, G. (1982, March 15). THE psychology of the CULT EXPERIENCE. Retrieved March 13, 2021, from https://www.nytimes.com/1982/03/15/style/the-psychology-of-the-cult-experience.html

Cults in our midst. (n.d.). Retrieved March 13, 2021, from https://culteducation.com/group/1273-recovery/17912-cults-in-our-midst-leaving-a-cult-and-recoverings.html

Lifton, R. J. (2004, April 13). Dr. Robert J. Lifton's Eight Criteria for Thought Reform. Retrieved February 15, 2021, from http://cultrecover.com/sites/default/files/pdfs/lifton8criteria.pdf

Griffiths, M. D., PhD. (2019, February 14). Love bombing. Retrieved February 04, 2021, from https://www.psychologytoday.com/us/blog/in-excess/201902/love-bombing

References

Detransitioners

Marchiano, L. (2020, January 12). The ranks of gender detransitioners are growing. we need to understand why. Retrieved February 12, 2021, from https://quillette.com/2020/01/02/the-ranks-of-gender-detransitioners-are-growing-we-need-to-understand-why/

Myers, F. (2019, February 24). My battle with the transgender thoughtpolice: James Caspian on the suppression of his research into people who detransition. Retrieved February 19, 2021, from https://www.spiked-online.com/2019/02/22/my-battle-with-the-transgender-thoughtpolice/

Ladyantitheist. (2018, January 18). I hated her guts at the time: A trans-desister and her mom tell their story. 4th Wave Now. Retrieved August 19, 2020, from https://4thwavenow.com/tag/ladyantitheist/

Bridge, L. (2020, January 09). Detransitioners are living proof the practices surrounding 'trans kids' need be questioned. Retrieved February 19, 2021, from https://www.feministcurrent.com/2020/01/09/detransitioners-are-living-proof-the-practices-surrounding-trans-kids-need-be-questioned/

Pique Resilience Project. (2019, February 5). *Detransition Q&A (#1)* [Video]. Retrieved February 13, 2021, from https://www.piqueresproject.com/newsfeed/detransition-qa-1 [9:20-10:03]

Erin Brewer (2021, March 25). *Insights from a Detransitioner.* [Video]. Youtube. https://youtu.be/1FaYBRpe9Ok

Gender Clinics & Transgender Health

Transgender Trend. (2020, January 20). The surge in referral rates of girls to the tavistock continues to rise. Retrieved February 06, 2021, from https://www.transgendertrend.com/surge-referral-rates-girls-tavistock-continues-rise/

John Money (1921-2006). (2011, November 11). Retrieved February 10, 2021, from https://www.goodtherapy.org/famous-psychologists/john-money.html

Colapinto, J. (2000) As Nature Made Him: The Boy Who Was Raised as a Girl. New York: Harper Collins Publishers.

Gaetano, P. (n.d.). The embryo Project Encyclopedia. Retrieved February 04, 2021, from https://embryo.asu.edu/pages/david-reimer-and-john-money-gender-reassignment-controversy-johnjoan-case

Boodman, S. G., & Boodman, R. (2000, February 29). A terrible accident, a dismal failure. Retrieved February 04, 2021, from https://www.washingtonpost.com/archive/lifestyle/wellness/2000/02/29/a-terrible-accident-a-dismal-failure/83850bc4-b27a-417e-ba85-3693a4cafdd0/

Day, M. (2016, November 15). How one of America's best medical schools started a SECRET TRANSGENDER surgery clinic. Retrieved March 30, 2021, from https://timeline.com/americas-first-transgender-clinic-b56928e20f5f

Smith, L. (2018, November 28). A bright new start for transgender health. Retrieved March 30, 2021, from https://www.hopkinsmedicine.org/news/articles/gender-affirming-treatment

MTF vaginoplasty: What patients need to know before choosing a technique. (2020, November 20). Retrieved March 31, 2021, from https://www.mtfsurgery.net/mtf-vaginoplasty.htm

O'Neil, T. (2021, March 12). Detransitioners open up about how transgender 'medicine' left them scarred for life. Retrieved March 31, 2021, from https://pjmedia.com/news-and-politics/tyler-o-neil/2021/03/12/detransitioners-open-up-transgender-identity-was-a-way-to-cope-with-my-trauma-and-body-hatred-n1432065

Keffler, M. (2020, December 02). All about the money: Sex reassignment surgery touted as "growth market". Retrieved February 04, 2021, from https://www.partnersforethicalcare.com/post/all-about-the-money-sex-reassignment-surgery-touted-as-growth-market

Transgender Trend. (2020, June 19). Johanna OLSON-KENNEDY and the US Gender Affirmative Approach. Retrieved February 05, 2021, from https://www.transgendertrend.com/johanna-olson-kennedy-gender-affirmative-approach/

655

References

Gender Dysphoria

Sundar, V. (2021, January 29). *Dysphoric: A Four-Part Documentary Series Part 01* [Video] (7:28-8:05). YouTube. https://youtu.be/w8taOdnXD6o

Shrier, A. (2020). Irreversible damage: the transgender craze seducing our daughters. In *Irreversible damage: The transgender craze seducing our daughters* (pp. 41-57). Washington, DC: Regnery Publishing.

Heyer, W. (2018, September 27). Childhood sexual abuse, gender dysphoria, and transition regret: Billy's story. Retrieved February 13, 2021, from https://www.thepublicdiscourse.com/2018/03/21178/

Eagle Forum (2019, November 10). *Erin Brewer: I was a trans kid* [Video]. YouTube. https://youtu.be/GFphNvRraLA

Dhejne, C., Van Vlerken, R., Heylens, G., & Arcelus, J. (2016, February 2). Mental health and gender dysphoria: A review of the literature. Retrieved February 13, 2021, from https://www.tandfonline.com/doi/abs/10.3109/09540261.2015.1115753?journalCode=iirp20

Heyer, W. (2016, November 16). Transgenders, 4 studies say it's mental disorders. Retrieved February 13, 2021, from https://waltheyer.com/transgenders-4-studies-say-its-mental-disorders/

Holt, V., Dunsford, M., & Skagerberg, E. M. (2014, November). *Young people with features of gender dysphoria ... - researchgate.* Young people with features of gender dysphoria: Demographics and associated difficulties. Retrieved May 5, 2022, from https://www.researchgate.net/publication/268879198_Young_people_with_features_of_gender_dysphoria_Demographics_and_associated_difficulties

Kaltiala-Heino, R., Sumia, M., Työläjärvi, M., & Lindberg, N. (2015, April 9). *Two years of Gender Identity Service for minors: Overrepresentation of natal girls with severe problems in adolescent development.* Child and adolescent psychiatry and mental health. Retrieved May 5, 2022, from https://www.ncbi.nlm.nih.gov/pmc/articles/PMC4396787/

Glidden, D., Bouman, W. P., Jones, B. A., & Arcelus, J. (2016, January). *Gender dysphoria and autism spectrum disorder: A systematic review of the literature*. Sexual medicine reviews. Retrieved May 5, 2022, from https://pubmed.ncbi.nlm.nih.gov/27872002/

Skagerberg, E. M., Di Ceglie, D., & Carmichael, P. (2015, March). *Www.researchgate.net*. Research Gate. Retrieved May 5, 2022, from https://www.researchgate.net/profile/Elin-Skagerberg-2/publication/273639503_Brief_Report_Autistic_Features_in_Children_and_Adolescents_with_Gender_Dysphoria/links/55238d180cf29dcabb0f0367/Brief-Report-Autistic-Features-in-Children-and-Adolescents-with-Gender-Dysphoria.pdf

Wiepjes, C. M., *et. al.* (2018, February 17). Define_me. Retrieved May 5, 2022, from https://www.jsm.jsexmed.org/article/S1743-6095(18)30057-2/fulltext

Hormones & Surgery

Anderson, R. (2020, July 21). Sex change: Physically impossible, psychosocially unhelpful, and philosophically misguided. Retrieved March 30, 2021, from https://www.thepublicdiscourse.com/2018/03/21151/

Kuhn, A., MD, Bodmer, C., MD, Stadlmayr, W., MD, Kuhn, P., MD, Mueller, M. D., & Birkhäuser, M. (2008, November 6). Quality of life 15 years after sex reassignment surgery for transsexualism. Retrieved March 31, 2021, from https://www.fertstert.org/article/S0015-0282(08)03838-7/fulltext#secd25081910e331

Mol, A., Laidlaw, M., Grossman, M., & McHugh, P. (2020, September 14). Correction: Transgender surgery provides no mental health benefit. Retrieved February 04, 2021, from https://www.thepublicdiscourse.com/2020/09/71296/

Dhejne C; Lichtenstein P; Boman M; Johansson AL; Långström N; Landén M;. (2011, February 22). Long-term follow-up of TRANSSEXUAL persons undergoing sex reassignment SURGERY: Cohort study in Sweden. Retrieved February 04, 2021, from https://pubmed.ncbi.nlm.nih.gov/21364939/

Shrier, A. (2021, February 11). Inside planned parenthood's gender business. Retrieved February 20, 2021, from

References

https://www.realclearpolitics.com/2021/02/11/inside_planned_parent hoods_gender_business_535705.html#!

Pilgrim, D., & Entwistle, K. (2020, July 27). *GnRHa ('puberty blockers') and cross sex hormones for children and adolescents: Informed consent, personhood and freedom of expression.* Taylor & Francis. Retrieved May 5, 2022, from https://www.tandfonline.com/doi/full/10.1080/20502877.2020.17962 57

Rapid Onset Gender Dysphoria

Littman, L. (2018, August 16). Parent reports of adolescents and young adults perceived to show signs of a rapid onset of gender dysphoria. Retrieved February 04, 2021, from https://journals.plos.org/plosone/article?id=10.1371%2Fjournal.pone. 0202330

Littman, L. (2018, August 16). Parent reports of adolescents and young adults perceived to show signs of a rapid onset of gender dysphoria. Retrieved February 12, 2021, from https://journals.plos.org/plosone/article?id=10.1371%2Fjournal.pone. 0202330

Updated: Brown statements on gender dysphoria study. (2019, March 19). Retrieved February 12, 2021, from https://www.brown.edu/news/2019-03-19/gender

Pique Resilience Project. (2019, February 5). *Detransition Q&A (#1)* [Video]. Retrieved February 13, 2021, from https://www.piqueresproject.com/newsfeed/detransition-qa-1

Shrier, A. (2020). Irreversible damage: the transgender craze seducing our daughters. In *Irreversible damage: The transgender craze seducing our daughters* (pp. 41-57). Washington, DC: Regnery Publishing.

Lloyd, J. C. (2020, August 11). Why a generation of girls is fleeing womanhood. Retrieved February 14, 2021, from https://www.thepublicdiscourse.com/2020/08/69452/

Anderson, R. T. (2018, February 20). Parents denied custody of child for refusing support of transgenderism: Here's what you need to know. Retrieved February 15, 2021, from https://www.lifesitenews.com/opinion/getting-a-sense-of-the-brave-new-transgender-world-how-parents-can-have-the

Marchiano, L. (2017, January 6). *Outbreak: On transgender teens and psychic epidemics.* Taylor & Francis. Retrieved May 5, 2022, from https://www.tandfonline.com/doi/full/10.1080/00332925.2017.1350804

Schools, Sex Ed, & GSA Clubs

American School Counselor Association. (2016). The school counselor and transgender/gender-nonconforming youth. Retrieved February 18, 2021, from https://www.schoolcounselor.org/Standards-Positions/Position-Statements/ASCA-Position-Statements/The-School-Counselor-and-Transgender-Gender-noncon

Newman, A. (2020, August 15). Teacher recruits "most emotionally unstable" kids for lgbt club. Retrieved February 04, 2021, from https://thenewamerican.com/teacher-recruits-most-emotionally-unstable-kids-for-lgbt-club/

Arlington Parent Coalition. (2020, February 08). The aps modus operandi: Ask us no questions, we'll tell you no lies. Retrieved February 13, 2021, from https://arlingtonparentcoa.wixsite.com/arlingtonparentcoa/post/the-aps-modus-operandi-ask-us-no-questions-we-ll-tell-you-no-lies

Keffler, M. (2021, February 08). Horrified mother gets front row seat to sex & gender indoctrination strategy meeting. Retrieved February 13, 2021, from https://www.partnersforethicalcare.com/post/horrified-mother-gets-front-row-seat-to-sex-gender-indoctrination-strategy-meeting

Arlington Parent Coalition. (2020, February 08). The aps modus operandi: Ask us no questions, we'll tell you no lies. Retrieved February 04, 2021, from https://arlingtonparentcoa.wixsite.com/arlingtonparentcoa/post/the-aps-modus-operandi-ask-us-no-questions-we-ll-tell-you-no-lies

Keffler, M. (2020, December 23). Transgender religion Codified & enforced at school. Retrieved February 04, 2021, from https://www.partnersforethicalcare.com/post/transgender-religion-codified-enforced-at-school

References

Goins-Phillips Editor, T. (2020, September 30). Judge bars wisconsin school district from HIDING students' gender identities from parents. Retrieved February 04, 2021, from https://www.faithwire.com/2020/09/30/judge-bars-wisconsin-school-district-from-hiding-students-gender-identities-from-parents/

Arlington Parent Coalition. (2019, May 27). Yes, They Taught Your Kids This. Retrieved August 19, 2020, from https://arlingtonparentcoa.wixsite.com/arlingtonparentcoa/post/yes-they-taught-your-kids-this

Paquette, A. (2014, July 10). Why peer-to-peer selling is taking off and what companies can learn from it. Retrieved February 13, 2021, from https://www.mediapost.com/publications/article/229737/why-peer-to-peer-selling-is-taking-off-and-what-co.html

Strange, V., Forrest, S., & Oakley, A. (2002, June 01). Peer-led sex education-characteristics of peer educators and their perceptions of the impact on them of participation in a peer education programme. Retrieved February 13, 2021, from https://academic.oup.com/her/article/17/3/327/658579

Paterson, J. (2018, May 31). Sex education in schools needs an upgrade. Retrieved February 13, 2021, from https://www.nea.org/advocating-for-change/new-from-nea/sex-education-schools-needs-upgrade

Planned Parenthood. (n.d.). Sex education tools for Educators: Sex education resources. Retrieved February 13, 2021, from https://www.plannedparenthood.org/learn/for-educators

Human Rights Campaign. (n.d.). Welcoming schools: Welcoming schools. Retrieved February 13, 2021, from https://www.welcomingschools.org/

Hoboken411. (2020, February 22). Most teachers quite disturbed about their unions' push for sexualization and indoctrination of school children. Retrieved February 13, 2021, from https://hoboken411.com/archives/137989

Arlington Parent Coalition. (2020, March 02). The state of the school 2020: Full Vigilance required. Retrieved February 13, 2021, from https://arlingtonparentcoa.wixsite.com/arlingtonparentcoa/post/the-state-of-the-school-2020-full-vigilance-required

Ruse, C. (2020). Sex Education in Public Schools: Sexualization of Children & LGBT Indoctrination. Retrieved February 13, 2021, from https://downloads.frc.org/EF/EF20E22.pdf

Arlington Parent Coalition. (2021, January 09). Model policies for the treatment of transgender students in Virginia's public schools. Retrieved February 15, 2021, from https://arlingtonparentcoa.wixsite.com/arlingtonparentcoa/post/model-policies-for-the-treatment-of-transgender-students-in-virginia-s-public-schools

U.S. Department of Education. (2020, December 15). Family Educational Rights and Privacy Act (FERPA). Retrieved February 16, 2021, from https://www2.ed.gov/policy/gen/guid/fpco/ferpa/index.html

Harvard University. (2021). What Is Title IX? Retrieved February 16, 2021, from https://titleix.harvard.edu/what-title-ix

Chen, G. (2008, March 26). Parental Involvement is Key to Student Success. Retrieved August 19, 2020, from https://www.publicschoolreview.com/blog/parental-involvement-is-key-to-student-success

Gladwell, M. (2012, September 17). In Plain View. Retrieved August 19, 2020, from https://www.newyorker.com/magazine/2012/09/24/in-plain-view

GLSEN. (2018, September). Model School District Policy on Transgender and Gender Nonconforming Students (p. 4). Retrieved February 16, 2021, from https://www.glsen.org/sites/default/files/2019-10/GLSEN-Model-School-District-Policy-Transgender-Gender-Nonconforming-Students.pdf

Miscellanea

Wright, C. (2020, March 04). Twitter Post. Retrieved February 18, 2021, from https://twitter.com/swipewright/status/1235302606819467265

References

Violante, C. R. (2016, August 30). Every cell has a SEX: X and Y and the future of health care. Retrieved March 30, 2021, from https://medicine.yale.edu/news-article/13321/

Kellaway, M. (2015, February 18). REPORT: Trans Americans four times more likely to live in poverty. Retrieved February 04, 2021, from https://www.advocate.com/politics/transgender/2015/02/18/report-trans-americans-four-times-more-likely-live-poverty

Herman, J. L., Flores, A. R., Brown, T. N., Wilson, B. D., & Conron, K. J. (2020, June 17). Age of individuals who identify as transgender in the United States. Retrieved February 04, 2021, from https://williamsinstitute.law.ucla.edu/publications/age-trans-individuals-us/

Family Policy Institute of Washington (2016, April 13). *Gender identity: Can a 5'9, white guy be a 6'5, Chinese woman?* [Video]. https://youtu.be/xfO1veFs6Ho

Shrier, A. (2020). *Irreversible damage: The transgender craze seducing our daughters.* Washington, DC: Regnery Publishing, a division of Salem Media Group.

Make Sense. (2020, November 01). False dichotomy - definition and examples. Retrieved February 06, 2021, from https://www.logical-fallacy.com/articles/false-dilemma/

Cretella, M., M.D. (2020, March 31). I'm a pediatrician. here's what i did when a little boy patient said he was a girl. Retrieved February 10, 2021, from https://www.dailysignal.com/2017/12/11/cretella-transcript/

Soh, D. (2018, October 31). Science shows sex is binary, not a spectrum. Retrieved March 30, 2021, from https://www.realclearpolitics.com/articles/2018/10/31/science_shows _sex_is_binary_not_a_spectrum_138506.html#!

Wright, C. (2020, November 25). JK Rowling Is RIGHT-SEX is real and it is not a "spectrum". Retrieved March 30, 2021, from https://quillette.com/2020/06/07/jk-rowling-is-right-sex-is-real-and-it-is-not-a-spectrum/

Transgender Trend. (2017, October 26). Born in the wrong body? Retrieved February 15, 2021, from https://www.transgendertrend.com/born-in-the-wrong-body/

Green, S. (2017, December 13). *Transgender: a mother's story* [Video]. YouTube. https://youtu.be/2ZiVPh12RQY

Dominican Hospital Foundation (2018, July 23). Diane Ehrensaft: *How to tell if babies are transgender* [Video]. Youtube. https://youtu.be/M7KBZeRC1RI

Hadro, M. (2021, February 22). Scholar Ryan Anderson's critique of TRANSGENDER Movement Reportedly de-listed by Amazon. Retrieved February 25, 2021, from https://www.ncregister.com/cna/scholar-ryan-andersons-critique-of-transgender-movement-reportedly-de-listed-by-amazon

Reilly, W. (2019, December 17). Are we in the midst of a transgender murder epidemic? Retrieved February 19, 2021, from https://quillette.com/2019/12/07/are-we-in-the-midst-of-a-transgender-murder-epidemic/

Backholm, J. (2020, May 05). Is critical theory practical? Retrieved February 19, 2021, from https://breakpoint.org/is-critical-theory-practical/

Chuck, E. (2016, August 26). University of Chicago: We don't Condone safe spaces or 'trigger warnings'. Retrieved February 19, 2021, from https://www.nbcnews.com/news/education/university-chicago-we-don-t-condone-safe-spaces-or-trigger-n637721

GLAAD. (2020, November 11). Transgender resources. Retrieved March 30, 2021, from https://www.glaad.org/transgender/resources

Aydin, B.K. et al (2019, June) Frequency of ambiguous genitalia in 14,777 newborns in Turkey. *Journal of the Endocrine Society,* Vol. 3, issue 6, pp. 1185-11985.

Ken, W. (n.d.). Changed: #ONCEGAY Stories. Changed Movement. Retrieved August 19, 2020, from https://changedmovement.com/

Cantor, J. (2018, October 17). *American Academy of Pediatrics Policy and trans- kids:fact-checking.* American Academy of Pediatrics policy and trans-

References

kids:Fact-checking. Retrieved May 5, 2022, from http://www.sexologytoday.org/2018/10/american-academy-of-pediatrics-policy.html

MacRichards, L. (2021, May 27). *Bias, not evidence dominates WPATH transgender standard of care*. CANADIAN GENDER REPORT. Retrieved May 5, 2022, from https://genderreport.ca/bias-not-evidence-dominate-transgender-standard-of-care/

OTHER BOOKS FROM
ADVOCATES PROTECTING CHILDREN

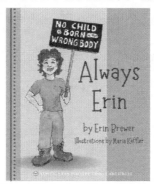

Always Erin, by Erin Brewer

When Erin was a little girl, two men hurt her. She thought that she got hurt because she was a girl, and if she became a boy, she would never be hurt like that again. But with the help of some wise and supportive adults, Erin learned that hurts can happen to anyone. She learned how to love herself as a girl again, and to know that no matter what, she was *Always Erin.*

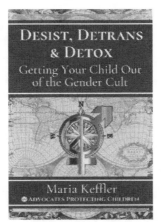

Desist, Detrans & Detox: Getting Your Child Out of the Gender Cult by Maria Keffler

Blindsided when a child suddenly announces a transgender identity, many parents today find their families under assault by an insidious predator: the billion-dollar gender industry. Nearly every parent whose child has fallen into the gender industry's clutches has heard the same emotionally manipulative threat: agree to your child's immediate social and medical transition, or prepare for the child's suicide. But there is a different—and saner—path. A growing cadre of parents are saying, "No," to the gender machine's unethical and deceptive narrative. Based on sound principles of psychology and child development, as well as on strategies used by parents who have pulled their children back from the gender cult's destructive ideology, *Desist, Detrans & Detox: Getting Your Child Out of the Gender Cult* provides a roadmap to help families navigate the treacherous terrain of gender indoctrination, and bring their children back to reality and safety.

Transing Our Children, by Erin Brewer with Maria Keffler

Children K-12 are taught that their bodies have nothing to do with their "gender identity" and that boys might really be girls and girls might actually be boys. Parents who hold biologically accurate views on sex and gender, and therefore refuse to capitulate to the medicalization of their children's healthy bodies, are undermined and vilified as "hateful, toxic, abusive, and transphobic." Teenage girls' healthy breasts and young men's healthy penises and testicles are removed in experimental procedures that irrevocably damage their sexuality and fertility. Gender therapists and doctors lie to parents and children, claiming that puberty blockers and cross-sex hormones are fully reversible and do no harm to young bodies and brains.

Transing Children is the fruit of a deep, wide, and horror-inducing investigation into the twisted world of childhood transgenderism. Brewer and Keffler have applied their analytic and critical-thinking skills

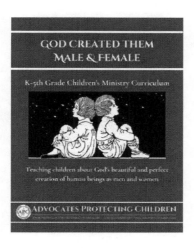

to unmask this beast of an ideology, producing this thorough and ground-breaking book.

God Created Them Male & Female:
K-12th Grade Children's Ministry Curriculum

Children today are bombarded with messages about embracing and participating in transgender ideology. Some schools are often actively involved in inculcating children into gender ideology. Many teachers are taught in continuing education classes that they must teach transgender theory and affirm children's "gender identities." Social media is replete with influencers and transgender groups that entice or coerce children into questioning their God-given sex, and gender clinics are popping up like weeds in cities across the country.

Gentle Leading: Meditations for Families with Transgender-Identified Children
by Lanya Kachannie

Within the pages of "Gentle Leading: Meditations for Families with Transgender-Identified Children," Lanya Kachannie addresses the spiritual issues that accompany a child's sudden transgender identification. Kachannie tackles fear; grief; anger; questions about God's sovereignty, goodness, & trustworthiness; as well as leads readers on a deep dive into what the Bible has to say about personhood and God's intention for his creation.

Whether you are the parent, family member, or friend of a transgender-identified child, or simply someone who wants to understand more about the myriad spiritual implications of the transgender narrative, "Gentle Leading: Meditations for Families with Transgender-Identified Children" offers a perspective on love and truth that culminates in renewed hope and faith.

"Each day of this devotional brings hope, healing, and knowledge with actionable items. With amazing spiritual insight the author gives simplicity to this deeply personal and complex issue. This would be a great devotional for any man or woman, even if you are not dealing with transgender issues."

--Pastor Robert Roper, First Baptist Church of Alva (FL) & Founder of Operation Millstone